The History of World Sculpture

THE HISTORY
OF WORLD
SCULPTURE

by

Germain Bazin

CHARTWELL BOOKS INC.

Published by Chartwell Books Inc.,
A Division of BOOK SALES INC.,
110 Enterprise Avenue, Secaucus, N.J. 07094.

Translated from the French by Madeline Jay

Library of Congress Catalogue Card Number 76-41583

© 1968 by Smeets Lithographers, Weert, The Netherlands

Printed by Smeets Lithographers, Weert, The Netherlands

© Sabam-Brussel 1976

ISBN 0-89009-089-0

Contents

The Origins

If I had to say which was the first basic artistic gesture – sculpting or painting, I would choose the former. For primitive man, painting was a luxury, whilst sculpting was a matter of life and death. The making of objects in the round was closely linked with the rudimentary industry which allowed man to perfect his way of life through the use of tools, thus multiplying his possibilities of action. The very first tool was probably not even made of wood, since to work on wood – unless it was a mere stick broken off from a tree – a cutting instrument was required, and only stone could provide it. Some loose piece of flint may have provided man with his first tool and from then on, he started splitting those pebbles which he had originally used as missiles; that was around the year 600,000 B.C., somewhere in Africa. Man was still only a *hominid*. Soon, he learnt to cut flints by hitting them with a stone, then with a piece of wood, and later by dropping them onto a stone anvil. He obtained bifacially flaked tools, and was content with them for four hundred thousand years. Such a long period of stagnation is as surprising as the miracle of invention. At last came a new wave of beings deserving the name *homo*, and evolution progressed faster. Through that first stone, picked and worked on, nature had found its master; man became *homo faber* and would one day transform the world, perhaps even destroy it. Around 100,000 B.C., Mousterian man could already make differentiated tools; he used bone and ivory obtained from animals. Finally, the great breakthrough which was at the start of an ever faster succession of civilizations came around the year 35,000 B.C., during the so-called Aurignacian and Perigordian periods. *Homo sapiens* (Cro-Magnon man) became so proficient in his working of stone that he could fashion all sorts of tools adapted to various needs: hand-axes, choppers, chisels, burins, rasps, end-scrapers, penknife blades, arrowheads, barbed and tanged points. Modern experimenters have endeavoured to rediscover all the gestures of primitive man and to reproduce his tools. What surprised them most was the speed of such workmanship – which explains why it has survived to this day: stone is the natural tool; it is more efficient than wood, and yet it is cut just as quickly. During the Solutrean period, the carefully retouched flaking of those forms which archaeologists have called "willow leaves" or "laurel leaves" was so perfect that one must assume some aesthetic intention on the part of the artisan. But by then, man had already produced works of art.

Some twenty-five thousand years later, around 7,500 B.C., another refinement was introduced in tool-making: polishing. With the Neolithic era, prehistory was on the verge of proto-history, which opened the door to history. The Pre-Columbians made their tools from polished flint; they were still using them at the time of the Spanish conquest in the 15th century.

Man is essentially a stone carver. The art of carving stone is the oldest human gesture. Nowadays, it may be on its way out, but it has remained a challenge to genius through the ages till our own century, when carving stone will soon be as rare an activity as cutting diamond.

The polishing of stone requires sedentary workshops, and time to spare, instead of a life made up of disconnected fleeting moments, like that of Paleolithic men. This transition from discontinuity to continuity implies some feminine influence, and in fact the dawn of agricultural civilizations in the Neolithic era coincided with women playing a more important role in patriarchic societies. But the change from rough to polished stone also had deeper implications.

A Solutrean "laurel leaf" and a Neolithic hand-axe are the two starting points of future developments, and of two widely different worlds of thought. Those two artifacts contain *ab ovo* the opposition between the intellect and the senses, the object and the subject, abstract ideas and outward appearances. They remain – even in our own age which prides itself on change – the two opposite techniques available to the sculptor. Man has used the one to fashion his gods, and the other to render human expression in its variety. From the beginning, the art of relief alternated between those two techniques and Michelangelo himself took part in the controversy, from the *S. Peter Pietà* to the *Rondanini Pietà*, he seems to have gone back through the ages to the original gesture of the creator who extracts the primeval form from inertia. Contemporary Mannerists, on the contrary, liked refined smooth shapes, polished like a mirror. Their chosen material was bronze, which Michelangelo did not use: he was a genuine stone carver, having had as a foster-mother the wife of a Settignano stone-mason.

It took humanity hundreds of thousands of years to progress from carved stone to polished stone. But in the following millenia, civilization evolved much faster. In the Middle East, the life of Paleolithic hunters was succeeded by the sudden flowering of agricultural civilizations, which brought about a whole range of technical inventions. The discovery of new materials caused a greater differentiation of tools and gave the artist a marvellous field for experimenting. For instance, the use of clay for making pottery utensils. As far as we know, ceramics were introduced as early as the sixth millenium B.C., in Anatolia, on the Syro-Palestinian coast. Clay was first modelled by hand, then, after various intermediary methods, the foot-propelled pottery-wheel was invented, probably at the same time as the cart-wheel. Progress was relatively slow, if we consider that in Mesopotamia wheel-turned pottery was contemporary with the invention of bronze, i.e. with the beginning of the fourth millenium. The two techniques are linked: both derive from modelling since, to cast an object in bronze, one first needs a model made of some malleable material, then a corresponding hollow shape into which the metal alloy – composed mainly of copper and tin – will be poured. Combined with copper in the proportion of 10 to 20%, tin has three characteristics: it makes the metal more resistant, it lowers its melting point, and it increases the flexibility of the moulten material. Therefore the invention of bronze provided new possibilities for sculpture; the previous technique of hammering metal leaves to produce a *repoussé* relief suggested yet another direction for human endeavour: the goldsmith's craft and the use of precious metals; as for wrought iron, it did not provide the sculptor with plastic material until the 20th century.

Already in the fourth millennium B.C., the whole range of techniques allowing man to carve, polish or model matter were known. Whilst the technique of painting developed very slowly through the centuries, the sculptor was in possession of all the resources of his trade from the very dawn of civilization. Which goes to show that carving is the original artistic gesture.

I Prehistoric Art

For a long time, Prehistoric art was merely a controversial subject for paleontologists. It crossed the threshold into archaeology rather late, and has only recently entered the domain of art history. Even now it often arouses a largely ethnological interest.

The childhood of art has nothing to do with the art of children. Nor is it related to the gropings for form of so-called primitive societies, whose outlook and way of life have been compared with those of Paleolithic men. Nothing in prehistoric painting suggests the conventions, stylizations, and distortions used to interpret nature by primitives cut off from naturalism by a whole system of thought that they project from within onto the outside world. Nothing is more direct, more "visual," than the prehistoric artistic rendering of animals, based as it is on an acuteness of observation achieved in later history perhaps only by a few Chinese or Japanese painters, by artisans from the steppes, or by Pisanello. More noteworthy still, this naturalism is not analytical: when Paleolithic men painted bison, mammoths, or reindeer on their rocky walls, they had not studied dissected dead beasts; they had observed the living animals in action. They were able to suggest that synthesis of successive stages of movement that alone can evoke life, where a too exact reproduction kills it. Although the Limeuil "sketchbooks" and other drawings after models prove that already at that time there were specialized artists, and even schools of art, such an intimate knowledge of animals could have been acquired only through the experience of hunting. The fluid line that the artist cast from his memory onto the rockface had to be as exactly calculated as the trajectory of an assegai aimed at a vital spot on the animal. Art was at first naturalistic and figurative. For the prehistoric artist – if his magic were to work – the image had to be as close to the model as possible, to be in fact its *double*. To be sure, contemporary primitives who paint or sculpt images in which nature is distorted or caricatured also believe they have achieved this quality of the *double*; sometimes even – as has often happened in the evolution of art – the magic power seems to grow stronger as the image moves further from its model, until the depicted form becomes a mere sign wholly charged with symbolic force. Such primitivist stylization is not a primary state, however, but the result of a different outlook. It presupposes an antagonistic attitude to nature, whereas naturalism expresses a kind of mystic oneness with his world on the part of man. A Paleolithic image shows the "naiveté" of its maker's direct communion with nature – the dimly remembered origin, perhaps, of historical man's nostalgia for a golden age. The animal from which man extracted his sustenance was for him not an enemy but a partner whose strength and agility he tried to secure for himself, perhaps by eating it, certainly by depicting it. Killing the animal implied no hostility at a time when the boundaries between life and death were not clearly established. When he painted a mammoth, Paleolithic man thought he gave it life and attracted it into the trap that he depicted in front of it; he thought that by the act of painting a mare pregnant, he made it become so. Thus reproducing nature, he felt that he was creating it. Leonardo thought along similar lines; but he believed that his intelligence made him a godlike and supernatural creator; prehistoric man could not have prided himself on his creative power – he lived too closely bound to natural phenomena, and in particular to the cycle of destruction and creation that is the great mystery of life.

That Paleolithic art was first practiced deep within the earth, in caves difficult of access, may indicate a wish to penetrate the mysteries of nature. Perhaps primitive man subconsciously identified those dark recesses with the womb in which life germinated. The mystery of conception appears to have led him first to suspect the existence of powers *other* than those he could sense, for it lies at the origin of what is probably the earliest religious cult, that of fertility, which centered on the fecundity of animals before taking on a more general significance.

For us, prehistoric man is first of all a painter. So famous are the great paintings of Lascaux and Altamira, of the Niaux and Trois-Frères caves, that we tend to overlook the rock engravings and reliefs, which are no less important. Aurignacian or Magdalenian painters often used the natural irregularities of the rock face to give relief to part or to the whole of the body of the animal represented, but true sculpture is much less frequent than paintings or drawings with engraved contour. This may in part be explained by the greater length of time that relief carving demanded, for the images may have been executed in a state of magic trance in which the artist-sorcerer could grasp the essentials of reality. Furthermore, the flexible contour line was better adapted to the artist's aim of capturing the animal in motion – that is, alive – whereas relief, with its greater weight and substance, suggests inertia and repose.

Paleolithic reliefs exist, however, both carved in stone and modelled from clay. Of those cut in stone there are three types, that may represent three stages of working: the engraved outline, the relief with the background cut away from a flat silhouette, and true relief. The relief is usually roughly hewn, but occasionally it is polished. Often polished, on the other hand, are the few little statues in the round that have been discovered – fertility figures with exaggerated female sex attributes, which may possibly have been based on the biological reality of the pregnant state. The two most famous Paleolithic fertility figures are the *Venus of Willendorf* (fig. 14) and the *Venus of Lespugue* (fig. 15); they embody two artistic styles which our time has called naturalistic and abstract. The sexual attributes of the *Venus of Willendorf* are represented purely naturalistically, but those of the *Venus of Lespugue* are expressed by carefully polished geometrical volumes that could have been created by a Brancusi. The Lespugue figurine is the only instance known of abstract representation in Paleolithic art; our knowledge of the period must have great gaps.

Since polishing appears to have been practiced on stone sculptures long before it was used for stone artifacts, we may be allowed to suppose that when axes or knives began to be polished, some aesthetic intention was involved there, too. We know that already in Paleolithic times man wanted to give a pleasing appearance to everyday objects, for he decorated some of his weapons, such as hooked spear-throwers (fig. 11), and rods (of unknown use) carved from reindeer antlers. The sculptor also provided body ornaments, pendants of amulets of various materials – the earliest examples of the jeweler's craft.

In the perspective of time, prehistory appears as an episode beyond all memory, and we never wonder at the long duration of Paleolithic art, practiced with very little change for nearly three hundred centuries by a civilization of hunters. Probably those little human groups remained content for a long time with the state of equilibrium they had achieved: they lived in isolation, separate entities rather than real societies. The break came around 10,000 B.C., with the transition period called the Mesolithic, when suddenly naturalistic art tended to congeal into stylized symbols. The evolution was completed in the Neolithic era, about 7,500 B.C., when a technical civilization began to develop through the rational practice of agriculture and the domestication of animals. Excavations of cities like Jericho in Palestine, Jarmo in Kurdistan or Khirokitia in Cyprus have revealed the existence in the seventh millennium of urban civilizations based on agriculture and animal husbandry, in which, as is indicated by the scarcity of cervidae remains found in the excavations, the hunter played a very minor part. This period saw the end of small isolated groups; men became more numerous thanks to the increase in basic sustenance; they formed communities and began to develop specialized skills.

Since stores of grain were now available and animal husbandry provided permanent reserves of meat, it might have been expected that man, no longer needing to hunt for his daily food, could devote some leisure to artistic creation. In fact the opposite occurred, as if human energy, completely absorbed by the developing technical civilization, were no longer available for any other activity. Wall paintings disappeared completely, and the word "artistic" seems hardly applicable to the undecorated utensils and roughly hewn idols revealed by excavations of late and middle Neolithic strata in the fertile regions of Syria and Palestine, where that civilization seems to have first emerged. As for stone carving, apart from the manufacture of flint tools it was practiced only in making bowls and fertility idols. During that pre-ceramic period, however – before some accidental fire had suggested the invention of fired heatproof pottery – man could still model the raw clay with which he built his dwellings. A kind of reproduction of the human form in the round appears in the skulls with their features reconstituted in plaster found at Jericho (fig. 17). The custom of preserving heads must go back to 80,000 years or so; but these skulls, apparently an attempt to represent the dead, are the ancestors of Egyptian mummies. The mother-goddess idols, no doubt because of their magic intent, remained fairly close to their female model; touches of paint probably represented the various details of figure and face, which would explain why the surfaces are usually quite smooth. On the whole, however, Neolithic art was non-representational, and the earliest pottery decoration, always geometric, whether painted or engraved, seems to have issued from an impoverished imagination. As man realized that he could exercise control over nature through the use of his intellect, he separated himself from the natural world; he broke the essential unity which made him one with the universe. Nature became for him the enemy he must tame and discipline to the service of man, forcing it to clothe and feed him, while trying to propitiate through magic and religion its mysterious forces, conceived as emanating from a "beyond" and "above" hostile to humanity. Magic, which in Paleolithic times was probably born of instinct, representing a spontaneous joining in with universal forces, was now exercised in complicated rituals, meant to capture the cosmic energies. Those rituals interposed between man and the outside world, and art no longer sprang from direct visual experience; it became abstract.

The type of figure most frequently found on Neolithic sites is the markedly steatopygeous female idol. As we have seen, it had appeared in Paleolithic times too – the first incarnation of the invisible; but it was so rare that the places where the few examples extant were found make but a sparse representation on the map. Neolithic figurines, however, made of the most various materials, have been unearthed by the hundreds. Around these female images crystallized the religious sentiment of those largely matriarchal civilizations founded on the fertility of animals and of the earth. The goddess in her universal power was beneficent to the living, and safeguarded the dead. She was the ancestor of that Great Mother whose cult was to be fundamental in Eastern religions in earliest historical times and who was later to emerge as Venus, whereas the mystery of the earth's alternately dying and reviving fecundity gave rise to the myths of Isis and Osiris, of Demeter and Persephone.

It would be interesting to make a typological classification of the numerous Neolithic fertility figurines that have been found around the Mediterranean and in the Balkans. They appear standing, sitting or recumbent; some are naturalistic, but most have schematized features, the earliest primitivist stylization in art: the proportions are sometimes elongated, or conversely swollen out, the bulges of the flesh exaggerated, the heads lengthened (perhaps as a phallic symbol), or the waist compressed to set off the expanding volumes of hips and breasts. In a progressive civilization, such stylization may result from a tendency to simplify after endlessly repeating a particular form.

Neolithic civilization lived on through the third and second millennia B.C. in certain regions like the Cyclades, when other regions had already entered history or proto-history. The Cycladic artists who carved the beautiful Greek marble from the Island of Paros and Naxos refined and polished the sculptured shape until it retained only the most tenuous resemblance to the original human model. The violin-shaped idols, or the heads like Neolithic hand-axes are sculptures responding not to material resemblances but to a sense of the magic residing in the created form as such; hence their expression of an elevated spirituality charged with the sense of magic. The idols of the Great Goddess found in the Cyclades are so stylized that the sex attributes, elsewhere exaggerated, have completely disappeared – a development typical for the Greek genius that constantly prefered the type containing within it all the separate possibilities of a given form.

A terminal date really can not be set for the prehistoric era; "prehistory" was prolonged throughout historic times, and in fact still exists in our day, for in the strictly etymological sense, the word applies to civilizations that have no writing, and hence, no written records. There are, however, cultures having no writing that are contemporary with other, historic civilizations that have left accounts concerning them; these are usually called proto-historic cultures. For our purpose, what matters is the persistence into historical times of artistic forms originating in prehistoric civilizations. The varying creative potential offered by bronze – which proto-historic societies usually learned from outside – did not materially affect the forms inherited from Neolithic art. During the Bronze Age, a so-called megalithic civilization developed around the Mediterranean and spread to the Nordic regions; it was characterized by huge monuments of rough-cut stone, fresh proof of the importance of stone for early men. Those stones are sometimes engraved, but rarely sculptured; yet in the most remote regions tombstones have been found bearing stylized human figures, or sometimes only a few human implements – weapons or tools.

The metal age appears not to have favored relief sculptures. It produced little other than figurines, and when these are of bronze they closely resemble those of the later Iron Age, contemporary with the historic civilizations developing in more favored regions. The little bronzes are sometimes figurative, but more usually stylized, often showing an elongation of proportions probably resulting from the requirements of primitive casting techniques. Clay statuettes follow the same pattern; their shape is coarse and childish, showing a regression in artistic invention.

In the steppes of Central Asia, groups of shepherds and hunters practicing only the most limited kind of agriculture continued the close association with animals that had characterized Paleolithic life. Since they led a nomadic existence, always moving on to find new pastures for their herds, the only artistic activities open to them were those involving portable objects: weaving or jewelcraft. Their gold jewels or ornaments for harnesses and saddlery mostly show animals, not realistically like the art of the Paleolithic hunters, but strongly stylized. Those small objects usually represent the animals locked in combat, their forms interlaced in a dynamic unity.

We glimpse the zoomorphic style halfway on its route to the West in a work like the Gundestrup cauldron (figs. 32–33), found in Denmark but probably produced by some Iron Age artisan from the Danube region rather than locally. The goldsmith used the *repoussé* technique to conjure out of the silver plates fixed to the cauldron a dancing ring of animals, some real, some fantastic, around the stag-horned Cervunnos, god of fertility.

In the Iron Age – sometime in the 8th century, or even as early as the end of the 9th – a people of horsemen from Southern Russia crossed the Iranian plateau and left on the slopes of the Zagros mountains megalithic tombs filled with bronze artifacts: axes, halbards, shields, quivers, jewels, harnesses, bridge bits, figurines representing men or hybrids (fig. 104) – all in a state of preservation indicating that they had never been used and were meant only as tomb furniture. This people of warriors and huntsmen was obviously under the influence of Mesopotamia. The conjunction of the fantastic style that had developed mainly in cylinder seals and of the zoomorphic steppes style engendered a multitude of imaginary forms, human and animal features combined into extraordinarily lively monsters reflecting their mystical beliefs. Transmitted by the barbarians who invaded the West, forms from this zoomorphic art followed obscure routes to reappear for the last time in Romanesque art.

After the fertile period that had produced the great Paleolithic picture book, there is in reality a dearth of large-scale artistic production. Man's creative activities again flowered in full only within a new type of society formed in historical times: the great urban civilizations that first appeared in the fertile valleys of the Tigris and Euphrates, and of the Nile rivers.

We must begin speaking of history, rather than of prehistory, at some time during the fourth millennium B.C., when what historians call the urban revolution was more or less accomplished, and men had grouped themselves together in the complex life of urban centers.

Cultural historians have not been in accord about the benefits of such urbanized existence. We may well agree with Lewis Mumford, in his *City in History*, that urban congregation engendered many of the evils that man has brought upon himself: the taste for wealth and power, and the consequent slavery, war, clash of empires and self-destruction of civilizations, by which the metropolis inevitably becomes the necropolis. But even if the Neolithic village were as idyllic as Mumford imagines, we cannot evaluate its art in terms of its style of life: aesthetic values cannot be measured by moral standards. Others, like Stryzgowsky, have voiced the (romantic) notion that city and empire crushed the well-springs of true artistic inspiration, which he felt coursed free and clear among nomad populations. Their simple and very little specialized way of life allowed – so he thought – full rein to imagination and intuition, whereas artists serving prince and priest in the great Mediterranean empires could produce only academic, formal work in obedience to their masters' tastes.

However, unless one is prepared to set a higher value on a Neolithic figurine or Ostragoth belt buckle than on the temple of Luxor, it is rejecting reality to deny that the first urban civilizations in the valleys of the Tigris and Euphrates and of the Nile favored the development of the arts. The organized and specialized life provided stability, continuity, wealth and leisure enough to make the prolonged development and enrichment of human thought and sensibility possible. The complex relationships engendered by urban association, and particularly by those two centers of city life, the temple and the palace, were the source of a whole matrix of ideas translatable into images; they also – a matter of some importance – provided a wide range of commissions, which encouraged diversified art forms.

It has been argued whether Sumer or Egypt first saw the dawn of true history, and which was the superior civilization. Opinions on the latter question depend on the historian's *parti pris*, but as to the first, the literal anteriority is most often conceded to Mesopotamia. In the Euphrates valley there existed during the fourth millennium a quite superior prehistoric (Neolithic) culture whose typical artistic products were the al'Ubaid clay figurines with curiously reptilian heads (fig. 34). Such spontaneously conceived and quickly manufactured terra-cotta creations continued to be produced throughout the evolution of Mesopotamian art in response to popular requirements. Prehistoric Mesopotamian civilization reached far afield: in the Indus valley, for example, centers of an advanced culture related to Mesopotamia were excavated at Mohenjo-daro and Harappa. The works of art found there are on a technical level far above a beginning awkwardness, though they are so few that we must assume the towns came to a violent end accompanied by thorough plundering. Upon Egypt, too, some daemonic wind seems to have blown from Asia, for in the beginning of Egyptian art we find examples of the fantastic ornamental animal style that flourished from earliest times on Mesopotamian seals.

At all times the development of sculpture in Mesopotamia was conditioned by the scarcity of stone in that land of alluvial plains. A gypseous alabaster, easy to carve, was to be found in many localities, but steatite and hard stone like diorite, dolerite, or granite had to be brought from the mountains. For executing his works the sculptor depended on flint tools, even after the introduction of bronze: chisels, and also drills for making surface ornaments, or for making holes intended to be widened later with a burin, were all of flint. Bronze was little employed in sculpture, and then only for figurines; in the large statue of Queen Napir-asu (fig. 55) we can see the artist hesitantly confronting a more monumental project in bronze (the figure weighs over a ton and a half). Architecture was grandiose, but elementary in form, since the scarcity of stone limited its design to what could be produced in sun-dried clay; palaces and temples bore few decorations and these were seldom of stone. The sculptor's most important market, from the beginning of the third millennium, was for statues of gods and ex-votos of various kinds.

During the third and second millennia, rough shapes were gradually replaced by more carefully finished objects which at the end of the evolution became somewhat mannered. The oldest statues worthy of the name are the group of alabaster worshippers and gods excavated from the Abu temple at Tell Asmar, who look as if conjured out of another world (fig. 39). Roughly hewn into cubist shapes, with gigantic inlaid eyes, they are probably the first manifestation of the belief in the magic power of the eye – a belief still alive nowadays in Italy as the fear of the "evil eye." During the second half of the third millennium, the empires of Akkad and Sumer brought to an end the civilization of the city-states, and art grew closer to nature; but the Neo-Sumerians created the most striking works in early Mesopotamia. There, for the first time in history, we can connect a style with the initiative of one man. In Lagash, a *patesi*, or local governor, had his portrait as a worshipper sculpted over thirty times in hard steatite. A feeling of concentrated strength emanates from these muscular, thick-set figures (fig. 48). The exaggerated ankles and wrists, the set jaws, and the hard forehead, show a stubborn refusal to communicate with or to accept the outside world – a refusal that also explains the inability of the artists to create that society of images: a composition. In these first attempts at monumental sculpture, the artist explores the basic forms under the individual features: the head is egg-shaped, the body a squared block of stone. Contemporary female figures are somewhat more human: one, wearing a horned headdress – the usual attribute of a goddess – displays a hint of a smile (fig. 51). Later, this austerity softened to the point of sensuality in representing nudes. The cult of the stele inspired an art that prolonged the Neolithic period: Hammurabi had the 285 laws of his code engraved on what is in fact a menhir (fig. 53).

Before the Assyrians, Mesopotamian sculptors conceived only isolated forms; we find no interest in compositions relating forms to each other, except on the cylinder-seals, where the artist's imagination was allowed an unusual freedom (fig. 44); we are tempted to consider these tiny works as the "major art" of the period. The reliefs are roughly carved, with characters lined up or juxtaposed in a confused manner instead of being linked by common action. This inability to connect forms is all the more surprising in that, during the fifth and fourth millennia, the pottery makers of Samarra and Susa had evolved an ornament using formal innovations worthy of Romanesque art.

The recent heightened admiration for Sumerian art has been determined in some ways by our contemporary preoccupations. On the one hand the taste for abstract and non-naturalistic art directs our appreciation to an art whose forms do not try to mirror natural forms; on the other hand, our disenchantment with the rule of reason, and the growing dominion of psychoanalytic notions prompt us to seek in man's art an explanation of what is obscure in man himself. The renewed prestige of the word "sacred" and of the idea of magic incite us to look for hidden truths in forms that, because they do not imitate the visible, appear to reflect the invisible. Herein also originates our sympathy with Mesopotamian religion, which is somber and abstruse as compared, for example, to the Egyptian – the first religion to introduce the idea of salvation. Our confusions and fears themselves may attract us to the civilizations of the Tigris and Euphrates valley, which witnessed so many bloody struggles and the collapse of so many empires, rather than to the peaceable kingdom of the Nile, whose art we may even blame for having followed so uninterrupted a course for so many centuries. Mesopotamian civilization seems to have suffered not only as a result of frequent irruptions of violence and the successions of peoples and rulers, but also from some inhibition. Haunted by thoughts of ever-present, inimical other-worldly forces, and by a conception of the afterlife as a miserable dark place where the soul could only vegetate, it could find no aim for life other than mere existence itself. Its art seems in the final analysis to have lacked the vitality and the rich all-inclusiveness that have characterized the arts of some other civilizations.

When we turn instead to Egypt, and if we look with an unprejudiced eye, Egyptian art must appear by contrast as far more truly precocious, richer, and certainly more sustained than the art of Mesopotamian cities and empires. In Egypt, art was first given that essential place in the human scheme of things that it maintained throughout the ebb and flow of later civilizations. By giving full scope to the creation of images, Egypt initiated the Western artistic tradition, while Mesopotamia, more haunted by the invisible than attracted by the visible, was the source of the Asiatic tradition.

The Egyptians were free from any terror of a dark world of shades, for they imagined an afterlife that was a replica of the world they knew; life simply resumed in eternity. For the Mesopotamians the world beyond was a cursed place, ruled by infernal powers; for the Egyptians, it was made up of the happiest moments of real life. To art the Egyptians assigned the task of recreating these moments truthfully, of assembling about the tomb, in enduring form, a faithful catalogue of the multiple good things and ways of earthly existence, confident that by magic translation into eternity they would be enjoyed by the dead forever in the afterlife. Hence, though almost all the Egyptian art that we know, from the earlier times at least, is funerary art, it impresses us with a spirit of cheerfulness and love for creation. Art will probably never again be endowed with such power: victory over death. Such a belief in the ability to recreate the world by simply reproducing its appearance had already moved Paleolithic artists. It implies a proud optimism, a faith in the efficacy of human actions, a self-confidence contrasting with the pessimism of the Mesopotamians, though the latter progressed further in science than the Egyptians, who were content with a pragmatic, empirical approach. The privilege of eternal life was at first the prerogative of the god-king, then of the courtiers whom he chose to take with him into the afterlife to look after him; and finally the Osirian faith extended immortality to all men, however humble – the first form of democracy in antiquity, though respecting only the afterlife, to be sure.

The nature of the ruler also differentiated the two civilizations. The inhabitants of the Nile valley believed themselves favored by a divine power; divinity was in fact present among them in the shape of their god-king. In Mesopotamia, the ruler was a mere man, a terrified intermediary between men and god.

Egyptian art is first of all the art of the sculptor. Stone was the most lasting material and therefore was used most, and preferably hard stone, even though it had to be extracted from the desert a long way from the Nile: diorite, basalt, porphyry, black granite, green and yellow breccia were fetched to the valley at great cost. Those near-precious materials were later exported by the Romans and by the Byzantines, until the Arab conquest of Egypt caused the quarries to be closed. Limestone, alabaster, sandstone and pink granite were found in the Nile valley itself. Wood was sometimes used, and became more frequent when the Osirian religion was extended to all, necessitating the manufacture of cheap funerary material in large quantity for the poor. The prestige of stone, dating back to the Neolithic period, was such that even the tools used to work hard stone were made of stone; later the Egyptians also used bronze implements, but they never learned to make strong tools out of iron. The skilled techniques of stone carving were transmitted from workshop to workshop throughout millennia. Apprentices had to copy models; models and copies have been kept to this day by the dry Egyptian soil which preserves all (fig. 78). Excavation of the workshop of the sculptor Tuthmosis, who lived in the Amarna period, has shown that to prepare for his portraits the artist took plaster molds of the faces of the living or dead model.

Egyptian art is primarily a mural art. There may even be some connection – although links are missing here and there – with Saharan rock engravings and paintings. Large relief panels actually appeared later than sculpture in the round, but the tenets of the Egyptian relief style appear already in a work of the Thinite period: the stele of the Serpent King (fig. 59). With its clever use of a frame, its firm silhouettes, its accurate modelling, this work achieves a fine equilibrium between realism and formal harmony. Mural art uses mainly profiles; it is born from the spectacle of the passing reality. Each form borrowed from perceived reality is not, however, registered as it is seen, but recomposed in the same spirit of synthesis as that shown by Paleolithic painters. The way the human figure appears in Egyptian reliefs demonstrates the wish, based on the requirements of magic, to represent the whole of a man, that is to say, a man in his ontological rather than optical truth: face and legs in profile, hips in three-quarter view, upper torso in front view, and also the eye, magnified as if to mirror the soul. What is most surprising is that the general effect does not shock us; the power of art makes us accept it as natural. In sculpture in the round, too, that principle of frontality, for which Egyptian art has been criticized as static, has a deeper meaning. The statue, facing the onlooker, motionless, goes beyond the immediate moment and tends to the eternal. The being confronting us may be Kephren or Amenhotep, but before all else he is the pharaoh, to whom Kephren or Amenhotep lends his features. The stark confrontation of statue and spectator is intended to present, not to represent, the concept of a being in his self-defining integrity – like the creator god Aton-Ra, "all in himself."

In our era of formalism and abstraction, Egyptian art has also been criticized as too realistic. But it rarely becomes naturalistic, except during the final decadence, or perhaps in the Amarna period; even then, when we look at the masks of actual Egyptian faces excavated from the workshop of Tuthmosis (fig. 72), we are surprised to find that they look so unlike the Egyptians depicted in a so-called realistic art.

Egyptian art, based on observation but bent towards an ideal, is the expression of a humanism born of a feeling of perfect harmony between god and man, between man and nature, between the visible and the invisible, between the present world and the world beyond. That humanism was strong enough to endure for millennia, miraculously surviving two periods of upheaval and invasion. Never has man held for so long to the conviction of living in an order without fault.

All human actions, all creatures of nature are sanctified in that sin-free world. If those hunted animals, those birds caught in nets, that cat watching young fledglings terrified by its approach – if all these creatures seem so alive, it is because the artist who created them was in deep sympathy with all living things. Even the "mystic naturalism" of the Christian Middle Ages did not express itself in such a pure outpouring of love for all creation. Looking at those hunting or fishing reliefs, we seem to witness "the adorable awakening of an April morning when the world was young" (to quote Christiane Desroches-Noblecourt). It is indeed a paradisiacal vision. All is new-made and pure in Egyptian art: each being, hunter or hunted, is pictured in his integrity, not mixed with his opposite, and therefore shown as ideal, without any accidental deformations. There is no worm within the fruit, no tree of good and evil.

Egyptian art gave a substantial place to women. A charming figure with supple gestures and firm, delicate breasts, woman is everywhere, princess, or slave fetching the geese from the marshes; indeed, the slave is sometimes more a woman – her compensation, for the princess must be dignified rather than natural. In this respect, the Egyptians surpass the Greeks; the latter deified female beauty and made of woman an erotic object; the Egyptians gave her a feminine soul. The chaste and graceful silhouettes remind us of the courtly ladies in Gothic illuminated manuscripts, or of quattrocento nudes, before Venice had rediscovered the weight of Eros in the female body. Egyptian art often represents woman as a wife or mother, sharing the life of man. In Mesopotamia she was allowed to appear only as a goddess; it was exclusively the female principle that was honored, that is, the power of fertility.

An unchanging conservatism has mistakenly been attributed to Egyptian art. It did preserve certain principles linked with religious beliefs, during its long life, but in fact it evolved much more than Mesopotamian art. The restless political state of the country of the two rivers gives a false impression of change, whereas the Egyptian empire, because it lasted so long, seems to have been immutable. But we tend to forget the progressively accelerated rhythm in which human evolution is measured: first in slices of a hundred thousand years, then of ten thousand years, then, on the eve of historic times, of one thousand years; only during the first millennium B.C., around the 7th and 6th centuries, does the century become the unit. Admittedly, at that time when other arts were evolving in the Mediterranean and in the Near East, Egyptian art was an empty survival; but it can hardly be considered stereotyped in its early and middle periods. The art-historical division into three "Kingdoms" in fact corresponds to the evolution of three broadly different styles. The austere, realistic style of the Old Kingdom characterized a period of discovery. During the Middle Kingdom, the pathetic realism of the South coexisted with a soft, graceful, noble style in the North. During the New Kingdom, traditon was brutally interrupted by the aesthetic revolution accompanying the religious reform of Akhenaten (Amenhotep IV), probably the first time in history that a sovereign left so personal a mark on the art of his time. The heretic pharaoh must have realized that to shake off the dominion of the priests of Amon, he must also destroy the artistic rules they dictated. The individual emerged from the limitations of the type. Even the pharaoh and his circle at Amarna were pictured as a middle-class family united by links of human affection; their physical characteristics were exaggerated, obviously as a protest against the archetypal canon which had been imposed until then. Akhenaten's aesthetic revolution was short-lived, but when Egyptian art returned to its tradition, some traces of the Amarna style remained: a heightened awareness of ordinary mankind, more feminine influence, more refined furniture and useful objects, and a taste for small statues.

In Ramessid times, to protect itself against invasion Egypt had to conquer others; as its horizons were enlarged it acquired a taste for luxury and a greatly expanded commerce with other peoples. But under those alien influences, academism began to affect Egyptian art. Statues became lifeless, and the hastily completed reliefs, although adding new warlike themes to traditional iconography, became conventionally decorative. In the Saite period, during the 7th and 6th centuries B.C., artists tried to halt that decadence; they gave a renewed and exaggerated impact to statuary by strong modelling of the heads and by the use of the hardest materials; but the Egyptian spirit seems irredeemably lost.

Next to the historical civilizations that flourished in the Near and Middle East between the fourth and second millennia B.C., there are others that remain more mysterious to us owing to the lack of written documents. In Crete for instance, only the latest script (Linear B) has yet been deciphered, and that recently; it was found to be an archaic Greek language, a fact which perhaps caused more surprise than it should have, since at the time the script was employed (1450–1400 B.C.) Knossos was ruled by Achaeans from the Greek mainland. There is little to be expected from the decipherment of tablets or stamp seals from previous periods, for like those in Linear B, they will no doubt prove to be only inventories, account books, or lists of civil servants. The cultures that succeeded each other on Minos's island seem to have differed greatly from the highly verbal civilizations of Mesopotamia and Egypt, where a feeling for history appeared concurrently with the development of cities and the worship of priests and rulers. Cities existed in Crete too, ruled over by kings surrounded by feudal lords, but no ruler is known to us individually; they are all confused under the name of Minos, whom the Greeks made into the King of Hades. These kings had a few soldiers who seem to have been required because of rivalries between towns; but Cretan art never reproduces the act of killing. Though extensive, the ruins at Knossos, Phaistos or Mallia do not prove the existence of a complex urbanized society: these palaces must have sheltered a culture very similar to that of the larger Neolithic villages, one based on agriculture and supplemented by resources from the sea. Those men seemed to sense not at all the tragic unrolling of time, the succession of lives and deaths that make up the warp of history. They seem to have evaded it by the cyclic conception of time characteristic of primitive agricultural civilizations, conceiving a world perpetually reborn, as is nature herself through the seasons. In contrast, man in the Middle East was haunted by a linear projection of time (which the Bible inherited and transformed into an instrument of terror) while the Egyptians, although they lived in history and made it, avoided the fear of mortality by imagining a duplication of time from life to afterlife.

Aegean art prolonged the prehistoric unconcern for monumental sculpture; it was content with small objects that, unlike the works from the Euphrates or the Nile valleys, do not obsess man with their presence. Cult objects were reduced to a few abstract symbols – the double axe, the sacred horns, the figure-eight-shaped shield, the sacred tree and the column (the last, an emblem of stability originating in baetylic stones), objects used simply as a focus for cosmic energy, and far less frightening than the personified gods of the Mesopotamia or Egypt, where man set up gods who turned against him and tyrannized over him. There is nothing of that kind in Crete; the most individualized deity is the snake-goddess (fig. 88), a charming incarnation of the Mother Goddess and the first benevolent aspect of that divinity conceived by men. Her worship was pleasant: priestesses with full, flounced skirts and bared breasts indulged in sacred dances while the men invited nature to procreate by processions and joyous songs. Acrobats, men or women, leaping over a bull, played a part in some mimed drama whose meaning is unknown to us.

The small objects found in Crete are beautifully shaped and polished. Their liveliness and perfection of form suggests a conception of life as one moment indefinitely repeated and free from the stigma of mortality. A feeling for monumental relief sculpture always seems to have been linked with a feeling for history, men wishing to leave on this earth lasting records of their existence, either on their own scale or on a superhuman scale – works that would act as man's double and immortalize him in enduring stone. These "imperishable monuments," these proud colossi cannot fool us; they were born of the greatest fear of all: the fear of death. Their huge mass weighs on human memory and leaves no escape from historical destiny; only the first man was free from that fear, and his freedom seemed such a wonderful privilege to those following that they called it the Golden Age. Archaic Cretan culture prolonged that Golden Age into historic times. Minoan beliefs in supernatural powers who tormented humans were very shadowy, as we can see from the fragility and small size of the cult figurines, which can be held in one hand. That people living from the export of bronze chose brittle clay for their own artistic creations, shows their entire lack of interest in transmitting to the future their own historical moment. The Cretans lived in a world of "being" rather than "becoming" – a state of grace witnessed by the charming statuettes of women, exquisite, elegant objects; by the stamp-seals on whose tiny stone field they engraved the forms of familiar animals, while contemporary Mesopotamian artists were indulging in monstrous evocations. Aegean representations of humans and animals are not, like those of the Egyptians, the result of close observation, but rather of an instinctive feeling for natural life on the part of an insouciant people, little given to metaphysical or historical speculation, seeing the world as a huge network of exchanges from which man benefited.

Divinity was incarnated in a woman, which seems to have given the keynote of that peaceful civilization and endowed its art with elegance. But as soon as figures of warriors were introduced from the mainland, everything collapsed. The idols with raised arms (fig. 89) created in the late Minoan period (1400–1200), when the island was invaded by the Mycenaeans, are a striking example of how a conquered nation's art may suddenly regress from the sophisticated to the popular. The sap has suddenly run dry; the mind proceeds through addition instead of synthesis, and the artist's hand, that skillful hand that had given life to so many graceful figurines, becomes a coarse and awkward instrument. To be sure, Minoan artists from the period of Mycenaean rule carved the ivory plaque excavated at Ugarit in Phoenicia, depicting a fertility goddess flanked by rampant goats (fig. 91); but even this charming little relief appears like a slightly confused and coarse redaction of the elegant works of the earlier Minoans. The art of the conquerors fed on the remnants of enslaved Minoan art; the most remarkable work of Mycenaean art on the mainland is the Lion Gate (fig. 90) at the main entrance to the citadel of Mycenae, where two lions, now headless, face each other on either side of a column, a cult symbol inherited from the Cretans.

About 2,000 B.C., at the end of the Bronze Age, a people of Indo-European origin – and therefore unconnected with the races previously inhabiting the region – invaded Anatolia in northern Asia Minor. Their art of small earthenware or bronze objects resembled that of other metal age cultures, until the later second millennium B.C., when these Hittites, as they are called, built grandiose structures which they ornamented with numerous reliefs. Soft limestone was available and they used it to form the lower course of their sun-dried brick buildings; the interiors were then faced with great sculptured reliefs representing gigantic figures, animals or hunting scenes. Those decorations, conceived in a somewhat clumsy, hieratic style, are of little artistic value; but they are interesting from a historical point of view since they were later imitated by the Assyrians. To their Hittite enemies, whom they finally conquered, the Assyrians owe also the paired lions or bulls set on either side of palace gates, and also their understanding of the art of fortification, which the Hittites had developed to a high level.

In the rival kingdoms that fought over Mesopotamia before the 9th century, the most important monuments were consecrated to the gods. An art devoted to the glorification of a sovereign, a true court art, waited for the unifying strength of an empire – Assyria, which for three centuries dominated the Middle East. The Assyrian king created the prototype of the autocrat, and to a greater of lesser extent, the various forms of imperialism that were to appear later in the Mediterranean and in the west were modelled on the Assyrian autocrat, around whose deeds and ceremonies everything gravitated. Even art was at his service – a new development. The kings of Egypt have left us only the dwelling places they built for their afterlife; their terrestrial homes were built of short-lived materials and did not last, but the kings of Assyria had a passion for grandiose palaces; each of them built at least one, and sometimes several, in each of the important towns of his empire. They inherited that habit from their predecessors, the despots who had ruled over the valley of the two rivers. These kings, although they claimed divine descent, were not god-kings like the pharaohs. In Egypt the divine king was the beneficent channel through which the forces nature reached the country and caused the work of men to bear fruit. The Assyrian king was a different kind of being – not god, but superman. His supremacy and his power over other mortals were expressed through strength. To reign, he had to be feared, and cruelty was for him a means of government as well as self-assertion; on cruelty were based his politics, his ethics, and his very survival. The texts discovered by excavators confirm the Biblical maledictions against those despots, who never tired of repeating how their hearts rejoiced over burned cities, massacred or deported populations (fig. 100), tortured enemies, and hecatombs of prisoners. During the three centuries of Assyrian rule, Mesopotamia and its surroundings lived in a perpetual bloodbath. The instrument of power was the army; therefore, the glorification of the hero-king in art took the form of representations of the battles in which he vanquished his enemies, the tortures that followed victory, and finally, the wild-beast hunts with which, in time of peace (that is, a period between wars), the king sustained his instincts for violence, the source of his regal power. Throughout the ages, from despot to despot, that royal iconography has been perpetuated: Louis XIV of France was a great hunter, and even the learned Hadrian went lion-hunting in Africa, conforming to the imperial ritual. But in Egypt scenes of war of hunting are found only in the era of decadence under the Ramessides, when Egypt burst its frontiers and gave way to the temptation of power for its own sake.

The kings of Assyria lived in immense, maze-like palaces. The main halls were decorated with low reliefs in a manner learned from the Hittites, and in a soft gypseous alabaster that facilitated the manufacture of those endless scenes depicting the mighty lord's ceremonies, wars and hunts, in which the despot himself is depicted as larger than other men, and isolated by his own impassive cruelty. From the moment the visitor crossed the threshold, he was subdued to the proper frame of mind by the awesome doorkeeping genii between whom he must pass, and who were designed to "maintain fear in the king's subjects, and so please his heart." Hybrids of man, lion, eagle and bull (fig. 98), these beings combined the attributes of strength based on instinct and on intelligence. Provided with five legs so as to look complete either full face or in profile, they demonstrate a lack of three-dimensional vision on the part of

Assyrian artists, who almost ignored sculpture in the round; and in fact, only very few Assyrian statues have been found. The exclusive use of profile is suitable for a narrative art showing passing forms in an ever-renewed action that knows no other cessation than in death. This art of the silhouette is interested only in gesture, showing men as well as animals in the midst of physical action. The animals are more lively, for they are free from the hieratic impassivity of the king, in whom only an awareness of the necessity of cruelty is expressed; no human faces have ever looked more inhuman, and even death leaves them untouched.

Needless to say, women are absent from these war-exalting themes with their exclusive virility, something quite alien to Egyptian art, whose repeated depictions of the divine royal couple evoke the ideally human in its two opposite incarnations. Classical Greek art emerges from its fierce primitivism with the kore's smile; and at all times art has become more fully human when representations of woman as man's companion are introduced, bringing man to a better understanding of his inner self – man who, left to himself, extraverted, always tries to be superman.

The awareness of surrounding space, which some Egyptian art attempted and which was to be the greatest achievement of Greek art, is totally lacking in Assyrian art. The characters are lines of puppets, each acting separately, not even linked with his neighbor in battle scenes, where one might expect an exchange of at least negative passions between two men trying to kill each other. When they attempted to depart from the usual alignment of successive forms, and to suggest depth, Assyrian artists could only superpose the forms in an inextricable muddle on the surface.

Minor arts confirm this inability to achieve unity, which I have already proposed as one of the characteristics of the demonomaniac ethics and aesthetics of civilizations that lived in perpetual fear of occult menace; for demonomaniac acts are essentially a disruption, something that separates while God is unity. Form is here defined by a heavy outline with jerky accents, the hard contours imprisoning the human essence. In those flattened reliefs, the ripple of muscles expressing violence in action is shown by sudden bulges on the surface (fig. 97), often with a harsh outline that seems to imprison this energy at the very moment of its release. We find for the first time in Assyrian art a stereotyped quality, which is one of the characteristics that have been called archaistic or primitive, but which has nothing to do with the art of the first men; it appears, rather, in derivative civilizations born of conflicting influences and trying to free themselves for a new start: in Greek art in the 6th century, for example, or in Romanesque art, or in the Buddhist art of the Chinese caves. The aesthetic created by Assyrian art combines stiffness of modelling with hieraticism, and was to emerge later as the true Asiatic tradition, which cast a gradual paralysis over the heritage of classical antiquity, to create what we call Byzantine art.

Before the creation of the Achaemenid empire, the Iranian plateau knew the art of two different peoples. One consisted of nomadic groups, whom some historians believe to have been the Cimmerians, and who settled along the Assyrian border, in Luristan, at the end of the 9th century. Although they had adopted a sedentary life, these horsemen and shepherds continued to make only small metal objects, mainly horse gear and chariot parts – a portable "minor" art practiced by migratory steppe nomads. In these pieces Mesopotamian mythology appears mingled with the indigenous nomad tradition, and new forms full of symbolic meaning proliferated in the Luristan bronzes. When first discovered, these works aroused interest because of their resemblance to Romanesque art. The recently discovered zoomorphic objects of Medean prehistory, however, seem far more likely to have contributed to Achaemenid art. Their soft, supple modelling is the very opposite of the harsh abrupt contours of Assyrian bas-reliefs. But from the Assyrians, Achaemenid emperors borrowed the basic tenets of the court art devoted to the greater glory of the ruler that ornamented their great palaces in Iran. This glory was no longer based on war: the Achaemenids had gone beyond the primitive stage of power based on force and exhalted a power based on justice exerted through the state – a civilizing instrument whose main representative was the King. The religion of the Medes and Persians was based on a sky-god and the first to isolate the metaphysical essence of divinity; religious rites were elevated by the prohibition of the sacrifice and of the soma-induced shamanist trance, leaving only the cult of fire. In their conception, two opposite principles were fighting over the universe, and the good would inevitably win. A new dawn was coming in an Asia so long crushed by fear; Mazdaism's leavening optimism was to be fully developed when Christianity, influenced by classical antiquity, separated it from Judaism, where it remained mixed with a fearfulness inherited from Babylonia.

A superficial comparison of the bas-reliefs at Achaemenid Persepolis with those at Assyrian Khorsabad might suggest only similarities in those endlessly aligned figures; in fact, all is different, beginning with the buildings themselves. Persepolis was not a fortress like the royal buildings at Nineveh or Assur, but an open palace, a symbol of the union of many peoples within the empire. At the end of the processional roads that led to the palace was a royal audience hall in which the monarch might show himself to his subjects. The iconography of the sculptured reliefs no longer celebrates the despot's cruelty in war, but his power, acknowledged by his subjects, to maintain peace. The processions depicted at Persepolis represent the New Year festivals during which high dignitaries, governors and provincial delegations came from all parts of the Persian empire to bring their offerings to the King of Kings. Outwardly, the same conventions exist as in Assyrian art: an endless repetition of attitudes and gestures, a monotony even more marked because the personages are not in action (fig. 110).

But the meaning is different. Those lined-up forms are still autonomous, but they are no longer separate; the spaces between them have become intervals, and there is a feeling of rhythm. All the forms are linked by a harmonious alternation of solids and voids; the series has become a sequence. The faces are set, but their rigidity is ceremonial dignity and not fierce impassivity. The modelling is softened and polished and the outlines make up a harmonious abstract design, with supple movements suggesting the existence of living forms.

It is very likely that the Achaemenids looked for models, and perhaps even for artists, in Ionian Greece, over which they ruled for a while, for Greek influence seems to soften the harsh forms borrowed from the Assyrians. Synthesizing the two influences, Persian art seems to testify to a sudden conversion of the Asiatic spirit from darkness to light.

III Greek and Roman Sculpture

1. *Greece*

"The world of classical Greece is dying before our eyes today. What neither invasion, nor the infiltration of Christian barbarians, nor the underhand intrigues of the coarse monks of the Thebaid, nor even time, that tireless destroyer, could achieve, is now accomplished under our very eyes by the ephemeral triumph of a few political demagogues." Thus in 1905 Péguy lamented the gradual disappearance of Greek from the curriculum of the French schools. Nowadays classical studies are almost everywhere a thing of the past; relinquished even by the Roman Catholic church, Latin is joining Greek in the sepulcher of discarded languages. But the spirit of Greece is not dead; it still has what Péguy called a "living existence," having survived the demise of Homer's language to extend its message in another form: art. As the world becomes more internationalized this nonverbal form for the communication of ideas is more and more appreciated; its prophetic value (in the etymological sense of the word prophet, that is, "spokesman") has nourished in modern culture a new interest in the past. Greece has never known greater prestige than she now enjoys through her art. Classicism, which she initiated, is the only aesthetic form to have survived the new barbarian invasions; in the name of primitive fetishes Raphael was dismissed, but not Phidias; and even Gauguin, in a passage often misunderstood because quoted only in part, paid homage to Greek art while trying to escape from its influence.

Our understanding of Rome will suffer more from the disappearance of her language, because the visual arts were but a secondary aspect of her genius. No amount of familiarity with Roman art can replace the knowledge of Latin, from which all European languages are more or less descended. The reality of Rome lies in the *Aeneid*, the *Commentaries*, or the *Pandects*, not in the Ara Pacis or the Pantheon; but Greece speaks to us through the Parthenon as much as through Sophocles.

The Greeks themselves thought differently: despite the admiration they accorded to their greatest artists they believed that the Gods made themselves heard through the voices of poets. To Greece we owe the preeminent place occupied by literature for so many centuries, and the corollary

that the language of the visual arts was for so long relegated to an inferior position as a technical or mechanical skill. The Greeks in this respect did themselves an injustice: thought, in their culture, expressed itself through visible forms as much as through words. Incarnating the absolute in the simplest kind of human ideal, their art assumed the value of a principle which, despite an occasional eclipse, has remained a constant in western culture and still rules us today, inspiring even those such as Picasso who seem most to transgress it.

The Greek ideal expressed itself best in sculpture. Under the Greek sun sculptural form reached a perfection never attained again, and one more complete than we can now know, since the color that originally enhanced the significance of the form has vanished. Writers on Greek art have evaded this matter of polychrome architecture and sculpture – as though Greek art were somehow tainted by the sin of realism (symbolized by the story of the Aphrodite of Knidos whose original colors were so lifelike, it is said, that she provoked an indecent assault); as though the truth of art had been sinned against by the very men who made it; and as though its beauty owed more to the work of time than to that of its creators. Describing a multi-colored Parthenon, the French Hellenist Raymond Picard termed it "baroque." It is hard to see why color should make a work baroque rather than classical – unless our vision has become biased by the time-stripped white statues that we know. Under the word baroque seems to lurk some pejorative allusion to a polychrome Spanish sculpture. But can we imagine the sublime spiritual images of Martines Montanez filed down, reduced to the original wooden core and deprived of the intense liveliness of color which gives them such radiance? The statues of the great Seville artist, though painted, represent one of the summits of classicism. The Greeks went as far as the Spaniards in their illusionism, and even made draped and articulated dummies with sculptured hands, feet, and heads – the acroliths, very similar to the *estatuas de vestir* carried through the streets of Seville during Holy Week.

If we pause to think, we will realize that the Greeks could not have done otherwise than to conceive their monuments in color. The many comments concerning the famous Greek light that "sculptures forms" come from philosophers, professors, or writers, who have transferred to Greek skies their own notions (preconceived in academic studios) of an abstract light that appeared to them a necessary corollary of the rationalism they attributed to Atticism. But the Greeks – it is too often forgotten – were a sea people. Who thinks of their light as a scalpel fit only for cutting out volumes has never seen it shining over the Greek sea, searching out each wavelet and transforming the waters into shimmering jewels. It would be surprising had the Greeks, a visual people, not been struck by the colorful intensity allied to the plastic values of their sea, which so little resembles the Atlantic's grey and misty fluidity. We must imagine in their full glory of color those temples now naked and scalped by the light; instead of the wind-corroded skeleton on Cape Sounion, picture a temple whose glow answered the liquid fire washing the promontory's foot. Far from detracting from the form, such polychromy must have enhanced it. The Parthenon's "gaudy colors" must have underlined the relationships between the various parts of the structure and exalted the life in space of its statues. The Parthenon today is probably as "absurd" as the nave of Amiens cathedral, where a cold light dissects an interior that its builders had intended to throb with the mysterious life still given Chartres by its stained-glass windows. In the history of art, periods in which architects did not use color are more the exception than the rule. But of Greek color, as of Greek painting, nothing is left; vase painting, with the stylizations proper to it, is likely to give us only mistaken or limited notions of Greek color. A whole aspect of Greek art has been lost forever, and we can only surmise that the Greeks were able to achieve a fitting synthesis of all the arts. Of that synthesis only *membra disjecta* are left, and when we study Greek sculpture we are constrained to a study of modelled volumes without the enrichment of the lifelike colors in which the artists had conceived them.

In the course of time polychromy was actually used less and less in sculpture, and it appears to have been largely abandoned in the later periods. The simplified masses of the pediment sculptures at Olympia depended upon color for secondary accents in the modelling; but already in the Parthenon, the forms are self-sufficient without the colors that once heightened their effect. In the 4th century the chromatic range became less bright, the hues less arbitrary and nearer to the refined nuances with which painters were then experimenting.

To understand the sculpture of Greece as it really was, we must not only reclothe the statues and buildings in lively colors, we must also attempt to reconstruct in imagination certain works for which the Greeks reserved their highest praises, the enormous cryselephantine Athena Parthenos or the Zeus of Olympia, both by Phidias (figs. 155, 156). The historian's mind has boggled at the attempt: apart from the fact that it may appear naive to have tried to represent the gods' greatness by gigantic statues, the use of goldsmithery on such a scale has offended admirers of Greek art as an incomprehensible lapse into barbarism. To the dim interiors of the temples these idols, for such they were, contributed the shining hues of their precious materials, of gold and ivory richly worked, of jewels. Yet their expressiveness was not sacrificed to the goldsmith's craft: the air of sovereign benignity that graced the head of the Zeus at Olympia, and which was so admired by those who saw it, can still be guessed at in the head from Cyrene which, experts tell us, most nearly resembles Phidias' conception of the god (fig. 157).

Perhaps what most inhibits our understanding of Greek statuary is the fact that so much of it is known only in copies. What could we understand of Michelangelo's art if all we knew of it were the Montorsoli copies, or imitations by even less gifted artists? The degradation suffered by Greek works is symbolized in this book by the juxtaposition the Erechtheion karyatids with a Roman copy from Hadrian's time and a 19th century restoration by Thorwaldsen! (Figs. 159–163.) In a way we are better acquainted with Egyptian or Mesopotamian art than with Greek, for there, it is the original that we study. The study of most Greek sculpture proceeds by a system of induction that attempts to work its way back through bastardized imitations – and even through literary descriptions – to the original forms. It is as if the historian trying to grasp the principles of Gothic sculpture had as his only material the 19th-century statues designed by Viollet-le-Duc and executed by Geoffroy-Dechaume for Notre Dame in Paris. However, we are not quite that badly off, for the principles embodied in Greek masterpieces were such that some trace of them survives even in vulgarized derivations. In fact, we seem to meet here with the Platonic concept that the truth of a form, be it in art or in nature, is not in its physical appearance, but in the idea that gave it birth. However lifelike a Greek statue may have been – and the marvel of Greek sculpture resided in the unity between nature and ideal – its supreme message was an abstract idea; that idea is what we search for, under the more or less coarse mold of matter in which it is now cast.

It is our great good fortune that, by the miracle of the Parthenon's preservation, we are able to apprehend the major achievement of Greek art not just through literary memories but in the tangible reality of a related body of architecture and sculpture. The course leading up to the Parthenon can also be mapped out with relative clarity, for archaic works did not particularly attract the antiquarian-minded collector, and many have been unearthed in their original locations. In the 4th century we become more uncertain; in the Hellenistic period increasingly so. It is here that the approach to Greek art becomes a kind of intellectual game, or creation of the imagination. Using the rare surviving texts as clues, we must interpret a crowd of copies and imitations left by the Roman empire. Their insipidity would soon discourage us if we did not each time make the effort to work our way back to the underlying principle, to the idea – which would have delighted Plato – to ensure our remaining within the *order* of things.

There is a gap in time between the last manifestations of Mycenaean art and the first of Greek; all attempts to fill it have been unconvincing. With a perfectionism no doubt inherited from his Greek origins, Christian Zervos has written a beautiful book entitled *The Birth of Greek Civilization*, but all the works which he has gathered in evidence around the Mediterranean area appear to represent endings, rather than beginnings. The notion that Greek art must perforce have resulted from a slow process of maturation originates on the prevailing conception that all history is one continuous evolution – a conception refuted by history itself. There was, in fact, a "Greek miracle," just as there was a Romanesque and a Gothic miracle. In the beginning of the 8th century, all around the Mediterranean, in Ionia as in southern Italy, in the Aegean as on the Greek mainland, forces were germinating which within one century would give birth to Greek civilization. It is as useless to seek explanations of that phenomenon as to try to settle just why, around 1100, some sculptor created the Miègeville portal (and with it a Romanesque style) at St. Sernin in Toulouse.

Can we agree with those who consider the smile worn by the first Greek statues a result of the sculptors' ineptness? That "heiroglyph of felicity" blooms on the stone faces as though welling up from an irresistible vital impulse; it animates even the dying warriors (fig. 138) from the Aegina temple pediments. It fades, then, in the first half of the 5th century, when the great trial of the Persian wars led the Greeks to a deeper awareness of their own forms of thought and life, and to an art of profounder import, both civic and theological – the art of Perikles and Phidias.

In the 6th century, Greek art became conscious of its own aims. Its great discovery was the statue as an autonomous organism and – what might seem contradictory – its adaptation to another organism of which it became an integral part: the monument. In Egypt and Mesopotamia sculpture in the round had made only a timid appearance, and the depicted human still clung to a supporting wall; or when he did stand free, he remained as rigid as the wall or as the block from which he had been carved. When, in Greece, shortly before 500 B.C., the statue won a mobility resembling that of its model, it was a parallel to the contemporary philosophers' concern with conciousness of self. From this time on a human being was to be a form inscribed in space; not just an outline, but a solid form occupying all three dimensions. This figure has neither back nor front, is not even to be viewed "from all sides," which would imply that it had "sides," but is self-defined as a unity of mass, volume, and direction organized within its own limits; this figure in the round is the first affirmation of humanity reduced to itself, stripped of any admixture of the divine or demoniac. The man knows himself to be other than the gods, to stand facing them not in a spirit of pride but in a spirit of acceptance of the fate willed by the gods – who in any case differ from humans only in their aboundingness, which in humans would be excess, *hubris*, and the road to perdition.

The sculptors did not arrive at their new conception of the free-standing statue through representations of the gods: they experimented first in their renderings of humans. For a long time, in fact, the cult statue of the god or goddess retained its fetish-like form of a *xoana* or baetylic stone, inherited from the original tree or rock, possessing the more mana for its indeterminacy of form. Even in marble the cult image still resembled the menhir-statue of early worship, or the column-statue reminiscent of the divine pillar held sacred by the Cretans and Mycenaeans. The Hera from Samos in the Louvre (fig. 127) has kept her columnar form, but she is an incarnation in metamorphosis: a blossoming human form issues from the stone, with voluptuous breasts and curving loins. When the idol finally assumed human form at the beginning of the 5th century B.C., it borrowed from the representations of the *kouroi* and *korai*, ideal youth and maiden figures representing mortals who wished their statues placed near a temple to attract the favor of the god. In these male and female figures the Greek sculptors defined the two poles of humanity, in whose dialectical opposition resides the life principle. The Greek mainland, more imbued with the Doric spirit, created the virile type, while Ionia is responsible for the feminine type. The Ionian influence entered Greece proper after 500 B.C., when the Greeks of Asia fled the advance of the Persians, and the confluence of Doric and Ionic styles produced Atticism. Until the 4th century the female statue remained clothed, the sculptors delighting in the study of drapery moving over the feminine forms, which are more salient than those of the male body. The male was represented nude, and allowed the sculptors to express that "corporeality" which is an essential element of Greek art. It is of interest to reflect in this connection on the development during the 7th and 6th centuries of the scientific spirit: science was no longer a technique by which men propitiated natural forces, but a search for pure knowledge; the sorcerer became a scientist; the magus became a philosopher. Such a development supposes that the thinking being defined first himself, then turned his attention to the surrounding world. It was the greatest revolution in human thinking since the technical leap forward of the Neolithic period, though operating in an inverse sense: the continuity linking all things and all beings – including man – was broken; nature became the object and each of its manifestations a phenomenon, hence observable. Reality was whatever was *tangible*; all things had a body, however minute, bounded by limits. At least that was so until Plato saw those appearances as a mirage and looked for reality beyond them. Even Pythagoras, although he conceived the universe as a sequence of mathematical relations, did not go beyond the bounds of that spirit of exact science. Plato carried it over into metaphysics; Aristotle was to bring the world back into the realm of the senses.

The aims of Greek art after the 6th century were very close to those of science: to discover the outward appearances of nature by reproducing them. Art, which had subsisted through centuries in a spirit of serene majesty, suddenly became alive with the rhythm of progress. Nature was best studied in her masterpiece, man: "Although there are many marvels in this world," Sophocles says in *Antigone*, "the greatest marvel of all is man."

It appears that pre-Hellenic art had so little to offer the early Greek sculptors that they turned to Egypt for the models for their first statues; but right away the undifferentiated mass of the Egyptian body was filled with muscular strength, compact at first, later sinuous and elegant. After form, movement had to be mastered. If painting showed the way, Myron's bronze *Diskobolos* (fig. 142) represented a decisive step: for the first time a complex set of movements was converted by analysis and synthesis into a shape molded in space, of which it takes possession in every dimension. That twisted shape has neither profile nor full-face, nor three-quarter view; it is modelling

in the round. Soon after, Polykleitos, in a spirit of aristocratic idealism perhaps inspired by Pythagorean theories, returned to the principle of frontality, and incorporated in his figures an ideal system of proportions. The Greeks' conquest of the individual form was always tempered by the search for the universal and typical; art, like science, must aim at general principles. The classicism that the Greeks first defined is badly understood in our time; we tend to forget that it rested essentially on naturalism, but a naturalism reaching for a truth deeper than that of the momentary and individual. It was the One that the Greeks sought in the unique; through men, they sought Man.

The speculative tendency, made possible by the individualism of a society in which subjects had become citizens, freed the artist from all kinds of limitations. From an obscure artisan destined to oblivion the artist is· transformed into a creator, promoted to glory. Alongside the name of prince or magistrate the work of art now bore that of its author. On many an akropolis the vicissitudes of history have left us pedestals no longer bearing their statues, but proudly signed, so that we are sure of the names of certain sculptors famous in ancient writings, like Kanachos or Pythagoras, whose works have disappeared.

From this time the artist had an important part to play in the city-state. Phidias acted as a sort of Minister of Fine Arts to Perikles, who shared his downfall when he was accused – wrongly it seems – of having embezzled part of the ivory intended for the statue of Athena Promachos. Lysippos, a favorite of Alexander, whom he probably accompanied to Asia, was the first court artist. Religious commissions no longer constrained the artist to observe certain rules; on the contrary, he was expected to invent, through his inspired genius, the forms most likely to incarnate divinity, or the feelings and passions of the human soul. Exercising his art, the sculptor was free to indulge in personal philosophy: Polykleitos conceived his *Doryphoros* (fig. 145) to satisfy an aesthetic ideal (and incidentally sold the statue for a high price). The artist began to suffer from the torments of creation: the 4th-century sculptor Apollodoros, nicknamed the Madman, was never satisfied with his own works and destroyed them as soon as he had finished them.

But the autonomy acquired by the statue did not lead to a declaration of complete independence. Freedom did not mean liberalism in those city-states where the government was mostly in the hands of the citizens. The statue, having achieved its individual existence, had yet to conform to the superior order imposed by a monument, the very heart of the city: the temple. The

6th-century Greek sculptor adapted his unit of sculpture to the architectural framework by the dynamism of line (as Romanesque artists were to do); the 5th-century sculptor (like the Gothic) by the balance of masses. Preserved almost intact, but deprived of their sculptures, the temples at Paestum demonstrate the essential importance of statuary in Greek architecture. The temples are like geometrical designs, too harshly outlined in space and refusing to relate to their surroundings. Although most of the Parthenon sculpture is no longer *in situ*, our imagination can bring together the scattered remnants and reconstruct a vision of the monumental synthesis in which structure and human forms enhanced each other in the expression of a civic and sacred ideal.

Before Greek art, the Mesopotamians, like the Egyptians, had been content with spreading their sculptures on flat surfaces with no other preoccupation than to pay tribute to a courtly or sacred hierarchy, or to relate a realistic narrative. Only the Persians, as we have seen, tried to introduce some rhythm in those endless processions – but that was under Hellenic influence. The Greeks gave rhythm to their buildings by the use of relief decorations at chosen points: the metope is inscribed on the entablature like a prosodic form, scanned by the triglyphs as if by caesurae. The frieze, in form probably originating in Ionia, might be descended from the Hittite or Assyrian processional reliefs, but the order of the figures is ruled by a definite rhythm, less strict than the regular alternation of triglyph and metope and as varied as life itself. During the 5th and 4th centuries the Greeks learned to link the forms in their friezes by rhythmic patterns of gesture underlined by drapery, and by the lines of action deployed in battle scenes. In the pediments crowning the structure appeared before the worshippers some epiphany of the gods, in vivid colors that the Mediterranean sun must have endowed with the metaphysical radiance of Byzantine mosaics. Although they look like very high reliefs, the classical pediment scenes are made up of groups of statues. Pediment figures had remained attached to the backgrounds in the archaic period, but in the 5th century they were carved in the round and simply set into the pediment.

The integration of the sculptures in the design of a monument may have been first achieved by the Italian Antenor, in a temple built at Delphi by the Alkmaeonidae, exiles from Athens. The pedimental groups from the temple at Aphaea at Aegina, sculptured in the first years of the 5th century, must have been arranged with a somewhat contrived rigidity, judging from the difficulties the Munich curators have experienced in attempting to discover their original order (fig. 138);

but the figures from the pediments of the temple of Zeus at Olympia more readily take their places in the reconstitutions of the pediments. In these figures from Olympia (figs. 134–137) is expressed for the first time an equilibrium between the divine and the human, though Apollo and Zeus on their respective pediments are still set apart by a shade of Olympian hauteur, something that melts away in the more humanistic harmony on the Parthenon, twenty years later.

All these compositions incorporate one of the fundamental laws of classicism: each form in its physical unity is autonomous, but it is associated by action or by an idea to the whole and is essential to its unity. In principle this reflects a democratic society in which public order was based on respect for individual freedom.

Games, in which individuals competed and submitted to the judgment of their equals, were one of the most fruitful factors of Greek life. Both the body and the mind took part: athletes performed on the palestra, men of letters wrote for the theater. The palestra provided the sculptor with models for the study of male nudes, but the theater offered a much wider field of experience. At first showing men acting in subservience to the will of the gods, Greek drama gradually turned to the study of human passions and, with Euripides, to problems of conscience. On the stage the sculptor could observe bodies moved by feeling and appreciate the plastic resources of drapery underlining and magnifying gestures and attitudes; there, too, could be seen movement of the dramatic theme, the train of episodes unfolding one upon the other, in a form that might offer inspiration for the composition of friezes.

When considering remote periods, the historian ought not allow himself to give undue importance to such monuments as have chanced to survive in imposing or complete form. To understand the 5th century we must look at the Parthenon in its contemporary perspective as the canonical expression, in some way, of the cult of the city. From it we may derive the notion that Olympian serenity dominated 5th century art to the exclusion of all else. However, already in the 5th century both sculptors and painters were attracted by the rendering of passionate life. It quivers in the vibrant bodies of the Nereids from Xanthos, molded by their wind-whipped draperies. Paionios of Mende boldly represented Nike in rustling draperies, lifted off the ground (fig. 170); the maker of the *Diskobolos* also sculptured a runner poised on tiptoe. The 5th century did not worship Apollo, Athena and Zeus alone: Dionysiac revels inspired Kallimachos' dancing maidens, whose forms are unfortunately known to us only through the numerous maenads reproduced for Roman amateurs (fig. 168;) their drapery expresses the exaltation filling their bodies, represented on the edge of trance, when ecstacy verges on orgy. The Nike adjusting her sandal from the temple of Athena Nike (fig. 169), whose body seems to throb in passage from action to rest, also belongs to an art which tries to fill the marble with life. Draped, rather than nude bodies, allowed these artists to explore new realms of feeling. The expressive resources of draperies are endless: in the above examples they show us the stir of movement; elsewhere they give a feeling of stability, as in Erechtheion karyatids, those descendants of the Cretan pillar-gods, who watch over the ancient relic of Kekrops.

Already in the 5th century many artists were inspired by the pathos of death and suffering. During the first half of the century, Pythagoras of Rhegion carved a lame Philoktetes. The theme of the wounded figure, collapsing, begging for his life from his attacker, or dying with a last cry, also tempted artists of this period. A competition organized by the city of Ephesos for a statue of a wounded Amazon brought together in competition Phidias, Kresilas, and Polykleitos, who emerged victor. We have some notion what the Amazons of Polykleitos and Phidias looked like; as for that of Kresilas, Pliny gives high praise to a *vulneratus deficiens* by his hand.

It is only through learned guesswork, progressing by induction and hypothesis through the enormous mass of marbles left to us by the Romans, that we can imagine what those original works were like. We rarely have an original to give us a direct contact with that art in all its truth. The remnants of a *Battle of Centaurs and Lapiths* and of a *Battle of Greeks and Amazons* from the temple of Apollo Epikurios at Bassae (fig. 173) show us how the choreographed contests of the west pediment at Olympia or the pediments from Aegina were transformed into an outburst of violence, a wild tussle. The despairing gesture of the woman with outflung arms will express centuries later the sorrow of Magdalen at the foot of the Cross. The fierceness of the Bassae frieze suggests some Peloponnesian influence, differentiating it from the Attic style in which everything, even death, is graceful.

In the 4th century, the Mausoleum at Halikarnassos, on the coast of Asia Minor, was as famous as the Parthenon had been in the 5th and was one of the Seven Wonders of the ancient world. Designed by Mausolus, a Graeco-oriental prince of Karia, and completed after his death in 353, by his wife and sister Artemisia, the gigantic tomb returns us to an atmosphere of Asiatic megalomania. It survived intact until 1452, when the Knights of St. John demolished it and incorporated its sculptures into a barricade against the Turks. The best preserved statue, which probably represents a member of the prince's family, if not the prince himself, gives an impression of oriental sensuality and weighty majesty (figs. 174, 175). To carve the decoration, some of the most famous artists of the time were called upon: Satyros, Timotheos, Bryaxis, Skopas and Leochares; specialists have vainly tried to distinguish their individual hands in the various surviving fragments of sculpture. The most expressive elements are from friezes representing the battles between Greeks and Amazons and between Centaurs and Lapiths, and a chariot race. They are scenes of violence, but executed with a harmonious restraint that suggests a fairly conventional official teamwork in which individual talents were subdued. Their elegant classicism expressed the ideals of an artistic school that has left us other typical examples, like the reliefs on the columns of the temple of Artemis at Ephesos, and the two sarcophagi from the Sidon necropolis: the *Sarcophagus of the Mourning Women* (fig. 191) and the so-called *Alexander Sarcophagus* (fig. 193). The latter is one of the most refined works of that century and the only Greek sculpture which has kept its original polychrome – intact when discovered, but now fading in the light of Istanbul Museum.

Although fragmentary, the mutilated remnants of the temple of Athena Alea at Tegea, rebuilt about 340 with Skopas as sculptor and architect, are much more eloquent. The pediment figures representing the Hunt of the Kalydonian Boar and the Battle of Kaikos express a strange melancholy, which may overcome a warrior in the midst of action, giving a languid look to his deepset eyes and pushing his head back in a pathetic attitude (fig. 176).

The 4th century was a great age for Greek sculpture, and its most remarkable achievements are to be found in statuary. Pliny attributed to Lysippos alone – who admittedly lived unusually long – over fifteen hundred statues. But unlike the previous century, the 4th was not a period of innovation; no 4th-century statue is as revolutionary as the *Diskobolos*. In the age of Alexander the most progressive art, the one which invented new forms, seems to have been painting. The 5th-century sculptors had discovered the beauty of man's body and the majesty of the gods; those of the 4th century instilled into their statues the breath of divinity, or of human passions.

The art of Praxiteles was for a long time considered a sort of genre sculpture, somewhat scandalous and possibly profane, if not outright sacrilegious. Charles Picard, however, has insistently pointed to the presence of a spirituality derived from Platonic philosophy in Praxiteles' figures. Several of them, closely linked with the sculptor's relationship to the courtesan Phryne, directly embodied the Platonic mystique of love. For the first time we are aware of an autobiographical element influencing artistic creation. Phryne inspired the Eros of Thespiai (fig. 180), the first example of a full-scale statue of the god of love; and the semi-nude figure of Aphrodite as a graceful, still-chaste young girl (known in a copy called the Aphrodite of Arles, fig. 181), is Phryne herself, for she served as a model for that sculpture, as well as for the later Knidian Aphrodite (fig. 182). The latter was conceived under the influence of Asia, where Praxiteles went about 365 to fulfill commissions in Kos and Knidos. It has been as much misinterpreted as Bernini's St. Teresa. Picard reminds us that, far from being sacrilegious, its senuousness was a poem to the divine beauty, incarnate in living and breathing flesh. Praxiteles' contemporaries believed that the goddess herself had inspired this "magically transcendent power of nudity," which caused in those who saw her, so an ancient author tells us, that shuddering sense of having looked upon something sacred.

After his return from Asia, Praxiteles was never again inspired by Aphrodite in the same way. But he expressed under other forms his new philosophy of the divine, based not in Olympian majesty but in the idea of a breath of life communicated from soul to soul. That breath could animate either the frenzy of Dionysios or the wisdom of Apollo, each beneficent in its way; or it could permeate even more subtly the form of Hermes bearing the infant Dionysios at Olympia (fig. 184), symbolizing the soul saved by pity, for the infant whom the messenger of the gods has rescued from the fury of Hera is to become a living pledge for the salvation of the human soul.

Though Skopas sometimes measured himself against Praxiteles, as when he sculptured the statue of Pothos, an incarnation of languid amorousness, he was mainly inspired by the pathos of life. The threat of death makes the athlete's strength meaningless and the hero is he who overcomes pain and death by the strength of his spirit. Doomed to be unhappy, persecuted by the gods he defied, transfigured by love and death, Meleager was a fitting hero for Skopas, who illustrated his legend at Tegea, and also portrayed him in a statue of which the melancholy head of the Ares Ludovisi seems a fairly faithful echo (fig. 178). We can also recognize the Skopasian pathos in the terror of death gripping the figures in a *Massacre of Niobe's Children*, known from a copy now in the Uffizi.

Lysippos was something of a universal genius,

comparable to Titian, and like him exceptionally long-lived. His art included all the tendencies of his age. Accomplished in the technique of bronze work, he explored all human passions, but since he moved in the circle of Alexander the Great, he devoted himself especially to the exaltation of virile heroism, of predestined genius. Some congenital weakness, as though from a surfeit of soulfulness, casts a pall over those over-elegant athletes with their elongated, counterpoised bodies. The arching of the back that expresses langour in Praxiteles' statues now seems a nervous reaction caused by profound lassitude. Even Herakles, whose hypertrophied muscles sag when at rest, seems to meditate on the vanity of his many labors (fig. 187). The interplay of curve on counter-curve makes the statue's contours vibrate and dissolve into the surrounding space. Such "impressionistic" sculpture was probably influenced by contemporary painting. Imitating originals by Leochares, the Diana of the Louvre and the famous Apollo Belvedere (fig. 189) are further examples of silhouettes more pictorial than sculptural; they were probably designed as garden decorations, for the Asiatic fashion of domesticating nature around the house had already reached Greece in the 4th century. The Skopasian type of head has reverberations also in the cult statue of Demeter from Knidos (British Museum), one of the rare 4th century originals. It is often attributed to Leochares and sometimes to Skopas himself. The tragic mother expresses through her eyes all the pathos of the loss of her beloved daughter. The elevation of human sorrow into a divine passion, that secret of the classical Greek genius, was rediscovered later by the sculptors of a few Pietàs.

Because of its preoccupation with emotion the 4th century was a great period for portraits of all kinds: portraits – either real or commemorative – of famous men, heroic effigies, character studies. The sculptors of that age immortalized the features of Aristotle, Plato, Socrates, Thucydides, Euripides, and Sappho. To Leochares, and even more to Lysippos (fig. 186), Alexander's image was the type of the man of destiny, the tragic hero whose various moods found their way into statues of many gods and semi-gods. Moist eyes, accentuated eyebrows, foreheads creased with worry, hair like a lion's mane or a tempestuous sea – such are the elements derived from that superhuman physiognomy. Artists such as Silanion, Apollodoros "the Madman," and Demetrios of Alopeke, who was called the Maker of Men, specialized in portraits. Their naturalism went so far that their imitators of the Hellenistic period could go no further. Silanion's bronze statue of the boxer Satyros of Elis with his battered face, or the wrinkled head of an old woman in the British Museum, whose original has been attributed to Demetrios, show how far those artists went in their search for characteristic features and individual marks left by life, age and trade.

In a general view of the history of sculpture, considering mainly the evolution of style, we might very well pass over most of the large Hellenistic production. If we strip from the Louvre's *Victory of Samothrace* (fig. 205) the prestige of its discovery and of its heroic mutilation, what meaningful addition does it make to Paionios' Nike or to the Nereids of Xanthos? Such a judgment would be unfair to the *Venus de Milo* (figs. 203, 204). The sculptors of the Hellenistic period were haunted by the memory of the Aphrodite of Knidos. Exercising their hands in all manner of artificial variations on the symbolic theme of the ritual bath, they succeeded only in debasing the divinity of the goddess a little more each time – not surprisingly, since they worked in a period when scepticism was already undermining belief. But the *Venus de Milo* has kept some of the magic virtue of the inimitable model, though her carnal magnificence reveals the influence of Asia, where the female attributes always tended to take on something of the generosity of the ancient agrarian fertility idol.

It was in fact in Asia that the great plastic discoveries of the 5th and 4th centuries were to be followed by true innovations. The Greek mainland sculptors inherited the formulae created by Praxiteles and Lysippos and maintained by their imitators. The most original manner in Greece proper at that time was a Neo-Atticism that looked backwards to pre-classical forms, probably in the hope of shaking off the yoke of classicism. (Later, in a similar way, the Nazarenes and the Pre-Raphaelites attempted to free themselves from an idealistic tradition gone stale by seeking inspiration in the Early, rather than in the High, Renaissance. In all cases the result was the substitution for one kind of academism of another still more sterile.)

The main contribution of the Hellenistic period was a broadening of the scope of sculpture, which, probably influenced by the more progressive art of painting, increased its range of expression. Sculptors no longer attempted to cast reality in the mold of ideal beauty, but explored the manifold individual aspects of nature. They developed an interest in the various forms and malformations of life, in exotic races and half-breeds, in dwarfs, cripples, clowns, beggars, and morons, in the signs of age and illness. Ignoring nothing that made part of the experience of life, they explored nature's unpleasant manifestations, but also

enjoyed the naive smile of a child, or the modesty of a graceful young girl. This aging world seemed to feel the need for extremes: man in his prime – the favored subject of the classical period – was no longer enough to give a feeling of life, which was sought in the child and in the aged, and in the marks of time and temperament on the human form.

With their passion for the human form as the product of the experience of life, at a time when many philosophers were investigating the human soul and wondering about its fate, Hellenistic artists multiplied individual effigies. The 3rd century completed the gallery of famous men, poets, orators and philosophers begun in the previous century. Whether imagined or taken from living models, these faces always radiate awareness, and old age ennobles without destroying their features. The rendering of character was practiced in portraits of the Diadochi, Alexander's successors. For a while, the portraitists were dominated by the Skopasian images of Alexander: the head with its ruffled hair and deep-sunk eyes leaning slightly towards the shoulder in a heroic movement. But it was not long before it seemed that the prince was best flattered by being represented just as he was, even ugly – that is, as a unique individual. Through their portraits of the Diadochi the artists explored the whole human soul and all its moods and passions. They represented all the qualities befitting a prince: warlike audacity, indomitable energy, the instinct to dominate, an unshakable self-confidence, perspicacity, scorn, stubborn will, self-control. But they also detected the human faults: hypocrisy, deceitfulness, soldierly brutality, lack of restraint, heavy sensuality, and even cruelty. The Greeks had more psychological penetration than the Romans, who may have gone further in the literal reproduction of reality, but who stopped at the gates of the soul, rendering only the more superficial aspects of character.

During the Hellenistic period sculpture invaded all of private, as well as public, life. It penetrated inside temples, palaces, squares, porticoes, libraries, and gardens. It even entered the more modest households in the shape of those terracotta statuettes, intended not for cult purposes but for domestic enjoyment, that were mass-produced from molds at Tanagra in Boeotia, at Myrina near Smyrna, at Tarsus in Cyrenaica on the shores of the Black Sea. It was in these statuettes rather than in monumental sculpture that classical forms were prolonged for a while, though to please their customers the makers also produced many naturalistic works. These statuettes often have considerable quality and have at least one advantage over their large sculptural models:

they are intact. Sculpture also took possession of furniture, creeping over tables, candelabra, fountains. The designers of these decorative pieces showed great ingenuity, inventing forms which were to be taken up again later by the artists of the Renaissance and Baroque periods. For the decoration of gardens dramatic groups set on rock foundations became popular. They were sometimes enormous, like the *Punishment of Dirke* sculptured by two artists from Tralles at the beginning of the 1st century B.C. The composition survives (rather confusedly) in the *Farnese Bull* (fig. 216), a much-mutilated and much-restored Roman copy in the Naples Museum. The rocky pedestal and the moving figures were intended to harmonize with their natural surroundings.

The athletic ideal was profoundly altered since the earlier days when sport was an exercise practiced by the aristocracy. The perfect athlete was no longer the discus thrower or the runner, but the wrestler with overdeveloped muscles and battered face. The amateur had become a professional, and it is surprising that such a man, who was despised socially, although his achievements were admired, should at one moment in time have imposed his Herculean shape even on representations of the prince. Such an exhibition of physical strength may have been a form of compensation for a hidden awareness of weakness.

One of the most expressive statues in the late Hellenistic style is the so-called *Borghese Wrestler* signed by Aphrodisias in the 1st century. It has been identified also as a gladiator, or as a torchbearer, but the question cannot be resolved, as the arms have been restored and only their general direction is known. The figure demonstrates the transformation of the Lysippean type in action. The projection of movement has distorted the form, which is no longer well defined in space; sculpture in the round reaches its extreme, with the solidity of the body – that "corporeality" of classical Greek sculpture – dissolved in the surrounding space. The sculptor borrows his technique from the painter, and the difficulty of achieving a "pictorial" sculpture becomes an end in itself.

The dying art of sculpture tried to revive itself through dilettantism or virtuosity, but its new lease on life came from contacts with barbarian styles: from Asia in the East, and from Rome in the West.

In Mysia, in the 3rd century, a family of satraps managed to free the country from Persian oppression and to create in Pergamon an independent principality which lasted until 133 B.C., when Rome intervened. The city they built is the Hellenistic center we know best. They used local

artists to design grandiose monuments, but also called upon artists from Ionia and from Greece proper. The seat of these philhellenic princes was for a while the last stronghold of Greek civilization, successfully resisting the Galatian barbarians, Gaulish tribes from the west who filled Anatolia with terror. Proud of his victories, Attalos I (247–197) celebrated them allegorically by consecrating to Athena at the foot of the akropolis of Pergamon a *Battle of Gods and Giants* and a *Battle of Greeks and Amazons*. But he also immortalized them more directly by building in Pergamon itself, in 228, an ex-voto made up of groups representing the defeat of the Gauls. It was the beginning of an imagery of barbarians with firm moustaches and unkempt locks, around whom evolved a whole iconography of suffering (fig. 198). Those mercenaries were followed by their families, and artists revelled in the representation of death ravaging their camp. Until the end of antiquity, there were numerous reproductions of statues showing a dying Gaul dropping his horn like Roland, or killing himself after having killed his wife to save her from slavery, or a Galatian child drinking from his dying mother's breast or fondling her corpse. Did the victors realize that by celebrating the bravery of those barbarians who offered their bare chests to the bronze-clad hoplites, they confessed their secret admiration for the primitive strength of their enemies? Admiration or even pity for the vanquished suggests a troubled conscience on the part of the victors; the Assyrians or the Egyptians never knew such sentiments. But Greek philosophers had taught even the great that a man is a man and has a soul, even if he is a barbarian.

In 180 B.C. Eumenes II (196–159 B.C.) celebrated in allegory style those epic struggles against the barbarians with a large altar consecrated to Zeus and to Athena Nikephoros, occupying the akropolis at Pergamon (fig. 196, 197). A team of sculptors completed a frieze 300 feet long and 6 feet high (only about 200 feet of it survive depicting all the episodes of the fight between the gods and the giants. Returning to the Asiatic use of a high plinth, the artist placed the frieze around the base of the altar that is to say at human level and no longer in the heights of the pediment where mythical exploits had formerly been celebrated. As a result, the figures, which are actually over life-size, appear truly colossal – appropriately for a war in which opponents hurled whole islands at each other. The giants are represented with human or animal features, or they are sometimes hybrids – men with lions' heads or snakes' bodies. The coils of the snakes and hydras, the flying drapery, the beating wings, the bounding horses of Helios, the wavy strands of manes, beards and hair all contribute to the composition's medley of forms. The Battle of the Gods against the Giants, represented through centuries on vases and on monuments, had been for the Greeks a symbol of the triumph of order over chaos, of intelligence over instinct. But at Pergamon the real heroes are the giants and not the gods. The conventional faces of the latter only express a sort of non-participation: they do not share in the action. The gods are impassive, and only the giants are alive in their tragic fury, fear, and pain (fig. 200). Ge, the Earth-Mother, begging Athena to spare her children (fig. 199), is a sort of *mater dolorosa*. She herself has been mortally wounded, though, by time, which has worn her face to a horrid ruin in which only the entreating eyes are left. The giants are very much in evidence as symbolic representatives of those barbarians who were threatening the Greek world, and who were soon to be held back only by other barbarians, the Romans. Here, the meaning of the theme is reversed: the longing of a menaced frontier people for strength has resulted in the glorification of primitive violence. This attempt to go back to primeval sources is typical of declining civilizations.

The Pergamon Gigantomachy frieze offers great novelties. The bodies pressed one against the other, closely united in battle, leave no room for the rhythmic intervals that in classical friezes had introduced a feeling of measure and cadence. This is the first appearance of the compositional principle later called "baroque" of which Rubens' works are the finest realizations: unity is achieved by a movement which seizes upon all the forms and sweeps them along together. At Pergamon the mixed assembly of gods, men, and monsters becomes one confused mass in which all the elements are bound by a unity of action. The vigorous relief with its exaggerated projections and deep hollows – a whole family of swallows could nest in one of those cavities! – gives a monumental impression fitting to the subject. The general impression is one of power, but a vividly coloristic power, with strong shadows contrasting violently to the projections struck by light.

Regenerated by contact with Asia, Greek art produced this last masterpiece, and Rhodes gathered up the inheritance of Pergamon; its artists specialized in the gigantic and the pathetic. They made a Colossus that towered over their harbor – a 60-foot high bronze statue celebrating Helios, the patron god of the island. A lucky find has brought to light, in a grotto at Sperlonga on the Tyrrhenian Sea, the remnants of a group which seems to represent Ulysses' ship braving the monster Scylla. It bears the signatures of three 1st-century sculptors from Rhodes, Hagesandros,

Polydoros, and Athanadoros, known from a text by Pliny as the makers of a Laokoön group. The frightened faces of Ulysses' seamen and the tense features of Ulysses (fig. 210) are reminiscent of the Pergamon giants. The most beautiful works from the end of the Greek period were those inspired by fear, suffering, and death. Two groups, very popular later, celebrated pain: the torture of Marsyas by Apollo (fig. 201), and the sufferings of the priest Laokoön and his innocent children (figs. 208, 209), who were punished by the same Apollo, the terrible, avenging god. Here again the meaning of the themes is inverted: the compassionate interest in the sufferings of the victims poses the question of a god's injustice; it is as if man were turning against god to call him to account. But already that injustice of the Olympian gods was being challenged by religions of salvation, who took as their σωτερ a demi-god or a hero and brought hope to men's hearts. Soon a sadistic people, heir to the frailties of the Pagan gods, would find pleasure in watching in the amphitheaters the agony on the faces of martyrs who sacrificed themselves to bear witness for the Saviour-God. Through the mystery of suffering, Greek artists, following the path traced by their tragic poets, discovered how deep was the human soul.

2. From Greece to Rome through the Mediterranean

From Ionia and from the Greek peninsula Hellenic art spread throughout the Mediterranean, encountering various other cultures and combining with them. All over the area old Mediterranean Neolithic aniconic styles still held sway in Greek times, in some remote regions continuing well into the Iron Age. The other principal current circulating in the Mediterranean area was a compound of Near Eastern traditions, which had remained alive even after the decline of the civilizations that had given them birth. At first these alien currents held Greek art in check, but then the Greek spirit combined with them to create hybrid forms, and in the Hellenistic period finally triumphed over them.

The Phoenicians, because of their rapid expansion throughout the Mediterranean, might well have offered cultural competition to the Greeks had they in fact had a true culture of their own. But the Phoenicians were traders capable of practical inventions but uninterested in abstract thought of any sort. For the ornaments of their daily life and for their religious objects they borrowed styles and themes from such surrounding civilizations as the Hittite, the Assyrian, and the Egyptian (fig. 93) – all of which came at various times under their power. The Phoenicians carried the bastardized art forms they had borrowed into their westernmost colonies, and in the 5th century, in those colonies and in the mother-cities of Asia, the Hellenic influence only added to the confusion of an eclectic art. As is always the case when a lesser culture is influenced by a greater one, the forms were transmitted with some time lag; thus a 4th-century Punic mask (fig. 227) shows itself to be a barbarian adaptation of the Greek 5th-century style. The curious iron helmet with a metal mask, found at Homs, probably made for a Syrian general towards the beginning of the Christian era (fig. 229), shows that Semitic ethnic types persisted concurrently with the Greek types in the hellenized East.

Carthage carried these mingled influences wherever she settled her colonies and trade outposts: to Malta, to the Balearic Islands, to Spain. It is impossible to define the style of an idol like the female statuette from Ibiza (fig. 230) other than to say that its rich ornamentation and its imagery seem to be Phoenician characteristics of Asiatic origin. The Asiatic aspect is less apparent in a work like the votive statue of Cerro de los Santos (fig. 231), a strange hybrid in which Egyptian frontality mingles with the archaic Greek style and the rigidity of a baetylic stone. The existence of a Phoenician *koiné* accounts for formal similarities in works from opposite ends of the Mediterranean, in Cypriote and Iberian sculptures alike.

But if Iberia was open to the oriental influences transmitted by Carthage, the native art of Provence, called Celto-Ligurian, was not (fig. 232). We do not know what the Greek art of Marseilles was like, for only insignificant remains survive from the ancient Massalia, colonized by the Phocaeans. It must have been but a small island of Greek civilization in the midst of the barbarian populations whose remains, going back to the 3rd and 2nd centuries B.C., have been found on the *oppida* of Roqueperteuse and Entremont (Aix-en-Provence). Entremont, seat of the confederation of the Salyes whose fractiousness threatened the Roman province of Narbonensis and the allied Greek city of Marseilles, was overcome in 123 B.C. by the Consul Gaius Sextius Calvinus. Excavations on those *oppida* have brought to light strange sanctuaries which seem to have been consecrated to deified dead heroes, and which appear to confirm the statements made by ancient authors concerning the cult of severed heads among some Gallic tribes. Although severely damaged, the Entremont warriors are still impressive (fig. 233). At the time when the artists who carved them were working, the only Greek style likely to have influenced them was the Hellenistic art of Marseilles. The formal power of their own art must have been strong, for when touched by refined Greek

forms, the Ligurian barbarians seem to have reached back to the source, to the severe art of Greece itself at the beginning of the 5th century. However, some "severed heads" from Entremont, with half-closed eyes, show a depth of suffering reminiscent of the art of Pergamon, and unusual in barbarian sculpture (fig. 234).

What curiosities might result from the penetration of Greek morphology into the very heart of the distant barbarian lands are apparent in the head from Mšecke Žehrovice (fig. 235) which in spite of its stylizations shows striking ethnic characteristics of a kind still associated with Central Europe.

The art of the Greeks themselves, practiced outside the main Greek centers, was not free from from provincial decadence. From remote Thessalia comes the early 5th-century relief excavated at Pharsalos (fig. 130), showing two women holding flowers, carved with a flavor somewhat rustic and archaic in comparison with contemporary works made at Olympia or Athens. The art of Southern Italy displays two main tendencies: a sophisticated one, linked directly with Greece, and an indigenous one. Although contemporary with the refined Greek classicism, the latter, nourished by the old Italiote popular art, produced a final version of the fertility goddess in the extraordinary ex-votos (fig. 239) recently excavated at Capua; Capua was, to be sure, on the southern border of the Etruscan country. The more sophisticated style appears in the reliefs executed for the great temples of Sicily and for the temple of Hera at the source of the Sele river, near Paestum. It directly reflects the style of the sculpture employed on the great contemporary Greek buildings, but nonetheless has a roughness emphasized by the coarse sandstone material in which the works are carved. Marble was scarce; imported from Greece, it was rarely used, save for the nobler parts of statues, such as hands or heads.

The most unexpected developments in the Hellenistic period resulted from the transmission of the Greek ethos along the route of Alexander's army, to the borders of Iran and India. At the critical moment it brought to the Buddhist world forms adaptable to the expression of the developing oriental religious ideas. What would more properly be defined as Greek art, however, appears mainly on the coins minted by the philhellenic princes in these remote provinces of Greek culture, whose sites have yet to be systematically excavated. At Begram, forty miles from Kabul (Afghanistan), about fifty small plaster reliefs have been found, which may have been intended as models for silver or bronze sculptures (fig. 238). These do not represent a genuine provincial art, however, for their very pure Alexandrine style indicates that they were imported, or at least were molded on Hellenistic originals.

The art of Etruria has provoked controversy for the last two centuries or more. Humiliated by the long foreign domination that Italy had just shaken off, Risorgimento scholars passionately sought justifications for a nationalistic pride in their newly recreated fatherland. Therefore, they tended to view Etruscan art as an indigenous and original art, superior to that of the conquering Romans, which they regarded as derivative from it. 18th-century English and Italian scholars had in any case launched a fashion for things Etruscan that had influenced the decorative art of the time, particularly in England. However the abundant materials discovered in recent excavations oblige us to dim this roseate view of Etruscan art. All through its development it appears to have reflected Greek art, to whose stimuli it faithfully responded, though adapting Greek forms to its own peculiar needs. In the 7th century, from which mainly bronze objects and jewels have survived, Etruria followed the orientalizing style of Corinth or the geometric Attic style. Larger sculpture was rare, but also imitated the art of those sources; the strange, plump-thighed Warrior from Capestrano (fig. 240) is a personage from a Dipylon vase who has emerged from his geometric chrysalis to take on a living shape. At the end of the 6th century, Etruria adapted the Greek archaic style to suit its own dynamic tendencies, contributing a heightened nervous tension. The Etruscans favored terra cotta and bronze, both materials well suited to a creative spirit that expressed itself through movement, through the arching forms of the smiling faces, through a mannerist taste for curves (fig. 241). So alien was Greek classicism to the Etruscan spirit that the archaic style was prolonged throughout the 5th century; it was not until quite late, in the second half of the 4th century, that Etruscan art adopted the developed classical style, only to discard it after a relatively brief period; and after the Roman conquest, the Etruscans of Umbria and Tuscany continued to practice their own separate art. The surprising tufa or alabaster relief sculptures from Volterra (figs. 245, 246) are popular derivations from Hellenistic Greek art; in the scenes of violence borrowed from Greek mythology with which they decorated these funerary urns the Etruscans felt at ease. The works that they produced between the 3rd century B.C. and the 1st century A.D. are much less stiff and academic than Roman art, and in fact rather resemble in their dynamic power the sculptures of Rhodes and Pergamon, recreated in a more rustic style. The cleverness of the compositions contrasts with the no doubt consciously careless execution – the artisans, working for a provincial clientele, did not bother with "finishing," and to a certain extent the polychromy with which they covered the reliefs allowed them to be less particular. The reclining figures decorating the lids of the funerary urns show a complete disregard for the organic structure of the body – but the faces are realistic, and the heads from these urns and from the recumbent effigies on the large sarcophagi found on other sites are intensely alive (fig. 247). This realism has been acclaimed as an indigenous feature afterwards inherited by the Romans; but it can also be shown that it reflects a parallel tendency in Hellenistic art. In fact, the Etruscan effigies differ from the Roman in that they are not really individual portraits, but strongly characterized types: the youth, the adult, the old man, the young or old woman, according to the age and sex of the departed. Even the *Obesus Etrusus* is a typical representation of the big landowner, at a time when eating rather more than one's fill was a sign of opulence.

Thus Greek aesthetic values collided with forms originating in earlier Mediterranean civilizations, which mingled with, and then capitulated to Hellenism. After the beginning of the Christian era, however, those popular artistic streams springing from old Neolithic sources or from the surviving orientalizing traditions flowed into Roman art and gradually pushed it further and further away from Greek formalism. These and other currents from Roman provincial art and from the barbarian world all converged finally in a veritable flood that submerged Graeco-Roman aesthetics and cleared the way for a new beginning in the history of western art.

3. Rome

While the general assessment of Greek art has not altered much since Winckelmann published his *History of Ancient Art* (1764), for the last fifty years art historians have been making efforts to re-evaluate the art of Rome. The verdict enunciated by the author of the first systematic study of ancient art went unquestioned for over a century; in Winckelmann's opinion, Roman art only hastened the decadence of Hellenism, a decadence which for him had begun after Greek art in the 5th and, to a lesser degree, in the 4th century had achieved certain absolute values that made it inimitable and that at the same time, so he felt, made its imitation the only possible road to salvation for future art.

Vienna-school historians like Wickhoff and Riegl wanted to rehabilitate Roman art. Riegl attempted to justify that aspect of it which in the eyes of the classicists was most unjustifiable – the awkward naïveté of the late-Empire styles, in which he found a positive value as a reaction against the classicizing Graeco-Roman illusionism that no longer suited the outlook of the peoples of the empire. Wickhoff, on the other hand, defended the originality of Roman art as compared to Greek art, and attributed to it the invention of spatial illusionism and of the realism expressed in portraiture, historical reliefs, and representations of scenes from daily life. There are still prejudiced Hellenists who would deny all originality to Rome; but even if it now seems clear that the spatial illusionism of Pompeiian and Roman art was derived from Greek painting, it is nonetheless difficult to take seriously the Hellenophile who, to prove the Greek origin of realism, finds the precedent for Trajan's column on the bottom of a 6th-century Laconian cup.

More recently, critics have seen in Roman art a dual character which they attribute to a dual inspiration from two superposed cultures: Italic and Greek. But the difficulty here is to define what is "Italic" Anything that occurred on the peninsula before the advent of Rome – particularly Etruscan art, which some have described as the source of Roman art – appears to Hellenists as a more or less late and provincial extension of Greek art. This same dualism, furthermore, has been interpreted as having had a social implication in imperial times: the classicism practiced by artists of Greek origin, that is, appealed to the upper classes impregnated with Hellenic culture, and took on the authority of an official art, while the indigenous style of less sophisticated creations was aimed at a middle and lower-middle class public of merchants, soldiers, and small officials. This class became more and more important in Roman history, and under Diocletian, at the very time when naïveté invaded official art, it emerged as the dominant one. In the last few years it has been thought that the "anti-classical" style, which some art historians had seen as the indigenous "Italic" contribution, in fact originated in all the provinces of the empire, rather than at its heart.

In all parts of the Roman world, and in Rome itself, excavations show that three sculptural styles existed concurrently: one dutifully following Graeco-Roman formalism in all correctness, and often a result of direct imports from Greece or Rome; a second awkwardly imitating the Graeco-Roman; and a third standing in some contrast to the Graeco-Roman. The last manner can be found throughout the Empire, showing that the Graeco-Roman style had not penetrated everywhere; but there is no art that can be called "Celtic," or "Iberian," "Dacian," "Berber,"

"Punic," or "Germanic"; all the provinces of the Empire alike offer the complete range of primitive or naïve styles, from abstraction to mere ineptness in copying the more sophisticated style. If these works appeal to us it is not only because our taste has become attuned to such forms over the last fifty years, but also because those humble and spontaneous native artists recaptured some freshness of feeling, some breath of the spirit that had long since vanished from the formalized Hellenic art, or had, in Rome, been quashed by an automatic realism. What classicizing artist could have expressed so directly the movements of Medea's frightened children hiding under their mother's skirts (fig. 298), or the despair of the weeping German captive (fig. 299)?

While Wickhoff and Riegl were rehabilitating the art of the late Empire, the Austrian historian Strzygowski was describing the decline of Rome and the triumph of the East, whose "spiritual values," he claimed, had furnished Byzantium with the inspiration for a new style. There was, to be sure, at the time of the Empire, a provincial art in Asia Minor that perpetuated a traditional oriental hieraticism, well-exemplified in the Palmyra tomb statues (fig. 306); but it can be shown that in Byzantium itself Early Christian artists took up the Hellenistic style again (fig. 322) and prolonged it until the 7th century, whereas in contemporary Rome, flooded with barbarians, truly new aesthetic values were being explored. Indeed, the Ravenna mosaics have been considered much closer to a "late Roman" style than to a Byzantine style.

All things considered, we come closer to the truth if we evaluate the Roman Empire on the basis of what it actually was: a union of peoples linked by a political and juridical concept rather than by a culture, an agglomeration of ethnic groups who did not even use a common language (the *pars orientalis* never gave up the use of Greek even for official documents), and who present an altogether less cohesive artistic *koiné* than the Greek world, which had never known political unity. While Hellenism pursued its course and the East its tradition, Rome elaborated an official art, which the conquered barbarians in turn translated into more primitive forms.

The picture is not so simple as that, however, for in Rome itself there were artisans practicing a naïve style, and throughout the Empire traveling workshops exchanged influences with one another. We can illustrate these cross-fertilizations in the case of sarcophagi brought to Rome from the East whose style, modified by Roman artisans, was then transmitted to the western part of the Empire; or with the example of the sculptors who came to Rome from Aphrodisias in Karia at the time of Augustus, and later can be traced as far away as Tripolitania and Spain. Too great importance should not be given to the fact that so many Roman artists were of Greek origin; to deny the originality of Roman art for that reason would be like denying that Sisley was a French Impressionist simply because he came from England, or to refuse to grant an indigenous value to 16th-century French painting because many among its artists were of Italian or Flemish origin.

The existence of a Roman art cannot be denied, though it might more justly be argued that in some way there was never a true Roman style; that the Romans created an imagery for which they found suitable forms but that they lacked the artistic impulse and even, through the mouths of some of their greatest men, expressed scorn for those who gave art an important place in the City; that they wanted to be known as a people of soldiers and lawgivers, not artists; and finally, that their passionate interest in classical Greek works, for which they paid large sums, was more the result of snobbery than of real taste.

What can be considered Roman sculpture, properly speaking, was first created in the Urbs, and later spread throughout the Empire at the will of the emperors. It embodied an official imagery that, in its semi-civilian, semi-religious ceremonial and ritual representations, guaranteed the legitimacy of the Roman *potestas*, whose virtue was entirely concentrated in the person of the Emperor through the special grace that devolved upon him with the *imperium* (fig. 251). Order in the civilized world depended on the adoption of the Roman political system by lands twice conquered, once by force and a second time by the beneficent powers of the *Pax Romana*. The most famous sculptures illustrating that propagandist iconography is the group believed (though this has been questioned recently) to have ornamented the *Ara Pacis Augustae*, or Altar of Peace, probably dedicated soon after 13 B.C. by Augustus, just returned from pacifying Spain (figs. 252–254). (The various pieces of this altar, discovered over the course of four centuries, were reassembled by the Fascist government on the banks of the Tiber, where the Campus Martius once lay.) In style, the altar has been called Pergamene, at least as far as the ornamentation is concerned; but it might more accurately be described as Neo-Attic, for the Ara Pacis meant to the Romans what the Parthenon meant to the Greeks. As on the Parthenon, classical forms are at the service of political order, but the Altar of Augustus celebrates men and individuals, and not gods, or even "citizens." A natural majesty, not unduly emphasized, seems to emanate from the persons of Augustus and his followers, but the sculpture of the frieze is a

consciously programmed art in which history and allegory replace myth. The Ara Pacis expresses the fullness of a historical moment, while the Parthenon transcends history.

This official and propagandistic classicizing style was kept up in Rome and in the Roman provinces, with many transformations, until the end of the Empire. It flourished under Claudius and Titus, and even under Trajan (98–117 A.D.). (Although Trajan favored another style, he did not neglect the classicizing manner, as proved by the reliefs from his triumphal arch; these were later incorporated into Constantine's arch. The greco-phile Hadrian (117–138) gave classicism a new lease on life, and the images of his oft-sculptured favorite, Antinous (fig. 276), pushed the Greek ephebe type one step further in its evolution towards the hermaphrodite. In the late Empire, Gallienus (253–268) imposed the official style still, and even in a period officially Christian, Theodosius (378–395) adopted it.

This classicizing style in which Roman officialdom became "nobilified" might be called the style of The State Triumphant; but there was another style competing for attention, one which might be termed the style of The State Militant. The imagery of works in this style reminded the citizen that the providential Roman order could be maintained only through ceaseless fighting against the thrust of barbarian forces, which had not only to be kept in check, but also to be won over to the cause of civilization. The Roman state rested on the principle of continuous expansion and conquest; when Rome was finally placed on the defensive, it was the beginning of her end. The Roman first came in the guise of a soldier; the soldier introduced to the conquered land the lawyer, the administrator, and the colonizer; these persons organized justice, administration, and the economy. It was Trajan, soldier by trade, who created an iconography expressing the force of the militant expansion of Imperial Rome. In the triumphal column that he had set up to celebrate his victories against the Dacians, the story of his campaigns is narrated without interruption in a spiraling relief, 215 yards long, wrapped around the column (fig. 271–272). The "continuous style" in which the reliefs are carved expresses an unfaltering fighting and conquering spirit far more effectively than could any Greek battle scene, where balanced reliefs portray contests between individual combatants who are symbols rather than persons, and are connected only by the requirements of visual rhythm. On Trajan's column the organized might of the marching legions clashes with the native violence of the barbarians in a relentless melee, until the final victory of the Romans. It is a purely Roman style: a new outlook has given birth to new forms. Abandoning the illusionistic and rhythmic elements of Greek classicism, the sculptors of Trajan's column have disposed the figures in ranges one above another, as if the spectator, like the commander-in-chief, dominated the scene from a high point, viewing the various episodes of the battle unfolding in isometric projection. They did not hesitate to alter the scale of human figures in relation to each other or to elements of the settings, which are treated as mere accessories though represented with great realistic accuracy. A dynamic composition irrevocably binds the actors of this tragedy into one single action and movement. Trajan's column represents one of the greatest achievements of ancient art; in that column Rome revealed her whole personality – her will for power supported by an awareness of her civilizing influence. That grandiose spiral frieze is the best expression we shall ever see of the clash of antagonistic forces that divide men and set them at each other's throats in war, that war which Rome held necessary to the safeguarding and extension of her greatest gift to the conquered countries: peace in the state.

The originality of this realistic Roman recording is undeniable: Hellenistic realism is quite different and anecdotal in character, and it was Roman positivism which discovered the plastic equivalent for a sense of history. It has even been suggested that the artist who designed Trajan's column must have had at hand some epic Latin poem that did not survive its illustration in marble. The column itself had in any case a votive and commemorative significance deriving from the triumphal monuments erected in Rome from the Republican period on to celebrate victories, as well as in the tableaux representing battles and campaigns that inevitably formed part of the triumphal processions accorded to victorious generals on their return to Rome. The column is a *monumentum*, a memorial, in the etymological sense of the word. The artist in no way reorganized the teeming thematic material of his reliefs so that the spectator could grasp their meaning more easily, nor did he made any attempt to correct the optical diminution of the figures as they wind higher and higher up the column. In fact not before the lapse of centuries and the advent of the modern telephoto camera lense could the reliefs on Trajan's column be really seen and accorded the admiration due their great quality.

To compare Trajan's column with the Pergamon frieze highlights the profound differences between the Greek and the Roman spirit. To celebrate a historical event, the Greek immediately linked it with some mythical, heroic archetype, his imagination overarching history to bind some essential form and idea that would raise man above the specific event; the Roman, on the contrary, represented the actual man, not heroes, recognizing only the facts, struck only by the actually experienced aspects of history. Rome gave us Tacitus; Greece gave us Homer. The same impulse that made the Greek artist go beyond events also helped him to move with ease in the world of formed concepts. At Pergamon, the artistic intention was primary, and the artist of the altar organized his colossal frieze into a grandiose spectacle; but in Rome, the imagery on Trajan's column escapes the eye's grasp. What the two monuments have in common is a certain conception of composition in which the individual actors are bound together by a continuous stream of movement. It is not surprising that the Romans adopted this style of composition, later called baroque, since one of their contributions to architecture is precisely that baroque quality of moving, coloristic surfaces; we can hardly appreciate this quality now, however, as the buildings have lost nearly all their ornament of columns, moldings, and panelings of colored marble.

Trajan's column is the starting point of a style which was to evolve more and more towards a sense of the tragic. Conceived three-quarters of a century later, but on the same principle, and designed to celebrate the victories of a philosopher-emperor who hated war and yet had to wage it throughout his reign, the reliefs on the column (fig. 273) of Marcus Aurelius (161–180) bear the marks of a spiritual unease that had begun to affect both private citizens and public men in the later 2nd century. The faces of the actors in Trajan's reliefs, adhering still to a classical tradition, express very little of the impulse that moves their bodies, and their dignified look makes them appear actors in some great historical drama. On the column of Marcus Aurelius the faces of both barbarians and Romans reflect the virulence of battle the relentless mechanical force of the legions turning to ferocity, the primitive violence of the barbarians turning to fury. With their flaming beards and hair, their coarse, ravaged features, and their burning eyes, the Samatians and Germans have an aura both "demoniac and pitiful," as Charles Picard has put it. The demon urging them on is rage against their invaders; all the evils that conquest brings upon them – torture, burned villages, razed towns, mass deportations – are fully pictured here. The *Pax Romana* advanced with cataclysm and misery. The victorious army took booty, not only of gold and precious materials, but even more, of human cattle. One result of the Roman victories was an enormous increase in slavery; Caesar is said to have sold a million Gauls. Many of those slaves had to fight again, but against each other in the arena, for the amusement of their conquerors. Some deep sense of remorse regarding so many outraged human lives must have tormented the Romans, for they depicted insistently the tortures inflicted on their enemies.

To the end of the ancient world the type of the vanquished barbarian remained for sculptors the paragon of human suffering (fig. 281). It was frequently represented on Roman sarcophagi, which are among the most original creations of the declining antique world, for in them all traditions from both East and West converge. On the sarcophagi may be found an expanded mythical imagery, drawn from traditional sources by the mystery religions and carried by them everywhere. This mythical imagery dwelt on themes of the spirit, of suffering, of afterlife, of spirit and sense: hunting myths (Meleager, Hippolytus, Adonis, the hunt of the camel, lion, or deer, Bacchic myths, nuptial myths (Alcestis), myths of the underworld (Hermes, Psyche, Persephone, the Nereids), moral myths (Achilles, Hercules), pastoral scenes, and groups of philosophers (fig. 283). (Philosophers were again in fashion, probably because of the influence of Plotinus in the second half of the 3rd century, when the ideal of *homo spiritualis* won out over the ideal of a life of action). In these funerary monuments the Romans often scorned allegory and had themselves pictured engaging in some military, religious, or civilian act of public life, or the deceased was represented with his right hand linked with that of his wife. Styles used on those sarcophagi, the manufacture of which was an important luxury industry, varied from the classical to what might be called the romantic, more or less according to the subject depicted. The assemblies of philosophers are direct forerunners of the apostle groups of the 4th century. In the lion hunts and in the themes of vanquished barbarians, a more "Roman" style, with the accentuated overtone of pathos found on the reliefs of Marcus Aurelius' column, was used for turbulent compositions in which the tragic barbarian faces take on the look of martyrs. Was not the stoic philosophy of Epictetus then spreading, with its conception of man as a "martyr," that is, bearing witness to the divine through suffering?

It has been in turn affirmed and denied that portraiture was one of the original forms of Roman art. An Italic origin for portraiture cannot be claimed because Etruscan effigies, however characteristic they may be, tend to follow a rather monotonous typology. On the other hand, the rare portraits of the Republican period, such as the beautiful bronze Capitoline Brutus (fig. 250), reflect the Hellenistic manner, although the physiognomies are typically Roman. But lest excessive analysis and speculation make us lose sight of the object, it should be stated that there is indeed a Roman form of portraiture quite distinct from the Hellenistic. The Romans conceived the portrait as a physical reconstitution of a person, represented without the psychological interpretation with which the Greeks endowed their most individual effigies. The Greek portrait is a character study, but the Roman portrait is a lifelike reproduction of the sitter's every feature, so faithful that it allows the spectator to speculate for himself on the person's character, viewing its marks in the plastic material of the face. This realistic tradition had its origin in the ancestor portraits that the Romans kept in cupboards in their houses and which served them as a genealogy. They were funerary masks molded in wax or plaster on the face of the dead, using a technique invented by Lysistratos, brother of the great Lysippos, at the end of the 4th century. The ancestral portraits were carried at funerals, receiving the honor of the *laudatio funebris* along with the effigy of the deceased, and they were also taken out for certain public ceremonies. Their possession was a right reserved to noble families by the *jus imaginum maiorum*, and those who had been subject to a condemnation were deprived of their right. To have a cupboardful of portraits was a sign of nobility – hence the practice of bust portraiture (the Greek portrait consisted of the head alone, set on a herme), and also the habit of truthful representation, typical of Roman psychology according to which every man was an individual in his own right and existence. Rome was affected only later by ontological problems, and then the faces began to exhibit the inner turmoil of a spiritual life, particularly in the eyes, which, however, tended to contrast with the straightforward realism of the face. In the east, in the so-called Fayum portraits stemming from the Greek tradition, the state of the soul imprints itself in the morphology of the face (fig. 305).

Paralleling the realistic series of portraits is another type: the official effigy, depicting a person in the performance and garb of his functions, either *togatus*, or clothed with the *laurica* and the *paludamentum* (fig. 251). The women of the imperial families have their own attributes and typology (fig. 258). Certain portraits of emperors triumphant took the form of equestrian monuments, though paradoxically, the only one in that form that has reached us is the portrait of the least warlike of all emperors, Marcus Aurelius, whose equestrian statue now stands on the Capitoline, in Rome, having been spared by medieval iconoclasts under the mistaken impression that it represented Constantine (fig. 274). Recent excavations at Cartoceto, near Pesaro, have brought to light the remains of what must have been an important imperial group in gilt bronze, dating from a period prior to the Aurelian and finer in execution and finish (figs. 262, 263). It is supposed that it represents Nero and his brother Drusus III on horseback, with Livia and Agrippina.

Since the excavations of Leptis Magna we know precisely the moment in time and space when Graeco-Roman sculpture began to undergo profound alteration (figs. 277–279). Under Septimius Severus, who came from Leptis, important sculpture workshops were opened to carry out the ornament for a triumphal arch, a basilica, and a forum in that town. To execute these large projects, artists were summoned from various corners of the Empire, but mainly from the East – not surprising on the part of an emperor who hastened the decadence of Rome and its aristocracy to the profit of the provincial bourgeoisie. The sculptural decoration reflects various styles, and most important, carvings on the arch, probably made by oriental artists, show a new style in which great use is made of the drill. The result is what has been called "negative relief," since instead of modelling the relief with the chisel, and bringing it out of the background in rounded form, the background is cut away by making incisions with the drill around the forms. Modelling is achieved mechanically and loses all its three-dimensional quality, no longer appearing to vary according to its direction in space and the intensity of the light. The sharp-edged raised areas appear rather flat, and are surrounded by deep black grooves. The figures are rigid, lifeless, and hieratic, initiating that trend towards the dehumanization of the figure which accelerated over the course of the 3rd century and ends in the flat, schematic representations of the early Middle Ages. The change is already complete in the reliefs of the arch of Constantine in Rome (fig. 284), and when the Emperor wished to celebrate his triumph over Maxentius, it appears that he could find in Rome only artists capable of this coarse and rather primitive style. He incorporated into the decoration of his arch reliefs borrowed from monuments of his predecessors, Hadrian, Trajan, Marcus Aurelius, so that we can follow in that one triumphal arch the progressive "degradation" of antique sculpture. Comparing the Constantinian reliefs to those on the Porta Romana in Milan, built in 1167, Maurizio Bonicatti stated that Constantine's artists had inaugurated medieval sculpture. All suggestion of realistic illusion is banished, all rounding of form in space; figures are spread monotonously on one plane; sharply detached from the background by the edgy silhouetting produced by the drill, they lose all organic connection with the whole; the proportions of one figure to another and of the various parts among themselves are no longer governed by nature, but by principles of moral hierarchy. The break is complete with the aesthetic of Phidias and Polykleitos, who had made the harmonious human body a symbol of truth. Corporeal beauty and physical existence as such had long been deprecated as inferior to the inner life, whose secrets men now sought in mystic communities, escaping from the shapeless and hard reality that burdened them. Instead of the religions of classical paganism, which had been practiced in the full daylight that glorified the bodies of gods as well as those of men, religions of initiation, secret religions, now flourished. Christianity, not the first mystery religion, took over the secret and initiatory form, and on becoming the official religion, drew to itself the provincial styles and eastern abstraction, from which to create the principles of a new art opposed to that of paganism. The Christians destroyed the pagan idols, and broke into a thousand pieces those divine bodies which men had so much admired. In the Sperlonga grotto we can see how huge sculptures were patiently reduced to dust by fanatics of the triumphant new religion, who were determined to annihilate even the memory of those myths that had enchanted men's minds, and to impose on them new ones concerned with spiritual salvation.

IV The Twilight of Sculpture in the West: The 4th to 10th Centuries

It is the convention to date the beginning of a new era in art history with the official recognition of Christianity under Constantine in the early 4th century. Like all overprecise dates for styles and trends in art, this one may cloud the issue rather than clarifying it – or, one might better say, prove confusing by overclarifying a situation that is actually muddled. It is true that Constantinian artists produced flat and weightless forms that seem to initiate a new, anti-natural and other-worldly art. Some critics (as noted already) have even placed the beginning of the new style as early as the 3rd century in what is still a fully pagan era. On the other hand, it is equally possible to regard the art of the 4th and 5th centuries as a last – though Christian – phase of antique art, to whose borrowed forms the new religion simply gave new meanings. The togaed figures that we find on sarcophagi or in mosaics of the 4th and 5th centuries are not Roman officials, but Christ and the Apostles, new iconographic personages robed in antique clothing; and in the effort to find a worthy semblance for Christ himself, these centuries hesitated between a beardless, youthful head inspired by the Apollonian image (fig. 318), and a sterner, bearded, partriarchal head adopted from the type of Jupiter (or Dionysios or Asklepios) – an image that eventually prevailed owing to the weight of oriental and semitic influence. It was not only in dress and facial types that the new art maintained antique appearances, but also in the style. In sculpture, in fact, there seems to have been a revival of the Graeco-Roman ideal in the second half of the 4th century, after the pronounced primitivism of the figures on the arch of Constantine; this revival, contrary to what was once believed, was most vigorous at Constantinople. The first Christian emperors, having shifted the base of their empire to that city, attempted to resuscitate antique forms in the service of the new triumphal, imperial, and theological art. Something of the measure and idealism of Greece remained in Byzantine art, especially in the court art, however far it departed from naturalism, persisting even up to the 11th century, when the Byzantine style clearly contrasts with the perfervid northern Romanesque.

The turn away from the ancient concept of beauty centered on the human figure in its harmonious, natural, and coporeal form, towards an aesthetic responding to the Christian ideals of the other-worldly was by no means definitive until later. Hence it is possible to interpret 4th- and 5th-century art as either a last phase in ancient art, or a beginning, for contradictory and overlapping stylistic currents actually do present themselves (as so often in troubled times, including our own) and had, for that matter, already been present in the art of the late Empire.

This fluidity of style must be borne in mind in approaching the monuments of the early Christian era. We find, for example, the same subject – the Entry of Christ into Jerusalem – treated on two contemporary sarcophagi; but where one demonstrates the disintegration of the ancient sculptural style (fig. 319), the other shows its continuation. The latter, the sarcophagus of Junius Bassus (fig. 320), is, in fact, one of the most accomplished monuments of late antique art. The two tendencies may also appear in one and the same work: the figures on a sarcophagus from Sidamara, for example, are modelled with the chisel in true relief form, while the architecture and ornament are worked with the drill, which produced a characteristic kind of bodiless lace-work. (Cf. fig. 323.) The latter was the style of the future; the former, of the past. Some figures have a kind of hybrid look, like the statue of an official from Aphrodisias (fig. 324), whose body is adopted from the antique manner, while the head conforms to the "modern" style, like the head identified as a portrait of Eutropius (fig. 321) which is already a saintly, emaciated, El Greco type. The 4th and 5th centuries produced an abundance of sculptures, in which the admixture of styles can be studied. For St. Helena's porphyry sarcophagus (fig. 317), clearly a work of great cost, an artist was still to be found who could emulate all the classical techniques of producing three-dimensional figures, in a deliberate effort to revive the great "neo-Attic" style of the time of Augustus; but the three-dimensional figures fall out of context, as it were, for there is no rhythmic unity among the various personages, each being treated as separate, and they float on the compositional field like astronauts in weightless state, neither action nor rhythm linking them. Though the artist reached for the sculptural volumes of Graeco-Roman forms, the spirit that moved him was no longer that of antiquity, and his solid forms are not set in space, but move on a single, abstract plane. The result is paradox, for all the artist's efforts to make the forms round and solid, working as relief forms, have only resulted in a bumpy surface. Other misconceptions of the spirit of the ancient style produced ridiculous results like the statue of the Emperor Marcianus at Barletta (fig. 326), which is a sort of blown-up dummy proclaiming on gigantic scale the death of an art. On the other hand, the two pairs of emperors embracing each other on St. Mark's in Venice (fig. 314), earlier by a century than the Barletta puppet, are masterpieces of the new style in which the reduction of reality to hieraticism is worked through a deft simplification of volumes and modelling. Two slightly later but similar groups, now in the Vatican, demonstrate the lack of consistency in the style of the time, for these appear to be grotesque puppets. Both sets are now believed to have been detached from triumphal columns.

What might be called a kind of rearguard action in the retreat of ancient forms was engaged in by the artisans practicing minor arts – the gem cutters, ivory carvers, and especially, the goldsmiths. These makers of luxury objects seem to have resisted for some time the evolution taking place around them. Metal workers in particular continued to employ the old mythological motifs on repoussé silver dishes for their rich clients; and even under Theodosius, those of the Roman aristocrats who had remained faithful to the old gods had this pagan imagery embossed on their richest table vessels. In the 6th and in the 7th century, in Asia Minor and in Constantinople, mythological subjects appear as diversions for those Christian aesthetes who retained a fondness for antique culture. The art of these workers in silver and gold is extremely important, for through it was transmitted to the West a technique of working in relief, a technique that was rapidly disappearing from sculpture in stone or marble.

If we try to imagine some marble or bronze group of sculpture in the round set in the atmosphere of Hagia Sophia in Constantinople or of St. Vitale in Ravenna, we realize how incongruous it would look, like a presence from a quite different world. By this period a new spirit had so transformed architecture as to exclude relief sculpture entirely from the role of architectural ornament. The evolution towards this moment had already begun in the late Empire, for surely only a group as huge as the Farnese Bull could have made an effect in the Baths of Caracalla (where it was found) while all the other statues that clustered in that building must have been dwarfed by its gigantic voids. It is impossible to conceive reliefs enlarged to the gigantic dimensions such buildings required. The ornament proper to these late Empire buildings was the decoration of mosaics and marble paneling that provided this new kind of architecture with a colored skin. The Greek temple, with its strict volumes and plain surfaces, presented itself in space with distinct dimensions, as a real presence, and called for relief sculpture to enrich its forms by articulating them under the light and tempering their contours with human images. The late Empire building, with its cellular structure, was not conceived for outward effect. It was instead a series of hollows excavated in a mass. The Romans' highly developed vaulting techniques allowed them to contruct a succession of enormous voids unobstructed by supports, and the architects delighted in varying the volumes of these interior spaces with curving planes that produced undulating, advancing, and receding surfaces unsuited to sculpture. Sculpture had perforce to be absorbed into the wall, as it were, taking on the quality of a kind of chasing on stone, so that the light would not be caught by too strong projections and break the unity founded on the spatial interplay of colored surfaces. The ultimate and logical end of this kind of symphonic unity was finally achieved not by Roman architects, but by Byzantine, in the great monuments of Constantinople and Ravenna. This logical evolution of forms is strikingly illustrated in minature by the evolution over the 5th and 6th centuries of the Byzantine column capital, based originally on the antique composite capital (figs. 335–338). The early examples still retain the original's profile and ornament in quite pure form, but worked with the drill, which turns the ornament from relief forms into a kind of fretwork. The inverse truncated pyramid serving as an impost block is merely a geometric simplification of the piece of entablature that in late Empire architecture was interposed between arcade and capital. The curving profile of the composite capital gradually became a truncated cone surmounted by volutes, then a kind of ribbed basket-form; finally it disappeared completely as the capital was reduced to the form of a reverse truncated pyramid similar to the impost block surmounting it, no longer a volume curving in space but an assemblage of four faces, flat planes, calling for a flat lacework decoration. The monotonous embroidery that ornamented the capital also covers the walls of the arcades, and nothing breaks the continuity of the luminous surfaces that merge one into another to make up the interior of a building like Hagia Sophia. One no longer stands before the monument to look at it as a spectator, a position implying a certain distance, both physical and intellectual, between spectator and object; the worshipper is immersed in a space bounded by vibrant, shifting colored surfaces flowing one into the other without interruption, and even the intervals open only onto other shimmering colored surfaces. The worshipper is no longer required to see clearly to or understand, but simply to allow the mystic luminosity to fill his soul as it submits itself to those effluvia of light symbolizing the world beyond.

The only kind of object that can be imagined set in the interior of a Byzantine church is one like the so-called Throne of Maximian in Ravenna (figs. 332–334). With the same kind of lacy, ornamental carving spreading over all the surfaces, it is a paradoxical monument and seemingly little suited to sitting. This unique piece, once regarded as Alexandrine but now believed to be from Constantinople, shows a fine balance between the antique sculptural style, still observable in the figures, and the flat, chased carvings of graceful foliated scroll ornament in the decorated panels, filled with animals symbolizing paradise – a kind of ornament that seems to have been characteristic also for the columns of ciboria. These subtle reliefs carved in soft ivory hues must have been invisible from a distance: enveloped in the semi-darkness of the church, they must have seemed a bodiless presence; the cold light of the museum robs them of this mysterious existence.

It seems clear why monumental sculpture fell into disuse by the 7th century in Byzantium. It did not absolutely disappear, for later Greek builders were in the habit of inserting sculptures in the outside walls of their churches, and a whole provincial school, the Armenian, continued to erect stone buildings and carve stone sculpture. The Armenian sculptors have been somewhat too hastily acclaimed as forerunners of western Romanesque art; they are perhaps more comparable to the fresco decorators of Serbian churches, for however profusely the low reliefs may ornament the exteriors of Armenian churches, they are as yet without organic ties relating them to their supporting architecture. The abundance of stone and the relative scarcity of wood and clay in that region, rather than the genuine sculptor's instinct, perhaps induced artists to carve stone figurative decorations.

The art that developed in the eastern capital of the Empire was a Greek art, and from the Greek mind Byzantium inherited the principles that led it to destroy the illusionistic Graeco-Roman style that, although already faltering in the late Empire, reigned over the Mediterranean for nine hundred years. The tendency of classical Greek art to reach for an ideal, which Plato raised to a philosophical principle, had set limits to illusionism – though never opposed to it, by obliging the creator to reject individual phenomena and appear-

ances in favor of a generalization within which all the multiple appearances could be included. Neo-Platonism, which was in a way an abuse of Platonism, incited the Byzantine mind to demand of reality only vague allusions or symbols, empty of corporeal substance, deprived of solidity, movement, expression, or life, and ultimately transforming reality into a transcendental and immobile sign. The forms Byzantine artists created owe nothing to observation; born of memory, they belong to an intellectual universe that was transmitted from age to age, and upon this world of remembered forms Byzantine art evolved without any reference to nature. Centuries were to elapse before an artist again turned a curious eye towards nature. In a penetrating article written twenty years ago, André Grabar demonstrated the remarkable similarities between Byzantine imagery and Plotinus' system of vision. Plotinus placed the seen phenomenon at the level of the object and not of the subject; the distinction between subject and object on which the Greek rationalistic system rested is thus destroyed in Plotinus. Perceived as if from within, instead of being considered as at a remove from the subject, the object is apprehended by direct intuition, which is what, for Plotinus, makes things intelligible. In an ivory such as the Consular Diptych of Anastasius (fig. 331), each part seems to be considered in itself and not in relation to the others or to the whole; the hierarchy regulating the relationships of the forms is of a mental, not a visual, order, and the composition as a whole, therefore, is a purely intellectual synthesis of various elements gathered around a theme, that is to say, an idea.

Subjected to ever more complicated speculation, this imagery might eventually have become entirely ossified had the artists not renewed it – not by looking at nature, but by a return to antiquity, whereby their forms acquired an element of truth giving the illusion of a new naturalism. This metamorphosis created a real renaissance in Byzantine art under the Macedonian dynasty (867–1056). After monumental sculpture finally disappeared, the successive stages in the evolution of relief sculpture in Byzantium must be followed in a study of ivories. Of a size suited to the hand, these ivories, both religious and profane, were not subject to the limitations that govern monumental art; like the miniature, therefore, they could evolve independent values. In the late 5th and 6th centuries, while the new intellectualizing style was providing such typical examples as the Anastasius diptych, the ancient illusionistic style was still used. In the 7th century however, the latter style was altogether given up in favor of the former, which became gradually more stereotyped. For reasons still not entirely clear, the art of ivory working seems to have been near demise even before the Iconoclastic Controversy; but it was brilliantly revived in the 10th century and saw two centuries of splendor. Among the most beautiful of ivories are those belonging to a well defined group of caskets all bearing similar ornament in the form of rosette borders. They were intended for profane use, and are exemplified at their finest by the Veroli casket (fig. 346), in which is apparent a vigorous revival of Hellenistic themes and even Hellenistic style, with naked figures modelled in a convincing half-relief. The style can also be observed in religious works, such as the plaque depicting the Forty Martyrs (fig. 350), whose artist, more like a Hellenistic Greek sculptor than a product of the Byzantine spirit, exercised considerable ingenuity in differentiating the attitudes and expressions of suffering in his various martyrs. The Christ Enthroned at the top of the plaque still has the traditional schematic look which we find unchanged in another Christ Enthroned in the Victoria and Albert Museum (fig. 347); but a bust of a Christ blessing in the same museum (fig. 344) is so free from convention that it would not seem out of place under the portal of a Gothic cathedral. The equilibrium between the divine and the human that had inspired Phidias seems again to animate the *Christ Crowning Romanos and Eudoxia* (fig. 345). An occasional artist was even emboldened by his feeling for life to make a sculpture in the round: a 10th-century Virgin (fig. 349), points forward to the French Virgins of the time of St. Louis. When we consider such ivories it might appear that Byzantine art, two centuries before French, was on the brink of the discoveries that gave birth to Gothic art. But ivory carving, which lacked the fruitful limitations of monumental art, failed to achieve other than a minor refinement; and even more defeating was the impossibility, owing to the very nature of the Byzantine mind, of a renewal through direct contact with nature. The Macedonian renaissance in the arts was ephemeral, and ivories soon returned to an elegant formalism and a mannerism betrayed in the elongated proportions of the figures. This was the swan song of that art; in the 11th century ivories practically disappeared, probably as a result of the economic decline of Byzantium. Ivory was replaced by steatite, a less costly material, and the sculptors who worked it only imitated and stereotyped the dead forms of the ivory workers. Sculpture disappeared from Byzantine civilization with the ivories, and even the mosaics began to decline. For economic reasons, the future belonged to painting. Its more fluid process was to allow the 13th and 14th centuries some progress towards naturalism, perhaps

with the help of western influences.

Inclined towards aesthetic as well as theological speculation, Byzantine art was in the main an erudite and sophisticated art; but it also had its provincial aspects. In painting, the rustic style is represented by the frescoes of the rock-cut chapels of Cappadocia, where monastic communities practiced a realistic and dramatic art in contrast to the principles of the then official art. In sculpture, the land richest in provincial orthodox art is Coptic Egypt, whose productions have recently acquired an exaggerated popularity originating rather in the anti-classical tastes of our era than in actual qualities in the objects admired (figs. 340–343). The imagery of Coptic art is very complex, mingling pagan and Christian themes. The preponderance of pagan themes in which Bacchic, Apollonian, and Aphrodisiac mythologies are prominent – in quite coarsely executed works of a heavy sensuality, and often representing women with accentuated sex characteristics – has suggested that pagan magic cults may have survived fairly long in the Egyptian countryside, while the Greeks of Alexandria had already adopted Christianity, and there, where the institution of monasticism was founded, Christianity was to undergo an individual development. In 451 the Council of Chalcedon condemned the Monophysites, and with them Dioscorus, Patriarch of Alexandria; Christian Egypt then broke with Byzantium and through nationalistic reaction entered upon an independent development. All the prerequisites to the birth of a popular art, whether Christian or pagan, thus coalesced. The resultant art interpreted and modified formal influences from all sides – from the depths of Egypt, from Palmyrene Syria, from the Hellenistic world of Alexandria, from the classical Graeco-Roman repertory, and also from Byzantium – mingling in the popular melting pot all the styles of sophisticated or non-sophisticated cultures. The forms of this art, unlike those of Roman provincial art, are popular, and not primitive. Among them can be found certain themes resumed in later western art, like the *gisant* (that is, the recumbent tomb figure), or the figure in a niche. Their vitality is unconstrained by limitations of style or form, though the execution is usually coarse and hasty, the artisans only roughing-out the shape and expending their efforts on the head, while the lower parts of the figures are left to atrophy. This popular trend was prolonged up to the Arab conquest and remains alive to our time in Ethiopian art, where its survival, however, affects only painting and not sculpture.

Towards the middle of the 8th century monumental art in the West entered on a long night. As a consequence of the Saracen and Frankish invasions, the last marble workshops in the Pyrenees closed down one after another; Gaul no longer received the capitals, the carved altars and the sarcophagi in which Gallo-Roman sculpture had proceeded by more and more degraded forms towards a kind of orientalism. The art the barbarians had practiced in their lands of origin, before they invaded the West, was not actually non-figurative, since it was inspired by animals, but it concerned itself not at all with the modelled relief form. The steppes metal workers who cast and chased the jewelry and dress ornament, or trappings for carts and harnesses, metamorphosed into linear ornamental variations the dynamic, non-human – almost frightening – vitality of the animals (fig. 352). This art of metamorphosis, seizing upon natural forms only to project them into an imaginary world, was to be one of the primary sources for Romanesque style. Once settled in the West the barbarians seem to have somewhat lost the impetus for their art, their metal work becoming more abstract; but the Vikings retained it in all its purity, producing their most beautiful chimeras at the very time when Carolingian artists in Europe were proposing the return to the human figure (fig. 355). In 11th-century Christianized Scandinavia, it was this barbarian spirit that still enriched and vitalized the interlace on the wooden door panels of the stave church at Urnes (fig. 356). This interlace is the later equivalent of that in the Irish miniatures, and the predecessor of the complicated Romanesque fantasies. As for sculpture in relief, the coarsely worked, cut-out figurations of Hornhausen or Niederdollendorf are the last manifestations of a completely degenerated monumental art (figs. 360, 361). The Irish sculptors, educated no doubt by their miniaturists, were skilled in endowing their compositions with a unifying rhythm, though their relief was no more refined (figs. 362, 363).

In the 8th century it seemed as though the human form, earlier apotheosized in western art, would disappear from it entirely. It was effaced in the art of Italy and Gaul, and in Byzantium encountered the prohibitions of the iconoclasts. Over the Mediterranean, from Syria to Spain, Islam spread a sort of desert spirit that reduced the human dwelling or place of prayer to a mirage covered with weightless, fretwork ornament. The beautiful Syrian rinceaux at Mshatta (fig. 367), in which relief still makes a play with light and shade, were soon to become a dry lacework; the sculptured capital followed an evolution similar to that of the capital in Byzantine art of the 4th and 6th centuries (figs. 370, 372); the few statues in the round produced by Islam clearly display the

Moslem inaptitude for expressing volume, resembling as they do wooden dolls rather than human beings (fig. 375). The animal forms that the bronze workers evoked in their aquamaniles or incense burners (fig. 378) conveyed more vitality, as do the famous Alhambra lions which are their stone equivalents (fig. 376). As for ivory, it lent itself in particular to the linear interlace combinations beloved of Islamic artists.

The fate of sculpture during the Dark Ages in the West has been debated for more than thirty years. The north of Italy, inhabited by the Lombards, offers more material for consideration than do other regions, for remains from that period are fairly abundant there. As during the Roman Empire, there seem to have been two prevailing currents, one more sophisticated and one more rustic. In the little town of Cividale, in Friuli, are two 8th-century stone altars with figures in relief. One of them, the Ratchis altar (fig. 379), is clumsily executed. On the other, the Sigwald altar (fig. 380), a technique like *champlevé* has been employed to produce a regular relief depicting the Cross with the symbols of the Evangelists (one of the earliest representations of the subject known), organized as a very effective composition. It probably imitates some embossed metal altar frontal, for it is ornamented with rosettes copied from the ornaments used to conceal the nails with which repoussé metal plates were fixed to a wooden core. Also in Cividale, in the church of Sta. Maria in Valle (fig. 381), are fine stuccos of elegant design and refined execution, whose date, much disputed, has been set as early as the 8th and as late as the 11th century. As is the case with the equally surprising frescoes at Castelseprio, it has even been suggested that a Byzantine artist might have worked for the Cividale court – although in fact at that time Byzantium had nothing of the kind to offer. It has been discovered, from a study of the remaining early medieval stuccos, most numerous in Spain and Italy, that the ancient techniques for working stucco – much easier than carving stone – were used throughout the early Middle Ages in ornament for buildings, until sculpture in harder materials was revived in the Romanesque period.

The Carolingian reform of the arts is one of the most striking instances in history of a civilization drawing from an awareness of its own decline the will to look back in search of the means for its regeneration. Charlemagne wished his palace at Aachen to be a *Roma Secunda*, and summoned from Rome, from Ravenna, from the East, and from the whole empire, materials, works of art, and also artisans, to create a worthy imperial culture in his metropolis. The invention of the

Caroline minuscule script as the vehicle for written thought (resumed after the interval of Gothic writing by the Renaissance humanists, who developed modern script from it) would be enough to prove that genuine progress does not always rest on gradual evolution. The political failure of the Carolingian Empire has somewhat masked the tremendous impulse given to culture by the Palace School (though German historians are perhaps more conscious of its cultural contribution, since the Carolingian achievement was prolonged without a break through the Ottonian empire until the start of Romanesque art.)

Today miniatures and ivories offer the only remaining evidence of what the arts were like under Charlemagne. The palace chapel at Aachen retains only its basic plan, having been rebuilt rather than restored. The only remaining original elements are the beautiful bronze balustrades in the galleries, ornamented with acanthus scrolls as graceful as those of antiquity (fig. 384). Little is left of goldsmith work from the time of Charlemagne. In the case of ivories, the late antique period had left in church treasuries many fine models of classical style so that Carolingian artists could reproduce them in all their purity. The art of stucco, already mentioned above in connection with the survival of antique techniques, could produce in Charlemagne's time the tondo supposedly portraying the monk Sola (fig. 386) which appears to point directly to the reliefs of Gilduin's altar in St. Sernin in Toulouse (fig. 518.) Sculptures in the round offer conflicting evidence. The bronze equestrian statuette in the Louvre representing the Charlemagne himself is such an accurate imitation of the antique that it was once believed to be a Renaissance work; on the other hand, the life-sized stone statue of the emperor, now in the cloister of St. John Baptist in Müstair (fig. 389), is so childish in style that it shows a complete lapse of all traditions, a sort of sculptural nullity. A head presumed to be that of Christ (fig. 387), found in excavations of Lorsch Abbey, is far better executed, betraying the influence of ivory carvings. The difference between a sophisticated art based on the antique and a provincial art was probably never more marked than during that period.

Ottonian art represents the ripening of Carolingian art, for Gaul itself was plunged into anarchy after Charlemagne's death. The Carolingian reliquary statue of St. Foy (fig. 397), a compound of parts done in various periods, including the gold head from the late Empire (5th century?), is a mere agglomeration of precious materials and far inferior to the goldsmith work produced in Germany at the time. At the beginning of the 11th century Ottonian art, nearing its end, produced its best sculptural works. The bronze workshop created at Hildesheim by Bishop Bernward was capable of casting in one piece such works as the 16-foot doors of St. Michael's cathedral (fig. 390, 391), or the 13-foot column (fig. 393) imitating Trajan's column, with a spiral relief representing twenty-eight scenes from the life of Christ – a noteworthy progress in technique if we consider that the Louvre equestrian statue of Charlemagne had to be cast in several pieces later soldered together. The two monuments with which Bernward decorated his cathedral are by two different men. The reliefs on the doors are more perfect and better finished, more alive and nearer to antique models; those on the column are harsher and more primitive, and anticipate the Romanesque spirit. In the column reliefs the background sets up a tension with the relief forms; but on the doors, the figures are placed on an inert surface as though simply applied. The doors of Augsburg cathedral (fig. 392), thirty years later, offer a sort of farewell to the past, on the eve of the flowering of Romanesque art, for they are made in strict imitation of Hellenistic figures. The gold antependium from Basle (fig. 399), contemporary with the St. Bernward doors, is undoubtedly the most perfect work of Ottonian art. The artist of the antependium rediscovered the dignity of the classical style, and through it expresses the divine world, transfigured into gold. Such works were the creation of two artists: a wood-carver who sculptured the wooden core, and a goldsmith who hammered the gold leaves applied to the core. What sculptural qualities the underlying wooden carvings might have can be seen in the Madonna (fig. 396) that Bishop Imad gave to Paderborn cathedral in about 1058: the gold leaves that covered it have been removed and melted down, and all that remains is the core of wooden sculpture in the round, as smoothly and softly carved as an ivory.

Thus, despite the vicissitudes and transformations resulting from its having been handed down through the centuries, the perennial classicism derived from the antique still inspired Ottonian art. If the mystique of the Germanic Holy Roman Empire was a political failure, it nonetheless succeeded on the artistic plane, for there it was able to recapture the principle of the antique. In such ways the world of the imagination may sometimes compensate for the insufficiencies of reality. Ottonian classicism stands in strong contrast with the expressionism that appears to have been a constant in German art of later periods: must it be concluded, then, that this romantic attitude, which may be detected in certain Carolingian miniatures, never touched Ottonian art?

Not, indeed, if the famous wooden crucifix (fig. 395) in the Cologne cathedral (which I have described elsewhere as "Schopenhauer crucified") was actually given by Bishop Gero (969–976). If so, it is the first surviving monumental crucifix in the West, a witness to earlier works that have not survived.

V Primitive Cultures

The word "primitive" is so broad in its connotations that it is difficult to define it accurately. How can we narrow down a term that might include both a Baoule mask and a painting by Duccio, or even one by Fra Angelico? One is tempted to reduce its meaning to the concept of "primary" – that which comes first – as applied to all human activities: thus alchemists would be the primitives of chemistry and astrologers the primitives of astronomy. But when we come to ethnology, our concern in this chapter, this limiting concept could no longer apply, for some primitive societies seem to be regressions of more evolved civilizations, and the most primitive of those still in existence usually reveal an ossified state of an earlier "primary" situation. Furthermore, the word "primitive" is not usually applied to the very first artistic products – those of the Paleolithic period. Finally, if we want to be understood when we use the word, we must be aware of contemporary reactions – those of young nations who have suddenly emerged from primitive societies to become democracies, and even more, those of Western thinkers whose self-punishment complexes make them consider the primitive thought and ways of life superior to those of more, advanced civilizations.

Although it has recently been disputed, there does exist such a thing as a "primitive mentality" characterizing both the so-called "savage" tribes still flourishing on this planet, and also the more advanced ancient societies, like those the Spaniards found in America on their arrival. Individuals from these societies differ from those of more advanced civilizations by their behavior in relation to themselves and to their surroundings. Western civilization developed when thinking man became able to differentiate between the knower and the known, which involves the definition of the former as an individual and the objectification of the latter, whose phenomena are linked by causal relationships in which only observed facts are taken into account. Western thought is based on this relationship between subject and object which with existentialism reaches a state of crisis in which neither term can free itself from the other, but each refuses the other. Indian thought, while transcending the subject-object distinction, admits it as a first stage of ontological meditation. The mental activity of a civilized man consists at the same time of taking apart and bringing together – of separating objects, then connecting them through chains of causality ever more inclusive; of generalizing more and more and freeing the object from its subjective wrappings to make it tend towards the idea (in the scholastic acceptation of the word). The idea in turn permeates reality like a fertilizing spring, promotes newly observed facts into the serial categories of registered phenomena, which they can alter or even reverse, for in the ever-active thought of Western man, the idea always has the value of a hypothesis, while with the primitive, it is immutable and stiffens into a dogma. The primitive does not distinguish among objects, any more than he separates himself from his environment; he thinks and behaves with the assumption that his ego is inseparable from the non-ego. His mental universe includes a conglomeration of odd facts which, since they are not "known" but only "perceived," are linked by mythical chains of causality in which the visible is only a sign of the invisible. In such a situation, man lives in fear, since he depends on an animate world which he can affect only if he enters it through magic ways, ways that are like traps designed to catch reality – and unreliable traps at that. Civilized man is led by the basic principles of reason and uses science to control the working of universal forces. The primitive is unable to defend himself against the primordial feeling of terror, whose survival in the more evolved cultures, like the Pre-Columbian, can be considered as a primitive feature.

Aesthetically, there is such a thing as primitive style, appearing as a lack of continuity in forms; we can find it in such apparently dissimilar works as a Negro fetish, a statue by a western folk artist, or an Aztec bas-relief. A Negro statue extracted from a wooden trunk with the help of an adze shows suddenly swelling volumes and abruptly arrested lines; the exaggerated swelling is a symbol of erection, of growth, of fertility. The work is conceived in separate parts whose cohesion is achieved by the intuitive feeling for rhythm, absent in the western folk artisan, who tends to put together disproportionate pieces. Michelangelo projected an idea into a block of marble; the work was complete in the artist's mind before it was realized in matter. The Negro sculptor extracts an image from a block of wood; the sequence of his gestures is like a ritual. An Aztec sculpture seems a puzzle of figurative or abstract fragments stuck together. All primitive works translate into stone or wood the drama of life for man oppressed by the plurality of phenomena: the primitive has not reached the state of awareness when man, faced with an interlocking network of data, isolates them and then includes them in a scheme of successive generalizations, ordering the properties of things according to the calm perspectives of reason, ruling over the chaos of appearances through intellectualized order, and translating the power that he feels surging within himself into the concept of a Transcendent Being, supreme light of the spirit, a God who banishes to the kingdom of shades the terrifying horde of wandering spirits, gods, and demons. It is clear why the revolutionary painters and sculptors of the early 20th century found so much to borrow from Negro sculpture. They wanted to break up the unity that characterized the traditional outlook of European art and to replace it by discontinuous forms that would express the anguish of western conscience faced with the rethinking of all its values.

A knowledge of Negro art, more than of any other, has allowed us to understand the primitive processus of artistic creation. Our understanding has come about with the help of observations collected by ethnologists, and particularly Marcel Griaulle's famous studies of a people whom he knew as still free from European influence: the Dogons. Those investigations are now part of history; the popularity of Negro art in the West and its industrial and commercial exploitation has debased its value. Decolonization, which gave independence to African peoples, has hastened the decline of African art even more than did colonization.

When he was carving a fetish or putting together the elements of a mask, the Negro artist had originally no other aim than to produce an object whose magical efficacy was guaranteed – an instrument, not a work of art. This magic power could be dangerous, and the masks through which communication with the other world took place used to be kept hidden when they were not exhibited in a ritual, in which only the initiated took part before it became a spectacle in which all the inhabitants of the village participated. In unspoilt societies like that of the Dogons, the concept of the artist as such was unknown: the making of masks was a sort of "public service" undertaken by all the men in the village; elsewhere, art was one of the prerogatives of the witch doctor In western and central Africa, it was the blacksmith who carved wooden idols,

since his being in permanent contact with the mythical world of fire made him the most valuable intermediary between society and the cosmic forces of fertility and death; he provided the tribe with all its material and spiritual tools. He lived somewhat apart, both honored and feared. In some societies the artist had a separate status, professional and corporate. It is interesting to note that this privileged social condition, which was accompanied by an *aesthetic* appreciation of the works, was found not in a tribal framework, but in societies where there was a ruler surrounded by an aristocracy, as in the ancient kingdoms of Benin (fig. 403) and Dahomey, where we find real palace schools. Africa, at the end of the 19th century presented al stages of artistic creation, from the tribal stage to court art.

Negro art is a peasant art. It only developed in a limited region of Africa, in the west and in the center, in societies based on agriculture. We do not find it in the parts of south or central Africa inhabited by pastoral, nomadic, or semi-nomadic populations. Even if the presence of Islam did not make it impossible to confuse Africa and "Negro culture," it would be wrong to think of what we call Negro art as the sole expression of the whole "black continent." Africa has revealed to European explorers some societies which have remained primitive, or become so again, but it would be as mistaken to consider a Congolese fetish or an Ivory Coast mask the deepest manifestations of the African soul as to evaluate western art on the basis of Polish folk sculpture. In Africa, empires and kingdoms have existed which produced advanced societies, and excavations – now just beginning – may one day recover their remains. To our present limited knowledge, the heart of Africa, the Mediterranean part aside, yields three chronological phases. The oldest is the prehistoric; it is characterized, as in the West, by rock-cut art, found in South Africa (fig. 10) and along the northern Sahara border. The second phase could be called proto-historic; it relates to civilizations excavated in the present territory of Nigeria, such as the Nok culture, before the Christian era, or the Ife culture, whose oldest remains seem to go back to the 12th or 13th centuries B.C. (fig. 400), and also the Kingdom of Benin, which reached its apogee in the 17th century (figs. 402, 403). It would be paradoxical to denominate the third phase as "historical," for the primitive societies of Africa colonized by the West are far removed from the sense of history; but nonetheless, those societies entered history through the Europeans who discovered them. The still rare finds from ancient Africa, and particularly the bronze sculpture of the Yoruba kingdom, show us a world very different from tribal primitivism. The German Leo Frobenius, who in 1910 first discovered works from the Ife culture, even believed them to be the production of a Greek artist. Others tried to explain the classical outlook of that art, inspired by the observation of nature, by assuming Egyptian, Roman, or Phoenician influences. External influence may certainly have brought into consciousness some indigenous tendencies, but the sequence of various cultures that flowered in the Gulf of Guinea indicates a clear internal evolution, not just a random stratification. Preceded by the lively Nok terra cottas, the serene beauty of Ife *cire perdue* bronzes was translated into more primitive forms in the Benin bronzes so much admired by our contemporaries; we know that these last derive from the Ife works, for in 1280 A.D. a king of Benin asked his liege in Ife to send him a specialist to introduce bronze art to his court. The degradation of classicism into neo-primitivism becomes more and more pronounced in Benin art the nearer it gets to the contemporary period; it is an example of how, in Africa, advanced civilizations could disintegrate and regress to a tribal state: works produced nowadays in Nigeria have returned to the "savage" stage of so-called Negro art.

While the Africans are farmers, the Melanesians and Polynesians are seafarers. The Africans are gifted for sculpture in the round obtained with the use of the adze, which is derived from an agricultural tool, the hoe. But islanders, who only leave the infinite world of the sea to enter the more impenetrable world of the forest, are not attracted by statuary. When they carve wood, they prefer cutting it out into lacework patterns, reproducing the design of the spirals which they like to paint on the facades of their dwellings or on their own bodies (fig. 415).

When Cortes' soldiers invaded Mexico, they were surprised to find a well-stocked market; there was even a shop which sold knives made of obsidian – strange meeting between the stone age and the age of firearms! When we look at the grandiose monuments built by the Maya and the Aztec, it is hard to believe that those gigantic structures were made with stone tools, without the help of draft animals or carts, or even pack animals, and that their potteries were made without any wheel. This strange technical lag of America, even in its highly organized ancient societies, is explained by the isolated position of those peoples, who were cut off from other civilizations. To progress, man needs other men, even if they are his enemies. The exchanges between Asia and the West were many, and even Africa never lost contact with the Mediterranean. But once

America had been populated by waves of immigrants from Asia and perhaps also from Oceania, the continent seems to have been closed to all outside influence; it had to be content with its own resources of fauna and flora, which were infinitely poorer than those of Eurasia. It is not surprising that the Mesoamericans should have deified corn since that plant was almost their only resource; they regarded it as miraculous. Deprived of the stimulation of a generous natural environment, the human spirit seemed to lack the ingenuity that in the rest of the world led it to increase the efficiency of effort through practical inventions. In any case, we know now that all the discoveries that tended to give man some control over natural forces were achieved in a privileged part of the Middle East, and from there spread to the whole world. But to reach America they would have had to traverse the insuperable barrier of the oceans, and at that time the continent seems to have already received its immigration quota.

Therefore, however developed they may have been, the ancient American civilizations were primitive. They still lived in the state of primeval fear; it seems to have been more acute there than anywhere else in the world. Nowhere had man found the earth so unproductive, nowhere the universe so hostile. The inefficacy of their actions, compared to their aspirations, fostered in these ancient peoples the frustrating sense of their own innate weakness and of the unreliability of a world subject to the blind power of invisible forces. To be, to endure, or to grow, everything demanded blood – human blood: the progress of time itself was secured only by the sacrifice of victims, as was also the growth of the corn. Priests walked in procession clothed in human skins from victims who had been skinned alive to symbolize the hulling of corn; children were tortured so that their tears might attract rain over the dry fields. Man was pledged to war to provide holocausts for the gods Alone in a hostile world, he was literally helpless and could only try to placate the invisible powers by magic. Far from weakening with time in an evolution such as occurred in all the great European and Asiatic civilizations, this terror grew through the centuries: the populations of America experienced a sort of evolution in reverse. Human sacrifices, still rare among the Maya of the Old Empire, became more frequent during the New Empire under the influence of the Toltecs. The Aztecs lived in a perpetual bloodbath; implacable divinities urged them to constant wars against their neighbors, to feed the altars. War had become a vital necessity, not for reasons of aggrandizement, but to keep the world's clockwork going! This progression of terror is reflected in art. Very ancient civilizations, before the Christian era, left funerary terra cottas which reveal them as optimistic people, enjoying the representation of details of daily life (fig. 419). At Tlatilco excavations brought to light "female and male figures, young and old, with thin or obese bodies, healthy or humped, sitting or standing, nude or half-dressed. Many of them are adorned with varied elegant hair-styles, long plaits, earrings, necklaces, little dancers' skirts or dresses. The latter have been called 'pretty women.' They are neither goddesses nor portraits, but may be representations with intended magic properties, designed to awaken or increase human or agricultural fertility... Some of the characters represented are carrying children, dancing, crying, playing with dogs, others are acrobats, dancers, ballplayers, magicians or fantastic creatures..." (The quotation, illustrating the variety in these figurines, is from the catalogue of the exhibition "Chefs d'oeuvre d'art mexicain," Paris, 1962.)

Excavations in the region of Los Remojadas, where the Totonac lived, have brought to light figurines depicting a whole population whose one aim in life seems to have been to play practical jokes on each other, to play on swings, wear fancy dress, tell funny stories, sing, dance, and roar with laughter. The children – who were numerous – laughed loudest of all. Did these people try to combat terror by a ritual of optimism?

These statuettes demonstrate that, as in prehistoric art, naturalism may be found at the origins, and stylization – which has been considered a sign of primitivism – may occur as a later development (contrary to the idea of a "life of forms," outlined by art historians from Deonna to Focillon, which can only be applied consistently to Western art). We are surprised by the freedom of these ancient figurines: they are really sculptured in the round, with limbs moving freely in three-dimensional space, and some of the dancers twist round in bold, spiraling movements. Modelled in soft clay by hand and fired once only, these figures can ignore the limitations of stone carving; but even figures carved in stone are sometimes animated by the same vitality. The Maya's organization of city-states brought about a great demand for monumental art to serve the aristocratic and religious hierarchies. That was the end of the freedom of expression and liveliness of archaic art; artists now had to submit to great sculptural programs for reliefs in stone or stucco to ornament buildings. The human figure was subjected to conventions similar to those of the Egyptians, who showed the body full-face and the legs in profile, and in the New Empire the Maya adopted a uniform, hieratic frontality and concentrated on the representation of gods

rather than mortals. During the Old Empire, the manner in which the figure is set in the center of the relief, surrounded by monstrous apparitions and hieroglyphic decorations pushed back towards the edges of the composition, still shows some feeling for design, but design is lacking in later periods, as Mesoamerican plastic art gradually became stereotyped. Aztec bas-reliefs are composite agglomerations of figures, ornaments, and truncated forms, all mechanically thrown together. In these inhuman compositions, jaguar snouts, snakes' jaws, death's heads, and fragments of dismembered human bodies are the terrifying tokens of a hostile universe governed by demonic forces. In no other part of the world was man so far removed from the soothing concept of God which pervaded all the civilizations of the Eurasian continent from Greece to China.

The cultures of the Andes seem to have been spared that philosophy of terror, thanks to the materialistic tendencies inspiring the Inca social organization, which was bound to the monotheistic cult of the sun. Less artistically gifted than the Mesoamericans, the Andean peoples rarely practiced sculpture. But they gave human faces to their pottery vessels, thus producing an extraordinary portrait gallery in which the sick, the deformed, the crippled and the tortured were not forgotten (fig. 427).

Folk art is not to be despised. It has aroused much critical controversy (including Berenson's invective against our present craze for it); the great Austrian historian Alois Riegl was among the first scholars to take it seriously Folk poetry had already attracted interest in the Romantic era, and towards the end of the 19th century this interest extended to everyday utensils and objects; the so-called folklore museums in the Scandinavian countries were founded at this time. As early as 1860, Kraszwski, in a study of Slavic art, demonstrated the indigenous character of Russian folk art. In 1871, however, the Englishman E. B. Tylor put forward an opposite theory; for him folk art represented the survival of universal traditions going back to the prehistoric period and persisting unchanged throughout the ages in the midst of advanced civilizations. This theory has now been generally accepted; André Varagnac has coined the word *archéocivilisation* to describe the sum of those popular customs which were born with the first agricultural cultures and resisted the great developments of history to die only now, killed by industrialism. In the case of artistic production, this hypothesis is least open to verification; however, a common decorative vocabulary made up of abstract ornaments used by folk artists in districts as remote from each other as Roumania and Portugal does seem to go back to the proto-historic period when these ornamental elements were signs possessing magic connotations. As for other folklore products, the fact that they are alike throughout the world proves mainly that there are feelings and frustrations, common to all peoples and all times, which influence the attitudes of the masses of ordinary people – for civilization is above all an effort to differentiate. Folk art is probably most original and most consistent in its use of color. A popular taste for polychromy reduced to a few strong, even acid, hues may be found alike in Mexico, in Poland, and in Spain. Fabrics and ceramics are the most appealing creations of popular art. Ancient fabrics of popular origin have rarely survived; some ceramics have. But it is sculpture, more enduring, that shows throughout the ages the unchanging uniformity of popular conventions. In sculpture may be observed, not originality, but the arbitrary simplification of forms obtained by hesitant hands trying to "reproduce" rather than invent. The artisan is not moved by that need to create that torments the artist and forces him to go one step further every time; the works of the artisan are analogous to industrial mass production. In all civilizations, alongside the skilled artistic creations, there has existed an almost universal form of "provincial" or "popular" art, in which a Punic sculpture contemporary with Rome (fig. 302) finds a strange kinship with Bogomil reliefs (fig. 432) from the Middle Ages or with an Italian 17th-century stele made by peasants at the time of Bernini (fig. 435). It is an art of timeless forms situated outside history.

It is told that just having completed the Kaila-sanatha temple at Elura, its designer exclaimed, "Could it have been I who made that?" He had so merged himself with his work that he was unable to see it as a thing apart from himself until the Vishvakarman had withdrawn. Only then did he regain consciousness of himself as an individual, an ephemeral being momentarily raised by the Creative Principle to the transubstantiated world and now fallen back into the universe of differentiated forms. His attitude is opposite to that of the Greek artist, for even when the Greek created sacred images (and in the classical period this was all he created), he considered his work from the beginning as the object, a product discovered by his mind searching for a concept in an external world; the divine spirit entered the sculpture after it had left his hands, when the god descended into the man-made form. In India, the god, the formless one, comes to the artist clothed in the form in which he desires to reveal himself to man; in the golden age of India men did not need to borrow from the world of illusion, for they contemplated the gods face to face, and art did not exist.

Herein may lie the explanation of why in this culture attracted to sculpture more than to any other art, to the point of allowing it to dominate architecture completely, there is so little attempt to create free-standing statues. The statue is an object. For the Greeks, it served to define man himself, as an *ego*, but this ego that in the Greek mind was the aim and end of being, in Indian ontology was only a transitory incarnation, destined in the perfect human being to be annihilated, merged in the Supreme Self, the universal One, the Absolute. In Indian art the sculptured figure is rarely treated as an isolated entity; it emerges from the stone but remains attached to the background – a background neutral, non-spatial, and as indeterminate as the infinite. The figure is usually linked with others, and even when it is alone, like the *yakshi* on the gate of the Sanchi stupa (fig. 448), the pulsations of the ecstatic state that twists the body suggest its interdependence with the sky behind it. In general, the multifarious beings invade the whole field, obeying no compositional principle, but simply accumulating all over the available surface; or they mass their twisting bodies over the flanks of the temples in an endless repetition of forms that mirrors the swarms of ephemeral beings engendered by the life process. Such groups as those on the Mamallapuram rocks (fig. 466) seem to have been conceived extemporaneously, unrelated in an overall plan. Indian thought is ruled by the impossible aim of synthesizing the many and the one: in the Hindu religion, the universe is a pullulating swarm of living beings – plants, animals, humans, gods and anti-gods – engendering each other in successive transmigrations that leave their souls unsatisfied and that endlessly delay the promised ultimate identification of all individual being in the Absolute. This sense of a germinating swarm inspired all Indian creations, whether of religious and philosophical sects, or in the arts and literature. The Purana poems relating the stories of the gods fill 1,600,000 lines, and India is said to have 300,000,000 gods!

Greek sculpture came into being along with Greek architecture, and was dependent on it; even the free-standing statue had to respond to architectonic laws. In India, on the contrary, it was the sculptor who was the architect. He hollowed the temple or monastery out of the mountain flanks, or opened a vast trench, reserving a rocky mass out of which he would carve a sanctuary like the Kailasanatha of Elura (fig. 467), where the rock was excavated to nearly one hundred feet to free the mass for the temple. Delving into the earth's entrails, the Indian satisfied a need to feel nature, the Holy Mother, immanent. The Kailasa, the temple of the Holy Mountain dedicated to Shiva, had to be extracted from a veritable mountain. At Mamallapuram the rocks along the coast were carved into temples or animals (fig. 465); but the designer of this sacred place preserved a few natural rocks, some of them close against the temples, so that the contact with the original earth-stuff should not be broken. After the classical period Hindu temples began to be built, rather than excavated, yet they were still conceived as the original mountain, as a heap of cut stones, in the heart of which the dim and narrow sanctuaries imitated the caverns of the primitive period. The Indian concept of architecture never moved beyond this heaping-up of stones; to be sure, the earliest architecture was constructed, but it was made of wood, and soon its forms, borrowed from Iran, were transposed, paradoxically, to caves hollowed out with chisels by the architects of the 2nd- and 3rd-century Buddhist sanctuaries.

Indian art begins where others end: with naturalism. Stylization and conceptualization, which have generally preceded the imitation of nature, and particularly in Greece, in India follow upon it. Attempts have been made to explain this anomaly by postulating the existence of an earlier, primitive and stylized wooden sculpture, since destroyed. As an argument in favor of this hypothesis its supporters point to two large statues dating from about 200 B.C., from Parkham, and now in the Mathura Museum. In fact, no such "explanations" of Indian naturalism are called for; Indian naturalism springs from the *genius loci*. It is already present in the prehistoric Indus Valley culture of 2500-2000 B.C., where it contrasts strongly with the entirely hieratic approach to art predominating in the coeval Mesopotamian civilizations, from which the Indus Valley culture largely drew its forms. Stella Kramrisch rightly saw in two sandstone statuettes from Harappa the two tendencies found in all Indian art. One figure is static, and represents life contained and at rest; the other, a dancer, has a vital, twisting body, unique at that stage in the history of art, and totally different from the block-like forms of the figures carved by contemporary artists at Telloh. The two Harappa statuettes are also distinguished from contemporary Middle Eastern works by their sensuously described nudity. This ingenuous sensuality was from the beginning characteristic of Indian sculpture. In both Greek and Hindu cultures, neither of which have made a "sin" of life, the body has been glorified. Unlike the Greek artist, the Indian was not interested in anatomical structure, representing it only very approximately; but the body of an Indian figure is shot through with a vital pulse, the essence of being itself, the breath of life. In the Hindu philosophy the body is not hostile; rather, it is the medium through which liberation is attained; ascesis is not the mortification, but rather the mastery, of the vital mechanisms, obtained through a complete awareness of body and soul. The sense of touch plays a basic role in the ritual of possession of the vital centers, and as for sexuality, one of the yoga methods exploits eroticism as a path to transcending the Ego and attaining unity with the Supreme Self.

It is understandable why the ideal type in Indian sculpture tends to the female, in contrast to the Greek, where the virile type came first and the appeal of the feminine only later. In Indian art, the characteristic female forms influenced the representation of the male body, and a viscerotonic type – that is, somewhat adipose – was favored, and became the type for the representations of the Buddha. In the female figures the female attributes – breasts, hips, fleshy folds – are strongly accentuated, as in the old fertility idols, and are emphasized by the s-curve (*tribhanga*) in which the body is twisted, and which accentuates its curves. The most characteristic of Indian female figures, the *yakshi*, appears again and again, with her rounding body ornamenting temples and gates. She is the guardian spirit of the vegetable sources of life. At Barhut, she barely emerges from her pillar and must deploy her movements sideways instead of out into space (fig. 445); at Sanchi, her body issues from the tree like a juicy fruit (fig. 448); at Mathura, her elegant, even affected, attitude reflects the refinements of the Emperor Kanishka's court, where poetry and philosophical subtleties flourished (fig. 449). In the Medieval temples of Bhuvaneshwara, Khajuraho, and Konarak, the female bodies are seized in an erotic frenzy (difficult to view simply as a symbolic union of essence and substance) that so contorts them that the bust manages to twist back completely over the haunches.

There are many Indias; the immense territory is divided and subdivided into sects and principalities, and all attempts at political unification have failed. Psychologically, there are certainly two Indias at least. The first is the heart of the country, the Deccan and the south, where pre-Vedic peoples were probably pushed back by the Aryan conquerors, but where was preserved the basic thread of the old proto-historic naturalistic civilizations that worshipped plant-life and the generative organs. That continental India gave to Vedantism its magic materialism, which continued to exist as a substratum of Indian spiritualism. The god Shiva, benevolent and terrible, is probably also a pre-Vedic survival. The other India, which might be called the international India, is that of the northwest, the India of the Indus and the Ganges, open to contact with Iran, the Hellenic lands, the world of the Scythian tribes, and through the oases of Tarim, with China. It was the path of the invaders who time and again attempted to remodel the Indian continent and the Indian soul. In that region, open to so many races and influences, Indian art was born. Paradoxically – though in India all is paradox, everything being both the thing itself and its opposite – it was Buddhism, religion of the Absolute, that gave India its art and its world of images. When the 3rd-century Emperor Ashoka, the Constantine of Buddhism, wished to celebrate the places sanctified by Buddha, he was obliged to borrow forms from Persian art; but already in the following century, an indigenous Indian art appears at Sanchi and Barhut. On these temples the figures telling the story of the Buddha are calm and smilingly graceful, the scenes diffused with a sense of peace; but near the Deccan, in the Kingdom of Andhra, on the Kistna River, Buddhist imagery took on a more dramatic aspect, in compositions crowded with figures which, seized as by a kind of sacred frenzy, writhe in ecstatic attitudes. These are the two principal stylistic currents in Indian art. The more serene style, expressing silence and an inward life, which Buddhism spread in the north, was enriched by contacts with Graeco-Roman art and communicated its spiritualistic optimism to China and Japan; the Amaravati style, of greater intensity and passion, was to be the source of Brahminic art.

In the earliest Indian art the image of the Buddha himself does not appear; at Barhut, Sanchi or Amaravati, in the stories about the Buddha, his figure was replaced by symbols. This aniconic tradition was perfectly orthodox, since once the Enlightened One had attained Nirvana he was "extinguished," that is to say, no longer an existence. Scholars of Indian art still dispute the source of the Buddha image, Indian historians holding to an Indian origin and giving Mathura as the place of its creation, while western scholars tend to believe that the idea of giving human form to the Buddha was inspired by Graeco-Roman anthropomorphism. It seems most likely that the idea of representing Buddha resulted from foreign contacts, and from historical evidence, these probably entered through the Gandhara region. In works at Mathura (fig. 459), contemporary with the Gandharan epoch, the Buddha is still represented with some reserve, as if the artist were tentatively practicing a strange custom. In the scene of Paranirvana which illustrates his death, for instance he is still present only as a symbol. In Gandharan art, on the other hand, the figure of the Buddha is never avoided. Not only does he appear in the scenes taken from his life, but the cult images depicting the Buddha, standing or sitting Indian-fashion in poses that were to become traditional, begin to multiply there, as do the Bodhisattvas of the Greater Vehicle, who now people the arcades of stupas and the corners of monastic cells. The *prahabmandala*, the halo, inherited from the Graeco-Roman world, also first appeared in Gandharan art.

Owing to the wave of Buddhist piety that swept the region in the first centuries of our era, the monasteries and stupas decorated with sculpture multiplied in the Gandhara area (now divided between Pakistan and Afghanistan, but then part of the Indian empire founded by the Scythian Kushan dynasty). On the eastern frontiers of Iran, Hellenistic influence had worked deeply into Bactria, and at Begram in Afghanistan, Greek and Indian works have been found hidden away together. In Bactria, the Graeco-Indian king Menander (Milinda in Indian), who reigned in the later 2nd and early 1st centuries B.C., was converted to Buddhism by a monk whom he had invited to his court; the conversations between monk and prince were collected in a famous work that became one of Buddhism's holy books.

The western influence exerted over Indian art has been called Greek, and yet it has been objected that at the time of the "Graeco-Buddhist" art of Gandhara (figs. 453-457), Rome, not Greece, held the power in the East. For the Indian, however, Rome and Greece were alike in their artistic approach, based on anthropomorphism; moreover, what Rome had to offer as an art form, especially on the eastern frontiers of western art, was Hellenism. Indian sculptors learned from the West what relief was; until then they had simply covered the surface before them by spreading out the figures all over it, like primitive artists. The Greeks taught them monumental art, and how a much more convincing image could be obtained by the use of a few figures linked together in common action and modelled in relief against a background over which they cast shadows, than by an all-over swarming of forms. Greece also provided an example of how to represent heads and bodies in order to emphasize the monumental aspect of a figure. Finally, they taught the Indian artists, who knew only the nude, how to exploit draperies in order to accentuate a gesture or to give the composition a feeling of rhythm. It has even been said that Apollo lent his features to the Buddha. Olympian anthropomorphic paganism seems, at any rate, to have appeared in the East just when the Indian sculptors felt the need to devise the image of a man who had attained divine serenity. The Gandharan Buddha heads, often preserved without their bodies (figs. 456, 457), express the varied moods of the Enlightened One, ranging from his indifference on the threshold of Nirvana to his infinite mercifulness, expressed in a radiant smile. The smile, which had appeared with the earliest Buddhist art, took on an enigmatic cast at Gandhara. The capacity to give the face a profound sense of life is another gift of Hellenism; until then, the head of an Indian sculpture had been only a part of the body, but now it became, as for the Greeks, the mirror of the soul. The various faces of the Buddha, of the Bodhisattvas or minor deities, of princes, soldiers, ascetics, and demons, of Greek, barbarian, and Indian ethnic types, might be considered as stemming from Hellenistic expressionism. Overtones of later Greek art are especially marked in the Gandharan stucco statues done later than the blue schist reliefs, which adhered more docilely to Graeco-Roman models (fig. 453). The malleability of stucco gave the artists a freer range and contributed to the creation of a specific style peculiar to the art of that time and place. The forms resulting from this encounter between a spiritualistic religion and the Graeco-Roman aesthetic are in some way comparable to those resulting from the rediscovery of antique classicism by Christian Gothic art, the expression of a religion of God-made-man.

In the 5th century the Chinese pilgrim Fa hsien counted one thousand stupas in Hadda and its surroundings. Unfortunately, the White Huns who repeatedly attacked India overran Gandhara, leaving nothing but ruins, as witnessed by the laments of another Chinese pilgrim, Sang Yün, in 520. Although entombed – and not brought to light until the 20th century – Gandharan art left a deep impression on India. Under the Gupta dynasty, which tried and failed to reunite the continent, a true Indian style developed in the north, in the 4th and 5th centuries, on the basis of Gandharan art. It appears incorrect to term this style "classical"; its tendency to stylization is, from both the classical and the naturalistic points of view, a regression, similar to that of Byzantinism in relation to Graeco-Roman art. In Gupta art the typology of the Buddha was definitively set (fig. 460). The attitudes of the Buddha were classed in categories and his gestures into types, as were those of the Virgin Mary in Byzantine representations: the Buddha *abhaya mudra* and *dharmachakra mudra* became established types like the Byzantine Virgin *theotocos* or *hodigetria*. In the perfectly oval, smoothly modelled, and impersonal faces, the pilgrim no longer could find the humanity that had given such mysterious appeal to the Gandhara figures. The breath of life that throbs in most Indian figures seems here to have withdrawn itself. The stylized mouths and half-closed eyes are geometric patterns, the eyebrows follow elegantly drawn curves, and the merciful smile is a mere formula. Transparent folds of clothing cover the smooth and impersonal bodies with thin, parallel ripples. It has been suggested that this "string-type" drapery might have come from China or Japan, but it is more likely that it was not imported but resulted from the same drive towards abstraction that turned the folds around the Buddha's neck into three perfect circles. Of all the images of the divine that man has created, these are among the most perfect expressions of a theological belief. They incarnate the state of Perfection, of the Supreme Self, the depersonalized being who has extinguished his will to exist and has therefore "realized" himself fully. Art has never invented a formula that so

adequately expresses a conception of what lies beyond life.

Not long after northern India created these images of silence, another religion was being elaborated under the Pallava dynasty, in the Deccan: Hinduism. At Mamallapuram, Elura, Ajanta, and Elephanta, 7th- and 8th-century artists cut from the rock thousands of images depicting the divine Power that moves the world, or illustrating the eloquent sacred poems. Coming into deeper India, Vedantism, once probably an aniconic religion, gave rise to an endlessly proliferating mythology describing a universe of whirling forms in perpetual migration, in a creation ceaselessly renewing itself. Out of the cosmic chaos emerge a few significant images, such as, the Dancing Shiva (fig. 475), and Vishnu asleep on the Serpent Ananta at Mamallapuram (fig. 462).

This creative vein persisted until the 13th century, moving, after the 9th century, into the northwest part of India, where Buddhism had at last been rejected. The gradual weakening of religious feeling made it necessary for the divine manifestations to assert themselves in more exaggerated spasms of activity and in neurotic repetitions. From the realm of Consciousness we have descended into that of mere Existence. The Mogul invasion completed the stereotyping of that powerful art, which survived only in a few bronze statues.

India eventually turned away from the religion of Buddha, but Buddhism, and with it the art it had created, spread throughout the Asiatic East under various forms: Ceylon, Siam, and Burma adopted the *Hinayana*, or Lesser Vehicle, while Cambodia, Java, China, and Japan took up the sense and imagery of the *Mahayana*, or Greater Vehicle. The art of Gupta nourished an international style, and transmitted iconographic themes which were variously interpreted in other centers, just as the Byzantine icon was transformed in the different western countries. But in China, which communicated with Gandhara and the Punjab through the oases of the Tarim basin, Graeco-Buddhist art retained some of its original strength, reinforced by traditional Iranian influences already marked in archaic China.

The severity of the Hinayana doctrine is reflected in the austere art of Ceylon and Siam, where the Gupta stylizations lost their elevated theological connotations to take on a more formal, and even mannered, character. But in Java, Buddhist art seemed to recover its youthful vigor. Though the seventy Dhyani Buddhas sheltered under the minature stupas at Borobudur are in the abstract Gupta tradition, the miles of high relief surrounding the terraces of the great monument narrate the endless stories of Buddha and his previous incarnations in a style of restrained naturalism almost classical in effect. The bodies that Gupta stylization had dematerialized were now brought back to life and roundness, though they lack the Indian sensuality. What is expressed in the figures' smiling grace, the suggestion of joy brought by retreat in meditation, the moderated curvilinear movements, the compositions limited to a few personages, the picturesque views of nature and human creations, is the harmony of all things and beings that stems from love.

In its great creative periods, both Buddhist and Hindu, Indian art was entirely dedicated to the figures of sages and gods. In Java, representations of the external world and of human life were introduced as a discreet background to Buddhist legends. Under the Khmers, Cambodian art was invaded by worldly subjects. In the vast galleries of the Ankor Vat temple, (figs. 480, 481) violence is unleased in gigantic battles: heroes clash weapons, dash their chariots at each other, and trample the dead piled up on the ground – all this in rather orderly affray, the sculptor observing the successive movements of the battalions, their progress, their clash, and finally the onslaught. Further along, evil rampages in Hell, with hideous demons inventing ingenious tortures for the damned, while nearby is the place of celestial sojourn, where beautiful palaces are inhabited by blissful creatures. In great historical triumphal processions infantrymen and horsemen parade, dominated by their chiefs mounted on elephants. All these animated scenes are staged as episodes from the legends of Shiva or Krishna or from the sagas of the Ramayana or the Mahabharata. But in fact they give us detailed information about life under the Khmers, illustrating the deeds of a warlike people governed by an absolute ruler. Like the Egyptian pharaoh, the Khmer ruler, the Devaraja, was a god-king. He is identified with Vishnu or Shiva, or with the Buddha, for in Cambodia Buddhism and Hinduism intermingled in an extraordinary syncretism that provided artists with a very rich iconography. Through the divine sagas the god-king proclaimed his own glory, as Louis XIV of France used to illustrate his through the myth of Apollo or the story of Alexander. In this art, no longer a theological but a theocratic art, we have moved from a land of the gods – India – to a world where it is the hero who is allpowerful. Like the Indians, the Khmers crowded their walls with figures, but unlike them, created well-ordered and rhythmically controlled compositions. The cosmic swarming beloved of the Indians repelled the Khmers, even when representing the World emerging from Chaos in the Churning of the Sea of Milk. Stylistic as well as historical comparisons with the West may be made; as in Egypt, the discipline that held the empire together also ruled art. Generally, Khmer artists arranged their relief scenes in superposed tiers, like the Egyptians, but, alone in the Indian world, they also made approaches to a western type of perspective. In the procession scenes the soldiers are silhouetted against a background of forests whose trees appear to move into depth, their size diminishing relative to their distance from the foreground where the human action takes place. Like western artists, and unlike the Indians, the Khmers also represented human bodies isolated in space – that is, they made true free-standing statues. Their figures stood vertically, in proud autonomy, not flexed in the contorted attitudes of Indian figures, which were possible only in relief and expressed the powerful pulses that merge the human being into the total life process. The Indians loved the soft texture of ripe flesh, but neglected anatomy; the Khmers modelled their bodies firmly, and polished the forms to suggest a dense muscularity. As was suitable for a race of warriors, their preferred physical type was somatotonic, robust and physical, rather than viscerotonic, and it was the male body that provided their canon of proportions and imposed its athletic forms on the female body. As a natural corollary, the Khmers were the only Far Eastern people to conceive architectonic orders and patterns for their monuments, or to employ articulating cornices. It is a matter for reflection that so small a kingdom, however aggressive, should have created an individual art closer in formal values to western art than to the Indian art that inspired it.

At Bamiyan in Afghanistan and at Tun-Huang in Kansu, over a thousand miles away from each other, two colossal rock-cut Buddhas keep watch over the opposite ends of the arduous silk route, which traverses the oases of central Asia to link China with India and Iran. Along that road Buddhism filtered into China. At the halting places for the caravans, numerous monasteries were established, thriving on the gifts of merchants who wanted to elicit from the divine powers protection against brigands. As earlier in India, Buddhist sanctuaries were excavated in the earth's heart; the progress of Buddhism in China is marked by a string of grottoes dedicated to the "thousand Buddhas" – sites like Tun-Huang, Yun-kang, Lung-Men, T'ien-lung Shan, and others newly discovered, like Mai-Chi-Shan.

Explored during the first third of this century by various German, French, English, and Japanese expeditions, the oases of Turkestan yielded rich archeological finds indicating a prolonged occupation from about the 3rd century, extending to the 9th century in western sites, and to the 11th in eastern sites. These were vital discoveries for the history of painting in the Far East, but the rock-sculptures are of mediocre quality. The finest specimens of sculpture are fragile models in unbaked polychromed clay, a popular art derived from the more sophisticated stuccos of Gandhara. The charmingly naïve figurines (fig. 490) represent a sampling of the various types produced by the mixture of races in this region situated at the crossroads between Iran, the Russian steppes, and China.

Monumental sculpture was introduced into China by Buddhism. Archaic China hardly knew the art of relief forms, though some of the Chou bronzes in animal shapes (fig. 493) suggest some capacity for sculpture. Under the Han dynasty, the human victims of burial sacrifices, the last of which occurred at the funeral of the Emperor Che-Huang-ti, were replaced by a whole range of terra-cotta objects and figures destined to furnish the tomb. In China as in the Middle East, art helped man to free himself from the cruel rites made necessary by the belief in an afterlife duplicating life on earth. From the Chou period we know only ritual vessels bristling with symbols, but the Han tombs have yielded a crowd of figurines evoking for us the busy life of the Chinese in the Great Empire. Unlike those of the later T'ang period, the Han tomb models are not overloaded with naturalistic details; a gesture, an attitude, or a movement is summed up in a single shape or silhouette (fig. 491). Artisan production of such high quality must be considered a reflection of a refined civilization, as was Greek pottery. Some of the horses' heads are as fine as those carved in marble by classical Greek artists – perhaps the resemblance is due to the fact that the Han emperors brought their horses from western Asia, from Samarkand. The quality of Han figurines might suggest the existence of a monumental sculpture, but the few statues that survive, which originally surrounded princely tombs, are inorganic masses of stone. On the other hand, the reliefs from the tombs, which we know mainly from rubbings, are delightful (fig. 494). Wandering through elegant palaces or in pleasant landscapes, the animated personages appear to comport themselves according to the laws of perspective; the line is nervous and full of life, particularly in the figures of horses, warriors, jugglers and hunters. However, these "reliefs" are hardly more than smooth, flat silhouettes, slightly raised against a gritty background, and they are really a kind of negation of sculptural qualities. This should not be surprising, for they are a transposition into the permanence of stone of now-lost painted scenes; the art of painting was born during the Han period and was destined to be China's major art form. These funerary scenes filled with picturesque details hint at a naturalistic phase in Chinese painting preceding the philosophical painting that developed later.

With the decline of the Han Empire the spread of Buddhism in China accelerated. Buddhist monasteries became the only institutions capable of maintaining some sort of order amidst the general disorder, just as, in the West, the monks of St. Benedict and St. Columbanus sustained islands of civilization in the barbarian flood that submerged the Roman Empire. When Turkish invaders from eastern Mongolia managed to establish a stable regime, called the Wei dynasty, in the north of China, they relied on Buddhism, which they made their state religion. Around the middle of the 5th century they employed thousands of sculptors to excavate rock-cut sanctuaries at Yun-kang, near their capital Ta-t'ung. When in 499 they transferred their capital to Lo-yang in the Honan, they again needed temples at the gates, and had them cut in the rock at Lung-Men. After the collapse of the Wei Empire at the end of the 6th century, political unity was again achieved temporarily by the Sui, who created a new group of rock temples at T'ien-Lung Shan. In these three groups of sanctuaries work continued throughout the following periods, and here we can trace the progress of Chinese Buddhist sculpture. At Yun-kang the Buddhas and Bodhisattvas still have the fleshy look and the rounded modelling of Indian reliefs and Graeco-Indian sculpture, whose traditions they incorporate (fig. 495). Lung-Men, before the art trade pulled it to pieces forty years ago, was one of the greatest of the world's sanctuaries (fig. 496). (Now, in private or public collections everywhere, the visitor may suddenly find himself facing a mutilated Bodhisattva from Lung-Men; though torn from its sacred context, the smile of the Merciful One still exerts its mysterious charm, and the figure takes on an even more unreal significance.) At Lung-Men the bodies have become thinner and the proportions more elongated; the frontal poses give the figures a hieratic aspect contrasting with the meditative faces radiant with the sense of mercy; the stylized draperies contribute to the disembodiment of these holy images. Hastily carved in grey-black rock, the Lung-Men sculptures are summary, even clumsy, but Wei bronzes still maintained the traditional Chinese artisan techniques from remote epochs. If the Indian art of Gupta gave the most profound interpretation of Buddhist theological inspiration, the divine message of salvation offered by the Mahayana received its most intense artistic expression in Wei China. The Chinese aptitude for mystic evocations was strengthened by a natural disinclination for relief form, and by an inclination towards metaphysical speculation, which found its natural outlet in the art of painting. The Chinese conception of the cardinal points as ordered in groups of four around a fifth at the center displays a feeling for a radiating space incompatible with sculpture, which is by nature a solid form bound within three dimensions. The progressive resorption of relief can be traced at T'ien-Lung Shan, where the style gradually became more and more linear. In the same way modelling became flatter in Quattrocento art, especially among the Sienese, who had certain spiritual affinities with China, as Berenson noted when he discovered Sassetta. Some of the T'ien-Lung Shan apsaras are reminiscent of Duccio angels.

In the T'ien-Lung Shan caves, the Buddhist figures of the T'ang period (fig. 501) contrast with the earlier ones in that they demonstrate a revival of the feeling for solid form. In that war-like dynasty, which achieved and maintained the unity of China for three centuries, Buddhism was still favored, but the T'ang artists were no longer moved by a spiritual fervor; their plump figures with apathetic expressions and inflated cheeks are no longer illumined by the flame of saintliness. The T'ang emperors turned their interest to profane subjects. Ceramic techniques were perfected, and painting gave rise to subtle intellectual speculation. Terra-cotta funerary pottery, often glazed, was plentiful – which shows to what extent Buddhism had become "paganized," for these pottery tomb figures were intended to provide for the dead in the afterlife, whereas the religion envisioned the complete abolition of all life for the Blessed. The T'ang figurines, inspired by the daily life of the time, have had such appeal for western collectors that the manufacture of fakes has flourished; but their self-conscious realism makes them in reality less attractive, less "true" than those of the Han period. The T'ang terra cottas (figs. 506–508) are difficult to study, as we lack precise chronological landmarks among the throngs of figures, but stylistic analysis seems to suggest an evolution of the elegant Sui style towards heavier and more naturalistic forms. The massive horses surrounding the tomb of the Emperor T'ai Tsung have been thought to be later copies – the tombs of the T'ang rulers, destroyed by rebels early in the 10th century, were restored by the first Sung emperor – but their weighty compactness seems very characteristic of T'ang materialism. In quality, none of the T'ang sculptures even remotely approaches the rare paintings preserved from that period.

Sculpture affirms a physical presence, and is therefore at odds with the sense of transitoriness that permeates Chinese thought. It was only for a brief period, under the first impact of Buddhist mysticism, that China was successful in creating a sculpture based in the idea of solid form.

Arrested in its westward progress by the frontiers of pagan or Christian civilizations, Buddhism expanded towards the east, and in the 6th century reached that Land's End of the Far East, Japan. After some struggle, the new faith was accepted as the state religion, and gradually won the whole country. Buddhism settled there, undergoing an evolution, but not being subjected to the persecutions and upheavals that afflicted its course in China. For that reason Korean, Chinese, and Japanese cult objects from the T'ang period have been preserved on the islands of Japan, while none are left in China, where we have to rely entirely on rock-cut sculptures and tombs contents.

Transmitted by Korea, then by China, the Buddhist themes adopted by Japan were illustrated with great refinement. From the beginning, Japanese sculptors handled hard lacquer, wood, or bronze with virtuosity. In Wei China, Buddhist art had throbbed with inner life; in Japan, it became intellectualized and assumed an iconological and theological character wherein it resembles Gupta art, but the Gupta stylization is absent, for already the Japanese tended towards the realism that was to reflect their indigenous artistic spirit. They painted portraits and were inspired by warlike themes. These last had already appeared in the proto-historic period in some of the Jomon figurines (fig. 509), with strongly magical overtones, and one personage of the Buddhist mythology served the taste for bellicosity: the "guardian of the faith," the *lokapala*, who defends the temple against the machinations of earth and hell. Represented as a samurai who blasts the evil-doer with his sword and terrorizes him with fierce grimaces, this St. Michael of Japanese Buddhism seems more akin to the demonic than to the angelic. The concentrated power of certain T'ang *lokapalas* (fig. 502), however, is more impressive than the display of force in the Japanese versions, where strength is dispersed in action. The Chinese artists always seem to keep some power in reserve, which gives their work a margin of mystery.

However perfect in technique, 7th- and 8th-century Japanese sculpture never reaches the heights of religious expression attained in the frescos of Horyu-ji – now only a memory because the were destroyed by fire in 1949. There the purity of line assumes a transcendental significance, and there, at the end of its tremendous expansion in the Far East, the Buddhist ideal of supreme detachment is fully expressed.

VII The Rebirth of Sculpture in the West

I. *Romanesque Sculpture*

Two almost exactly contemporary art works from opposite ends of Europe, the gold antependium (ca. 1020) from Basle on the Rhine (fig. 399), and the lintel on the church of St. Genis des Fontaines (1022) at the foot of the Pyrenees (figs. 514, 516), give the measure of the great cultural gap separating the last works of Ottonian art from the first of Romanesque. The calm figures on the Basle antependium, still responding to antique "illusionistic" aesthetics and standing comfortably in the spaces allotted to them, are in considerable contrast to the figures subjected to a purely ornamental treatment at St. Genis des Fontaines. Here, the personages on the central panel of the lintel are linked in complex compositional interrelationships, while the apostles at either side are tightly fitted into the arcades, which in fact impose their form on the human figures. The lintel is among the first works in which the sculptured forms are clearly adjusted to an architectural framework. In its flattened relief forms the lintel may still partake of the spirit of the early Middle Ages, but its compositional precocity points forward to the coming art.

The St. Genis lintel remains an isolated work, however, for the experimental phase of the Romanesque, lasting through the years from about 1020 to 1070, revolved largely around an architectural element which until then had elicited rather uninteresting treatment: the capital. Early medieval artists had attempted to rescue its monumental function through a revival of the antique types, or had simply reduced it to an elementary cubic shape; but now the capital became the first architectural form to be "sensitized" to stylistic novelty. The very recalcitrance of its shape proved a stimulating challenge to artists. No compulsory iconographic program restricted the sculptors of the 11th-century capitals at Tournus (fig. 515). St. Benigne in Dijon, the Trinité in Caen, St. Benoit-sur-Loire, Bernay Chatel-Sensoir, St. Hilaire in Poitiers, or other churches in Spain and Germany, and the artists indulged freely in juggling imaginative and imaginary elements. They combined forms from middle eastern civilizations, from classical antiquity – such as it was known to the barbarian world – and even from the depths of Asia. The wellspring of French Ro-

manesque sculpture is this play with forms multiplied and metamorphosed in which the sculptor indulges a sense of competing with the demiurge in his creation of "monsters" (analyzed and discussed by Henri Focillon and Jurgis Baltrusaitis). In the first overpowering impulse to create new forms and images, after a long period of stagnation, the sculptors began by establishing between themselves and the outside world the protective screen of a fictional universe populated with imaginary beings, which took on reality as they were embodied in three-dimensional form. The concreteness of the sculptured volumes in turn sustained the artist's creative power – indeed, painting and the minor arts, and even the wooden statues that imitated goldsmith work, remained within the scope of the earlier aesthetic, which they prolonged until the height of the Gothic period. The bronze workers of the Meuse region perpetuated the classicizing Ottonian manner up to the 12th century, and the baptismal font of St. Bartholemy in Liège, cast by Reyner of Huy between 1107 and 1118, nearly a century after the the lintel of St. Genis des Fontaines, reflects a serenity totally dissimilar to the seething Romanesque dynamism then prevailing in the rest of the land which had been Gaul (fig. 571).

The first artist to employ a frank and vigorous relief, though softened by shadows from undercutting, was Bernard Gilduin, who signed the St. Sernin altar in Toulouse (fig. 518), which was consecrated in 1096, and who was also responsible for the remarkable figures of apostles and angels accompanying the Christ in Majesty surrounded by the symbols of the Evangelists, in the ambulatory of the same church. Details in Gilduin's work show the influence of goldsmithery: the decorative rosettes on the blind arcades and the modelling of drapery folds, imitating repoussé metal work. In the first Romanesque works, the volumes seem so pronounced and so solid that one would expect that the relief figures would next take on a separate existence in space, as statues; the development was, in fact, the contrary. On the slightly later Miègeville portal of St. Sernin (fig. 521), each figure, without entirely renouncing its individuality, is linked to the others in an overall compositional scheme. This first attempt to impose unity on a monumental group of sculptures was characteristic of the Languedoc school. Contemporary Spanish artists were content with juxtaposing disconnected relief panels, but at Moissac, where the volume of relief is even further reduced to become a kind of swelling of the wall surface, the undulating linear forms constitute an intensely vital ideological as well as architectural focal point on the building, for the figures are disciplined by a deeply significant unifying iconographic scheme (fig. 522).

Forty years after the starting point of the revival of sculpture, we find ourselves proceeding in a direction opposite to the original one. The Isaiah at Souillac is already hardly more than a wavering flame compared to the older figures in the cloister, immobilized against the wall that holds them stonebound. In the figure of Isaiah (fig. 525), the animated rhythm becomes frenzy, and on the trumeau from the dismantled portal of Souillac monsters swarm like knots of vipers (fig. 526). At St. Etienne in Toulouse, the apostles on the jambs simulate with their crossed legs a feverish gait matched in the rhetorical quality of their gestures and expressions (fig. 527).

The beginnings of the Burgundian school have been all but lost in the almost total destruction of the great abbey of Cluny, the work of St. Hugh. The apse capitals (fig. 532), miraculously preserved, have given rise to a lively polemic. Are they earlier than the Toulouse reliefs, as Kingsley Porter thought, or do these refined works date from a later period, as the French school believes? Some light is shed on the earliest Burgundian Romanesque sculpture by the few remnants of the west portal of Cluny identified or excavated by Sumner Crosby. One of these, a head with empty pupils that originally contained lead inlay, is smoothly shaped and somewhat archaic, despite the quivering life of the mouth (fig. 531); it tells us nothing, however, about the composition of the tympanum from which it came, carved about 1100. To judge from the portals of Autun and Vézelay, the Burgundians were not so expert in the art of composition as the Languedoc masters. Less attracted to formal experimentations, they slid easily into a vein of expressionism; it could be demoniac, as on the Vézelay capitals (fig. 535), or humorous, as in the work of Gislebertus at Autun. The sculptors of Aunis, Poitou and Saintonge, however, introduced a rhythmic grouping in the swarming forms in which they sheathed their facades, and to them is due the invention of a particularly successful form, later adopted by Gothic art: the figured voussoir.

In the Romanesque period, endless variety went into the melting pot: subtle creations like the *Juggler* from St. Pierre-le-Pucellier, Bourges (fig. 530) are contemporary with coarse, popular reliefs like the Cluny *Cobbler* or such for-

malistic academic works as the head of Lothar in Reims, from that king's cenotaph at St. Remi.

In Provence (St. Trophime at Arles), in the Rhone valley area of Languedoc (St. Gilles du Gard), may be found a quite different approach to monumental sculpture (figs. 539, 541). Relief is replaced by statues, or almost-statues, standing against an architecture of forms borrowed from the remnants of antique art still found in those regions. It was a different world, turned towards the Mediterranean and linked to the Italian school. In Auvergne too the tympanum (Conques-en-Rouergue) (fig. 538) was composed of statuary masses balanced like weights in the two pans of a scale – a principle of monumental composition that was to become characteristic for Gothic tympana.

The Romanesque school of northern Italy, once considered a minor one, has recently been studied in many publications. These somewhat invalidate Kingsley Porter's thesis, which tended to minimize the influence of French Romanesque sculpture in Italy. The Emilian workshops, however, were apparently nourished by the main currents of Romanesque France, springing from the schools of Languedoc and Burgundy, and from Chartres – particularly the last, which seems to have had close links with Emilia. However, Italy imposed its native genius on the imported forms, so much so that their origins are sometimes unrecognizable, the adopted motifs being clothed in utterly alien style. Emilia, where the liveliest branch of Romanesque art developed, persistently elaborated and pursued certain forms basic to Italian sculpture up to the time of Donatello, forms utterly divergent from the French.

Roughly speaking, two main currents prevailed in northern Italy. The first is the Lombard, which tended to develop barbarian elements, its artists showing little interest in human figures but indulging instead in endless repetitions, in frieze-like arrangements, of the old migration period zoomorphic or ornamental motifs. San Michele in Pavia shows the final stage in that tendency, the columns and the arches around the portals covered with these designs as if by tattoo or embroidery. Inflated to monumental scale, this barbarian heritage could give rise to such strange and powerful works as the ambo in the basilica of Isola San Giulio (fig. 546), Orta. The second current can be found in Modena, Piacenza, Parma, and Ferrara. Its main aim was to resuscitate the human figure. The evolution begins in the work of Wiligelmo's school on the facade of Modena Cathedral (fig. 547) (1099 to 1166 according to Roberto Salvini; 1106 to 1120 according to René Jullian); it reached its height at the end of the 12th century in Benedetto Antelami, whose art looks forward to the Dugento, and who was responsible for a complex of sculptures at the Parma Baptistry, which were continued by his workshop into the 13th century (figs. 551, 552).

The revival of form in sculpture developed along divergent paths in France and in Italy. In France, sculpture tended to express itself as relief, adhering to the wall and closely linked with the architecture. Emilian sculpture, on the contrary, unhesitatingly favored statuary, from the beginning on. The contrast between the two approaches is nowhere more evident than in Italian works directly inspired by French sculpture. The Eve in the Lodi Cathedral (fig. 553), for instance, is obviously inspired by a Languedoc model; but the instinctive Italian tendency to render full justice to the volumes works at cross-purposes with the artist's awkward imitations of the clinging drapery folds that give surface animation to the French sculpture. The crossed legs, which in the Toulouse reliefs suggest a dance movement, have become a heavy stamping. Burgundian sculpture, according to Roberto Salvini, inspired the strange reliefs in the museum at Modena, which look as though they might have been excavated at Selinunte, and which, by analogy with some Greek works, have been called "metopes"; but if that is the case, their maker has created the most static works in all Italian sculpture, and far removed from the supple style of Cluny or Autun (fig. 550).

The very essence of Italian Romanesque sculpture is inertia, while the French school tends towards movement. The anarchic dynamism of barbarian art, disciplined by stylistic rules which have been defined by Baltrusaitis, produced monnumental rhythms. The lack of architectonic feeling on the part of North Italian Romanesque or even Gothic artists is revealed in their disinclination to design facades decorated with other than monotonous bands of Lombard ornament – blind arcades row on row, or naively juxtaposed series of reliefs in cases where figurative elements were introduced.

The favorite motif of the Italian Romanesque sculptor was the human figure. Desiring to give it its full individuality, he was unwilling to distort it by imposing architectural rhythms upon it; even less was he inclined to mix it with animal forms in chimerical combinations like those produced by the French sculptors; even the Emilian school, the most open to French influence, preferred borrowing its beasts from antique models, while the Lombard school directly perpetuated the barbarian tradition of monsters, but still without subjecting them to the endless metamorphoses that delighted French artists. To be sure some parts of France were also interested in the statue, particularly Provence, which exchanged motifs with

Emilia, and was in some ways closer to it than to the rest of France. Still, the Provençal school was not cut off from other French schools, but shared with them the linking of sculpture and architecture, with the difference that at Arles or St. Gilles the statuary dominated the organization of the architecture, rather than submitting to it. Moreover, if the Provençal sculptors obtained their effects by balancing masses rather than by modulating their surfaces in linear rhythms, they still employed drapery to create subtle, almost pictorial effects; nor were their figures' volumes so brusquely static as those of Emilian artists, for Romanesque vitality links the stocky forms in continuous rhythms. In Provence as in Emilia, Romanesque sculpture drew copiously on the antique. Ancient remains were especially plentiful in Italy, of course, and the digging necessary to establish cathedral foundations frequently uncovered more of them. In southern Italy, which remained isolated from the Romanesque stylistic trends, the imitation of the antique style went on without interruption up to the 13th century. Capitals like those in the church of Monreale (fig. 558) belong to the pure classical tradition.

French forms traveled to Spain along the pilgrimage routes, which meandered through the countryside on the way to Compostela, to allow the faithful to visit various sanctuaries on their way; in the northern provinces of the peninsula, Oviedo, Leon, and Compostela became centers of a Spanish sculptural revival. There seem to have been exchanges in both directions, for certain works at Leon and Oviedo, apparently dating earlier than St. Sernin, may even have influenced the beginnings of Romanesque there. Spanish sculpture differed from the French mainly in its lack of architectonic discipline. A feeling for monumental forms first appears during the second half of the 12th century, develops in the Silos cloister, at San Vincente of Avila, and finally produces the rigorously architectonic Portico de la Gloria at Santiago de Compostela (fig. 569), the work of Master Mateo, done from about 1169 to 1188. Its relation to the first great Romanesque Gothic portals is so close that a French origin has been suggested for this artist; some Spanish historians believe him to have been a pupil of the French artist Fruchel, to whom the facade of San Vincente of Avila is attributed. Compostela sculpture also reveals the first organized iconographic program in the French manner to be found in Spain. Many different influences meet in the Portico de la Gloria, for we also find reminiscences of the Romanesque art of Poitou. Nonetheless, the architectonic order here constricts the statuary rather than giving it a rhythmic unity.

Catalonia offers no such monumental sculptural

ensembles as those of northwest Spain. But in the remote Pyrenean valleys may be found a few examples of an art that has largely vanished elsewhere, that of altar frontals. In the richer monasteries these might have been magnificent products of the goldsmith's art, of the type surviving in the gold antependium from Basle and the paliotto of Sant' Ambrogio in Milan; but in Catalonia we find imitations of stucco or wood, made for poor churches and preserved from destruction by their very lack of value and by their isolation in the mountains (figs. 567, 568).

During the 12th century, Romanesque sculpture spread in successive waves through Europe; brought by the Crusaders, it even spread to Palestine, where it took on a strangely Asiatic cast. In Germany Romanesque sculpture evolved without the French concern for architectonic rhythms, as shown by the decoration of the portal of the Jacobskirche in Regensburg (fig. 575), for instance. It continued, however, up until the 13th century, and the Prophets around the choir at Bamberg (fig. 576) are but slightly earlier than the first works from the High Gothic Reims workshop. The impassioned dialogue of these figures of apostles and prophets expresses the dialectical spirit of early medieval apologetics, and contrasts with the evangelical serenity of the apostle groups on contemporary French cathedrals. It also reveals the beginnings of the German expressionistic tradition.

Maintaining itself rather apart from the main stream of Romanesque art, the art of bronze casting continued to yield works of art, especially various objects of liturgical furniture, in various parts of Europe – in the Meuse region, in Germany, and in Italy. Founders' workshops cast several notable doors for churches during the 11th and 12th centuries. At the end of the 11th century in Verona, a very primitive artist, little affected by contemporary developments, made the doors for the church of San Zeno (fig. 580). The easternmost products of the bronze-workers' art can be found in Novgorod, in Russia, and Gniezno, in Poland, in doors from a Magdeburg workshop (fig. 581). The doors made for Monreale and Pisa (fig. 582) by Bonannus of Pisa at the end of the 12th century show the latest developments. Such doors were often export objects: Byzantium exported doors to many parts of South Italy, and there they were imitated by local workshops. Stone was the artist's favored material in France, but Italy and Germany never lost the tradition of bronze-working, which in Italy was to undergo a magnificent revival at the time of the Renaissance.

2. *Gothic Sculpture*

"Lord, let me know through love what I sense through knowledge; let me feel with my heart what I apprehend with my mind... Catch me up in your love, possess me wholly! Take me into the sanctuary of your love, I ask that grace, I entreat that favor. I knock at the door of your sanctuary and beseech you to open it... O comfort my soul hungry for your love! Let love of you fill it, let your love fill it; take hold of me and possess me entirely..."

Thus stammered the ecstatic St. Anselm, discovering "the very sweet Jesus, the beloved friend." Not since the passionate St. Augustine six centuries earlier had like cries of love risen from the soul to God. Night had ruled in men's hearts; the Christian religion of love had become a religion of precepts under which the faithful bent in fear. Western culture was to be reborn in the return to the sources of the Gospel, in the rediscovery of God made Man. A new love and knowledge, mysticism and philosophy, came from it; creation and all its creatures were to be justified by the rediscovery of the truth that in identifying himself with human nature, God had sanctified all of nature. As a result, the veil that had hidden the world since the end of antiquity was torn away. The sculptors in the cathedrals could again carve out the forms of the human body, since that *corpus verum* was the body of God himself. As once before, when the free-standing statue took form under the Greek sun, it was in sculpture that the body was first rediscovered. Three-dimensional form tends to lure the artist closer to nature, while painting may tempt him to ornament and abstraction. Sculpture in the Gothic period became an open-air pursuit, done in a yard, sometimes even done from the model, whom the sculptor could see face to face with the created work. Pygmalion breathed life into a statue – not a painting. Manuscript illumination, painting, stained glass, and enamels still clung to Romanesque formalism, but in the earliest years of the 13th century Christ and the Virgin stepped down from the tympanum onto the trumeau of the church door, showing to the faithful merciful faces in human likeness.

It was logical, then, that the human figure first returned to natural form in sculpture; but before that occurred there were many conditions that were long in being fulfilled When St. Anselm uttered his burning prayers sculptors were only just attempting their first clumsy figures in the great abbey of Cluny or at St. Sernin in Toulouse. Figurative sculpture had to serve a long apprenticeship through the 12th century before the image of the benign Christ could be born. Art had to emerge from the cloister, a seeming paradox, since it was in the cloister that mystic speculation was born and developed. Yet in the religious community the mystic could be disruptive; dedicated to self-abnegation, he was yet an individual whose behavior might transgress community discipline – the ecstatic trance might seize him just when the bell summoned the brothers to common prayer. The greatest among those called to mystic union with God, men like Johannes Eckhart or St. John of the Cross, all had trouble with the ecclesiastical hierarchy. The faith of the convent was a faith based on order. For centuries, liturgical duty was the sole motivation for the monastic vocation. Until the time of St. Anselm (ca. 1033–1109) and St. Bernard (1090–1153) a monk entered the cloister to praise God, not to love Him. The monastery imprisoned a mortified soul and body in the never-ending round of the liturgical years, as the monk endlessly circled his cloister, cut off from the world. From his very isolation mysticism was born, a bridge traversing the forbidden world of existence to reach the essence. As long as art remained in the hands of monks in the overheated mental world of the cloister, it ignored nature and reveled in monsters incarnating those obscure terrors called sin. In the shadow of the monasteries, privileged places isolating men from life, all the old symbols, all the archetypes deposited in the collective unconscious of humanity, throve and found expression in the stone monuments, until that radiant figure appeared who would put all the chimaera to flight.

Before this voice of love, first heard through a few exalted monks, could find its echo in the world of images, the monastery workshops had to be replaced by those of the cathedrals, the abbey by the immense open church to which the worshipper came not simply as a pilgrim-guest but as one of the faithful who had contributed to the building with his own hands, with his own faith, love, and self-confidence based on a trust in God made Man. Most important, the artist was no longer necessarily a member of the cloistered, all-male society, but was a man who often went home from the workshop at night to embrace his wife and play with his children, children he might take walking in the fields or woods to pick flowers; in his house lived an old father who might serve as a model for the prophets. The framework of his life need no longer be the monkish ranks, but that human microcosm mingling sexes and ages, the family, and beyond that, that wider family of the town, no less a City of God for being an earthly city.

Once the impulse had been given, the evolution was rapid. Before the death (1226) of St. Francis of Assisi, who celebrated with such overflowing love the sun, the moon, the animals and plants of God's creation, the cathedral sculptors had already turned to nature. Though many years were to pass before they manifested much interest in animals, in 12th-century Ile de France they had already discovered delight in the flowers and plants that each spring brought life to the countryside around the towns where the cathedrals were rising, their lofty vaults visible from every point in the surrounding plains. For those who have long known these churches intimately, nothing is more moving than the springlike vegetal ornament, still intact where other decorations have been destroyed, that gradually crept over the stone building. As we know through a lover of botany who devoted her life to the study of this ornament, Denise Jalabert, the sculptors at first borrowed from nature only generalized floral forms, which they adapted to an architectural function. Then gradually, from the first quarter of the 13th century, they began to copy the distinct species: lilac, violet, oak, hawthorn, ivy, grape, trilobate hepatica, holly, fig, walnut, watercress, thistle, hops, buttercup, arum lily, fern, maple, sweetpea, hollyhock, rose-mallow, briar, crowfoot, plantain, mugwort... the cathedral became a huge stone herbarium. The monsters entirely lost their prominent place on the capitals, which they had occupied for more than a century. Put to flight by nature, they took refuge in the cathedral's upper parts, where they made themselves useful as gargoyles spitting out rainwater – a sad end for images that had occupied a place of honor within the sanctuary.

The Ile de France in the 13th century offered a combined political and cultural progress paralleled only in 5th-century Athens. France would crystallize around the nucleus of the Capetian Kingdom. There more than anywhere else the monarch was mindful of his duties towards his subjects. Louis VII, the king under whom St. Denis, Sens, Laon and Notre-Dame de Paris were built, said: "Divine kindness has decreed that all men, since they have the same origin, should be gifted from birth with a sort of natural freedom. But Providence has allowed some of them to lose, through their own fault, their original dignity and to fall into a servile condition. It belongs to our Royal Majesty to elevate them to freedom again." The freeing of serfs, the emancipation of the communes, and in general, the protection of their subjects against feudal brigands were the ruling policies of the kings of France, supported by the bishops. There was no question of divine right at that time, as on the other side of the Rhine; the king was only an agent, delegated by Providence. Louis IX, St. Louis, went further. This is how he admonished his son: "My son, I beg you to win the love of your people. For I would prefer that a Scotsman come from Scotland should govern the Kingdom well and loyally, rather than that you should govern it badly." This love comes from the same source as the love of God: "Dear Son, I teach you first of all to love God with all your heart and all your might, for without love, nothing is worth anything."

Like the Greek temple, the cathedral is the monument of the city; marvelous expression of unity, it was born of the aspirations of the people, grouped around the bishops and king. As Robert Branner wrote, the art of St. Louis' period was a courtly art, from a court where sanctity did not exclude elegance. Chartres was a country cathedral, while Paris, Amiens, and Reims reflect the the aristocratic graces of a society where feudalism no longer ruled, a society open to the influence of southern France, where woman was made an ideal being whose beauty and virtue were celebrated by the poets. Influencing religion, this courtly love spread the cult of the Virgin Mary next to the cult of Christ. The Virgin, once elevated unattainably in that theological symbol, the tympanum, came down to preside over the trumeau; there, though she kept her sternness for a while, she soon became a courtly lady. We like to imagine Marguerite of Provence, the dainty wife of St. Louis, with the features of the Virgin on the north portal of Notre-Dame de Paris – a figure spared, possibly because of her beauty, when the *sans-culotte* of 1793 destroyed all the other statuary of the cathedral (fig. 617).

Born in the Ile de France, of elements borrowed from Languedoc and Burgundian art, the Gothic church portal achieved its definitive form as early as 1150, at Chartres. Sculpture was longer submerged in the architecture: it created its own mirror of architectural forms. On the tympana, lintels, or arches, equilibrium was reached by a static balancing of statuary. Column-statues were no longer the ornament for the supports, but became the columns themselves – a development which is also symbolic. Standing solemnly, they are courtiers and ladies, clothed in rich contemporary dress instead of in the conventional draperies of the Romanesque period (figs. 583–588). Their heads are no longer schematized but are real human faces, some with a hint of the smile that in St. Louis' time bloomed full, and even affectedly, on the faces of the statues at Reims, whence it spread to the rest of France and Europe. The first to mention that very French facial expression was the Capetian king who reigned when the Chartres Royal Portal was built. To his cousin Henry II of England, who had taken Aquitaine from him by marrying the wife he had repudiated, Louis VII wrote insolently: "We are

not rich! We own only three things: bread, wine, and a smile."

After 1200, the great cathedral workshops opened one after the other, developing their separate traditions, but influencing each other. This created a very complex situation from the historiographic viewpoint, since in the Gothic period the sculptural style, like the architectural, underwent such rapid transformations that no building program was completed in the style in which it had been begun, however speedy the work. From one statue to the next, the sculptor pursued his search for new forms and expressions, and new artists constantly brought fresh ideas. The avant-garde reigned in that golden age of Gothic classicism.

Despite reciprocal influences, until about 1250 each workshop tended to keep its own style. The sculpture at Chartres shows a strange mixture of rough rusticity and asceticism; it embodied theological aspirations, and as a result, when its style became less rigid, around 1215, it produced one of the most beautiful of all representation of God made Man, the human and the divine combined in perfect unity (fig. 591). The Amiens workshop is distinguished by a natural grace tempered with religious serenity: the *Beau Dieu* of Amiens (fig. 607) is more human than divine. The Paris atelier was characterized by a nobility of style befitting the royal metropolis; without any direct imitation of antiquity, it achieved quite spontaneously the most beautiful classical rhythms, nearest to those of 5th-century Greek art. At Reims, the book of stone is the most difficult of all to decipher, successive changes of program having resulted in puzzling crosspaths in the statuary. The thread through the stylistic labyrinth of Reims has been unraveled by fifty years of patient research, mainly by German scholars. (The first was Wilhelm Vöge, a man of genius so devoted to Reims cathedral that his health and his morale were deeply shaken by his countrymen's persistence in trying to destroy the sublime building during the first World War. As if in retribution, he left his chair at Freiburg University, giving up his research and interrupting a career which would have made him one of the pioneers of art history.) We now know that the famous classicizing atelier of Reims belongs to the beginning and not to the apogee of the evolution. To it belong the angels on the chevet, set in place as early as 1221, and statues of Christ and various apostles and saints; these were adjudged of inferior workmanship by Jean le Loup, the second *maître d'oeuvre*, who demoted them to the north transept. From the same workshop came other pieces which were considered fine enough for the west front: notably the Visitation (fig. 604). The elegant draperies falling in clinging folds may be derived, as has been claimed, from an antique tendency in the 12th-century art of the Meuse and Rhine regions, best exemplified in Nicolas of Verdun, which links up with Ottonian and even Carolingian art: the similarity of these draperies to the harmonious draperies of the Lorsch Gospel covers has been noted earlier. However, some statues, notably the figures of the Visitation group, undeniably wear Greek chitons and himations, which the artists cannot have seen in local examples. It is more logical to suppose that some Reims artist saw the Greek originals that were still above ground in Athens. After all, a Reims artist brought back from Greece the Byzantine motif of the angels bearing the instruments of the Holy Liturgy, unusual in the West, which he transposed into statuary in the angels of the apse buttresses. Such a contact was historically possible after the capture of Constantinople by the Crusaders. In 1205 Athens was conquered by Othon de la Roche, whose lands in France were near Champagne, and Guillaume de Champlitte, from Champagne, conquered Morea (the Peloponnesus). Othon de la Roche was made a duke and used the Propylaea as his palace and the Parthenon as a cathedral. Thus a meeting occurred at least once between Greek classicism and the new Gothic classicism.

But the Reims "first manner," because of these antique influences, and because it was rooted in the traditions of the early Middle Ages, was considered outmoded by Jean le Loup, who became master of works about 1228. To rejuvenate the Reims workshop, he turned to the more modern workshop of Amiens, whose facade had been begun about 1225. The Reims Virgins of the Annunciation (fig. 610) and Presentation, in contemporary costumes, and Simeon (fig. 609) are inspired by the Amiens style. Their more elongated proportions, their drooping shoulders and oval faces, tend away from the antique towards that Gothic verticalism which began in the column-statues of the Chartres Royal Portal. But the drapery is no longer a mere ornament; its broad movements and deep folds set off the shape of the bodies. The Gothic canon moved rapidly towards a refined elegance of which the Reims Queen of Sheba, reduced to a stump during the first World War, was the most perfect example. An elevated theological tone allied to classical nobility was maintained in the monumental statues on the upper parts of the north transept (the Church and the Synagogue; Adam and Eve). Owing to civil disorders, the Reims workshop was closed in 1233. Reopening in 1236, its style began to evolve towards a somewhat affected grace, which was accompanied by the appearance of the famous

smile; over-emphatic and mannered on the St. Nicasius angel (fig. 611), it is more subtle and human on lesser-known statues. One of these was the Bathsheba from the great rose-window, whose head, found among the rubble and unfortunately now fixed into place with an iron clamp, miraculously survived the destruction of her figure and the entire group to which she belonged.

The workshops of the large cathedrals were active until the second half of the 13th century. Then differences became less marked, and individual manners tended to merge into one style in which the Reims manner was predominant. The *Vierge dorée* of the Amiens north transept (fig. 618) is directly derived from the St. Nicasius angel and has become so human that she has lost her transcendental character, to become merely a happy, if elegant, young mother playing with her baby. The large Bourges workshop, source of a magnificent set of portals, produced a very elegant Last Judgment, while the apostles of the Sainte Chapelle (fig. 616) best exemplify a sculptural perfection devoid of inspiration. From the end of the 13th century classicism inevitably ossified into academism; artists were no longer able to render the subtle psychological meaning of the smile, which appears as a mere convention in the Virgin at St. Amand-les-Pas (fig. 631). During the 14th century, sculpture became completely stereotyped and mannered. A few artists, like the sculptor who made the tomb of Cardinal de Lagrange at Avignon (fig. 634), could still recapture the grand style. Apostle groups of the type made famous by those in the Sainte Chapelle in Paris (fig. 616) became essential to the ornament of episcopal and princely chapels. A southern French artist working in Rieux between 1324 and 1328, however, could still use that formula to make a series of powerful statues whose expressionism looks forward to Sluter: the features of his St. Paul (fig. 632) suggest to us Sluter's Moses.

We must picture the workshops of the great French cathedrals as schools of apprenticeship which provided the whole of Europe with young artists who could bring the new artistic forms to the numerous workshops set up everywhere by bishops desirous of rebuilding their cathedrals. Thus, the Gothic style born in the Ile de France and in Champagne spread in successive waves as far as Scandinavia. Its infiltration into Germany is most interesting. The influence of Reims over the Bamberg workshop, for instance, has been stressed and denied and has provoked passionate controversies between French and German art historians. Investigations at Bamberg, proving that all the statues were *in situ* for the dedication in 1237, have pushed back the date of the Reims statues to some years earlier than 1250, a date which had been generally accepted by French historians. The Bamberg sculptors impressed their own strong personality on the French models. As interpreted at Bamberg, the classical clothing of the Reims Visitation becomes a turmoil of baroque folds, and the gentle face of the Reims Virgin is replaced by a plump, naturalistic face from a very different world – the world of Germanic expressionism, which was born at Bamberg (fig. 638). On the portal, the *Fürstentor*, the artist meant to endow the elect with the smile of Reims, but their expression can hardly be distinguished from the satanic grin of the damned (fig. 637). A few years later, sometime between 1249 and 1270, this naturalism came into its own in the west choir built by Bishop Dietrich at Naumburg cathedral (figs. 640-641). The iconographic theme is unusual; in a very Germanic show of feudal pride, twelve barons and baronesses from the Saxon Marches, early benefactors of the church, stand around the choir, among them the margraves of Meissen, Bishop Dietrich's own family. The stress on individualism and on psychological accuracy is remarkable, all the more so as these historical portraits are purely imaginary. The artist even gave one of them the face of a rogue because Timo was known to have been a traitor. In the Crucifixion on the choir screen, Mary is for the first time shown weeping at the foot of the cross, her face twisted in grief (fig. 642). In the 14th century and until about 1430, German art begins to display that typical oscillation between the extremes of a somewhat affected feminine charm and a cruel expressionism – the eternal torment of the Germanic soul in search of equilibrium.

Set halfway between France and the heart of Germany, Strasbourg assimilated much more faithfully the spirit of Chartres and Reims, adding a touch of exquisite elegance to the latter style in the statues of the Church and the Synagogue (fig. 628), while the Germanic influence is more obvious in the expressions of the Virtues (fig. 629) and Vices of the west facade. In the Dormition of Mary, south transept (fig. 627), the faces of the apostles are inspired by Chartres, but the supple drapery is typical of the "antique manner" once prevalent in the Meuse and Rhine districts.

Gothic Spain was more closely dependent on the French workshops. The most faithful imitation of the Chartres column-statues is to be found on the way to Compostela, at Santa Maria la Real de Sangülsa. By the 13th century artistic forms were no longer transmitted along the route followed by Compostela pilgrims. Public life had become laicized, and international exchanges were no longer dominated by monastic orders, but by political expediency. There were numerous exchanges at that time between Castile, strengthened by the *reconquista*, and France, for the French queen-mother was a Castilian. The great center from which the French Gothic style spread through Spain was Burgos Cathedral, whose workshop dominated Spanish art until the end of the 15th century. A master from Amiens sculptured the Sarmental Portal (fig. 648) where a Christ like the *Beau Dieu* gives his blessing, surrounded by archaic and awkwardly naturalistic symbols of the evangelists; clearly in those times of humanistic classicism, monsters were no longer acceptable. On the Coroneria Portal, whose composition shows considerable uncertainty, we find a noble *apostolado* also inspired by Amiens, and in the upper parts of the towers, monumental statues in the style of Reims. In the upper cloister, the statues of the founders, St. Ferdinand and Beatrice of Swabia (fig. 650), reflect mundane aspects of the Reims style. In Leon, the west facade has a porch with doors that seem inspired by the north and south transepts of Chartres, but the workshop used Spanish sculptors familiar with the new style and capable of working out artistic forms of their own (fig. 647).

In England there was little interest in monumental sculpture; tombs (fig. 646) were the most original English productions of the 13th century.

Italian sculptors prolonged the Romanesque style well into the 13th century, particularly in Emilia. The Parma Baptistry (fig. 552) shows the continuation of Antelami's workshop gradually replacing Romanesque by Gothic. Elsewhere in the Parma area, in the Veneto, in central Lombardy, imported Gothic regressed towards Romanesque, or sometimes even became Byzantine. In southern Italy the Romanesque style was even more persistent, dominating the Ravello ambo as late as 1272 (fig. 652); only the hint of a smile in the head surmounting the ambo shows some Gothic influence.

In Italy as in France, the new style appeared in districts other than those in which Romanesque art had flourished. During the second half of the 13th century, in painting as in sculpture, Tuscany assumed leadership of the cultural movement in the peninsula, creating the first really Italian style, a style which was one day to dethrone the Gothic even in France where it had been born.

The sources of Nicola Pisano's art are obscure. Historians too facilely explain his style by citing a document stating that he came from Apulia. The literal imitation of the antique practiced by a few sculptors under the patronage of Frederick II of Hohenstaufen has left only the impoverished works from the Porta Capuana (Capua museum), and was probably as ephemeral an influence as the inspired policy of the Emperor himself, so progressive for his time that it was misunderstood. (The cruel Charles of Anjou, who became King of Naples in 1266 soon drowned in blood Frederick's dreams of universal harmony.) Those few examples cannot have influenced Nicola Pisano. The stamp of antiquity is so strong in his work that it can only have been impressed in Rome. It has been suggested that he was inspired by sarcophagi, but their real relationship to his art is not so simple; searching for antique forms Nicola Pisano found Early Christian sarcophagi that derived from them, but where could he have found, in either pagan or Christian sarcophagi, compositions as orderly as his reliefs on the Pisa Baptistry pulpit? (Figs. 654–656). Paradoxically, it is the rather confused reliefs on his Siena pulpit, under a different influence (fig. 657), that suggest the entangled compositions on late Roman sarcophagi. In 13th-century Rome so many relics of paganism still remained above ground that there was no need to dig for them. Nicola Pisano must have gone directly to the antique sources and not to the bastardized forms of Early Christian art. In the latter he could have found no model for the Hercules representing Fortitude in the Pisa Baptistry – a magnificent study in anatomy, with the sex clearly represented, which exemplifies the marked difference in approach compared to French statuary, which always remained deeply religious: here the theme only is theological, while the spirit remains pagan.

Only in the Pisa pulpit do we find that revival of the antique relief, that interest in the corporeal reality of the human figure. Against a borrowed Gothic architectural structure the grandiose cadences of the reliefs and the quiet authority of the statues give an impression of strength which must be understood as springing from an underlying humanism very different from Gothic humanism, in which flexible bodies are molded by the soul. The Siena pulpit is entirely different from that at Pisa. The compositions are encumbered with a tangle of characters, curved folds replace the fluted folds of Pisa, the bodies are restless – the whole spirit is altered. This new style may be due to Giovanni Pisano, son of Nicola. His share in the Siena pulpit was important enough for him to have received a fee half as large as his father's. Surprisingly, the two pulpits are fairly close in date, that at Pisa having been completed in 1260 and that at Siena begun in 1265 and finished in 1269. Giovanni Pisano's birthdate is unknown, but when the Pisa was commissioned he was probably only a young apprentice. When he had become his father's main assistant a few years later, his personality was certainly strong enough to have influenced Nicola's style. In 1284 he under-

took, alone, the pulpit in Pisa Cathedral, and in 1295 that of Sant'Andrea in Pistoia. Developing his own style, he remained aware of antique art, but rejected his father's limiting paganism; if we look at Giovanni's interpretation of the figure of Hercules (fig. 660), we see that his father's athlete has now undergone a course of asceticism, emerging as a lean hero whose head suggests that of a prophet rather than that of a demigod. Giovanni had been converted to Gothic. How did he come in contact with it? Probably through ivories: the confusion of his compositions is understandable if they were an imitation of the scenes on ivories, narrative scenes intended to be read at close range. Entirely different from his father's, Giovanni Pisano's genius tended towards dramatic action. An apocalyptic vein runs through his work, twisting the shoulders, lowering heads, bringing passion to the faces. That is why his masterpieces are the Old Testament figures on the upper part of the facade at Siena (fig. 663): they are even more prophetic and visionary than the sculptures of the Bamberg choir, and express a mood recaptured by Sluter, Donatello, and Michelangelo. Italy was to excel in the rendering of the suprahuman symbolized in the herculean power of bodies and the unleashed force of action. The dialogue between mother and child which French sculptors had depicted with such human tenderness became dramatic with Giovanni Pisano. The strange Virgin of Prato (figs. 661, 662) stares passionately at the young colossus on her arm; the draping of the heavy folds of her garment expresses the pent-up violence in her body. This Virgin is a direct precursor of Sluter's Virgin on the portal of the Chartreuse of Champmol. As at Champmol, Virgin and Child are linked in the same tragedy: that of the human condition.

Giovanni Pisano's tormented genius found no imitators, as though he had offered only an interruption in the true tradition of Tuscan art, represented in the second half of the 13th century by Nicola's style as it had appeared in all its purity on the Pisa Baptistry pulpit. Tino di Camaino and Fra Guglielmo, who made the Arca di San Domenico in Bologna, followed Nicola docilely; Arnolfo di Cambio, who had worked on the Siena pulpit, interpreted him more freely. At Orvieto Cathedral a talented artist, probably Maitani, assimilated Gothic flexibility and combined it with Hellenistic grace (fig. 667). The lesson of nobility taught by 13th-century French art would have remained without sequel in Italy had it not been for Andrea da Pontedera, known as Andrea Pisano, who made the first of the bronze doors for the Florence Baptistry (figs. 669, 670). It took Italy one century to overcome both the Olympian humanism of Nicola Pisano and the dramatic instinct of Giovanni, and to assimilate finally the rhythmic cadences of Paris, Amiens, and Reims. This late assimilation was to become, three-quarters of an century later, the source of one of the great traditions of Italian sculpture, but during the latter half of the 14th century it appeared to dry up; Andrea di Cione, known as Orcagna, was as conventional in sculpture as in painting.

Northern Lombardy fostered families of architects and sculptors who, from the early Middle Ages to the 17th or even 18th century, handed down through the generations the traditions derived from abroad. From the 12th to the 14th century, the sculptors known as the *Maestri Campionesi* remained faithful to the massive Romanesque style, even when they attempted a few Gothic innovations. Nicola's style was brought late to the north, in the 14th century by the Pisan Giovanni di Balduccio, who worked about 1335 on the Arca di San Pietro Martire at St. Eustorgio in Milan. In the second half of the 14th century, the workshops of the colossal Milan Cathedral were initiated; they produced innumerable statues, fully Gothic, but of a purely formal style that in its worst examples was stereotyped into senility.

Like ancient art, Gothic represents a principle rather than a style. Romanesque art was born, reached its flowering, faded, and died within a relatively short period, without going beyond the limits of a style that would have ended in hollow rhetoric had it been prolonged. But the vital force within Gothic never died completely, and has sequels in western civilization until the 20th century. The possibilities of Gothic style were so all-encompassing that it soon turned into its contrary. This is perhaps more obvious in architecture than in sculpture, for under the seemingly frivolous ornament, 15th-century religious buildings are more solidly constructed than the bold churches of the 13th. Only the study of the historical sequence and continuous evolution that links the serene French portals of the 13th century with the tormented sculpture of the 15th can explain how the one could have engendered the other, apparently its opposite – revealing the truth that Gothic art, like Greek art, contained within itself the limitless possibilities of life itself. (In 1913 the classical archaeologist Wladimir Deonna pointed to the analogous historical developments of Greek and of Gothic sculpture; both evolved from classicism to baroque. From this analogy Henri Focillon deduced the principles of a system of evolution leading from primitivism to baroque through the various stages of classicism, academism, and mannerism. But, as has already been observed in connection with prehistoric and primitive art, this process which he called "the life of forms" applies fully only to Greek and Gothic art.)

By the end of the 14th century in France, its country of origin, Gothic sculpture had become static and stereotyped, in spite of the new life infused by Flemish art, just then beginning to assert its individuality. Gothic inspiration seemed to have run dry when a Netherlander from a region previously barren of artistic talents, took advantage of a favorable combination of circumstances to bring about the revolution needed to revive this dying style. Claus Sluter, working at the end of the 14th century at the Chartreuse of Champmol, built by the Dukes of Burgundy as their pantheon, liberated statuary from all architectonic limitations and gave it a new compactness and solidity. Through an almost theatrical exaggeration of gesture and expression, through acutely naturalistic observation, and through the force of action in the sculptured bodies, he gave his statues an intensely material presence that Gothic art, for doctrinal reasons, had always avoided. That body which had been only an outer wrapping suddenly became a prime reality. The workshop formed at Champmol, which first executed the statues for the base of the Calvary (figs. 673, 674) (now called the "Well of Moses"), for the church portal, and for the tomb of Philip the Bold (figs. 675, 677), continued to be active well into the 15th century. It is now thought that Sluter's nephew, Claus de Werve, played an important part in the workshop, particularly in the making of the tomb of Philip the Bold: he probably not only carved but also designed the *pleurants* (mourners), in which dramatic feeling is brilliantly expressed by masses of drapery alone – for that is all that is visible in these figures.

During the 15th century, while the stone carver's art was evolving on the basis of Sluter's style, another style was developed in Flanders and in Brabant by the wood carvers, transposing the style of Roger van der Weyden into relief. Their compositions are filled with a confusion of elongated, mannered figures quite unlike Sluter's powerful, massive forms; the draperies are broken by innumerable folds, and the background is tangled lacework. The most beautiful example of this Brabant style is in stone: the funerary church of Brou, at Bourg-en-Bresse, dating from the beginning of the 16th century (fig. 696).

The history of sculpture in northern Europe divides into these two currents, which sometimes mix. In France, the Brabant style invaded Champagne, where unknown artists carved some of the most moving expressions of the Passion; it was known also in Burgundy, clearly influencing the Semur Entombment (fig. 681). But Burgundy was the main center of Sluterian art, which through the Rhone valley reached as far as southern France and inspired the Provençal school and the statues around the choir at Albi. Sluter's style also penetrated to the Loire region under the Bourbons and gave a solid foundation to the Loire school, which during the second half of that century created many wonderful works, buried in country churches and anonymous, and therefore less famous than many contemporary Italian statues of lesser artistic value.

After 1460 the Sluterian style was progressively softened, and religious imagery became less dramatic. Drapery was more supple, expression – even the expression of pain – less intense, physiognomic types were less individual, and the pathos more restrained – shown, in the French manner, by a concentration of inner life and not by its physical effects. As in the 13th century artists were attracted by femininity and again inspired by the group of the Virgin and Child; sculptors no longer selected models from the aristocracy but from the ordinary people, thus giving their characters a simple, human flavor, devoid of vulgarity and typical of French art.

A century of that tradition resulted in a masterpiece once attributed to Michel Colombe but now anonymous: the Solesmes Entombment, a liturgical work of profound and noble pathos figs. 693, 695). Gothic art had gone back to its own source: the dead Christ with serene features has the same face as the *Beau Dieu* of Amiens.

In Germany, the Sluterian and the Flemish trends met and mixed in a tumultuous conjunction. A few artists, such as Nikolaus van Leyden, working in stone, tried to preserve the autonomy of the free-standing figure, but polychrome wood-carving invaded the whole of Germany, with the resultant reign of the *Zackenstil*, the "broken style," with cut-out, broken, involved forms reminiscent of the interlace of medieval Irish illuminators; the structure of a garment, for example, becomes impossible to decipher. In the works of of Veit Stoss, Sluter's influence is still visible, through this entanglement, in the weight of the clothes and the depth of the heavy folds. A passion for naturalism introduced into the imagery the most vulgar popular types: cripples, idiots, deformed or diseased characters – medical specialists have delighted in diagnosing the various illnesses represented by Veit Stoss in his Cracow altar (fig. 704).

This *Spätgotik*, as the Germans term it, continued into the first third of the 16th century. Its dying gasp produced even more exaggerated works, like the Niederrotweil Altarpiece (fig. 706), in which the draperies are tangled around the convulsed forms as if by a blast of madness.

Expressionism, unrestrained, piles exacerbation on exacerbation and ends by destroying itself with it own excesses. Beyond a certain point, the only way to render the patient conscious of his soul is by torturing him: the Gothic German sculptor became a torturer of the form which he cut up, clipped, and tore to pieces. Art was an outlet for his cruel instincts. This tendency to torture form is characteristic of schools of art which were not, like Italy, Flanders, or France, involved in the search for new forms, and on receiving forms from outside, they could only exploit them to "express" their own temperaments, eventually deforming them entirely.

Thus, that passionate century which in France ended in a renewed serenity, in Germany finished with torments. A Würzburg artist contributed a soothing melancholia to that tense style; the profound sadness of Roger van der Weyden was revived by Tilman Riemenschneider. Bent heads, long noses and emaciated features, lean bodies, draperies drooping as if dislodged, soft, sad Madonna faces, the pained gentleness of the Saviour – everything is a translation into wood of the ascetic imagery of Roger, who was the genuine founder of the Flemish style that, eclipsing the style of Van Eyck, invaded the whole of northern Europe and penetrated even to Spain.

In fact, 15th-century Spain seems a province of northern art. German, French, and Flemish artists all went there, attracted by workshops offering numerous commissions. We are not sure of the nationality of Gil de Siloë, who worked at the Charterhouse of Miraflores, near Burgos, where he carved in wood the main altar (fig. 713), and in alabaster the tombs of Juan II and Isabella. According to some documents, he might have come from Antwerp. The style of the tomb, in which the garments of the Virtues fall in noble folds like those of Sluter's figures, is very different from the style of the main altar – a triumph of the *Zackenstil*. In the latter, the mannered style reminiscent of 15th-century Germanic saints and madonnas suggests a German origin for Gil de Siloë. The Spaniards were to delight in huge, elaborate altarpieces set against the windowless wall of the *capilla mayor* in their churches. Not intended to be deciphered, but rather to rise like a permanent prayer in images, figures and details blurred by the twilight reigned over a sanctuary closed to the worshippers and glimpsed from a distance as a vague and mysterious glow of gold and colors. Such accumulations of sculptured forms appear as a mirage replacing reality, which for the Spaniards had no actual existence, in a universe of mere creatures – that is, of nothingness.

Those huge altarpieces could be realized in

stone as in wood. In the Isabelline style, architecture, covered with a network of sculpture, resembles some aspect of nature, a forest or a grotto. On the facade of the Colegio San Gregorio in Valladolid, even man reverts to nature and becomes hairy like a savage (fig. 716). Wherever *Spätgotik* reigned, that is, in most parts of Europe, architecture admitted its failure by returning to natural forms: columns were replaced by trees, moldings by rocks. This tendency was particularly marked in Portugal, in the excesses of the Manueline style, artists desperately piling up creatures and plants, agricultural or fishing tools, as if they had lost all power of creating forms.

VIII The Renaissance

The course of Italian art, by nature highly inventive, was punctuated by returns to traditional sources whenever the development of new forms led it too far from those sources. In sculpture, its essential tradition is a grasp of the corporeal reality of the human body which Italian artists – Guglielmo in the Romanesque period, Nicola Pisano in the 13th century, and Nanni di Banco in the Quattrocento – repeatedly sought in the art of antiquity. But at the beginning of the 15th century, after the Gothic style had run its course, it appeared possible to demand rejuvenation from the Gothic itself. Ghiberti, making the second door of the Baptistry in Florence, quite naturally looked at the door cast three-quarters of a century earlier by Andrea Pisano, and found there the principles of a classicism which Andrea had borrowed from French 13th-century art. For that reason Ghiberti has been considered a medieval artist. The author of an outstanding work on Italian sculpture, John Pope-Hennessy, has placed him in the volume devoted to Gothic while giving Donatello right of place in the Renaissance volume. In reality, the distinction between Gothic and Renaissance is nowhere less operative than in Italy, even though it was the humanists themselves who invented it, and it must be set aside if we want to understand the spirit of Italian art. That distinction is particularly artificial if the criterion used to differentiate one style from the other is the degree of imitation of the antique. The Florentine sculptors who created the Renaissance style in the years before 1430 sought to imitate the antique, not as an end in itself (even if they themselves believed so), but as a means to find nature, which they considered to have been lost by medieval art. Such is the aim Alberti claims for sculpture in his *De Statua*: "to make works so that they resemble as much as possible the real bodies created by nature." That imitation of the antique did not always result in a closer resemblance to nature: Nanni di Banco's group of the *Quattro Santi Coronati* (fig. 719) exhibits a mere pastiche of the ancient forms, and at the end of his short life he reverted to the Gothic style in the Porta della Mandorla of Florence Cathedral.

There are two ways to reach nature: through its essence, or through its reality. Ghiberti illustrates the former, and Donatello the latter; the former tends towards classicism, the latter towards what would be called naturalism, if that name had not been appropriated by a 19th-century concept alien to our present subject. Donatello based his formal research on an acute observation of nature, including a study of the nude and even of anatomy in corpses (though not through systematic dissection, which awaited Leonardo), to discover the structure, the rhythms of action, and the play of axes in the human body, so that he might bring that body to life in palpitating relief and vibrant contours. Ghiberti's bent towards the classical, on the other hand, enabled him to apprehend beyond all the singular features the real form, which includes all the particular possibilities of a gesture or an expression. He had a predilection for drapery because it allowed him to exteriorize the rhythms of action and also to link together the various forms in a composition. For Ghiberti worked towards the total unity of his compositions; no artist after him knew how to create in reliefs a world so vivid, a world no less animated for being ruled by order; nobody could bring bronze to life as he did. With unsurpassed virtuosity he exploited the whole range of relief, from figures almost in the round in the foreground, to elements worked in very flat relief in the backgrounds, effectively suggesting infinite recession into depth. Donatello, on the other hand, was a maker of statues; creating isolated forms and studying the human body and the human soul, he gave "character" to all his creations, borrowing the faces of his prophets from live models. In all honesty, from the purely formal point of view, the reliefs from the Santo in Padua (fig. 732) and those of the north pulpit in San Lorenzo must be counted as semi-failures. He exploited the flattened relief, which Ghiberti had used to obtain nuances in perspective, to suggest a medley of pictorial effects that are actually anti-sculptural; and his perspective is unclear. The rhythm of a Ghiberti composition may be seized at a glance, after which the eye may dwell on its lively details; Donatello's relief forms are confused, less clear even than those of Luca della Robbia, as can be seen by comparing Donatello's doors in the old sacristy of San Lorenzo with Della Robbia's doors for Florence Cathedral. In fact, Donatello, always so precise in his statuary, eluded the problems of relief by a *non finito* or *bozzetto* technique which appeals to us because we find it more "modern," but which hides a weakness. On the other hand, the free-standing statues by Ghiberti, his St. John the Baptist and his St. Matthew at Or San Michele, are admittedly conventional. Owing to a kind of instinct of sociability, he could conceive a form only in relation to another; he belongs to the same artistic family as Raphael and Mozart. He gave his full measure only in the third set of Baptistry doors, the Porta del Paradiso. (Figs. 721–724). Here he was allowed to discard the proposed division into twenty-eight small reliefs, a repetition of the scheme of the two earlier doors, which would have tied him to a limited space and few characters, and to adopt instead ten larger panels grouping several scenes in each relief; the new scheme gave his vision a much wider field, and allowed him to create in each panel a self-contained microcosm.

The two tendencies of Quattrocento Florentine sculpture are already visible in the two surviving works out of the seven entered in the competition organized in 1401 by the *arte di Calimala* for the second Baptistry doors. One, by Brunelleschi, represents the naturalistic style later adopted by Donatello; the other, by Ghiberti, to whom the contract for doors was awarded, represents the more classical style. Brunelleschi abandoned sculpture for architecture, and it was Donatello who continued the experimental studies of humanity in all ages and with all expressions.

If one artist could be singled out to exemplify the prolongation of the medieval spirit in the Quattrocento, it would be Luca della Robbia. In his bronzes as in his facile, polychrome terra cottas, he remained within the limits defined a century earlier by Andrea Pisano, but his art is softened by the influence of Fra Angelico, whose mysticism he changed into piety – a transformation similar to that which Memling wrought in the art of Roger van der Weyden. Jacopo della Quercia, in contrast, through his dramatic intensity and his powerful rendering of the human body, took the first step on the road leading to Michelangelo's tragic humanism (figs. 734, 735).

In Florence in the first part of the Quattrocento, sculpture was the pioneering art. It was not until around 1425 that painting embarked upon the "modern" style, reaping the benefit of experiments already realized in sculpture; it remained dependent on sculpture, so much so that certain painters, Andrea del Castagno, or later the Paduan Mantegna, created pictures illusionistically imitating reliefs. Architecture was slower still to develop, and it was the painters who first experimented with classicizing architecture in the backgrounds of their pictures. For twenty-five years the sculptor bore the responsibility of creating new forms, His art was now once more autonomous, emancipated from architecture and even commanding it: it was the sculptors, not the architects, who invented the tabernacle niche for statues, and from them came the new type of funerary monument, the baldachin tomb decorated with reliefs whose iconography celebrated the virtues of the dead "hero" in a manner more pagan than Christian. Venice took that idea further and made the tomb into a triumphal arch.

The architect gave an important place to sculpture until the end of the century, when Bramante, at the *Canonica* in Milan, following the path marked out by Brunelleschi in San Lorenzo and Santo Spirito in Florence, had rationalized architectural design and restored to the architectural orders the place they had occupied in antiquity. The sculptor's art flourished especially in the decorated pilasters and capitals which, inspired by antiquity, offered a great variety of imaginative forms. The finest are those in the sacristy of Santo Spirito in Florence (fig. 760), made by Giuliano da Sangallo, who himself sculptured the ornament for the buildings he designed. Throughout the 15th century sculptors enjoyed experimenting with a decoration inspired by antiquity and exhibiting this richness of invention reminiscent of the fully developed floral ornament of the Gothic period. Antique grotesques, discovered in the last third of the century, also inspired artists; schools of decorators were formed in Florence and Rimini, then in Milan and Venice. The purest forms are found in the castle of Urbino, created by teams of decorators from Florence and Rimini. This inventiveness came to an end when the austere regulation of the architectural orders eliminated figures from the ornament.

The new conceptions of the funerary monument, which tended to make an antique-style hero of the deceased, revived a type of commemorative monument that had virtually disappeared since antiquity: the equestrian statue. It is true that during the 14th century sculptors in Verona, Venice, and Milan had represented a man on a horse, but the horse was only a lifeless accessory. At the funerals of *condottieri* the catafalque was often decorated with an equestrian statue made of some temporary material; Jacopo della Quercia made such a statue in Siena for the burial of Giovanni d'Azzo Ubaldini, and Vasari describes the making of it in great detail. Agnolo Gaddi also made one in Florence for the funeral of Piero Farnese in 1390; it was soon destroyed, and so it was decided that Piero Farnese and his companion, Sir John Hawkwood, should be commemorated in Florence Cathedral by frescoed images, also commissioned from Agnolo Gaddi. A quarter of a century later the Gothic painting of Sir John Hawkwood seemed out of fashion, and in 1436 the young Paolo Uccello was asked to renew it; wanting to give the illusion of a statue in bronze, he painted it as a kind of monochrome, a demonstration of the geometry of illusionistic perspective. Uccello had already been in Venice and seen there the 4th-century horses of San Marco, which he used as models for his own horse. A marble equestrian monument planned in 1435 for the condottiere Niccolò da Tolentino in Florence Cathedral was not executed – no doubt because of lack of money – but it was partially realized twenty years later in a monochrome fresco by Andrea del Castagno (fig. 733), quite similar to Uccello's.

Painters, as we can see, preceded sculptors in exploiting the equestrian theme. In 1444 in Ferrara, Lionello d'Este commissioned a statue of his predecessor Niccolo, but we do not know what it looked like, for although it was put up in 1451, it was destroyed in 1796 It was the work of Baroncelli and earned him the nickname Niccolo del Cavallo. Pisanello, on medallions and in paintings and sketches, brought his considerable skill to the rendering of the horse; the horses tossing their heads in the fresco of Sant'Anastasia in Verona are very lifelike. The earliest equestrian statue to have survived is that of Erasmo da Narni, called il Gattamelata, captain-general of the Republic of Venice, who died in Padua in January 1443. Donatello was then in Padua working on the main altar of the church of St. Anthony. A statue was commissioned from him, first intended as a funerary monument to stand inside that church. But the monument, completed in 1450, was erected outside, in the square (figs. 730, 731). It is usually said that this work was inspired by the the horses of San Marco and by the Marcus Aurelius now on the Campidoglio in Rome. Those monuments could have given the artist only a very general idea for his equestrian statue; Donatello did not start from the antique, but worked from nature to recapture the antique, and both man and horse are the result of intensive study. The group gives the impression of self-assured power, of a strategist whose clever manoeuvres have won him victory. Although the general is wearing armor, he is represented bareheaded, like the *Imperator* in a triumph, and intelligence radiates from his uncovered forehead. Later, in Venice, Verrocchio portrayed the Colleoni as a tense warrior gathering up the reins before launching his mount into battle; this is not an *Imperator*, but a bully. These two statues express the divergent theories of war held by opposing factions named after two famous *condottieri*, the *bracceschi* and the *sforzeschi*. The former believed in strategy, the latter sought victory in unexpected, violent action. Verrocchio's quasi-romantic statue is in-

ferior to Donatello's serene group, which has never been equalled. Leonardo resumed the theme of a man on horseback, calmly triumphant or caught up in the thick of action. In a first version of the monument to Francesco Sforza, he posed himself the problem of bringing equilibrium to a rider on a rearing horse. His numerous sketches for this group inspired a host of statuettes (fig. 750), but like most of the attempts of that experimenter of genius, they came to nothing, and sculptors dropped the theme of the equestrian statue until the Mannerist period.

Youth was one of the favorite subjects for Early Renaissance sculptors. Luca della Robbia and Donatello competed on that theme on the two *cantorie*, or singing galleries, for Florence Cathedral, now in the museum of the Opera del Duomo (figs. 729, 737). Luca's figures are a too-literal imitation of living models, but Donatello, in the frenzied dancing of his *putti*, expresses the dynamic vitality of Eros, symbol of universal life. The *putto*, his creation, was destined to grace all the monuments of the end of the century, bearing garlands, inscriptions, or medallions, as an Eros or as an infant angel. Around those naked children are robed angels (the specialty of the Rossellinos, particularly Bernardo), youths in the flower of adolescence, who flutter or alight, holding candelabra around a tabernacle (figs. 740, 740A)

The resuscitation of the portrait bust cannot be credited to Donatello, as it once was: the earliest works of that kind to reach us are those portraying Piero de' Medici (1453) and Niccolà Strozzi (1454), by Mino da Fiesole. Reviving an ancient procedure described by Pliny, the Florentines took plaster casts from life; often the result was a gross naturalism which defeated its own purpose, for art and nature are two different things and the former can only render the latter (when it aims to) if it interprets reality in a manner appropriate to itself. Those portraits are indeed lifelike – but "horribly so," as Cézanne would have said. They force us to see as ordinary persons, not only physically imperfect but also characterless, those Florentines whom we imagine as princes of the spirit. Portraiture represents the false note in Italian Quattrocento sculpture. The only genuine character studies are Donatello's prophets for the Campanile (fig. 727), which retain from the living models only what outwardly expresses the inner soul. Sculptors were not sure how far down they should represent the bust: they sometimes took it right down to the waist, showing too much of the arms, which looks awkward. The busts of laughing children by Desiderio da Settignano are affected (fig. 743), and female portraits were no better than those of the male; Francesco Laurana's are the exception (fig. 744).

In the second half of the century, the famous Florentine *soave austero* degenerated into academicism; grace turned to affectation, realism to vulgarity. Verrocchio and Pollaiuolo, trained as goldsmiths, were sidetracked into surface effects; Donatello's near-pagan art produced as its offspring the bronze statuettes of Bertoldo (fig. 745) and Pollaiuolo, and the Venetian Riccio, that are pastiches of the antique, or sometimes even attempts to fake it; they are mere collectors' curios.

Siena made its contribution to the Florentine relief production with Agostino di Duccio, who worked on the decorations of the Tempio Malatestiano in Rimini (fig. 741). To the Florentine definition of contour he added a sort of Gothic dryness characteristically Sienese. His talent was for line, and relief for him was only a pretext for surface undulations and linear variations reminiscent of 12th-century French Romanesque art, which gave his figures a feverish liveliness. However, until the 16th century Siena also sustained her tradition of polychrome wooden statues, deriving from the art of Nino Pisano in the 14th century and attractive in their archaism.

Artists from Florentine workshops continued to spread the new style all over Italy. At the beginning of the 16th century the style exported by Florence was a sort of classicizing formalism, probably influenced by Leonardo; Andrea Contucci, known as il Sansovino, took it to Genoa, Rome and Loreto; reaching Sicily, the style was kept up for a long time by the Gaggini family.

Lombardy modified the Florentine style in the most interesting way by interpreting it as Gothic. Accustomed to consider sculpture as an applied decoration on buildings, the Lombards deprived that art of its autonomy, its very essence, and treated it as ornamentation. In this spirit Amadeo, architect and sculptor, designed the Colleoni Chapel in Bergamo, its facade a jumble of polychrome marbles and decorative and figurative sculpture. The huge workshop of the Certosa of Pavia, begun about 1464, became one of the main centers of the Lombard style; through the works of the Certosa shop, and not through good Florentine examples, the Renaissance was revealed to northern European artists – still Gothic spirits, to whom the Lombard mixture was, in any case, more comprehensible than the revolutionary Florentine experiments. The decoration of the Certosa, begun in terra cotta in the cloisters, was continued in marble for the interior of the church and the facade (fig. 749). The latter is entirely covered with columns, candelabra, foliated scrolls, classical ornamentation, statues and reliefs, with no interval of wall left bare; it is neither architecture nor sculpture, but an enormous piece of goldsmith's work. Amadeo worked on it with the

brothers Mantegazza, who influenced him. Renaissance art interpreted through this exaggerated Gothicism resulted in an anti-classical mannerism anticipating by more than half a century the strained art of Alonso Berruguete. Imported from Lombardy into Venice, this style mixed with direct Florentine influences and became more subdued under the impact of ancient inspiration, still alive there. Tullio Lombardo's Adam (fig. 754) announces Michelangelo's Bacchus, from which it seems less removed in time if we consider that in 1493 Tullio was still working on the Vendramin Tomb, for which he made the Adam, while the Bacchus was made between 1496 and 1501. In the whole of Italy at that time, no artist had so closely imitated the antique.

Antonio Rizzo, Pietro Lombardo, and Tullio Lombardo developed the funerary monument in the direction of the ancient triumphal arch, creating structures adorned with numerous statues and reliefs of a slipshod, classicizing finish; these had a largely decorative value, subordinated to the architecture (fig. 752).

The history of sculpture in Florence could be summed up in five statues, all illustrating the theme of David, the perfect symbol of the hero since it shows the weak served by intelligence triumphing over brute force. The first of the five is that carved in marble by Donatello in 1408 and 1409, an amiable clothed adolescent whose listless attitude and effeminate face are somewhat equivocal; his own triumph seems to leave him indifferent.[1] Donatello's bronze David (fig. 728), probably cast about 1450, appears in heroic nudity. His left wrist still rests on the hip in a noble attitude inherited from the Middle Ages, but his right hand now grips a sword. The adolescent stands relaxed after action, his bones showing through the flesh of the thin muscular body, and a broken outline boldly defines the figure in space. Verrocchio, in his bronze David, completed before 1476, exaggerates the slender tautness of a feverishly nervous *ragazzo* (fig. 748).

Between 1501 and 1504 Michelangelo carved the marble colossus of the Piazza della Signoria (fig. 764) from a block roughed out years before by Agostino di Duccio; when he did so, he abandoned the myth of childhood that the Quattrocento had exploited to stress the contrast beween the hero and the giant. He represented David at the moment preceding action, as a wrestler standing on guard for the attack: he will owe his triumph not to skill but to his muscles. But in this transitional work, the muscles seem grafted onto

[1] The attribution to Donatello of the unfinished marble David in the National Gallery in Washington, seems dubious to me, although Janson (Pls. 21-25) accepts it.

the bony structure; the pectoral muscles do not seem to correspond with the athletic anatomy proposed; no more does the musculature of the too-slender arms. When he carved the Slaves for the tomb of Julius II, Michelangelo for the first time exchanged the intellectual for an overtly physical type, represented in genuinely powerful bodies. The last stage in the evolution of the athlete is the marble David carved by Bernini in 1623–1624 (fig. 875). Represented dramatically, in mid-action, his body twists through space in the act of casting the stone from the sling; he is no longer a hero: like the Borghese Wrestler from the 1st century B.C., he is a professional.

Michelangelo was a Florentine and a maker of statues. His attempts at relief were few and date mostly from his youth. His statues are isolated forms tormented not by action, but by passion, and hopelessly imprisoned in their marble solitude. Even in the statues most carefully finished – in the Florentine manner – like the Bruges Virgin or the Pietà in St. Peter's (fig. 762), we are aware of the block from which those statues were hewn, but the very material throbs under the stress of myriad pent forces. This epiphany of superhuman power is best illustrated in the frescoes of the Sistine Ceiling, from which certain figures reappear in marble a little later, around 1513–1516, when Michelangelo carved the first figures for the tomb of Julius II: the Louvre Slaves and the Moses. The latter (fig. 765), indeed very near in spirit to the Sistine Ceiling, is the last of Michelangelo's creations to affirm an inner force, a power born of Yahweh's anger. The power in the Slaves (fig. 766) is held captive, a symbol of the human condition in which the soul is chained to the body. In the Medici Chapel sculptures (figs. 767–770), all energy seems drawn off by death; the powerful bodies fall in upon themselves, or twist on their own axes in a last spasm of agony. The four allegories of the times of day probably represent the greatest effort ever made by a sculptor to invade with a single form all the dimensions of space. The bodies of the two princes, however, are elongated, as though Michelangelo had been affected by the Mannerism dominating Florentine art at the moment when he was working on those statues. This elongation may also be the first sign of a tendency to spiritualize matter, less pronounced just after Michelangelo's return to Rome in 1534, but later resumed more strongly. The Slaves formerly in the Boboli grotto, with their gigantic athletic forms still unfinished and half-imprisoned in the block, seem to have been turned to stone by some divine curse (fig. 771); their tremendous struggle symbolizes the struggle of the spirit against matter. In the later Leah and Rachel, made around 1542–1545 for the Tomb of Julius II, the modelling became drier, more abstract, possibly as a result of short-sightedness. As if aware of it, Michelangelo more and more often left his works unfinished, according to the *non finito* procedure invented by Donatello in his Paduan bronzes. Practiced by Michelangelo in his youth as a way of bringing marble to life, it later became his way of spiritualizing matter. The bodies of the Florence Cathedral Pietà (fig. 774) are longer, more emaciated, almost skeletal. The crumpled, lifeless body of Christ and the weeping creatures around him are empty of power. The Rondanini Pietà, two merged and drawn-out forms, is a yearning, not a state of being (fig. 773).

Michelangelo despised bronze, considering its apparant hardness a deception, since the building up of the clay and wax models from which the bronze is cast is an easy technique; only direct carving in stone seemed to him worthy of a great artist, for he conceived it the artist's end to liberate the forms and forces hidden within a block of marble. He exerted over his period a sort of fascination that paralyzed other sculptors, who only emerged from that trance after his death, with the second generation of Mannerists.

The Frenchman Michel Colombe is known to us only in sculpture from his old age, as all the earlier works mentioned in documents have disappeared. The tomb of the Duke of Britanny in Nantes Cathedral (figs. 777, 778) is not entirely by his hand, since it was designed by Jean Perréal, another famous unknown. The recumbent figures and the four Cardinal Virtues are of a high quality, but the figures on the base must be by an assistant. The St. George from Gaillon (fig. 779), from his own hand, exhibits a rather feeble Italianate inspiration. For masterpieces dating from the beginning of the 16th century we must look elsewhere than to the workshop of this aging artist. The admirable Vierge d'Olivet (fig. 780) belongs to the naturalistic tradition born in France in the later 15th century, but reveals an idealistic touch showing Italian Renaissance influence. That native trend of naturalism found expression in many works, such as the first sculptures around the choir in Chartres Cathedral by a man whose name, Jehan de Beauce, reveals his origin. But after about 1535 Mannerism was brought to France by the Italians whom Francis I called to Fontainebleau. The frame of Michel Colombe's St. George is Italian; in France, Italian art was at first known mostly as ornament, produced by transalpine artists or directly imported from Genoa or Lombardy.

The Renaissance spirit was assimilated more quickly in Germany. From the second third of the 15th century Nuremberg was a center for humanists, poets, philosophers, and scholars; it is therefore not surprising that a bronze monument such as the Shrine of St. Sebald in Nuremberg, dating from the early 16th century, should have been invaded by the new manner. This is true largely for the figures (fig. 785); the intricate architecture, although generally Renaissance in style, is still dominated by the first design, known from a project dated 1488, which shows a sort of Gothic church forty feet high. This ensemble is a forest of forms in the true German manner, but the individual nude or draped figures, as well as the ornament, are so closely inspired by ancient and Italian statuary that they presuppose a direct knowledge of it, obtained on the spot. The messenger who brought the new style across the Alps was probably Peter Vischer the Younger, who had probably traveled in Italy in 1507–08. He was twenty-one when the shrine was commissioned from his father, Peter Vischer the Elder, in 1508. His older brother, Hermann, who crossed the Alps in 1515, reinforced this influence even more.

The extravagant project for the tomb of Maximilian at Innsbruck, conceived at that time by the founder of Hapsburg glory, synthesizes several ideas. The idea of a gathering of ancestors in a church issued from family pride, as had the benefactor statues in the west choir of Naumburg. The medieval theme of the burial procession, illustrated by Sluter on the tomb of Philip the Bold and brought back to Innsbruck by the humanists, merges curiously with the memory of the ancestor portraits that accompanied the funeral cortege at patrician burials in Roman times (see above, p. 36). Dynastic pride never inspired a more grandiose project; it was to have included forty statues larger than life, a hundred statuettes, and thirty-two busts of Roman emperors. Begun in 1509, it was set up only in 1593 in the Hofkirche (figs. 786–789), built from 1553 to 1563 by the Italian Andrea Crivelli in the form of a *Hallenkirche*, whose wide interior was particularly well suited to the unrolling of such funeral display in bronze. The project was continued by the Emperors Ferdinand I and Leopold I, but in the end the monument had only forty statues, twenty-three statuettes, and twenty busts; not only the ancestors of Maximilian and his wives, but also his relatives, and a gathering of historical heroes as well were to have been grouped around Maximilian's tomb. The monument is actually a cenotaph, since the Emperor was finally buried at Wiener-Neustadt. It was the first great expression of the Hapsburg imperial concept which, inherited from the Germanic Holy Roman Empire, claimed to be universal, whereas the French concept of royalty was exclusively territorial and dynastic. Many artists worked on the monument;

we know that Peter Vischer was paid for two statues after sketches by Dürer, but they are not specified, and therefore the two best are usually attributed to him: those of King Arthur and of Theodoric. The other statues, loaded with sumptuous robes, lacework, precious stones, and the parade and tournament armor which was worn then, resemble barbaric heraldic trophies, though they display extraordinary virtuosity on the part of German bronzecasters, traditionally expert in metalwork.

In the 16th century, Spain continued to borrow from the rest of Europe to provide sculptors for its workshops, in great demand particularly for the making of tombs, altarpieces, and church furniture. Artists already impregnated by the Renaissance spirit came to join the Spaniards, and very soon, at the end of the reign of the Catholic kings, the peninsula adopted the new style, which it used almost exclusively for religious ends. At that time many Italians were working in Andalusia: Domenico Fancelli, Torrigiano, Francisco Fiorentino, Jacopo Fiorentino, known as *el Indaco*, and Giovanni Moreto.

In Burgos, it was the Frenchman Felipe Bigarny, "from the diocese of Langres," who introduced the Renaissance. In 1498 he was given a commission for three reliefs for the *trasaltar* of the Cathedral, and he made them in the style typical of the Loire region (fig. 791). Spanish artists also went to Italy to study. Two men from Burgos, Bartolomé Ordóñez and Diego de Siloë, the son of the famous Gil de Siloë, worked together in Naples in 1517, where several of their works have survived. Alonso Berruguete, the son of the Castilian painter Pedro Berruguete, stayed in Rome and in Florence, where we find evidence of his presence in 1508 and 1512; we know that he copied the Laocoön and that he knew Michelangelo. Returned to Spain, Bartolomé Ordóñez was asked to take over from Domenico Fancelli, who had just died, the uncompleted commission for the tomb of Philip the Handsome and Joanna the Mad in the Capilla Real in Granada (fig. 792). In October 1519 he went to Carrara to fetch marble and to carve on the spot the figures for the tomb, in a workshop he opened with Italian assistants. He died in December 1519. This beautiful work is in a late 15th-century Florentine style.

Italian and French influence met and joined in Burgos in 1523 when Felipe Bigarny and Diego de Siloë received a joint commission for the altarpiece for the Du Guesclin Chapel in the Cathedral (figs. 793, 794). It is just possible to distinguish the two hands, although Felipe's somewhat heavy style softened in contact with the freer manner of his colleague Diego. The latter is much more modern; he was influenced by Donatello, the main source of Spanish Renaissance sculpture, and from Michelangelo he borrowed a feeling for the majestic. In 1528 Diego again worked as an architect in Granada, where he created a new type of building, imitated even in America. Experienced in both arts, he conceived sculpture as integral to architecture and created a type of monumental sculpture particular to Andalusia, making a great use of columns and statuary, mainly caryatids. The masterpiece of that style is the San Salvador Chapel at Ubeda (fig. 800), a church designed by Diego and commissioned from him and Andrés de Vandelvira. The latter opened the sculpture workshop responsible for the admirable facade and the statues inside the church and the sacristy. The iconography of San Salvador is a harmonious mixture of Christian imagery and pagan themes; it is filled with an enjoyment of life, no doubt the result of the freedom granted the artist to create according to his inspiration, which was very rare in Spain. San Salvador is typical of Andalusia, which tends to a classicizing taste, in contrast with the tormented art found in Castile with Alonso Berruguete and Juan de Juni. Castilian architectural decoration is completely different; the most representative example is the mysterious facade of Salamanca University (fig. 796), of which we know only that it was already completed in 1533. The arabesque motifs and the grotesques covering the facade are of French origin, and the Lombard influence that can be noticed may have been brought by French artists from the Loire working in Spain; if so, they were completely assimilated to Spanish art. The facade of the Colegio San Gregorio, Valladolid, (fig. 715) shows similar qualities in another style. Its or-namentation is very free, as the building imposes no structural limitations. The eye roves over the whole facade without finding any landmark; always attracted by new accents, it feels the pull of the infinite. This impression is reinforced by the flatness of the relief, which casts only very faint shadows. The quality of the sculpture is such that the spectator becomes irritated at his own inability to fix those images, which elude him like a mirage. The name Plateresque, which means goldsmith's style, often generally applied to Spanish art of the 16th century before the Escorial, should be restricted to Castile; in Andalusia, sculpture often remained dominated by architecture.

The main ornaments of Spanish churches, from the 15th century onward, were the great altars rising at the back of the *capilla mayor* like high cliffs covered with sculpture. Plateresque sculptors carried over into the new repertory of statuary and ornamentation, in wood or in stone, the spirit of the Gothic altarpiece, a sort of Jacob's Ladder put up for God, enthroned above it on his Cross, accompanied by the mourning figures of the Virgin and St. John.

In Portugal, after the exaggerated lyricism of the Manueline period, Frenchmen like João de Ruão and Nicolas Chanterene introduced the peaceful style of the Loire Renaissance. The Portuguese were faithful to that style, and the melancholy serenity of their Virgins and Saints remained a tradition until the end of the 17th century. Another Frenchman, Hodard (Odarte), created in Coimbra exceptional terra-cotta works directly influenced by the Lombard style of Guido Mazzoni or Niccolo del' Arca (fig. 850).

IX Mannerism: The Anti-Classical Reaction

It has taken nearly three-quarters of a century to reverse the concept of Mannerism propounded by Romain Rolland in 1895, to make it positive instead of negative. What Rolland and so many others considered as the decline of Renaissance painting is now viewed as an independent and worthwhile phase of Western art. The many studies published during the last thirty years have revealed Mannerism as an expression of a neurosis, of a state of anxiety, and also as a deep-rooted reaction against classicism, finally resolved not in a return to classicism, but in the Baroque introduced through the divergent styles of the Carracci and Caravaggio. A reaction against the Renaissance had begun in Florence even before the death of Raphael; in some cases it paralleled a kind of classicism, as in Spain, where Alonso Berruguete was the contemporary of Diego de Siloë.

The Mannerist revolution was initiated in Florence between 1515 and 1525 by painters who soon found a following. In sculpture, Mannerism came later, developing about 1535 as an interpretation by others of Michelangelo's style: one of the focal points of Mannerism was the Medici Chapel and its tombs, completed between 1525 and 1534.

Mannerism in sculpture was inaugurated in Florence by Bandinelli, a rival of Michelangelo, who managed to take from him the commission for a monumental group intended as a companion piece to the David in the Piazza della Signoria; the marble block was delivered from Carrara in 1525 and subsequently passed from Michelangelo to Bandinelli. The result was Bandinelli's Hercules and Cacus, completed in 1534, an inflated colossus which from the moment it was set up to our own day has provoked endless jeers from amateurs, critics, and tourists alike (fig. 807). It is a negation as sculpture, the product of a puny talent. Luckily, ten years later Florence again had a real artist when Benvenuto Cellini returned from France after making his famous saltcellar for Francis I. In 1545 Grand Duke Cosimo I commissioned from him the bronze Perseus, which was set up in the Loggia dei Lanzi in 1554 (fig. 809). Cellini is one of the few artists of his time who did not imitate Michelangelo. The sinewy body of his Perseus shows the influence of Verrocchio and Pollaiuolo, and the careful finish came naturally from his goldsmith's hand. The theme of the conquering hero is renewed in Cellini's figure, presented at the dramatic moment of triumph, holding aloft the Medusa's bloody head. The arms reach out from a body outlined against space rather than twisting to occupy it; the work was meant to be seen in profile. In his bust of Cosimo I (fig. 808), Cellini put an end to the deadlock of naturalism in which the Quattrocento portrait had stuck fast and inaugurated a new genre, revived from antiquity: the heroic portrait. The prince is represented in action, his head turned to the right, his hard eyes expressing command; the modelling subtly indicates the successive planes and the chasing of the armor is remarkable. The arms and the bust are cut at the right level and are well balanced on the small pedestal.

The 16th-century bronze was unaffected by the irrevocable decline of stone carving. The latter was too straightforward to express all the subtle nuances to which the artists were attracted. Working in bronze, artists were also freer of Michelangelo's influence, which reappeared in marble works as exaggerated, bulging muscles and blown-up proportions. Bronze was the medium suited to the flowing, smooth, feminine shapes that sculptors preferred in reaction against the athleticism of the Michelangelesque male bodies. Sculptors of 16th-century Italy expressed better than any before or since the suppleness and grace of the female body. Following in the wake of the painters, they elongated that body to make it more flexible and more elegant; with the double contrapposto of the hips and bust emphasizing the body's curves, they created the *linea serpentina*, the line that doubles back on itself after describing a capricious arabesque and gives a flowing beauty to the forms. Michelangelo saw in the human body a reflection of divine beauty; but for him, as for Quattrocento artists, that beauty was an attribute of the male body. Cinquecento sculptors found it in the female body, less easily analyzed and containing secret harmonies that led them towards the goal of their art: the discovery of the *disegno*, or rather of the *disegno interno*, an intangible intellectual quality, a divine shadow of the tangible. It could most surely be apprehended in the nude, and therefore the nude was the main subject of study for painters and sculptors. Beauty was no longer thought to reside in a system of proportions, as in the Quattrocento. Alberti, in his *De Statua*, had worked out for the sculptor a complete table of measurements, but Michelangelo had said one must have a compass in one's eye and not in one's hand. As for the study of nature, it became a mere stimulus for the imagination; it induced the artist to draw from memory and to find within his own imagination the creative spark.

In Michelangelo's work, woman borrowed some of man's strength; in Mannerist bronzes, on the contrary, the male body derives its qualities from female anatomy: Giovanni da Bologna's Apollo and Mercury are androgynous. The idea of force, inherited from Michelangelo, more generally found expression in stone carving. One subject particularly interested Mannerists: the combat between two wrestlers. Michelangelo first used the theme in a figure intended for the Tomb of Julius II, Victory, who pins down a subdued enemy with his knee. He again proposed to render the forces of conflict in a group of Samson and two Philistines (the commission taken from him by Bandinelli). His sketches for the project, some still surviving, inspired Pierino da Vinci when he made a statue on the same theme (fig. 806). Michelangelo also wanted to carve a Hercules and Cacus, which we know from a damaged model. All through the century sculptors made marble groups illustrating figures locked in combat: Vincenzo Danti made an Honor triumphant over Falsehood, Ammanati a Victory, Vincenzo de' Rossi a Hercules and the Centaur; and Giovanni da Bologna used the theme four times – for Florence triumphing over Pisa, Samson slaying the Philistine, the Rape of the Sabine (fig. 816), and Hercules and the Centaur. Exploiting the *linea serpentina* to enclose the supple surfaces of the two bodies – in the Rape of the Sabine, of the three – he alone was able to unite the figures into one contorted composite form symbolizing effort. A twisting shape, penetrating space like a gimlet, was achieved by Giovanni da Bologna in his famous Mercury (fig. 815); the statue is no longer boxed-in within its own space; it moves in all directions and creates around itself a living space. The Mercury was the boldest attempt a sculptor had yet made to defy the laws of gravity. It is the opposite of Michelangelo's statues, which bore down into the ground with all their weight. There is nothing material in that body of Mercury; it is an abstract work made to enchant the mind.

Feverish experimentation went on in the workshops that sustained Florence's leading role in sculpture after she had lost it in painting. They created the princely portrait and a modern type of commemorative monument illustrating the theme of glory. Giovanni da Bologna's equestrian statue of Cosimo I (fig. 817) – compared with the works by Donatello and Verrocchio – embodies the abstract concept of the prince. Tribolo, Giovanni da Bologna, Ammanati and Buontalenti (who was not a sculptor, but a *projettista*) elaborated the motifs of the fountain and the tomb with an expanded use of statuary. They created a new figurative vocabulary for garden decoration, rich in the fantastic and the grotesque, and sometimes made their works look like rock to express nature in the rough. Buontalenti placed Michelangelo's unfinished Slaves in the rockery of a grotto. We must think of 16th-century Florence not as a dead town, but rather as a sort of laboratory for experimentation in modern sculptural forms. When the Fleming Giovanni da Bologna settled in Italy, he chose the court of the Grand Dukes as the most likely place to develop his talent as a sculptor; he worked there for half a century, making of Florence a rival to Rome. But in the 17th century Florence declined into a nostalgia for her past: Pietro Tacca, a pupil of Giovanni da Bologna, ignored the new Roman Baroque to imitate his master's manner (figs. 821, 822).

A Tuscan, Leone Leoni, established a workshop in Milan, afterwards continued in Madrid by his son Pompeo, who produced the finest series of princely portraits in Europe: the bronze statues of Charles V, Philip II, and their wives, for the tombs in the Escorial (fig. 823).

The Mannerist experiments continued in central European bronze workshops. At the end of the 16th century and at the beginning of the 17th, Hubert Gerhardt, Hans Krumper, and Hans Reichle cast commemorative monuments, allegories, and garden statues for the court of Munich. They also made fountains in the Florentine fashion: Hans Reichle even designed one for Danzig in 1619. The greatest of those sculptors, and the real heir to Giovanni da Bologna's art, was the Dutchman Adrien de Vries (fig. 831). In Italy when he was called to the service of Emperor Rudolph II, he brought Florentine Mannerism with him to Prague. He was particularly intrigued by the theme of two wrestling figures, which he treated several times as a mythological subject. Wanting to exceed the virtuosity of Giovanni da Bologna's Mercury, he represented in his Hermes abducting Psyche not one, but two, figures supported by the tip of a single foot. Hubert Gerhardt took up the same theme and imitated Gianbolongna's group of three figures (the Sabine) in a Hercules abducting Dejaneira; he also transposed the wrestling theme in his Horses Fighting. More eclectic than Adrien de Vries, he also imitated – somewhat clumsily – Benvenuto Cellini's Perseus.

In the Low Countries, stone carvers apparently rejected all feeling of solidity in their statues or reliefs; their loose modelling seems to look forward to the soft fleshiness of Rubens' nudes. When Cornelis Floris designed the choir screen in Tournai (fig. 862), he was inspired by Sansovino's *loggetta* in Venice, which he transformed into a Mannerist facade with statues and reliefs arranged as if by chance, and quite unrelated in scale.

In the Mannerist epoch, architects employed sculptors to decorate building interiors. For the Villa Madama in Rome, Raphael and Giovanni da Udine had invented a stucco decoration drawn largely on the grotesques discovered in Nero's *Domus Aurea* and still very close to the spirit of antiquity (fig. 776). Stucco ornament, which could be rapidly executed, became a normal type of decoration for palaces and especially for villas and country houses. It spread even over the exterior and sometimes covered a whole facade with its figures and ornaments. In the north, such decoration was usually cut in stone, and facades bristled with herms, caryatids, and imitations of the paper or leather scroll work used in decorations for festivals. Engravers like Dietterlin in Germany, Vredeman de Vries in the Low Countries, or Hugues Sambin in France acknowledged no limits to their graphic inventions; their frenzied ornamentation, spread by printed books, was taken up by sculptors who transposed it into stone. The carvers of altarpieces were also inspired by it; this paranoiac, overloaded style comes not from the 16th century, but from the early 17th, in those places where Mannerism continued up to the Thirty Years' War; just as the Spätgotik produced its most extreme examples in the 16th century during the Renaissance, the Uberlingen altarpiece by Jörg Zürn (figs. 834–836), echoed a century later that of Niederrotweil (fig. 706).

The destruction of the church of San Benito y Real in 1842, an aftermath of the French Revolution, brought Alonso Berruguete's works out of the gloom of a *capilla mayor* and down to eye level in a museum, where they could be – and were – appreciated (figs. 837, 838). But it was the handsome exhibition of his works in 1933 in the Colegio San Gregorio, transformed into a museum, that brought Berruguete's name to a position second only to that of the somewhat later El Greco, with whom he has certain affinities.

His contemporaries evidently realized the revolutionary character of Berruguete's art, for after he had completed the San Benito altarpiece in Valladolid, after six years' work, it was rejected by the committee of experts convened on July 29th, 1533, to declare, according to custom, whether the work fulfilled the terms of the contract. The committee asked for several altera-

tions, but we do not know whether the artist had complied with their wishes when the abbot finally accepted the work on January 14th, 1534. This criticism – of which no detailed account exists – may have sprung from professional jealousy. It may have been directed not at Berruguete's aesthetic approach, but at the technique, which even now some historians consider "hasty" or "popular." But that is probably the crux of the matter: Berruguete's genius expressed itself through the form as well as through the conception. The technique he chose for that altarpiece was polychrome sculpture, which was widely used in Spain throughout the 16th century. After the wood had been carved and all the cracks had been filled with stucco, the forms were coated with a mixture of plaster and clay. They were then completely covered with gold leaf, and afterwards *estoffado*, that is, colored. Sometimes the painted layer was engraved to reveal the gold, meant to suggest ornaments on the clothing; silver was also used. Emerging on the surface through engraving, or underlying the color, the precious metal gives a mysterious reverberation to the forms. This technique exploits the possibilities of both relief and painting; Berruguete, who had been trained as a painter by his father, understood it so well that he handled relief as a painter, summarily, so that it retained a fluidity that would lend its movement to the colored end product. The technique evolved by Berruguete remained very popular during the whole of the 16th century, a period during which the sculptors themselves were responsible for the polychromy of their statues. In the 17th century the situation was different: the statue completed by the sculptor was afterwards handed over to a painter, and therefore the sculptor was more inclined to treat it as a pure work of statuary; when he carved it, he could not envision its final, colored state. The sketchy carving of Berruguete at San Benito is certainly intentional, as is proved by careful finish he gave to the reliefs for the choir of Toledo Cathedral which were never meant to be polychromed (fig. 839).

Berruguete had been schooled during a long stay in Italy, where he knew Michelangelo and studied the works of Donatello; but he placed himself in violent opposition to the Renaissance spirit as early as the first quarter of the century, just when another Castilian, Diego de Siloë, was beginning to spread it throughout Spain. Diego may have sensed that Castile was not favorable to his aesthetic approach, and while Berruguete was working on the San Benito altarpiece he moved to Andalusia, where the Italianate style was to prosper. Berruguete, on the contrary, laid down at Valladolid the foundations of a truly

Spanish art, of which Old Castile remained the sanctuary. Those figures bent by a stormy wind, their souls seeming to be thrust outside the matter of their bodies, are a passionate affirmation of Christian spiritualism in the face of the Renaissance cult of Man. Human beings are not intended to enjoy this earthly realm, but must rather strive desperately and at all times towards a state of ecstasy in which the soul, freed from the body, can hope to approach the divine principle. The 16th-century revival of mysticism in Spain produced saints, but also sects with a following of illiterates, such as the *alumbrados*, derived from Arabic mysticism and preaching a direct contact with the divine mind through a sort of conditioning of the soul intended to reduce all the faculties to passivity. It was to combat those sects that in 1527 – just when Berruguete was working on the San Benito altarpiece – Francesco de Ossuna published his *Tercio Abecedario Espirituale*, which was to influence St. Teresa of Avila so deeply. Written in ordinary language, it unfortunately popularized mystic thought, thus encouraging the very excesses it was meant to suppress.

Berruguete has been called "Gothic"; I do not agree. Just as the classical Gothic style contained its opposite, the Flamboyant style, so the rich vein of Renaissance classicism could provide material for the style that would react against it. Berruguete used all the forms he had learned in Italy, but he interpreted them as a Mannerist, that is to say, out of context. His characters are seized by a trance which dislocates the whole organization, just as Pontormo's and Rosso's feverish figures engender chaos in their compositions, each character wrapped in himself, quite detached from his companions – something typical of mysticism, which produces the individual turned wholly inward, cut off from the world in an attempt to get closer to God.

In reality, the Plateresque style, of which Berruguete was the greatest exponent, was much more than the late transformation of another style; it was the first original artistic form created by Spain, until then under the influence of other countries. Spanish art historians have understood this, since they consider *Plateresco* one of the high points of their own art.

Berruguete never surpassed the San Benito altarpiece; his later works seem rather mass-produced. Working on the choir of Toledo Cathedral, he adopted the elegant, aristocratic style of the Renaissance and indulged in "formal" experiments quite alien to the ideas of his youth. But the revolution he had started spread all over Spain. Even Damian Forment, from Catalonia, who had not much personality of his own, became a convert; starting as a Gothic artist, he went on

in a Renaissance style and finished as a Mannerist. The chosen land for Berruguete-imitators was Navarre. In that remote province, this passionate style later produced some remarkable altarpieces which have been studied by a great scholar – the first to "discover" polychrome Spanish sculpture – Georg Weise.

In Valladolid, Berruguete's style was made even more dramatic by Juan de Juni (fig. 844), said to be of French origin, but obviously trained in Italy. He was very much influenced by Michelangelo and by the Laocoön, whose face he borrowed for his Christ. With Juni, interior drama becomes theatrical and a cry of pain takes on the overtone of rhetoric. But his technique is admirable, even superior to that of Berruguete. In his reliefs he used the Italian *schiacciato* technique and produced works which are not painted sculpture, but a genuine combination of sculpture and painting, the color adding life to the relief. Unlike Berruguete, Juni gave his statues heavy, powerful, Michelangelesque bodies, expressing tragedy through physical effects: his style might more truthfully be called proto-Baroque (figs. 841, 843).

Juan de Juni's passionate style, like Berruguete's, gradually calmed. He was influenced by the Romanizing tendency in Spanish art after 1560, which developed as a reaction against Mannerism. The more subjective style was replaced by a solemn, impersonal, and abstract art imitating High Renaissance formalism, a change similar to that instigated by the Carracci in Italy. It was not only Herrera's reforms that caused this change, as has been claimed; the stylistic reversal had already begun by about 1550, when the *Plateresco* was still in full bloom. Before Herrera designed his Escorial altar of 1579, Esteban Gaspar Becerra had submitted his overall designs to an architectural discipline, and his sculptures to the new Roman formalism, in his high altar for Astorga (1558). He was closely followed by Esteban Jordan in the Valladolid altar (figs. 848, 849), and in the altar for Santa Maria de Mediavilla at Rioseco.

While Spain became more deeply Christian under the impact of the Italian Renaissance, France, on the contrary, turned pagan. When he built Fontainebleau, Francis I called upon Italian artists to create a court art capable of serving his purpose of modernizing culture. From then on, French art negated its tradition to become more profane than religious. Francis I summoned one of the founders of Florentine Mannerism, the painter Rosso, who created an original work, a completely new kind of court decoration, in the Galerie des Réformés. He combined stucco with painting – which Giulio Romano had already done in the Palazzo del Tè in Mantua – but he gave the stucco figures the importance of real statues (fig. 852). Unfortunately the very flat painting of the artists who worked under Rosso's direction conflicts with the three-dimensional effect of the stucco. The lack of unity between the paintings and the sculptured frames is characteristic of Mannerism. Rosso, Benvenuto Cellini, and Primaticcio introduced to Fontainebleau the elongated female nudes smoothed into flowing curves which were to become a traditional French genre until the 18th century. The most famous work of that kind is the Diane d'Anet by an unknown sculptor (fig. 854). Under Henry II the new style was assimilated and France produced original architects and sculptors. While painting continued to bear the stamp of Mannerism, sculpture tended to shake if off. Goujon's forms leaned towards classicism; his Nymphs of the Fontaine des Innocents (fig. 855), with their clinging draperies symbolizing flowing water, are reminiscent of such late 5th-century Greek statues as those on the temple of Athena Nike in Athens. For the second – and not the last – time, French sculpture bowed to classical Greek art across the centuries, whereas Italian sculpture always remained closer to Roman or Hellenistic art. The psychologically penetrating portraits by Clouet or Corneille de Lyon had no equivalent in sculpture; but Germain Pilon endowed his funerary portraits with traditional French naturalness (fig. 859) and added to his models a restrained dignity that looks forward to the 18th century.

In the Ile de France and in the Loire district a style of architecture developed that required no ornament, but in other parts, in Toulouse or Burgundy, Mannerism inspired sculptor-architects like Hugues Sambin and Nicolas Bachelier to produce those decorations of caryatids and herms so popular in the Low Countries and Germany at the same period (figs. 856, 860).

The relationship between architecture and sculpture has been constantly shifting throughout the history of art; in some periods the architect has laid down the law to the sculptor and in others the sculptor's work dominated architecture. An extreme at one pole is the Escorial, where the stone-carver's contribution is limited to a few austere moldings, but this severe limitation followed upon half a century during which the opposite extreme was the rule, when proliferating statuary had been allowed to smother the architectonic structure of buildings. The most fruitful periods for sculpture, however, have not been those allowing the image-makers such unbridled freedom; the finest statues, the most impressive reliefs, have been created during periods of classicism, when the sculptor has accepted a self-imposed discipline and even contributed, with his work, to an orderly architectonic scheme.

The 17th and 18th centuries made great use of sculpture, as indeed of all the arts. After the ascetic catharsis of the Counter Reformation, which in any case was fully effective only in Spain, sculpture once more invaded the monuments, and in countries where the Baroque triumphed, began to overrun them inside and out. The earlier part of this epoch produced the last of the great sculptors. Masters like those of Chartres, Paris, or Reims, like Nicola Pisano, Ghiberti, Donatello, Michelangelo, or even Giovanni da Bologna, saw their last great descendants in Bernini and Montáñez. In the later 17th and 18th centuries sculpture tended more and more to degenerate into a merely ornamental art, though it was subservient to architecture only in appearance, and in fact lent itself, as did painting, in support of the architects' experimentation with interior space. Sculpture exists in great quantity in Rococo buildings like Ottobeuren or Neubirnau, but each statue or relief is nothing in itself and counts only as an element of the total symphony of forms in which architecture, painting and sculpture all combine in the swansong of a civilization. Understandably, the museum setting is fatal to Baroque sculpture, which always appears impoverished when detached from the surroundings within which it was conceived, from that coordinated whole that the Germans have termed *Gesamtkunst*. Even the masterpiece of Bernini, his Apollo and Daphne, might lose some of its magic if it were to be removed from the Villa Borghese, where it has always stood, to some clinical museum decor.

Once more it was Italy that invented the new style which all of Europe eventually adopted as its artistic language, though sometimes giving it an opposite interpretation – an evolutionary development common in all great stylistic creations, as we have seen.

Florentine Mannerist sculptors had concentrated their efforts on making the statue self-sufficient, even when it involved two or more figures. At the end of the 16th century sculptors in Rome had turned their efforts once more to an attempt to reintegrate sculpture, and particularly the relief, with architecture. Among the earliest important works in this vein were the Sistine and Borghese chapels of Santa Maria Maggiore, which proved veritable laboratories for experiment in Baroque decoration.

The end of the Mannerist period in Rome also saw an archeological movement that led to a revival of imitation of the antique in an altogether literal manner. Nicolas Cordier, from Lorraine, admired ancient art so passionately that he even made up statues from excavated fragments. Gianlorenzo Bernini, who received his grounding from his father Pietro, learned directly from antiquity by restoring antique works, the most famous of which is the Ares Ludovisi, to which he added an *amorino* in Hellenistic taste. At the age of fifteen he carved the statue of the goat Amalthea, whose attribution was soon forgotten; it was taken for a genuine antique, and was only recently discovered to have been carved by Bernini. The four groups and statues commissioned from the young Bernini by Cardinal Scipio Borghese, and still in the Villa Borghese, show marked Hellenistic influence. The David (fig. 870) is reminiscent of the Borghese Gladiator, and the slender body of Apollo in Bernini's Apollo and Daphne (figs. 871, 872) looks back to the Apollo Belvedere, though the Aeneas and Anchises and the Rape of Proserpina also show a strong Mannerist inheritance. The Apollo and Daphne was probably the most beautiful group sculptured during the 16th and 17th centuries; since Michelangelo, no one had been able to endow marble with so much life – a life which is shown just as it is arrested in a cry, the ultimate act of this being who is about to enter forever the world of silence.

The four works dating from Bernini's youth were still conceived somewhat in the Mannerist spirit, that is to say, with the statue considered as a selfsufficient entity, but when Urban VIII ascended the papal throne and began to employ Bernini on monumental works all over Rome, the sculptor gave up his interest in free-standing statues. From then on his work was designed to be seen in an architectural setting – an outlook characteristically Baroque. In later years the architect and sculptor completely merged within him. Bernini, like Michelangelo, approached architecture as a sculptor, composing buildings in masses, and when he created sculptures (except in the portraits) it was for the purpose of animating an architectural or natural setting. Even the Ponte Sant' Angelo angels (fig. 878) are designed with the background of the Roman sky in mind, and it is better, therefore, to see the copies on the bridge than to see the originals in Sant' Andrea delle Frate, where they were placed because Clement VII, who commissioned them for the Ponte Sant' Angelo, found them so beautiful that he refused to expose them to the inclemencies of the weather.

Bernini's statues appear to move with the purpose of breaking out of their limiting contours – those contours that had enclosed all Mannerist statues in a kind of prison symbolized by the *linea serpentina*, the artificial condensation of the statue's life and pulse within which all movement was rigidly contained. The human beings Bernini represents appear to long for escape from their self-sufficiency – that is, from their loneliness; a Bernini statue always implies an invisible antagonist or interlocutor – God, in the case of the religious statues. The portraits, imaginative evocations or life studies, show the model caught in the midst of conversation, as was Costanza Buonarelli, the artist's mistress, whose image is quivering with passion (fig. 875). Even in the face of death there is no silence: on the tombs of Urban VIII and Alexander VII (fig. 881), the Virtues are witnesses called to God's Tribunal to plead for the deceased. Nor is the spectator allowed to remain passive before Bernini's work: he is caught up, appealed to. With Bernini we are at the theater, and sometimes the spectators even appear, as in the Cornaro chapel in Santa Maria della Vittoria, where members of the Cornaro family watch from stage-boxes the representation of St. Teresa's Ecstasy, chatting among themselves, some even turning their backs on the sacred drama (figs. 873, 874).

One must talk, shout, act, run, fight, love, pray – anything rather than remain alone, face to face with oneself, questioning the needs of the inner life. Such was contemporary Rome, capital city of the Church, a community of believers which had become a defensive association against pessimism. Since the 16th century Italian mystics like St. Philip Neri or St. Mary Magdalen dei Pazzi had lovingly tendered to the faithful their assurances of a God "more Father than Judge." This optimism was rooted in the humanists' beliefs according to which human nature, created by God, could clearly be only good. There was no question of repressing natural tendencies, but only of directing them towards God. The Augustinian anguish that tortured the Spanish mystics, demanding a terrifying confrontation between man and his conscience, was most violently rejected in Rome. The Italian saints preached happiness as a genuine sign of sanctity. "My children, be cheerful," said St. Philip Neri, the most amiable of saints, "...a cheerful spirit is closer to Christian perfection than a melancholy spirit." St. Mary Magdalen dei Pazzi asserted that "God does not like sad hearts. He wants free and joyful hearts." Maulde La Clariere wrote in his *Life of St. Gaetano* that for Italian humanists, "Christianity is less a final knowledge of things than a link uniting men with God and with one another, a link of love and grace. The role of religion is to touch the feelings, to soften men's hearts, and therefore to give them a genuine personal incentive and other social virtues such as kindness, unity – in other words, happiness." All these saints lived in a constant state of emotional uplift, echoed in their verbal and written outpourings. During her ecstasies St. Mary Magdalen dei Pazzi preached so volubly that she had to be provided with six secretaries, who wrote under her dictation for hours and sometimes for whole days.

Michelangelo had led sculpture into a path which none could follow, and thus led it to sterility: Bernini brought it back to life. Few artists have had such a following and few have been so fully understood by their imitators; it was impossible to work in the manner of Michelangelo, but easy to be Berninesque. Some artists in Rome resisted his influence, however; the most stubborn of these was Algardi, whose avoidance of Bernini led him to a cold classicism derived from Mannerism. While Bernini's star climbed in Rome, Francesco Mochi in Piacenza worked for thirteen years on equestrian statues of two Farnese princes; in these monuments rider and horse were caught up together in the same impulse of movement, rather than rider dominating horse (fig. 867, 868).

Jacques Sarrazin lived for a long time in Rome, but when he left for Paris in 1628 he brought with him, not the influence of Bernini, who, younger than Sarrazin, had not yet produced his greatest works, but rather the influence of the antique. Like Bernini, Sarrazin had restored numerous antique sculptures; but while the Italian artist had been interested in Hellenistic works, the Frenchman turned to the classical style. Through his many pupils Jacques Sarrazin was the real founder of the French classical school (fig. 883).

Simon Guillain, with his bronze statues of Louis XIII, Anne of Austria, and Louis XIV as a boy, a group intended for the Pont-au-Change in Paris (fig. 884), is representative of French humanism, which stands for an act of conscience translated into deed through control of self. French classicism blossomed in what was called the "School of 1660"; peopled with antiquities and copies from the antique, the gardens of Versailles became a huge workshop which put artists on their mettle. In his Apollo tended by the Nymphs (fig. 886), François Girardon revived the noble art of Phidias. French sculpture having always remained close to Greek classicism, 17th-century French artists felt that the genuine sources of antique art were in Greece and not in Italy. La Teulière, director of the French Academy in Rome, dreamed of creating a school in Athens, in that city "where there are still beautiful remains," as he wrote.

The art of Versailles, dominated by Le Brun and regulated by and for the king, favored sculpture rather than painting; the latter sank to the level of mere decoration while a group of talented young sculptors was forming in the Versailles "nursery." For the monument of Louis XIV in the Place Vendôme, Girardon created the prototype of the royal statue, representing the sovereign in antique dress, serenely triumphant on a pacing horse. Unfortunately, we have been robbed of that masterpiece by the revolutionaries, and we know it only through the reduced models which have survived (fig. 887).

Undoubtedly the bust of Louis XIV that Bernini sculptured during his sojourn in Paris in 1665 was the model for many later French state portraits, carved or painted. In it Bernini duplicated the proud attitude of his earlier Francesco I d'Este (1650) (fig. 876), but gave the French king a truly sovereign appearance. Coysevox, in portraits of artists or magistrates done early in his career, retained the sobriety of the French manner which characterizes his busts of Louis XIV (1679–80 and 1681); but he was inspired by Bernini's heroic style in his posthumous portrait of the Prince de Condé (fig. 889), commissioned by the Prince de Conti in 1688.

French 17th-century sculptors evolved a type of funerary monument with numerous figures grouped around the deceased – represented in his death throes, or awakening to eternal life, or taking leave of his family, or praying. These tombs are reminiscent of contemporary funeral orations, which rank among the most beautiful literary expressions of the time. The passionate rhetoric of death is restrained by a self-control that slows the gestures and forces them to conform with the classical laws according to which the forms must be completely self-sufficient.

In this classical concert there were a few discordant Baroque notes. These were sounded most noticeably by the Marseillais Pierre Puget, who had a taste for representations of effort or pain. The muscular contractions of his statues (figs. 892) contrast with the smooth surfaces modelled by other French 17th-century sculptors.

In Spain, most sculpture was designed not for the open air, nor for large, well-lit cupola churches, but for gloomy chapels, where often only the polychromy and gilt covering the sculptures enable them to be seen in the darkness of the sanctuary. These sculptures were not the work of sophisticated artists who had traveled to Rome, but of artisans who, shut up in their workshops, considered the exercise of their trade as an act of prayer. As before, sculpture centered around the altarpiece, which now obeyed a strict architectural organization designed to include statues and reliefs. Spain was divided into two artistic schools: in Castile reigned the Baroque, introduced by Berruguete and Juan de Juni; Valladolid remained the capital for sacred images, its principal exponent, Gregorio Fernandez, practicing a rhetorical style much less moving than the profoundly meditative style of Juan Martínez Montáñez of Seville. The classicizing tendencies of Andalusia were inherited by Montáñez, and they also found their way into the art of Zurbaran; there are some indications that Zurbaran was deeply influenced by the older Montáñez. The masterpiece of Montáñez, the main altar in the church of San Isodoro del Campo at Santiponce (1609) (fig. 906), dates from the beginning of his career. The faces of his figures are full of deep sadness, of commiseration for the human condition; the sculptor expresses a mood opposite to the optimistic Catholicism of Rome, a mood prevailing in a country where Augustinism predominated, where man, sensing himself unworthy of divine solicitude, examined the depths of his soul with anguish and found there only nothingness. In Granada, Alonso Cano, a reluctant priest, chose less earnest subjects; his graceful statues look forward to the 18th century (fig. 908).

To understand 18th-century Italian sculpture, it is essential to see the convent-palace of Mafra in Portugal, built by King João V in emulation of Philip II's Escorial. More than fifty statues from Italy were ordered to decorate the church – a type of exchange common in 17th- and 18th-century Europe. These sculptures are in the moderated Berninesque style that was practiced in Rome and Florence at the time. In Naples and in Sicily more interesting developments were taking place. Neapolitan sculptors illustrated the theme of death with frenzied statues in the Cappella Sansevero (figs. 913, 915), using illusionistic devices and even *trompe l'oeil*; virtuosity appeared the only possible way of being original. More convincing are the works of Serpotta, from Palermo, at the end of the 17th century. Serpotta decorated several oratories with stuccoes in which may be seen all the elements of the Rococo style that was to flourish in Germany (fig. 912). Serpotta was the Guarini of sculpture. In Naples the fashion grew for the Nativity scene, the *presepio*: numerous figures of terra cotta, or more usually, of wood, dressed in real fabrics, were assembled in crowds teeming with natural life around the scenes of the Nativity or the Adoration of the Magi (figs. 916, 917). In Naples the naturalistic content of these scenes was exploited, but the elegant style of the statuettes greatly influenced Spanish art. Southern Italy had been in close contact with Spain since the 15th century. The facades of Sicilian buildings in Apulia and in Campania were often sheathed in a carved decoration compounded of deliriously contorted vegetable, human, and fantasy shapes.

The flight from reality which is Baroque art suited the Spanish temperament. Artists created in the churches in Spain theatrical structures like the famous *trasparente* in Toledo cathedral (fig. 920), which delighted their contemporaries. The name for this type of structure, *trasparente*, is significant; in Italy, Germany, and Spain the statuary groups, pierced and open, were often given a setting in which the light came from behind, blurring the contours and mingling further the already complicated forms. The Spanish altarpiece now reached the apogee of its evolution. During the last years of the 17th century José Churiguera designed the colossal altar of San Esteban in Salamanca (fig. 919), in which powerful twisting columns symbolize the aspiration of the whole towards heaven. In Portugal carved wood decor spread over the walls and ceilings of the churches, so that the interiors resembled caskets for precious jewels. The altarpiece was such an important element of Spanish art that from the 17th century on it influenced the decoration of the church facades as well.

Reaching New Spain – that is, South America – the Baroque forms proliferated like a plant transplanted to the tropical climate, though native stone carvers sometimes seem to rediscover spontaneously forms reminiscent of Pre-Columbian.

In Spain after Montáñez art declined into a naturalism which lost all nobility; Pedro de Mena turned Montáñez' idealistic expressions of faith into mere devotional images. In the 18th century Francisco Salzillo brought from Naples to Murcia the graceful art of the Neapolitan *presepio*, which he transposed into a type of sacred imagery that later spread to Portugal. Portuguese sculptors, however, still maintained a tradition of restraint, of interiorized reaction. This tradition echoed in Brazil where, at the end of its evolution, it produced the last great Christian image-maker, Antonio Francesco Lisboa, called o Aleijadinho ("The Cripple"). In the spirit of this mulatto, instinct combined with deep faith, and he refreshed the etiolated Rococo with a primitive strength in his scenes of the Passion of Christ (fig. 926), which are as powerful as the works of Montáñez.

The true heirs of Bernini throve in Central Europe and in Germany, where his theatrical compositions combining architecture, painting, and sculpture were imitated and expanded. Painting and sculpture tended not so much to develop within a framework imposed by the architecture as to become associated arts and to merge with it. On ceilings where carved decoration continues painted decoration and figures grow out of an animated architecture, it is often impossible to define where one ends and the other begins. The building interior becomes a shifting, moving world created by the sum of the parts. These interiors are often the work of a family whose members shared the responsibility for the various techniques, as did the brothers Asam in Bavaria, or the brothers Zimmermann in Swabia.

Any material could be used for relief effects: stucco, wood, marble, stone, or bronze. Adopting Italian stucco techniques, the Germans exploited stucco as a principal element of their interior decoration. The town of Wessobrunn, in southern Bavaria, specialized in training stucco workers who were then employed throughout the German-speaking world. Their stuccos are painted in bright colors that appear unreal and facilitate the transition between relief figures and paintings – though in any case the moving, jagged, Rococo framing elements constantly lap over into the painted scenes. All these lavish and spectacular reliefs do not have as much feeling for sculptural form as a single mutilated Greek statue in a museum. An occasional statue or group does stand out, and somtimes the whole decoration of a church may be organized around that one statue. In Bavaria, Egid Quirin Asam produced some very effective compositions: his Virgin of the Assumption (fig. 933), suspended in space in the church at Rohr, is a triumph over the law of gravity, a law that true sculpture obeys.

At the end of its evolution the excesses of the Rococo produced a sort of anarchy in which the unity of the decoration was destroyed, but which gave back some individual value to the separate statues, as exemplified in the Zweifalten monastery. At that time Josef-Anton Feichtmayr found an intensity of expression worthy of Alonso Berruguete. In the pilgrimage church of Neubirnau, a kind of madness seems to seize the figures: propelled out of the sacred scene, they circle like dancing dervishes, desperately contorting their bodies without managing to establish any connecting link with one another (fig. 941).

According to a Christian aesthetic requiring that the soul be closed to alien influence, the church so effusively ornate on the interior was decorated on the exterior almost exclusively by architectural motifs. Palaces were quite another matter: they might be covered with stone reliefs. Atlantes supporting the weight of the balconies, staircases, or upper floors were the favorite motif of princely dwellings – a significant display of captive strength. Just as the glorification of religion overlay a growing unbelief, this royalist rhetoric preceded the overthrow of kings. In an art apotheosizing a way of life that was rapidly nearing its end, princes and churchmen wrapped themselves in a screen of make-believe that hid the impending upheaval of society; they intoxicated themselves with a dream whose realities were already fading. It is interesting to note that it was the enlightened King Joseph II who closed the Baroque workshops in Austria.

Amidst this riot of images it is difficult to find a genuine sculptor, an artist devoted to the eternal problems of three-dimensional form. A rare example in Austria is the bronze sculptor Raphael Donner (fig. 947), and in Prussia, Andreas Schlüter, who made one of the proudest equestrian statues of a period swarming with them – that of the Great Elector in Berlin (fig. 931), inspired by Girardon's Louis XIV, which Schlüter might have seen during a visit to Paris before the statue was erected in the Place Vendôme.

France, unlike Central Europe, produced sculptors still faithful to the basic tenets of their art. A few were influenced by the Baroque, such as Lambert-Sigisbert Adam or Pigalle; most remained classicists, and most noteworthy among these is Bouchardon. Houdon brought back naturalism in his portraits, and in his nudes returned to the smooth, elegant style traditional in France. With Pajou and Clodion that style degenerated into sugary statuettes and clock ornaments. The rest of Europe, in the throes of the Baroque, realized that France alone had sustained the spirit of sculpture; whenever important monuments were needed, French artists were called upon to provide them. Falconet, who in his own country had produced only minor works, was called to St. Petersburg, where he set up on a rock a vivid equestrian statue of Peter the Great, reviving the little-used theme of the rearing horse (fig. 951).

French 18th-century sculpture is full of charm and liveliness; it produced graceful figures and portraits sparkling with wit. Nonetheless it remained fairly superficial, an art without a vital spirit to animate the smooth and accomplished silhouettes.

The 19th century saw the course of art divide into two paths: one, that of official art, was strewn with honors; the other, that of the vital, creative art, was heaped with opprobrium. Posterity has reversed this judgment, treating with scorn all that once attracted medals and commissions, while celebrating those artists who progressed along a road filled with pitfalls to make the 19th century one of the greatest periods in art history. But it was primarily a century of painters. One could, if necessary, live in poverty, painting continuously, filling one's cupboards with unsold canvases. But this kind of experimentation was impossible for sculptors, for their art requires an accord between the artist and society. Not that sculptors lacked public commissions during this century: public buildings and squares were crowded with statues and bas-reliefs, but these only revealed the sculptors' inability to grasp the basic principles of their art. Paradoxically, it was at this moment when plunged in mediocrity that sculpture exerted its greatest influence, for in the first half of the 19th century sculpture dominated painting. At the end of the 18th century a new revival of the antique had put an end to the pictorial liberty of the Baroque style and prevented a spontaneous outburst of Romanticism; painters were required to compose their canvases like bas-reliefs and to polish the imaginary volumes of the painted subjects. With the *Oath of Horatii* and the *Brutus*, David had produced models of archeological painting; Ingres, like a sculptor, showed a preference for cameos and Greek vases. Even Géricault could not rid himself completely of recollections of the antique. It was Delacroix who broke the spell, but only at the risk of losing the most elementary sense of anatomy.

The antique was the ideal of the Italian Canova (figs. 958, 959), who was a sculptor after Winckelmann's heart; two of his statues had the supreme honor of confronting the two most celebrated sculptures of antiquity, the *Laokoön* and the *Apollo Belvedere*, in the Vatican's Museo Pio-Clementino. This was the limit of the sculptors' ambition at that time: to imitate the antique to the point of deception. Yet for our eyes, at least, the sculptures of Canova are easily distinguished from genuine antique sculptures – these are the marbles of the sun, while Canova's glacial nudes seemed bathed in moonlight. It is this wan light that injected Romanticism into his art, for the Moon, daughter of the Night, haunts the early Romatic painters: the Frenchman Girodet, the Swiss Fuseli, the Englishman William Blake.

In Europe at the time of Canova, sculptors of every nationality propagated a style *à la Romaine:* the Englishman John Flaxman, the Dane Bertel Thorvaldsen (fig. 960), the Prussian Gottfried Schadow (fig. 956), the Swede Johan Tobias Sergel, the Frenchman Chaudet – some of them inclining towards grace, others towards virility. They practiced an art that owes its cold appearance not to antique sculptural models but to the plaster casts that represented them in every academy of art. The Greek originals that entered the museums in London, Paris, Munich, had no effect. Greece was seen through the screen of Rome. Thorvaldsen, for example, kept in his studio in Rome the sculptures found in 1816 at the temple of Aphaia in Aegina. Commissioned by King Ludwig I of Bavaria to restore them, he ended by Romanizing them.

The Romantics, such as Préault (fig. 965) and Duseigneur in France, did indeed try to animate their statues, but they succeeded only in creating gesticulating, grimacing mannequins. Barye's attempt to recapture nature through the observation of animals was no more successful; he lost himself in details of anatomy, and the beasts seem frozen in their roaring. He was more fortunate in his rare figures, in which he was less slavishly representational, and he found a kind of truth in seeking the equilibrium of the statues of classical Greece.

The only sculptor of the second quarter of the century who had any real sense of sculptural volumes was the Frenchman François Rude. Undoubtedly his Burgundian origin was the source of his healthy naturalism, a naturalism that often made him break the bonds of antique models. A fervent supporter of the Revolution and faithful to Napoleon (he was a voluntary exile in Brussels from 1814 to 1827), Rude had the epic sense; he knew how to fix a commemorative statue firmly in the changing light of the open air, or to evoke some great historical event, such as the *Departure of the Volunteers of* 1792, known as *La Marseillaise* (fig. 963).

Rude was the son of a coppersmith; Jean-Baptiste Carpeaux, born in Valenciennes, was the son of a mason, and he began work as a plasterer's assistant. For him, as for Rude, manual labor was the rule from childhood; it left its indelible mark upon both men, and through it they escaped the intellectualism that dried up the academies. For them sculpture was above all working with the hands. Rude, who had learned to forge iron, could draw robust volumes from a block of stone. The plasterer Carpeaux remained a modeller (fig. 968). He loved to handle clay, and bronze also suited him well, but his marbles preserve the fluidity of petrified modelling. Drawing upon the Flemish Baroque tradition to free himself from the domination of the antique, Carpeaux conscientiously treated each work as having its own special problems. The group of *The Dance* for the Paris Opera (fig. 967) recalls the explorations of the 16th-century Florentine Mannerists into movement developing upon itself.

Many painters also worked in sculpture: Géricault's rare essays in this medium are very fine. Daumier, with his powerful hands, modelled a few busts in addition to the famous *Ratapoil* and *The Emigrants* (fig. 966), but this genius was only a sketcher, and his sculptures are very few. (One must reject his authorship for the series of statuettes made after lithographs that have recently been attributed to him.) Degas, when almost blind, turned to sculpture so that he could feel the volumes of his favorite figures of horses and dancers. Renoir's sculptures are, in fact, painted subjects transposed into three-dimensions by other hands (fig. 975). As for Gauguin's sculptures in wood, they attempt to interpret the art of carving in terms of primitivism.

At the end of the century, Dalou in France (fig. 969) and Constantin Meunier in Belgium (fig. 970) sought to regenerate the art of sculpture through injecting social content. In painting, a giant, Courbet, had taken this direction, but in the sculpture of these two men it was less fruitful.

Then Rodin appeared. He seemed destined to renew the art of sculpture, but he strayed from his path. Possessing a faultless technique acquired through long study, Rodin exhibited the *Age of Bronze* at the Salon of 1877, when he was 37; for the first time in long years the human body lived in bronze. The work caused a tremendous scandal, for the public was not ready to renounce its beloved mannequins – the artist was even accused of trickery, of having cast his model from a living figure. Rodin had been in Italy and he followed the steps of Donatello and Michelangelo in seeking the antique, but through nature. Unfortunately, he thought himself Michelangelo and forced his talent, and thus, ten years later, he fell into pathos with the *Burghers of Calais*. Finally, in his late marbles, he adopted a fluid style similar to that appearing at the same time in Italy in the works of Medardo Rosso (fig. 973); the fluidity of modelling was related to Art Nouveau, as was the eroticism of these late Rodin groups (fig. 972). It is sad to see such mastery end in these lumps of butter. Rodin's portraits in bronze, however, whether after life or commemorative, are always excellent. His Balzac is like a brilliant snapshot, conceived in a sort of trance in which the artist identified himself with his ideal model.

One might indeed have believed that Rodin would restore sculpture to its rightful place; all Europe passed through his studio, but instead of understanding him, sculptors merely imitated him. Rodin's most assiduous student was Antoine Bourdelle (fig. 974), who felt that he was going back to the source in creating pastiches of Greek art of the early 5th century; but he was aware, at least, of monumental sculpture. Then Maillol appeared, a man of genius who brought the false hope of a renewal of figurative sculpture just as it approached its nadir. This Mediterranean, creating colossi of marble and bronze after female models, affirmed one last time the radiant splendor of the human body (fig. 976). Despiau (fig. 977) was another who made successful sculptures of the nude, but then he turned to the portrait, seeking a truth which eluded him. During the past half-century of abstraction, a school of figurative sculpture has continued to exist, served by men of talent such as Wlérick in France, Francesco Messina and Manzù in Italy (fig. 1009), and Franco in Portugal.

Cubism was invented by two painters; it is essentially a reduction to an art of the surface. Moreover, for one of these painters, Picasso, sculpture is always developed in relation to his painting. Some consider his sculptures more significant than his paintings, but it is my belief that he prefers to let his imagination explore in painting, and that he then rethinks his inventions in three dimensions. In the Blue Period he transposed some of his figures in bronze; at the end of the Cubist period (1912–1914) he created compositions with polychromed wood elements that were analogous to his painted still lifes. (These Cubist compositions influenced Henri Laurens [fig. 988].) Later Picasso assembled iron elements in his sculpture (fig. 995), attributing the value of objects of art to casual discards, used as he found them, as ready-mades, or assembled with other elements. In this he followed Marcel Duchamp and the Dadaists, and also anticipated the most recent developments. "The image-maker," said Georges Salles, "works most creatively in the disorder of the bureau drawer." These experiments in *forme brute*, however, have not prevented Picasso – who is free of any prejudice – from occasionally creating expressive figurative bronzes (fig. 1005).

Artists of various nationalities have put sculpture to the test of the Cubist aesthetic. The Hungarian Czaky was the first, in 1911; then followed the Ukranian Archipenko (fig. 986), the Frenchmen Laurens and Raymond Duchamp-Villon (figs. 984, 985), the Russian Ossip Zadkine (fig. 999), and the Spaniard Julio Gonzalez (figs. 996, 997), who, like his compatriot Pablo Gargallo (fig. 994), used cut sheet-iron. In Italy Umberto Boccioni, signatory of Marinetti's *Futurist Painters' Manifesto*, created a sort of cinematic Cubism to show the development in space of a form in motion (fig. 989).

At this time, in Moscow, a revolution whose importance would not be discerned until much later had begun with the signing of the *Realist Manifesto* in August 1920 by the brothers Antoine Pevsner (fig. 1010) and Naum Gabo, and with the creation of Tatlin's project for the *Monument to the IIIrd International* that same year. These men invented a totally abstract sculpture, called Constructivist. Made up of metallic elements, it no longer worked with opaque volumes but with a transparent network that made space and light vibrate.

Other artists, while continuing to transcribe reality, will use it only as an allusion. In the work of the Roumanian Brancusi, in which natural data are reduced to their purest forms, sculpture based on nature is transported into the realm of ideas (figs. 980, 981). In the sculptures of Hans Arp there is an element of Dadaism, but the forms are derived from Brancusi and transformed in their meaning by Arp's expressive intention (figs. 990, 1000). The art of the Englishman Henry Moore is linked to Surrealism, although this derivation is not generally recognized. The stretchings, moldings, hardenings, softenings, the arbitrary juxtapositions that he imposes on the human body, suggest the manipulations of Dali; in the open air his sculptures become challenges to their environment (fig. 1001). These monsters seem to evoke the sudden mutations that atomic radiation might cause in human genes. Giacometti's Surrealism, more generally recognized, is less evident. His skeletal anthropomorphism is more Expressionist than Surrealist; his elongated, flayed figures tremble in space like stalks of wheat (fig. 1002). In this style of the écorché, Germaine Richier created huge, pathetic, bronze images, searing, throbbing figures, like survivors of napalm bombing (fig. 1006).

America entered the international scene of contemporary sculpture with Alexander Calder. With his "mobiles" he introduced the new element of motion into three-dimensional art. "The art of Calder," said Marcel Duchamp, "has the sublimity of a tree in the wind." In the mobile, which borrows its basic feature from a scale – a multi-dimensional scale - palette-like discs, balls, or spoon-shapes are arranged to canalize the air currents. Shuffling, grazing, caressing, they compose with space a kind of ballet of forms, endlessly recommencing (fig. 1003).

In the most recent developments – Pop, Kinetic, Minimal art, as so on – one witnesses a sort of promotion of sculpture, which for a half-century had been more or less subjugated to painting. The art of the painter seems to have exhausted the possibilities of the state of permanent revolution that is the goal of the present direction. Sculpture has the advantage of being one degree less removed from reality. It has reality in its hardness; it is a raw fact confronting actual space. Sculpture has come out of the studios and the museums; in its latest forms it is part of the environment in which contemporary man lives; it decorates his gardens, public monuments, office buildings, and factories. In Italy, at the Spoleto Festival, a spatial dialogue between modern sculptures and an ancient town has recently been created.

There are still unbelievers who see intentional mystification in the strange creations of recent sculpture. But the destruction of the sculptural plasticity that dominated the civilizations of the Mediterranean and the West for millennia occurred internationally, proving that the sculpture of today is a response to destiny, and that it is linked to a civilization in which the concepts of space and time – upon which the life of man has always been based – have been deeply shaken.

The artists of today work as if, starting at zero, they wish to give themselves up to new experiences; they seek inspiration in completely untraditional materials: ores, rough stones, roots, wood eroded by water, household utensils, light bulbs, mechanical objects, crushed metals (sometimes even entire automobiles [fig. 1007]). They avoid any allusion to nature and by seeking substance in basics hope perhaps to revive dried-up sources.

Delivered from the prison of relief, sculpture dilates in space, offering itself, but treacherously – it cuts, batters, pierces, and condenses the space. The artist plays a subtle game of volumes and voids, of abrupt stops and sudden surges, of polished surfaces and opposing planes. Entirely free of all illustrative requirements, the sculptor has certainly never before gone so far in experimenting with the basics of his art.

As for the moral significance of the sculpture of the 20th century, it is infinitely complex. As I wrote in 1946 in *Le Crépuscule des Images*, one can see in the movements derived from Cubism and Constructivism a projection from the artist's subconscious of the abstract universe discovered by modern science. But, in fact, one finds nothing in modern art that would suggest – as is too often said – that it is a documentation of the machine age. The universe of the machine is an exact world, ineluctable, implacable. The ethereal creations of Pevsner, Gabo, and Lippold (fig. 1016) are less evocative of the machine than of speculations in higher mathematics. The most aberrant-appearing sculptures of the past few years translate a sort of plastic anarchy and move us as protests against the dehumanization introduced by the mechanization and standardization of industrial society. They are three-dimensional materializations in space of those alienations denounced by certain sociologists and philosophers, notably in the United States, against which at this moment an instinct for revolt seems unleashed throughout the world.

Whatever some critics may think, contemporary artists have not failed in their mission; the man they reveal to us is only the man we are. These strange works are sounding an alarm. Let us hope it is not a prophecy.

Chapter XI translated by B.M.C.

1 *Bifacially flaked point* · Paleolithic, Acheulian, 300,000 B.C. · Musée des Antiquités Nationales, Saint-Germain-en-Laye, France.

In the 15th century, the painter Jean Fouquet represented one of these stones in the hand of St. Stephen in his painting of Etienne Chevalier. They were then considered of mysterious origin and were called *pierres à fendre* (splitting stones). This one was chipped out by a pithecanthropoid some 300,000 years ago, with the help of a hammering tool made not of stone, but of wood or bone, which produced thinner flakes. The maker of the object must have been aware not only of the functional value, but also of the beauty of this finely worked implement.

2 *Dagger from Hindsgavl* · End of Neolithic, after 2,000 B.C. · Nationalmuseet, Copenhagen.

Just as the sailing ship reached perfection in the late 19th century when steam had already arrived, so did stone working achieve a high degree of virtuosity at the beginning of the metal age, as this dagger shows. That the artisan used the material to imitate metallic prototypes can be seen clearly in the shape of the blade and the form given to the pommel. It appears as though the stone has softened to adapt its hardness to metal's ductility.

3 *Polished stone axe* · Neolithic · Musée des Antiquités Nationales, Saint-Germain-en-Laye, France.

The polishing of stone was only one among many Neolithic innovations, but it resulted in a new aesthetic approach to stone. After hundreds of thousands of years, faceted volumes were replaced by perfectly smooth shapes.

4 *Elk-shaped ritual axe* from Uppland · Neolithic, 4,000 B.C. · Statens Museum, Stockholm.

The polishing of ritual objects could be particularly refined. Sometimes the tool was shaped like an animal, clearly indicating an artistic intention.

5 *Bone harpoon* · Paleolithic, Magdalenian · Musée des Antiquités Nationales, Saint-Germain-en-Laye, France.

Bone tools were to become quite widespread during the Upper Paleolithic period. Most characteristic, perhaps, are the harpoons - "marvelously precise fossil missiles," as the Abbé Breuil described them. The first harpoons, with simple saw-tooth edges, appeared in the middle of the Magdalenian period, around 13,000 B.C.; later came beautiful harpoons adorned along one edge with recurring barbs. The latest type, with barbs on both sides, is often less perfect in its shape, as the barbs tend to become thicker. At the end of the Magdalenian and after, harpoons became flatter and the profile of the barbs coarser still.

6 *Bronze spear point* with engraved decoration · Northern Bronze Age, 9th or 8th century B.C. · Nationalmuseet, Copenhagen.

Elegance of design and beauty of ornament are combined in this weapon. Note the tapering towards the end. Deep scorings outline the edges and meet towards the top, in the middle rib. The same finish is apparent in the typical Northern Bronze Age decoration engraved on the socket: between two zones of horizontal hatchings, high vertical bands alternate with delicate spirals arising from each other.

7

7 *Bison* · Rock engraving in the la Grèze cave · Paleolithic, Gravettian, ca. 21.000 B.C. · Les Eyzies (Dordogne).

Drawn with a deep, firm line, this single bison at the entrance to the small cave of La Grèze is among the earliest rock engravings in Paleolithic art. The horns are seen frontally, while the rest of the animal appears in profile. Through a change in scholarly terminology, the work is no longer connected with the Aurignacian phase, but with the Gravettian, a term now used to identify a time chronologically equivalent to the final phase of Aurignacian culture as it was defined at the beginning of this century.

8

8 *Neighing horse* in the Montespan cave · Paleolithic, Middle Magdalenian, 13,000 to 10,000 B.C · Montespan (Haute-Garonne), France.

Climatic conditions similar to those prevailing in the cave at Tuc d'Audoubert insured the preservation of a horse drawn in damp clay in the Montespan cave. Engraved on the soft material with swift, precise strokes, it shows a masterful and sober draughtsmanship which we still admire. Access to the cave is difficult, and it seems to have been visited by only a few generations of men, probably in the Middle Magdalenian period.

9

9 *Clay bison in the Tuc d'Audoubert cave* · Paleolithic, Middle Magdalenian, 13,000 to 10,000 B.C. · Tuc d'Audoubert (Ariège), France.

Needless to say, Paleolithic artists were not content with carving hard materials. But only an exceptional pattern of circumstances allowed their more fragile works to survive, as for instance this bison at the bottom of the grotto at Tuc d'Audoubert. It is about 23 inches long, modelled in a crude clay that cracked as it dried. This bison has been preserved by a deposit of stalagmitic material; nearby are the formless masses of other works which did not survive.

10 *Antelope* engraved on the rock · African Paleolithic · Transvaal Museum, Pretoria.

Only the Bushmen live in the Kalahari desert. These dark little men with their yellowish skin and Mongoloid eyes have been gradually pushed into that desolate area by the expansion of other African peoples. Matchless hunters, they stalk their victims armed with bows and poisoned arrows. Trusting in their natual agility and cleverness, their magic rituals and formulae, they fearlessly hunt even the biggest game. This masterly rock engraving of an antelope reveals the gifts of observation of a people living close to untamed nature.

10

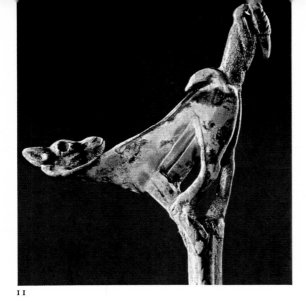

11

11 *Fawn with a bird* · From a spear-thrower found in the grotto of Mas d'Azil (Ariège) · Paleolithic, Magdalenian · Saint-Just-Péquart Collection, Saint-Brieuc, Côtes-du-Nord, France.

This strange and charming group was carved by a Magdalenian artist on the end of a hooked spear-thrower cut from a length of reindeer antler. Such implements seem to have been used to add impetus to the spear's flight. The fawn, poised as though perched on a rock, turns round towards the dropping he is evacuating, on which two birds are billing and cooing. Early Gallic wit, perhaps? A spear-thrower decorated with the same scene, of somewhat less accomplished art, was found in another grotto, at Bedeilhac (Ariège).

12 *Venus of Savignano* · Paleolithic · Museo Ethnografico Pigorini, Rome.

Paleolithic "Venuses" are rarely found in Italy, if one disregards the group discovered near Menton. However, this statuette (height, 9 inches) in green serpentine, from Savignano, near Modena, offers a beautiful study of volumes through grouping of the area of hips and torso. The strange elongated form serving as a head may represent a cowl, or it may be a formal element intended to echo symmetrically· the tapering of the legs. Faces interested Paleolithic sculptors very little, but this figure, like the Venus of Lespugue, betrays a very active taste for symmetry.

12

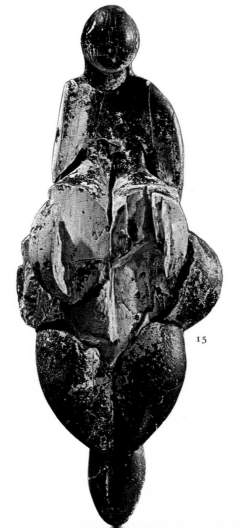

15

13 *Venus of Laussel* · Paleolithic, ca. 21,000 B.C. · Laussel (Dordogne), France.

At Laussel, a whole open-air sanctuary has been found. Sheltered by a rocky overhang, it is situated between the cliffs and the fallen rocks below, and decorated with a series of bas-reliefs. The main sculpture, in relief on the rock, is a female figure about 15 inches high, represented full-face, holding a bison's horn as an offering (?). The treatment of the figure is the same as in the small contemporary Gravettian figurines. To represent the buttocks, the artist has shifted them to the sides. Traces of red ochre, which was frequently used in Paleolithic rituals, have been found on the limestone flags.

14 *Venus of Willendorf* · Paleolithic, ca. 21,000 B.C. · Naturhistorisches Museum, Vienna.

This limestone statuette, 4½ inches high, from Lower Austria, belongs to the first known school of statuary art. This school, formerly referred to as Aurignacian, is now attributed to a more clearly defined age, called "Gravettian." The very full female body with abbreviated limbs, its head featureless below curly-looking hair, must not be regarded as a faithful representation of reality. It reflects, rather, an aesthetic ideal and a religious symbolism. The intention of such works was, it seems, to promote human fertility as that of animals was promoted by animal representations. Later examples from the Neolithic Age, however, probably embodied the Earth Mother.

14

15 *Venus of Lespugue* · Paleolithic · Musée de l'Homme, Paris.

The architectonic composition of this wonderful six-inch ivory from Lespugue (Haute-Garonne) contrasts with the expressionistic realism of the Venus of Willendorf. The legs, shoulders and head are made smaller to accentuate the middle part of the body, where the very low breasts, the buttocks pushed forward to the sides, the abdomen and the thighs are grouped in symmetrical volumes. Despite the stylistic differences between the Lespugue and Willendorf Venuses, the same stress on sexual forms, the same suppression of facial features, the same positioning of the arms distinguish both and demonstrate their iconographic kinship.

13

16

16 *Seated female figure*, from Anatolia · Late Neolithic, 6th millennium B.C. · Archeological Museum, Ankara.

This female figure, about three and a half inches high, of unfired clay, was found in 1962 at Catalhüyük, one of the first important fields excavated in Anatolia. It has been dated by Carbon 14. Judging from such idols as were discovered there, fertility goddesses were worshipped at the time this figure was made. They appear either seated or standing, but are almost always obese and massive, with the arms bent at a sharp angle to bring the hands to rest on the breasts. The nose and ears are usually carved in relief, while the eyes are indicated by slight hollows.

18

18 *Small female figure* from Mamariyya (Egypt) · Painted clay · Predynastic, 4,000 to 3,000 B.C. · Brooklyn Museum, New York.

At the dawn of civilization, in the predynastic era, sculpture made its appearance in Egypt in the form of male or female figurines in clay or ivory. The prehistoric heritage is evident in the theme: the highly schematized image is a symbol intended to evoke thoughts of the Great Mother, and such a widespread cult needed only cursory allusions to call to mind its chief deity. The simplicity of forms, the elegance of the curves, the feeling for organic synthesis, and the discretion in representing sex attributes make the figure already characteristically Egyptian.

19 *Marble head* from Amorgos · Cycladic · 2,600 to 2,100 B.C. · The Louvre, Paris.

Among the funerary effects brought to light in the Cyclades were several of these heads. They belonged to large statues hewn from marble and then broken up so that they could fit in the tomb. This one, measuring 14 inches, came from a statue over six feet high. The face takes the form of an elongated oval, and the features are not carved in relief except for the ears and the triangular nose; the latter, strongly defined, evokes for us the absent facial parts, which were probably originally added with a brush.

19

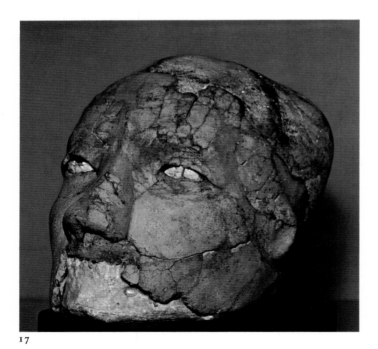

17

17 *Human skull modelled in plaster*, from Jericho · Neolithic, 5th millennium B.C.

In 1953, in a stratum of the excavations of Jericho dating from the 5th millennium B.C., Kathleen M. Kenyon discovered seven skulls in various states of preservation. The features have been "reconstituted" in plaster over the skulls to produce individual portraits. The eyes are made of pieces of shell and the skull cavity is filled with clay; in one case, the plaster is tinted to simulate the color of skin. It has been suggested that these heads may have been the skulls of venerated ancestors, or, perhaps, the heads of enemies killed in battle. Whatever their origin, they are the first known attempt at figurative sculpture that uses the skeleton as a point of departure.

20

20 *Marble figure* from Keros · Cycladic · Early Bronze Age · The Louvre, Paris.

On this little island near Amorgos, Koehler unearthed in 1883, among other things, this statuette of a lyre player. It was found in a square, covered tomb 39 inches deep. The human outline, the instrument, and the chair are reduced to cylindrical forms. The harmonious perfection of its finely modelled structure and its extreme stylization place the lyre player at the apogee of Cycladic figurative art, of which it constitutes the most complete expression. Beautiful in workmanship, it stands apart from all other artistic efforts of its era, and marks a clear break with prehistoric art.

21

21 *Seated mother with child*, from Thessaly · Terra cotta · Neolithic · National Museum, Athens.

During the Neolithic period, the image of the Great Goddess underwent a transformation: In the early Neolithic, she appeared as a headless idol with atrophied arms and legs and hypertrophied female attributes; in the late Neolithic, she became more human and carried in her arms the infant that had made her flanks swell. This mother tenderly hugging a child to her breast (height: 6½ inches) was found in Thessaly, in Northern Greece, on the site of the acropolis of Sesklo. Clearly visible there are both the early, pre-ceramic Neolithic strata and the late Neolithic strata in which appear remains of the pottery that began to be used in Greece about 5,000 B.C. This figurine is covered with a sort of black tattoo on an ochre background, with traces of red. Body paint was probably thought to have magic properties; it may have been a custom of the period as a protection against evil influences.

22

22 *Marble figure* found at Naxos · Cycladic · Early Bronze Age · The Louvre, Paris.

Almost without exception, the Cycladic idols symbolize the Great Mother Goddess, that powerful deity from whom stems every form of life, human, animal, or vegetable. They are unique in that they are usually carved from the local island marble, and they are of a completely different type from the Paleolithic and Neolithic female figurines. The idea of fertility is no longer insisted on by means of obesity, but is merely hinted at. There is a striving towards simple plasticity, as much in the construction of superposed geometric volumes as in the great simplification that eliminates all detail.

23

23   *Head of a large figure* in terra cotta, from Yugoslavia · Neolithic.·
Pristina Museum, Yugoslavia.

Images of the Great Goddess of fertility illustrate the influence in
Yugoslavia of the Near-Eastern cult, transmitted by Greece; and they
are evidence, also, of the prestige that Greek civilization enjoyed on
the banks of the Danube. But while in Greece Neolithic sculpture is
represented only by small statuettes - in which some attempt is made,
however, to humanize the features - in the Balkans late Neolithic
figures increase in size (the Pristina head is 7 inches high) and take on
a dramatic flavor, especially through the great enlargement of the
eyes and the rather expressionistic stylization.

24

24   *Reclining woman* from the hypogeum of Hal Saflieni (Malta) ·
2,300 to 1,450 B.C.·

This is one of two figurines of sleeping priestesses discovered in a room
with a painted ceiling. The figure is stretched out on a couch whose
shape suggests a wooden framework covered with reeds. With its Ma-
tisse-like disproportion of the head, small in relation to the rounded
arms, this figurine is one of the most beautiful pieces modelled by the
early inhabitants of the island of Malta. Dressed in a long fringed skirt
which distends still further the enormous volume of the hips and
thighs, it resembles Cretan figurines with their naked breasts and
their long, flowing skirts.

25   *Mother Goddess* from Cyprus · Late Bronze Age, 14th to 13th
centuries B.C. · The Louvre, Paris.

During the last period of the Bronze Age, the island of Cyprus entered
on the era of its greatest prosperity, having become one of the chief
centers of the Mycenaean world and the intermediary between Asia and
the Aegean. Cypriot art tended to become schematic, as can be seen
in this curious statuette discovered at Alambra, quite flattened, made
in red-varnished terra cotta. The head, with its bird's beak and its
huge ears pierced with moveable rings, recalls an Asiatic type. The
subject is probably a fertility goddess holding a child in her slender
arms. Examples of the type have been found throughout the Aegean-
Anatolian region.

25

26   *Chariot with solar disc*, from Trundholm · Ca. 14th century B.C. ·
Nationalmuseet, Copenhagen.

Animal sculpture died out in Europe after the last Paleolithic age.
The Neolithic had produced scarcely anything but small female idols.
The bronze Trundholm horse, discovered in a peat-bog in the northwest part of the island of Seeland, is perhaps the first example of a
revival of animal art. The gold-covered disk is sumptuously ornamented with the concentric spiral motifs native to Nordic bronze art.
Mounted on wheels, the work doubtless symbolizes the sun being
drawn across its heavenly course by a celestial steed.

26

27

27 *Statuettes* of cast silver, ornamented with gold leaf · From Ugarit · Late 2nd millennium B.C. · The Louvre, Paris.

Excavations of the ancient town of Ugarit (now Ras-Shamra), situated on the Syrian coast almost opposite Cyprus, have brought to light an important site dating from the second half of the 2nd millennium. Among the finds are these two cast silver statuettes, each supported by a heavy, conical pedestal. They are largely flattened and elementary in form, adorned only by gold leaves forming loincloths, and by necklets of gold thread; only the heads are treated in some detail. The deeply hollowed eyes appear to gaze at the worshipper, to whom the outstretched hands perhaps presented some now-vanished attribute.

28 *Female figure* from Boeotia · 8th century B.C. · The Louvre, Paris.

This terra-cotta statuette is distinguished by a bell-shaped tunic inside which the moveable legs are suspended. Details of dress and ornament are picked out in reddish-brown color. The hair trails down the inordinately long neck in wavy tresses; a necklace carries a pendant that falls between the breasts; the short arms are decorated with swastikas and the half-open hands have painted palms. The feet are painted with high, laced footgear, while the tunic is ornamented with rosettes and a row of dancing women. (33 inches high.)

29

28

29 *Warrior* from the Hallstatt era · Early Iron Age, 8th to 5th centuries B.C. · Naturhistorisches Museum, Vienna.

Between the 8th and the 5th centuries B.C. the first Iron Age flourished in and around the Alps: eastern France and southern Germany represented the "primitive Celtic" region; further east were the Raetian tribes; Illyrian-Venetian tribes inhabited the western Alps and northern Italy. Among a wealth of other metal objects displaying strong Italic influence, are squat, assertively modelled little figures in the round, decorating the handles of bronze receptacles. Most of these represent animals, but there are also human figures, like this little bronze warrier, 3 inches high.

30 *Menhir*, with a representation of a male figure · 7th century B.C.
· Musée des Antiquités Nationales, Saint-Germain-en-Laye.

This type of megalithic stele seems to have been produced over the
course of about a thousand years in Liguria or South France. The
upper part is carved in a crude low relief, schematically representing
human figures, with accompanying equipment or clothing. The
figures are sometimes male and sometimes female. The male figures
bear some kind of accoutrement which has been interpreted as the
bow and tinderbox used to make fire.

30

31

32 *The Gundestrup Cauldron* · Celtic · 1st century B.C. (?) · Nationalmuseet, Copenhagen.

The "cauldron," about 28 inches in diameter, is made up of a group of
gilt silver plates, seven outside and five inside, with a disk at the base.
The pieces were collected from a peat-bog in northern Jutland. This
mysterious object, of a fierce art filled with religious symbols, is
certainly Celtic in origin. The sacred personages represented on it,
the warriors clad in breeches, the trumpets and torques, all proclaim
that origin. It is not known, however, whether it was made in northern
Gaul, in the Celto-Ligurian region, or in the Danube valley. Some of
the figurations, like the curious representations of elephants, reveal
unexpected oriental influences. The work seems to date from the last
centuries before Christ, rather than the 3rd or 4th centuries A.D., as
was once thought.

32

31 *Statuette of an archer*, from Sardinia · Nuraghic, 7th to 5th
centuries B.C. · British Museum, London.

The warrior, dressed in a short tunic and carrying his quiver on his
back, is protected by a helmet and greaves; on his chest is a sort of
breast-plate, probably part of a cuirass; beneath this hangs a short
dagger. The small nuraghic bronzes can be classed according to three
distinct styles: that of Uta, with clean, stripped volumes; that of
Abini, with ragged forms; and finally, the "barbaricino" group, simple
and very direct. This work (7½ inches high), with its sober volumes and
restrained pose, belongs to the Uta group.

33

33 *The Stag-God* · On an inside plate of the Gundestrup Cauldron (see number 32).

Seated in a Buddha-like pose, the horned stag-god Cervunnes, whose name we know from a bas-relief on the Gallo-Roman monument of Nautae Parisiaci, brandishes in one hand a torque, in the other, a serpent. He is surrounded by animals, dominant among them a wolf and a stag. The stag's branching antlers could be a divine symbol of regenerative power. A link has been seen (though the notion appears of dubious validity) between Cervunnes and the very ancient cult of stag-worship evidenced by the Paleolithic "sorcerer" in the Trois-Frères cave (Ariège).

II Development of Sculpture in the Near and Middle East

34 *Woman and child*, from Ur · Terra cotta · Mesopotamia, al 'Ubaid Period, 4000 to 3000 B.C. · Iraq Museum, Baghdad.

A number of these terra-cotta figurines, mostly representing women as symbols of fecundity and fertility, were found at Ur. The broad shoulders, slim hips and legs placed close together form a quite elegant body; but the head is scarcely human and resembles that of a frog or a snake. Incisions cover the pubic triangle and a high headdress of bitumen ornaments the head. Characteristic of these figurines is the decoration of flattened pellets, placed somewhat at random, doubtless representing tattoos. The principal interest of these idols is that they show us the 4th-millennium fertility goddess type was represented as nude, or almost nude.

34

35

35 *Crescent-shaped tablet* · End of the 4th millennium · British Museum, London.

This shale tablet, along with others known by the name of Blau Monuments, was at one time considered inauthentic. In reality, these documents provide precious evidence of the evolution of writing at the end of the 4th millennium from pictographic to linear writings. Similar tablets from Susa show us, moreover, that this transformation is contemporary with the appearance of proto-Elamite writing, which in the late 4th millennium also abandoned pictography . The engraved scene shows a bearded figure holding out a votive offering a vase or a statue (possibly a lion's head); he is accompanied by a woman.

36 Detail of reliefs on a *vase* from Warka (Uruk) · Alabaster · Mesopotamia · Jamdat Nasr period, 4000 to 3000 B.C. · Iraq Museum, Baghdad.

In the photograph appear two registers of the reliefs on a big alabaster vase from the Uruk period. The whole vase has four registers, with figurations related to the cult of Inanna, a Sumerian goddess of love and fertility. Above on the right, a servant dressed in a loin-cloth holds the fringed belt of a high dignitary who has come to pay homage to the goddess. Behind him - this part would represent the back of the sanctuary, for the relief runs right round the vase - baskets, cups, and animal-shaped vessels brim over with offerings, first fruits of the harvest; and yet more are borne by a file of naked servants, on the register below: this ritual vase tells us that no one approached the goddess empty-handed.

36

37

This group of alabaster statuettes, discovered together in the little Sumerian town of Tell Asmar, bears quite definitely the mark of inexperienced local workmanship: there is no grace in the square shoulders, the trapezoidal chests, and the legs, reduced to the role of props. This clumsiness, however, may yet suggest a deliberate choice, for these are worshippers; face to face with the god, the poor human form is reduced to a gesture of offering, to the expression of a dazed, enraptured soul. The group's attitude of fervent adoration makes clear the mainspring of Sumerian art: its primarily religious inspiration.

37 Fragment of a ceremonial *palette* · Schist · Egyptian, Late Predynastic, ca. 3000 B.C. · British Museum, London.

Palettes of green slate date from the end of the Predynastic Age (about 3000 B.C.). In the center of one side a circular cavity has been hollowed out, probably to hold cosmetic to be applied to the statue of the god or king. The fragment shows a battlefield strewn with corpses, over which birds of prey are squabbling; a lion, perhaps representing the king, tears at one of the bodies. A little higher, a figure dressed in a long, embroidered robe leads a prisoner. The artist has attempted to depict movement in a realistic and energetic style.

38

39

38 *Knife from Gebel el Arak*. Flint blade set in an ivory handle · Egyptian, Predynastic, ca. 3300 to 3000 B.C. · The Louvre, Paris.

The figurations on the ivory handle illustrate the relations between predynastic Egypt and the East at the dawn of history. On this side of the handle, a battle unfolds: warriors confront each other in the upper part, while in the lower, Eastern ships with raised prows engage crescent-shaped Egyptian vessels. On the other side, a hero - an Egyptian transposition of Gilgamesh, legendary king of Uruk and Sumer - tames two rearing lions, while below appears a hunting scene with a lioness, dogs and wild sheep.

40 *The God Abu*, from the temple of Abu at Asmar · "Mosulmarble." · Mesopotamia, al'Ubaid Period, 3000 to 2500 B.C. · Iraq Museum, Baghdad.

These two large statues were in the group of worshippers found in a pit in the square temple at Tell Asmar. The extremely schematized features of the God Abu - the abstractly patterned mouth, nose and eyebrows, and especially the enormous eyes that seem to consume the face - give rise to a concentration of all expression in the rapt, intense gaze. Some scholars are inclined to interpret the figure as an effigy of a god, considering the size of the eyes as the sign of his omniscience; others believe these inhumanly staring eyes would be equally appropriate to a worshipper gazing into the divine light.

40

42 *Head of a bull* · Bronze · Sumerian, Early Dynastic period, 3000 to 2500 B.C. · City Museum of St. Louis.

The beginning of the 3rd millennium B.C. saw metal entering into general use in Mesopotamia. A great many masterpieces resulted from the exploration in art works of the new materials. This bull's head, of unknown origin, is fascinating with its terse, intense expression, and the restrained force of its patterned, yet vital, nostrils and jaw. The sharp, fixed glance is enlivened by the polychrome inlay of shell and lapis lazuli. A curly beard, partly preserved, has the effect of investing the animal with an almost human appearance; the artist takes a middle course between the bestiality of other animal representations and the complete humanization seen in the man-headed bulls so numerous in Mesopotamian art.

42

41 *Stele of King Naram-Sin*, from Susa (originally from Babylon) · Red sandstone · Mesopotamia, Akkadian period, 2500 to 2000 B.C. · The Louvre, Paris.

The stele represents a victory of the king of Akkad, Naram-Sin, grandson of Sargon, over mountain-dwellers from the east. In order to ensure the unity of the subject, the artist has discarded the traditional compositional method of dividing the scene into superposed bands. Larger than the soldiers and wearing the horned helmet of the gods, the monarch stands aloft near the summit of a mountain. The enemy are fleeing and falling while the victorious army climbs the slopes in pursuit. The part played by the gods in the victory is recalled at the top by celestial symbols of Shamash and Ishtar.

41

43 *Head of a man* · Alabaster, with shell and lapis lazuli inlay · Mesopotamia, Akkadian period, 2500 to 2000 B.C. · Oriental Institute, Chicago.

The ethnic type of this head, found at Bismayah (ancient Adab), is Semitic: elongated skull, small mouth, aquiline nose. The beard, trimmed to a point, is an equally distinguishing feature, and characteristic of Akkadian custom, for the Sumerians were always shown clean-shaven. The surprisingly lifelike expression of the eyes was produced by filling the eye cavity first with bitumen, and setting into this small pieces of shell, and finally a little disc of lapis lazuli to form the iris. The modelling, which is both tender and subtle, makes us appreciate the Akkadians' immense contribution, on the level of human sensibility, to the Sumerian tradition.

43

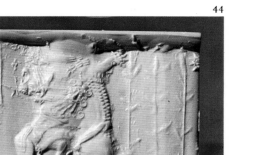

44 *Impression from a cylinder-seal* · Mesopotamia, Akkadian period, 2500 to 2350 B.C. · British Museum, London.

The combat between the traditional hero Gilgamesh - who is always victorious - and a savage beast, in this case a lion, remains the essential theme in gem-cutting, predominating over other religious and mythological subjects. In carving these miniature scenes, the Akkadian artist attains a remarkable skill, owing to his originality as much as to his improvements on tradition. Severe composition and an incisive quality are the dominant features. Here, in each group, two diagonals suffice to create the illusion of energetic movement: the body of the lion, arched in a spasm of agony, thrusts to meet the powerful counter-thrust of the hero, whose head is wonderfully placed at the point where the converging forces meet.

45 *Man-headed bull* · Black soapstone · Mesopotamian · 2400 to 2300 B.C. · The Louvre, Paris.

Appealing in its fine workmanship, its good proportion, and the firm handling of volumes, this docile bull lies with his forelegs tucked beneath him, his benignly gazing human head crowned with a horned tiara. A richly patterned fleece covers his shoulders and rump, and wavy locks curled at the end frame the face. To maintain the expressive unity of the whole the artist has invested the features with a certain animality, which is nevertheless transformed by the supernatural force manifest in the horns, emblem of divinity; the transition from animal to god is thus imperceptibly worked, and in the image, the friendly spirit whom the bull represents becomes fully convincing.

46 *Lion-headed demon* · Terra cotta · Mesopotamian, 2200 to 2100 B.C. · The Louvre, Paris.

This statuette, with its freely modelled lion's head set on a vaguely human body, grasps a bird in its hands. The image arises directly from the intricate world of Mesopotamian magic, which, whether "black" or "white," existed on a level quite separate from that of the great gods. Demons were its mediums, both good and bad - for man could not act in either direction save through the will of the ever-present supernatural powers. It might be noted that the Telloh (Lagash) field has yielded very similar worshipping figurines from the same period as this statuette, with human heads, but holding small animals in the same fashion, as offerings.

45

46

47

47 *Male head (Gudea?)*, from Lagash · Steatite · Neo-Sumerian, ca. 2100 B.C. · Metropolitan Museum of Art, New York.

In the 23rd century B.C., the Guti nomads invaded Mesopotamia and settled there, but without trying to reconstitute the Akkadian Empire under firmly centralized rule. This situation allowed such Sumerian cities as Ur or Lagash to acquire, very quickly, great independence. The Louvre possesses a remarkable series of portraits of the princely governor of Lagash, Gudea. They exemplify the sculptural perfection attained at that time; this head is only one example among many, but it displays the firmness of volumes, the understanding of the composition, the refined taste for continuous but varied surface modelling that mark a highly accomplished art.

48 *Votive statue* of Gudea, from Lagash · Diorite · Neo-Sumerian, ca. 2100 B.C. · The Louvre, Paris.

This is the only complete seated effigy of the governor of Lagash among the numerous portraits of him in the Louvre collections. The turbaned figure makes clear that, after the Amorite invasions, the Sumerians revived their traditional canon for the figure, using a very short body, only four or five heads high. Economy or lack of skill have been alleged as reasons for the stocky proportions, but this can hardly be accepted if we consider either the high quality or the great quantity of the statues recovered. This indifference to realistic proportion was intentional, like the even more complete indifference to the realistic human form displayed by the sculptors of the Tell Asmar worshippers. Only the expression of religious fervor mattered.

49 *Gudea's libation vase* · Steatite · Neo-Sumerian, ca. 2100 B.C. · The Louvre, Paris.

The cup takes the form of a horn with a pouring-spout. Rearing up the sides to the spout, as if to consume the liquid being poured out, are two intertwined snakes, symbols of the chthonic gods. Their undulating bodies might appear to trace the course of the streaming liquid. Behind each snake stands a demon, half-eagle, half-snake, crowned with a horned tiara. These composite figures are attributes of Ningizzida, personal god to Gudea, and also guardians of the temple; the ringed staff which they grasp in their claws symbolizes the temple door.

49

48

50

51 *Head of a female divinity* · Terra cotta · Mesopotamia, Akkadian period, ca. 2300 to 2100 B.C. · The Louvre, Paris.

The Sumerian civilization, of a hardy character, was capable of assimilating every influence without significant disruption of its own cultural tradition; the various invasions seem but to have enriched it with a new vitality. Thus, the establishment of the Akkadian empire brought to Mesopotamian art the feeling and the imagination that it had lacked. With the Guti invasion and the Neo-Sumerian reaction that followed, these new elements did not disappear, as is demonstrated by the head shown here. The Sumerian horned tiara surmounts a woman's face of tender sensuality; but the intent eyes, a little too large, are nonetheless intended to express, in the traditional manner, her divine nature.

50 *The goddess Nin-Sun* · Black steatite · Neo-Sumerian, 2200 to 2100 B.C. · The Louvre, Paris.

The charming young woman on this relief, a few inches high, clearly represents the goddess Nin-Sun, to whom, the inscription tells us, the bas-relief was dedicated. The goddess has long hair confined at the temples by a band, and a necklace composed of multiple strands encircles her neck. The flounced robe that hides the shape of her body is the old Sumerian *kaunakes*, made originally from sheepskin, with long hanging strips of woolly hide. After Mesopotamian fashion had rejected this type of dress, it remained the characteristic garb for gods and goddesses. Therefore, despite the absence of the horned tiara, the figure certainly represents a deity, but a secondary deity, who played only a minor role in the Sumerian pantheon.

51

52

52 *Winged goddess* · Terra cotta · Neo-Sumerian, 2000 to 1800 B.C. · The Louvre, Paris.

Excavations have revealed a great number of figurines from the Larsa epoch, terra-cotta plaques depicting all sorts of scenes of everyday life, and religious figures. The relief reproduced here gives us an important variant of the well-known type of the nude goddess. She is crowned with a horned tiara which asserts her divine nature. The admirably proportioned body is that of a woman, but she has wings on her back, and on her feet, rapacious claws that grip the two ibexes on which she stands. Because of her gesture of blessing, she can be placed among the friendly deities in the band of grimacing spirits that make up the Mesopotamian pantheon.

53

54

53 *Stele bearing the Code of the Babylonian King Hammurabi* · Black basalt · Neo-Sumerian, 1800 to 1700 B.C. · The Louvre, Paris

For their steles, the Babylonians often made use of blocks of stone left more or less in their original form. Such is the case with this stele, on which King Hammurabi (1793-1750 B.C.) caused the 282 laws of his famous Code to be engraved. It was removed from Babylonia by a conquering Elamite, probably Shutruk-Nahhunte, towards the end of the 2nd millennium B.C. Although it is well-known that Hammurabi was neither the first nor the only ruler to have conceived such a code, the work remains remarkable nonetheless - as much for its content, deciphered by Schiell, as for the quality of its execution.

54 Detail of upper part of fig. 53: *King Hammurabi* before the god Shamash.

At the top of Hammurabi's Code stele, the bearded king, dressed in a robe closely resembling that of Gudea, and wearing a turban, stands before Shamash, god of justice, with his right hand raised in an attitude of prayer. The divine nature of the god is indicated by his long tiered robe (based on the Sumerian *kaunakes*), his horned tiara, and the flames leaping from his shoulders. King and god look each other full in the face and speak freely, the one without cowardice in submission, the other without tyranny in authority. We are reminded of the Book of Exodus (XXXIII, 11): "And the Lord spoke to Moses face to face as a man is wont to speak to his friend."

55

55 *Statue of Queen Napir-asu,* from Susa · Bronze · Mesopotamia, Elam, Kassite period, ca. 1250 B.C. · The Louvre, Paris.

During the Kassite era, Elam enjoyed a very real material prosperity which in turn gave rise to an abundance of art works, foremost among them this large bronze statue of the wife of King Untash-Huban. Once its completed form had been cast, it was furnished with a core intended to strengthen it; the whole is a remarkable achievement in view of the primitive technical means available for the task. The queen, her hands crossed in an attitude of prayer, is dressed in a tight-fitting bodice and a wide skirt decorated with embroidery, which the artist has attempted to represent faithfully, marking that strong taste for ornamental surface detail recurring periodically in Eastern art.

105

56

56 *Seals from Mohenjo-daro* · Steatite · Indus Valley culture, 3000 to 2000 B.C. · Museum of Central Asian Antiquities, New Delhi.

The site of Mohenjo-daro consists of a group of burial mounds situated on the banks of the Indus in Central Sind. There, and at Harappa, have been discovered the finest remains of the Indus Valley culture, which has been dated by correlation with Mesopotamian chronology to about the second half of the 3rd and beginning of the 2nd millennia B.C. It is known particularly for the steatite amulet-stamps, square in shape rather than cylindrical, depicting an animal (most often a bull) accompanied by an inscription. Here, a horned ox stands before an unidentified object, an altar or manger. The semi-pictographic writing on the seals, which in some ways resembles proto-Elamite writing, has not yet been deciphered.

57 *Statuettes of animals* from Mohenjo-daro · Terra cotta · Indus Valley culture, 3000 to 2000 B.C. · National Museum of Pakistan, Karachi.

The excavations at Mohenjo-daro have unearthed a number of figurines of gods or of animals, modelled in terra cotta and sometimes covered with a red color. One statuette reproduced here represents a humped ox which, in spite of its mutilation, has retained a vivid strength in the representation of the drawn-back muzzle, the bright eyes and the folds of the heavy neck. The brightness of the pupil was produced by making a small slit in the head and enlarging it to make the eye-socket, then inserting a clay pellet. The care with which the statuette is made suggests that it was a religious offering, but we do not know whether the animal itself was held as sacred.

58

58 *Statuette from Mohenjo-daro* · Limestone · Indus Valley culture, 3000 to 2000 B.C. · National Museum of Pakistan, Karachi.

This bust, formal and ceremonial in character, may represent a deity, priest, or high official. The trefoil motif that adorns the drapery is an astral symbol, very widespread in the ancient Orient, and it leaves no room for doubt as to the sacred implications of the role in which the figure is depicted. A narrow band embellished with a circular ornament holds the short hair. The low forehead, the thick lips, and the nearly closed eyes give the face an enigmatic and awe-inspiring expression, which must have been accentuated by the original incrustation of white shell in the eyes.

59 *Stele of the Serpent King*, from Abydos · Limestone · Egyptian, Archaic Period (1st Dynasty), ca. 2900 B.C. · The Louvre, Paris.

The stele of King Wadji, sometimes called Zet or the Serpent King, was discovered at the First Dynasty necropolis at Abydos. The decoration is essentially symbolic: the divine falcon, radiant with power, is the dynastic god Horus. He protects the king's name, embodied in the hieroglyphic of the serpent inscribed in a rectangle possibly depicting a plan of the throne-room, placed above the conventional representation of a palace façade. This façade, decorated with niches and pilasters, is pierced by two doors recalling the dual nature of Upper and Lower Egypt.

59

60 *Portrait panel of Hesy-ra*, from his tomb at Saqqara · Wood · Egyptian, Old Kingdom (IIIrd Dynasty), 2780 to 2680 B.C. · Egyptian Museum, Cairo.

In the mastaba (tomb) of Hesy-ra at Saqqara, Mariette discovered three wooden panels at the back of niches that usually held statues of the deceased. On one of them is represented Hesy-ra himself, an important personage from the epoch of King Zoser. Hesy-ra is shown in a walking pose, wearing a long flaring wig, his loins covered by a cloth with a pleated end tucked into the waist. In his right hand he holds a baton, in the other a staff and his scribe's implements. The intensely energetic and aristocratic face is treated with the powerful realism characteristic of Old Kingdom works.

61 *Prince Rahotep and his wife Nofert*, from Medum · Limestone, painted · Egyptian, Old Kingdom (IVth Dynasty), ca. 2650 B.C. · Egyptian Museum, Cairo.

These large statues were discovered in the statue-chamber of Rahotep's mastaba at Medum, one of the necropolises of Memphis, the Old Kingdom capital. A vivid life emanates from them, owing to the colors, which have remained miraculously intact: red-ochre for the male, Rahotep, and yellow-ochre for Nofert, whose shoulders, revealed by the hieratic white cloak, show a lighter flesh tint. Rahotep's face leaves an unforgettable impression in its striking realism, but the candid expression lacks subtlety.

62

62 *Prince Khufu-khaf and his wife receiving offerings*, from his tomb at Giza · Egyptian, Old Kingdom (IVth Dynasty), ca. 2650 B.C. · Egyptian Museum, Cairo.

The funeral offering, whose regularity alone guaranteed survival in the afterlife, was naturally of great importance. In the Old Kingdom, those privileged to have been in the service of the king while alive were recognized as his dependents after their deaths as well. Offerings consecrated in the royal temple of the necropolis were distributed in the mastabas, as is shown by innumerable funerary inscriptions beginning with the words: "Offering given by the king . . ." Khufu-khaf, son of Cheops, is depicted beside his wife, who holds his hand and fondly slips her arm under his.

63 *The great Sphinx at Giza*. · Egyptian, Old Kingdom (IVth Dynasty), 2680 to 2565 B.C.

When his funerary complex was being built, King Chephren had this figure of a sphinx carved from a great outcropping of natural rock rising beside his granite valley-temple at the beginning of the ramp leading up to his pyramid. This gigantic, human-headed lion, 185 feet long and 65 feet high, represents the god Harmakhis - Horus-of-the-Horizon - with the king's features. Uniting, in one majestic form, animal, king, and god, the sphinx is a form of the solar deity; serene guardian of the other world, and guarantor of resurrection, he defends the necropolis.

63

64

64 *Seated Scribe, from Saqqara* · Limestone, painted · Egyptian, Old
Kingdom (IVth Dynasty), ca. 2680 to 2565 B.C. · The Louvre, Paris.

The scribe, disciple of the ibis-god Thoth, who according to Egyptian
myth invented writing, was possessed of a science that rendered him
indispensable in the bureaucratic Egyptian society, where a complex
hierarchy of officials administered the country under the Pharaoh's
divine authority. A literate man could hope to attain the highest posts,
and popular Egyptian tradition often praised the merits and the
advantages of the scribe's profession. The following lines come from a
Chester Beatty papyrus:

Make me a scribe and keep this in your heart . . .

A book is more use than a well-carved stele . . .

It takes the place of the chapel and the pyramid . . .

(P. Gilbert, *Egyptian Poetry*, p. 98).

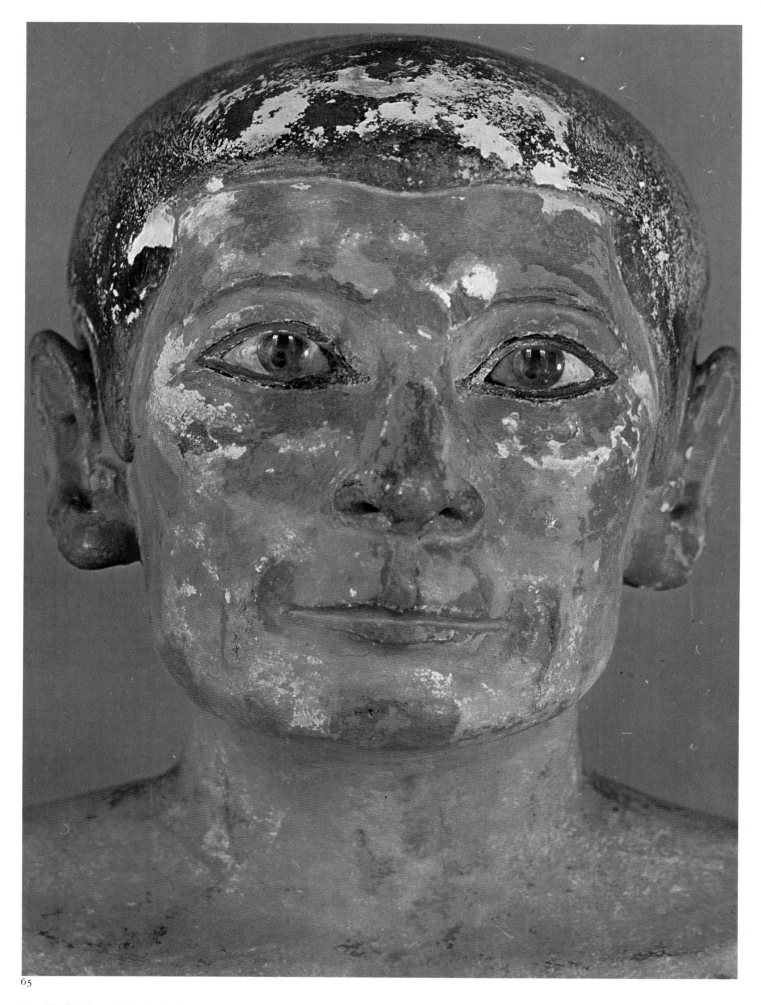

65

65 *Head of the seated scribe* in fig. 64.

The statue type of the seated scribe appeared in Egypt at the beginning of the IVth Dynasty and remained in use until the end of Pharaonic art. The example often designated as the "Louvre Scribe" is the most famous from this long series. The face, marked by experience and years, seems to be turned towards some invisible speaker. The intelligence and liveliness of the glance are suggested with skillful incrustations; the eye-socket is filled with a mixture of black and white enamel, and a little strip of silver set behind the glass iris reflects light.

66 *Statue of Ranofer*, from his tomb at Saqqara · Limestone, painted · Egyptian, Old Kingdom (Vth Dynasty), ca. 2500 to 2400 B.C. · Egyptian Museum, Cairo.

In the Vth Dynasty Ranofer fulfilled important religious functions at Heliopolis, the greatest religious center in Egypt at this time. In his tomb at Saqqara were discovered two over-life-size painted limestone statues, identical in carving, pose and form. They differ only in hairstyle and dress. In this one, Ranofer wears a short loin-cloth and a flaring wig. The idealization of the serene visage has not suppressed the portrait's individuality; in this respect the statue is a prime example of the incomparable balance achieved in Vth Dynasty statuary between the expression of immediate life and a sense of the permanent.

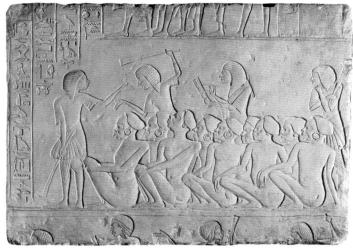
68

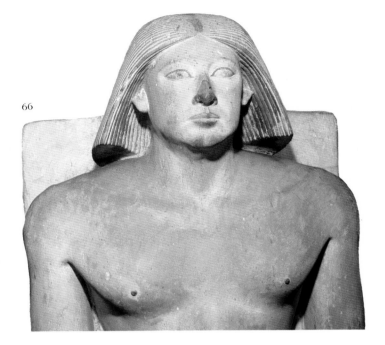
66

68 *Procession of prisoners*, bas-relief from the tomb of the Pharaoh Horemheb · Egyptian, New Kingdom (XVIIIth Dynasty), ca. 1350 B.C. · Museo Civico Archeologico, Bologna.

This bas-relief adorned one side of the funerary chapel of the Pharaoh Horemheb. Although the bodies are modelled in the round, the mural character of the relief is emphasized by the incised contours. Several panels represented war prisoners. Those depicted here are Negroes; they listen to the orders of the foreman while two guards, armed with sticks, stand ready to enforce the orders and a scribe writes on his tablet. In this relief harsh realism is softened by elegant draughtsmanship.

67 *Herding donkies*, from the mastaba of Akhuthotep at Saqqara · Limestone, painted. · Egyptian, Old Kingdom (Vth Dynasty), ca. 2500 to 2400 B.C. · The Louvre, Paris.

The Old Kingdom tombs, or *mastabas*, grouped around the royal pyramid, appeared above ground as rectangular masses of compact masonry; below these, usually excavated in the bedrock, were the actual burial chambers. In the masonry a chamber, a kind of chapel, was reserved, which served as a place of contact between the world of the living and the world of the dead; it was there that the cult of the dead was carried on. Innumerable reliefs decorated this room, and the things depicted were believed to be magically translated in the other world, for the benefit of the deceased. These picturesque and charming scenes revive for us a whole world of bucolic charm.

67

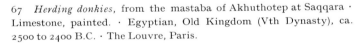

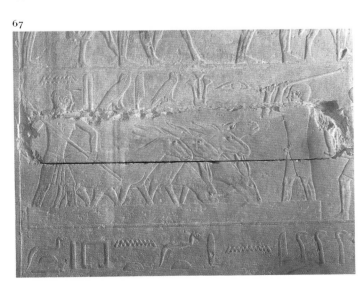

69

69 *Atum greeting Sesostris I*, from Karnak · Egyptian, Middle Kingdom (XIIth Dynasty), ca. 1900 B.C. · Egyptian Museum, Cairo.

On this limestone pillar from Karnak, the great Heliopolitan god Atum, father of the gods, usually identified with the setting sun, greets Sesostris I. Having taken the king by the arm, he puts his hand behind the king's head in sign of protection. God and king are crowned with the double crown of Egypt, in which the white mitre of Upper Egypt and the red crown of Lower Egypt are symbolically united. The pure line of the contour and the charm of the subject allow us to overlook somewhat the scene's conventional character.

111

70

70 *Portrait of Amenemhetankh.* · Sandstone · Egyptian, Middle Kingdom (XIIth Dynasty), ca. 1800 B.C. · The Louvre, Paris.

This portrait of a contemporary of King Amenemhat III is one of the finest examples of Middle Kingdom private statuary. The hands are placed flat on the apron in a somewhat stiff attitude, but the figure's rigidity does not impair the high quality of the fine modelling of the bust and the delicacy of the idealized face. Amenemhatankh was a priest of the crocodile god Sobk at Shedet - the Krocodilopolis of the Greeks - at Fayum. This oasis, irrigated by a branch of the Nile, was the object of jealous care by the XIIth Dynasty princes, who established a residence there.

72

72 *Death mask of Amenhotep III*, from Amarna · Plaster · Egyptian, New Kingdom (XVIIIth Dynasty), ca. 1370 B.C. · Staatliche Museum, Berlin.

In the reign of Amenhotep III Egypt attained the height of her imperial power and was in military control of Syria and Palestine. The influence of the East penetrated the Nile valley, where the Pharaohs themselves willingly married Asiatic princesses; a need for reformation appeared in the religion, ill-adapted to the new conditions. At the end of Amenhotep III's reign there were already clear signs of the religious and artistic crisis that was to occur during the following reign. An example is this mask, probably molded on the lifeless face of Amenhotep III, which was found in the workshop of the sculptor Tuthmosis at Amarna, the new capital of Amenhotep IV.

71

71 *Amenhotep II under the protection of Hathor*, from Deir El Bahari · Egyptian, New Kingdom (XVIIIth Dynasty), ca. 1450 B.C. · Egyptian Museum, Cairo.

Discovered in the funeral temple of Deir El Bahari, this statue represents the goddess Hathor in the form of a cow. The head, framed by papyrus, bears the solar disc and two ostrich plumes between the horns. Amenhotep II appears twice: crouching, he drinks the milk of the goddess; with his back to her powerful chest he walks under her protection. Hathor was worshipped at Thebes as a goddess protecting the necropolis; she was also often identified with Isis, mother of Horus, sheltering in the reeds of the Delta. It is in the double role that she appears here in a funeral temple, guarding the king, who was descended from Horus.

73 Head of a colossal statue of *Amenhotep IV*, from his temple of Aten at Karnak · Sandstone · Egyptian, New Kingdom, XVIIIth Dynasty, ca. 1360 B.C. · Egyptian Museum, Cairo.

Immediately on his accession in 1372, the young Pharaoh broke with the all-powerful priesthood of Amon at Thebes. He replaced the traditional cults with a religion of monotheistic tendency in which the cult of Aten, the solar disc, held a dominant position. Amenhotep IV took the name of Akhenaten and established a new capital at El-Amarna, in central Egypt; but before leaving Thebes, he built, at nearby Karnak, a temple to Aten, from which a few colossal statues remain; the head of one of these appears here. The ambiguous and disconcerting facial expression, the elongated, exaggerated features combine into a new harmony; and despite its curious ugliness the face gives an impression of passionate force and mystical liberation.

73

112

74

75

74 *Amenhotep IV (Akhenaten) with his wife (Nofretete) and daughters* ·
Egyptian, New Kingdom (XVIIIth Dynasty), ca. 1360 B.C. · Staatliche Museum, Berlin.

In Akhenaten's new religion, the divinity of the sun, Aten, is conceived
as radiating throughout creation; and official art celebrated, in
obedience to the King's desire, both the all-creating sun and the
flower blossoming in its rays. Akhenaten (whose name means Blessed-
of-Aten) rejected traditional iconography, and had his family life
depicted in its most intimate and happy moments. Here the Pharaoh,
whose unpleasing physical appearance is evoked with systematic
exaggeration, embraces one of his daughters, while rays from the
sun-disc hold out symbols of life (the *ankh*) to parents and children.

75 *Queen Nofretete*, from Amarna · Limestone · Egyptian, New
Kingdom (XVIIIth Dynasty), ca. 1360 B.C. · Staatliche Museum,
Berlin.

Nofretete's origins are obscure; some believe her to have been the
sister of Amenhotep IV (Akhenaten); others identify her as the
Mitannian princess Tadukhepa who came to Egypt to marry Amenhotep III, after his death becoming the wife of the new Pharaoh. This
courtly bust, found at Amarna in the workshop of the sculptor Tuthmosis, has been the subject of many commentaries. It is striking with
its elegance, of a rather decadent nature, and the contrast of the
enormous weighty headdress balanced above the slender, fragile neck.

113

76

76 *Head* from the period of Amenhotep IV (Akhenaten) · Wood ·
Egyptian, New Kingdom (XVIIIth Dynasty), ca. 1350 B.C. · The
Louvre, Paris.

76 *Head* from the period of Amenhotep IV (Akhenaten) · Wood ·
Egyptian, New Kingdom (XVIIIth Dynasty), ca. 1350 B.C. · The
Louvre, Paris.

This energetic little wooden head, which must have had some inlay in
the eyes, was acquired on the art market. No insignia adorns the
headdress, but the elongated jaw and skull seem to identify it as a
portrait of a member of the royal family. In Amarna statuary the
heads were sometimes added separately, and this head may have been
designed as part of a statue, but the extreme lengthening of the neck
suggests that it was perhaps intended to decorate the end of a harp -
which would render all identification impossible.

77 *Head of a jackal* reclining on a chest · Wood with inlay · Egyptian,
New Kingdom (XVIIIth Dynasty), ca. 1340 B.C. · Egyptian Museum,
Cairo.

In the treasure of Tut-ankh-amon (ca. 1354 to 1345 B.C.) was a gilded
wooden chest, decorated with symbols of Isis and Osiris, containing
substances used for embalming. The jackal surmounting it is none
other than the great god of the dead, Anubis. Having, according to
myth, mummified the god Osiris himself, Anubis became the patron
of embalmers. Invoked since the earliest times as protector of the
necropolis, he also led the deceased into the other world. The chest of
Tut-ankh-amon is a translation into three-dimensional form of the
soul-guiding god's hieroglyphic, showing a large black jackal lying on
a mastaba.

77

114

78 *Sculptor's model of falcons*, from Tanis · Egyptian, New Kingdom
· Egyptian Museum, Cairo.

During his excavations at Tanis (now San el Hagar) in the eastern
Delta, Pierre Montet brought to light, south of the great temple, two
brick constructions from the time of New Kingdom that must have
been used as sculptors' workshops. Numerous models were discovered
there, small square or rectangular plaques, often squared off for
greater ease in establishing the proportion of the figures. Here, the
upper falcon shows three stages of work: the claws are only blocked
out, the back and the wings are more elaborately worked, and the
head has been given its final appearance.

79 *Dog*; tomb statue from Assiut · Limestone · New Kingdom
(XIXth Dynasty), ca. 1314 to 1200 B.C. · The Louvre, Paris.

The age-old god Wepwawet, "He-who-clears-the-way," was honoured
in the form of a jackal or a black wolf-dog at Assiut in central Egypt.
The living animal, in which the god was believed to be present, was
venerated in the temple enclosure. All animals of the same species,
sacred throughout the region, were the object of popular devotion,
especially in the late epochs, and at their deaths they were mummified and carefully interred. This large and beautiful statue of a wolf-dog
comes from the dogs' burial ground at Assiut.

79

80 *Queen Karomama* · Damascened bronze. · Egyptian, Late Period (XXIIth Dynasty), 950 to 730 B.C. · The Louvre, Paris.

About 950 B.C., profiting from the opportunity offered by the weakness of the central power, Libyan mercenaries took possession of the Egyptian throne. To control the powerful priests of Amon, they installed members of their own family in the office of High Priest at Thebes. This marvelous statuette represents Karomama, wife of the Libyan king Takelot II, and daughter and mother of a High Priest. Dressed in a robe whose rich embroidery depicts the great wings of protective goddesses, the queen is offering a libation; in her hands she held a vessel or sistra. Still Theban in its subdued charm, the figure of Queen Karomama is nonetheless a transitional work, pointing towards Saite art in its sleek, refined modelling.

80

81 *Upper part of a statue of Mentuemhat*, from Karnak · Granite · Egyptian, Late Period (XXVth Dynasty), ca. 660 B.C. · Egyptian Museum, Cairo.

During the XXVth Dynasty, of Ethiopian origin, King Taharqa (689-663 B.C.) entrusted the administration of Thebes to an official called Mentuemhat. For nearly thirty years this man was the real master of Upper Egypt. He succeeded in safeguarding his privileges throughout a troubled epoch that saw the fall of the Ethiopian dynasty, the Assyrian conquest and the sack of Thebes by Assurbanipal, and finally the accession of Psamtik I, prince of Sais, founder of the XXVIth Dynasty (663 B.C.). The hard, polished granite unflatteringly describes the deeply-wrinkled negroid features of the clever governor at the end of his career.

81

82 *Petamenopet* as a seated scribe · Egyptian, Saite Period (XXIVth Dynasty), ca. 730 to 715 B.C. · Egyptian Museum, Cairo.

The Saite kings of the XXIVth Dynasty rescued Egypt from chaos and gave the country a century of political and economic renaissance. Their more liberal laws opened up Egypt to the Hellenic world then in the making. Art, however, returned to the traditions of the great Memphis era, but stripped of creative dynamism, it generally produced works that are cold, if pleasing. Statuary faithfully copied the ancient types, but it is in the meticulous care taken in producing facial likeness that this somewhat deadened art excels.

83 *Female figurine*, from Petsopha · Terra cotta · Minoan, ca. 2000 B.C. · Archeological Museum, Herakleion.

Petsopha, one of the "peak sanctuaries" typical of the era of the first palaces, yielded up this figure of a praying woman, placed there as an offering. This five-inch figurine sums up quite well the characteristics of Cretan sculpture, which was concerned not so much with realistic representation of the body as with a general form, which it enlivened with certain concrete details. The thin waist and the bell-shaped skirt are pleasantly naturalistic, but the face, hardly more than a rough outline, is expressionless. The Cretans, who did not leave much large-sized sculpture, produced many smaller works that, taken all together, create a picturesque and homely imagery.

82

83

85

85 *Cow suckling its calf*, from Knossos · Polychrome terra cotta · Minoan, 1700 to 1500 B.C. · Archeological Museum, Herakleion.

This earthenware plaque comes from the treasure of the sanctuary at Knossos. It depicts a cow suckling her young, an obvious allusion to the Great Goddess, source of all plenty, who nourishes all beings. The composition, stamped with gracious facility, is based on an interplay of curves which link together the movement of the feeding calf with that of the mother, who lowers her hindquarters to help him. In religious and secular art alike, Cretan inspiration is direct and familiar.

86 *The Harvester Vase* · From Hagia Triada · Steatite · Minoan, ca. 1600-1500 B.C. · Museum, Herakleion.

Plastic art on a large scale is uncommon in Minoan art, but in carving soft steatite for vases or ritual objects, Minoan artists showed a feeling for three-dimensional form easily translatable into monumental sculpture, had there been any demand for such. The Hagia Triada vase probably represents a ritual procession of farm workers, grateful for a good harvest. Their joy is conveyed with Dionysiac abandon; they are singing, with chests thrust out, and one of them, intoxicated, falls to the ground. Animating all Cretan art is this same fervent vitality, which was to be found in Greek vase paintings as well. (Width 4½ inches).

84 *Male figurine*, from Petsopha · Terra cotta · Minoan, ca. 2000 B.C. · Archeological Museum, Herakleion.

This almost nude man, poised in suppliance to the deity, is the male pendant to the praying woman wearing the bell-shaped skirt, reproduced in fig. 83. Like that work, it is modelled with a small-scale, generalized technique, simple but effective, the arms and the legs rudely blocked, the face scarcely outlined. On the silhouette thus sketched, the few defined details become most important: the frontal sheath and the dagger worn in the belt.

84

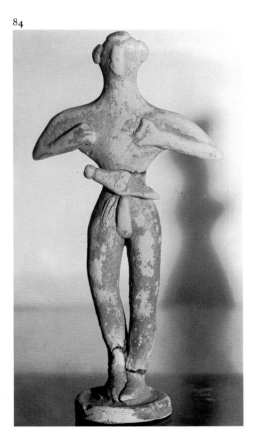

86

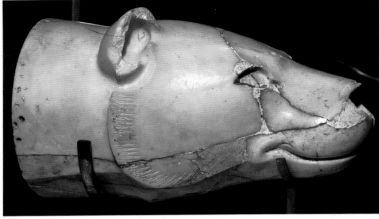

87

87 *Rhyton* in the form of a lioness's head · Limestone · Minoan, ca. 1500 B.C. · Archeological Museum, Herakleion.

The rhyton, an imitation of the animal's horn used by the ancients as a drinking vessel, played an important role in ritual in Crete, where it appears in various forms. This example, 11 inches long, is in the form of a lioness's head; it was doubtless intended for use in libations to the Great Goddess of Crete, who was also the protector of wild beasts. Highly stylized, but modelled with great delicacy, this feline head conveys the synthetic but extremely evocative vision of the Cretan animal sculptors.

89

89 *Figurine of a goddess*, from Knossos · Terra cotta · Crete, Period of Mycenaean occupation, 1400 to 1200 B.C. · Archeological Museum, Herakleion.

This figurine, 8 inches high, is an example of a curious series of rather coarse idols found throughout Crete and dating from the Mycenaean occupation. This particular one comes from the sanctuary of the Double Axe at Knossos. A cylindrical base takes the place of the traditional bell-shaped skirt. The arms are raised in a ritual gesture. A dove crowns the head, and by allusion to the prolific nature of this particular bird, evokes the fecundizing power of the goddess. Essential details of the anatomy and of the ornament are outlined in color.

90 *The Lion Gate at Mycenae* · Mycenaean, ca. 1250 B.C.

The gate opens in a wall that ancient Greek tradition ascribed to the mythical Cyclopes. Four enormous blocks frame the gate, and the relieving triangle above the lintel is occupied by the famous sculpture showing two rampant lions facing each other on either side of a column surmounted by an entablature. Their heads, now lost, were made separately. Almost 10 feet high, these lions are the first known example of monumental sculpture in Greece. Though the inspiration comes from Crete, the volumes are nevertheless treated with a vigorous feeling for mass in which superfluous details are disregarded. This taste for the monumental distinguishes the Mycenaean from the Minoan civilization.

90

88

88 *The Snake Goddess* from Knossos · Polychrome terra cotta Minoan, ca. 1540 B.C. · Archeological Museum, Herakleion.

This figurine, 11 inches high, comes from a sanctuary in Knossos. Its principal interest lies in the information it gives us about Minoan religion and costume at the beginning of the 15th century B.C. The Cretans frequently paired the snake with their goddess for symbolic reasons, as the snake was associated with fertility, regeneration, and immortality. The young woman wears a long skirt with tiers of flounces. The very low-cut, close-fitting bodice reveals the breasts and is prolonged, front and back, by a rounded apron.

91 *Fertility Goddess*, from Ugarit (Ras-Shamra) · Ivory · Phoenician, 1400 to 1200 B.C. · The Louvre, Paris.

From a tomb at Ras-Shamra (ancient Ugarit) comes this ivory pyxis cover. In the center the fertility goddess, identified by the ears of corn that she holds in her hands, is seated on an altar of a Mycenaean type flanked by rampant ibexes - a frequent theme in West Asian art. The uncovered breast, the wide, flounced skirt and the hair held by a band are characteristic of the Cretan style, and the facial features recall the "Parisienne" of Knossos rather than Semitic types. In all, the work has a strongly Mycenaean appearance and shows how important was Aegean influence in Phoenicia at the end of the 2nd millennium.

91

92 *Ashtart* · Bronze · Phoenician, 1400-1200 B.C. · The Louvre, Paris.

Dressed in a long robe and adorned with spiral-form jewels, the Great Goddess sits on a throne She lifts her right hand in a gesture of peace; the left hand must have held a scepter. With its eyes deeply cut, probably to hold some now-lost inlay, the head has a strange, fascinating expression. The goddess is called Ashtart (the pronunciation is confirmed by the correspondence discovered at El Amarna, and also in the Greek transcription, Astarte). Ashtart is one of the great figures in the Phoenician pantheon, and one of the many names given to the Great Mother, goddess of motherhood, of fertility, whose cult spread through the whole of western Asia, and who reappears in Greece with the names of Aphrodite and Cybele, among others.

92

93

93 *Stele* from Ras Shamra Phoenician, 1300–1200 B.C. · The Louvre, Paris.

The Phoenicians combined artistic elements taken from their various neighbors into works of a hybrid nature. On this stele Baal, god of storms, is depicted brandishing a mace in one hand and a thunderbolt in the other (unless the latter is a tree symbolizing vegetation). The general pose is taken from Hittite reliefs, the pointed cap is of Egyptian origin, the horns indicating divinity are a Mesopotamian motif, and the little worshipper beside Baal is dressed in Syrian fashion. This stele comes from Ugarit, the most northerly Phoenician city, which owed its prosperity to its proximity to Cyprus, rich in copper and wood.

94

94 *Idol* · Bronze · Phoenician, 1200 to 800 B.C. · The Louvre, Paris.

Excavations in Syria have yielded many small bronzes that demonstrate the skill in metalwork acquired by the Phoenicians, although, on the artistic level, the mass production of certain types perhaps diminished the quality.

119

95 *Warriors* on a tile from a frieze; from Pazarli · Painted terra cotta · Phrygian, 6th century B.C. · Archeological Museum, Ankara.

Having perhaps helped to overthrow the Hittite empire, the Phrygians, from Thrace, founded a short-lived kingdom in Anatolia towards the end of the 8th century. Phrygia held power only until the invasions of the Cimmerians (beginning of the 7th century B.C.), but remained for long afterwards a lively cultural center. Close study of their art is of particular importance for an understanding of the sources of Archaic Greek art. The two warriors on this terra-cotta plaque, for example, wearing crested helmets and greaves, and carrying lances and round shields, very much resemble hoplites; they seem to find their nearest parallels in contemporary Greek ceramics, but it should be noted that their armor is that of the Syro-Hittite soldiers. Such tiles, molded in relief and then colored, were most often intended as elements of friezes running beneath the eaves of a building.

96

95

96 *Lion* from Marash · Basalt · Hittite · 9th century B.C. · Archeological Museum, Ankara.

The Hittite empire, created in the 14th century by Suppiluliumas, fell in about 1200 to an influx of iron-armed invaders from the north. But Hittite traditions were kept alive in various little states in southern Anatolia and northern Syria, such as Marash, Sinjirli, Carchemish and Sakje-geuzi. In these areas developed a later Hittite art, provincial in character and clearly influenced by Assyria. This 9th-century basalt lion, covered with Hittite hieroglyphics, comes from Marash. Its mediocre quality and traditional treatment illustrate the degree to which the great Hittite art had survived to the beginning of the 1st millennium.

97 *Relief of Assurnasirpal hunting*, from Nimrud · Alabastrine limestone · Assyrian, 9th century, B.C. · British Museum, London.

The hunt ranked with war among the major themes imposed upon the Assyrian artist. It is also the theme which he treated with the greatest success, continuing a rich tradition of animal art. Here Assurnasirpal stands in his chariot and turns to shoot an arrow at a lion, which has already placed one foot on the axle-bar. The charioteer drives his three horses over another lion in its death throes. Bringing up the rear are musicians and soldiers whose indifference shows us that the king combats these ferocious animals singlehanded, and that he is invincible. Admirably summing up the event, all narrative incident excluded and the background mute, the scene is raised to a symbolic, didactic plane.

97

98

98 *Winged, man-headed bull*, from Dur Sharrukin (Khorsabad) ·
Chalk alabaster · Assyrian, 8th century B.C. · The Louvre, Paris.

The winged bull with a man's head, carved from a single block, comes
from the gateway of the palace built by Sargon II at Khorsabad, not
far from Nineveh. These terrifying beasts, man, eagle, and bull all at
once, were placed on either side of the doors as guardian spirits, and
were called in the texts *shedon* or *lamassu*. The forms are hard and
powerfully defined under the sheathing of minutely detailed surfaces.
The artist has sought to express not life, but rather a kind of pitiless
machine capable of crushing any hostile visitor. The five legs are intended, in accordance with the convention, to present the beast as truly
complete, from whatever angle it might be viewed.

99

99 **The hero Gilgamesh**, from the palace at Dur Sharrukin (Khorsabad) · Alabaster · Assyrian, 8th century B.C. · The Louvre, Paris.

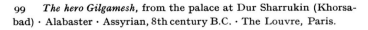

Gilgamesh is one of the figures that Mesopotamian art loves to depict.
But, whereas his epic legend could have provided artists with a great
variety of subjects, the hero's iconography tends to be limited to the
same few themes, endlessly repeated. Pre-eminent among these is the
scene of his combat with wild beasts. The Sumerian hero survives in
Assyria in this relief from the palace of Khorsabad. Bearded and
long-haired, and dressed in an Assyrian-style fringed tunic, Gilgamesh
tames a lion - one far too small to be in the least frightening. The artist
uses the convention, well-known in Egypt and common also in
Assyrian reliefs, of the body seen frontally, the feet in profile.

121

100 *Deportation of populations*; detail of a relief · Alabaster · Assyrian, 7th century B.C. · The Louvre, Paris.

The detail reproduced is from a scene of deportation after one of Assurnasirpal's victorious campaigns. The cruel practice of transplanting civil populations in order to deprive them of their alliances was practiced everywhere and in every age throughout the East. Bands of men, women and children, with their wagons and livestock, stretch out along the road to exile. The artist's skill enables him to give his bas-relief scene three distinct successive spatial planes: two oxen walk side by side; behind them, men follow each other, walking in line. As though, in a brutal world, the artist could express only violence whatever his theme, the forms are hard and the muscles appear tensed, though the pace is calm.

100

101

101 *A king in his chariot of state*; detail of a relief · Alabaster · Assyrian, 7th century B.C. · The Louvre, Paris.

The king, recognizable by his tiara and his regal stature, stands in a chariot with a huge spoked wheel and woven bodywork. A parasol with a hanging flap protects its three occupants from the sun. Servants walk behind. Clearly displayed here are both the shortcomings of Assyrian art and its virtues. The relief is carved with assurance, the clearly defined silhouettes outlined against a perfectly plain background, and then treated to a profusion of ornamental surface detail. The technique results in a pleasing balance between plain and decorated surfaces, but it also gives rise to the lifelessness of the figures, which remain flat and without substance.

102

102 *The demon Pazuzu* · Bronze · Mesopotamian, 1000 to 500 B.C. · The Louvre, Paris.

Depicted in the form of a lean, naked man, with fiercely grinning jaws, two pairs of wings, and predatory claws, is the demon Pazuzu, "the king of the evil spirits of the air, who comes fiercely from the mountains in a high rage" - so the inscription tells us. This is a personification of the southeast wind, bringer of storms and malaria; one of the Sumero-Akkadian evil spirits, along with the "Seven," and Labartu, terror of pregnant women. The figurine, with a ring attached to the head, was meant to be hung round the sick person's neck to exorcise and destroy the power of the demon.

103 *King Assurnasirpal II* · Alabaster · Assyrian, 9th century B.C. ·
British Museum, London.

The Assyrian era was characterized by a prolific artistic production
intended mainly as political propaganda: the Assyrian kings, absolute
monarchs of a kind new in history, wanted to immortalize their least
and greatest deed in writings and in images. Representations of the
king as an all-powerful being multiplied; but once the superman type
had been codified it became fixed and unchanging, and the man
himself disappeared behind the symbol of his power. Without the
inscription, there would be no way for us to recognize in this cold,
majestic statue a portrait of Assurnasirpal II, for all Assyrian kings
seem strangely alike to our eyes.

105 *Statuette of a god* · Bronze · Iran, Luristan, 8th to 7th century
B.C. · Archeological Museum, Teheran.

The god here represented is the protector of a city, as we are told by
the cuneiform inscription on his skirt. Carried off as booty during a
war, the figure was reinstalled "in its place" by one Marduk. The
inscription was made several centuries later than the work itself (which
dates from the 8th to 7th centuries). Besides being of unusual size
(about 14 inches high without the feet, which have been lost), this
work is striking for the studied refinement of the volume and for a
certain plasticity, evident in the face and the arms. The costume and
the weapons are carefully detailed; the god wears the overlapping
tunic found much later among the Parthians.

105

104

104 *Idol,* from the Zagros mountains · Bronze · Iran, Luristan, ca.
9th to 8th centuries B.C. · Cinquantenaire, Brussels.

In the high valleys of the Zagros mountains in western Iran were
discovered, in 1928, megalithic necropolises containing bronze and
iron objects of striking originality. The work of a race of nomadic
horsemen who had settled in Zagros during the 2nd millennium B.C.,
they introduce us to a world of fantasy, in which imagination has re-
arranged forms in bold combinations. Impaled on a votive spike and
flanked by cock's heads, this multiple-headed hero, taming two monsters, must be Sraosha, the god of justice, whose attribute is the cock.
Production of these bronzes reached its peak in quality and quantity
during the 8th and 7th centuries.

106 *Rhyton in the form of a bison* · Terra cotta · North Iran, 9th to 8th century B.C. · Foroughi Collection, Teheran.

For some years there has been a demand for this pottery. Discovered during fortuitous and often clandestine excavations, examples of it come from megalithic tombs of the 9th and 8th centuries B.C., located in the mountainous area southwest of the Caspian Sea, and reveal a most original art. This rhyton in red terra cotta, of very fine paste, has the form of a bison, the animal which, with the stag, most often inspired the coroplastes of Amlach. Too fragile for normal use, these rhytons perhaps had a votive purpose; they may have been used for funeral libations.

107

106

107 *Rhyton in the form of a gazelle's head* · Bronze · North Iran, 8th to 7th century B.C. (?) · Foroughi Collection, Teheran.

Of unknown origin, this bronze goblet would seem to date from the 8th or the 7th centuries B.C., the time of the rise of metallurgy in the mountains of northwest Iran. It must have been among some funeral effects similar to those found in Scythian tombs. Scythian bronze workers were to take up the theme of the zoomorphic rhyton, which is also common in Achaemenid carvings. The eyes and the eyebrows were inlaid. Incised detail defines the muzzle and the corrugations of the horns. A graven decoration of Mesopotamian inspiration enlivens the smooth surface between the horns, where can be seen two ibexes rearing up on either side of a tree of life.

108 *Rhyton in the form of a ram's head*, from Ziwiye · Iran, Scythian, 7th century B.C. · Sekilowitz Collection, New York.

This rhyton was part of the treasure placed in the tomb of some Scythian prince. It is known that Scythians moved into northern Iran in the 7th century, and were annexed by the Medes, with whom they had allied themselves against the Assyrians. The characteristics of Scythian art - a taste for the synthesis of forms, and a sure skill in animal art - already had indigenous Iranian antecedents in the art of Amlach, and in the Luristan bronzes; moreover, they herald Achaemenid art. The frequent use of precious materials, of ivory, gold, and silver, shows how wealthy were these nomadic bandits.

108

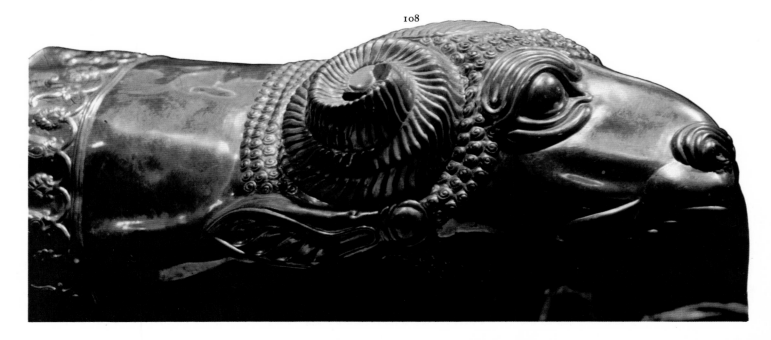

109 *Plaque from a revetment*, from Ziwiye · Gold · Iran, Scythian, 7th century B.C. · Archeological Museum, Teheran.

Repeated in several repoussé reliefs is the scene well-known from Mesopotamian art - a hero overcoming a wild beast, in this case a rearing lion, threatening with his claws a figure in Assyrian dress who makes ready to stab him. The hero's dress and the beard, and also the treatment of his muscular calf, are typically Assyrian; but the technique with which the ornament is handled, the main forms being embossed and then retouched with an etcher's needle, seems to be local. One imagines that the prince buried at Ziwiye had had these objects made in a workshop which copied models from the whole Eastern catalogue of the 9th to the 7th centuries B.C.

110

110 *East staircase of the apadana* of the royal palace at Persepolis · Persian, Achaemenid, late 6th- early 5th centuries, B.C.

Begun under Darius I at the end of the 6th century B.C., Persepolis, the royal Achaemenid town, is a grandiose showcase of an official art created for the court. The king went there at the time of certain festivals to receive the homage of the "twenty-eight nations" subject to the Empire. The decoration of the staircase leading to the *apadana*, the royal audience hall, depicts a whole procession of courtiers all fixed in stone. In the center, eight guards bear a royal inscription; at the angles, a lion bringing down a bull symbolizes the defeat of Evil by Good. On the rear wall is arrayed, on several registers, a long cortege of tributaries and courtiers.

111 *Capital with bulls*, from the palace of Darius at Susa · Persian, Achaemenid, late 6th to early 5th century B.C. · The Louvre, Paris.

The private palace of Darius was still built in Mesopotamian fashion, with apartments placed around three central courts. Its original feature was the *apadana*, an immense pillared room, with numerous columns which allowed the enclosure of vast areas. The architects show considerable boldness in capping their very slender columns, over 60 feet high, with these monumental capitals, which were placed on the fluted shaft over a cruciform section decorated with volutes. The roof beams rested on the necks of the bulls. The whole work was painted yellow to imitate marble and to conceal faults in the stone.

111

112 *Archers of the royal guard*, from the royal palace at Susa · Glazed brick · Persian, Achaemenid, early 5th century B.C. The Louvre, Paris

On this frieze, which adorned the walls of the *apadana* of his palace, Darius caused his "immortals" to be represented. One can imagine in this very guise the warriors whom the Spartans braved at Thermopylae. Herodotus adjudged their long tunics to have been troublesome in battle; but here they are attractive, with their brilliant, decorative appearance, originally enhanced by rich drapes, refined and barbaric in equal measure, in characteristically Achaemenid taste. Scarcity of stone and proximity to the Mesopotamian plain are two factors explaining both the use of glazed brick, and the Neo-Babylonian influence, more marked at Susa than at Persepolis.

112

113

113 *Procession of Dignitaries*; relief on the staircase of the royal palace at Persepolis · Persian, Achaemenid, 5th century B.C.

This detail from a bas-relief decorating the staircase of the *tripylon*, a council hall adjoining the palace of Darius, represents Persian dignitaries, holding lotus flowers, on their way to an audience. The reliefs in the *tripylon* still bear traces of polychrome. Sculpture at Persepolis remained subject to the principle of the decorative frieze, uniform, and always dependent upon the architecture. This formula the Achaemenids adopted from the Assyrians, but made more flexible. Restrained and orderly, the figured scenes take on a subdued tone, and the smiling dignity of these vassals paying homage to their sovereign differs greatly from the stiff servility of the courtiers at Nimrud or Khorsabad.

114 *Rock-cut tomb of Darius*, at Nagsh-i-Rustam (Laristan) · Persian, Achaemenid, 5th century B.C.

In opposition to the Mazdean custom, the Achaemenid kings revived a tradition of Medean princes and were interred in tombs excavated directly in the impressive cliff at Nagsh-i-Rustam, near Persepolis. The façade of Darius' tomb, about 73 feet high, takes the form of a Greek cross. The sculptured part imitates the entrance to a palace, with its columns surmounted by bull-shaped capitals. The architrave supports a throne held by the twenty-eight nations conquered by Darius. On it stands the king, in adoration before a fire-altar, under the protection of Ahuramazda, whose winged emblem appears in the center.

114

116

116 *Aeolic capital from Larisa* · Limestone · Greek, 7th century B.C. · Archeological Museum, Istanbul.

The surviving capitals of this type have come from Larisa near Smyrna, or from Lesbos and Neandria in the Troad - all regions where the Aeolian dialect was spoken, whence their designation "Aeolic." They are generally considered as the ancestors of the Ionic capital. Unlike the Doric capital, which derived from the thick, robust Mycenaean capital, the Aeolic capital originated in the vegetable ornament crowning oriental columns. The high shaft spreads out into curling volutes, and a double ring of leaves marks the transition between column and capital, the space between the volutes being filled with more stylized leaves.

115

115 *Mare suckling her foal* · Bronze · Greek, Geometric, 750-700 B.C. · National Museum, Athens.

Found at Olympia, this group is a charming example of the small bronzes made during the Geometric period. On a rectangular base the mare stands straight, firmly poised on her strong legs. The foal, however, draws back as it raises its head to suckle, and the diagonals traced by its legs temper the rigidity of the mare's stance. The masses are stylized into simple volumes: cylinders for the bodies, heads, lower legs; swelling triangles for the upper legs. The simple silhouette incorporates the barest essentials of form, with only the ears and knees as sharper accents.

117 *Lion from the monument of Menekrates* · Limestone · Greek, 7th century B.C. · Museum, Corfu.

This lion was found near the tomb of Menekrates in the necropolis of ancient Kerkyra (modern Corfu). Menekrates was a Lokrian, the *proxenos* of the people of Kerkyra, according to a metric inscription on the grave monument. This inscription must be one of the oldest of its kind, for according to the style of writing it dates from about 600 B.C.; and if the lion, which lies on a rectangular base with its head half turned away, really belongs to the monument of Menekrates, it is the oldest known Greek example of an animal on a tomb. In any case its robust, highly stylized forms show it to belong to the Proto-Corinthian tradition of the 7th century B.C.

117

118 *Gorgon and other figures* from the west pediment of the temple of Artemis at Corfu · Limestone · Greek, Archaic, 600-580 B.C.· Museum, Corfu.

In the evolution of pediment decoration the composition of this relief, made from local conchitic limestone, marks a transitional phase. An enormous running Gorgon with a belt made of snakes looms in the center, her head projecting over the cornice; she seems a gaudily magnified version of an apotropaic acroterion motif, but here she is flanked by her children, Chrysaor (at her left) and the winged horse Pegasos (of which a fragment is visible at her right). Panthers watch over her, and illustrating the battle of the Gods and the Giants at the sides, are figures which are telescoped to accommodate the narrowing slant of the cornice, and still paired as they might have been on metopes.

118

This was found with three other metopes of identical dimension (33 by 23 inches) in the fortifications of the Selinunte Akropolis. They came from a small Doric temple that has not been identified. Their very archaic style points to a date in the second quarter of the 6th century B.C., and they are among the oldest known sculptured metopes. A coarsely beaded molding surmounts the representation of Europa being carried off by Zeus in the form of a bull. The relief is very flat, with sharply cut contours, and the composition is awkward: the bull, tightly squeezed within the frame, must hollow his back to make room for Europa.

119

From a Boeotian sanctuary comes this votive statuette with an inscription, engraved on the thighs in Theban characters, informing us that it was dedicated to Apollo by a man called Mantiklos. The god is represented standing, naked, and must have held a bow in his left hand. The forms are still close to the geometric style; but already the facial details and the anatomical structure of shoulders and chest are more defined, the waist narrow and the thighs well rounded. The interest in anatomical structure displayed by this figure anticipates later sculptural developments.

Excavations at Delphi revealed, on the base for these robust figures, the incomplete signature of a sculptor from Argos, (Poly)medes, who, around 600 B.C. carved the sculptures in an island marble to commemorate two Argive youths, Kleobis and Biton. They were recompensed by the gods for having harnessed themselves to the chariot of their mother, a priestess of Hera, and drawing it to the temple. The heads are flattened, and the strong faces, symmetrically framed by long curls, are expressionless; but the bodies are striking in their athletic strength. The anatomy is represented according to the general conventions of the time, but the artist has modelled his details with an intent to express vigour and power: necks thick, pectorals massive, legs muscular, arms tensed, and fists clenched ready for action.

120

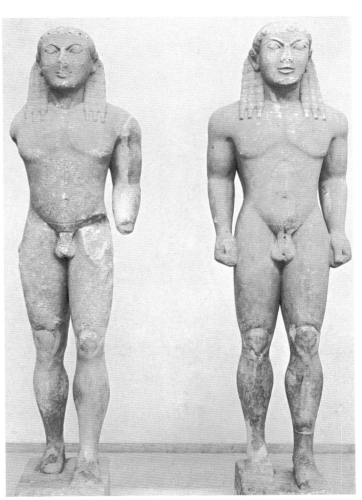

121

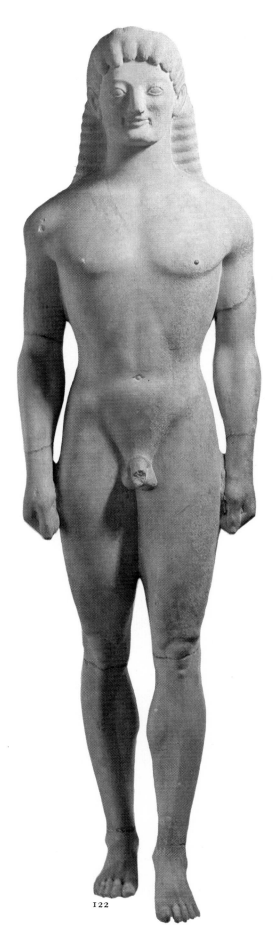

122

122 *Kouros from Tenea* · Parian marble · Greek, Archaic, ca. 550 B.C. · Staatliche Antikensammlungen, Munich.

Around the middle of the 6th century B.C., the kouros type shows a development towards refinement and grace in this beautiful ephebe from Tenea. He is represented frontally, somewhat smaller than life-size, and the simply delineated elements of the body's structure are accented by the pattern of muscles. Long slender legs, narrow waist, and wide shoulders fine down the figure's silhouette, while the sharp features express intelligence and enjoyment of life. The statue recalls figures on late Corinthian vases, and, since Tenea depended from Corinth, may reveal characteristics of Corinthian workshops.

129

123 *Kouros from Piraeus* · Bronze · Greek, Archaic, ca. 520 B.C. ·
National Museum, Athens.

In 1959, workmen digging sewers in a street in Piraeus, Athens' sea-
port, brought to light the oldest known bronze kouros. The youthful
figure (76 inches high) held a bow in his left hand, and probably a
patera in his right. His body is sensitively modelled in firm volumes;
the representation of the legs already shows a deep knowledge of
anatomy. The perfect stateliness of the body finds its complement in
the grave awareness of the head, in which the features are sharply
delineated, the eyes slightly downcast, the nose straight and lips
compressed.

123

124

124 AFTER KRITIOS AND NESIOTES · *Harmodios and Aristogeiton.*
Marble. Roman copy of an Early Classical Greek bronze of ca. 460
B.C. · National Museum, Naples.

The bronze original of this marble group (height, 78 inches) represented
the two tyrannicides who killed Hipparchos, son of the tyrant Pisis-
tratos and became symbols of freedom. It was set up in Athens in
477 B.C. to replace an earlier group removed by the Persians three
years before. The figures have been conceived as complementary parts
of the whole: Aristogeiton puts his left leg forward, Harmodios his
right; one is giving a cut and the other a thrust; the elder holds out
his arm, covered with a cloak, to protect his young companion.
Nonetheless, each hero has been treated in his own right and the
eyes and movements of each are directed towards his separate action.

125 *The "Omphalos Apollo"* · Marble · Roman copy from a Greek
bronze of ca. 460 B.C. · National Museum, Athens.

This marble statue (height, 70 inches) was found in the theatre of
Dionysios in Athens, not far from a marble *omphalos*, with which it had
no connection but which nonetheless gave it its name. It may be a
replica of the Apollo Alexikakos ("who-averts-misfortunes") by
Kalamis. The archaic stiffness of the kouros has newly given way here
to a timid attempt at asymmetry: the left leg is bent, the left hip and
the right shoulder slightly lowered. The rendering of muscles is a
compromise between the earlier monumental stylization and a more
realistic approach.

126 *Female figure, formerly in Auxerre* · Limestone · Greek, Archaic,
ca. 650 B.C. · The Louvre, Paris.

Found in an attic of the Auxerre museum by Collignon, who published
it at the end of the 19th century, this female statuette (26 inches high)
is of unknown origin, but it must be attributed to Cretan art of the
end of the 7th century B.C. It illustrates clearly the first phase in
Greek statuary. Standing rigidly encased by her tunic, blocky curls of
hair framing her face in the Egyptian manner, she holds her right arm
pressed against her chest. A wide belt draws tight about her waist, and
a cape covers her shoulders; her costume is adorned with geometric
designs.

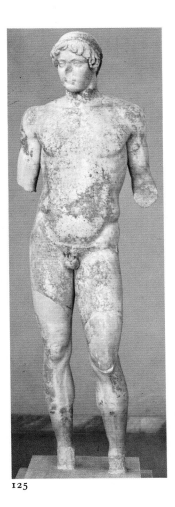

125

128 *Kore 675* from the Athens Akropolis · Marble, polychromed Greek, Archaic, ca. 530-520 B.C. · Akropolis Museum, Athens.

In the lovely procession of kores dedicated to Athena, this one stands out because of the astonishingly well-preserved polychrome painting. The tunic, of a uniform bluish green, molded on the torso, is partly covered by a mantle of natural light color strewn with red and blue designs which hangs from the right shoulder. This becoming style of costume, imported from Ionia, lends itself better than the old rigid Dorian peplum to a play of draperies in which the main concern is decorative effect rather than realism. In the same way, long plaits, undulating tresses and spiral curls make up an elegant coiffure in an ingenious translation into marble of the hair-style of the time. The height of the figure as preserved is about 28 inches.

128

127 *Hera from Samos* · Marble · Greek, Archaic, ca. 570-560 B.C. · The Louvre, Paris.

Taller than life (6 feet 4 inches high), the goddess, with her radiant dignity, stands as a brilliant climax to the series of female statues made on the island of Samos shortly before 550 B.C. Dedicated by Kheramyes to Hera, divine wife, patron and protector of legitimate unions, she seems to sum up the delicate refinement of Ionic art, which was represented at its most accomplished on Samos. The artist, working his marble with great technical mastery and sensitivity, reveals a statuesque body close-molded by a finely pleated linen tunic, a woolen mantle with wider pleats and a long smooth veil.

126   127

129

129 *Running maiden* · Limestone · Greek, Late Archaic, ca. 480 B.C. · Museum, Eleusis.

This charming, swift-running figure (28 inches high) is all that remains of a small pediment from Eleusis. One could imagine her one of Persephone's companions, fleeing from the sudden apparition of Hades, who abducted Demeter's daughter. The thickset body, broad shoulders and massive head give an impression of robust stockiness; yet an astonishingly light and vivacious movement flows through the figure, with the long, curving folds moving diagonally down the draped peplos from right shoulder to left foot. The traditional abduction theme is newly keyed to an elegance wholly unsentimental.

130

130 *Two women holding flowers*, relief from Pharsalos · Marble · Macedonian, early 5th century B.C. · The Louvre, Paris.

This stele, broken off at top and bottom (preserved height, 22 inches), was discovered near Pharsalos in Macedonia. It dates from the beginning of the 5th century B.C. Two women face each other, the right one sitting, the other standing. Each holds a flower in her right hand, and the woman on the left also holds a purse - symbolic gifts that, in this scene of exchange, take on a funerary meaning. The firmly drawn folds of the peplos reveal the arms, and in the center, the hands overlap in an intricate and harmonious pattern.

131 *Head of a telamone*, from the Agrigentum Olympeion · Greek, Archaic, early 5th century B.C. · Museo Civico Archeologico, Agrigento.

The enormous (333 feet by 168 feet) temple to the Olympian Zeus, begun at Agrigento in the beginning of the 5th century B.C. and never finished, marks both the taste of the south Italian Greeks for monumental constructions and their disdain for the canons of religious architecture. The peristyle was replaced by a solid wall enlivened by half-columns alternating with telamones and karyatids. These figures were 25 feet high, and were built up, like the wall, of blocks of stones in superposed tiers. The coarse but powerful modelling of this rigorously symmetrical head suits its functional role.

131

132 *Head of the "Charioteer of Delphi"* · Bronze · Greek, Early Classical, ca. 480-475 B.C. · Museum, Delphi.

Only the charioteer survives of a bronze chariot with four horses offered to the sanctuary at Delphi by a prince of Syracuse to commemorate a victory at the Pythian Games. Now he stands alone in proud dignity but modestly. It is a youth's face, naive and entirely absorbed in an ardent desire to win. The eyes are set in with enamel and onyx and lend the gaze a concentrated fixity. The tightly curled hair is bound with an engraved headband from which a few stray locks escape.

132

133

134

134 *Apollo, and battling Lapiths and Centaurs*, from the west pediment of the temple of Zeus at Olympia · Marble · Greek, Early Classical, ca. 460 B.C. · Museum, Olympia.

A superb Apollo in the pediment's center towers over the centaurs and Lapiths battling at the wedding of Pirithoüs and Deidameia. His body is seen frontally, but his head turns to follow with his glance the imperious gesture of his right arm, which appears to command the heroes round him to defend order and virtue. On his right, a centaur attempts to abduct a woman, who offers strong resistance, while Theseus (?) advances to her rescue. The hero's expression of calm determination is in strong contrast to the centaur's bestial grimace. The brutal passions of the scene are suggested largely by the conflicting lines of the grouped bodies.

133 *Athena, Herakles, and Atlas*, metope from the temple of Zeus at Olympia · Marble · Greek, Early Classical, ca. 470-460 B.C. · Museum, Olympia.

This metope is one of the twelve which, in the pronaos and the opisthodomos of the temple of Zeus, illustrated the labors of Herakles. It shows the hero holding up the heavenly vault while Atlas brings him the golden apples of the Hesperides. The well-balanced composition is the work of a sculptor aware of the powerful architectural rhythm of the temple building itself. Expression is conveyed solely by the three actors' gestures, which temper the repeated verticals of their bodies. Athena is represented frontally but her head is turned in profile; she looks at Herakles and, one arm raised, assists him with the majestic impassivity befitting a goddess. The other two figures express heroic power and human action.

135

135 *Apollo*, from the west pediment of the temple of Zeus at Olympia · Marble · Greek, Early Classical, ca. 460 B.C. · Museum, Olympia.

Almost ten and a half feet high, Apollo dominates the pediment not only through his size but also through his regal self-assurance. His head is full, blunt, and noble, with its heavy eyelids, straight nose, thick lips, and heavy chin, capped by the more conventionally treated hair. With the neck and shoulders cut in the very pattern of athletic strength, the figure is a perfect image of the helpful god who, armed with calm willpower, presides over the triumph of good and order.

136

137

137 *Lapith woman*, from the west pediment of the temple of Zeus at Olympia · Marble · Greek, Early Classical, ca. 460 B.C.

A young woman, standing (we are shown here the upper part of her body), is ravished by a centaur who is grabbing her left breast. She is trying to free herself from his hold, but their gestures are represented with a classic restraint which softens the violence of the scene. The drapery with conventional, but harmonious curves gives enough fulness to balance the figure. The faces are a mixture of roughness and sensitivity, willpower and serenity

136 *Head of a Lapith*, from the west pediment of the temple of Zeus at Olympia · Marble · Greek, Early Classical, ca. 460 B.C. · Museum, Olympia.

The young Lapith is being bitten in the arm by the centaur whom he is trying to overcome. To express his pain, the sculptor has made the features more human, scoring the forehead with two long creases, widening the eyes, and drawing back the corners of the half-open mouth in a slight twist. The conventional rendering of the hair, in tight round curls forming a kind of helmet, does not diminish the sense of power emanating from this figure - as, indeed, from the whole pediment group.

138 *Wounded warrior*, from the temple of Aphaea at Aegina · Marble. · Greek, Archaic, 500-480 B.C. · Staatliche Antikensammlungen, Munich.

In the west pediment of the temple of Aphaea at Aegina were sculptures illustrating the battle between the Greeks and the Trojans engaged in struggling groups on either side of a central Athena; this figure of a wounded warrior occupied the right-hand angle. Divested now of Thorwaldsen's 19th-century restorations, it is an interesting example of Aeginetan sculpture in the early 5th century. It is handled in the manner of bronzes rather than stone carvings, the anatomical forms being carefully studied and their contours conscientiously delineated, producing a rather cold effect. The conventional smile and some awkwardness in the figure are the clearest notes of persisting archaism in its style.

138

139

139 *Zeus from Cape Artemision* · Bronze · Greek, ca. 460 B.C. ·
National Museum, Athens.

One of the rare original Greek bronzes to have come down to us, this
over life-size statue was found in the sea off Cape Artemision. The god
no doubt brandished his thunderbolts in his right hand, his glance bent
on the adversary to whom he points with his outstretched left arm.
His weight rests mostly on his left leg, and the right is slightly flexed,
ready for the recoil. Dominating the athletic vigor of the body is a
proud head that radiates intelligence. The figure's hard-drawn outline
is softened by the supple curls of the beard and hair.

140

140 *Flute player* from the "Ludovisi Throne". (See fig. 141).
Museo delle Terme, Rome.

On one short side of the "Ludovisi Throne" is this relief of a naked
young woman who sits on a cushion with her legs crossed, playing the
double flute. She may represent profane love, of which Aphrodite
(whose birth the central panel seems to represent) is the patroness, as
she is of sacred love, symbolized on the relief opposite this one by a
veiled woman. The flute-player's attitude is awkward, but her dimpled
body is full of charm, with its curves and its soft modelling echoed in
the folded cushion. The work probably came from an Ionian workshop
in southern Italy.

141 *Birth of Aphrodite* (?), from the "Ludovisi Throne" · Marble ·
Greek, Early Classical, ca. 470-460 B.C. · Museo delle Terme, Rome.

The so-called Ludovisi Throne consists of a marble block about 39
inches high, roughly rectangular in shape, with reliefs carved on the
two narrower ends and on one long side. It was found in the Villa
Ludovisi in Rome and its exact purpose is unknown. This is the relief
from the long side, probably representing the birth of Aphrodite: the
goddess is just risen from the sea waves, for her tunic clings wetly to
her body, and the pebbly shore is suggested under the feet of the
Horae on either side of her. They modestly hold before her a cloth
whose beautiful dipping horizontal folds complement and flow into
the vertical pleats of their own clothing. The composition, symmetrical
but not rigidly so, is centered on Aphrodite's soft profile.

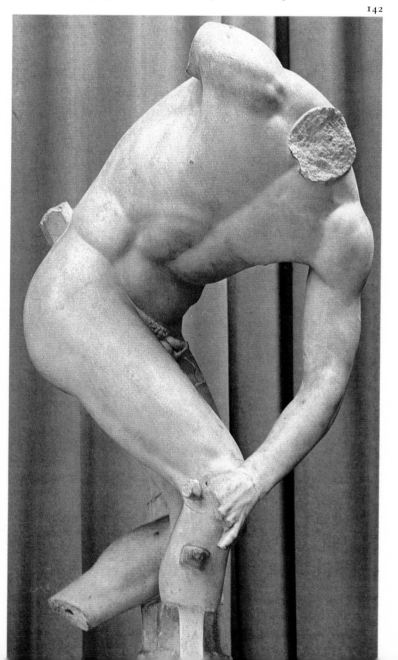

142 MYRON. *Diskobolos* · Roman marble copy of a classical Greek
bronze of ca. 460-450 B.C. · Museo delle Terme, Rome.

The bronze original of the discus-thrower by Myron of Eleutherai
(Attica), as famous in antiquity as it is now, represented the high point
in the sculptor's career. It is known to us only through various marble
replicas, of which this one, formerly in the Lancelotti Collection, is the
most complete. The athlete is shown at the moment of arrest just
before he swings the heavy disc forward to throw it. The body suggests movement through studied, abstract curves, while the serene
head indicates concentrated effort. In this already classical masterpiece, physical reality is transformed to serve the ideal conception.

143 MYRON · *Diskobolos* seen from the back · Plaster copy of a
classical Greek bronze · Musée des Beaux-Arts, Paris.

Seen from this view, Myron's discus-thrower is no less interesting than
in profile. Echoing the half circle formed by the arms, the sinuous line
of the body performs like a coiling spring ready to release its energy.
The musculature is boldly plotted in broad planes, such details as
there are being handled with an eye to compositional effect rather than
to anatomical accuracy; for the artist has approached both the bodily
structure and the representation of motion by analyzing nature and
then recreating it in his mind, adapting reality to the ideal in order to
compose a harmonious whole.

145 AFTER POLYKLEITOS · *Doryphoros* · Marble · Roman copy of a
lost Greek bronze of ca. 440 B.C. · Museo Nazionale, Naples.

Polykleitos from Argos was the first to define, in a treatise which has
been lost, a set of ideal proportions for the human body. He materialized this "canon" in his famous bronze statue of a spear-bearer - also
lost to us save in numerous copies from antiquity, among which this
one (height, 6 feet 6 inches) is accepted as an adequate replica of the
original. The naked athlete stands with his lance over his shoulder.
The shift of weight to the supporting right leg sets up in the body a
series of rhythmic responses: the flexing of the left leg, whose heel is
lifted; the contraction of the right side of the torso which lowers the
shoulder on the side of the supporting hip; and the corresponding
expansion of the opposite side of the torso where the hip is dropped
and the shoulder raised. All these are worked with a mathematically
precise understanding of weight movements and counterpoise, and
no rigid verticals disturb the impression of moving, yet timeless,
equilibrium.

144 *"Mourning" Athena* · Marble · Greek, Early Classical, ca. 460 B.C. · Akropolis Museum, Athens.

Leaning a little forward, the goddess rests her forehead against her spear, her right hand on her hip, and crosses one leg over the other. To the impression of graceful ease, the faintly diagonal folds of her peplos - apparently ignoring the law of gravity - add a suggestion of arrested motion. The lower end of her spear is set against the base of an upright block of stone which may be the boundary marker of a sanctuary, or perhaps an allusion to the recently built wall of Kimon. This accomplished low relief (25 inches high) is free of archaic conventions and already attains classical equilibrium.

143

144

145

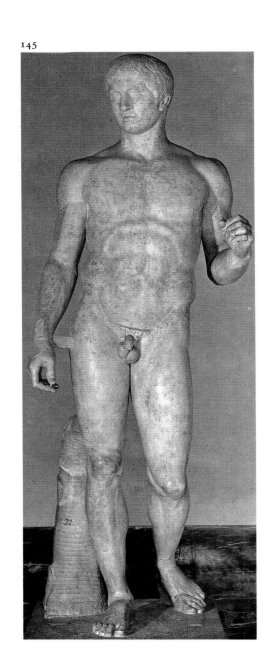

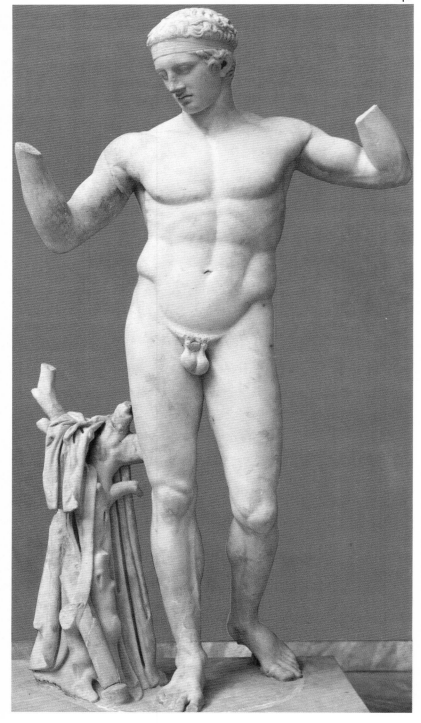

146 AFTER POLYKLEITOS · Marble · Roman copy of a lost Greek bronze of ca. 430 B.C. · National Museum, Athens.

As famous as Polykleitos' Doryphoros was his slightly later Diadoumenos, known, again, only through replicas, of which this marble from Delos is one of the best (height, 74 inches). It betrays the influence of the more graceful style that came to dominate Greek art in the last quarter of the 5th century B.C. The pose is quite similar to that of the Doryphoros, but the raised arms with which the young athlete ties a fillet round his head break the tight spatial framework in which the earlier figure was inscribed, and movement is now more important than stability. The slimmer forms foreshadow the taste for youthful nudes that characterizes 4th-century sculpture.

148 *Wounded Niobid* · Marble · Roman copy from a Greek original of ca. 440 B.C. · Museo delle Terme, Rome.

This beautiful statue, found in the gardens of Sallust in Rome, has been connected with two other statues of similar origin now in the Copenhagen Museum. It has been suggested that those three works were copied from a group of wounded Niobids made by an artist of the Parian school working in Athens after 440, perhaps Agorakritos. The strong, naked body is represented realistically, in an expressive attitude. The young Niobid is arrested in her flight by the celestial arrow that has struck her back; she is falling, her left knee nearly touching the ground, her torso stiffening with pain, and her mouth half open in a cry which is interrupted by death. With her right hand she tries to pull out the arrow, while her left holds up her peplos. Already in 5th-century Greek art the human body could become a vehicle for suffering.

147 *Wounded Amazon* · Marble · Roman copy of a Greek bronze original of ca. 440 B.C. · Museo Capitolino, Rome.

According to a not altogether trustworthy anecdote from antiquity, Polykleitos, Phidias, Kresilas and Phradmon each made a bronze statue of an Amazon for the sanctuary of Artemis at Ephesos. Three of those Amazons are known to us through marble copies, but no agreement has been reached as to their attribution to the various competitors. The type represented by this statue (height, 81 inches) signed by the copyist Sosikles is often attributed to Polykleitos, but is more likely to have been by Kresilas. The wounded warrior, leaning on her lance, displays her wound. Her attitude is reminiscent of the style of Polykleitos, but the composition is less refined, more realistic.

149

149 *Aphrodite, Dione, and a third goddess*, from the east pediment of the Parthenon · Marble · Greek, Classical, 438-432 B.C. · British Museum, London.

Despite serious mutilations, the Parthenon pediment sculptures constitute the most impressive ensemble that classical Greece has left us; and perhaps for this reason the name of Phidias has always been attached to them, though the attribution leads to certain serious chronological difficulties. Nevertheless, it is certain that the masters of the Parthenon sculptures were deeply influenced by Perikles' adviser on artistic questions. The east pediment represented the birth of Athena, who sprang fully armed from the forehead of her father Zeus. Here, the semi-recumbent Aphrodite (56 inches high) reclines in a posture of divine ease next to her mother Dione - two among the assembly of gods and goddesses who witness Athena's miraculous birth.

150 *Demeter and Persephone*, from the east pediment of the Parthenon. · Marble · Greek, Classical, 438-432 B.C. · British Museum, London.

Corresponding to the group of Dione and Aphrodite, harmoniously framed in the right hand angle of the pediment, is the group of Demeter and Persephone (height, 59 inches) in the left. The more restrained treatment of the drapery suggests another hand at work: while Aphrodite, Dione and the third goddess rise in a froth of sharp-edge folds that gather and flow over their bodies with masterly ease, the robes of Demeter and Persephone fall in broader, less sinuous and more conventional patterns. But the composition shows the same care in linking the figures rhythmically.

151

150

151 *Head of a horse from Selene's chariot*, from the east pediment of the Parthenon · Marble · Greek, Classical, 438-432 B.C. · British Museum, London.

In accord with the symbolic interpretation favored in Periklean times, the birth of Athena depicted on the east pediment of the Parthenon was flanked on one side by Helios, the rising sun, and on the other by Selene, the moon, seen as she plunges downward toward the western horizon. The same deities flanked the births of Pandora and of Aphrodite on the pedestals of Phidias' Athena Parthenos and Olympian Zeus, as well as the Fall of Troy on the northern metopes of the Parthenon. Of the horses of Selene's chariot, no more emerged from the corner of the pediment than their heads which are of a vigorous and compelling realism.

139

152

152 *Horsemen from the Parthenon frieze* · Marble · Greek, Classical, 442-438 B.C. · British Museum, London.

154

154 *Maidens from the Parthenon frieze* · Marble · Greek, Classical, 442-438 B.C. · The Louvre, Paris.

The sculptural decoration of the Parthenon, executed in Pentelic marble as is the rest of the temple, is richer than is usual for Doric temples: in addition to the metopes and pediments there is a 40-inch-high frieze, borrowed from the repertory of Ionic temple decoration, unfolding across the upper part of the cella wall, on the outside. The frieze has always been thought to represent the quadrennial Panathenaic procession, which culminated in the ceremonial donation of a new veil to the goddess. The veil would have been woven in the years intervening since the last Panathenaea by maidens such as are here portrayed walking forward with shy dignity under the eye of the two marshals.

153

153 *Parthenon frieze* Akropolis, Athens.

The cavalcade of youthful Athenians that took part in the traditional Panathenaic procession occupies a major part of the Parthenon frieze. No less than a hundred and forty-three horsemen advance along the north and south sides, by ones and twos, in overlapping groups, bunched or spread out, the horses moving in different tempi that effectively vary the rhythmic advance of the procession. It was perhaps for this that the designer used so many of these figures in diverse attitudes ranging from motionless waiting to furious gallop; and certainly, he was skilled in the rendering of the nervous animal bodies, the snorting nostrils and proud necks, which only the best sculptors were able to recreate without falsifying their movement and harmony.

155 *The "Varvakeion Athena,"* a 2nd-century copy of Phidias' Athena Parthenos · National Museum, Athens.

This marble statuette, 42 inches high, found in 1880 near the Gymnasium of Varvakeion in Athens, probably dates from the 2nd century. It is a coarse but fairly faithful replica of the huge cult statue that Phidias made between 447 and 438 B.C. for Perikles' Parthenon. Traces of polychromy help us to imagine the vivid appearance of the original statue - a gigantic assemblage of gold and ivory elements (on a wooden framework), further brightened by color. The proportions of the figure and its wide, low base - when considered together with several other documents - must also be taken as repeating those of Phidias' colossus.

155

156 AFTER PHIDIAS · *The Zeus of Olympia*, represented on a 2nd-century Roman coin · Museo Archeologico, Florence.

Executed soon after the Athena Parthenos of Athens, Phidias' colossal ivory-and-gold statue of Zeus in the temple of Olympia was unanimously hailed in ancient times as the masterpiece of masterpieces, one of the seven wonders of the world. Removed by the Christians to Constantinople, it perished there in a fire, and all we know of it comes from literary descriptions and from this tiny copy on a bronze coin issued by the Emperor Hadrian at Elis in 137 A.D. to commemorate the 230th Olympic Games. The original colossus stood some forty-five feet high and represented the god seated on a throne adorned with innumerable sculpted and painted figures, its great bulk filling the entire rear part of the cella of the temple.

156

157 *Head of Zeus* · Marble · Roman, 3rd century A.D., probably inspired by the Zeus of Olympia · Archeological Museum, Cyrene.

This head in Pentelic marble (height 15 inches) belonged to a statue, now lost, dedicated at Cyrene under the Antonines. It was probably inspired by the chryselephantine Zeus of Olympia by Phidias, but if so, it was a free adaptation. In spite of its academic style, which emphasizes power rather than grandeur, it gives us an idea of the serene, gracious majesty that according to ancient writers characterized Phidias' colossal statue. The calm, smooth face contrasts with the ruffled hair and beard; in the original this contrast was stressed even more by the use of different materials.

157

158 *The "Athena Medici"* · Marble · Roman copy from a Greek original of ca. 450-420 B.C. · The Louvre, Paris.

This heavily draped female figure once stood in the gardens of the Villa Medici in Rome; and since Ingres caused her to be transported to France, she has sometimes been called the *Minerve Ingres*. She wears a heavy peplos, through the opening of which we can see a finer tunic, and a military cloak is thrown over her shoulder. The statue is the finest of a series of replicas of a lost original attributed to Phidias or his school and is sometimes wrongly identified as Phidias' Athena Promachos, who stood in a rather different attitude.

158

159

159 *Karyatids from the Erechtheion* · Marble · Greek, Classical, ca. 417-409 B.C.

The graceful karyatid portico was built about 420 B.C.; the maidens themselves were *in situ* in rough form before 417, and by 410 to 409, were finished. The robust young women (height, 92 inches) in Pentelic marble who support the architrave revive a type of support created by the Ionian architects of the Archaic period. Each maiden's peplos falls along her supporting leg in vertical folds which suggest the flutings of a column; but the reference becomes clearly human where the transparent material molds her breasts and her other, bent, leg. Coiffed by elegant sculptured capitals serving both as headdress and architectural elements, the karyatids successfully combine strength and elegance.

160

160 *Karyatid from the Erechtheion* · (See also fig. 161).

The monumentality that their architectural role confers on the karyatids - and which is emphasized still more by the present mutilation of their arms - is tempered on closer observation by various details that evoke their grace and their femininity. Since 1952, when copies of them were found in Hadrian's Villa (see fig. 162), we can in imagination restore to them their arms heavy with bracelets, and the artistically crumpled folds of material that they held in their left hands. But their most remarkable ornament was certainly their long hair, elegantly arranged in falling clusters of braids. (see 161).

163 *Roman copy of an Erechtheion karyatid, restored by Thorwaldsen ·* Vatican Museum, Rome.

Long before the karyatids of Hadrian's Villa were discovered, other antique copies had been identified. They were not, however, retained in their fragmentary state for their documentary value, but instead seem to have fired the zal of restorers. In this example, we see the interpretation of a Roman imitator, reinterpreted by a 19th-century sculptor. The liveliness and elegance still evident in the Tivoli replicas has been replaced by the disembodied coldness of neo-classicism.

163

162

162 *Copy of a karyatid from the Erechtheion ·* Marble · Roman, of the time of Hadrian · Villa Adriana, Tivoli.

Already in antiquity the perfect beauty of the Erechtheion karyatids aroused the admiration of art lovers and their desire to own something as like them as possible. The most eminent of Roman Grecophile amateurs, Emperor Hadrian, had replicas of them made for the gardens of his villa at Tivoli; and there they were unearthed in 1952. Their academic accuracy shows more skill than sensitivity on the part of the 2nd-century copyists; but in their good state of preservation they reveal for us details, previously unknown, that must have been present in their originals - the bracelets, the *paterae*, the gathered-up drapery held in the left hand - which complete our knowledge and deepen our understanding of the Akropolis statues.

143

164

164 AFTER KRESILAS · *Bust of Perikles* · Roman copy from a bronze Greek original of ca. 445 to 440 B.C. · Vatican Museums, Rome.

Kresilas of Kydonia, a Cretan sculptor working in Athens, was the author of a bronze statue set up on the Akropolis which portrayed Perikles full-length in heroic nudity. The bust pictured here was probably inspired by Kresilas' statue which must have been done at the high point of the statesman's political career around 445-440 B.C. when he was aged about forty-five or fifty. Perikles wears here the Attic helmet with movable cheek-guards, symbol of the function of *strategos* he exercised for fifteen years in a row - but also perhaps a clever means of covering up the congenital skull deformation which earned him the nickname of "Onion-Head."

165

165 *Funeral stele of Hegeso* · Marble · Greek, Classical, ca. 410-400 B.C. · National Museum, Athens.

Among the most beautiful of Attic steles is this one (height, 59½ inches) from the end of the 5th century B.C., with its mood of serene and aristocratic acceptance of death. The dead woman, seated on a harmoniously curved chair, is gravely decking herself out before the great journey. With her right hand she lifts aside her veil - so thin that it is hardly visible - repeating the ritual gesture of the bride. Standing in front of her, a young servant girl proffers a jewel casket. The refined and restrained treatment of the draperies and the calm purity of the faces give this marble relief an atmosphere of charming melancholy

166 *Carved decoration on the wall of the Erechtheion cella* · Marble · Greek, Classical, ca. 420 B.C. · Akropolis, Athens.

To enliven the long bare wall that faces the Parthenon and whose surface is broken only by the projecting karyatid porch, the architect carried all across it the ornament of the capitals on the angle pilasters. Under the three fasciae supporting the frieze are a cyma reversa molding with Lesbian leaf ornament, an ovolo carved with egg and dart, and a band of alternating palmettes and lilies. The traditional motifs are treated here with the most beautiful delicacy and refinement.

166

167 *Capital in the north porch of the Erechtheion* · Marble · Greek, Classical, ca. 420 B.C. · Akropolis, Athens.

The Erechtheion's architectural decoration is characteristic of the ornamental style which, at the time it was built, appealed to those who commissioned the building: the pietistic conservatives who formed the entourage of the general Nikias. The capitals on the east and west façades and on the north porch are an important part of that decoration. They are the most richly ornate of all Greek Ionic capitals. Between the fluted shaft and the strong volutes which hug it closely, in accord with Attic tradition, the usual egg and dart molding is supplemented by a band of alternating palmettes and lilies.

167

168 *Maenad with goat* · Marble · Roman, perhaps after a Greek original of the late 5th century B.C. · Palazzo dei Conservatori, Rome.

This graceful marble bas-relief (height, 57½ inches) is among the finest examples of a Dionysiac motif often reproduced by Roman sculptors. The Maenad is brandishing the hindquarter of a wild goat which she has torn apart in the paroxysms of her orgiastic dance. But the furious action - which is contradicted by the grave, religious expression of her face - serves mainly as a pretext for the riot of swirling, transparent draperies, probably inspired by a model from the end of the 5th century B.C. This kind of dextrous calligraphy characterizes a group of works usually attributed to the Athenian sculptor and goldsmith Kallimachos.

169 *Nike untying her sandal* · Marble · Greek, Classical, ca. 410-407 B.C. · Akropolis Museum, Athens.

The parapet (height, 56 inches) formerly surrounding the small temple of Athena Nike at the entrance to the Akropolis is a masterpiece of the style that triumphed in Athens during the last quarter of the 5th century B.C. It is enlivened by a graceful series of Victories preparing a sacrifice. This one is removing her sandals preparatory to entering the sacred enclosure. The sculptor's chief concerns seem to have been the virtuoso play on the figure's nudity under her transparent robe, and the ornamental combinations of drapery folds, which make up a quasi-abstract pattern of light and shade. The firm design and broad curves of the figure give an impression of elegance and weightlessness.

170 PAIONIOS · *Nike*, from Olympia · Marble · Greek, Classical, ca. 420 B.C. · Museum, Olympia.

Paionios of Mende (Thrace) won the competition organized at Olympia to provide the temple of Zeus with gilt bronze acroteria. This Nike may have been a replica of one of them, repeated in marble by the artist himself, and placed atop a high base in the same sanctuary to celebrate the victory of the Messenians over the Spartans in 425 B.C. The goddess (height, 90 inches) is represented with her wings still outstretched, just touching foot to the ground. The calligraphic arrangement of the draperies is borrowed from Attic art, but the sensuous body visible through the material, and the bared right leg betray the artist's Ionian origin.

169

170

171

171 *Marching soldiers*, from the Nereid monument at Xanthos ·
Marble · Greek, Classical, ca. 420 B.C. · British Museum, London.

Built as the tomb of a Lycian prince, the monument consists of an
Ionic temple set on a high podium and was distinguished by the
Nereid statues that probably originally stood between the columns.
From the smaller (height, 25 inches) of the two superposed friezes that
decorated the base this picturesque sculptured fragment has been
preserved. It represents an obliquely viewed row of warriors marching
forward. The artist creates an impression of large numbers and rapid
movement through an effective and decorative linear scheme. To the
Greek feeling for form was here added the Eastern narrative gift.

172

1571

172 *Female head*, from the west pediment of the Heraion at Argos ·
Greek, Classical, ca. 420 B.C. · National Museum, Athens.

This life-size (height of face, 6½ inches) head of a young woman is one of
the few remaining fragments from the sculptured decoration of the
new Heraion at Argos. After a fire in 423 B.C., which destroyed the
earlier Heraion made of tufa, a new temple was built at the end of the
5th century B.C., and decorated on the east pediment by a Birth of
Zeus, on the west pediment by a Fall of Troy. The sobriety of style
suggests that this head may be a work from the school of Polykleitos,
who made the chryselephantine statue of Hera herself for the same
temple.

173 *Battle of Lapiths and Centaurs*, from the frieze of the temple of
Apollo at Bassae · Marble · Greek, beginning of the 4th Century B.C. ·
British Museum, London.

At Bassae in Arcadia stands the Doric temple of Apollo Epikurios.
A groundless tradition attributes it to the Parthenon architect, Iktinos.
Begun about 460 B.C., it was finished only after an interruption, at
the beginning of the 4th century. At that time it received an inside
Ionic colonnade, which bore a sculptured frieze in high relief representing battles of Greeks and Amazons, of Centaurs and Lapiths. This
frieze (height, 25 inches) is somewhat heavy in execution, and in its
use of semi-transparent draperies reveals the influence of late 5th-
century Attic art.

174 *Portrait statue*, from the Mausoleum at Halikarnassos · Marble ·
Greek, ca. 350 B.C. · British Museum, London.

Bryaxis, probably Karian by birth, after a period of study and work
in Athens was called back to his own country about 360 B.C. to colla-
borate with Skopas, Timotheos and Leochares on the sculptural
decoration for the monumental tomb that King Mausolus was building
at Halikarnassos. Of this sumptuous building, one of the Seven Wonders of the ancient world, only a few fragments are left, among which is
this statue from Bryaxis' shop, long mistakenly considered a portrait
of Mausolus. It is 120 inches high and stood on the north side, between two columns of the peristyle.

175 *Head of the portrait statue in fig. 174.*

The sculptured decoration of Mausolus' tomb included a number of
portrait statues of relatives, ancestors or dignitaries standing round
the dead king like a last guard of honor. This figure is robed in heavy,
theatrical folds of drapery and the head is powerfully individualistic.
The fleshy face, oriental in type, has an imperious forehead and nose,
a slightly scornful mouth; its short beard and long hair are rendered
somewhat summarily, since owing to the placing of the statue it would
have been seen only from a distance and from below.

173

175

174

147

176

176 SKOPAS (?) · *Head of a warrior*, from the temple of Tegea ·
Marble · Greek, ca. 370-350 B.C. · National Museum, Athens.

Some time around 360 B.C. the Tegeans asked the sculptor Skopas
from Paros to build and probably also to decorate with sculptures a
temple to Alea, a local goddess assimilated to Athena. French excavations have revealed fragments from marble pediments representing,
on the east, the chase of the Kalydonian boar, with Meleager and
Atalanta and others, and on the west, the battle of Telephos against
Achilles. This warrior's head (height, 12 inches) with its powerful
square jaw and pathetic upward glance is handled in a rough, massive
style directed more towards general effect than towards attractive
detail - a style well suited to the needs of architecture.

178

178 · AFTER SKOPAS (?) · *The Ares Ludovisi* · Marble · Roman copy
of a Greek 4th-century original · Museo delle Terme, Rome.

In a temple dedicated to Mars by L. Junius Brutus, near the Circus
Flaminius in Rome, there was a colossal seated statue of Ares by
Skopas. The Ares Ludovisi (height, 62 inches), a work of considerable
quality, has sometimes been considered a copy of that original. The god
of war is represented sitting on a rock in a casual pose, his left foot
lifted and resting on a helmet, his hands crossed over the flexed knee.
The little Eros who seems to be playing at his feet may have been a
Hellenistic addition to the original. The figure's proportions are
altogether "Skopasian," and the dreamy expression is characteristic
of Skopas' style, though here it has a somewhat academic cast. In the
17th century, Bernini restored the work, which was then in the Villa
Ludovisi; he remade the right foot, the head of Eros, the left arm and
the right forearm.

177

177 AFTER SKOPAS · Head of Meleager · Marble · Roman copy of
a Greek original of ca. 340 B.C. · Villa Medici, Rome.

There exist several Roman marble copies that record Skopas' lost
bronze statue of Meleager, Atalanta's unhappy lover who conquered
the Kalydonian boar. The most beautiful and probably the most
faithful reflection from the original is a head placed on a quite unrelated body in the gardens of the Villa Medici in Rome. The face, with
its rectangular forehead, weighty orbital arch, pathetically upturned
eyes, and powerful jaw, is consistent with the style of Skopas, who
had already represented the hero on the east pediment of the temple
at Tegea.

179 AFTER SKOPAS · *Maenad* · Marble · Roman copy of a Greek
4th-century original · Albertinum, Dresden.

The theme of the maenad gripped in the frenzy of Dionysiac dancing
was probably created by Kallimachos at the end of the 5th century
B.C. (See fig. 168), and it was used again by Skopas about 350 B.C. in a
Parian marble statue of which this is a reduced copy (height, 18½ inches). The suave and composed line has been replaced by a sensuously
modelled, tense body, arching backwards in the grip of emotion, hip
and thigh bared by the flying drapery. The ancients admired above all
the long floating hair, caught up, like the body, by the impetus of the
disordered movement.

180 AFTER PRAXITELES · *Eros of Thespiai* · Marble · Roman copy
from a Greek bronze of ca. 350 B.C. · The Louvre, Paris.

According to an ancient tradition, Phryne was given by her lover
Praxiteles her favorite among his works: an Eros in Pentelic marble,
which she dedicated in a temple of Eros in her native town of Thespiai.
This is the least incomplete copy of that original, though the head,
the arms, the larger part of the legs, and the tree trunk have been
restored The back of the slender boy's-body was enfolded by two long
wings. The raised right arm towards which the head is leaning shifts the
weight slightly, creating that counterpoised stance characteristic of
the later Praxitelean works.

179

180

181 *The Aphrodite of Arles* · Marble · Roman work of the 1st century
B.C., reflecting a Greek original of ca. 350 · The Louvre, Paris.

This Aphrodite was discovered in 1651 in the Roman amphitheatre of
Arles. It was over-restored by the French sculptor François Girardon
who added the apple and the mirror, attributes of the beauty contest
Paris judged on Mount Ida. The fact is, we have no idea what the
original gesture of the arm was. The tender and modest nudity of the
body, the grave sweet expression, the counterpoise of shoulders and
pelvis all have much in common with the works of Praxiteles' youth.
(Height 77 inches.)

181

182 AFTER PRAXITELES · *Aphrodite of Knidos* · Marble · Roman copy after a Greek work of ca. 350 B.C. · Vatican Museums, Rome.

For the ancients, the masterpiece of Praxiteles was the statue of Aphrodite in Parian marble he executed for the Knidians around 350 B.C. Set up on a low base in the center of a rotunda, she received the homage of innumerable visitors, and poets poured out epigrams in her honor. The fame of this lost marvel is proved by the great number of copies which have come down to us. This copy is admittedly somewhat academic, but it permits us to glimpse something of the beauty of the original in which Praxiteles united the vibrant sensuality of the female nude with a god-like majesty.

182

183 AFTER PRAXITELES · *Apollo Sauroktonos* · Roman copy of a Greek bronze of ca. 350 B.C. The Louvre, Paris.

This statue is a plaster copy of a bronze original created by Praxiteles. The doughty Apollo, slayer of the monster serpent, Python, has become an amiable youth slyly watching a lizard. The typical Praxitelean S-curve, the head inclined towards the bearing leg and turned towards the flexed leg, gives the body a graceful, sinuous line. The slender, soft forms, and the fine featured face suggest the supple vitality of a very young body momentarily stilled in watching.

184 PRAXITELES (?) · *Hermes from Olympia* · Greek, ca. 340 B.C. (or Ancient Greek copy) · Museum, Olympia.

This group in Parian marble (height, 85 inches) is often considered as an original work by Praxiteles dating from about 340 B.C., but it is more likely an antique copy. Hermes must have held in his right hand a bunch of grapes, coveted by the small Dionysios sitting on his left arm, which rests on a tree trunk hidden under drapery. There is here the same tender dialogue between adult and child, the same awkwardness in rendering infant anatomy as in the group by Kephisodotos, Praxiteles' father (fig. 188); but here the curve of the body is more marked, and there is an intentional contrast between the play of light over the softly modelled nude bodies and the deeply cut, folded masses of drapery.

185 AFTER LYSIPPOS · *Apoxyomenos* · Marble · Roman copy of a Greek work of ca. 330 B.C. · Vatican Museums, Rome.

After his gymnastic exercise, the athlete is scraping the dusty oil from his right arm with a strigil. The slim, lively, relaxed figure (total height 82 inches) stands firmly but at ease, resting his weight on his left leg the right slightly outstretched and bent. His face displays physical weariness and a certain melancholy; but the body is all harmony, with the balanced distribution of the weight between the two legs, the calculated rhythm of the arms boldly occupying space. Even in this copy of Lysippos' original bronze we are made aware of the sculptor's innovations in the direction of three-dimensional movement and a more sharply individualized emotional and physical presence.

184

185

186

186 AFTER LYSIPPOS (?) · *Bust of Alexander* · Marble · Roman copy of a Greek original of ca. 330 B.C. · The Louvre, Paris.

This marble herm, usually known as the "Azara bust" after its donor, was found near Tivoli. In spite of dilapidation and restorations it seems to be the most authentic Lysippian portrait of Alexander the Great (total height, 26 inches). The hair is represented as supple, ruffled locks, the full mouth is slightly open, the chin well marked. His glance is moving because of the melancholy gravity of the eyes, set deep and shadowed by the orbital arch and eyelids. Among the long series of portraits of Alexander, this one is the most convincing in its sincerity.

187 *The Farnese Hercules* · Marble · Perhaps inspired by a 4th-century Lysippian bronze. Greek, 2nd century. B.C. · Museo Nazionale, Naples.

The 2nd-century Athenian Glykon signed his name to this more or less faithful imitation of a type created in bronze by Lysippos in the 4th century B.C. Leaning on his club, which is draped in the lion skin, the hero appears astonishingly massive (height, 127 inches). After the baroque fashion of his own time, Glykion has given him superhuman, swollen muscles, probably exaggerating the bodily power of the original statue; but if Lysippos had conceived Hercules as great, he had also wanted to depict his humanity; from Lysippos must come the sad, downcast glance and the lax athletic body, leaning slightly off-center, revealing the conquering hero in a moment of weariness, thinking back on his past exploits.

187

151

188

188 AFTER KEPHISODOTOS · *Eirene and Ploutos* · Marble · Roman copy after a Greek bronze of ca. 370 B.C. · Glyptothek, Munich.

About 370 B.C., the sculptor Kephisodotos set up in the Athenian Agora an allegorical bronze statue representing Peace holding the infant Wealth in her arms. In this antique copy (height, 79½ inches) Eirene is dressed in a heavy peplos, and wears her hair in the long tresses required by classical tradition. Her right hand held a scepter. On her left arm, Ploutos, rather coarsely represented (infant anatomy was as yet imperfectly studied in sculpture), stretches out his arm towards his protectress with a charming gesture to which she responds in the tender smile on her serene face. Through a very human rendering of emotion, Kephisodotos created a type heralding a new style.

189

189 AFTER LEOCHARES (?) · *The Apollo Belvedere* · Roman copy of a Greek work of the late 4th (?) century · Vatican Museums, Rome.

Found near Anzio in the last years of the 15th century, this famous marble Apollo (height, 88 inches) aroused tremendous enthusiasm on the part of Winckelmann and other 18th- and 19th-century connoisseurs of neo-classical bent. It is a marble copy of a Greek bronze that has been attributed, on good grounds, to the Athenian sculptor Leochares; it may reflect the Apollo Alexikakos which he sculptured about 335 B.C. as a counterpart of the one by Kalamis (see fig. 125) in the temple of Apollo Patroos. The god, in motion, seeming hardly to touch the ground, held the Avenger's bow in his left hand and in his right the Healer's laurel branch.

190

190 *Head of a youth, from Antikythera* · Bronze · Greek, 375-350 B.C. · National Museum, Athens. (see also fig. 192).

This bronze ephebe was fished out of the sea just off shore from Antikythera in 1900, together with other works of art which made up the cargo of a sunken ship. The nude young man raises his right arm, hand turned palm downwards, fingers spread out: is he Paris offering the apple of discord? or perhaps Perseus holding up Medusa's head by its hair? The head is slightly turned to the right and the face with its noble, energetic features gives an impression of gentleness, accented by the searching gaze of the deep-set eyes.

191

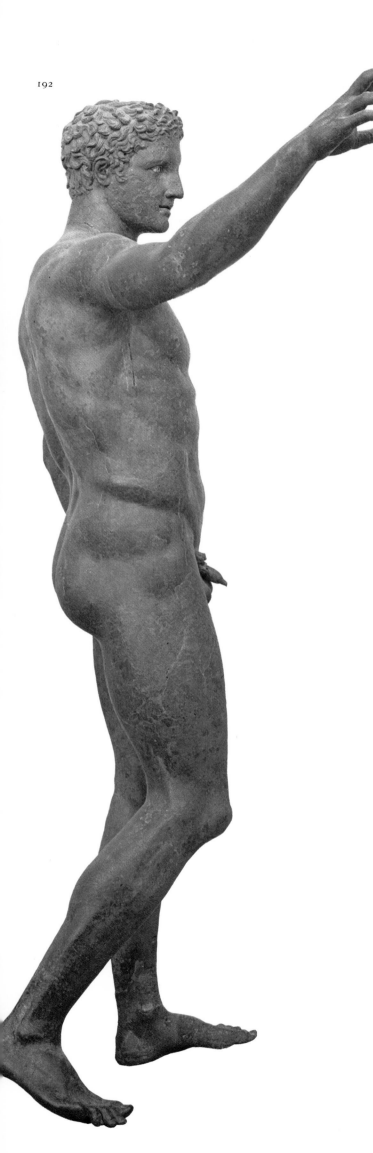

191 *Relief from the Sarcophagus of the Mourning Women*, from Sidon · Marble · Greek, ca. 350 B.C. · Archeological Museum, Istanbul.

This remarkably well-preserved sarcophagus was found in the royal necropolis at Sidon. It imitates the shape of an Ionic temple without frieze (total height, $71\frac{1}{2}$ inches). Carved in very high relief, the mourning women dressed in peplos, tunic, and cloak stand between columns, three on the short and six on the long sides. Their bare feet signify mourning. Monotony in the repeated matronly figures is skillfully avoided by subtle variations in their attitudes and expressions. An illusion of depth is given by the parapet running between the columns.

192 *Statue of a youth, from Antikythera* · Bronze · Greek, 375-350 B.C. · National Museum, Athens.

193 *So-called Alexander sarcophagus* · Pentelic marble · Greek, Late 4th-century style · Archeological Museum, Istanbul.

This sarcophagus was found in the royal necropolis of Sidon, in a remarkably good state of preservation. The rectangular chest is covered with a lid imitating a roof and is richly decorated with polychromed marble reliefs in which appear hunting scenes and Greeks battling Persians. An expert chisel has carried out the vigorously imaginative conceptions of the sculptor, who was also a goldsmith and a painter. This sarcophagus, made for some rich Phoenician prince, bows to the oriental tradition but is Greek in spirit and material.

193

194 *So-called Alexander sarcophagus* - (detail) Hunting Scene.

194

195 *Dancing girls from the Acanthus column* · Marble · Greek, late 5th-early 4th century B.C. · Museum, Delphi.

This marble column, over 30 feet high, was among the offerings erected at Delphi. It must have suggested an enormous trunk terminating in a cluster of acanthus leaves; and it supported a metal tripod whose bowl rested on the heads of the three girls sculptured in high relief (height, 83 inches). They wear short tunics which show off their firmly modelled legs; and in the graceful, restrained rhythms of their dance, they are perfectly suited to their leafy setting.

196 *Crouching Aphrodite* · Marble · Roman copy of a Hellenistic bronze of ca. 275 B.C. · Ny Carlsberg Glyptotek, Copenhagen.

The crouching Aphrodite made in the first half of the 3rd century B.C. by the sculptor Doidalses of Bithynia for King Nicomedes enjoyed great fame - judging from the numerous Roman copies and replicas. The original was made of bronze, and the marble adaptations require supports to ensure their stability. The goddess is intimately seen in the usual position of the Greek woman at her bath. Her opulent and realistic curves are disciplined by the closed triangular composition. The sculptor has exploited the painterly contrast of heavy locks of damp hair against the smooth flesh surface.

195

196

197

197 AFTER POLYEUKTOS · *Demosthenes* · Marble · Roman copy after a Hellenistic bronze of ca. 280 B.C. · Ny Carlsberg Glyptotek, Copenhagen.

After Alexander's conquests, Athens lost her artistic leadership in the expanded Hellenic world; and in 3rd-century Athens a sober style, faithful to tradition and hostile to innovations, developed, of which the most representative work was Polyeuktos' bronze statue of Demosthenes, erected on the Agora in 280/279 and known to us through many replicas. It is a posthumous portrait of the orator, who died in 322, a nostalgic evocation of the last great Athenian democrat. The well balanced composition centered on the folded hands is enclosed in the hexagon outlined by the bare arms. The orator's face expresses a deep inward suffering.

198 *Head of a Gaul*, from Fayum (?) · Marble · Hellenistic · Museum, Cairo.

Founded in 331, Alexandria had become, by the 3rd century B.C., the most important city in the Mediterranean world. The colorful, cosmopolitan crowds of the great port were an endless source for exotic types and models suitable to realistically treated artistic trends. This head of a Gallic mercenary in the ptolemaic armies has the same pathetic, hirsute visage as the Galatians on Pergamene ex-votos. But with its impressionistic technique and fluid, unfinished appearance, it is one of the most revolutionary of Hellenistic art works.

198

200 *Head of the Giant Klytios*, detail from the great frieze on the Altar of Zeus from Pergamon · State Museums, East Berlin.

The use of obscure mythological figures (whose names are given on the border of the frieze) and of rare iconographic details, elaborations of an erudite nature, remind us that Pergamon owned a library second only in importance to that of Alexandria. Nonetheless, the exuberant genius of the anonymous creator of the great frieze has given the work both tremendous vividness and great unity, though there are variations in execution suggesting the hands of several sculptors. Over the faces, drawn with pathos, the tormented anatomy, the violently swirling draperies, light and shadow play in dramatic contrasts that heighten the titanic battle's theatricality.

200

199 *Athena and Alkyoneos*, from the Altar of Zeus from Pergamon · Marble relief · Hellenistic, ca. 180 B.C. · State Museums, East Berlin.

The generosity of the kings of Pergamon attracted artists from all over, and this kingdom in Asia Minor became one of the most brilliant centers of Hellenistic civilization. It was under Eumenus II (197-158 B.C.) that artistic activity reached its climax with the construction of the great altar of Zeus, an immense structure with a sculptured frieze covering its entire exterior base. The subject of the frieze was the traditional gigantomachy, the war between the Olympians and the giants. In each section the battle centers around one of the Olympian gods. Here, Athena triumphs over the giant Alkyoneos while Ge, the Earth-Mother, half-emerges from the ground to beg mercy for her son. (The frieze is 7½ feet high and over 426 feet in total length.)

199

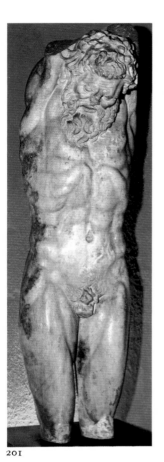

201

201 *Punishment of Marsyas* · Copy of a Hellenistic original of ca. 300-250 B.C. · Archeological Museum, Istanbul.

The Hellenistic artist has chosen to illustrate the legend of the Phrygian satyr Marsyas in its most dramatic moment: the old Silenus, sentenced to be flayed alive, is tied to a tree, his body tense with horror at the approaching torture, his staring eyes bent on the executioner sharpening his knife. The various copies of the Marsyas all show his face more or less violently convulsed with terror. Owing to the dramatic emphasis in the subject and the accentuation of the muscles revealed in fluctuating chiaroscuro patterns, the original may be dated somewhere in the first phase of Pergamene baroque.

202 *The Scythian executioner* ("*l'Arrotino*") · Roman copy of a Hellenistic original of the 3rd century B.C. · Uffizi, Florence.

The Scythian executioner sharpens on a stone the knife with which he will flay Marsyas alive; he is known only in this one, well executed, highly polished copy. Placed on a rectangular base, the figure is meant to be seen from all sides, forming, from whatever viewpoint, an ingeniously devised pyramidal composition. The artist has endeavored to render the ethnic characteristics of the Scythian type. Shown with receding forehead and gaping mouth, the executioner looks up at his victim with the stupid expression of a sadistic torturer. A seated Apollo, a beautiful and datached spectator, probably completed this group, so exceptionally rich in forms and contrast.

202

204

203 *Aphrodite of Melos* · Parian marble · Hellenistic, 2nd or 1st century B.C. · The Louvre, Paris.

204 *Head of the Aphrodite of Melos* · Detail of fig. 203

Bought on the island of Melos (Milo) by the French ambassador in Istanbul in 1820, the Louvre "Venus de Milo" is as controversial as it is famous. In general form she belongs to the tradition of classical Aphrodites, and was earlier thought to be an original 4th-century work. However, the twist of the body on its axis - head and shoulders turned to her right, legs to her left - the complex tilting of the different sections of her torso, the slipping draperies, and the sensuousness of the nude body are all non-classical features, and she is now generally considered an eclectic late Hellenistic creation.

The stylistic resemblance of the "Venus de Milo" to a statue found on Delos, in which J. Charbonneaux recognized the idealized features of the last king of Pontus, Mithridates VI Eupator, suggests an artist working towards the end of the 2nd and the beginning of the 1st century B.C. There has been passionate controversy as to the gesture her lost arms might have made; the most likely hypothesis is that with her right hand the goddess held her slipping draperies and with her left, an apple, the symbol of the island of Melos. The small head, with its melting glance, belongs to the Praxitelean tradition.

205 *The Victory of Samothrace* · Marble · Hellenistic, ca. 190 B.C. (?) The Louvre, Paris.

In the sanctuary of Samothrace, this Victory stood on a base formed like the prow of a ship, in a pond which reflected her image. The figure commemorated a naval victory and has been related to the Nike blowing a trumpet on coins issued by Demetrios Polyorketes (336-283); but the discovery in 1950 of the statue's empty right hand has invalidated that identification, and she is now believed to have been an ex-voto from the Rhodians after their victory over Antiochus III of Syria, about 190 B.C. With her impetuous, rushing movement and the complex rhythms of her drapery, she is one of the most powerful among Hellenistic "baroque" creations.

206

205

206 *Ram* · Bronze · Hellenistic · Museo Archeologico, Palermo.

The earlier Greeks were interested principally in the human figure but they did not neglect the representation of animals, who often appear in art, as in mythological tales, as companions or enemies of man. In the Hellenistic period representations of the animal as an independent subject became more widespread, no doubt because of the increased interest in life in all its forms. Replacing the earlier generalized rendering were more detailed and realistic images like this bronze ram, which was intended as decoration for a building in Syracuse. It reminds us that Theocritus, inventor of that genre of bucolic poetry, the Idyll, lived at the court of the 3rd-century Sicilian Tyrant Hiero II.

207

207 *Hellenistic prince* · Bronze · Hellenistic, ca. 160 B.C. · Museo delle Terme, Rome.

In its heroic character, its proportions and the classicizing rendering of the hair, this powerful figure seems inspired by Lysippos' lost statue of Alexander bearing a lance. But the altogether open composition, the mobile, realistic face, and the theatrical attitude indicate a date no earlier than the 2nd century B.C. This "Hellenistic Prince" cannot be identified with any certainty: it has been suggested, comparing him to Republican coins, that he was Sulla or Lucullus, but the most convincing hypothesis is that he was prince Demetrius I Soter (162-150 B.C.), son of Seleucus.

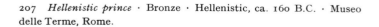

208

208 *Laokoon and his sons* · Marble · Hellenistic, late 2nd, or 1st century B.C. · Vatican Museums, Rome.

The theatrical group representing the death of the Trojan priest Laokoon was, according to Pliny's testimony, the work of three Rhodian sculptors, Hagesandros, Polydoros and Athenodoros. The group of three figures closely entwined by coiled snakes was clearly meant to be seen from the front; and since recent research by F. Maggi has allowed us to restore Laokoon's right arm to its original flexed position, the triangular composition appears even tighter than the traditional restoration had led us to believe. But within its framework conflicting tensions are set up as the father and the younger son sink to the left, dying, against the altar behind them, while the elder son pulls to the right in his attempt to free himself.

209 *Head of Laokoon* · Detail of fig. 208.

The artists who carved the group have demonstrated their technical dexterity by endowing the marble with the different textures of the bodies, contrasting the powerful maturity of Laokoon's torso to the smooth body of his younger son. The faces express the same paroxysm of pain that grips the giants of the Pergamon frieze, where we find quite similar melodramatic chiaroscuro effects produced by the same sunken eyes, mouths half open in an agonizing cry, and tortuous strands of beards and hair. The date of the Laokoon, found in 1506 in the ruins of the Golden House of Nero, is controversial: 2nd century B.C. according to some scholars; about 50 B.C. according to others.

209

210

210 *Head of Ulysses*, from the Sperlonga cave · Marble · Hellenistic, late 2nd, or 1st century, B.C. · Museo Archeologico Nazionale, Sperlonga.

The most striking element in the decoration of the Sperlonga grotto must have been the large Rhodian marble group representing Ulysses' ship attacked by the monster Scylla. Such fragments as have survived give us an idea of the exceptional quality of that animated work. Only recently discovered, the group bears the signatures of the three sculptors of the Laokoon group; hence new fuel has been added to the controversy concerning the dating of those Rhodian artists' activity. This bearded head wearing the conical sailor's bonnet has been identified as Ulysses. In its tormented, expressionistic rendering, it is closely akin to the famous Vatican group.

211 *Child's head* · Roman copy of a Greek Alexandrine model(?) · Museo Archeologico Nazionale, Sperlonga.

The child Eros and little *erotes* ("loves;" *putti*) were among the favorite subjects of Hellenistic and Roman artists, who were attracted by their impish charm and plump bodies. This little figure from the villa of Tiberius in Sperlonga differs from the usual representations in its elaborate hair style, the strands being parted in the middle and drawn down across the forehead into puffy ringlets over each ear. The coiffure, similar to that generally employed for Harpokrates (the Hellenistic version of the Egyptian Horus [or Hur]-the-child), seems to point to an Alexandrine model.

211

212 *Young girl* · Marble · Hellenistic · Museo Archeologico Nazionale, Sperlonga.

Since 1963, excavations have been carried on in the so-called "villa of Tiberius" at Sperlonga, on the Tyrrhenian coast between Gaeta and Terracina. The great residence appears to have been not only a country seat but also an important fish-breeding center. Among the very numerous marble statues unearthed there is this young girl with the sophisticated, melon-shaped hair style. Under her heavy and elaborate draperies the girl's body appears very slender, exemplifying the Hellenistic ideal of feminine grace expressed in a more popular form by the numerous terra-cotta figurines from Tanagra and Myrina.

212

213 APOLLONIUS (?) · *Belvedere Torso* · Marble · Hellenistic, 1st century B.C. · Vatican Museums, Rome.

This mutilated torso - hailed as a miracle when unearthed at the beginning of the sixteenth century - has been variously identified as Hercules, Marsyas and, most recently, the wounded Philoctetes. No immediate prototype for it is known, and it seems to be an original creation of the Athenian sculptor Apollonius, son of Nestor, whose signature appears on the rough-hewn base. Author also of the bronze Boxer in the Museo delle Terme, Rome, Apollonius appears to have been among the most important of the Neo-Attic sculptors working at Rome in the 1st century B.C.

214 *Boxer* · Bronze · Hellenistic, 2nd or 1st century B.C. · Museo delle Terme, Rome.

Engraved on the *cestus* of this resting pugilist's left hand is the signature of Apollonios, son of Nestor. The figure takes approximately the same position as the "Belvedere torso," and is endowed with the same bulging muscles. The head is that of a professional boxer - face scarred, nose broken, ears damaged - and its brutal realism combines oddly with such classical stylistic elements as the treatment of the beard and hair. The contrast points up this boxer's actual remoteness from the idealized representations of athletes in the Classical period.

215 *The Borghese Warrior* · Marble · Greek, 1st century B.C. copy of a 2nd-century original. · The Louvre, Paris.

The artist who carved this young warrior exploits to the full the possibilities of the third dimension, which had been introduced into Greek sculpture by Lysippos. The warrior's body thrusts forward along a forceful diagonal; he holds up a shield to protect himself, and the figure takes complete possession of its surrounding space. The body suggests an *écorché* figure (an artist's anatomical model), for the whole network of muscles and veins is clearly apparent under the taut skin. On the tree trunk appears the signature of the Ephesian artist Agasias, son of Dositheos.

216 *The "Farnese Bull"* · Marble · Roman copy of a Hellenistic work of the 1st century B.C. · Museo Nazionale, Naples.

To avenge her ill-treatment of their mother Antiope, Amphion and Zethos tied Dirke to the horns of a furious bull, and left her to be dragged to her death. The event was represented by Apollonios and Tauriskos of Tralles, adoptive sons of Menekrates of Rome, in the 1st century B.C.; but their composition has reached us only in the form of this 3rd-century Roman copy, the largest of all known ancient statues, found in 1546 in the Baths of Caracalla and heavily restored. The copyist has added two characters, Antiope and the *genius* of Cythera, thus spoiling the pyramidal composition. Intended to be seen from all sides, the group of figures clustering on their rocky base is shot through with the fiery drama of action.

213

214

216

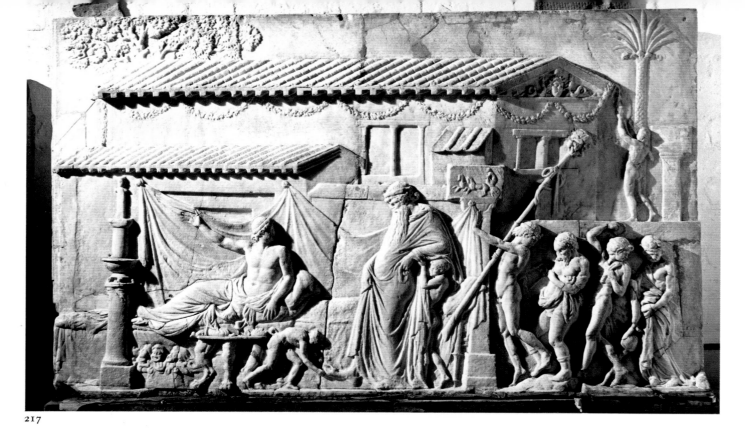

217

217 *Dionysios visiting Ikarios* · Marble · Perhaps a Graeco-Roman copy of an original of the 3rd century B.C. · British Museum, London.

This relief, of which several versions are extant, represents Dionysios visiting a mortal. The reclining host - probably a dramatic writer, for masks lie at his feet - has sometimes been identified as Dionysios' friend Ikarios, who introduced the culture of the wine in Greece. The scene is set in front of a continuous architectural background, with landscape elements. An interest in landscape first arose in Alexandrine circles, but such pictorial reliefs as this one probably owed their popularity during the 1st century B.C. to the naturalistic tastes of the Roman clients who patronized the Greek artists.

218 *Youth and dolphin* · Roman copy of a Hellenistic original. Museo Nazionale, Naples.

In their Campanian summer villas, wealthy Romans surrounded themselves with numerous art works, mostly inspired by Hellenistic models, but often of very high quality. This young Eros embracing a dolphin, one of the minor figures often depicted in the marine *thiasos* of Neptune and Amphitrite, was intended as the central element of a fountain. The interlaced bodies of dolphin and boy are inscribed in a spiral-shaped composition whose dynamism raises the work above decorative banality.

218

219

219 *Dancing Pygmy* · Bronze · Hellenistic · Musée de Bardo, Tunis.

This pygmy playing castanets comes from a sunken ship found off Mahdia on the Tunisian coast. The ship must have sailed there in about 80 B.C., carrying its assortment of Greek art works destined for the capital of the empire. Pygmies had already been represented during the archaic period (a combat between pygmies and cranes is depicted on the François vase), but they became particularly fashionable in the Graeco-Roman period. To the "Nilotic" scenes so frequent in mosaics and paintings, they imparted much appreciated exotic flavor, while allowing the artist to ridicule human behavior through their grotesqueness.

221

220 *Draped, standing woman,* from Tanagra · Terra cotta · Hellenistic · The Louvre, Paris.

In 1870-71, clandestine excavations in the necropolis of Tanagra in Boeotia awoke collectors and archeologists to the artistic interest and copious diffusion throughout the Hellenistic world of small clay statuettes. The Tanagra workshops concentrated their activity on the single theme of the draped young woman, but there are numerous variations in their gestures, attitudes and draperies. Their elegance and their slightly affected grace reflect larger works, particularly Praxitelean ones. After being fired, the statuettes were retouched and covered with bright colors of a sometimes doubtful taste.

221 *The Titeux Dancer,* from Tanagra · Terra cotta · Hellenistic · The Louvre, Paris.

The products of Boeotian workshops (which included Thebes, Thespiae, and Elatea as well as Tanagra) were very popular already in the 4th century B.C. Their figurines were exported far afield and were imitated in minor centers. In these statuettes, aesthetic appeal was more important than the religious significance that had made earlier terra cottas mere utilitarian objects. Tanagra figurines were household ornaments, even if they seem occasionally to suggest religious significance. This secularization of small objects, which were now considered as ends in themselves, connotes the great religious and social changes that had occurred in the Hellenistic world.

222 *Draped woman,* from Myrina · Terra cotta · Hellenistic · The Louvre, Paris.

After Tanagra, the most important center for the production of terra cotta figurines was the small city of Myrina in Aeolis, halfway between Pergamon and Smyrna. It rose in importance from the 3rd to the 1st century B.C., as Boeotian workshops declined. The repertory is more varied than that of Tanagra, but the influence of Boeotian models and types is everywhere obvious, as in this graceful figure of a woman walking. The great number of different signatures and workshop marks point to a highly organized industry, and it is now believed that the neighboring town of Kyme was actually responsible for a great part of Myrina's production.

222

220

223

223 *Man's head*, from Asia Minor · Hellenistic · The Louvre, Paris.

In Asia Minor, alongside the Myrina workshops with their graceful creations, there existed smaller artistic centers whose utterly different production was marked by a fierce realism and a taste for caricature. This head (12 inches high) is typical of those grotesque and dramatic works: it represents a bald man with markedly negroid features, the lower part of the face appearing as though deformed by some disease. The skull is decorated with a band on which are fixed two clusters of ivy berries. The work, vividly alive, was not cast, as were most such small objects, but modelled.

224

224 *Deformed man*, from Smyrna · Terra cotta · Hellenistic · The Louvre, Paris.

Their taste for anything bizarre or exaggerated prompted Hellenistic artists to investigate physiological malformations. This inclination is particularly marked in the Smyrna figurines, such as this deformed little man (3 inches high). The enormous head with its beaky nose is attached directly, without any neck, to a body with an exaggerated hump and atrophied legs. Among the Hellenistic centers producing terra-cotta statuettes, Smyrna was one of the most interesting owing to the technical researches pursued there concerning clays, glazings and colors.

225 *Figure of an actor*, from southern Italy · Terra cotta · Hellenistic · The Louvre, Paris.

This (9 inches high) represents an actor in an exaggeratedly rhetorical pose, wearing a false nose and a false belly. Hellenistic terra cottas are a mine of information on the antique theater in the epochs of the Middle and New Comedy. Since this lively figurine came from a south Italian workshop, it must represent a traditional character from one of the largely improvised popular comedies called *Atellanae* (after the little town of Atella in Campania), which were a species of ancestor to the Commedia dell'Arte.

225

226 *Horse* · Chalcedony gem-stone · Greek, 350-300 B.C. · Museum of Fine Arts, Boston.

Engraving on gem-stones was a minor art, but an extremely refined one, owing to the demanding miniaturist technique it required. This chalcedony (6 inches high) is shaped like Egyptian scarabs, examples of which the Phoenicians had spread through the Mediterranean countries as early as the 8th century B.C. It is remarkable for the harmonious solidity of the figure cut from the middle of the surface and for its exceptionally delicate finish. It has been attributed to Dexamenos of Chios, the most famous of Greek engravers.

226

227 *Glass mask* from Carthage · 8th to 4th centuries B.C. · Bardo Museum, Tunis.

Pliny attributes the invention of glass to the Phoenicians; in fact it did appear in the Near East in the middle of the 2nd millennium, and if it was not invented by the seafaring traders of Phoenicia, it at least owes its spread to them. The production around Carthage from the 8th to the 4th centuries B.C. is practically limited to the making of amulets in terra cotta and glazed paste. Most typical are these little masks in colored glass, intended to be hung up to drive away the evil eye. Shoddy goods of this nature were exported in great quantity.

227

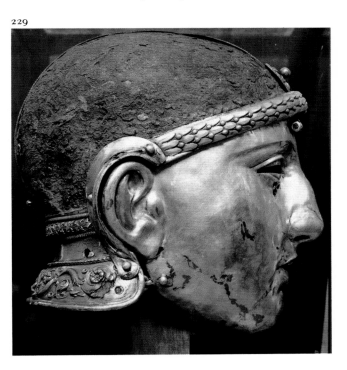

229 *Parade helmet in the form of a portrait* · Iron, gold, and silver · Syrian, 100–50 B.C. · National Museum, Damascus.

This full-dress helmet in silvered iron, with gold as well, was discovered during clandestine excavations at Homs, the ancient Emesa, in Syria. Helmet and portrait-mask combined, it protected the head completely; a hinge on the forehead allowed the opening of the face part, which could be fastened shut below the ear. The very narrow slit for the eyes was supplemented by a trefoil aperture that enlarged the visual field. The diadem decorated with a rosette, and the neck guard, are delicately chased. A work at once barbaric and refined, this helmet must have belonged to a member of the Greco-Arabic dynasty that ruled at Emesa under the patronage of Rome.

229

228 *Syrian musicians on a camel* · Terra cotta · Syro-Roman · The Louvre, Paris.

The somewhat coarse figurine, 9 inches high, comes from the Damascus region (possibly Palmyra). It represents two women sitting on a camel, under a kind of hood; one plays a double flute, the other rests her hands on a flat object, probably a tambourine or a zither. They are two musicians following in the train of one of those Syrian divinities whose cult spread throughout the Roman empire, particularly in the 3rd century, at the time of Syrian empresses. Apart from the camel, the oriental character of the work is marked by the frontal representation of the two priestesses.

228

230 *Female statue* from Ibiza, Balearic Islands · Terra cotta · 2nd–1st century B.C. · Museo Arqueologico Nacional, Madrid.

Ibiza, the largest of the Pithyusae Islands and a regular port-of-call for ships between Sicily and the Iberian peninsula, was one of the most important bases of the Phoenicians in the western Mediterranean. Excavations there have turned up vestiges of Punic burial grounds and sanctuaries dating from the 7th to the 5th century B.C. A great many terra-cotta votive statues of rather stylized form have been found. They are remarkable for the extremely lavish decoration of the clothing and jewelry. Skillful workers in wrought metal, the Phoenicians played a prime role in spreading the techniques and designs of Eastern goldsmith work.

230

165

231

231 *Votive statue* from Cerro de los Santos (Albacete) · Museo Arqueologico Nacional, Madrid.

The metal-bearing resources of the Iberian peninsula made it a prize hotly disputed between Greeks and Phoenicians. Under their combined influence a new civilization came into being in southeast Spain, flourishing, from the 5th to the 3rd centuries B.C., in the region lying between Alicante and Cordova. Iberian art owes the existence of its stone statuary to the Greeks, while Punic influence is clear in the minute detail of dress and jewelry. Although lacking the same hieratic monumentality, the "Dama del Cerro," a priestess or holy woman holding a ritual vessel, recalls the famous "Lady of Elche" in her richness of dress.

232 *Two-headed Hermes* from Roquepertuse (Bouches-du-Rhône) · Celto-Ligurian, 3rd to 2nd centuries B.C. · Musée Archéologique Borély, Marseilles.

The monumental portico of the sanctuary at Roquepertuse, formed by three jamb-posts on which appear representations of severed human heads, is surmounted by a lintel dominated in the center by a large bird of prey, probably a funerary symbol. The two-headed "Hermes," carved in stone and 12½ inches long, was positioned at one end as an acroterium. The tenons appearing on one side show that it was set in profile. Between the two "Hermes" heads loomed a bird of prey whose sharp beak is still visible. This work, as indeed the whole portico, was painted.

232

233 *Warrior's head* from Entremont (Bouches-du-Rhône) · Stone. Celto-Ligurian, 3rd–2nd cent. B.C. · Musée Granet, Aix-en-Provence.

In the wake of Celtic infiltration, two major sites of Celto-Ligurian civilization flourished from the early 4th century to the north of the Greek coastline of Provence: Roquepertuse and Entremont. Many remains of sculpture were discovered on the sites of sanctuaries with propylaea that had been destroyed about 125 B.C. during the Roman conquest of Provence. The influence of Mediterranean art is evident in this emaciated head (12 inches high), particularly in the treatment of the hair, the exophthalmic eyes, and the outline of the nose and of the forehead.

233

234

234 *Severed head*, from Entremont · Stone · Celto-Ligurian, 3rd to 2nd centuries B.C. · Musée Granet, Aix-en-Provence.

According to the Greeks, the Celts used to embalm the heads of important enemies they had slain. In the Celto-Ligurian civilization, the role of severed heads seems to have been especially important. Real, engraved, or carved, they adorned the sanctuary pillars and lintels, and within there were to be found statues of crouching men placing their left hands on lifeless heads. A victory sign, perhaps? Or are they deceased men who, in the beyond, lay hands upon a head which contains their soul? Whatever the meaning, this limestone head (9 inches high) with half-closed eyes, projecting cheek bones and turned-down lip-corners, exudes a tragic sense of death.

236

235

235 *Head* from Mšecke Žehrovice (Prague) · Limestone · Celtic, 2nd century B.C. · National Museum, Prague.

Outside the Celto-Ligurian realms, Celtic sculpture is scarce. One of the few examples that has appeared east of the Rhine is from Bohemia. This curious head, 10 inches high, is much more stylized than Celto-Ligurian works, but the use of the spiral is a typically Celtic feature. The ears and the hair – which is reduced to a band surmounting the forehead – are likewise treated ornamentally. The neck is decorated with a Celtic torque. It is probably the figure of a hero from some sanctuary, and must be from the 2nd century B.C., when Celtic power was at its height in Bohemia.

237 *Head of the God Zeus-Ahuramazda*, at Nimrud-Dagh (see fig. 236).

The colossal statues erected on one of the summits of the Antitaurus Mountains by Antiochus I were probably toppled by an earthquake. Their iconography and style reveal a combination of Greek and Iranian elements.

237

236 *Sepulchral sanctuary of Antiochus I at Nimrud-Dagh* · Anatolia, 1st century B.C.

Commagenia, a little kingdom lying northwest of the Parthian Empire, was governed in the 1st century B.C. by a prince who styled himself a lover of Greece while proclaiming his Achaemenid ancestry: Antiochus I (69-34 B.C.). The monument he set up to the glory of his deified father in the Antitaurus mountains in Turkey reflects this dual adhesion: on two terraces situated to the east and west of a high artificial hill were erected seated colossi representing Antiochus surrounded by his protecting deities taken from the Greco-Iranian pantheon: Zeus-Ahuramazda, Apollo-Mithras, Hercules-Verethragna, and the goddess Commagenia. Both as to religious ideas and style, here materialized is Alexander's dream of unity.

238 *Medallion with young man's head*, from Afghanistan · Plaster · 1st century B.C. · National Museum of Afghanistan, Kabul.

At Begram, the ancient capital of Kapisa (possibly the Nicaea mentioned by Arrian), situated northwest of Kabul, the French Archeological Delegation in Afghanistan discovered an exceptionally important group of art objects in two walled-up rooms of a palace. There were plaster models, glass and bronze objects of Mediterranean origin, Indian ivories and Japanese lacquer. The rooms appear to have been walled up about the middle of the 3rd century A.D. Among the plaster models was this fine medallion in high relief.

238

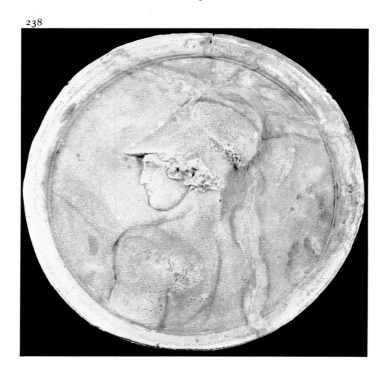

240

240 *Warrior* from Capestrano · Limestone · Etruscan, late 6th century B.C. · Museo Archeologico, Chieti.

This over life-size representation of an armed chieftain comes from a necropolis hidden in the mountains of Picenum (near Aquila). The curious armor and the faithfully detailed weapons would seem to date from the end of the 6th century B.C. The figure wears a metal mask beneath his great crested helmet. The two side supports (one with an undeciphered inscription) have suggested to some that the statue illustrates the primitive custom of exposing the deceased at his funeral, standing, and supported by his weapons. This custom appears to have been followed for a long time by the Roman patrician families in Rome, for it provoked the astonishment of Polybius the Greek as late as the 2nd century B.C.

239 *Statue of mother-goddess* · Tufa · Italic, 4th to 3rd centuries B.C. · Museo Provinciale Campano, Capua.

This tuff-stone statue, representing a mother-goddess sitting on a throne and holding several infants in her arms, is one of the numerous ex-votos found in the Italic "Matres" sanctuary that was discovered at Fondo Patturella, near Santa Maria di Capua Vetere. The earlier ex-votos were clearly influenced by Greece, but later works, like this one, show by their expressive qualities a local, Italic, approach to sculpture. The goddess's imposing seated posture, the drapery folds angularly cut, the number of stylized infants, combine to make this coarse work a powerful evocation of maternity.

239

241 *Apollo*, from Veii · Terra cotta · Etruscan, ca. 500 B.C. · Museo Nazionale di Villa Giulia, Rome.

This terra-cotta statue of Apollo stood with other statues as an acroterium on the roof of the temple of Veii. The god advances irresistibly towards Hercules, to take from him the hind of Mount Cerynea. His Ionian garb – chiton and himation – clings to his body in the strong wind. The figure's extraordinary vitality is accentuated by the rich polychrome. It is tempting to attribute this masterpiece of ancient art to the only Etruscan artist whose name tradition has preserved for us: Vulca of Veii, who worked in Rome during the last years of the 6th century.

242 *Chimera*, from Arezzo · Bronze · Etruscan(?), 5th–4th centuries B.C. · Museo Archeologico, Florence.

The chimera, a monster of Eastern origin made up of a lion's body and a dragon's tail, is depicted with muscles tensed and back arched in a last desperate effort; but the goat's head growing from its back is already dying from a wound on its neck. The sculpture of the chimera's attacker, Bellerophon, has disappeared. Despite the stylization of the locks of hair and the ornamental character of the head, the bronze forms quiver with life and pain. The statue's origin and the date have been much disputed: some consider its powerfully expressive quality as the mark of an authentically Etruscan creation; others regard this chimera as an imported Greek work.

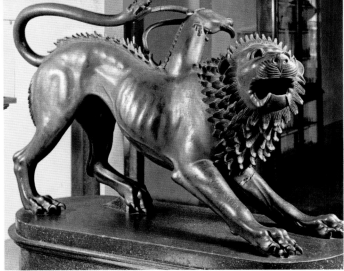

242

241

243

243 *Husband and wife*; sarcophagus from Cervetri · Terra cotta ·
Etruscan, late 6th century B.C. · Museo Nazionale di Villa Giula, Rome.

The Etruscans often used terra cotta to produce large-scale works, as
in this famous sarcophagus depicting a dead couple reclining. Their
tender and intimate pose reveals the exceptional consideration that
women enjoyed in Etruscan society. The pointed shoes and the dome-
shaped cap *(tutulus)* are typically Etruscan. The decoration of the
kline (couch) and the delicate, smiling faces with their incisive profiles and almond eyes reveal the Ionian inspiration in this work, which
is a splendid example of the vivacity and refinement of archaic Etruscan art.

244 *Funerary urn decorated with reliefs*, from Chiusi · Stone · Etruscan, late 6th century B.C. · Museo Archeologico, Florence.

During the archaic era, Chiusi produced characteristic urns shaped like
little houses; here the lid imitating a pitched roof has disappeared.
These urns were usually made in *pietra fetida*, with decorations carved
in very low relief. The subject most often represented is the funeral
banquet; lying on couches and surrounded by servants, entertainers
and domestic animals, the deceased take part in an endless feast. The
costumes and the very heavy forms reveal strong Ionian influence;
according to the most generally accepted tradition, reported by Herodotus, the Etruscans originally came from Asia Minor.

244

245 *The death of Actaeon* · Alabaster · Etruscan, Hellenistic period · Museo Guarnacci, Volterra.

During the Hellenistic era the northern towns of Etruria, particularly Volterra, produced great numbers of alabaster urns elaborately carved and enlivened by color. The carved decoration is inspired by Greek mythology, but shows a marked preference for violent scenes. On this urn is depicted the punishment of Actaeon, who was changed into a stag and torn apart by his own dogs. On the right, balancing the scene, is a draped figure, a stereotype from the Hellenistic repertoire, which proves that model books were used. Such workmanlike pieces as this were rapidly executed; here, the deeply cut relief accentuates the dramatic character of the scene with shadow-filled hollows.

245

246 *Tydeus*, one of the Seven against Thebes (detail of a relief on an urn) · Alabaster · Etruscan, Hellenistic period · Museo Guarnacci, Volterra.

This detail, from an alabaster urn depicting the siege of Thebes by seven allied chiefs, shows the hero, Tydeus, beneath the walls of the city, gripping a severed head – a bloody episode not to be found in the Greek literary tradition. Both the gate and the powerful, arched body of the hero are shown at an angle, in an attempt to create an illusion of depth. The great originality of this piece lies in the attempt to transpose into sculpture the spatial conquests of painting, thereby initiating the illusionistic relief that was to be developed in Roman art.

246

247

247 *Head of a tomb figure* · Etruscan, Hellenistic period · Ny Carlsberg Glyptotek, Copenhagen.

On the lids of Etruscan urns and sarcophagi the dead person was represented in reclining position partaking of an eternal banquet. The realism typical of such sculpture in the round during the Hellenistic period contrasts with the heroic character of the decoration on the sarcophagi themselves, and it seems that the lids and urns must have been made quite independently of each other. The bodies are flaccid and stereotyped, and the entire interest is concentrated on the heads, which are individualized with powerful realism. The dead man here has no illusions, he is resigned and serene, and this in itself is quite exceptional because usually these funerary portraits are almost painfully hyper-realistic.

248

248 *Tomb with stucco reliefs*, at Cervetri · Etruscan, 3rd century B.C.

Illusionism in sculpture is pushed to an extreme in this famous carved tomb at Cervetri, where the overall form imitates a house interior, and the painted stucco reliefs create an illusion of many domestic objects hanging from nails on a wall. The central *loculus* flanked by Aeolian capitals takes the form of an alcove bed with carved legs. It was doubtless intended for a woman, judging by the objects which surround it: vessels, a fan, a necklace, and sandals set on the low table. The decoration of this tomb is of considerable interest for a knowledge of everyday life in Etruria in the 3rd century B.C.

249

250 *The Capitoline Brutus* · Bronze · Etruscan or Roman, 3rd century B.C. · Palazzo dei Conservatori, Rome.

Since the Renaissance, many have believed that this magnificent bust represents L. Junius Brutus, who in 509 B.C., according to tradition, liberated Rome from the Etruscan yoke and became the first consul of the Republic. The handsome, bony face animated by an intense inner life would in this case have to be a reconstituted portrait, for the work could date from no earlier than the 3rd century B.C. It is interesting to note, however, that the delicate features and disheveled beard and hair are not without resemblance to the profile, on coins of 59 B.C., of Marcus Brutus, Caesar's future assassin, who claimed descent from the illustrious 6th-century patrician.

249 *Family stele of L. Vibius* · Roman, 1st century B.C. · Vatican Museums, Rome.

The concern with likeness and the detailed realism that characterize late Republican Roman portraits doubtless owe much to the tradition of commemorating deceased ancestors by means of wax masks, which in patrician homes were kept in a special room and exhibited at ceremonies. The faces of L. Vibius, his wife, and his child recall death masks. The frontal presentation of these half-length figures is characteristic of a popular trend which continued to exist in Roman art parallel with the official, classicizing art.

251 *Augustus as Pontifex Maximus* · Marble · Roman, 27 B.C. – 14 A.D. · Museo Nazionale Romano, Rome.

Official statues of Augustus usually represented him carrying out one of his two main duties: that of *imperator*, commander of the Roman army, or of high priest. This statue found in the via Labicana shows a mature Augustus, clad in a toga, preparing to sacrifice to the gods; his bearing is majestic, and his face expresses *gravitas*. The head was carved separately (as were the right arm and left hand, now lost) and fitted onto the body; its workmanship is remarkable. There are traces of polychromy on the toga.

250

251

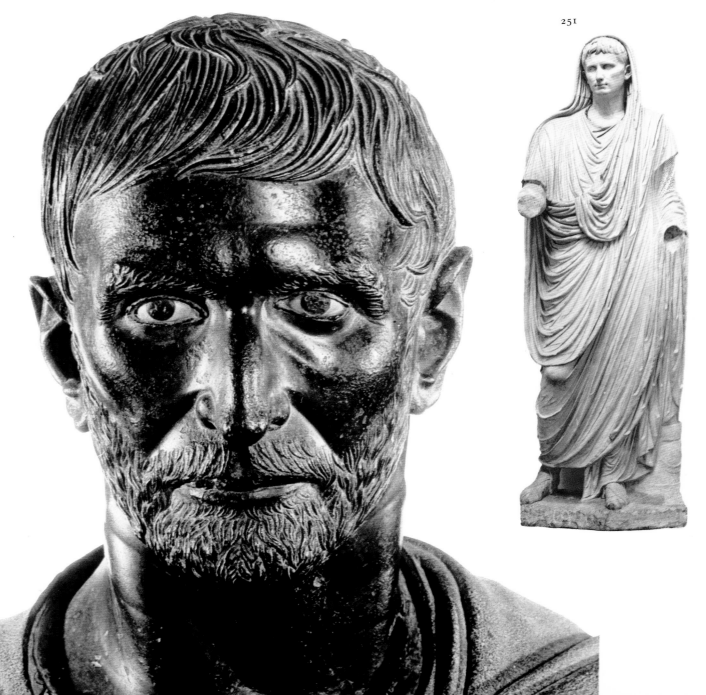

171

252

252 *Procession* on the north wall of the Ara Pacis · Marble · Roman, 13-9 B.C. · Lungotevere in Augusta, Rome.

On the long surfaces of the north and south walls a procession unfolds, probably depicting that which took place when the monument was consecrated. Identification of the figures is in dispute; the heads have to a large extent been recarved. On the north wall, the senators who voted this altar in homage to the emperor are slowly walking, laurel-crowned and hieratically draped in their togas. Official Augustan art rediscovered the classicism of Greek reliefs, from which it borrowed the neutral background and isocephalic representation of the figures. However, a rather formal solemnity, which is characteristic of Roman *dignitas* emanates from the scene.

253 *Allegory of the Earth*, on the Ara Pacis · Marble · Roman, 13-9 B.C. · Lungotevere in Augusta, Rome.

The enclosure-wall of the Ara Pacis was pierced by doors on the east and west ends, and on either side of the doors were reliefs of allegorical and legendary characters. The best-preserved depicts a buxom young mother sitting on a rock. She is generally identified as Tellus, the Earth, flanked by personifications of Air and Water; others regard her instead as the image of Italy. The theme of Earth pacified and rendered fertile is developed in parallel fashion in literature, as poets and sculptors collaborated in the great program of return to tradition, originated by Augustus.

253

254 *Ornamental relief* on the Ara Pacis Augustae · Marble · Roman, 13-9 B.C. · Lungotevere in Augusta, Rome.

The Ara Pacis Augustae, erected on the Campus Martius from 13 to 9 B.C. was intended to commemorate the restoration of peace throughout the Empire after Augustus, victorious campaigns in Gaul and Spain. Its sculptural decoration reflects the Emperor's desire for order, which in official art is marked by classic discipline. The lower part of the marble wall surrounding the altar is covered with an extended floral design; acanthus rinceaux burst forth in pliant but symmetrical foliated scrolls between which moves a host of little animals. Natural fantasy and ornamental severity are balanced in this lively creation which has assimilated the discoveries of Hellenistic art.

255 *Sacrificial procession* · Roman, late 1st century B.C. - early 1st century A.D. · The Louvre, Paris.

This bas-relief shows the Suovetaurilia, the traditional sacrifice performed on great occcasions of an ox, a lamb and a pig. This ceremony, characteristic of Roman religious pragmatism, is a frequent theme in official art. The classicizing purity of this relief obviously derives from the Ara Pacis friezes. It has sometimes been suggested that the principal figure, who carries out the preliminary libations at the altar, is the Emperor Tiberius, successor to Augustus (the face is largely a modern restoration). The trees behind the altar may represent the two laurels solemnly planted before Augustus' house on the Palatine in 28 B.C.

255

256 *Gemma Augustae* · Engraved cameo (sardonyx) · By a Greek artist working in Rome in the 1st century A.D. · Kunsthistorisches Museum, Vienna.

As a result of the war led by Sulla (99-80 B.C.) against Mithridates, King of Pontus, which devastated Asia Minor, the artisans who had been working there for a luxury clientele emigrated to Rome. In the reign of Augustus, Dioskurides the engraver founded there a whole dynasty of gem-cutters. Rightly or wrongly, the Gemma Augustae, an exceptionally large cameo (8 by 9 inches), has been attributed to him. The scene commemorates the triumph of Tiberius after the surrender of Dalmatia and Pannonia in 9 A.D., and it offers a veritable manifesto of official Augustan mythology.

256

257

257 *Head of the young Augustus* · Marble · Roman, 27 B.C. - 14 A.D. · Musée Lapidaire, Arles.

Supreme master after the battle of Actium in 30 B.C., Octavian set up the system of the Principate and three yards later took the name Augustus. His effigies, discovered in great numbers (more than a hundred have been counted) in all parts of the Empire, demonstrate the importance attached to emperor worship. They all show the same regular, delicate face; according to his contemporaries, Augustus was, indeed, a handsome man, but the idealism with which his official portraits are marked is the result of a conscious intent to place before all eyes a serene image of the master of a pacified world.

258

258 *Head of Octavia* (?) · Basalt · Roman, ca. 40 B.C. · The Louvre, Paris.

The subject of this coldly elegant portrait, carved from Egyptian basalt, is thought to be either Livia, the second wife of Augustus, or, more probably, her sister Octavia, the wife of Antony. The strictness of the family customs reintroduced by the Emperor is reflected in the austere, dignified faces of the great Imperial ladies. The "Octavia" hair style, with the broad roll of hair over the forehead and wavy bands drawn down into a bun on the nape of the neck, is characteristic of the time of the second Triumvirate. Feminine hair styles in Roman art provide an invaluable guide to dating.

259 *Bust of young boy*, from Pozzuoli · Marble · Roman, 1st century A.D. · Museo Barracco, Rome.

During the Julio-Claudian era, under the influence of imperial iconography the portrait tended to become idealized; individuals had themselves represented in the same fashion as the princes. In this bust of a young boy can be seen the delicate features and short, casually arranged locks of hair common in portraits of Augustus; however, the artist has succeeded in expressing the charm of his young model's visage, as yet not stamped with a definitive personality. During the Julio-Claudian period, the portrait bust stopped at a rounded line just below the collarbone; later, as the torso became increasingly important, the portrait also included the shoulders.

259

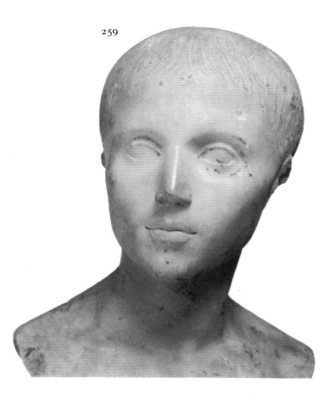

260 *Bust, called "Clytie"* · Marble · Roman, 1st century A.D. · British Museum, London.

This bust, which still recalls the grace of Hellenistic female representations, is related to the classicizing movement of the 1st century. It has been thought that it might portray the beautiful Antonia Minora, wife of Drusus I, who appears on the Ara Pacis Augustae. However, it might be an allegorical representation, for the bust rises from a corolla of flowers. In the 18th century this was the most famous work in the Townley collection in London; it was called Isis, or, by Townley himself, Clytie. The nymph Clytie was loved by the Sun and deserted by him for the love of Leucothea; she killed her rival, but was punished by the Sun; she pined away and turned into a heliotrope, the flower that always turns its face toward the sun.

260

261

261 Landscape scene · Stucco · Roman, ca. 30 B.C. · Museo delle Terme, Rome.

The houses of wealthy Romans were ornamented with ceiling stuccos, as well as floor mosaics and frescos on the walls. In the gardens of the Farnesina near the Tiber were discovered the decorated vaults of an exceptionally well-preserved residence dating from the beginning of Augustus' reign. Foliated scrolls frame mythological scenes and light, airy architectural landscapes peopled by lively little figures. These fragile reliefs, swiftly and impressionistically executed on a preparatory drawing, reveal the same note of fantasy, the same unreality, and the same escapist taste as contemporary painting.

262

262 Horseman, from the Cartoceto di Pergola group · Bronze, gilt · Roman, 1st century A.D. · Museo Nazionale, Ancona.

Discovered in a border district, this major sculptural group poses a problem of identification. S. Stucchi has suggested that the two horsemen represent Nero Caesar and Drusus Caesar, sons of Germanicus and Agrippina. Heirs to the Empire, they were banished during the reign of Tiberius, in 30 A.D., and the destruction of the group might be explained by this *adamnatio memoriae*. This hypothesis, however, is difficult to accept; the horseman with the wide, balding forehead bears only a very slight resemblance to other portraits of Nero Caesar. The work does appear to date from the Julio-Claudian era; but the view that it depicts members of the Imperial family probably must be discarded.

263 Horse's head, from Cartoceto di Pergola (Pesaro) · Bronze, gilt · Roman, 1st century A.D. · Museo Nazionale, Ancona.

This head was among the fragments of a gilt bronze group found in 1949 in a ditch at Cartoceto di Pergola in the district of Pesaro. The whole composition, in spite of patient efforts at restoration, has still not been entirely reconstituted. It comprised at least four figures larger than life-size: two women and two horsemen. The statues, made of separately cast bronze pieces welded together, seem to have been purposefully and methodically destroyed. The importance of the figures represented is demonstrated by the sumptuous trappings of the horses, who wear *phalerae* decorated with busts of the gods.

263

175

264 *Bust of L. Caecilius Jucundus* · Bronze · Roman, 1st century A.D. · Museo Nazionale, Naples.

When the Flavian dynasty, which was of plebeian stock, came to power in 69 A.D,, realism reasserted itself in the art of portraiture. The bust format typical of work done in Rome was the ultimate stage in the Etrusco-Italiote tendency to concentrate all interest on the face as most revealing of expression and personality. Here, the sculptor strove to capture, down to the finest detail, both the intelligence and the homeliness of the banker he portrayed. Despite this emphasis on individualism, the work preserves all the organic coherence of Hellenistic portraits. The bust done at the commission of a freedman was found in the banker's villa in Pompeii.

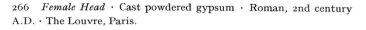

265 *Hadrian* · Marble · Roman, 2nd century A.D. · Museo delle Terme, Rome.

Of Spanish origin, Hadrian was adopted as successor to Trajan in 117. Great pacifist and tireless traveller, he managed to stabilize the Empire after the conquests of his predecessors. His reign, and in fact the whole Antonine era, represents the golden age of the Roman Empire, seen as a huge and homogeneous world state. This marble bust, a little larger than life-size, reproduces the emperor's mobile face in rather idealized fashion. An impassioned admirer of Hellenism, Hadrian was the first ruler to adopt the short beard of the Greek philosophers, thereby establishing a fashion which was to become quite widespread.

266 *Female Head* · Cast powdered gypsum · Roman, 2nd century A.D. · The Louvre, Paris.

This life size bust (17 inches) is nearly complete; one can in fact make out at the base the rounded shape with which it ends. It shows a woman in the prime of life, whose characteristic hair styling places her in the 2nd century A.D., although the detail on the eyeball - the hollowed pupil and the iris circumscribed by a line - could point to a later date. The complicated hairdress is formed by hair pulled up at the back in fine strands (visible on the rear of the skull), then formed into braids that are wound and crossed over each other making a kind of turban. The rather rare medium is a sort of gypsum powder, set with a bonding element, formed in a mold. The process of modelling suited the realism of the Roman portraitists even better than direct carving in marble.

267

267 *Group from St. Ildephonse* · Marble · Roman, 1st century B.C. · Prado, Madrid.

The conquest of Grecia Magna first, then of Asia Minor and of Hellas itself in the mid-2nd century B.C., increased the flow of Greek art works to Rome. The fascination that Greek art held for the Romans is shown by the innumerable copies that were made of famous Greek sculptures, copies that very often provide us with the only form we know of those pieces. The work of art, having become simply a luxury item, provided an excuse for a skillful manipulation of diverse forms. Characteristic of the resultant eclectic style is this group, which combines an archaistic karyatid, a Praxitelean youth, and a Polykleitan youth.

268

269

269 *Pan* · Marble · Neo-Attic work of the Roman period · British Museum, London.

After the sack of Athens by Sulla in 86 B.C., the Neo-Attic art workshops were transported to Rome where their leading role in the spread of Greek models continued until the Antonine era. The skillful craftsmen (who usually preceded their signature with the epithet "Athenaios") were inspired by all the phases of Greek art, archaic, classic, or Hellenistic. This stylistic indifference resulted in creations that are coldly decorative, with virtuosity replacing inspiration. The statue of the god Pan belongs to the mode for archaizing works that took their models from the academic art of the end of the 5th century rather than from true archaic prototypes.

268 *Dionysios and the Graces*, from Leptis Magna · Roman, early 2nd century, A.D.

The excavations at Leptis Magna have brought to light a number of statues showing what rich and diverse styles might converge in a Roman city situated on the borderline between the Empire and the Orient. Elements of Berber, Greek, and Roman styles may in fact be seen in the abundant surviving sculpture. Leptis Magna was already a center of intense artistic production, and attracted specialists from all the countries surrounding the Mediterranean. This relief shows an archaizing taste, of a kind that had led the Hellenistic Greek amateurs to seek out for their collections Greek art from the 6th century. The Roman world followed the Hellenes, creating imitations in an archaizing style reminiscent of the "Etruscan" manner invented by late 18th-century English decorators.

177

The arch at Benevento, built in 114 in Trajan's honor, marked the junction of the Via Appia and the new Via Traiana. This new road, cutting short the route to Brindisi, was intended to improve communications with the East, where Trajan continued his conquests up to his death in 117. The difficult balance between architectural structure and applied decoration is admirably maintained here; the dynamism of the carved reliefs, separately framed and coordinated on the façade, is balanced by the high smooth bases and the great unified mass of the dedicatory inscription on the attic.

271 *Column of Trajan* · Marble · Roman, 106–113 A.D. · Forum of Trajan, Rome.

Trajan, a soldier-emperor, created an iconography appropriate to the militance of Imperial Rome. The triumphal column celebrating his victory over the Dacians is decorated with a continuous spiral of reliefs which expresses the conquering spirit far more effectively than battle scenes in the Greek tradition, in which individual combatants are opposed as symbols. Here, the figures are placed in superposed ranks, as if the viewer, like the commander, surveyed the battlefield from a high viewpoint. The dynamic composition binds the participants into a single action.

273 *Marching army*, relief on the column of Marcus Aurelius · Marble · Roman, 180–193 A.D. · Piazza Colonna, Rome.

The two campaigns waged by the Emperor in the Danube district against the Quadi and the Marcomanni in 172–3 and against the Sarmatae in 174–5, are represented on the column erected in honor of Marcus Aurelius on the Campus Martius in Rome. Imitating the design of Trajan's column, this monument is decorated in a very different spirit. The balance of the composition is broken up by a medley of hectic shapes; the high-relief, worked with a drill, expresses in a dramatic chiaroscuro the sufferings caused by a ferocious war.

272 *Soldiers climbing a stockade*, bas-relief on Trajan's column · Marble · Roman, 106–113 A.D. · Forum of Trajan, Rome.

In its long, spiral-shaped decoration (23 turns, over 600 feet), Trajan's column tells the story of the two victorious campaigns of Trajan in Roumania against the Dacians from 101 to 106. The relief is very low and does not break the architectural unity of the monument. The scenes are linked in a lively, continuous narration, with the figure of the Emperor recurring as a leitmotiv. This clear, harmonious composition is the outcome of a very learned art. It was probably through the influence of paintings used for triumphs that Hellenistic relief developed into the sober, realistic historical art of Rome.

272

274

274 *Equestrian statue of Marcus Aurelius* · Bronze · Roman, ca. 170-180 A.D. · Piazza del Campidoglio, Rome.

During his long reign, Marcus Aurelius (161-180) saw the stability of the Roman Empire shaken - for the first time the force of the barbarians made itself felt on the borders as a real danger, and the philosopher-emperor was obliged to lead a soldier's life. This large equestrian statue in gilded bronze probably adorned the upper part of a triumphal arch. The emperor is depicted with his right arm raised in the *ad locutio* gesture. Miraculously preserved (the early Christians believed it to represent Constantine), the effigy was placed by Michelangelo at the center of his Piazza del Campidoglio. Its influence over equestrian monuments of the Renaissance was considerable.

275 *Sacrifice of Marcus Aurelius* · Marble · Roman, 2nd century A.D. · Palazzo dei Conservatori, Rome.

This monumental relief very probably comes from a triumphal arch. It represents Marcus Aurelius, who with veiled head makes the preliminary libations of a sacrifice. The scene takes place before the façade of a temple, probably that of Jupiter Capitolinus at Rome. By fulfillment of the rites, the emperor ensured the proper functioning of the universe - an idea fundamental to the imperial mystique that developed during the 2nd century, which explains why this scene recurs so often in official art. The composition still falls within the classicizing tradition of Hadrianic times, but the heads, with their incised pupils and tumbled hair, have a new expressive intensity.

275

276

276 *Head of Antinous* · Marble · Roman, ca. 140 A.D. · Museo Nazionale, Naples.

The death of his young favorite, Antinous, drowned in the waters of the Nile in 130, left Hadrian inconsolable. He established an official cult to him and caused numerous effigies of the departed to be carved; in these he found an opportunity to give expression to his taste for Greek art. Commissioned for the most part from Asiatic artists, these statues belong to the tradition of classical ephebe sculpture; but the sensual, melancholy face of the young Bithynian is always quite recognizable. The contrast between the polished flesh surfaces and the complex locks of the hair is characteristic of portraits from the Antonine era.

277 *Frieze* from the Triumphal Arch of Septimius Severus, Leptis Magna (detail) · Roman, beginning of the 2nd century A.D.

Four marble bas-reliefs with figures two-thirds life-size decorated the triumphal arch erected by Septimius Severus shortly after 202 at the crossroads of the *cardo* and *decumanus* of the city of Leptis Magna in Tripolitania. These bas-reliefs show a completely new orientation in Roman plastic art. Under Augustus, an official classicizing tradition was formed in Rome, continuing under Trajan and taking on a refined and somewhat morbid character under Hadrian. The period of the Antonines, between 180 and 190, saw the beginning of a shift in emphasis from sculptural to coloristic effects. At Leptis Magna the evolution was accelerated; the artists who carved the imperial bas-reliefs made extensive use of the drill, which imparts a marked dryness to the relief and a rigidity that almost turns the folds into fluting.

279

279 *Medusa head*, from the Quadri-Portico of the Severian Forum at Leptis Magna · Roman, beginning of the 2nd century A.D.

In each of the spandrels between the arches of the great Quadri-Portico in front of the Severian basilica at Leptis Magna, there was a Gorgon or Medusa head in *imago clypeata* – that is, in the form of a shield. There are seventy of them, either still in place, or in the Castle Museum in Tripoli. These Gorgon heads, in Asiatic marble, had not only a decorative but also a propitious function. They must have been carved from a model by sculptors of varying ability. The most beautiful of them, like this one, exhibit a sense of grandeur which makes them masterpieces of antique monumental art.

278

278 *Pilaster showing the Dionysiac cycle*, in the Basilica of Septimius Severus at Leptis Magna · Roman, early 2nd century A.D.

The twisting vine tendrils, among which appear small frolicking animals and figures of gods and demigods, are a symbol of life borrowed from the cycle of Dionysiac legends, which were mingled with the cult of Liber Pater, Roman god of vegetation. As sculptured ornaments, these magnificent scrolls show a vigor and a refinement in modelling that is in strong contrast with the dryness of the reliefs on the triumphal arch. The drill was employed in conjunction with the chisel, however, and on some of the pilasters the sculptor shows a predilection for pictorial effects.

280

280 *Sarcophagus* · Marble · Roman · Museo Nazionale Romano, Rome.

The Barbarians represented in battle scenes on sarcophagi are the only ones shown dying under the blows of the victorious Romans. Their bearded faces, framed by thick hair, express mental as well as physical suffering. (See also detail fig. 281.) Through the iconography of the barbarian, pathos was introduced into Roman art.

282

282 *Portrait of Gordian III*, detail from the sarcophagus of Acilia (fig. 283) · Museo delle Terme, Rome.

An unusual modification has been worked in this symbolic representation: the head of the corner philosopher has been carved separately, and Prof. Bianchi Bandinelli has identified it as the young Gordian III, Emperor from 238 to 244. This obvious portrait contrasts with the other heads, which are "types" of philosophers in the Hellenistic tradition; but the pathetically tense expression of the figure bending forward just behind it makes it appear to be the very embodiment of meditation. The sculptor has contrasted the hair, which is worked with a drill, to the polished flesh textures.

283 *Sarcophagus of Acilia* · Marble · Roman, mid-3rd century A.D. · Museo delle Terme, Rome.

This sarcophagus - unfortunately very fragmentary - was discovered in the neighborhood of Rome, on the road to Ostia. Carved in high relief from a single block of Greek marble, the exceptionally large figures (47 inches high) have an effectively sculptural quality. The oval form allowing decoration in a continuous frieze is of Hellenic inspiration, Roman taste tending towards more discontinuous compositions. The subject - in accordance with one scheme of funerary decoration typical of the 3rd century - is a group of philosophers (there are *rotuli* at their feet) who, encircling the deceased man, ensure his immortality by their knowledge. The nine muses form a counterpart to them on the other side.

283

281

281 *Sarcophagus* (detail of fig. 280).

284

284 *Arch of Constantine*, in Rome · Roman, 315 A.D.

The triumphal arch celebrating Constantine's victory over Maxentius
at the Mulvian Bridge was inaugurated in July 315. Its decoration is
largely made up of reliefs taken from monuments of Trajan, Hadrian
and Marcus Aurelius. However, there is a long frieze that was executed
in situ when the architectural sections of the arch were completed,
which relates the final campaign of Constantine up to his entry into
Rome and his speech to the people there. These reliefs, formerly
painted, demonstrate the appearance of a popular, narrative genre in
official art. The harshness of the faces and the simplification of outlines and of masses echo the style of sculpture made during the
Tetrarchy.

285 *Façade of the Khazneh*, Petra, Jordan.

Situated at the crossroads of the caravan routes of Arabia, Syria and
Egypt, the capital of the Nabatean kingdom, Petra, enjoyed considerable prosperity from the 2nd century B.C. until it was annexed
by Trajan in 106 A.D. Its opulence was displayed in monumental
tombs hewn out of high rocky cliff-faces. The finest of these façades
in *trompe-l'oeil* is that of the Khazneh Firaoun, the "Treasure of the
Pharaoh," some ninety-eight feet high with two stories decorated
with friezes and sculptures. The architectural vocabulary employed
had remarkable variety - Corinthian columns, circular domes, broken
pediments - and was borrowed from Hellenistic sources. The vivacity
of this architecture, at one and the same time lightly graceful and
grandiose, and its scenographic character indicate some sort of
relationship to the *frons scenae*, the fixed façade used as permanent
stage set in Hellenistic-Roman theatres.

287

287 *Composite capital with a figure of Hercules* · Roman, early 3rd century A.D. · Terme di Caracalla, Rome.

The composite capital is formed by replacing the top row of leaves of the Corinthian capital with an echinus decorated by an ovolo molding and the volutes from an Ionic corner capital. It appears for the first time on columns in the Arch of Titus. In the baths begun in Rome in 217 by Caracalla, the composite capital carries an added complication in the form of a central figure: a resting Hercules in the tradition of the Lysippian figure, a famous replica of which, known as the Farnese Hercules, was found in the same baths. This capital is characteristic of the decorative richness of works from the time of the Severi.

286

286 *Candelabrum with storks* · Marble · Roman, 1st century B.C. - 1st century A.D. · Museo Nazionale, Naples.

In the 1st century B.C., Neo-Attic workshops produced for the Roman luxury trade tall marble candelabra with triangular bases, decorated over their entire height with workmanship of remarkable delicacy. This sort of refined and costly object seems to have been particularly popular during the Julio-Claudian period. Decorative palm leaves, naturalistic foliated scrolls, winged lions, rams' heads, all combine in a decoration that is composite, but truly elegant. The rare and refined motif of the stork recalls the long-necked swans which, during the same era, animate the foliated scrolls of the Ara Pacis.

289 *Drunken Silenus* · Bronze · Roman, 1st century B.C. - 1st century A.D. · Museo Nazionale, Naples.

With their conquests, the Romans developed a taste for luxury. The towns of Herculaneum and Pompeii in Campania, buried in 79 A.D. by the eruption of Vesuvius, give us some idea of the imagination and refinement in the furnishings and decoration of the dwellings of rich Romans. This bronze candelabrum depicts a Silenus crowned with vine leaves, drunkenly obstinate in his attempt to stand firmly and support his burden. This humorous creation demonstrates the consummate technical mastery of the Hellenistic-Roman bronze workers in their minor arts.

289

288

288 *Bas-relief decorated with a gryphon* · Roman, 2nd century A.D. · Museum of Fine Arts, Boston (Francis Bartlett Collection).

This bas-relief was part of the decoration of Trajan's Forum in Rome. The winged gryphon with an eagle's head and a lion's body terminates in plant-like scrolls; in some of the frieze elements belonging to the same work there are putti whose bodies turn into foliage in the same way. Of great decorative richness, this relief is the expression of a pompous and florid official art. The gryphon, a motif of Oriental origin, was used by the Romans to decorate friezes, armor and sarcophagi; it sometimes carries a symbolic meaning, but usually its value is, as here, strictly ornamental.

290

290 *Female head*, found near the source of the Seine · Wood · Gallic, probably 1st century B.C.

Most of the ex-votos discovered at the source of the Seine were carved from local stone. In the course of excavations in 1963, wooden sculptures of exceptional interest were discovered: they confirm the existence of the wooden *simulacra* made by the Gauls that Caesar mentions. Executed with very simple technical means by local artists working for pilgrims, this head displays a sense of volume and a gift for stylization out of the ordinary.

292 *Recumbent figure*, from Meroe · 1st - 3rd centuries A.D. · Ny Carlsberg Glyptotek, Copenhagen.

The kingdom of Nubia, long held within the orbit of Egypt because of its wealth in gold and rare woods, asserted itself independently in the 7th century B.C., when the Pharaoh's power began to wane. Despite the Roman expedition that in 23 B.C. destroyed Napata, their ancient capital, the prosperity of the Sudanese dynasties continued to reveal itself in their sumptuous golden jewelry, and in the surge of building activity on which they engaged, in the 1st and 3rd centuries A.D. at their new capital, Meroe. The best preserved of the constructions are the royal baths, whose stone façade was adorned with statues. In this distant African province, Ptolemaic influences combined with an indigenous tradition to create works of an extremely lively, hybrid style.

292

291

291 *Samnite gladiator brought down by a lion* · Provincial Roman · Musée Denon, Châlon-sur-Saône.

Gladiator scenes enjoyed considerable success in Gaul, which might be explained by the survival of ancient Celtic rites of sacrifice. This forcefully stylized group, of a late period, depicts a lion throwing a Samnite gladiator, recognizable by the semi-cylindrical shield upon which his foot is placed, and by the plumed helmet whose folded-back visor is decorated on either cheek with a dolphin. Besides being a simple *venatio* scene, this group must have echoed the more general theme of the ravening wild beast that often appears in funerary sculpture.

293 *Horsemen and soldiers*, from the frieze on the Arch of Augustus, at Susa · Gallo-Roman, 9 B.C.

The Arch of Susa was built in 9 B.C., at the end of the war waged by Augustus to conquer the Alpine peoples and to clear the route to Gaul through the Mont Cenis pass. The frieze describes the treaty of friendship concluded between the emperor and Prince Cottius, who became Prefect of the district. The relief has no other aim than a faithful narration of the successive events. In its mediocrity, the sculpture, of local workmanship, offers a considerable contrast with the architecture's learned harmony.

293

185

294

294 *Stele of Bellicus the Blacksmith* · Gallo-Roman · Musée Archéologique, Sens.

The characteristic production of Gallo-Roman sculpture is the funerary stele. The deceased usually wanted to be depicted engaged in their daily activities, and these realistic and entirely candid scenes reflect the hard-working, prosperous life of Roman Gaul. The blacksmith Bellicus is shown ready to bring his hammer down on the iron bar that he steadies on the anvil; he wears the heavy woollen tunic of Gaul. The craftsman has ruthlessly depicted his enormous bald head. In its naiveté and spontaneity Bellicus' stele is a good example of this popular art, unpolished but full of life.

295

295 *Stele with four deities* · Gallo-Roman, early 3rd century A.D. · Musée Archéologique, Strasbourg.

This type of base, decorated with four figures of divinities, was very widespread in Gaul. It reveals the adoption of the Roman pantheon by Celtic tribes, but in a rather free interpretation. The monument was discovered in 1954 at Strasbourg, ancient Argentorate, which was first an important garrison, then an interior base of operations behind the defensive system of *limes*. The principal face, depicting Juno leaning on a torch in front of an altar, is of a greatly superior execution when compared with the other sides. The hair of the goddess, parted down the middle, is in the style fashionable under the Severi; the work can be dated precisely, from the reign of Caracalla.

296 *Cippus decorated with female dancers* · Stone · Gallo-Roman · Archeological Institue of Luxemburg, Arlon.

Besides the direct representation of family life that is the most original aspect of their inspiration, Gallo-Roman craftsmen employed on the side faces of their monuments more conventional motifs that denote the spread of model books. The female dancer who decorates this cippus found in the *vicus* of Orolanum, near Trier, derives from a Greek prototype, but the rationalized Hellenistic model finds a new vitality in the smooth volumes of this provincial version. Carved from a somewhat coarse local stone, the cippus retains traces of vivid polychrome.

296

297

297　*Female bust* · Gallo-Roman · Musée des Antiquités Nationales, St. Germain-en-Laye.

Because of the purifying and curative qualities attributed to spring-water, the source of the Seine (25 miles northwest of Dijon) was the object of an indigenous cult that arose during the Gallo-Roman era. Excavations have brought to light the whole complex of buildings where worship and medicine were combined, under the invocation of the Dea Sequana. The very large number of ex-votos discovered proves that this place was a center of pilgrimage frequented for more than four centuries; among the ex-votos was this head, about 5 inches high, of a young girl of robust beauty.

298

298　*Medea* · Gallo-Roman, 2nd century A.D., inspired by a Greek model · Musée Lapidaire, Arles.

The Narbonne district of Gaul, pacified and made into a province from the end of the 2nd century B.C., was the most completely "Romanized" district in the Empire. The wave of Greek art, and the great number of replicas discovered there, must also owe something to the Greek history of this region, which was colonized in the 6th century by the Phocaeans. The group depicting Medea pulling out the sword meant for her two children, who cling fearfully to the folds of her drapery, derived from a Greek model; but through his simplification of the volumes, the native sculptor has created an intense expression of restrained grief very different from the lively pathos of Hellenistic art.

299

299　*German prisoner* · Provincial Roman, 1st century A.D. · Sammlung des Altertumsvereins, Mainz.

With the permanent installation of military contingents along the Rhine, considered the Empire's natural frontier after the end of Augustus' reign, workshops for carved funerary steles developed in that region. Their production throughout the 1st century was conditioned by military realities. This relief from the legionary camp at Mainz (Mogontiacum) depicts a female German prisoner, her head sorrowfully resting on her hand, in the traditional pose of allegories representing conquered provinces. Through the simplification of the volumes within the closed curve of the drapery the artist has succeeded in expressing his compassion for the grief of the vanquished.

300　*Embarkation on the Moselle* · Roman provincial, 2nd-3rd centuries A.D. · Landesmuseum, Trier.

The necropolis of Neumagen (Noviomagus), in the district of Trier, has yielded some of the finest reliefs in provincial Roman art; they are noteworthy for their restraint and their originality in composition. The town owed its prosperity to the river traffic along the Moselle, which was particularly heavy during the 2nd and 3rd centuries. In all probability, this stele, in the form of a ship loaded with heavy casks, was intended to commemorate a shipowner. While simplifying the composition by depicting only six members of the crew, the artist has still shown the ship's twenty-two oars, which give a rhythmical movement to the bas-relief.

300

301

301 *Stele with horseman*, from Thrace · 2nd–3rd centuries A.D.
Archeological Museum, Sofia.

A very large number of steles bearing the image of a mounted figure
have been discovered in Thracian territory; they appear to be a creation characteristic of this region during the 2nd and 3rd centuries A.D.
Such reliefs could be either votive, or funerary, as is the case here:
portraits of the three deceased persons are sculptured on the lower
part. Modest in size and generally of coarse workmanship, these monuments demonstrate the popularity enjoyed by the "Thracian horseman." Under the influence of the Greeks settled along the Black Sea,
this ancient deity, a local protector, took on the appearance of a young
hero on horseback, borrowed from the Hellenic repertoire.

302 *Stele of a priestess of Ceres* · Limestone · Punic-Numidian, 1st
century A.D. · Bardo Museum, Tunis.

Rivals of the Greeks in the western Mediterranean, the Carthaginians
nevertheless came under their influence from the beginning of the 4th
century B.C. This stele discovered near Maktar shows that the Carthaginians had adopted the worship of the goddesses of Eleusis. Flanked
by torches, the priestess exhibits the initiatory ear of corn and the
cista; below her is the *calathos*, between snakes. The presence of instruments (blade, cutlass, tongs) indicates the persistence of the Punic
tradition of bloody sacrifice. An expression of Neo-Punic art, this
monument remains essentially symbolic, but the repertoire has become less abstract under the influence of Graeco-Roman anthropomorphism.

302

303

303 *Hornblower*, from Osuna · Stone · 1st century B.C. · Museo Arqueologico Nacional, Madrid.

The Romans occupied Spain early in the course of the conflict that set them against Carthage, that is, towards the end of the second Punic war, about 206 B.C. The "Romanization" of Spain, initiated already in the Republican era, went very deep. From the 1st century B.C. comes a group of curiously disparate sculptures found at Osuna (ancient Urso), elements of a frieze carved from local stone. Several hands can be made out, most of them rather clumsy; the warrior-hornblower stands out from the rest for his restrained, classical treatment. It has been suggested that these reliefs made up a monument commemorating Caesar's victory in 45 B.C. over Pompey's son, in Spain.

305

305 *Mask from a mummy* · Graeco-Roman · Egyptian Museum, Cairo.

From the time of the Old Kingdom in Egypt it had been the custom to cover a mummy's face with a mask, produced in some precious medium for the Pharaohs, and for others in wood, in stucco or in some other plastic material. The mask was intended to serve the deceased as a head, should his own be destroyed. Between the 1st and 5th centuries the Greeks and Romans adopted this custom, but they transformed these masks into true portraits, produced with paint on wood or on linen, or modelled in plaster. In this small mask (8½ inches) representing an orientalized type, the eyes are made with inlaid calcite and black glass; the face is painted a dark reddish-brown, the hair and eyebrows black.

304

304 *Funerary relief* from Ghirza (Fezzan) · Archeological Museum, Tripoli.

The Fezzan desert (ancient Phazania) was crossed by important caravan routes which brought to the markets of Tripolitania all kinds of equatorial products sought by the ancient world: gold, ivory, ebony, black slaves. In order to keep these routes safe, the Romans, under Cornelius Balbus, subdued the Garamantes in 19 B.C. Among the garrisons subsequently established to defend the narrow cultivated areas, Ghirza has left important remains from the 3rd and 4th centuries. From the south necropolis on this site, at the furthest edge of the Empire, comes this very rudimentary relief, depicting in schematic fashion a deceased couple.

306

The ethnically mixed population of Palmyra paid honor to gods of a thoroughly syncretic nature in which a Semitic element predominated. The three gods Aglibel, Baalshamin and Malakbel are represented on this bas-relief, oddly combining coiffures made up of astral elements with the uniforms of Roman generals. Congealed in a hieratic pose three times repeated, the gods are shown frontally, their symbolic immobility emphasized by a neutral background enlivened only by some inscriptions in Palmyrene writing; the denial of any concern for space is a characteristic of Palmyrene art.

308 *Detail from a funerary relief* · Palmyrene · Museum, Damascus.

The deceased woman sitting at the feet of her husband is, like all Palmyrene female figures, heavily adorned with jewels. A wealth of ornaments, like the hierarchy of proportions, was a convention asserting the importance of the figure represented. With their frontal positions and wide-open eyes earnestly gazing at the spectator, these figures are an attempt at symbolic representation quite opposed to the naturalistic and illusionist tendencies of Graeco-Roman art. At Palmyra, the West's bridgehead in Asia, were developed the conventions and motifs that would appear one or two centuries later in the art of the Late Empire.

308

306 *Tomb of Yarkai* · Palmyrene, 175–200 A.D. · Museum, Damascus.

The remarkable stylistic and iconographic unity in Palmyrene sculpture is particularly noticeable in the numerous funerary reliefs used to close the *loculi* in which the mummified bodies were placed. The deceased are represented as busts, in a stereotyped frontal pose, the men in draped garments, the women drawing aside their veils. In the main niche of the hypogeum of Yarkai, the image of the dead man, dressed in the baggy trousers and the footwear of Parthia, lies on a richly embroidered bed. The members of his family surrounding him are depicted in a frozen, frontal pose that engages the spectator in direct communication.

307

309

309 *Veiled women*, on the Temple of Bel, Palmyra · 1st century B.C.

An oasis in the Syrian desert, halfway between the coast and the Euphrates, Palmyra owed its prosperity to the passage of caravans from Iran and Central Asia. As an intermediary between Rome and the Parthian kingdom, it played a major role owing to its neutrality, which made it indispensable to both sides. If its grandiose architecture is inspired above all by Graeco-Roman models, the sculpture is marked by strong Parthian influence. On this fragment from the great temple of Bel, the linear stylization that causes the faces to disappear beneath the convolutions of the veils demonstrates a strong bent towards abstracted forms.

310 *Sanatruces II, King of Hatra* · Marble · Iran, Parthian, 2nd century A.D. · Iraq Museum, Baghdad.

Situated near present-day Mosul, Hatra enjoyed great prosperity in the 2nd century A.D., when it was the capital of a small kingdom on the Upper Tigris. This statue, found in a temple, represents King Sanatruces II in prayer, one hand raised, and holding in the other a sacrificial palm. The praying gesture does little to alter the stiffness of the frontal pose; no more does the position of the left foot, placed a little forward. The king is wearing a diadem surmounted by an eagle, and his face is framed by the two tufts of curly hair characteristic of Parthian monarchs. The details of dress are minutely carved, trousers and tunic are richly embroidered, and the belt is highly worked.

311 *Head of a man* from Hatra · Iran, Parthian, 2nd century A.D. · Iraq Museum, Baghdad.

Among the statues dating from the 2nd century A.D. recently discovered at Hatra are some marked by a vigorous analysis of physiognomy, despite certain elements suggesting stylistic impoverishment, such as the incised details depicting wrinkles on the forehead, or waves in the beard. Remarkable for its strength of modelling and the spirituality in its expression, this head strangely evokes the western Middle Ages; it could have belonged to a figure from the portal of some Gothic cathedral. An original artistic expression blossomed in this city, set on the silk route and therefore open to the cultural exchanges carried between China and Syria.

310

311

191

312

312 *Triumph of Shapur I*, sculptured in the rock, near Bishapur · Iran, Sassanian, after 260 A.D.

On the walls of a gorge near Bishapur, Shapur I (241 to 272 A.D.) had a series of bas-reliefs carved to record his glory. This one celebrates the triumph of the "King of Kings" over the Roman emperors Gordian III, Philip the Arab, and Valeriano. Philip the Arab kneels and begs the conqueror's mercy, while the latter seizes Valerian's hand in token of capture. A winged spirit, typically Hellenistic, bears a diadem for the king. The presence of Valerian on the bas-relief allows the work to be dated after the battle of Edessa (260 A.D.).

313

313 *Colossal statue of Shapur I*, at Bishapur · Iran, Sassanian, 250 to 300 A.D.

In a cave near Bishapur, a town he founded in the second half of the 3rd century A.D., Shapur I had this gigantic statue carved, the only example of sculpture in the round in the whole of Sassanid art. It was carved from a natural rock pillar almost 23 feet high, with its feet set in the rocky ground and the bulky tiara cut away from the vault. It gives an impression of serene, but stereotyped majesty, despite the life given by the artist to the flowing curls of hair and the folds of the tunic, which are treated like moving pennants. The torso is stiff, though the artist has attempted to give movement to the arms.

315 *Figurine* from the Pamphilus catacomb · Ivory · Early Christian, 3rd-4th centuries · Vatican Museums, Rome.

Cemented into the masonry of the *loculi* are to be found many small objects: ancient coins, intaglios, cameos, ivories, and such. Most are of pagan origin, but were used by the Christians to decorate and identify their tombs. Ivory dolls with bronze articulations have also been found in the tombs, but these are generally rather stiff and quite unlike this dainty figurine representing a child in a Phrygian bonnet. It is unusual and must relate to some oriental myth.

IV The Twilight of Sculpture in the West:
The 4th to 10th Centuries

314

314 *The Tetrarchs*(?) · Porphyry · Roman, late 3rd - early 4th centuries A.D. · Southwest corner, façade of St. Mark, Venice.

Perhaps an image of the Tetrarchy founded by Diocletian in 292, this porphyry group of four Roman generals bestowing the accolade on each other, two by two, could have been brought back from the East during the 13th century. If it represents the Tetrarchy, then the two Augusti, Diocletian and Maximian, here greet the two Caesars, Galerius and Constantius Chlorus. This hypothesis would account for the presence of four figures, and also, in dating the work to the late 3rd century, would in part explain its stylistic vigor - the large, simple forms, and the faces conforming to types rather than individuals. The hardness of the porphyry also contributes to the severity of the style.

315

316

316 *Sarcophagus of Constantia* · Porphyry · Roman, early 4th century A.D. · Vatican Museums, Rome.

Porphyry, echoing the sumptuousness of the imperial purple, was frequently used in court sculpture up to the middle of the 5th century. The grape-trampling putti surrounded by vine-tendril volutes on Saint Constantia's sarcophagus appear also on a fragment of carved porphyry preserved at Constantinople in a collection of imperial sarcophagi from the period between Constantine and Marcianus. That fragment is probably from the sarcophagus of Constantine, which inspired that of his daughter Constantia. The subject is derived from the symbolism of the funeral art of antiquity. Such subjects gradually become secondary, then disappear altogether from later Christian sarcophagi.

317 *Sarcophagus of Saint Helena* · Roman, early 4th century A.D. · Vatican Museums, Rome.

On a bare porphyry field, quite without landscape features, horsemen pursue and capture barbarians - very realistic figures doing battle on an imaginary terrain. Is this a real battle or is it a symbolic struggle between defenders of the faith and infidels? The arbitrary spatial arrangement of this early 4th-century composition already foretells some aspects of Byzantine painting. The sarcophagus was very probably that of Saint Helena, or of her husband Constantius Chlorus. Sarcophagi in porphyry were no longer made after the middle of the 5th century when relations between Constantinople and Egypt became strained.

317

318 *Head of Christ*; detail from the Sarcophagus of Junius Bassus ·
(fig. 320) · Vatican Grottos, Rome.

The Christ who sits enthroned as law-giver between Peter and Paul is
a descendant of the youthful gods of antiquity. His outline forms the
axis of the sarcophagus' upper register; his face, framed by the largest
open area, radiates majestic youth. The light, flowing hair, the wide-
set eyes, the straight nose, the full cheeks and the fleshy mouth all
bring to mind certain Apollo types. Through its central position and
its radiance, this figure sheds a religious aura over the series of narrative scenes set about it.

320 *Sarcophagus of Junius Bassus (detail)* · Marble · Early Christian,
ca. 359 Vatican Grottos, Rome.

The sarcophagus of Junius Bassus, the Prefect of Rome who died, a
new convert, in 359, is one of the finest creations of post-Constantinian
art. The figures, set off by thoroughly classical architecture, have a
new fullness, an independence as regards the background of the relief
which makes them almost sculpture in the round. The quality of the,
drapery with its broad, elegant movements is particularly noticeable on
the figure of the youthful Christ entering Jerusalem. Once victorious,
Christian art moved away from the lively popular tradition that it had
followed under Constantine

320

318

319

319 *Sarcophagus of Valerius and Adelphia (detail)* · Marble · Early
Christian, 330-340 · Museo Nazionale, Syracuse.

Its popular character, the lack of any strong accent in sculptural
rhythms, the stocky figures, the clumsiness in rendering drapery — all
these features characterize the sarcophagus at Syracuse, which must
date from the decade 330-340. It appears to offer a last echo from the
long friezes on the Arch of Constantine. Christ entering Jerusalem has
a young, handsome face, but it is much too big for his squat body. The
draperies are heavy masses scored by long drill marks. The charm of
the work rests in its naive spontaneity.

Two angels, of a rather cold beauty, decorate each of the long sides of this sarcophagus, made for a very young Byzantine prince of the time of Theodosius. In gentle flight scarcely disturbing the folds of their robes, they bear a leafy crown framing the monogram of Christ. On the ends of the sarcophagus are Peter and Paul, flanking the Cross. Found in the necropolis of Sarigüzel (Constantinople), this work demonstrates the classicizing Greek tradition prevalent in the Imperial workshops during the second half of the 4th century, reacting against the coarser art of the Constantinian era.

322

321

323

323 *Sarcophagus from Psamathia (Constantinople)* · Marble · Early Christian, ca. 400 · Staatliche Museum, Berlin.

This sarcophagus fragment was discovered in Constantinople in the Psamathia quarter; its form was inspired by the pagan funerary sculpture of Asia Minor, the most famous example of which is a sarcophagus found at Sidamara. On the latter, as on a sarcophagus now at Melfi, from the same group, the figures are inscribed in a rhythmic architecture of twisted columns surmounted by a triangular pediment, and framed by architraves and conches. The Psamathia sarcophagus employs only the central part of this composition, showing Christ flanked by two disciples. The figures are very classical, but numerous pictorial effects are introduced in the drilled ornament.

321 *Portrait of Eutropius(?)* · Marble · Early Christian, 5th century · Kunsthistorisches Museum, Vienna.

Although still bearing the stamp of Roman realism, this remarkable head also possesses that glance seeming to penetrate a world beyond the spectator, and those stylized, even schematized, features characteristic of portrait art from the 4th century onwards. Found at Ephesus, it was at first believed to be part of a religious group, doubtless because of its intense spirituality; but it is nowadays connected with a base that bears an inscription praising a certain Eutropius, citizen of Ephesus, who had the town's main thoroughfare resurfaced with marble.

325 *Crucifixion*, on the door of St. Sabina in Rome · Wood · Early Christian, ca. 430.

Totally unknown before the 4th century, the subject of the Crucifixion became widespread in Early Christian art after the theologians began to emphasize the dogma of incarnation in their struggle against Docetism (the doctrine that Christ's appearance and deeds were not accompanied by bodily reality). The Crucifixion on the door of St. Sabina is one of the very first examples of this scene, which remained triumphant for centuries thereafter in religious art. Christ, alive, is shown on a cross that is suggested rather than actually represented. Wearing only loincloths, Christ and the two thieves are crucified before a building with a triple façade, perhaps an evocation of Jerusalem, such as appears on some Western sarcophagi and ivories.

325

324 *Statue of an official*, from Aphrodisias · Early 5th century A.D. · Archaeological Museum, Istanbul.

Statues of dignitaries from the Aphrodisias workshops are massively carved large marble blocks, and show the new trend in Roman sculpture at the beginning of the 5th century. In this statue found in the baths of Aphrodisias, the broadly handled cloak enveloping the body contrasts with the features, which are stylized and yet sensitively studied as to psychological content. The spirituality emanating from the face is still of a very human variety, not yet transcendental, as in the portrait of Eutropius of Ephesus (fig. 321).

324

326 *Colossal statue of an Emperor, at Barletta (Italy)* · Bronze, 5th century.

All the power of the emperor-strategus is displayed in this gigantic statue (13½ feet high). It was shipwrecked at Barletta as the Venetians were bringing it from the East, after the capture of Constantinople. The head has the nobility produced by that stylized realism characteristic of Roman and Byzantine portraits from the 4th century onwards. It results in the creation, not only of an individual, but also of a type—which explains why this sovereign, here identified as Marcianus (450-457), has been taken for almost every emperor from Valentine I to Heraclius. The legs and arms were remodelled in the 15th century.

326

327

327 *Twisted column* in St. Peter's, Rome · Marble · Probably 3rd century.

During the reign of Constantine, six twisted columns in Greek marble were placed around the altar of St. Peter's; six more were added in the 8th century. Later they were all redistributed in Bramante's new building, and again by Bernini; one of them has disappeared. The medieval legend says that they came from the temple of Apollo at Troy; then from the temple of Solomon, whence their epithet "Solomonic." The one placed by Bernini in the gallery of St. Helena, probably from the Greek Orient, is decorated alternately with a register of spiralled fluting, then a register of putti frolicking among vine leaves.

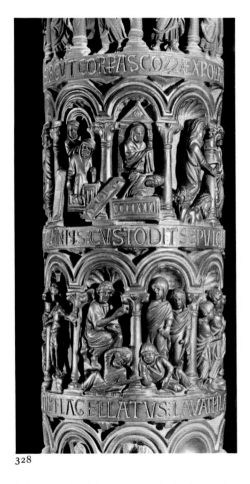

328

328 *Column of a ciborium* · Alabaster · 13th century (?) · San Marco, Venice.

The alabaster columns of this ciborium are no longer thought to be Early Christian: the inscriptions between the successive levels are certainly medieval, and most scholars now concede that the columns to the rear must likewise be. Currently, however, the idea is gaining ground that the entire ciborium may very well be a Venetian pastiche done during the proto-Renaissance of the 13th century. This seems to indicate that in Venice prototypes handed down from the earliest Christian art continued to be copied for a very long time. The Christ in Limbo and the Holy Women at the Tomb pictured here come from the right front column, whose scenes from the Passion are Early Christian in style but, in certain respects, medieval in their treatment of subject matter.

197

329

329 *Hercules and the Nemean Lion* · Silver plate · Byzantine, 6th century · Cabinet des Médailles, Paris.

Even more than the Romans, the Byzantines had a liking for gold and silver vessels. Right up to the reign of Heraclius, large silver plates, called *mensoria*, were worked in repoussé and engraved with a technique and feeling very close to Hellenistic models. The plate showing Hercules strangling the Nemean lion is conceived like a medallion, the figures perfectly composed within their circular frame and the movements of Hercules and the lion locked together in perfect balance. Although classically restrained, the scene nevertheless shows a tendency towards stylization, and a love of detail. (Some scholars consider this work to be Gallo-Roman.)

330 *Head of an Empress* · Marble · Byzantine, 4th to 6th centuries · Castello Sforzesco, Milan.

Like many portraits displaying a similar synthesis of realism and idealization, this head has been dated between the 4th and 6th centuries. The intense and burning glance, the thin face with its delicate nobility, and even the hair style, would seem to suggest an identification as Theodora; but the curious flatness of the face and the modelling of the cheeks strongly recall the head of the Barletta emperor (fig. 326), which adds weight to the suggestion that the subject is Pulcheria, wife of Marcianus. That such different datings are possible emphasizes the continuity in portraiture style from Late Imperial to Early Byzantine art.

331 *Diptych of Anastasius* · Ivory · Byzantine, early 6th century · Cabinet des Médailles, Paris.

From 399 onwards, a consul was appointed annually for each capital. At his accession to power, the consul sent to his acquaintances ivory diptychs fitted with wax tablets. The inscriptions on them were usually in Latin up to the end of the Consulate. In a splendid robe decorated with a rosette pattern, the enthroned Flavius Anastasius (appointed consul in 517) holds a scepter and the *mappa* which he will throw as a signal for the beginning of the games celebrating his entry into office. He sits enthroned on a rostrum with a pediment surmounted by medallions depicting the Emperor Anastasius, and probably Empress Ariadne, and Pompeius. The excellent workmanship suggests that the diptych was made in Constantinople.

330

33²

332 *The throne of Maximian* · Ivory · Byzantine, mid-6th century ·
Archiepiscopal Museum, Ravenna.

Several hypotheses have been put forward concerning the origin of
this splendid ivory throne. According to the most widely held opinion it
belonged to the Bishop Maximian, as the monogram visible on the
front part of the seat would seem to show. It may have been a gift from
Justinian, perhaps for the enthronement of Maximian in 545, for the
throne was probably produced in Constantinople. It is possible that
the various panels composing the throne were carved in different
workshops, or, at least, by different artists, as would seem indicated by the stylistic differences between the scenes from the story of
Joseph and those from the life of Christ.

333

333 *St. John and another Evangelist* · Detail of Maximian's throne
(fig. 332.)

The four evangelists on the front of the throne, turning towards the
central figure of St. John the Baptist, have the authoritative stance of
ancient philosophers. Each stands before an aedicula with twisted
columns, a scallop shell haloing his head, to emphasize his sacred nature. Of the two on the right, the younger, who is beardless, is doubtless John. Despite the classicism of the architecture, the monumentality of the figures, and the broad sweep of the draperies, the tendency of Byzantine sculpture to compress volumes between two planes is
already felt.

334 *Evangelists, St. John the Baptist, and ornament* · Detail of
Maximian's throne (fig. 332).

Broad bands filled with vine-scrolls and animals suggest the structural elements of the throne, while also uniting and framing the figured panels. The finest of the decorative bands is on the front, beneath the Evangelists. Its composition is symmetrical: on either side
of a vase, from which vine tendrils fall and which is flanked by two
rearing lions, are birds of several species, deer, and hares, enfolded
within the curling rinceaux. The elegant orderliness of the antique
foliated scroll is imbued with a feeling for contrasts of light akin to the
art of lacework.

334

In its development through Early Christian times the capital reveals a progressively more pictorial treatment of the sculptured elements, tending to arrive at new forms entirely different from those of the classical Corinthian capital. At S. Costanza in Rome, doubtless built by Constantia, daughter of Constantine, as a baptistry and transformed after her death into a mausoleum (354 A.D.), the capitals are still true composite Corinthian capitals, but they lack the opulence of the heavy forms of antiquity, and appear rather dry. The abutment of the arches on the capital necessitated a stout entablature with divers moldings; in this entablature originated the impost block, which was then finally reabsorbed into the capital.

335

337

337 *Capital* in the gallery of Hagia Sophia, Istanbul · 6th century.

In some cases, as for example in this Ionic capital from a gallery at Hagia Sophia, the impost has been kept, but for aesthetic reasons the combined capital and impost were intended to give the illusion of a single block. Over the splayed form the incised decoration, unmodulated in depth, runs in parallel registers, like strips of light against the dark background hollowed out by the drill. Pressing apart the acanthus leaves in the front part, the monogram of Justinian takes its place in this ornamental frame of abstract leaves. Unlike this one, most of the capitals at Hagia Sophia move, without the transitional impost, directly into the decorative patterns of the arches.

336 *Capital* in St. John Studion, Istanbul · Byzantine, ca. 453.

During the 5th century, an ever-increasing use of the drill led sculptors to produce linear, spiky plant forms no longer resembling the pliant acanthus of antiquity, with its widely opened leaves. They blocked out the foliage roughly with the chisel and then cut the contours with the drill. This capital is referred to as "Theodosian" for it was originally believed to have been made at the time of Theodosius II; in actuality the type did not appear until about 450, and became widespread in the second half of the 5th century. The oldest dated example is this one from St. John Studion (built in 453), which still supports an architrave.

336

338

In the church of San Vitale, pilasters of green porphyry divide and accent the marble panels below the famous mosaics of Justinian and his Empress. The capitals crowning these pilasters are carved in very low relief, and the plant decoration of which they are formed is treated in a strictly two-dimensional, symmetrical manner. Here, sculpture tends towards drawing, and the structure of the capital is reduced to a play of balanced lines.

340 *Male bust* · Coptic, beginning of the 3rd century · Coptic Museum, Cairo.

Besides the steles in the Egyptian manner, there exist others clearly imitating provincial Roman art. Such is the case with this funerary monument, whose overall form is like an obelisk, but whose sculptural relief displays all the characteristic Roman elements. The bust of a man of mature years, doubtless a Roman citizen, stands in a niche hollowed out of the pillar. He is dressed in a tunic and *pallium*. His face is individualized and realistic, and does not display the schematization of Coptic portraits.

340

339 *Transenna* from San Vitale at Ravenna · Byzantine, late 5th century · Museo Nazionale, Ravenna.

From the second half of the 5th century, and particularly under Justinian, the carved parts of Byzantine edifices tend to evolve into a fine marble lace-work, where the spiky acanthus creates a continuous rhythm of foliated scrolls over the surfaces. In this section of the choir screen, or *transenna*, from San Vitale, a feeling of discontinuity is given by the repeated interlacing of the bands that sketch out lozenge-shaped frames for the stylized acanthus blossoms. These last sometimes suggest Greek crosses; one actual cross, and two doves, are the only Christian symbols to be found on this screen.

339

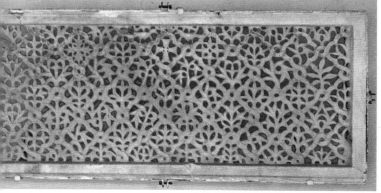

Funerary stele · Coptic, late 3rd - early 4th centuries · Ikonen-museum, Recklinghausen, Germany.

The sarcophagus was unknown in Egypt during the first centuries A.D.; steles in both the Roman and Egyptian traditions are therefore very numerous. In the necropolis of Kom Abu Billu, several hundred of them have been discovered, and they can be dated, through coins, between 268 and 340. The stele of one "Kollouthion" and his daughter, both depicted in prayer, owes much to ancient Egyptian art, from which it had inherited the subtle use of sunk relief, the beauty of finely pleated fabrics, and the convention of the combined frontal and profile views. These steles were doubtless enlivened by colors.

341

342 *Venus in a shell* · Architectural niche fragment · Coptic, ca. 400 · Coptic Museum, Cairo.

Despite the sharp division between the Greek spirit reigning in Alexandria, and the Christian and monastic attitudes prevailing over the rest of Egypt, mythology remained in favor throughout the land, and especially at Ahnas, where this niche was found. In a delightful gesture stressing her nakedness, Venus spreads behind her a mantle hanging in broad, curving folds, like a falling wave. The Ahnas artists' independence from Byzantium, and even from Alexandria, allowed full play to individual tastes for more robust and less aristocratic forms. This Venus belongs to a group of works dating from about 400, characterized by a soft, gentle style.

342

343

343 *Virgin of the Annunciation* · Wood, polychromed · Coptic, 5th to 6th centuries · The Louvre, Paris.

With the naiveté and also the spontaneity characteristic of Coptic art, the young girl perched on a high stool makes a gesture of surprise, turning her wondering face towards the spectator. In her left hand she holds a basket. The right side of this polychrome wood relief has been destroyed; one can still make out the bottom of a tunic and a foot. The subject must have been an Annunciation, though Gabriel has almost completely disappeared. Mary, seated, is placed at the left of the scene, according to the iconography favored in Egypt during the 5th and 6th centuries. Of the eyes, there remain only holes that were originally inlaid with colored stones.

344

346

346 *Putti and animals*, from the Veroli casket · Ivory · Byzantine, 10th century · Victoria and Albert Museum, London.

The altogether pagan insouciance of these naked children sporting with animals is part of the return to antiquity observable in various aspects of 10th century Byzantine art. Many ivory caskets were then decorated with mythological scenes inspired by manuscript illuminations. This plaque ornaments the long side of one such casket (formerly in the Veroli cathedral), one of the most important examples of the genre, owing to the many mythological subjects decorating it and also to the lively style of the figures, so round and firmly modelled.

344 *Christ as Pantocrator* · Ivory · Byzantine, 9th century · Victoria and Albert Museum, London.

On this face of Christ, with its regular features and grave expression, can be seen the severity characteristic of works produced during the reign of Leo VI (the Wise). The same austere and somewhat coarse beauty is found in the figures in the lunette of the outer vestibule of Hagia Sophia, in those of the enamelled crown of Leo VI (Treasury of St. Mark), and in those of the jasper relief in the Victoria and Albert Museum. This 9th-century ivory may be the pendant of a plaque, in the same museum, depicting the Virgin and Child.

345 *The Crowning of Romanos and Eudoxia by Christ* · Ivory · Byzantine, ca. 950 · Bibliothèque Nationale, Paris.

In the art of ivory carving, especially during the 10th century, the Byzantines best showed their understanding of ancient, and in particular of Greek, sculpture. The Christ who crowns these two young sovereigns is a Hellenistic god, with grave face and stately bearing. Because of its style, and also because it closely resembles the ivory depicting Otto and Theophano (Musée de Cluny), which is probably an imitation of it, we may conclude that this plaque depicts Romanos II and his wife Bertha of Provence, who took the Greek name of Eudoxia.

347 *Christ blessing* · Ivory · Byzantine, 10th-11th centuries · Victoria and Albert Museum, London.

Seated on a voluminous cushion placed on a throne, this majestic Christ gives a blessing with his right hand and in his left holds a book. His robe falls loosely in regular folds, closely resembling the dress of the Christ crowning Romanos and Eudoxia (fig. 345); its similarity to the Bibliothèque Nationale ivory dates this work as 10th or 11th century. It was obviously detached from a book cover, for three holes still mark the point where the clasp closed. Traces of polychrome also remain.

345

347

348 *Openwork plaque with Christ and saints in medallions* · Ivory · Byzantine, 11th century · Victoria and Albert Museum, London.

This pierced ivory plaque is quite representative of the delicacy and elegance in ivory carving during the 11th century. In contrast to the sober classicism of the preceding century, the shapes have become more elongated, and certain mannerisms begin to make their appearance, foreshadowing the tormented linearism of the 12th century. The drapery folds, long and narrow, are treated with nervous tension rather than monumentality. The faces, however, with their smooth, subtle modelling, retain an expression of austerity. Around the large central medallion depicting St. John the Baptist are arranged the smaller medallions showing SS. Philip, Stephen, Andrew and Thomas.

349 *Virgin and Child* · Ivory · Byzantine, late 11th century · Victoria and Albert Museum, London.

The 10th and 11th centuries have given us many beautiful ivores depicting the Virgin Hodighitria ("Guide"), but this statuette is the only known example produced as free-standing sculpture. The expression, the pose, and the way the garment hangs in long, elegant folds - all very classical in style - reappear in several triptych panels. Sometimes the figures from such panels have been cut out and reworked in order to give them independent existence; but only the London statuette possesses that finished beauty of a work originally created to be seen from different angles.

350

348

349

350 *The Forty Martyrs* · Ivory · Byzantine, 12th century · Staatliche Museen, Berlin-Dahlem.

This ivory depicting the death agony of the forty martyrs of Caesarea is usually dated in the 10th or 11th centuries. The elegance of the style, a certain affectation in the poses, a taste for pathos and for the human - as opposed to the supernatural - have caused this work to be placed alongside 12th-century Constantinopolitan art. Christ enthroned, worshipped by six angels, hovers over the group of soldiers condemned to die of cold on a frozen lake for refusing to recant. The representation of some of the martyrs is inspired by ancient sources; thus the bearded old man embracing a young man derives from Pan instructing Daphnis.

351

351 *Little Metropolis*, church in Athens · Byzantine.

The Greek school of architecture remained faithful to the taste for fine display. The Little Metropolis, also known as St. Eleutherea or as the Church of the Virgin of Gorgoepikoos ("of speedy fulfillment"), is a typically Byzantine creation, which reuses ancient materials in a new spirit. Blocks of Pentelic and Hymettus marble and of *poros*, as well as ancient and Byzantine sculptures, have been assembled in a coherent and harmonious whole. Byzantine reliefs from the 9th and 10th centuries often depict Oriental themes; animals either gripping their quarry or rampant on either side of the Tree of Life. This church is dated from the 11th or the 12th century.

352 *Tiger and gazelle* from Ordos · Bronze · Art of the Steppes, 4th - 1st centuries B.C. · Musée Cernuschi, Paris.

The peoples of the Ordos steppes, situated between Mongolia and China, developed metalwork similar to that of the Russian steppes. The culture from which these objects derive, as well as their dating, which varies between the 4th and 1st centuries B.C., is still puzzling. Depictions of animals make up most of the production, in a style lying somewhere between Chinese art and the abstraction of the Scythians and Sarmatians. Combat scenes, stags, horses and leopards are reminiscent of Scythian plaques. The twisted pose, and the dynamic, contorted lines furrowing the animal's body are characteristic of this barbaric art, in which idea and symbol take precedence over naturalistic representation.

352

354 *Griffin holding a stag head in its beak* · Wood · Siberian Scythian art, 6th–4th centuries B.C. · The Hermitage Museum, Leningrad.

The site of Pazyryk in the Altai mountains, southwest of the Minussinsk basin, has been repeatedly excavated by Russian scholars. It has yielded Scythian tombs containing a large amount of funerary material, in a perfect state of preservation because of hard frost. Only gold objects have disappeared, stolen by tomb-robbers. Most of the objects – saddlery and harnessing equipment – are made of wood, leather, felt, or stag-horn. The shapes are inspired by animals, but interpreted in a fanciful manner. This object, which may have been a war-standard, was found in the second *kurgan* in Pazyryk, excavated in 1947–48.

354

353 *Engraved gold stag*, from Kuban · Pontic Scythian art, 7th–6th centuries B.C. · The Hermitage Museum, Leningrad.

The Scythians settled in southern Russia (Pontic Scythia), and from there they spread in various directions. They were buried in large tumuli, called *kurgans*. They loved gold ornaments and jewelry, and their art was confined to those small objects, created under the contradictory influences of Greece and Asia. The Asiatic flavor is obvious in this engraved gold piece representing a stag found in the Kostromskaia *kurgan* in Kuban. The horns of the animal are stylized into spirals. The object, about 12 inches long, may have been the umbo of a shield.

353

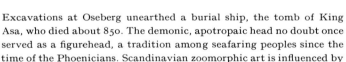

355 *Head* from Oseberg · Wood and metal · Viking, ca. 850 · Oslo University.

Excavations at Oseberg unearthed a burial ship, the tomb of King Asa, who died about 850. The demonic, apotropaic head no doubt once served as a figurehead, a tradition among seafaring peoples since the time of the Phoenicians. Scandinavian zoomorphic art is influenced by that of the steppe nomads, the Scythians in particular. From 400 on, invasions swept over Europe. The Germanic tribes borrowed their art from the Scytho-Sarmatian peoples; the Vikings extended their raids down to the Caspian Sea and up along the Volga, reaching southern Russia by the 9th century. They brought back the iconography and the ornamental vocabulary of the steppes, assimilating zoomorphic mixtures and hybrid creatures, and perpetuating the vision of the barbarians through the High Middle Ages in the West.

355

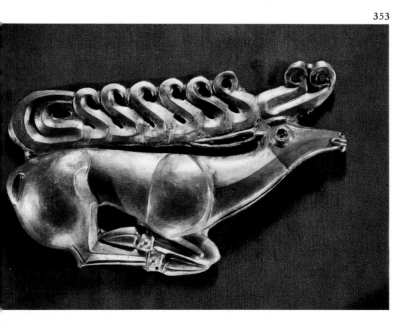

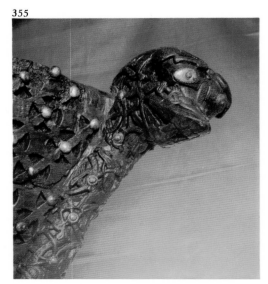

356

356 *Sculptured portal* on the Stave Church at Urnes · Wood ·
Scandinavia, ca. 1050.

357 *Prow ornament of a boat*, from Gokstadt · Late Viking, 10th
century · Oslo University.

Norway was converted to Christianity in the reign of King Olaf, in the
11th century. There was as a result a great upsurge of architecture.
The first Christian art is characterized by the *Stavekirke*, churches
built entirely of a wooden frame and rubblework. The decoration on
the portal of the church at Urnes has given its name to a style and is a
focal point for the development of Norwegian Romanesque art. The
style of Urnes is the latest incarnation of a zoomorphic art. Through
Viking art, it is the Christianized heir to barbarian art. The interlace
and the zoomorphic imagery, treated with great flexibility and elegance, bring to mind the refinements of *art nouveau*.

Simpler in style and coarser in technique than the example from Oseberg (fig. 355), the Gokstadt figurehead illustrates once more the influence of Scythian art on these nomadic sailors; the Scandinavian
woodcarver has imitated the theme of the horse used by the steppe
bronzeworker. Less frightening than the Oseberg dragon, this creature
is perhaps more realistic; the artist, succinctly summing up the idea of
a horse, satisfies our eye by his figure's resemblance to the model, and
our imagination by its interlacing patterns, which work like a synthesis of the animal's galloping movements.

357

359 *Capitals* from the crypt at Jouarre (Seine-et-Marne) · Marble · Merovingian, 7th century.

The two crypts at Jouarre are all that remains of the late 7th century Abbey of St. Columbanus. The columns and capitals are true examples of Merovingian aesthetic, not reused elements from ancient edifices. Carved in white marble from the Pyrenees, they are the product of local workshops that had maintained ancient ornamental traditions through the height of the barbarian invasions of the 5th to 8th centuries. Starting with the Corinthian capital, these workshops produced capitals carved with confidence and flexibility, interpreting and exploiting all the ornamental possibilities of the antique, but never falling into dry and stereotyped repetitions.

359

358 *Stele* from Larbro (Gotland) · Scandinavia, 7th or 8th century · Historika Museet, Stockholm.

Alongside the zoomorphic style, there existed in Scandinavia also a figure style best exemplified in a series of painted steles. The oldest group, dating from the 5th and 6th centuries, shows the influence of the later Roman style; another group displays characteristically Scandinavian iconography and style in its nautical funerary scenes; a third group, dating from the 7th and 8th centuries, to which the Larbro stele belongs, represents the full flowering of the genre. Arranged in superposed registers, figure scenes cover the whole face of the stele, which is outlined by a band of interlace ornaments. The interpretation of the scenes, in which appear drakka, combats and duels, is in doubt; some writers regard the scenes as illustrations of Norse sagas.

358

360 *Tombstone* from Hornhausen · Frankish, 7th - 8th centuries · Landesmuseum für Vorgeschichte, Halle, D.D.R.

The Frankish domain was more subject to the influence of late antiquity than were other parts of Europe at the time of the invasions. The Franks, Burgundians, and Alemanni mingled Christian symbols and Gallo-Roman recollections with the early, zoomorphic style, as well as with the geometric interlace style produced by the cultures of Halstatt and La Tene. The Hornhausen tombstone depicts a warrior, bearing lance and shield, mounted on a stylized horse. From the 6th century onwards, numerous items of minor art can be seen decorated with this figure in persistently similar form: the same stylized man and horse, the slanting lance, the horse's head thrust forward and small in relation to the body.

360

361

361   *Tombstone* from Niederdollendorff · Stone · Frankish, 7th century · Rheinisches Landesmuseum, Bonn.

The art of sculpture in the round disappeared in the West with the barbarian invasions. Reduced to imitating minor arts such as gold-smith work, embroidery and jewelry, sculpture was confined to relief carving in purely ornamental forms. True, here and there an anthropomorphic motif still cropped up on these shallow flat reliefs, as on this seventh-century Frankish funerary slab. No longer was there any attempt at realism; modelling and perspective had been forgotten, and the artistic conventions were derived from the aesthetic of primitive civilizations. Here, accessories such as the sword are given as much emphasis as the personage himself, and he is reduced to no more than a symbol in which the swordsman is confused with the themes of a Christian iconography which was only just beginning to take shape.

362

362   *The Moone cross* (Kildare); detail of base · Granite · Ireland, 6th century.

Towards the end of the 6th century, the carved Irish stele developed into a monumental cross carved in very shallow relief, with biblical and evangelical scenes in compartmented tiers. The Moone cross, set up during the 8th century, is of this type. The twelve apostles are arranged in three superposed symmetrical rows on the pyramidal base. The artist shows no concern with composition or reality. The harsh simplification results in an ideogram, and the apostles are no longer human beings, but merely summary symbols: enormous heads, rectangles for the bodies, two feet each. These simple granite figures have a strong suggestive force bordering on the magical.

363

363   *South cross of Castledermot* (Kildare) · Ireland, 9th century.

The structure of Irish crosses developed very little: a pyramidal base, a rectangular shaft, and arms linked by a circle. With the passage of time, pure ornament disappeared and carved scenes covered the cross completely. Erected in the 9th century, the one at Castledermot is of the same type as the Moone cross. Its iconography, centered on the theme of the Crucifixion and Redemption, is more coherent. Interest in composition is also evident in the various compartments, whose scenes present themselves more legibly than do those of the Moone cross. But the aim of the sculptor was still the expression of an idea rather than the narration of a story.

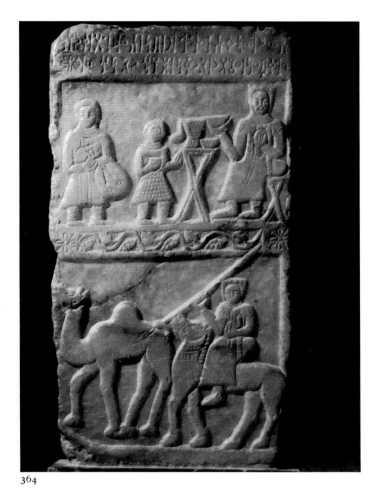

364

364 *Stele with camel-driver* · Nabataean, ca. 1st century A.D. · The Louvre, Paris.

Although the origin of this stele is uncertain, it probably comes from the Yemen. Of the two superposed reliefs, the upper one, in an archaic style of Mesopotamian origin characteristic of Yemeni art, is an offering scene, explained by the inscription above it. The band of stylized scroll patterning typifies the Roman element that found its way into all the Arabian provinces, and particularly into the region occupied by the Nabataeans. The lower relief shows a scene taken from the life of camel-drivers. The artist has taken pains to render accurately the camel-driver's clothing and hair style, and also the details of the animal's harness.

365

365 *Head* from South Arabia · Limestone · 2nd century A.D. · National Museum, Rome.

Sketchily modelled as it is, this head is closely related to the famous heads found in the Yemen early in this century by Müller, who published them, and which are now in the Kunsthistorisches Museum, Vienna. Worthy of note are, on the one hand, the treatment of the nose and eyebrows, and on the other, that of the mouth. The elongated head, characteristic of those Yemeni figures influenced by Rome, can be found in all these works, but the realism we usually associate with Roman art is more marked in the figures brought back by Müller. The Yemen was a dependent territory of the Empire in the 1st, 2nd and 3rd centuries A.D.

366

366 *Karyatid* from the Palace of Khirbat al-Mafjar (Jordan) · Stucco · Islamic, Ommayad, 8th century · Palestine Archeological Museum, Jerusalem.

This graceful figure stands in the pendentive formed by two arches banded in scroll and palm-leaf ornament of a Hellenistic type common in Byzantine Syria. With both hands she supports the cornice that links the crowns of the arches. In its clearly pagan style as well as in its supple movement, the figure relates to paintings at Qusayr'Amra, the summer palace – or rather, the hunting pavilion – of the Ommayad Caliph al-Walīd I, which is more or less contemporary with this palace at Khirbat al-Mafjar. The reciprocal influence of motifs from paintings, sculpture and even mosaics should be noted here, and also the prolonged survival, evidenced by this small monument, of the art of stone-cutting that had flourished in southern Syria during the late period of Roman domination.

211

367

367 *Fragment of a frieze*, from Mshattā · Islamic, Ommayad, 8th century · Staatliche Museum, East Berlin.

The Ommayad castle of Mshattā was built by Al Walīd II (743–744) in the middle of the desert, 15 miles from the Jordan River. It was planned as a vast square, 130 yards on each side, with only one doorway, that in the middle of the south side. Workmen requisitioned in Mesopotamia and in Syria were employed on the building, which remained unfinished. The ornament is closely related to that lavished by Byzantine craftsmen on the Dome of the Rock (Mosque of Omar) at Jerusalem, and on the *intrados* of the arches surrounding the *saha* of the great mosque in Damascus. It is a type of ornament largely inspired by Persian forms, and executed by cutting away the background in a technique like champlevé. The delicate scrolls of the mystic vine – not given any particular significance here – wind in and out, forming a moving background that sets off the figures of griffins, lions, peacocks, and bustards. Characteristically for this Syrian art of the Ommayad dynasty, the whole surface is amazingly varied and rich in details, full of images whose further development appears to have been cut short by political catastrophe.

368

368 *Fragment of a wall panel*, Medina az-Zahra (near Cordova) · Islamic (Spain), 10th century.

The Ommayad sovereign Abd al Rahman III began building this city as a luxurious retreat in 936. It soon became a capital city, though in 1010 a civil war destroyed a large part of it. The geographers Idrisi and Makkara tell us that in the city, in their time, there were numerous art works of diverse origin, Byzantine or Persian, as well as works of local artists (these last including the statue of Abd al Rahman's favorite that welcomed visitors at the entrance to the city). Local artisans expended all their art here to surpass, in virtuosity and delicacy, the orniment of the Mosque at Cordova. This example is characteristic in the highly inventive elaboration of details, which led, however, to a rather thin and insubstantial quality in the whole. The attempt is made to avoid the simple balanced and symmetrical schemes that distinguish the art of Cordova.

369

369 *Detail of the piers of the mihrab*, Great Mosque, Cordova · Islamic (Spain), 10th century.

Characteristic of sculptured ornament of North African origin are marble or stucco panels filled with patterns based on scrolls, thyrsi, palm leaves, rose motifs and little flowers, carved in shallow or deep relief. The panel reproduced, from the time of the Ommayad Caliph al Hakim II, shows the feature this ornament shared with Syro-Byzantine ornament (which already, well before the time of Islam, had been influenced by Persia): the rigorous symmetry of areas situated on either side of a stem, a trunk or a thyrsus that divides the panel exactly in half. The Cordova mosque, with its almost over-lavish ornamentation in this style, shows what great prestige the style enjoyed in the 10th century. It was then that the art of the countries adhering to the Sunnite faith definitively renounced figurative art in favor of stylized ornamentation, though an occasional statue was to be made, but never one organically related to the decoration of a building. The Shi'ite countries never experienced this restriction on plastic expression; nor (from the 10th to the 12th centuries) did the countries subordinated to Fatimid authority.

370 *Capital* in the *Salón Rico*, Medina az-Zahra (near Cordova)·
Islamic (Spain), 10th century.

It is worth comparing the preceding capital with this one, which is
characteristic of the art of a city distinguished by creative originality
and a concern with new decorative motifs. The Medina az-Zahra
architect has retained the structural outline of the composite capital,
but he has endeavored to enhance it with stucco or marble. In the
Oratory of al Hakim II the decoration centers on ornamental panels
bearing floral and palm leaf motifs, but in the Salón Rico entire surfaces are masked with delicate sculptured ornaments that endlessly
develop the acanthus motif. The capital shown here is completely
enveloped, volutes and all, in a pattern of thorny stems that cover its
cylindrical part.

370

372

372 *Capitals* from the entrance to the Villaviciosa Chapel, Great
Mosque at Cordova · Islamic (Spain), ca. 970.

The oratory of al Hakim II was completed in about 966. The capitals
have summary volutes and a double ring of foliage. The springing of
the main vault rises from a plain abacus, and that of the other arches,
directly from the capitals. A sense of effortless lightness is perhaps due
to the plain and robust ornament of the capitals, on which nothing
has been detailed, or reworked in undercutting, and these capitals
thus form a contrast to the highly worked arches resting on them.
This type of capital is found again in the central nave and *mihrab* of
the great Mosque, as well as in the oratory of Abdal Rahman II (833)
and in those parts of the mosque added by al Mansur (987); the tradition followed here is that of stonecutters of Ommayad Spain.

371

373

371 *Stucco panel* from Nishapur (Iran) · Islamic, 10th century · Metropolitan Museum of Art, New York.

The site of Nishapur, in Khorasan, which was excavated by a team
from the Metropolitan Museum, has yielded a number of stucco decorations from the 9th and 10th centures. The most important of these
panels came from a *liwan*, an area of a mosque. The panels were originally painted white, yellow, blue and red. The decoration consists of
palm leaves – so stylized that they are reduced to abstract schemata –
inclosed in multifoil forms, with all the intervals filled and the surface
perforated. Since there is no relief, the complete polychrome panel
must have looked more like a carpet than a sculpture.

373 *Wooden door* · Islamic, Seljuk, ca. mid-13th century · Archeological Museum, Istanbul.

From the Konia region comes this door made up of three planks, joined
on the inside by two cross boards now held by nails fastened by rosettes. Over the top part of the door is an inscription in Seljuk. The
work is characteristic of the profoundly original and creative aspect of
Seljuk art. Its main decorative element is the ornate central panel,
whose motifs are grouped around a circle decorated with interlace on
a background of flowerlets stemming from the Fatimid fleurs-de-lis.
The interlace motifs form a series of twelve-pointed polygonal star-
shapes whose symmetry gives the panel a sense of firmness and equilibrium. In the four corners are two lions of a Persian-Mesopotamian
type, and two *simurghs*. The decoration – quite distinct in style from
the Syrian and Egyptian carved panels, and even more so from inlaid
woodwork – is reminiscent of ivories, and especially Persian ivories,
that were to be found almost everywhere between the 11th and 13th
centuries.

213

374

The two turbaned figures, standing one on either side of a bush bearing three flowers arranged in a tidy triangle, wear full-length tunics under coats with embroidered sleeves. They are soldiers: one leans on a long sword, the other wears at his waist a short, straight sword, and holds on his right shoulder the classic mace of Iranian arms. Considering restrictions imposed by the material, the deliberate roundness of the faces is worthy of remark. They seem to be of the North Iranian type frequently found in 12th and 13th century manuscripts and ceramics. The other side of the piece – of which this is the back – is decorated with the figure of a woman, seated on a dais between two vases of flowers and playing a tambourine. The fragmentary character of this carved ivory plaque allows only vague speculations as to its intended destination.

375

375 *Statue of an Iranian prince* · Stone · Islamic, Seljuk, 13th century · Metropolitan Museum of Art, New York.

In this example of Seljuk art, the headdress, with its horns rising at either side of a central motif, closely resembles that of Chosroes in the fresco at Qusayr'Amra representing the caliphs' victory over the princes. Again, the way in which the image is treated recalls miniatures of the Baghdad school, as well as the Rhages ceramics with their metallic highlights. The craftsman has interested himself primarily in a careful description of the details of the state robes and the headdress, and similarly he is intent on showing how richly decorated are the materials of the undergarment. Each shoulder bears a Kufic inscription giving the titles of the prince, and his cloak is edged with heavy embroidery in epigraphic patterns. The human forms are very generalized, and the face and hands are treated schematically: the figure clearly exemplifies an art more concerned with producing symbols than with representing human figures.

376 *Lion* on the fountain of the Harem Court in the Alhambra, Granada · Islamic (Spain), 1350–1400.

Twelve lions support the basin of a monumental fountain in the great court believed to have formed the center of the harem quarters of the Alhambra, which was built in the second half of the 14th century under Yosuf I (1333–1354) and Mohammed V (1354–1391). The lions are near relations to those that may be seen supporting columns in cities of the maritime republic of Amalfi. Their forms are quite general, and they represent lions only in a conventional way, as indicated by the inscription: "These lions have no soul; have no fear, they cannot assuage their anger." The fountain is of a type commonly made everywhere in North Africa up to the beginning of the nineteenth century, and the type was then repeated in the consciously "Islamic" art of the French colonial period.

377 *Hen and chicks* · Silver gilt · Lombard, 8th century (?) · Monza Cathedral.

This delightful little group in gilded silver highlighted with semi-precious stones, is, for the barbarian era, astonishingly delicate in execution. It is said to have been presented by Queen Theodolinda to the cathedral at Monza in the 7th century, but some art historians, refusing to accept this as the original, state that such technical skill and such competence in modelling the forms could belong only to an 11th-, 12th or 13th century copy. Some have even claimed for it an Arabian origin. A lack of comparable material - most of the goldsmiths' creations of this time have disappeared - makes the question difficult to decide. Lombard art was open to all influences, from exquisite Hellenistic refinement to barbarian simplification.

377

378

378 *Detail of an Incense-Burner* from the Gurgan region · Bronze · Islamic, Seljuk, 11th–12th centuries · Archeological Museum, Teheran.

This incense-burner, $11\frac{1}{2}$ inches long, represents a quadruped with a feline head, its mouth half open, tongue out, and ears pricked. The tail, formerly straight up, is now bent down over the back. The back, the chest, and the neck are all perforated, the openings appearing as part of a kind of grillwork of scrolls formed by stylized fleur-de-lis. On each ear a palm leaf is engraved. The decorative areas are set off by a double line edging their surfaces, and by a central dotted motif. On the animal's chest is an inscription in the decorative Kufic script characteristic of 11th and 12th century Fatimid and Persian bronzes. It says: "Valor, power, and glory." In its composition this piece may be compared with the griffin of the Camposanto in Pisa, and with a number of bronze lions of the Fatimid epoch which are quite similar although intended to be used as ewers and therefore not perforated.

215

379 *Adoration of the Magi*, from the Ratchis Altar · Lombard, mid-8th century · San Martino, Cividale.

Decorating one side of the altar presented about 745 to the church of San Martino in Cividale by the Lombard King, Ratchis, is an Adoration of the Magi - a frequent 8th century theme. Among disparate stylistic elements combined in the altar (the influence of Irish miniatures, Scandinavian ornamental motifs, reminders of Byzantine and even of Coptic art), the basic formula is barbarian. The composition is made up of superposed figures, sized according to their religious importance, and so stylized that the folds of the garments and other details are almost mechanically repeated.

379

381

381 *Procession of female saints*, in Sta. Maria in Valle, Cividale · Stucco reliefs · 8th (or 11th) century.

Lombard art attaches great importance to the interior decoration of churches, as may be seen from the frescoes and stuccos of the *tempietto* of Santa Maria in Valle at Cividale. For stylistic reasons - their affinities with the post-iconoclastic Byzantine style - and because comparative material is lacking, it has sometimes been suggested that these stuccos, generally dated about 750, in fact come from the 11th century. Seeming directly inspired by the endless rows of figures in Byzantine mosaics, these stucco figures have little in common with 8th century Lombard art, and might be the work of Greek or Byzantine sculptors working at the court of Cividale.

380 *The Sigwald Altar* · Marble · Lombard, ca. 730 - 760 · Cathedral, Cividale.

The old marble altar-frontal, reused in the decoration for a baptismal font in the Cividale Cathedral, was presented by the Patriarch Sigwald in the mid-8th century. The carver has exactly imitated cloisonné metalwork forms, to the extent of carefully reproducing even the flower-shaped heads of the nails that would have fastened the metal plates. In subject matter, one relief is a kind of abstract picture-puzzle, with the cross, the Tree of Life, and the symbols of the Evangelists - all inspired by Eastern motifs - mingling with age-old monsters and ornamental plants and lacework.

380

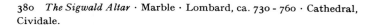

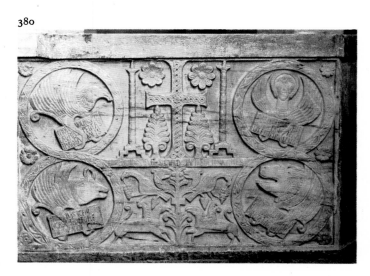

382

382 *Stucco capitals* from the Oratory of S. Benedetto at Mallés · Carolingian, late 9th century · Museum, Bolzano.

Stucco was often used during the Dark Ages as a material for architectural ornament, for it was easy to work. Columns and capitals in the apse of San Benedetto at Mallés did not perform any structural task, but hid the rubblework walls and created the illusion of a sumptuous building. On the capitals are orant busts, the heads framed in the foliage parted by the hands in their gesture of prayer. The boundary between the vegetable and human worlds is undefined, and both seem to share in the same kind of growth. During the 9th century, human figures gradually invaded the composite foliage capital inherited from antiquity.

383

383 *Capital* from the nave of St. Rémi at Reims · Pre-Romanesque,
mid-11th century.

The capitals of Saint Rémi, consecrated in 1049, are of stucco, carved
with a chisel. This technique is rare in 11th-century France, being more
characteristic of Carolingian and Ottonian art. Some of these capitals,
as for example the one depicting a scene from the story of Samson,
have sometimes been regarded as Romanesque; but L. Grodecki has
shown that they are pre-Romanesque in feeling. Samson and the two
birds set back to back are detached from the background, and the
scene unfolds all around the capital's bell but quite unrelated to its
structure. The neighboring capitals show the hollows intended to hold
the stuccos, which have fallen.

384

384 *Pulpit* of Santa Maria Maggiore, Tuscania · Panels are Lombard,
8th century.

In the study of medieval Italian sculpture the pulpit occupies a special place; in Italian churches it was not merely a piece of liturgical
furniture, but an independent structure of monumental character and
often lavishly ornamented. The pulpit in Santa Maria Maggiore at
Tuscania, reconstructed in the 12th century using 8th-century sculptural panels, is one of the last offshoots of Lombard art in Latium. The
whole surface is covered with interlace in various forms, probably of
Germanic origin. Confronting his marble, the sculptor appears to have
been seized with the same *horror vacui* as the illuminator before his
page; like him, he created a world of continual linear movement, of
ceaselessly self-gestating forms in perpetual metamorphosis.

385

385 *Bronze grille* (detail), Palace Chapel, Aachen · Carolingian, ca. 800.

As the architecture of the Palace Chapel at Aachen was completely renovated during 19th-century restorations, the eight bronze grilles that close off the tribunes are particularly precious, for they are practically all that is left of the original decoration of the edifice built between 795 and 810. These grilles, which were originally gilded, demonstrate the skill of bronzeworkers of that time; they were cast in a single piece. Curiously, they show a certain development of a style corresponding to the Frankish and Lombard tradition towards the classicism of the Palace School; some were inspired by the marble screens in the churches of Rome.

387

387 *Head of Christ* from Lorsch · Carolingian, early 9th century · Landesmuseum, Darmstadt.

This head, discovered in the monastery at Lorsch an der Bergstrasse, is without doubt Carolingian, and comparison with the Ada ivories dates it in the beginning of the 9th century. Its mutilation has accentuated the rather weak modelling in this face of Christ, with its full and robust forms, its calm, tranquil expression. Closer to ancient than to Byzantine art, the head in some ways recalls the head of Christ on the sarcophagus of Junius Bassus. In reaching back once more to antiquity, Carolingian artists made a break with the current of barbarian art.

386

386 *Stucco tondo*, Church of Solnhofen (Bavaria) · 819–842 (?).

The date of this tondo is disputed; some historians place it no earlier than the 11th century. According to Christian Beutler, it represents Sola, an Anglo-Saxon monk who died a hermit in 794 in a valley of the Almühl and was buried beneath a basilica consecrated in 842. The striking resemblance of the head to that of the Christ in the ambulatory of St. Sernin in Toulouse probably stems from a common imitation of ivories, which transmitted ancient traditions interpreted in the Byzantine manner.

388

388 *Crucifixion* · Intaglio on rock-crystal · Carolingian, 9th century · Cabinet des Médailles, Paris.

Like the Greeks and Romans, the Byzantines and the barbarians were attracted by engraved gemstones, but the delicate technique needed to create them fell into disuse during the 4th century, and in the following century the practice of carving in cameo - that is, in relief - lapsed entirely. The emperors collected mainly ancient stones. It is not until the Carolingian era that good gems are again found and these are almost always intaglio on rock-crystal. One of the most famous is the Crystal of Lothair, which stylistically resembles this Crucifixion; and an almost identical Crucifixion, mounted in a flamboyant monstrance, is now in the Diocesan Museum of Freiburg (Germany).

390

390 *Adam and Eve banished from Paradise*, detail of the St. Bernward door, church of St. Michael, Hildesheim · Bronze · German, ca. 1015.

The Archbishop Bernward of Hildesheim commissioned these famous doors and also provided their iconographical theme – Sin and Redemption. The first doors cast in one piece (in 1015) in the West since Roman times, they rank as masterpieces of Ottonian art. The sculptor or sculptors seem to have worked from a painted model or to have been inspired by Carolingian miniatures. The background, conceived in a pictorial manner, provides a setting, its very low relief giving an illusion of space; the figures, on the other hand, are carved almost in the round, the upper parts of the bodies standing away from the background and the vigorous modelling accentuating the dramatic tension, so that the panel takes on the quality of full three-dimensional relief. (About 23 × 43 inches.)

389

389 *Statue of Charlemagne* from the church of St. John the Baptist in Müstair · Stucco, Carolingian, 9th century · Cantons des Grisons, Switzerland.

This life-size statue once stood against the wall of the monastery church, which Charlemagne is said to have founded; it was removed during the 15th century, at which time it was damaged, then restored (mainly the hands, the scepter and the orb); an inscription from the end of the Gothic era, probably reproducing an earlier one, gives the date 801, when the Müstair Monastery was founded. The work appears to be the simple production of an isolated artist working without models and without guidance from traditions.

391

391 *St. Joseph*, detail of the Nativity, St. Bernward door, Hildesheim (see fig. 390).

The figure of St. Joseph seems to bend out from the background with a very natural movement, leaning towards the Virgin with pride and admiration. Despite the panel's size, the sculptor has treated the little figure as though it were a large-scale statue in the round, without either neglecting or simplifying any of the details. The supple folds of drapery, the simple and natural gestures, the successful handling of the face, round and full without being too soft, all allow the action its full expressive value.

219

393 *Column cast for Archbishop Bernward of Hildesheim* · Bronze ·
Ottonian, ca. 1020.

The Archbishop of Hildesheim, St. Bernward (993-1022), was a humanist and an artist. He was tutor to the Emperor Otto III, and made
several journeys to Rome. No doubt inspired by what he saw there,
he commissioned for his cathedral a pair of bronze doors, a cross, and
various other objects in bronze and gold. It was said that he himself
designed these works. The bronze column, which is actually an outsize
paschal candlestick, is obviously inspired by Trajan's column, and
illustrates the prestige that antiquity persistently enjoyed in the eyes
of German artists. But whereas the Roman column celebrated imperial
triumphs, Bernward's was dedicated to the triumph of Christ on
Earth, the band of sculptures spiraling up it recounting the life of
Christ.

393

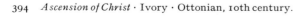
392

392 *Panels of a door*, south portal, Cathedral of Augsburg · Bronze·
German, ca. 1050–1060.

The two leaves of this door appear to have been composed from the
reassembled remains of two other doors executed about 1050–1060.
Divers allegorical and mythological figures, one to each panel, make
up a rather confused theme that is difficult to decipher. Imitation of
antiquity is obvious. Each panel is carved with a sensitive relief and
subtle modelling reminiscent of the graceful charm of Hellenistic
cameos. The Augsburg doors are akin to those at Salerno and to Italo-
Byzantine art, which together with Ottonian art has provided the
most beautiful examples of the classicizing trend in the Middle Ages.

394

394 *Ascension of Christ* · Ivory · Ottonian, 10th century.

It was natural that Ottonian art, a preeminently imperial art, should
lay claim to the heritage of antiquity and Byzantium. Not only the
style, but also the techniques and artistic genres were imported, as is
the case with the ivory plaques, based on Byzantine, as well as on
Carolingian, models. The Ascension of Christ from the Bamberg
Treasury, attributed to 10th century Lorraine workshops, has all the
characteristics of the Carolingian art that it seeks to propagate.
However, the Ascension scene is conceived with great expression, like
a human, not an other-worldly, drama. The roundness of the figures,
the animation of the group formed by the Virgin and the mourning
apostles, and the rising figure of Christ, literally drawn up by God's
hand, are characteristically German features.

395

396

395 *Christ on the Cross (Gero Crucifix)* · Wood, gilt and polychromed · Ottonian, late 10th century · Cathedral, Cologne.

Ottonian art exploited the principles of Carolingian art right up to the 11th century. Regarded as the oldest monumental crucifix in Europe, the wooden cross said to have been made for Gero, Archbishop of Cologne (969-976), is a remarkable example of imperial Germany's renewed interest in monumental sculpture. The type is derived from Carolingian miniatures, onto which is grafted a Byzantine influence. Although the date is disputed, this Christ certainly has all the characteristics of Ottonian art: a firmly confident modelling; a thorough study of anatomy, though with details kept subordinate to the whole in an incipient stylization; a realism in the physical representation that invests the work with a sense of the drama's actuality.

396 *The Imad Madonna* · German, ca. 1085 · Diözesanmuseum, Paderborn (Westphalia).

This Virgin was given to the Treasury of Paderborn Cathedral by the builder-Bishop, Imad, in about 1058. It was originally covered in gold leaf, like similar Virgins in the rest of Europe, but the basis for the metal sheathing, instead of being a crudely carved core, was a finished statue. It is a fully Romanesque sculpture, as opposed to the barbarian Virgins in Majesty or the imperial Virgins of the beginning of the century. The handling is restrained, almost severe, and the Mother of God has a sovereign dignity. The placing of the Christ Child in profile marks the beginning of an evolution; the Virgin was soon to hold her son naturally in her arms.

221

397

397 *Reliquary statue of St. Foy enthroned* · Carolingian · 5th (?) and 9th centuries · Treasury, Church of St. Foy, Conques.

Scientific study has solved the problem of dating this work: the head dates from the late Empire (5th century?), and the body of the statue is from the last quarter of the 9th century. This figure is perhaps the prototype of all reliquary statues. Consisting of a wooden core entirely sheathed in gold set with enamel, gemstones, cameos, and precious stones, its aesthetic value must be calculated by the goldsmith's measure rather than the sculptor's. It is really an idol, more symbol than figure; enthroned, with arms outstretched, the saint attains magical force. Reliquary statues were rejected by some contemporary clerics.

399 *Two archangels*; detail of an antependium from Basle · Gold and precious stones · Ottonian, 1002-1019 · Musée de Cluny, Paris.

A humanized style of representation and an understanding of drawing and relief reappeared in the north first in metalwork, and from there found their way into stone sculpture. In Ottonian Germany the understanding of three-dimensional form had been kept alive through the techniques of repoussé metalwork, many examples of which are to be found in church treasuries. This splendid gold antependium, presented by Emperor Henry II to the Cathedral of Basle between 1014 and 1022, was probably made in Mainz between 1002 and 1019. The two archangels, who stand out boldly against the background, are treated with a classical feeling for plastic form.

398

398 *The Romsey Christ* · England, beginning of the 11th century.

Not only on the Continent, but also in England, monumental sculpture began to be made again in the late 10th and 11th centuries; there too, it tended to derive its forms from illuminated manuscripts. The Romsey Cross, executed between 1000 and 1020, is the transcription in stone of models from a Winchester school manuscript. The environment was favorable for the new types, for, leavening the native barbarian and Irish tendencies, there was in the English monasteries a spirit of cultivated renascence, particularly evident in the art of miniatures. The Saxon sculptor here created work inspired by continental models in which Byzantine influence predominated over native characteristics, and the Romsey Christ has been likened to a 10th-century ivory.

399

400

401

400 *Head of a woman* · Terra cotta · Nigeria, Ancient culture of Ife, 11th–15th centuries. Museum für Völkerkunde, Berlin.

Ife, the religious center of the Yorubas, enjoyed a moment of great splendor in the 13th century when it contained several hundred sanctuaries. Even today many rites are celebrated there in homage to the Oni, the sovereign descended from a long line of divine kings. The Oni governs his people and watches over their prosperity through the intermediary of a hierarchy of priests and notables. The sober and delicate modelling of this small commemorative head (6½ inches), with its network of grooves undoubtedly meant as tattoo marks, permits us to glimpse, over and beyond its obvious naturalism, the serenity and dignity that characterize the aristocracy of this Nigerian people.

401 *Female head known as "the Princess from Benin"* · Bronze · Nigeria, Benin, 16th century · Property of the Government of Nigeria, on loan to the British Museum, London.

This bronze female head, cast by the lost wax process, belongs to the first classical period (16th century) of Benin art, when it was still under the influence of the idealized realism inherited from Ife. In the palace of the *Oba* there was an altar used for the official cult rendered to that divine king, and on which effigies of the queen-mothers, similar to this face, were also honored. This commemorative bronze is still restrained and does not display the ostentatious luxury which characterizes 17th-century Benin works. The royal head wears a high coiffure adorned with a network of coral beads, and around the neck there are several necklaces made of the same cylindrical beads.

223

402

402 *Leopard* · Bronze · Nigeria, Benin · Museum für Völkerkunde, Munich.

During the 17th century European bronze was imported by the rulers of the kingdom of Benin. The result was an intensified production from the foundries, and the fabrication of works of increased dimension. This leopard, intended for the *Oba* (ruler), figures among the more refined objects; it is one of the most successful bronzes of this "middle period" in Benin art. The powerful dignity felt in this sculpture is in keeping with the symbolism associated with the leopard. The Oba kept real leopards in his palace as living emblems of the strength of royal power.

403 *Royal head; pectoral mask* · Ivory · Nigeria, Benin, 16th century · Museum of Primitive Art, New York.

This pectoral mask representing an Oba is in the style of the classical period of the kingdom of Benin and dates from the 16th century when it attained its greatest political power. The royal visage has hair in a tight pearly pattern, necklaces of grains of coral, and two additional ornaments in the form of friezes made up of tiny heads, bearded and wearing round hats. The latter were meant to portray emissaries from Portugal, and these effigies of diplomatic envoys from a distant and powerful king were used in these ornaments, in combination with the fish-tailed genii who were the protectors of the Oba, to raise the prestige of the ruler in the eyes of his people. (Height 8¼ inches.)

404 *Mask of Nimba* · Wood and straw · West Africa, Baga · British Museum, London.

Shaped like an enormous carved wooden bell, this Nimba mask, 3 feet 8 inches high, in the form of a female bust, was carried on the head and shoulders of a dancer. The dancer, completely veiled by the full straw skirt, saw through an oblong opening made between the elongated breasts. The mask evokes Nimba, spirit of fertility, favorable to women. It is one of the sacred objects used by the Simo secret society, which presides over the Baga tribe's ritual ceremony initiating the rice gathering time at the end of the rainy season, as well as over the funerals of the members of this Guinean sect.

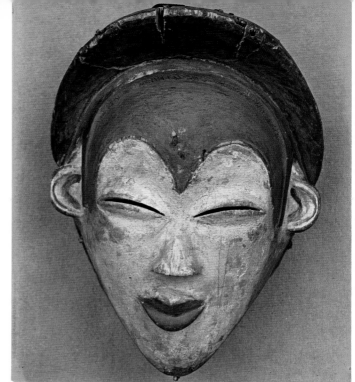

405

405 *Spirit mask* · Wood, coated with clay, and painted · Lower Congo, Gabon · Pitt Rivers Museum, Oxford.

Many people of the lower Ogowe river valley, in the wooded Gabon region, exploit the art of the mask as part of their worship of the dead. The artists of these matrilineal groups represent the ancestral guardian spirits with feminine characteristics. The idealized face with slanting, slit eyes is coated with sacred white clay and heightened with red. Identifying scar marks and headdress vary from one specimen to the next. To intensify their mysterious aspect, these supernatural spiritual evocations were occasionally carried on stilts. This beautiful example of Gabon art is strikingly subtle and delicate in modelling.

406 *Dance mask* · Wood · West Africa, Cameroon, 19th–20th century · Rietberg Museum, Zürich (E. von der Heydt Collection).

The peasant populations of the high Cameroon plateaus live organized into small states. Their imposing royal palaces on quadrangular ground-plans are enhanced with monumental statues on the pillars and surrounds of the doors. Art works from these regions combine a realistic character with a formal dynamism quite exceptional in Africa, and each court has its individual style. This large dance mask is elaborated according to a rhythmic conception of volumes which confers on it an astonishingly architectonic quality. It is attributed to an artist of the Bacham, a group of the Bamileke people in the Bamenda region. (Height 26½ inches.)

406

403

404

409 *Mask* · Wood, polychromed, and straw · Central Congo, Bushongo · Smithsonian Institution, Washington, D.C.

Formed in the 17th century in the heart of the Congo, the Bakuba kingdom consists of separate populations, politically confederated. They acknowledge the military supremacy of the Bushongo tribe, ancestors of their ruler, who has divine rights. He is the nation's unifying element, owing to the general belief in his supernatural power over the country's prosperity: the fertility of the women, the abundance of the fruits of the earth and of game. This helmet-shaped mask (13 inches high) is the work of the Kete people, linguistically related to the Baluba of the Kasai, but deeply influenced in their art by the ruling Bushongo tribe. The Kete interpretation of the mask type borrowed from the heart of the kingdom tends towards a simplification of the features and an accentuation of morphological characteristics.

407

408

409

410 *Standing figure* · Micronesia, Caroline Islands, Nukuoro · Musée de l'Homme, Paris.

Micronesian art is characterized by extreme simplicity; it achieves its highest expression in the wooden statuettes or "tinos" representing protective deities. Though small (13½ inches), this one gives the impression of being much larger, owing to the purity and severity of forms and to the broad, yet delicate treatment, in the modelling. Its "cubist" appearance sometimes suggests affinities with contemporary sculpture. The head, a simple egg-shaped volume, its pointed end forming the chin, the straight, hanging arms, the position of the legs, and even the shoulders, all show a subtle use of asymmetry.

407 *Chief's stool* · Wood · Eastern Congo, Baluba · Royal Museum of Central Africa, Tervuren.

The seat borne by a crouching figure is a sign of authority for a Baluba chief. The female figure represents the protective ancestor of his line, assuring prosperity to the people through the intermediary of her heir on the throne. Baluba sculpture is generally characterized by the eurythmy of its rounded forms. The kneeling figure under this throne (20½ inches) exhibits the same formal traits as the *Kabila* holding a bowl in fig. 411: slender forms, and accentated features in an elongated face. The existence of a dozen other works in the same style, found at Buli in the northern Baluba region, suggests the work of a single artist or workshop.

408 *Mother and Child* · Wood with reddish patina · Congo, Mayumbe · Royal Museum of Central Africa, Tervuren.

When Diego Cão discovered the mouth of the Congo in 1482, and landed in an inlet on the river's left bank, he learned from a vassal of the Manikongo that he had entered the territory of a sovereign, fifth in line of descent, who ruled a vast and well organized state. Diplomatic relations began between the kings of Portugal and the Manikongo, which resulted in the arrival of missionaries and technicians. After the conversion of the Manikongo in 1491, Christianity was adopted by the aristocracy, who became educated and assumed European modes of life and dress. Despite subsequent vicissitudes, this cultural contact made itself felt in Congolese art. A successful example of this is the beautiful ancestral statuette of mother and child. The woman's headdress is shaped like a mitre and she wears a necklace and trousers. (Height, 9 inches.)

410

411

Kneeling woman with a bowl · Wood · Eastern Congo, Baluba · Royal Museum of Central Africa, Tervuren.

The famous Kabila figurine (19 inches high) known as "The Beggar Woman" is one of the most highly esteemed works of African art, in part owing to the sensitive expression on the dramatic face. The motif of a woman with a bowl is characteristic of the Baluba people in the southeast Congo region. Formerly called "mendicants," these kneeling figures are now understood to be connected with the art of divination: the female figurine represents a guardian spirit; the bowl held in her hands is for the sacred white clay, the source of life and symbol of peace. Diviners are consulted with a view to understanding the cause of some misfortune – sterility, illness, death – or the chances of success in some undertaking, such as travel, business, intrigue, or war. Offerings slipped into the bowl attract the attention or blessing of the spirit.

413 *Statue of a man* · Wood, tinted black · Eastern Congo, Baluba · Ethnographical Museum, Antwerp.

From the 16th century onwards the people in the southeastern region of the Congo came under the political domination of the Baluba tribe, a haughty aristocracy of hunters and fighters boasting a sacred blood-line that linked them with the empire's heroic founders. The qualities of the leader are seen exalted in the statue (height 34 inches) of a man, standing proudly, conscious of being invested with the supernatural power, inherited from his ancestors, over the land's fertility and its people's welfare. The rhythmical treatment of the forms, with their elliptical syntax, and the characteristic crisscrossing on the back of the headdress, indicate the hand of a master-sculptor from the Baluba tribe of northeastern Katanga.

412 *Tiki* · Wood · Polynesia, Hawaiian Islands · British Museum, London.

The wooden figure is characterized by its mouth cut in a kind of drooping figure 8, vigorously treated muscles and relatively large size (height, 30 inches). It represents Tiki, instrument of Tane (the male element, and creator of all forms of life), and also the first man; he always evokes virility and fertility. He assumes human, phallic or foetal forms, in every substance and size, so much so that the word "Tiki" has become a common noun. He is everywhere, either in the form of a guardian effigy or schematized into a symbol; he is the prime source of inspiration for statuary, decoration and tattoo designs.

412

413

414 *Stone images* · Easter Island (Polynesia).

Whether intended as images of gods or of the dead, these statues once stood on altars in sanctuary-tombs. The gigantic monoliths – some as much as 49 feet in height – were hewn out of volcanic rock in three or four weeks' time. From the foot of the Rano-Raraku volcano where the sculptors' workshops were set up, the completed statues were dragged to the seashore. Typically, the face is carved on an oblique concave plane; the shadow from the overhanging brow gives the impression of a piercing gaze, the mouth is indicated by thin protruding lips. Only the features on these great narrow masks framed by long ears remind us that the statues are not two-dimensional, and they seem hacked out by two or three blows of a gigantic ax.

414

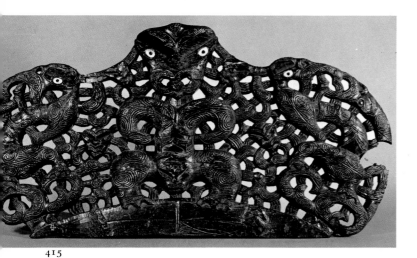

415

416 *Headdress of war-god* · Feathers on wooden frame · Polynesia, Hawaiian Islands, Kukaili-Moku · British Museum, London.

Red kiwi feathers, collected over a number of years, are fixed one by one on a basketwork frame to form this headdress, which has mother-of-pearl eyes. Hunters capture the bird, pull out about fifty feathers from its tail and set it free. The headdresses are carefully preserved in treasure-chests, for they have an important symbolic significance: at major ceremonies a tuft of a small red feather ensures the presence of some supreme deity whose representation is forbidden. The art of working feathers was highly refined, and also provided kings with magnificent cloaks and casques formed like the hoplite helmet.

415 *Sculpture from a counsel-house door* · Wood · New Zealand, Maori · British Museum, London.

Figures of great ancestors and guardian spirits are incorporated into the "House of Men" so that they may impart their wisdom to those holding meetings there. These sculptures are so closely bound up in tribal warfare that, in case of defeat, they are burned to prevent them from falling into enemy hands. The Maori tribe favors sculpture in high relief, sometimes perforated, and woods lightly tinted with ochre. Also characteristic are dramatic compositions that intermingle birds, masks, and spiral motifs coiled round every joint of the body, and mouths forming a figure 8, the tongues protruding (as a sign of strength in battle or perhaps of the wisdom of the deceased).

416

417

417 *Mask* · Tortoise shell · Polynesia, New Guinea, Island of Dewar · Nationalmuseet, Copenhagen.

This mask from the islands in the Torres Strait is typical of the art produced there in its use of tortoise shell. Tortoise-shell plaques, carved with pierced motifs of leaves, stars, and dots, are attached like pendants to the upper parts of the mask, which is made of pieces of bark sewn together. The eyes and mouth are a pretext for an engraved decoration of fine serrated motifs, the excisions filled with chalk and touches of red. This process and the choice of colors resemble those used for bark belts made in the Papuan gulf not far away. The mask, adorned with selected shells, is the intermediary through which supernatural beings communicate with the living.

418 *Laughing child* · Terra cotta · Mexico, classical period of Vera Cruz · Collection C. Lienhard, Zurich.

In the state of Vera Cruz, the culture of the classical period of the 6th to 10th centuries helped to diffuse the urban civilizations of Teotihuacan and Tula but later was itself absorbed into the Aztec culture. This laughing child, arms spread wide in an animated asymmetrical gesture, represents Xochipilli, the god of renewal, of flowers, poetry, music, dance and sunrise whose idol the Aztecs covered with the flayed skin of the sacrificial victim to ensure that once again the world would be reborn to life.

420 *Lintel with a mythical subject*, from a temple in Yaxchilan (Chiapas) · Mexico, Mayan, 692–726 A.D. · British Museum, London.

A mythical serpent with curling scales rears up before a high dignitary who is gorgeously arrayed, wearing a magnificent headdress and adorned wit jewels. From the monster's wide-open mouth emerges a human head with the same cranial deformation as appears on the seated dignitary. This flattened skull, achieved by binding the head between small boards, was much in vogue with the Mayans. The serpent-apparition rises above a large vessel, which, like that held by the ecstatic scholar before him, contains written scrolls. Three cartouches with hieroglyphics occupy the background of the composition. Dating from the classical Mayan period, the relief is carved with delicacy.

418

419 *Seated Child* · Clay · Mexico, Olmec, 3th–7th centuries B.C. · Private collection, Mexico.

This clay figurine (14¼ inches high) is covered in a white slip. The suppleness of the modelling, the naturalness of the pose, the feeling of life emitted by the statuette, testify to a simple humanity in the civilizations of the archaic epochs; later the empires of the Mayans, Toltecs and Aztecs will engender an increasing cruelty, expressed by a progressively inhuman stylization.

419

420

421 *Atlante*, from Tula · Mexico, Toltec, 10th–12th century A.D.

Four such Atlantes, supports for the wooden architrave bearing the roof, stood at the entrance to the sanctuary on top of the pyramid at Tula, the religious city of the Toltec people. This five-stepped pyramid was devoted to the worship of the sun and of death. The sanctuary piers, each fifteen feet high and composed of four stone drums, are carved to represent armed warriors, wearing the traditional butterfly-shaped shields on their chests. All four colossal statues, identical in attitude and expression, are executed with great care and precision as to their ornamental details and attributes. A feeling of power emanates from this figure, which symbolizes the sun-warrior armed with shafts of light.

421

422

422 *Mask of Quetzalcoatl* · Turquoise mosaic inlaid on wood · Mexico, Mixtec, 1300–1450 · British Museum, London.

A culture hero of the Toltecs, the erudite prince who in the tenth century built his capital at Tula established there the cult of Quetzalcoatl – the mythical serpent covered with feathers of the firebird – and considered himself the incarnation of that fertility god who ruled over sun and water. The tradition went that, exiled from his country as a result of palace intrigues, Quetzalcoatl disappeared but promised to return at the dawn of a new golden age. That messianic hope explains the spread of his cult among all the peoples of Mexico. This very fine funerary mask may very well have been meant to represent the hoped-for divine benefactor.

423

423 *Decorative reliefs* in the inner court of the Palace of Columns at Mitla · Mexico, Mixtec, 13th century.

The culture of the warlike Mixtec people is renowned for its gold and silver work, distinguished by a wealth of highly inventive motifs; and also for the turquoise, coral, and jade mosaics, inlaid with delicate precision on their ritual wooden objects. The Mixtecs' technical virtuosity in stonecarving and their taste in decoration are also manifested in these ornate reliefs, which lighten the imposing mass of the building with their regular Greek key patterns.

229

424

424 *Hunting with a snare* · Volcanic tufa · Ecuador, Manabi culture. Musée de l'Homme, Paris.

The Manabi culture of Ecuador developed on the Pacific coast. Their sculptured works were almost always carried out in volcanic stone. This relief has a bird-hunt as its subject: the bird-catcher is shown in a rigidly symmetrical frontal position, in the middle of complicated geometric patterns. Only the essential features of the face are represented; more detail, however, is introduced into the pectoral and loin-cloth which relieve the figure's nudity. A bird appears at either side of the bird-catcher's feet below the nets that he holds. His form more or less responds to that of the volutes crowning the scene's decorative framework.

425

425 *Stele* from San Agustin, Colombia · Stone.

A monumental stele, rather than a statue modelled in the round, this strictly symmetrical figure portrays a deity or a high dignitary. Extreme schematization is achieved by a reduction of anthropomorphic elements to a minimum, giving the massive silhouette the appearance of a pillar. The face becomes a mask; the features combine to form geometric figures, as the staring eyes combine with the eye-sockets to form rectangles. In this face recomposed in two dimensions, the nose seems to stretch horizontally to the width of the wide-open, grinning mouth, which, like the eyes, has assumed a rectangular form. The culture of San Agustin spread to the mouth of the Magdalena River in Colombia. These megaliths are considered extremely old, and are found in company with ceramics of a very archaic nature.

426

426 *Llama* · Silver · Peru, Cuzco style · American Museum of Natural History, New York.

The Central Andes gave rise to civilizations of high level in which work in gold and silver reached real artistic and technical heights of varied quality and expression. In the Andes the llama was valued not only as a beast of burden but also for flesh and wool, and it became the ideal animal for sacrifices. This statuette of a llama is made of silver leaves assembled with great ingenuity. The parallel lines formed in relief by beating the metal from the reverse side cleverly capture the appearance of the animal's pelt with its long wisps of woolly hair. A fine example of metalworkers' art, it came from Cuzco, capital of the empire established by the Incas in the first half of the 15th century.

427 *Jar in the form of a deity* · Pottery · Peru, Mochica culture · Museum of Archaeology and Ethnography, Cambridge.

The Mochica culture originated in the first centuries A.D. It is known for its funerary materials, among which the painted ceramics take pride of place. The most famous works are vase-portraits but the artists of this race of fishermen and maize-farmers were inspired by very diverse subjects and by religious themes in particular. Living in the valleys of the northern coast of Peru, they continued to favor the ancient feline god whose cult had spread after the ancient civilization of Chavin. This red and white jar, 16 inches high, represents the deity in anthropomorphic form, seated, holding a human head and a copper axe.

427

428 *Great totem pole* · Wood · North America, Northwest coast Indians · Musée de l'Homme, Paris.

Along the fishing coast of northwest America, cut off from the rest of the continent by the Rocky Mountains, flourished a civilization peculiar to the "salmon fishers" which produced numerous works of art and particularly woodcarvings. According to tradition, the inhabitants lived a communal life in large halls built from cedar planks and ornamented with polychrome carvings. Each line of descent had its own heraldic symbols, illustrating its mythical origins. The aristocrats were proud of their status and prestige and were bound by tradition to offer the solemn feast of *potlatch;* this obliged a family to make a display of honor and wealth by heaping precious objects upon the other clan. The erection of a huge pole, such as this one, decorated with clan's emblems, most frequently animals like the crow, bear, beaver, shark, or eagle, gave the signal for these grandiose celebrations.

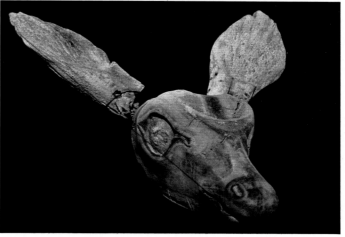

429

428

429 *Head of a deer* · Wood tinted with ochre · North America, Florida, Mound-builder culture · University Museum, Philadelphia.

In southeast North America, the wooded plains of Florida and the Mississippi Valley first saw the rise of what was termed the mound-builders' civilization, which flourished from the 11th to 17th centuries. A Central American influence seems to have found its way to these maize farmers, who built mounds in the shape of animals (tortoises, snakes, etc.), or of pyramids. Some mounds served as pedestals for temples. These mounds were sometimes real tumuli, with funerary furniture which included objects demonstrating skilled craftsmanship: pottery, stone pipes and bowls, engraved shells and wooden figurines. This graceful deer head (5½ by 7½ inches) is one of a series of masks found at Key Marco in Florida.

430

430 *Ancestor mask* · Wood, painted · Borneo · Nationalmuseet, Copenhagen.

Primitive cultures showing common characteristics developed in the group of islands situated in southeast Asia, between the South China Sea and the Pacific Ocean. For the natives of Borneo, as for most primitive cultures, masks represent the figures of ancestors. In the south of the island, they have human or demon faces; in the west they often assume an animal appearance. The mask is painted, and decorated with feathers and other materials.

431

Funerary sculpture is the most interesting artistic manifestation in southern Ethiopia. Commemorative effigies in the form of wooden posts surmounted by carved heads are raised to the glory of important deceased men and famous warriors. They are set beside megalithic monuments bearing symbolic figures. This stele shows a half-length figure in a totally conceptual representation; particular importance is given to the arms of the deceased, raised in a fervent, imploring gesture.

433

431 *Female mask* · Wood · Vietnam, Sedang · Musée de l'Homme, Paris.

The value of a ritual object lies more in its magico-religious qualities than in its artistic merits. This female mask was used in agrarian rites in central Vietnam by the Sedang people. To ensure fertility of the land, the two sexes are associated, and during the ceremonies the female mask, worn by a woman, is accompanied by a male mask, worn by a man. Black lines trace the forehead, eyebrows, eyelids, and chin; the mouth has teeth set into it.

432

432 *Monument to the little Voivode*, Radimlja (Herzegovina) · Stone · Bogomil art.

On the banks of the Radimlja River, in eastern Herzegovina, stands a funerary group unique in Europe, composed of upright stones, sarcophagi, and small houses for the dead. It was a cemetery for the members of the heretical Bogomil sect, established about the middle of the 10th century. Its doctrine, part Manichaean and part Pauline, enjoyed great favor in the Balkans during the 12th century. The monument to the little Voivode is representative of their art – that of the local stonecutter, who was often also the village blacksmith. The lord, portrayed standing and wearing an embroidered coat, raises his right hand, which transmits a great feeling of power because of its disproportionate size; it represents a solemn magic gesture of supplication to higher powers. The rosette, the interlace and the trefoil motifs, the circle of the sun, the bow fitted with an arrow – all these are common elements of the Bogomil decorative vocabulary, which was in effect a symbolical language accessible only to the initiated.

434

434 *Female figure* · Stone · Pagan Slavic · Coll. Charles Ratton, Paris.

These mysterious life-size statues of female figures have been found over a vast area from Galilee to Siberia, and even in the steppe regions, where there is no stone. Archeologists have termed them picturesquely *kamenya baba* ("stone goodwives"). For the most part they are naked, or dressed in a simple tunic, and show a development, in a realistic direction, that would seem to suggest their having been produced over quite a long period of time. Continuing the type of the fertility goddesses from prehistoric times, they may be a vestige from pagan Slav art, prior to the conversion to Christianity; or they may have been worked by some Asiatic tribe, which set them along its migration routes

435

436 GISLI GUDBRANDSON · *Detail of a carved wood chair* · Iceland, ca. 1600 · Museum, Reykjavik.

The kinds of distortions wrought by folk artists are remarkably consistent all over the world. They may be found, too, in far-off Iceland, but in certain aspects of its folk art there are rude survivals of ancient Viking art in more or less bastardized forms. While most works of folk art are anonymous, the name of the author of this one is known: Gisli Gudbrandson from Hvammur, who lived between 1584 and 1620.

436

435 *Stele of Saint Valentino* · 1662 · Museo di Castelvecchio, Verona ·

The thirteen Veronese communes have posed many ethnological problems. Their population was composed of very ancient Latin or Germanic stock, joined in the 14th century by mountain dwellers from Bavaria. The autochthonous art that sprang to life in these lands produced steles and crosses, made for centuries in the same popular style and set up at intervals along the roads. The little stele of St. Valentino, dated 1662, exemplifies the stonecutters' decorative bent; simplification and geometrical rendering of the forms make the figure a perfectly legible ideogram.

233

437

437 *Stone stele* · Basque · 1646 · Musée de l'Homme, Paris.

In the formal repertory of ornament used on stone sculptures in the Basque country, the rosette is the most frequent motif. This ancient design had appeared no less frequently in Celtic silverwork, and in France it may also be seen, cut in stone, in Brittany or Auvergne, where stone sculpture was in high favor. This Basque funerary stele bears the date 1646. On the circular upper part is a cross with arms of equal length, their ends ornately worked. The cross is surrounded by four solar symbols, two of which display the rosette motif in its most classical form.

438 *Calvary of Saint Thegonnec*, detail · Brittany, 1610.

The Breton type of large crucifix, accompanied by numerous statues of saints and scenes from the Passion, appeared at the very end of the 15th century and enjoyed its greatest popularity in the 16th century. The representation of mystery plays doubtless contributed to the formulation of these complex religious monuments, which were set up in the open air, and which are unique in Christendom. The calvary of Saint Thegonnec includes a cross with two horizontal arms, flanked by the gallows of the two thieves. On the platform are nine skillfully arranged scenes. Here, just below the Pietà group, is the Deposition, with the body of Christ surrounded by the Holy Women, Mary Magdalen and Joseph of Arimathaea, who holds the crown of thorns. The variety of attitudes and facial expressions reproduced in stone endows this peasant sculpture with a strikingly lifelike quality.

439

439 *Gingerbread mold*, from Torún, Poland · Wood · Musée de l'Homme, Paris.

Wood sculpture is the favorite medium of Polish folk artists. It is used for all sorts of things, from votive statues to carved furniture and even for humble household objects in which the workmanship is masterful and, at times, of great finesse. This gingerbread mold shows what patience and skill are required of the folk artist. A woman of the wealthier class is depicted, right hand jauntily placed on her hip, her left arm holding a child who snuggles tenderly against her shoulder. She is decked out in all her finery, and not the tiniest detail is missed in the painstaking rendering of her plumed hat and richly decorated gown.

438

440 *Saint Anthony of Padua* · Wood, polychromed · Lithuania · Musée de l'Homme, Paris.

The Baltic region was less affected than eastern Europe by the art of icons inherited from Byzantium, and in its religious wood sculptures exhibits an engaging, peasantlike robustness. In this votive statue, Saint Anthony of Padua is portrayed holding – rather clumsily – the infant Christ, who is conceived as a small adult. An attempt at variation in the arrangement of the folds of the tonsured saint's coarse soutane somewhat relieves the heaviness and overriding frontality of this work.

440

441

441 *Funerary statue* · Wood · Afghanistan, Kafiri peoples · Museo Nazionale di Antropologia, Florence.

Outside Europe distinctions between great, folk and tribal art are difficult to make, especially as adequate studies have not been made. This funerary sculpture is the work of the Kafiri, an Asiatic people living in the Biri valley, isolated in the mountainous region of Afghanistan. The carved wooden effigy represents the deceased, standing, and richly attired. His headgear takes the form of a mitre; he wears a torque around his neck and a sash or sword-belt. The rosettes and interlace shown on his clothing are universally employed ornamental motifs.

442 *Monument of the Postman Cheval* at Hauterives (Drôme), France · ca. 1879–1900.

The country postman Ferdinand Cheval wrote that as he daily climbed the paths of the Drôme region, "in order to entertain my thoughts, I built a fairy palace in my dreams…" In 1879, when he was in his forties, he undertook the realization of those dreams. He began by building a tufa waterfall, and this was later flanked by the Temple of Nature and the Barbary Tower. The work was completed by thirty-three years of hard labor, often done at night, by candlelight. Building in an era when architects were investigating and reviving all manner of styles, this inventive man took the Angkor Vat temple as model for his structure, thus evoking the splendor of exotic countries. Built with winding staircases that lead from floor to floor, the temple, combining carved stone and cement, is built up, cut, and modelled in astonishingly fantastic forms, within which hides a whole, entirely consistent symbolism.

442

444

443 *Capital with lions* · Polished sandstone · India, Maurya period, ca.
274–237 B.C. · Archaeological Museum, Sarnath (Uttar Pradesh).

This capital, which bears the Buddhist symbol of the Wheel of the Law
(*dharmachakra*) on its plinth, has now become the emblem of the Indian Republic. It surmounted a column erected by the Emperor Asoka
in the park at Sarnath, where Buddha first preached. The influence
of Achaemenid architectural sculpture is obvious here. The same type
of capital is found also – with more or less important variations – in
Gandhara sculpture, which precedes it by at least three centuries. The
smooth polish of the surface is typical of the Maurya Dynasty, although it also appears at other periods.

443

445

444 *"Mother-Goddess"* „ from Mathura · Terra cotta · India, 2nd century
B.C. · Prince of Wales Museum, Bombay.

The dating of terra-cotta female figurines, like this example from Mathura (Uttar Pradesh), is still controversial. The figure probably goes
back to about the 2nd century B.C., for it displays remarkable analogies with the "baroque ladies" typical of the northwest frontier,
which as a result of the excavations at Charsada can be dated 250–100
B.C. The object of these statuettes has not been determined either;
they are certainly of the fertility goddess type, but they may have lost
their original significance and become mere charms.

445 *Yakshi on an elephant*, and railing elements, from Bharhut · Red sandstone · India, Shunga period, 2nd century B.C. · Indian Museum, Calcutta.

An inscription enables us to identify this yakshi from the Stupa of Bharhut (Madhya Pradesh) as Chulakoka Devata – "the goddess Chulakoka." The attitude is typical of the female human and divine figures that appear on the balustrades and the torana of the stupa. It reflects the belief that a tree will come into flower when touched by a beautiful woman's foot. The figure stands upon an elephant whose trunk is coiled around the tree. Perhaps this animal, and all those that perform the same function on the Bharhut reliefs, should be identified as the precedents for the *vahana* ("vehicles") characteristic of later Buddhist and Hindu iconography.

447 *The Dream of Queen Maya;* pillar medallion, from Bharhut · Red sandstone · India, Shunga period, 1st–2nd centuries B.C. · Indian Museum, Calcutta.

The episode of the miraculous conception of Siddhartha is depicted on a medallion which decorated one of the pillars of the balustrade of the Stupa at Bharhut (Madhya Pradesh). The artist has set down one figure beside another, inventory-fashion: the sleeping queen, the elephant coming down towards her, and the attendants. Only in the two little figures with their backs turned is there any attempt to indicate – for practical rather than stylistic reasons – recession in depth from one plane to the next. Each element is defined with great calligraphic precision.

447

446 *North Gate of Stupa No. 1* (The Great Stupa), Sanchi (Madhya Pradesh) · India, Early Andhra period, 1st century B.C.

The *torana* (gates) of the Great Stupa at Sanchi correspond with the cardinal points and lead into the corridor intended for the ritual circumambulation of the stupa – that is, symbolically, the Path of Life around the World Mountain. The north gate appears to have been executed second of the four gates. The relation between the jambs and the architraves goes back to wooden architecture, just as the relief technique is derived from carving on wood or ivory. The sculptured areas, completely filled by figures of animals or ornament, are conceived as though sandwiched between two absolutely parallel planes: the background and the original surface of the block.

446

448 *Yakshi*, East gate of the Great Stupa, Sanchi (Madhya Pradesh) · India, Early Andhra period, 1st century B.C.

Placed as a bracket for the lower architrave of the east torana (done just after the north torana), this yakshi was only technically a free-standing statue; in fact, the artist conceived the figure as largely confined to a frontal plane. Carved in extremely accentuated relief form, the yakshi was silhouetted against the sky or the stupa, which offered a background parallel to the plane of both the figure and the compact mass of foliage of the tree. The twisting movement achieved by the pose of the arms and the strongly out-thrust hip is noteworthy. Here, as in later Indian monuments, the presence of yakshis, ancient fertility deities, testified to the persistence of pre-Buddhist religious phenomena.

449 *Pillar with a yakshi*, Bhutesar, Mathura · Red sandstone· India, Kushan period, 2nd century A.D. · Indian Museum, Calcutta.

This pillar from a stupa at Bhutesar is one of the most famous works of Mathura (Uttar Pradesh) sculpture. Just what role these female figures played in the context of Buddhist stupa decoration is not clear, but they are ever present. The yakshi stands upon a dwarflike yaksha symbolizing earthly powers. There is a smaller scene above the yakshi which represents couples in the attitude of people at a banquet; the significance these couples is not clear either, but they are often found on cosmetic palettes in the northwest. This pillar has obvious iconographical precedents at Bharhut.

449

239

450

451 *Ivory plaque*, from Kapisi (Begram) · Afghanistan, 2nd century
A.D. · National Museum of Afghanistan, Kabul.

At Begram, northwest of Kabul, the French Archeological Delegation
has brought to light the ancient Kapisi, which was probably the
Kushan souvereigns' summer capital. The French excavation found in
a palace an exceptional collection of art works, including plaster
models, glass, Hellenistic bronzes, Indian ivories, and Chinese lacquer.
This ivory plaque, part of the decoration for a throne, represents a
woman in the pose of a yakshi under a portico resembling the gate of
a stupa. The chronology is still uncertain, but stylistic aspects would
seem to preclude a date prior to the 2nd century.

451

450 *Standing couple*, from the façade of the *chaitya*, Karle (Bombay) ·
India, Andhra period, early 2nd century A.D.

Like other works from Karle, these figures, probably of donors, reveal
surprising affinities with contemporary Kushan works, in particular
the sculpture from Mathura (Uttar Pradesh). They are also reminiscent
of certain ivories from Begram (Afghanistan) and of some of the earliest pieces from Amaravati (Deccan). Such affinities are noticeable
not only in composition and in iconography, dress, and jewelry, but
also in the style, which nevertheless retains much of the art of Sanchi.
One can see from this time onwards the formation of an Indian stylistic
koinè, which attains full bloom in the "internationalism" of Gupta art.

452 *The Enlightenment of Gautama* · India, 2nd century A.D. · Freer
Gallery of Art, Washington, D.C.

This is the culminating moment in the life of the Buddha: the Blessed
One, sitting in the shade of a pipal tree on a grass-covered seat, lowers
his right hand towards the Earth, which he calls upon to witness his
quality as Buddha. All around him demons from the army of Mara,
who try to prevent his attainment of Enlightenment, make vain attempts to distract him. Figures in high relief, conventionally disposed
in several rows, fill the whole area, producing lively light effects.

452

453 *Bust of an ascetic*, from Hadda · Stucco · Afghanistan, 4th century A.D. · National Museum of Afghanistan, Kabul.

The identification of this figure, with its dramatic expression, is uncertain: it probably represents an ascetic, although there is no characteristic *jata* (coil of hair over the forehead). This work is one of a series of stuccos found at Hadda, Afghanistan. It was certainly part of a sculptured ensemble, but one cannot even form a rough idea of the whole, so fragmentary are the remains of the stuccos from this locale (as from Gandhara in general). This head is justly famous for its effective contrasts of light and shade, which appear to dissolve the material solidity of the figure in a manner owing much to Hellenistic influence.

453

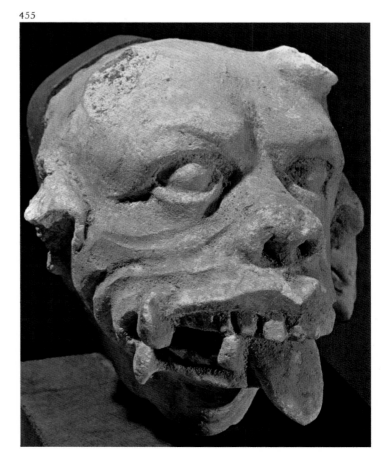

454

454 *Spirit with flowers*, from Hadda · Stucco · Afghanistan, 4th–5th centuries A.D. · Musée Guimet, Paris.

Among the many fragments of Gandharan stucco art found during French excavations at Hadda, on the borders of Afghanistan, this bust has enjoyed special popularity. It obviously has its origin in some Roman work such as the statue of Antinous-Vertumne now in the Lateran Museum. It probably represents a genie offering flowers to Buddha. Despite a certain calligraphic facility typical of Gandhara art, the fluidity of the planes calls to mind the stucco medallions at Begram, which were imported from the Mediterranean.

455

455 *Head of a demon*, from Hadda · Stucco · Afghanistan, 3rd–5th centuries A.D. · National Museum of Afghanistan, Kabul.

Scenes of demonology seem to have interested Gandharan sculptors as much as they did Bosch and Breughel. There are many schist reliefs showing Buddha vainly tempted by the demon Mara, accompanied by packs of demons of terrifying appearance. In the stuccos – particularly in those from Hadda – these demoniacal figures were endlessly multiplied and varied during the evolution of Buddhism, exploring all possible human and animal aspects and producing very effective combinations.

456

456 *Head of Buddha*, from Gandhara · Limestone composition · India, 5th–6th centuries A.D. · Victoria and Albert Museum, London.

This head is typical of the images of Buddha in the later phase of Gandhara art, the so-called Stucco Period. The classical reminiscences of the earlier Gandhara sculptures in stone are evident, but there is also some relationship to works of the same time done in Sarnath (Uttar Pradesh), especially as concerns the clarity of transitions from one plane to another and in the sinuous form of the eyes. Like all Gandhara stucco sculptures, this work was originally painted.

457

457 *Head of Buddha*, from Hadda · Stucco · National Museum of Afghanistan, Kabul.

The Chinese pilgrim Fa-hsien, who visited the site of Hadda (not far from present-day Jalalabad) in the 4th century A.D., spoke of a great Buddhist sanctuary there with 1,000 stupas. The site was demolished by an invasion of Huns shortly after another Chinese pilgrim, Sang Yün, had visited it in 520. The French archeologist Barthoux excavated the ruins of 531 stupas, most of whose remains are now in the Kabul museum or in the Musée Guimet in Paris. The stucco statuettes found on the site, such as this head of Buddha, are molded over a core of chalk and straw that makes them extremely fragile. The Hadda period dates between the 2nd and 5th centuries A.D., but between these limits the chronology of the works is difficult to establish.

458

458 *Buddha taming the Maddened Elephant*; railing medallion from the Stupa of Amaravati · Marble · India, Andhra period, late 2nd century A.D. · Government Museum, Madras.

Though contemporary with the Gandhara and Mathura schools, the school of Amaravati (Andhra Pradesh) evolved stylistic themes and motifs that have a more purely Indian appearance. Some scholars have maintained that it was this school that "created" the Buddha image, but it is more likely that Amaravati derived it from outside influences. In this medallion from the Stupa of Amaravati the strongly spiraling movements that generally characterize works of the school are entirely absent. In composition the work relates to the medallions from Bharhut, but it differs from them profoundly in the employment of a far more sophisticated visual perspective.

459 *Standing Buddha*, from Mathura · Red sandstone · India, Gupta period, 4th–6th centuries A.D. · Indian Museum, Calcutta.

Found in Mathura, this Buddha, whose hands originally made the *abhaya mudra* (gesture of reassurance), is only a gentle reflection of the Kushan images. Formal unity of the work is achieved by the curving lines of the face, the edges of the gown and the stringlike drapery folds, whose sinuous movement is emphasized by the deep shadowing round the thighs. The Enlightened One is portrayed with the characteristics of an ephebe, responding to established iconographical canons, and the artist has created particularly subtle *sfumato* effects in his modelling. The excellent state of preservation of the *prabhamandala* (halo) augments the importance of the image.

459

461 *Bodhisattva bathing in the Nairanjana*, from Amaravati · India, Andhra period, 70 B.C.–300 A.D. · Museum of Fine Arts, Boston.

Amaravati, situated in the eastern Deccan, was the capital of the Andhra kingdom, which lasted from about 70 B.C. to the beginning of the 3rd century A.D. The voluptuous and powerful Buddhist style from Sanchi and Mathura has affinities with the Amaravati style, particularly towards the end of its development, when the figures become more elongated and more sinuous, the poses more animated, and the compositions more confused and dynamic. It was at Amaravati that the future Medieval style of India was formed.

460 *Budda Preaching his First Sermon*, from Sarnath · Sandstone · India, Gupta period, 5th century A.D. · Archeological Museum, Sarnath.

One of the most beautiful works of Gupta art is this image of Buddha giving his first sermon in the Deer Park, his hands in the *dharmachakra mudra* – the gesture of the turning of the Wheel of the Law. Composed in a triangle, the figure's forms are utterly simple, almost geometric, and the image is rendered supremely effective by the great circular *prabhamandala* (halo) set above the massive square forms of the throne. Beneath the throne are portrayed disciples in attitudes of adoration, three on either side of the Wheel of the Law which symbolizes the first prayer. The earliest Siamese and Cambodian Buddhas derive from this type, as do those from Borobudur (Java).

460

461

462

462 *Vishu Anantasayana*, rock-cut relief at Mamallapuram · India, Pallava period, mid 7th century.

The Pallava dynasty was established in the region of Andhra in the southeast Deccan; Mamallapuram, near Madras, was its port. In the various rock-sculptured sanctuaries created there in the middle of the 7th century, Hindu mythology received one of its purest expressions. This granite relief represents Vishnu resting on the coils of the serpent Ananta; Brahma the creator rises from his navel. The clear, restrained style conveys the presence of divinity in which the creative power is concentrated.

464 *Room in a vihara*, Cave 33 at Elura, India.

The great complex of rock sanctuaries at Elura in the Maratha country evolved over several periods. After the Buddhist caves, which were excavated up to the 6th century, came the Hindu caves, and finally Jain caves. The groups of caves form the *viharas*, or monasteries, composed of cells around large rooms used as refectories or meeting places. Cave 33 was part of a Jain monastery and belongs to the last period, after the Elura Kailasanatha temple was built. The Jain sect, based on the preaching of the jainas (wise men), developed parallel to Buddhism. The rock-cut room is conceived like a constructed building, the pillars with fluted shafts, bases and capitals seeming to perform the same role as they would have in a wooden hall.

463 *The Wedding of Shiva and Parvati*, Dhumar Lena, Cave 29, Elura · India, Chalukya period, 580–640 A.D.

The *panigrahana* ceremony (the *dextrarum junctio*) of Shiva and Parvati is carved in Cave 29 at Elura. Though dated in the Chalukya period, it has rightly been compared with works from the more recent Rastrakuta period sanctuary at Elephanta (Bombay). Owing to their composite nature, the reliefs in this cave are undoubtedly closer to those of the Kailasanatha temple at Elura (8th century) than to those of the Gupta temple at Deogarh (ca. 500 A.D.).

463

464

465

465 *Rock-cut beast and one of the five Ratha*, at Mamallapuram · India,
Pallava period, early 7th century.

On the banks of the Mamallapuram near Madras are granite rocks
which in the early 7th century were sculptured into various forms.
Illustrated here is one of the five *ratha* (chariots), replicas of temples
of the period and named for personages of the *Mahabharata*. Other
rocks are cut in the forms of animals, such as the great beast seen here.

466

466 *The Descent of the Ganges*, at Mamallapuram (Madras) · India,
mid-Pallava period, 630–668 A.D.

Carved on two enormous granite outcroppings at Mamallapuram is
one of the greatest masterpieces of Pallava art, from the reign of Nara-
simhavarman I, Mamalla. It represents the miracle granted by Shiva:
the Ganges' descent from the heavens. In the center of the composition
is a split in the rock through which flowed the actual water at flood
time, performing in the sculptured scene the role of the waters of the
sacred river coming down to earth. A multitude of people and animals,
real and fantastic, cluster all around like a microcosm of the living
universe. Stylistic elements derived from the Kistna Valley and especially from Amaravati are present, but, recast in the Pallava mode,
certain elements cede much of their calligraphic quality to plastic or
coloristic effects.

467

467 *The Kailasanatha*, at Elura · India, Early Medieval period, ca.
750–800 A.D.

This Kailasanatha (a temple of the Holy Mountain Kailasa, dedicated
to Shiva) is carved out of the living rock, like the *ratha* at Mamallapuram. The temple was offered to the god by one of the rulers of the
Rashtrakuta dynasty in the second half of the 8th century. Although

there appear close similarities to the temple of Virupaksha at Pattada-
kal (ca. 740) and to the Kailasanatha of Kanchipuram (ca. 700), the
derivation from Pallava architecture at Mamallapuram remains in-
disputable. This is an advanced example of the type of temple crowned
by a stepped pyramid and ornamented with vestigial model shrines
that is found later in the sanctuaries of southern India.

468 *Flying Devata*, Kailasanatha Temple, Elura · India, Medieval
period, 750–800 A.D.

Originally, the rock-cut Kailasanatha temple was probably coated
with plaster and painted, so details of this flying spirit must have been
carried out in the stucco. Although in its anatomy the figure differs
little from the Pallava images, a novel note is introduced with the
body's violent twist, which is almost an anticipation of the spiraling
figures at Khajuraho (fig. 476). But the relationship to the plane of
the wall remains unchanged from the time of Pallava and Chalukya
art: the figure seems cut into by the background plane, and does not
give the impression of being able to move freely in depth.

468

469 *Stories from the Mahabharata*, Kailasanatha Temple, Elura · India, Medieval period, ca. 750–800 A.D.

On the Kailasanatha Temple, sculptured friezes arranged along
superposed registers trace the narratives of the two great Indian epic
poems, the Mahabharata (on the north wall) and the Ramayana (south
wall). The Mahabharata tells of the struggle between the two clans
of the Pandava and the Kaurava. The battle themes lend themselves
well to the intermingling of forms favored by Indian sculptors. From
scene to scene figures follow on in continuous action, without relaxation or interruption, expressing the unending flow of things and beings
in an eternal process of renewal. These bas-reliefs may originally have
been covered with a layer of painted stucco; when the Moslems conquered the Deccan in the beginning of the 16th century, they called
the Kailasanatha the Painted Palace.

470 *Interior of the chaitya*, Cave 26, Ajanta · India, ca. 600–642 A.D.

The *chaitya*, or naved Buddhist temple carved out of the rock, appeared
in the 1st century B.C. In its original state it was an imitation of
the wooden constructions which were in turn related to Iranian prototypes. This type of cave-temple continued until the 7th century at
Ajanta, but reminiscences of the wooden construction (still seen in the
vault here) gradually disappeared, giving way to a style that is more
properly Indian, and sculptural rather than architectural. At the end
of the central nave there is a stupa or *dagoba* commemorating the
Paranirvana or the supreme state reached by the Buddha, whose
teaching was directed towards the achievement of this state.

469

470

471

471 *Façade of the chaitya*, Cave 19 at Ajanta · India, Gupta period, first half of the 6th century A.D.

In the Maurya period, the façades of these rock temples were decorated with a system of arcades and niches inspired by wooden constructions (*kudu*). In the Gupta era, they took on a sheathing of sculpture; here, only a small bay is kept to light up the *chaitya* nave, which in early times opened directly to the outside. Despite the carved surfaces, however, the architectural structure is still strongly emphasized and the sculptured reliefs are fitted into the intervals of this structure. The figures represent Buddhas, repeated to the point of monotony, or else guardian-kings.

472 *Mother and Child* · India, Medieval period, 11th century · Indian Museum, Calcutta.

This group, said to be from Bhuvanesvara, seems to resemble more the sculpture of Khajuraho. The initial architectonic function is felt through the rigorous superposition of the component parts, which contribute to the twisting movement of the whole. The compact vegetable mass at the top – something found also in the torana at Sanchi (fig. 446) – is intended to create a spatial illusion – a kind of niche that surrounds the figure with strong chiaroscuro effects. The shape of some of the jewels, especially of the bracelets, is still in fashion in India today.

472

473 *Vrksaka (Tree Goddess)* · Stone · India, Medieval period, 8th–10th centuries A.D. · Archeological Museum, Gwalior.

This work comes from a Hindu temple at Gyaraspur in Madhya Pradesh. Although in its iconography the figure hardly differs from the Sanchi yakshi (fig. 448), earlier by almost a thousand years, it seems to be completely freed from the spatial conventions that persisted down to post-Gupta times. Further, certain typological similarities with Khajuraho sculpture suggest a date from the end of the 10th century. However, some experts place this figure in the 8th century. The sinuous rows of pearls and the material pulled tightly around the thighs make it a very effective composition.

473

474 *Tara* · Stone · India, Medieval, Pala period, 11th century A.D. Indian Museum, Calcutta.

During the period from 730 to 1197 A.D., under the Pala and Sena dynasties, a style was created in Bengal and Bihar that incorporated a number of motifs and stylistic elements from classical Gupta art. From Bengal and Bihar this classical tradition was transmitted to Nepal and Tibet, on the one hand, and on the other to Burma and Java and even to Yunnan. The Pala rulers were conscientious protectors of Mahayana Buddhism, one of whose favorite deities is Tara, portrayed under different aspects deriving from the Bodhisattvas. This figure from Bihar shows characteristics typical of Pala art in its maturity: a fairly pronounced *tribhanga* (S-curve, of the body), minute attention to detail, and exuberant floral ornamentation.

475 *Shiva as Nataraja* (Lord of the Dance) · Bronze · India, Chola period, 12th–13th century A.D. · Museum van Aziatische Kunst, Amsterdam.

Apasmara purusa, the demon personifying oblivion and ignorance, is trampled on by the god Shiva in his role as Lord of the Dance (Nataraja), dancing the cosmic dance within the orb of the sun, represented by the circle of fire. Such representations of Shiva as universal destroyer and regenerator are typical of the schools of southern India and are among their most strongly dramatic expressions. The god is holding the tambourine and the flame, his two traditional attributes, which symbolize the birth and destruction of the universe.

476 *Love scene*, Chitragupta Temple, Khajuraho · India, Northern Medieval, 11th century.

Phallic art and sexual representations appear in India only with the Hindu era as, in the West, they appear with the Hellenistic era: eroticism is always a late offspring, therefore, and one absent from the art of the great classical civilizations. Many of the Medieval temples of India show erotic scenes endlessly multiplied on the various levels of the *vihara*. In the Indian mystique the physical union between two people has a philosophical meaning. It is a pantheistic act that leads to communion with the universal harmony; creatures joined in the ecstasy of the flesh experience for a moment a unity with that essential harmony. Every skilled practice was employed to give the experience the greatest possible intensity, and the promotion and perfection of it are the aims of the *Kama Kala* teachings.

477

477 *Statue of Hari-Hara* · Cambodia, Early Khmer, ca. 7th century A.D. · Musée Albert Sarraut, Phnom-Penh.

This composite deity unites in one figure the bodies of Shiva (Hara) on the right and Vishnu on the left. From the 6th to the 9th century, the so-called pre-Angkor era, Cambodian imagery was profoundly impregnated with Hinduism. At this time Khmer art endowed the forms that it had received from India with an architectonic quality, emphasizing the structural power of the human body and its muscular system. The figure was portrayed by preference free-standing and upright, showing even details of anatomical structure – something quite foreign to the spirit of India. Free-standing statues dominate the development of Khmer sculpture.

479 *Female deity* · Cambodia, First Angkor period, 11th century A.D. · Musée Guimet, Paris.

Khmer sculpture evolves in the direction of an ever-growing concern with perfection in modelling, based on a profound knowledge of anatomy; the knowledge is not asserted obviously, as in the pre-Angkor period, but is evidenced in a mastery over the body's muscular equilibrium. The Angkor Vat period produced some admirable partly draped female statues, equalling classical Greek sculpture in the beauty of their modelling – an analogy even more marked because, for the most part, these figures have reached us in a mutilated state, with head and arms missing. The drapery of this example is unfinished.

478 *Head of a Bodhisattva* · Cambodia, Second Angkor period, 11th–12th centuries A.D. · Musée Guimet, Paris.

In the Second Angkor period of the 11th and 12th centuries, Khmer art became more naturalistic and rid itself of the earlier stylistic conventions. The smile of Buddhist figures lights up faces of a native type, with half-closed eyes, prominent cheekbones, heavy features and thick lips. Spiritual light animates human flesh; the face symbolizing beatitude and supreme wisdom becomes more accessible to the worshippers because of its more human appearance.

478

479

480

480 *Marching army*, gallery relief from temple of Angkor Vat · Cambodia, Second Angkor period, ca. 1112–1153 A.D.

Angkor Vat, perhaps the high point in Khmer art, was dedicated to Vishnu by Suryavarman II (ca. 1112–1153). The low-relief sculptures in the galleries appear to be subjected to all manner of subtle stylistic devices that strive to transform human figures, animals, and plants into moving, patterned arabesques, exploring all possible variations. The sculptors did not aim at rendering realistic spatial effects, but the infinite variations of light give an illusory depth to the compositions, enhanced by surprisingly pictorial effects. Every available space in the relief is filled with foliage or figures. The scene is taken from the great epic poem of India, the *Ramayana*.

481

481 *Towers with faces*, the Bayon Temple, Angkor Thom · Cambodia, Second Angkor period, late 12th–early 13th century A.D.

Angkor Thom, built by Jayavaram II, is a Buddhist monument. The central edifice, the Bayon (which gives its name to a stylistic phase of Khmer art), is characterized by the great towers with human faces. These probably represent Jayavarman himself, deified and identified with Lokeshvara, the Bodhisattva to whom the temple is dedicated. But the religious concept reflected in these curious pieces of sculptured architecture is Hindu rather than Buddhist: one could compare them to enormous *caturmukhalinga*, the symbol by which the god-king reveals himself in every direction.

482

482 *Celestial dancer*, from Mi Son · Sandstone · Cham school, 10th century A.D. · Musée Henri Parmentier, Da Nang, Vietnam.

In the kingdom of Champa, a type of art was produced that has been rightly distinguished from Khmer art, although the latter often influences it. Until the 10th century, the capital was in the Quang-Nam area, near the holy city of Mi Son, where the village of Trakieu now stands. This dancer comes from there. The natural twist of the body contrasts effectively with the rigid profiles of the cornice. This work, like the sculpture of Borobudur, shows how Pallava art spread outside India.

483

483 *Head of a Buddha* · Bronze · Thailand, Sukhodaya period, early 14th century A.D. · Musée Guimet, Paris.

While Indian and Khmer Buddhas have a quite human appearance even in the Gupta era, the Buddha figures made in Thailand during the Sukhodaya era appear like crystalline abstractions of Buddhist wisdom, so stylized have the facial features become: the head a beautiful oval, the features thoroughly refined, the nose sharp-ridged, the hair arranged in numerous patterned curls, ear lobes elongated out of all proportion, eyebrows pronounced and eyelids lowered over slit eyes. The sacred protuberance, the *ushnisha*, is often surmounted by a flame symbolizing spiritual life.

484 *Buddha*, on the Stupa of Borobudur · Java, late 8th century A.D.

The stupa of Borobudur is the most important Buddhist monument in Java. In addition to the representations of the Karma doctrines, the Jatakas, and the Avadana, the stories of Maitreya and Samanthabhadra, Buddha of the future, Borobudur presents a series of portraits of the Enlightened One, some of which are half-hidden in their miniature stupas with perforated walls. A derivation from the Gupta Buddhas of Sarnath and Mathura has often been proposed, but must in any case be considered as indirect. The contribution of the Javanese artists is the softening of the strict geometry of their prototypes and a marked interest in *sfumato* effects.

484

485 *Sudhana and his Ladies drawing water from the lotus pool*, gallery of the Stupa of Borobudur · Lava stone · Java, late 8th century A.D.

The geometrical schemes of Borobudur reliefs often seem so regular and so over-simple as to suggest a tired academism. The essential lines of the composition, the edges of the reliefs, and the architectonic structure are contained in a rigid order of parallel and orthogonal lines. Again the derivation from Gupta sculpture is clear, but here the scenes are more richly ornate and light plays a more important role. The reliefs in the various galleries of the stupa are arranged in accordance with the principles of the Mahayana Buddhist cosmogony.

485

487 *Decorative tiles* from Harvan, Kashmir · Indo-Iranian, 4th century A.D.(?) · Musée Guimet, Paris.

In this plaque, as with all those in terra cotta that bear the mark of the Harvan monastery (Kashmir), Indian and Iranian influences are evident; they are mixed with local elements hard to identify precisely – Turkish, perhaps? These plaques are generally dated 4th century, but they show analogies with Sanchi art of the 7th century. Though less obvious than the elements characteristic of Parthian Iran, there are other stylistic elements here that go back to Sassanian art. The letters on the lower listel are from the *kharosthi* alphabet, typical of the northeastern region of India.

486

487

486 *Female torso*, from Fondukistan · Terra cotta · Afghanistan, 7th-8th centuries, A.D. · Musée Guimet, Paris.

A group of particularly important sculptures, datable for the most part to the 7th–8th centuries, has been brought to light by the French Archeological Delegation in the monastery of Fondukistan, between Bamiyan and Begram (Afghanistan). The figures are of an extremely linear design and produce subtle calligraphic effects elaborating on motifs from Pala India. From the stylistic point of view one might equally compare them with work from Chinese Turkestan, with which they share certain technical characteristics, such as the use of rough clay mixed with vegetable or animal fibers, as at Tumsu (Chinese Turkestan), Bamiyan and Tapa Sardar (Afghanistan).

488 *Head of a Bodhisattva* · Stucco · Central Asia, 7th century A.D. · Musée Guimet, Paris.

This head was found in thirteen pieces in a monastery on the site of Duldur-Akhm in Central Asia. Modelled in stucco, it was baked by a fire in the monastery. Set on the hair with its thick curls is a laurel circlet like that of a hero from classical antiquity. The Greco-Buddhist smile of beatitude is expressed with exquisite delicacy; that smile spread from one monastery to the next along the routes of Central Asia to China.

488

489

489 *Bodhisattva*, from Fondukistan · Terra cotta · Afghanistan, 7th–8th centuries A.D. · Musée Guimet, Paris.

This Bodhisattva is a perfect illustration of the refined linearism characteristic of the Indo-Iranian style of Fondukistan and which finds an echo on the one hand in the sculpture of Tumsu (Chinese Turkestan) and on the other in the terra cottas of Huksar (Kashmir). From the iconographical point of view, this art was evidently susceptible to numerous influences, which it has nevertheless not exploited to the full, doubtless on account of the interruption caused by the Moslem conquest. These sculptures in rough clay, painted and sometimes gilded, were supported by a wooden core. Some parts were done separately with the help of molds and then applied to the figures.

492 *Bodhisattva*, from Kumtura · China, ca. 7th–8th centuries A.D. · Musée Guimet, Paris.

The centers of Kucha art, while linked with Indian or Indo-Iranian traditions, gradually departed from them after the Chinese conquest in the 7th century. Contact with models of T'ang art is evident in this Bodhisattva, which comes from the rock sanctuary at Kumtura. One must not lose sight of all that T'ang art owes to Indian art of the Gupta era; compared with the works found at Fondukistan, this torso seems almost archaic. The perfect preservation of the color makes the piece a precious document.

492

490 *Kneeling worshipper*, from Kumtura · China, 7th century A.D. · Musée Guimet, Paris.

This devout kneeling figure, holding an offering, comes from Kumtura, a religious and artistic center whose activity extended over almost five centuries. It is done in mud mixed with straw and hair and is supported by a straw core. The excellent state of preservation of the polychrome makes the work exceptionally important. The simplified structure, reduced to a few essential volumes, and the rounded features of the face relate the work to certain Chinese funerary statuettes of the T'ang Dynasty: it is therefore a relatively late work, doubtless of the 7th century.

491

490

491 *Statuette of a woman* · Terra cotta · China, Han Dynasty, 202 B.C.–220 A.D. · Museum of Fine Arts, Boston.

An austere, serious expression characterizes this lady draped in a long robe; her attitude is of withdrawal, almost of reverence. The figure is a *ming-ch'i*, one of a type of Chinese funerary terra cottas which include statuettes of human beings and animals, reproductions in miniature of houses, rice fields, boats, chariots, and other objects of common or ritual usage. The living dedicated them to the dead in memory of their past existence, as funerary furnishings intended for use in afterlife.

493 *Tiger* · Bronze · China, Chou Dynasty, 10th century B.C. · Freer
Gallery of Art, Washington, D.C.

This object, coming in all probability from Pao-ki-hien (Feng-siang-
fou, Chensi), is stylistically related to the Middle Chou period, although
it dates from an earlier time. The large opening on the back has led
some scholars to believe that this bronze was a vase, but it was more
probably the foot of a canopic vase or of a throne. (Length 30 inches.)
The soft, heavy forms, lacking any details of muscular structure, are
freighted with hook and spiral decorations (*lei-wen*, thunder motifs),
which cover the whole surface and emphasize the schematization of
the planes.

493

494 *Funerary relief* · Stone · China, Han Dynasty, 114 A.D. · Rietberg
Museum, Zurich (Coll. von der Heydt).

This plaque, which was part of the Tai family tomb, situated in Lieou-
tch'eng-chan (Shantung), may be dated from an inscription on it. It
belongs to a kind of funerary art particularly fashionable in China
during the Han dynasty. Carved or engraved plaques decorated the
walls of the sepulchral chambers and vestibules in the tumulus tombs,
and sometimes also the rooms of the small temples that stood near the
tombs. The decoration is worked in extremely shallow relief, hardly
rising above the background. It is divided into three horizontal bands.
As in all reliefs of this type, the subjects are scenes from everyday life,
mixed with mythological themes relating particularly to Taoist tradition.

494

495

495 *Bodhisattva* · Stone · China, Wei Dynasty, 5th century A.D. ·
Musée Guimet, Paris.

This figure in very high relief is one of the most important works
from the Yun-kang caves. In the mountains of Yun-kang, near P'ing
Ch'eng, the capital of northern Wei province, numerous grotto-sanctu-
aries were created through the efforts of the monk T'an-yao, who was
named curator of the monasteries of the empire in 460. These grottoes
were decorated with innumerable figures of Buddha or of Bodhisattvas,
in all sizes. In the first half of the 20th century these grottoes, like
those of Lung-Men, were stripped of their reliefs, which were sold in
the Occident. The smiling face of this Bodhisattva expresses the infinite mercy of one who, to save others, has consented to delay his
moment of entrance into supreme beatitude.

496

496 *Stone relief* from Lung-Men, Honan · China, ca. 495–550 A.D. ·
Museum of Fine Arts, Boston.

This is the portrait of the prince Siddhartha, future Sakyamuni
Buddha, seated in an attitude of contemplation. The position was to
become characteristic for the iconographical type of the Maitreya
Buddha. From the stylistic point of view, the work belongs to the
first phase of Chinese Buddhist sculpture: the body and limbs are
thick-set, the smile archaic, and the treatment of the drapery rigid as
it spreads into dovetail arrangements of rich folds at the lower edges.
The figure nevertheless expresses an intense spirituality.

497 *Flying spirit (apsaras)* · Stone · China, Wei Dynasty, 385–535 A.D. · Fogg Museum of Art, Harvard University, Cambridge.

This relief originally decorated Cave 2 at T'ien-lung Shan (Shansi), the most beautiful of all Buddhist rock temples in China. It represents an *apsaras* (*t'ien-nu* or *fei-t'ien* in Chinese) in a flying position, with clothes loosened and long tags of drapery flapping in the wind, stylized like tongues of flame. The figure represents a celestial nymph considered in ancient Indian mythology as a goddess of nature and fertility, skilled in the art of disturbing the contemplation of ascetics by luring them with her beauty. It was incorporated into the Buddhist pantheon as a *deva* (*t'ien-shen* in Chinese), a spirit still subject to the cycle of rebirth.

497

499

499 *Base for a statue* · Grey limestone · China, Wei Dynasty, 385–535 A.D. · University Museum, Philadelphia.

The base is in the form of an inverted lotus flower resting on a square plinth decorated with scenes in extremely low relief. Represented is a procession of personages bearing offerings, led by a donor who has dismounted from his horse and holds a censer in his hand. The participants in the procession carry emblems and standards denoting the donor's rank: scepters, parasol, and flag. A groom holding the reins of a richly harnessed horse brings up the rear of the procession.

498 *Chimera* · Stone · China, Wei Dynasty, ca. 500 A.D. · University Museum, Philadelphia.

The skill that Chinese art had already achieved in its earliest phase in representations of animals is illustrated by this sculpture of a fabulous beast. Like others of his type, the beast was intended originally to guard the *shen-tao* (paths of the spirits) – the paths that led to the tombs. The most frequent representations are of lions guarding princely tombs, and of chimeras, considered the noblest of beasts, guarding the tombs of the emperors. Chimeras are portrayed as hybrids of lions and winged dragons, with goats' horns on their heads.

498

500

500 *Base for a statue* · Grey limestone · China, Wei Dynasty, 385–535 A.D. · University Museum, Philadelphia.

The relief represents a genie emerging from a lotus flower and holding with both hands a large perfume-burner on his head. At either side crouch lions with thick manes, in almost heraldic positions. Above them are phoenixes. Floral motifs fill the empty spaces of the composition. Like the previous one (fig. 499), this relief is characterized by its essentially graphic style.

501 *Torso of a Bodhisattva* · Stone · China, T'ang Dynasty, 618–907 A.D.· Collection A. Patino, Paris.

This statue comes from the rock temple of T'ien-lung Shan (Shansi), which may be termed the type-site for T'ang stone sculpture. The body bending slightly forward from the bust, the elegantly proportioned limbs, the manner in which the drapery is arranged, and the richness of the bracelets endow this figure with the realism and worldly ease typical of Chinese Buddhist iconography during the T'ang era, influenced by Indian art and the late Gupta style. The absence of any hieraticism is combined with a strained rhythmical movement of the body, reminiscent of the *tribhanga* (S-curve) in Indian statuary. (Height 3 feet 5½ inches.)

501

502

502 *Head of a lokapala* · Stone · China, T'ang Dynasty, 618–907 A.D. · University Museum, Philadelphia.

This detail of the head of a lokapala, from the same group as the previous statue, illustrates an even more violent aspect of T'ang art. The facial features recall the Central Asiatic origin of its iconographical type, but also discernible is the influence of Indian Tantric sect models, combined with a feeling for caricature that is specifically Chinese.

503

503 *Horseman* · Stone · China, T'ang Dynasty, 7th century · University Museum, Philadelphia.

This realistic T'ang relief represents an armed horseman trying to remove an arrow which has stuck in his horse's chest. The minute rendering of details is reminiscent of Parthian and Sassanid art. The theme was very popular in T'ang China and is connected with the militaristic, epic-loving spirit of the period. It is also a reworking of old central Asian and Romano-Persian motifs, assimilated into a local tradition of animal art. This relief was part of the group, the "Six Horsemen" of Emperor T'ai-tsong (who died in 640), which decorated a building near his tomb. According to an ancient tradition, the relief was executed after a drawing by the scholar and court painter Yen Li-pên (about 600-673).

504 *Guardian figure* · Stone · China, T'ang Dynasty, 618–907 A.D. · University Museum, Philadelphia.

From T'ien-lung Shan comes a group of statues of *lokapalas* (*Hu-shih-che*, *T'ien-wang* in Chinese), portraying the guardians of the four points of the compass. They were appointed to defend the world from attack by evil spirits. The inspiring force behind them created an iconographical type, peculiar to Buddhist art, whose pitiless and terrifying expression denotes the zeal with which the guardians fulfil their task. By its attitude of authority, immobility, and menacing facial expression, the figure reproduced was intended to inspire fear in the evil spirits, to make them desist from their attacks.

504

505

505 *Bodhisattva* · Wood, polychromed · China, Sung Dynasty, 960–1279 A.D. · Museum van Aziatische Kunst, Amsterdam.

The statue represents the Bodhisattva Avalokiteshvara (*Kuan Yin* in Chinese) seated in the position called the *maharajlila* ("the repose of the great king"), his right arm hanging relaxed on the raised right knee. It is an iconographical type characteristic of Chinese Buddhist art of the Sung era, and is related to the better known type of the standing Kuan Yin, with its typically feminine appearance. In this work the figure of the merciful Bodhisattva is still draped in masculine robes, but the richness of the costume, the softness of the face and limbs, give it an ambiguous and effeminate look.

506

506 *Equestrian statuette* · Glazed terra cotta · T'ang Dynasty, 618–907 A.D. · Alberto Giuganino Collection, Rome.

With the exception of the face and hair, which are painted in crude colors, the statuette is covered with iridescent yellow and green glazes. The rider's costume seems to be of Persian style; it is, in fact, not unusual to find T'ang statuettes showing influences from Central Asia and Iran, or inspired by western Asiatic iconography. Iranian models can sometimes be detected in the figures of jugglers, dancers, and concubines, but the influence of Central Asia is clearest in the representation of animals, particularly camels and horses; it is known that certain animals were in fact imported into China from countries to the west.

507 *Female figurine* · Terra cotta · T'ang Dynasty, 618–907 A.D. · Musée Cernuschi, Paris.

It is difficult to date works created in the three centuries of the T'ang Dynasty. In this statuette there is still a dynamic stylization, a quality of synthesis tending towards the simplification of forms, and an élan characteristic of work of the Han period. The figure is an exquisite image of femininity.

507

508

508 *Statuette of a dancer* · Terra cotta · China, T'ang Dynasty, 618–907 A.D. · British Museum, London.

This T'ang figurine, supple and sinuous in form, represents a dancer, her body curving and her head turned to the left. The arms are elongated by the flowing sleeves whose floating movements convey the idea of the dance rhythms. Modelled of grey terra cotta, the statuette bears traces of white paint and decoration in unbaked colors.

509

509 *Female figurine* · Terra cotta · Japan, Jomon period, 1st millennium B.C. · Takeo Nakazawa Collection, Tokyo.

This female figurine is one of the many terra-cotta idols from the late Neolithic culture of the Japanese archipelago; it emerged during excavations of a mound of shells near Iwatsuki (department of Saitama). The treatment of the figure – a woman wearing a three-lobed headdress – is schematic; her facial features have been stylized and rendered by small terra-cotta pellets. Like all the terra-cotta statuettes of the Jomon group (named after the "cord-pattern" that decorates the pottery), it is interpreted as a symbolical portrait of a mother-goddess, and part of a cult of abundance and fertility.

511

511 *Kwannon* · Lacquered wood · Japan, Asuka period, 7th century A.D. · Chuguji Convent, Nara.

This statue, carved in camphor wood and blackened by smoke from cult ceremonies, dates from the first phase of Japanese Buddhist art. It represents the Bodhisattva of Mercy, Avalokitesvara (*Kwannon* in Japanese), in a seated position, with right leg placed over left and right hand close to chin in the gesture of meditation. According to legend, the work was executed by the famous Shotoku Taishi (572–621). Some authorities identify this figure as Maitreya Buddha (*Miroku* in Japanese).

510

510 *Head, from a haniwa* · Japan, Kofun period, 4th–6th centuries A.D. · National Museum, Tokyo.

This specimen of human head, from a *haniwa*, is a typical product of Japanese art in the Kofun era, that is, the "ancient tombs" era, which lasted from the 4th to the 6th–7th centuries A.D. The *haniwa*, which were originally probably simple terra-cotta tubes (the name in fact means a circle of clay), later were surmounted by heads, or figures of humans and animals, models of houses, boats, and objects of daily or ritual use. Though almost certainly influenced by the tradition of the Chinese *ming-ch'i*, they were intended for a different use: instead of adorning the inner chambers of the tombs, they stood closely spaced in rows following the outline and over the top of the monumental funerary tumuli.

512

513

512 *Great Amida Buddha* · Kotoku, Kamakura · Bronze · Japan, Kamakura period, ca. 1250.

Known as the Great Buddha (*Daibutsu*) of the city of Kamakura, the statue represents the Buddha Amitabha (*Amida Nyorai* in Japanese – "Buddha of the West"). It stands within the outer walls of the Kotoku temple compound at Kamakura, where it was originally housed in a building that was later demolished. According to tradition, the 37-foot figure was cast by Ono Goroyemon or by Tanji Hisatomo in 1252. From the stylistic point of view it reveals the influence of the sculptors Kokei and Unkei, who worked in the later 12th and the early 13th centuries.

513 *The guardian spirit Shitsukongoshin*, from the Sangatsudo (Hokkedo) of the Todai-ji, Nara. Painted clay · Japan, Nara period, mid-8th century A.D.

A *Sukongoshin* (*Vajrapani* in Sanskrit), a Buddhist guardian spirit, is here portrayed as a terrifying creature. According to the tradition of the Todai-ji (the temple where it is preserved), it was made in 733. Because it inspired such fear, it acquired the reputation of possessing miraculous powers; in fact, one popular legend tells how, during the period of the civil wars, the statue turned into a great bumblebee and succeeded in putting down the rebels. Because of the atmosphere of magic that still surrounds it today, it is cited as one of the "secret statues" (*hibutsu*). It is kept in a closed shrine that is opened only on rare occasions, during solemn ceremonies. (Height, 68½ inches.)

514

514   *Lintel*, Saint Genis des Fontaines (Pyrénées-Orientales) · French, 1019–1020.

The first hesitant step in Romanesque sculpture is movingly attested in this lintel, dated exactly by an inscription placing it in the "twenty-fourth year of King Robert." From this point on, the primacy of the achitectural frame is established; the contours of the apostles are literally defined by the surrounding keyhole arches and columns. This flat relief technique is closer to engraving than to sculpture, and the treatment of the drapery folds is a translation in stone of graphic models. The lintel gives an idea of what Romanesque sculpture was to become, but it is still impregnated with the spirit of barbarian art.

515   *Capital*, Saint Philibert, Tournus (Saône-et-Loire) · French, late 10th century.

A sculptured double capital supports the eastern arcade on the north side of the vault in the upper narthex of St. Philibert. The squared block surmounting the composite capital is decorated on one side with a palmette and on the other with a grimacing, bearded head. The technique is crude, the art unpolished, but this first appearance of the human figure is striking; it is probably the first portrait in French art. It is matched by the figure of a mason, signed "Gerlannus," on the south side of the same arch; it may be that the one figure represents the architect and the other the abbot who promoted the work.

516   *Christ, angels, and apostles*, detail of fig. 514.

This is one of the oldest sculptural examples of the theme of Christ in Majesty. The image of Christ teaching, seated on a throne in the center of a mandorla, was developed by miniaturists interpreting a text of Saint Matthew. The two angels holding the mandorla are reminiscent of winged spirits on ancient sarcophagi. Their spread wings and twisting bodies entirely fill the space allotted to them; Romanesque sculptors could not tolerate empty space.

516

517

517 *Virgin and Child* · Wood, polychromed · French, 12th century · The Louvre, Paris.

The Vigin enthroned and holding the blessing Child on her lap, the Virgin in Majesty, and the Virgin *Sedes Sapientiae* or *Theotocos* are all iconographic types frequent in Romanesque art. Traceable to pre-Romanesque prototypes like that at Conques, they were repeated everywhere in the 11th, 12th and 13th centuries, and especially in Auvergne. At times executed in precious metals, at times in polychromed wood, the Virgin is treated as a noble figure, distant and hieratic, the Child as a sober theologian, not a human infant; the pose is stiff and frontal and no imaginative detail is allowed to relieve the monotony of the straight-falling folds of the robes. The Louvre Virgin is already more lifelike: her face with its slightly petulant expression is more individualized, and the Infant hesitantly moves his legs.

518

518 *Christ and angels*, altar frontal, Saint Sernin, Toulouse · French, ca. 1095.

Bernard Gilduin was responsible for the sculptures of the altar of Urban II, consecrated in 1096. The central area of the shrine displays a mandorla with Christ in Majesty, borne up by two symmetrical figures of angels. It is treated in the same way as the funerary portraits on Gallo-Roman sarcophagi, or the portraits on oriental ivories. This vision of Christ as a detached and powerful god was to prevail throughout Romanesque art. In form it is a transposition into sculpture of the gold altar frontals laid over wooden cores. The linear treatment of the elliptical folds of drapery, rather than the hesitant modelling, gives the indications of the figure's anatomy.

520 *Apostle*, detail of fig. 519.

The apostle's face with its protruding eyes, low forehead, firm nose, and projecting lower jaw, under the cap of short, tightly curled hair, is not very far removed from Gallo-Roman stele images. Its formal simplicity is accentuated by the manner in which the head is reserved against the cut-away background, the face lacking any interior modelling but handled rather as a single rounded mass. Although it is in relief, the figure is without a true third dimension, which could have been obtained only by presenting a succession of planes modulating the forms in space, or by a greater naturalism. Psychological analysis and naturalism are sacrificed in favor of monumentality – an approach to the human figure indicating a primitive or archaic phase in art.

519

519 *Apostle*, Saint Sernin, Toulouse · Marble · French, late 11th century.

The Languedoc school witnessed an early revival of monumental sculpture. This apostle occupies one of seven panels that now adorn the screen around the choir of Saint Sernin. Attributed to the sculptor of the altar (fig. 518), they can be dated in the very end of the 11th century. The classical type of a figure in an arched niche is here worked like a Byzantine ivory: the draperies fall stiff and straight, save for the rigid curves of the part drawn diagonally across the body; the saint's pose is static; the figure conforms entirely to the limited space defined by the frame. Transmitted by 5th-century Christian sarcophagi, by miniatures and by goldsmith work, the type became common in Romanesque sculpture.

520

263

521

521 *The Ascension of Christ*; tympanum of the Miègeville portal, Saint Sernin, Toulouse · French, ca. 1115.

In style this tympanum is already more evolved than the previously described sculptures. The same types of personages are portrayed, but this time greater importance is given to composition and poses. The sculptured scene is an integral part of the architecture, fitting exactly into its allotted space. The gestures of the protagonists and the more detailed treatment of the draperies create an animated surface and show a real effort to represent movement. Languedoc sculpture, asserting itself at an early date in French art, has some relation to the contemporary sculpture of northern Spain.

522 *The Second Coming of Christ*; tympanum of the south porch, Saint Pierre, Moissac · French, 1110–1120.

One of the most famous tympana in Romanesque art, this one was executed for the west porch of Saint Pierre and soon after (between 1120 and 1131) moved to the south porch. The iconographical theme, the Apocalyptic Vision, is taken directly from the *Commentaria in Apocalypsin* of Beatus, as Emile Mâle has pointed out. The fierce and majestic Christ is surrounded by the symbols of the four Evangelists; gazing up at Him, the twenty-four Elders assume animated postures, their bending, twisting movements accentuated by the broad, agitated folds of their drapery. In its monumental size and in such details of execution as the flat, curving drapery folds, the composition is characteristic of the art of Languedoc.

522

523

The Prophet Jeremiah is represented in a dance-like posture on the trumeau of the south portal of Moissac. This figure, with its fine head, is testimony to the stylistic evolution of Languedoc sculpture. In less than half a century the works of this school developed from the squat, heavy, inexpressive figures at Saint Sernin (fig. 519) to the vital, elongated form of Jeremiah, whose expressive head suggests contemplation.

524 *The Apostle Peter*, cloister of Saint Pierre, Moissac · Marble · French, 1100–1110.

In technique and in general iconography the apostles in the Moissac cloister are closely akin to those in the ambulatory of Saint Sernin (fig. 518), but they are stronger and more vigorous in style. The pier is conceived as a stele, and the standing figure, completely incorporated into its support, is confined within the spatial framework of the arched niche. The face seen in profile is more realistic in effect than the frontal visage of the apostle from Saint Sernin; and here the apostle's attributes are clearly shown.

524

525

525 *Isaiah*, church of Souillac (Lot) · French, ca. 1130–1140.

The figure of Isaiah prophesying the advent of the Virgin occupies one of the jambs of the portal devoted to the legend of the Deacon Theophilus that was erected about 1130–1140. While the figure is still gripped to the plane of the block, its fragile, attenuated forms nevertheless express a characteristically Romanesque febrility. Legs crossed in a violent twist, limbs and drapery tensed in conflicting motion, face haggard, beard and hair flying in the wind, Isaiah seems caught up in prophetic ecstasy. In the fleeting, ruffling draperies the Romanesque artist gives free rein to an extraordinary play of linear patterns and exuberant decorative and rhythmic details. The sculpture at Souillac issues logically from that at Moissac.

265

526

527

527 *Saints Peter and Paul*, from Saint Etienne, Toulouse · French, ca. 1110–1150 · Musée des Augustins, Toulouse.

Eight such reliefs representing the twelve apostles originally ornamented the portal of the chapterhouse of Saint Etienne. Like the figures in the Saint Sernin choir, these two apostles shelter under an arcade; but in their attitudes very little remains of the Saint Sernin apostles. Peter and Paul are attenuated, animated and sinewy; their crossed legs suggest a walking movement, and the statues seem to break away from the plane of the wall to assume a life of their own. The drapery falls in complex and rather agitated folds, the limbs, and especially the joints, hugged by arbitrarily patterned swirls of pleats.

528

526 *Trumeau* of the old portal, church of Souillac (Lot) · French, 1130–1140.

The depiction of fantastic beasts can be traced to a very early eastern origin. Romanesque art absorbed Asiatic elements and created a new vocabulary from them. These swarming, intermingled forms rarely have any religious justification; they have a symbolic value and play a decorative role. Animal imagery in Romanesque churches is found mostly on the piers, columns and capitals. The artist of this trumeau dizzily piled up his creatures to cover the whole surface, obedient to the demands of both symmetry and *horror vacui*; intoxicated with forms and volumes, the sculptor bends and twists his feline creatures' bodies as he will.

528 *Herod and Salome*, capital from the cloister of Saint Etienne, Toulouse · French, ca. 1120 · Musée des Augustins, Toulouse.

St. John the Baptist's fate is narrated on this capital: on the right is the beheading scene and on the left, the feast with the dance of Salome, treated in intimate, anecdotal fashion. Herod strokes the face of the child Salome, who in turn sketches out a dance step. The style is supple and nervous, the many tight folds outlining the bodies; Salome seems to sway, and Herod resembles a *raffiné* prince. In respect to gesture and feeling the scene's realism is striking and is accentuated by the very minute treatment accorded to details.

530

530 *Juggler*, from Saint Pierre-le-Pucellier, Bourges. French, late 12th–early 13th century · Musée de Lyon.

This fragment of an archivolt from the portal of Saint Pierre-le-Pucellier is characteristic of Romanesque art towards the end of the 12th and the beginning of the 13th centuries. The juggler assumes a contorted position within a framework that encloses but does not imprison him. Whirling, dynamic forms, linear arabesques, and the fantasy natural to Romanesque invention here combine with a 13th-century sense of realistic observation, creating a work where accurate analysis of movement fuses with Romanesque fervor.

529

529 *Women with Signs of the Zodiac*, from the south door of the transept of Saint Sernin, Toulouse · French, ca. 1150 · Musée des Augustins, Toulouse.

This bas-relief symbolic of the signs of the Lion and the Ram has been dated, not without much controversy, around 1150. In it one senses a genuine striving after three-dimensionality, and the composition tends to capture a rhythmic feeling. The pose with legs crossed – possibly of Oriental provenance – was submitted to infinite variations in Romanesque sculpture. The proportions of the two female figures are elongated, the bodies are more supple than in the past, and there is even faintly, timidly still, a suggestion of a breeze lifting a bit of the lower edge of the tunic.

531 *Head of the Virgin*, from the portal of the Abbey of Saint Pierre, Cluny · French, before 1115 · Musée du Farinier, Cluny.

The very moving remains from the portal of Cluny, terminated in 1115, are filled with a sense of elevated spirituality. The small head of a young and beautiful Virgin, from the lintel, is one of the most refined in Romanesque art. Confidently carved, it unites mystical purity with monumental grandeur. The subtle modelling of details enlivens the simple mass of the face, which reflects a humanism alien to the usual dramatic conception of faith. The almost classical aesthetic of the Cluniac school results from the conjunction of a well-tried technique and a lofty iconographical inspiration evincing a preoccupation with theology.

531

532 *The Four Rivers of Paradise*, capital from the Abbey of Saint Pierre, Cluny · Musée du Farinier, Cluny.

The sculpture from the abbey at Cluny has provided art historians with one of their thorniest problems in chronology: for the orthodox French school the capitals date from 1120–1140; for the American school and for some French historians, they were carved before being put into place – that is, before 1095. According to the American thesis it was the Cluniac masterpieces that inaugurated the Romanesque revival of monumental sculpture, a revival whose beginnings have traditionally been ascribed to Languedoc. In either case this capital remains a beautiful piece, with sinuous, boldly formed foliage swollen with sap, and an allegorical male nude representing a river at each corner. On each face of the capital the composition is finely balanced, and the decorative elements are raised in true relief modelling.

532

533 *Eve with the Forbidden Fruit*, Saint Lazare, Autun · French, 1120–1135 · Musée Rolin, Autun.

The Eve of Autun originally formed the right half of the lintel of the north portal of Saint Lazare. The sculptor, possibly Gislebertus (see fig. 536), was in no way hampered by the lintel form that obliged him to arrange his figure horizontally; on the contrary, he has exploited it in creating an Eve of exceptional femininity and subtlety in Romanesque art. Gathering the fruit with her left hand, she turns from her tempter with a charming movement to impart her secret to Adam; she moves with grace and ease in an idyllic world of vegetation, floating in an unreal space. The artist shows a knowledge of anatomy, complete technical mastery and a remarkable feeling for linear elegance.

533

534 *Head of Christ*, from the *Ascension and Mission of the Apostles*, tympanum in narthex, La Madeleine, Vézelay · French, ca. 1125–1130.

The portal leading from the narthex into the nave was executed by the "Master of the Tympanum" and his school. The Christ at Vézelay is of a type halfway between the terrifying avenger-prince at Moissac and the man-God of Chartres. By isolating the head and bust against a plain background, the master gives the image its full importance, centering Christ's regal head with its elongated but regular features against the crossed halo. In type the head is still Romanesque, but it is already animated by an inner spirituality, bringing the Son of God, preoccupied with his evangelical mission, closer to mankind.

534

536

535

535 *Profane Music and the Demon of Licentiousness*; capital no. 6 of the nave, La Madeleine, Vézelay · French, ca. 1130–1145.

Attributed to the "Master of the Tympanum" at Vézelay, or perhaps, rather, to a pupil, is this scene in which a grimacing devil seduces a naked woman; she is charmed by the sound of a flute played by a juggler and by the scent of poisonous flowers. Certain features of the demon's head are noteworthy: his flamelike mane of hair serves as the capital's corner motif, and his twisted, expressive mouth is in keeping with the medieval conception of the devil – horrible, but not too disquieting or mysterious. The composition is extremely free, yet clearly ordered to carry out the anecdotal as well as the architectural function.

536 *The Weighing of Souls*: detail from the Last Judgment tympanum of Saint Lazare, Autun · French, before 1147.

The Saint Lazare tympanum is from the hand of the mysterious "Gislebertus," about whom we know nothing other than his signature on the work. The presentation of the Last Judgment with its accompanying themes is a little confused, but the detail of the Weighing of the Souls displays features characteristic of the Autun style: figures exaggeratedly elongated, the realism of gesture and expression overstated, a predominantly picturesque mood, and the clear influence of mystery plays. The execution is somewhat dry, subordinated as it is to both the spirit of invention and the urge to fill all available space. The result, however, is an extraordinary and truly expressionistic work of art. The devils casting the terrorized sinners into hell have a power rarely achieved.

537 *Wedding at Cana (or Last Supper?)*, tympanum of Saint Fortunat, Charlieu (Loire) · French, ca. 1150–1175.

The theme of the feast is easily adapted to an architectural framework; the table can be rectilinear on a lintel and circular on a capital. Here, the table is semicircular, adapting itself to the tympanum form and becoming the basic coordinating element of the whole composition. The compositional firmness of the scene somewhat restrains the fervor and restlessness that Burgundian sculpture displays in other mid-12th century sculptures, and which is here seen in the voussoirs, where the figures gesticulate freely.

537

538

538 *Last Judgment*, tympanum of the west portal of Saint Foy, Conques (Aveyron) · French, 1125–1150.

This tympanum is the most important ensemble of sculpture in Auvergne. While the arrangement and the division of the scenes into registers reveal the perfect sense of compositional balance inherited from the Languedoc conception of the scene, the style comes closer to popular art: thick-set figures with noble but stereotyped features, static attitudes, and the inclusion of the local legend of Saint Foy in the Last Judgment scene. More naive and descriptive than the Autun Last Judgment, it has, nevertheless, just as much expressive force.

540

540 *Saint James the Less and Saint Paul*; west portal of Saint Gilles du Gard · French, first third or second half of the 12th century.

The west portal of Saint Gilles offers one of the largest ensembles of Provençal Romanesque sculpture, but the uncertain dating makes it difficult to place the work in the evolution of Romanesque art. These two apostles might well be considered not precursors but southern versions of the Chartres west portal Kings and Queens, while also having points in common with Lombard art – the crouching lions gripping their prey on which the figures stand, for example. In style, both figures and decorative elements are markedly influenced by classical antiquity, and the strong feeling for relief has its roots in Roman models.

541 *Cloister*, Saint Trophime, Arles · French, late 12th–14th century.

The Saint Trophime cloister was built in the second half of the 12th century. Its sculptural decoration was done at various stages, at times in marble and at times in stone, and was completed only in the 14th century. The statues against the piers, the high reliefs, and the foliage capitals constitute a typical scheme illustrating the direct influence that antique art sometimes exercised on Romanesque art. Roman and Gallo-Roman examples and Early Christian sarcophagi were frequently found in Arles, where the tradition of modelling in the round seems never to have been lost. The influence of the freer style of the Ile de France can already be discerned in some of the more slender and elongated 13th-century figures.

541

539

539 *Façade*, St. Gilles du Gard · French, begun 1116.

At St. Gilles du Gard, which was begun in 1116, imitation of classical antiquity was carried to the point of pastiche. The portal is a Roman triumphal arch with three doors linked by a colonnade. Not only is the architecture Roman in style, but its statuary also is impregnated with classical influences. Dating the structure is far from easy because it has undergone many transformations. There are two opposing theories, one holding out for the first third of the 12th century, the other for the second quarter or latter half of the same century. St. Gilles has much in common with Italian architecture: a very similar iconography, a repertory of ornamentation drawn from antiquity, and the same independence of the sculptor from the architect.

542

542 *Capital*, from a church in Arles · French, late 12th century · Museum, Arles.

The theme of this late 12th-century capital has its origin in a distant eastern prototype. But the modelling, with its assertive relief and its plasticity, belongs to Roman sculpture. The two monsters, male and female, are in no way frightening or enigmatic; their supple, free bodies and amiable faces are a far cry from the traditional representation of beasts. The composition is perfectly balanced but its arrangement has more in common with that of a frieze or a bas-relief than with the more compact, blocklike decoration appropriate to a corbel or a capital.

543

543 *Façade* of Notre-Dame la Grande, Poitiers · French, 1100–1150.

The two extremes between which Romanesque art fluctuates – "Asianism" and "Atticism," the East and Rome – are reconciled in the façade of Notre-Dame la Grande at Poitiers. Onto the predominantly Roman structure, based on the triumphal-arch type of façade, is grafted a sculptural ornament in which eastern and barbarian elements are prominent. Quite in contrast to the classical Romanesque portal, the tympana take a minimal place, and the carved decoration spreads out into a frieze moving over the wall above the doors and over and around the blind arcades. The iconographical theme, the Mystery of the Incarnation, is unusual and probably came from a mystery play.

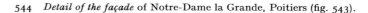

544 *Detail of the façade* of Notre-Dame la Grande, Poitiers (fig. 543).

Scenes from the life of Jesus – the Visitation, the Nativity and the Bathing of the Infant – succeed each other in the carved frieze. The blind arcades are entirely covered with exuberant ornament in which motifs from classical antiquity mingle with barbarian or eastern themes. The obsessional fear of emptiness which engendered this seething mass of forms, mingling geometric ornament with anthropozoomorphic combinations, is characteristic of the Poitevin school. No longer is the architect master over the sculptor; instead, the latter sees in the structural façade before him nothing more than a wall to be filled in, treating the church as a reliquary to be decorated in the manner of a goldsmith.

544

545 *Voussoirs* from the portal of Saint Pierre, Aulnay (Charente-Maritime) · French, 1150–1200.

Saint Pierre at Aulnay seems to reflect the art of Poitou. The decorations on the voussoirs of the central door are of exceptional richness. The four successive round arches that frame the doorway, each projecting beyond the one below, are adorned with dynamic narrative figures that sum up the whole of Romanesque iconography and technique. Closest to the door are foliated scrolls in low relief, followed by a ring of Saints; the Elders of the Apocalypse are next, and finally, fabulous monsters, rampant along the axes of the radially placed blocks on which they appear. The little figures are arranged in a harmonious synthesis of all influences and with a keen awareness of compositional values. In some of the modest country churches, the final stages of Romanesque art produced its finest masterpieces.

545

546

546 *Pulpit*, San Giulio, Orta · Italian, early 12th century.

The pulpit on the island of San Giulio, in Lake Orta, is rightly considered one of the major works of Lombard sculpture in the beginning of the 12th century. The "barbarian" strain in Italian Romanesque art produced few works of such expressive force and such powerful vitality, employing means of such economy. Fabulous monsters, legendary characters, and highly imaginative foliage motifs are handled with great restraint in broad areas of flat relief carving. An intense life and a wild, spirited force lie under the apparent monumental solidity of the decoration.

547

548 *The Prophet Ezekiel*, portal, Cremona Cathedral · Italian, ca. 1107–1117.

The Master of the Cremona Cathedral is a contemporary of Master Guglielmo. Employing a style more in the mainstream of western art than Guglielmo's, he introduced the theme of the jamb-statue into Italy. The jambs of the porch are not so much columns as piers with statues modelled in the round set against them, in a manner resembling that of the great Provençal groups, whose prototype they may in fact be. The idea of the free-standing figure, inherited from antiquity, remained a living tradition in Italy.

548

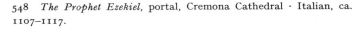

547 GUGLIELMO (or WILIGELMO) (Italian, active first decades 12th century) · *Daniel and Zacharias*, Cathedral of Modena · Italian, 1106–1120.

Guglielmo's portal for Modena Cathedral is one of the most important surviving examples of Romanesque sculpture in Italy. The ornament is conceived as a series of relief plaques, which cover the façade without becoming an integral part of the architecture. Provençal and Languedoc reminiscences can be found in the figures of the prophets Daniel and Zacharias, particularly in the drapery, but the influence of antiquity is the decisive one. Because of their simple and broadly handled volumes, their naturalistic conception, and their tendency to take on a separate existence as free-standing statues, the figures seem restricted by the narrow frames of their niches. In all these aspects they are far removed from the prophets at Moissac and Souillac with their flat, linear dynamism.

549

549 *Main portal*, Verona Cathedral · Italian, 1140–1150.

At Modena, Piacenza, Ferrara, and Verona, Guglielmo and a Lombard sculptor whom we know only as Niccolo developed the chief element of the Italian Romanesque façade: a light porch sheltering the reliefs around the door and supported by colonnettes resting on two crouching lions. The façade of Verona Cathedral (consecrated in 1187) was restored in Gothic times, and Niccolo's portal also underwent some alteration. With its tympanum dedicated to the theme of the Nativity and its sculptures of Roland and Olivier on the piers, the portal has more in common with French art than with native Italian types.

550

550 SCHOOL OF GUGLIELMO, *Antefix*, from the south portal of Modena Cathedral · Italian, ca. 1125–1130 · Museo del Duomo, Modena.

The lateral portals of Modena Cathedral, the Porta della Pescheria and the Porta dei Principi, were decorated by the school of Guglielmo. The iconography is very original, deriving from a mixture of literary sources and hagiography. The various sculptors working at Modena gradually gave up the rigidity and forcefulness of Master Guglielmo for the sake of picturesque charm. This delicately finished antefix, or "metope," from the buttresses on the south side of the nave is conceived like an antique metope. The very Italian design is based, in contrast to the linear French style, on a balancing of large masses, here obtained with the curious inversion of one of the figures.

551 BENEDETTO ANTELAMI (Italian, 1150–1230) · *The Descent from the Cross*, on the pulpit of the Cathedral of Parma. 1178.

The first known work by Antelami is this Deposition at Parma. Antelami's rigorous and severe style has roots in Provençal sculpture and particularly in the conception of statuary inherited from antiquity. The Virgin, St. John, and the Holy Women, standing one behind the other, are clearly set off from the background, and the drapery folds are chiselled into the marble with a precision suggesting the art of the bronzeworker or goldsmith. Antelami disregards picturesque, anecdotal, or formal devices; his compact, firm forms have affinities with classical antiquity. Only the bowed heads and a restrained gesture of the hands evoke the pathos of the scene.

551

552 ANTELAMI · *The Last Judgment* · Tympanum from the Baptistry, Cathedral of Parma · Italian, ca. 1196.

In 1196, Antelami undertook the construction and decoration of the Parma Baptistry. French influence is no doubt present in the choice of subject for the tympanum of the west portal: the Last Judgment – an iconographical theme hitherto unknown in Romanesque Italy. Antelami successfully assimilated the art of antiquity and of Byzantium, as well as French Romanesque art and even Gothic art from Chartres, and from the mixture created a personal style of considerable monumentality. The tympanum is perfectly arranged and logically composed, while at the same time each figure, each statue, is one organic entity – a strong contrast to the Romanesque type of tympanum, in which the separate figures tend to merge in a dynamic overall turbulence.

552

553

553   *Eve*, portal, Lodi Cathedral · Italian, 12th century.

Although the Eve of Lodi Cathedral is a statue set against a pier, a column-statue in the Italian manner, in execution it is close to the French style. Some consider this sculpture to be a work by Antelami from the second third of the 12th century; it was more probably carved by an Antelami follower, one of the group that Jullian has termed the Master Stylists. The expressiveness of the sorrowful face, the dynamic movement emphasized by the folds of the contemporary dress, and the linear formulations are all characteristic of the 12th-century Lombard school, in which the tradition of antiquity is enlivened by an awareness of transalpine, and especially Provençal, style.

554

554   *Door knocker*, from the Cathedral of Susa (Piedmont) · Italian, 12th century · Treasury, Susa Cathedral.

Door knockers were traditionally made in the form of animal heads, either lions or oxen. This one, from the door of Susa Cathedral, is unusual. It has been considered a Lombard work containing elements of German art, but in motifs and style it is typically barbarian. The hybrid head, the ring in the shape of a serpent, the lions, and the jumble of arabesques on the supporting plaque are closer to a Merovingian or Irish jewel than to Italian sculpture. If the 12th-century date frequently suggested for this piece is accepted, then the persistence of pre-Romanesque traditions in the minor arts must also be accepted.

555   *The Descent from the Cross*, Cathedral of Tivoli · Italian, 13th century.

Among the numerous schools of wood carving active during the 13th century, an "Antelami" trend opposed to French or Byzantine tendencies may be distinguished. The Virgin and St. John at Tivoli translate into a popular and more naturalistic idiom the refined models of the Parma Deposition (fig. 545). Contrary to what occurred in other countries – in Spain for example – the art of these popular image-makers borrows from the more sophisticated forms without altering their spirit. In Italy, the taste for statuary and for a certain type of classicism was perpetuated in pious images and in the ornamentation of church furniture.

555

556   *Façade* (lower central part) of San Pietro di Spoleto (Perugia) · Italian, 12th–13th centuries.

The convent church of San Pietro di Spoleto was completed in the 13th century and altered in the Baroque era. The central part of the decoration must date from the beginning of the 12th century, except for the upper reliefs, which are from the 13th century. It reveals Armenian and Syrian influences in its architectural structure. The six large horizontal reliefs, scenes of fierce combat in which beasts are paired with men, birds, or other animals, are Roman in handling and Oriental in inspiration. The others are directly inspired by the antique. Religious iconography is absent from this sober and hieratic ensemble – one of the most remarkable creations of Italian Romanesque art.

556

557

557 *Altar frontal* · Stucco, polychromed · Italian, 12th century
Siena Pinacoteca.

The altar frontal, or *palliotto*, which fills the space above the altar
table, underwent an evolution in technique. In this example, decorated
with the Romanesque theme of Christ and the symbols of the Evangelists, the painted stucco was probably used as a substitute for goldsmith work, which at the beginning of the Romanesque era had
replaced sculpture in the round in the decoration of altars. Later,
painted scenes were in turn to take the place of sculpture.

558

558 *Capital*, Monreale Cathedral · Italian, ca. 1180.

The Monreale basilica in the hills outside Palermo was built from
1174 to 1182 under the auspices of the king of Sicily, William II, who
had artists brought from all over the world. The result is an extraordinary combination of styles. The architecture is composite, half-
Norman, half-Byzantine; a triple Byzantine choir crowns a nave
designed on a basilical plan. The mosaic decoration is Byzantine, while
the ornamental sculpture derives from antiquity. The composite
capitals in the nave are directly inspired by Hellenistic models, and are
the work of a classicizing Campanian workshop employing Roman,
Apulian and Byzantine sculptors.

559 *Paschal candlestick*, Cathedral of Gaeta (Campania) · Italian,
13th century.

The monumental Paschal candlestick, conceived as a column with its
shaft entirely covered with carvings, was a major theme in 13th-
century Campanian art. This coastal region gave its own interpretation
to themes and styles from antiquity, from Lombardy, and from Byzantium: the result is a narrative art bristling with action and movement. The characters jostle each other in each register, acting out
episodes in the life of Christ, and the overall effect is like an illuminated manuscript – which must in fact have been the direct source of
inspiration for these marble reliefs. Despite the apparent disorder of
the composition, there is a strong feeling for relief derived from antiquity, which foreshadows the Hohenstaufen's premature (that is to
say, pre-Renaissance) revival of antiquity in Sicily.

559

560 *Crucifix* · Ivory · Spanish, ca. 1063 · Museo Nacional Arqueologica, Madrid.

This crucifix, given to San Isidoro de Leon Cathedral by Ferdinand I of Leon and Castile, marks the first known appearance of the theme of Christ on the Cross in Spanish art. The decoration on the cross itself and the frieze of intertwined animals and foliage around the edges recall Cordovan or Mozarabic ivories, while in the body of Christ, Ottonian and Italian types mingle. Characteristics of a truly Spanish style can already be felt through this Byzantinism. Black onyx inlay indicating the dilated pupils accentuates the intense expression of this lifelike Christ.

561 *Deposition and Ascension*, tympanum of the south transept portal, San Isidoro, Leon · Spanish, 1090–1095.

The "Master of las Platerias" worked at San Isidoro, burial church of kings, between 1090 and 1095. To him is ascribed this simple and well-balanced tympanum, with its unusual iconography: the Deposition from the Cross, associated with the Ascension. Spanish art here draws away from the influence of Toulouse to assert its native qualities. The iconography, the ample volumes, the masterful carving, the treatment of the faces, all exemplify the development of a Spanish tendency parallel to the contemporary French, but resulting in a more expressionistic and more popular style.

561

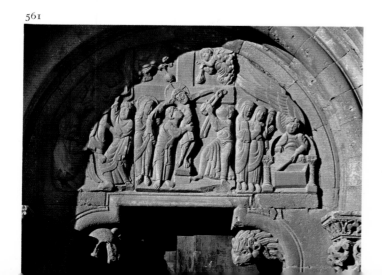

562

562 *Saint Vincent*, south transept portal, San Isidoro, Leon (see fig. 561).

The Portal of the Lamb at San Isidoro is decorated with a series of sculptured plaques assembled at random above the archivolts; its tympanum, perhaps also of reused material, reveals the sculptor's clumsy effort to adapt this semi-circular surface to its monumental role. On each side of the arch are statues, one of Saint Isidoro, the other of Saint Vincent, his feet resting on a corbel decorated with the head of a bull. The figure is modelled with a strong three-dimensionality, characteristic of early Spanish Romanesque sculpture.

563

563 *Woman with a skull*, Puerta de las Platerias, Santiago de Compostela · Spanish, 12th century.

The silversmiths' portal of Santiago is made up of elements in different styles assembled at random within an architectural frame; they surely came from other ensembles. The woman with a skull was placed in such a way that it was necessary to cut into her head to give room for the voussoir. The figure is a symbol of Luxury, "who holds the fetid head of her lover, decapitated by her husband; she kisses it twice daily as her husband requires." The salient modelling of this relief is characteristic of the first style of Compostela.

565

564

564 *King David*, Puerta de las Platerias, Santiago de Compostela, Cathedral · Spanish, ca. 1100.

A work by the Master of las Platerias – probably the same personality as Master Esteban, son of the Cathedral architect – the prophet David is still impregnated with elements from the art of Toulouse almost contemporaneous with the Puerta de las Platerias, carved at the very end of the 11th century. However, the less numerous folds, the more strongly affirmed relief, and the general simplification result in a more realistic, if less refined, art than the Languedoc models.

565 *Portal* of the monastery church of Ripoll (Gerona) · Spanish, 12th century.

The marble porch of the monastery church at Ripoll is typical of 12th-century Catalan art. The façade, entirely covered with sculptures, is treated like a picture book – the Bible translated into stone images comprising scenes from the Old Testament and from the lives of the apostles, mingled with fabulous beasts. A number of influences, particularly from Italian art, are mixed with local Catalan and Roussillon traditions and can be discerned in the clearly differentiated styles on the various registers. The pictorial treatment that is carried to the point of disorder in the upper registers contrasts with the more architectonic composition of the lower parts and of the jambs.

566 *Majestad de Batllo* · Wood, polychromed · Spanish, 11th–12th centuries · Museo de Arte de Catalunya, Barcelona.

This Majestad – Christ on the Cross, wearing a tunic, and honored as the King of Kings – is one of the most original expressions of Catalan art. Its iconographical theme is Oriental and first appears in miniatures and the minor arts. In style the sculpture belongs to the transition period between the 11th and 12th centuries. It is the finest of a group of Majestades from a single atelier, either that of Ripoll or that of Cuxa. The excellently preserved polychromy suggests the "colored splendor" of the Romanesque world, and the rich tunic emphasizes the conception of the Christ-King victorious despite his torment.

566

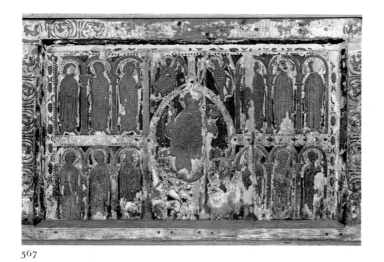

567 *Christ in Majesty and Apostles*, altar frontal, Ginestarre de Cardos · Stucco, polychromed · Spanish, 1251 · Museum, Barcelona.

In Spain the early Romanesque tradition of gold or silver altar frontals was carried through to the 13th century in the frontals of polychromed stucco or wood. That of Ginestarre de Cardos is one of a mass-produced series which invariably treats the theme of Christ set among symbols of the Evangelists and surrounded by the apostles. The popular image-makers, cut off from the great sculptural works ornamenting architecture, merely crystallized the formula, alternating between hieratic and realistic interpretations. Here the polychromy, darkened by chemical reactions, only accentuates the sculpture's mediocre and stereotyped aspect.

568 *Christ in Majesty and Apostles*, altar frontal from Santa Maria de Tahull · Wood, polychromed · Spanish, early 13th century · Museo de Arte de Catalunya, Barcelona.

The Tahull frontal, from a local workshop, is of higher quality than those in painted stucco. If the effect of the whole is one of uniformity, owing to the repetitive traditional theme, the individuality of the Tahull school asserts itself in details of the execution. Each figure is a small statue, in which accurate anatomical observation and a firm sense of relief alternate with a schematized ornament. But in a final analysis the decorative spirit is stronger than the narrative realism.

568

570

570 *Head of St. Metronus*, Abbey Church, Gernrode · German, 10th or 11th century.

The dating of this head of St. Metronus, now part of the decoration of the Holy Sepulcher in the Gernrode abbey church, is much discussed. German historians have suggested dates fluctuating between 980, which seems rather too early, and 1100, or even later. It is one of the most extraordinary heads in northern Romanesque art. With great economy of means the sculptor has created a face of astonishing realism; the expression is powerful and the chin and forehead suggest will and determination. A sense of deep, all-encompassing faith radiates from this head, which is already imbued with German expressionism.

571 *Baptismal font* · Brass · Saint Barthelemy (Liège) · Mosan, 1107–1118.

Fonts of this design, cast in brass and chased, have been attributed to Rainier of Huy; this one was made on commission from Abbot Hellinus (1107–1118) for the church of Notre-Dame-des-Fonts in Liège. Around the font appear in turn the Baptism of Christ; the baptism of the centurion Cornelius and of the philosopher Crato; John the Baptist preaching to the publicans; and the baptism of the publicans. Twelve oxen alluding to the apostles adorn the support. This work represents the logical issue of the art of the 10th- and 11th-century Mosan ivory and bronze workers. The poses and the handling of the drapery presuppose a deep understanding and total assimilation of antique models.

569

569 *Prophets and other figurations*, Portico de la Gloria, narthex of the Cathedral of Santiago de Compostela · Spanish, 1168–1188.

Influenced by French art and still impregnated with Romanesque elements, the Portico de la Gloria belongs at the very beginning of Spanish Gothic art. Conceived and carried out between 1168 and 1188 by Master Mateo, it combines Spanish traditions with a new conception of the church portal. The figures decorating its piers are column statues. Modelling in the round asserts itself, sculpture frees itself from the architecture. The short, thick-set figures adopt conventional attitudes, but the surprising realism of the faces breaks with the Romanesque type. Master Mateo inaugurated for the prophets a physical type that was to spread up to the time of Sluter.

571

572 *The Raising of Lazarus*, Chichester Cathedral · English, 11th or 12th century.

The dating of the two reliefs at Chichester representing the Raising of Lazarus and Christ in the House of Martha and Mary depends on whether they considered post-Norman-conquest works, or typically Saxon. The approximate date of 1080, suggested by some English historians, has the merit of taking into account the Saxon as well as the French elements in this Norman work. On the other hand, several authorities believe the panels to have been executed as late as the 12th century, while yet others place them as early as the middle Saxon period. The decidedly expressionistic style of the emaciated, angular face suggests an attribution to a Saxon sculptor.

572

573 *Apostles*, Basle Cathedral · German, late 11th century.

The apostle relief originally decorated a pulpit in Basle's earlier cathedral, but was incorporated into the walls of the new cathedral's transept at the end of the 12th century. The apostles are set in arcaded niches, following the scheme often employed by ivoryworkers and goldsmiths. The sculptor's innovation was to group them two by two and to make them talk and gesticulate freely, so that they look like monks or scholars discussing a point of doctrine in the dim cloister. This picturesque naturalism is far removed from the original Byzantine and Carolingian imperial versions of the theme, and differs from the Henry II altar frontal (Musée de Cluny, Paris), one of the more sophisticated examples of this style in the second half of the 11th century.

573

574

574 *Two apostles*, choir screen, Cathedral of Bamberg · German, early 13th century.

The choir screen of Bamberg Cathedral is decorated with a series of prophets and apostles in a late Romanesque style, executed before the dedication in 1237. The apostles dispute, two by two, in a succession of niches, the earlier pairs standing under arches that are still semicircular, the later under trefoil arches. Although Germany has little feeling for monumentality, these apostles carry on the Ottonian traditions inspired by antiquity. The thick-set sturdy bodies are revealed by the curving folds which emphasize the bodily forms. In the broad modelling and the expressive pathos given the faces, the apostles are close to Roman models.

575

576

575 *North portal*, Jakobskirche, Regensburg · German, late 12th century.

Irish and Scottish monks founded an abbey at Regensburg in 1100. The church, dedicated to Saint James, and the cloister were completed in 1180. The north portal follows the rigidly clear architectural scheme of Ottonian churches. The decorative sculpture is applied to the triumphal arch façade without really being integrated into the architecture. The strange iconography, with its monsters and sphinxes, has not yet been convincingly interpreted; it has been described as the struggle between Good and Evil, or even as an evocation of the Twilight of the Gods! The style is a curious amalgam of Irish, Lombard, and Byzantine elements.

576 *Head of the Prophet Jonah*, choir screen, Cathedral of Bamberg · German, early 13th century.

This image of the prophet Jonah is one of the finest examples of German statuary in the first quarter of the 13th century. The square head with shaven skull, the gathered brows, the intense, haunted glance, and the half-open mouth, forcefully convey the prophet's tension and dramatic vision. Compared with Bamberg sculptures from the Gothic workshops that began to operate around 1230, the statues on the choir screen display their Romanesque inspiration in their drapery, and it is clear that when the Gothic style was imported into Bamberg it found there a still-flourishing Romanesque art.

577

577 *Virgin of Mosjö* · Wood, polychromed · Sweden · ca. 1150 · Nationalmuseet, Copenhagen.

Romanesque art gradually made itself felt in post-Viking art in the Scandinavian countries, as a result of influences coming from north Germany and from England. This statue still retains something of the barbarian stylizations of the Viking era, but there is probably, too, some influence from the art of English miniaturists who, during the same period, favored these elongated forms, plaited hair and sleeves falling almost to the ground.

579

579 *Virgin Mary* · Metal · Scandinavian, 11th or 12th century · Nationalmuseet, Copenhagen.

The barbarian art of the Vikings was not impervious to Byzantine influences. Later, in Romanesque times, numerous contacts with France and the Mediterranean countries had a decisive effect on Scandinavian art. In this small metal figure of the Virgin, found in Randers Fjord in Denmark, linear stylization dominates. The Nordic artist transformed the French type of Virgin in Glory by a style compounded of plane surfaces and angles to produce a work in which severity and a tendency toward abstraction create a remarkable formal beauty.

578

578 *Capital*, from Nazareth · Palestine, late 12th century · Museum of the Greek Patriarch, Nazareth.

French art had a profound influence on the art of the Near East. Nazareth, where this late 12th-century capital comes from, was the most important center for the diffusion of Romanesque art in Palestine. The two bearded heads decorating the capital are in the French tradition; the elongated faces, the eyes, and the hairstyles all recall those on a capital in the church at Plaimpied, in the Berry region. This is a very simple and easily readable type of capital, with figures set in a fan-shaped composition round a vertical axis.

580

Dates as far apart as the 9th and 13th centuries have been suggested for the doors of San Zeno in Verona. In fact, these doors have undergone a number of transformations after suffering through various wars, fires, and earthquakes. It seems that the oldest panels are from the 11th century and the most recent from the 12th century. A primitive, barbarian technique predominates in the former. A résumé of the earliest forms of human affliction is given in the figures placed at random over an empty space: Eve plies her distaff, while Adam pulls the plough, and Cain has just murdered his brother. Through the awkward forms of the strange, crude style can be felt a strong evocative force.

581 *The young St. Adalbert and his parents*, south portal, Cathedral of Gniezno (Poland) · German(?), 1st half of 12th century.

The origin of the doors of Gniezno Cathedral is mysterious: they have been pronounced in turn Polish, Bohemian, Byzantine, or even Crimean. The most likely theory is that the door, cast in one piece, came from Magdeburg. The entirely Germanic iconography and the depictions of the life of St. Adalbert (a friend of Otto III) support this attribution. The distortions in form, the linear treatment of the draperies, the low relief, the faults caused by clumsy casting and removal from the mold, mark it as a Romanesque work. Byzantine and antique elements remain dominant, however, in the composition and in the proportions of the bodies.

581

582

582 BONANNUS OF PISA (Italian, mentioned 1174–1186) · *Nativity*, doors of the Cathedral of Pisa · Bronze · Ca. 1175–1180.

Bonannus of Pisa, architect and sculptor, created the doors of Pisa Cathedral after having worked on the bell-tower in about 1173. These doors have many points in common with those at Monreale, which are almost certainly the work of Bonannus. Twenty-four panels trace the lives of Jesus and of the Virgin. The scene of the Nativity, set in a cave in accordance with Byzantine tradition, is skillfully composed and achieves real monumentality. Influences from antique and Byzantine sculpture are mixed with realism in the rendering of the shepherds. A. Boeckler has stressed the links between sarcophagus decoration and Bonannus' art, which has its roots in antique sources.

583

583 *The Royal Portal*, Chartres Cathedral · French, ca. 1150–1170.

This portal, begun in about 1150, offers an iconographical and technical conception of sculpture that is partially inherited from Romanesque portals. The theme is a résumé of the Christian doctrine and an illustration of the links between Old and New Testaments: on the jambs are the prophets and the precursors of Christ, and on the tympana, from left to right, are depicted the Ascension, Christ of the Apocalypse, and the Mystery of the Incarnation. In spirit, the portal is Gothic; tympana and lintels are recessed under the arches, which are decorated with series of statuettes, and each jamb is occupied by a single figure whose core it becomes, to form the famous column-statue.

584 *Christ of the Apocalypse*, central tympanum of the Royal Portal, Chartres (see fig. 583).

Christ in Glory, surrounded by the symbols of the four Evangelists, was a usual theme after 1150. In this example, the tympanum space is occupied only by the mandorla and the symbols of the Evangelists, without any of the multiform confusion of a Romanesque tympanum. Instead of an ornamental sculpture applied to a wall surface, we now have a composition conforming to the architectural framework, to which the iconographical program is subordinated. The serene, majestic Christ has a well-proportioned body, and an authoritative, slightly aloof visage.

584

585 *Jamb statues*, Royal Portal, Chartres (see fig. 583).

These column-statues are completely integrated into the architecture. Their elongated proportions and the symmetry of the attitudes is in keeping with their function as supports. The absence of architectural canopies over their heads enhances their upward movement. But whereas the stiff poses and orderly draperies may have been intended to adapt the figure to its architectural function, the sculptor has given his imagination free rein in rendering the faces, which are naturalistic and of an extraordinary variety. This concern with realism is evident from the care with which he has handled the contemporary dress, faithfully describing the embroidery, the belts, and the hairstyles.

585

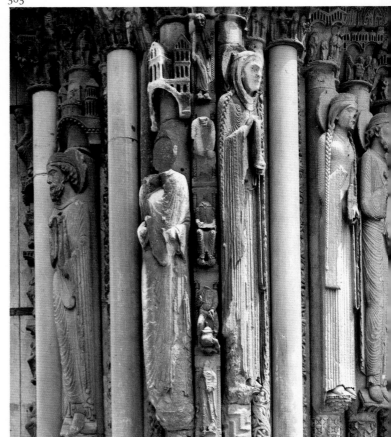

587

586 *Jamb statue*, detail, Royal Portal, Chartres (see fig. 585).

586 *Jamb statue*, detail, Royal Portal, Chartres (see fig. 585).

This detail is a good illustration of the classical concepts that were to underlie Gothic art. The light flickers over the projections and hollows and enlivens the geometric exactness of forms, achieved through a realistic observation of clothing and hairstyle. The line is controlled and now obeys the artist's will. The perfect precision of the carving is proof of the degree of skill that French art had achieved at the dawn of the Gothic era. The sculptor, a follower of the Burgundian school, created a work which is both the culmination of all Romanesque art and the promise of a new style.

586

587 *Head of a jamb statue*, detail, Royal Portal, Chartres (see fig. 583).

This head of a prophet or patriarch is no longer a symbol or an abstraction but a real, living portrait. The long, bony face, characteristic of the first school of Chartres, and the calm expression are the very opposite of the contorted features of Romanesque heads. The wavy hair and carefully arranged beard are treated as forms and substances of a particular kind, not just as decorative elements. The head frees itself from the jamb and the sculptor takes a step away from relief conceptions and towards statuary fully in the round. It was at Chartres that the new ideal in French sculpture first appeared, in which keenness of psychological observation combines with asceticism, and spirituality is balanced by a humanistic feeling.

588

588 *Head of a jamb statue*, Royal Portal, Chartres (see fig. 583).

This young King of Judah could easily be a Capetian prince. His face, modelled in broad planes, is that of an intelligent, self-confident man. A fleeting smile, foreshadowing the Reims smile, illuminates and softens his strong features. The personages of Holy Scripture are no longer mysterious and unapproachable; they are made more human and are identified with contemporary society.

589

589 *Isaiah, Jeremiah, Simeon, St. John the Baptist, and St. Peter,* north transept portal, Chartres Cathedral · French, ca. 1230.

The 13th-century sculptures at Chartres are still within the tradition of the master responsible for the Royal Portal. Chartres provides a fine example of the autonomous development of a style. The prophets – Isaiah, Jeremiah and Simeon – and St. John the Baptist and St. Peter are still conceived as column-statues: the legs still dangle, the straight and close-set drapery folds and the stiff gestures are still comparable to statues from 1150. The faces, on the other hand, are individualized and diversified. This series of portraits, with beards stressing the elongated ovals of the faces, is one of the most beautiful embodiments of Christian mysticism in art, the expression of a calm faith, of confidence in a God who is master of human destinies.

590 *Voussoirs* of the north transept portal, Chartres Cathedral · French, ca. 1200–1235.

The tympanum of the central portal of Chartres' north transept is devoted to the Triumph of the Virgin. It is encircled by five rows of voussoirs, on which are ranked statuettes of standing angels, patriarchs, prophets, and the ancestors of the Tree of Jesse. The Gothic artist exploited the archivolts for figurative sculpture, while the Romanesque artist had used them primarily for decorative bands on which he gave range to his fantasy. The sculptures of the Gothic voussoirs are no longer mural relief, but have become three-dimensional statuary.

590

591

591 *Christ Teaching,* south portal, Chartres Cathedral · French, ca. 1200–1230.

The lateral portals at Chartres are decorated with the most beautiful sculptures from the fully classical period of the Chartres school. Realistic expression is tempered by compositional restraint and balance. A reminiscence of the Royal Portal's column-statues can be found in the body of Christ and in the ordered drapery folds, but his face is that of God-become-Man. The image ceases to be a symbol and becomes the human embodiment of the Son of God. A handsome, intelligent man with an elongated and bony countenance, fine hair and beard carefully arranged, he is both a merciful and a rather sorrowful figure, expressing the duality of his nature, divine and human.

592

592 *St. Theodore,* south portal, Chartres Cathedral · French, ca. 1230.

St. Theodore, in the embrasure of the right door of the south transept, is stylistically among the later figures at Chartres, probably dating from the last period of the work there – that is, about 1230. By then, Gothic art had completed its evolution towards the mastery of three-dimensional form and truth to nature. Bare-headed and wearing the costume of a 13th-century warrior, the saint is the embodiment of the ideal knight. Gothic statuary had reached perfection. The thin, oval face is still of the great Chartres family, but has a more marked virility, confidence and sobriety than have the faces of the prophets.

593

593 *Nativity*, from the former jubé of Chartres Cathedral (now in the Cathedral crypt) · French, ca. 1250–1260.

The jubé (choir screen) at Chartres, completed before the dedication of the Cathedral in 1260, was dismantled in 1763. This fragment representing the Nativity gives some idea of the beauty of the lost work. The reclining Virgin rests her weary body, and with a very human maternal gesture, pushes aside Jesus' swaddling-clothes to look at him, while Joseph leans tenderly over her. The master has recorded the scene with insight and restraint. The loose, supple drapery, the charming face of the Virgin, the placid calmness of the ass and the ox, all contribute to an impression of peace and relaxation.

594 *Virgin and Child*, north transept, Reims Cathedral · French, last quarter of the 12th century.

Certain elements belonging to the original Romanesque-style cathedral of the 12th century were successfully incorporated into the doorway to the Reims cloister in the 13th century. The Virgin enthroned beneath an architectural baldaquin was originally designed for a recessed wall tomb. Its style is that of the last quarter of the 12th century, but the drapery is fuller and the position of the Child resting on the Virgin's right arm is more natural, more human than in the Romanesque prototypes, and differs from the traditional type found in Chartres or Paris. It may be that this new type of Virgin enthroned was influenced by the art of the Meuse Valley.

594

595 *The Dormition of Mary*, tympanum of the west portal, Senlis Cathedral · French, 1180–1190.

The west portal of Senlis marks a new stage in the emancipation of sculpture. Dedicated to the story of the Virgin, it consecrates the triumph of the cult of Mary. The sculptor has at his disposal a new iconography in the illustration of which he can give his creative spirit full freedom, unhampered by outdated and empty formal tradition. Fluttering angels cluster around the body of the Virgin with a mixture of joy and curiosity that shows a keen sense of observation. The scene is well balanced and the third dimension is exploited as a matter of course.

595

596

596 *Virgin in Majesty*, tympanum of the St. Anne Portal, Notre-Dame, Paris · French, ca. 1170.

Some of the sculptures on Notre-Dame, commissioned by Sully in about 1170, were reincorporated into the St. Anne portal about 1230–1240. The Virgin is carved from a Romanesque model of the "Virgin in Majesty" type. The attitude, the stiff pose, the fluting of the drapery folds, recall the Virgin in Majesty from the Royal Portal at Chartres Cathedral. But the elongated oval of the face, the long, slender proportions, and some details of the drapery are new elements, making the Paris Virgin more sober and monumental than the Chartres model, and further removed from the Romanesque style.

287

597 *Dormition and Coronation of the Virgin,* tympanum of the Portal of the Virgin, west façade, Notre-Dame, Paris · French, ca. 1210–1220.

The tympanum of the Paris Virgin Portal, contemporary with the north and south portal sculptures at Chartres, combines architectonic harmony with the art of the sculptor. Its theme is the glorification of the mother of Christ. The tympanum is strictly organized and divided into three registers. On the lintel, which is incorporated into the tympanum, are three kingly ancestors of the Virgin and three prophets; the two themes of Mary's Death and of her Resurrection are combined in a single group in the central part, where the figure of Christ stands just behind Mary; finally, in the upper part Christ crowns his mother in Paradise. The work synthesizes the elements of the future classic style of sculpture: simplicity and clarity of composition, high relief modelled fully in the round, and a harmonious adaptation, but not subordination, to the architectural framework.

597

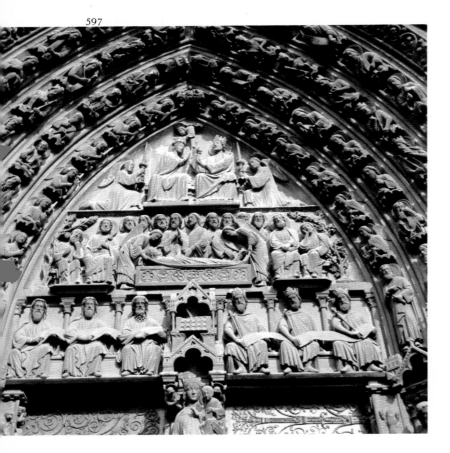

599

599 *St. Michael Slaying the Dragon,* Portal of the Virgin, Notre-Dame, Paris · French, ca. 1210–1230.

The dado of the Portal of the Virgin is decorated with bas-reliefs representing scenes from the lives of the Saints. St. Michael slaying the dragon is the subject of one of them. In Romanesque times, this scene would have been portrayed as a terrifying and fantastic episode; the Gothic artist has retained the allegorical and symbolical aspect, but he has treated the theme in a calm, balanced style. The volumes move easily within the frame, and the relief possesses the equilibrated beauty of a metope from the distant Greek era.

600

598

598 *Interior of arch,* Portal of the Virgin, Notre-Dame, Paris · French, ca. 1220.

The voussoirs of the Portal of the Virgin are decorated with half-length figures forming a choir of angels, kings and prophets. At the lower end the prophets continue the frieze of heroes of the Old Testament on the lowest register of the tympanum. The sculpture of the arch is no longer simply a decorative element but now is linked in theme and style to the tympanum. Rather than a frame limiting the sculpture, the arch enlarges the tympanum like an aureole, enhancing the monumental sculpture and creating a subtle link between architecture and sculpture.

600 *The Month of August* · Portal of the Virgin, Notre-Dame, Paris ·
French, ca. 1210–1230.

The piers of the doorway dedicated to the Virgin are decorated with
twelve small bas-reliefs. The labors of the Months are associated with
the signs of the Zodiac. Sowing appears here as the labor for the
month of August. The Gothic sculptor, taking as his themes such simple
actions of everyday life, treats them as admirable little scenes where
realistic observation is combined with sobriety of expression and noble
simplicity. There is nothing of the irreverent picturesqueness of Romanesque art. The artist seeks inspiration in reality and portrays it in
a naturalistic way, while masterfully controlling the compositional
elements. These little compositions match the great tympana in their
refined sense of balance.

601 *Virgin and Child*, portal of the church at Longpont-sous-Mon-
thléry · French, ca. 1220.

This statue adorns the trumeau of the 13th-century portal of a Cluniac
priory near Paris, forming part of a group dedicated to the glorification of the Virgin and inspired by the Coronation Portal at Notre-
Dame in Paris. Although damaged (the heads of mother and child are
modern), it is interesting because it undoubtedly echoes a similar Virgin,
destroyed during the Revolution, who once stood on the Paris Cathedral. The movement of the drapery folds is still rather stiff, but the
dress is contemporary; the sculptor's effort to give life to his statue
is at odds with the architectonic rigidity that still grips body and
drapery.

601

602 *St. Etienne*, trumeau of the central door, west front, Sens Cathedral · French, ca. 1215–1220.

Sens Cathedral was rebuilt after a fire in 1184. The statue of St. Etienne,
patron saint of the church, is still a column-statue, but the figure is
further developed than those at Chartres. The young saint's refined
and slightly elongated head is full of charm and delicacy. This is an
intelligent young deacon, sure of his faith, the pattern of the intellectual in an age when philosophical thought supported belief. The 13th
century was not to advance many years before such finely adjusted
balance between idealism and naturalism was lost.

602

603

603 *St. Peter*, Portal of the Last Judgment, north transept, Reims
Cathedral · French, ca. 1220.

This apostle, like the others near him, belongs to the first group of
sculptures made for Reims, and was originally intended to decorate
the main façade designed by Jean d'Orbais. It must, therefore,
have been executed about 1220. St. Peter is much further removed
from his Chartres origins than are his companions. The draperies are
agitated and the folds crumpled; his height, the breadth of his shoulders, the powerful head and fierce expression all represent something
new in Gothic sculpture. The first, the "classicizing," school of Reims
may have been influenced by the art of the Meuse region, especially by
Nicolas de Verdun, as well as by models from antiquity.

Art historians now believe that the figures at Reims that owe a strong debt to antiquity were produced about 1220 by the workshop responsible for the first façade, and not by that responsible for the final façade of about 1250. Some of these statues were eventually placed on the transept portals, others, like the beautiful Visitation group, on the west façade. The figures are rather thick-set, with short legs. The pose, the faces, and the moving, broken folds clinging to the bodies all suggest very strongly the flowing drapery of ancient statues. This renewal of the antique must have been brought about by a master acquainted with the art of the Meuse Valley and with Greek and Roman marbles, and possessing a talent able to adapt these models to local traditions.

606

606 *Annunciation and Visitation*, west façade, Amiens Cathedral French, 1225–1236.

Carved between 1225 and 1236 under the guidance of Robert de Luzarches, the sculptures on the west façade of Amiens show a remarkable unity in iconography and style. The statues are still frontal and closely connected with the piers; the folds are deep but somewhat stiff, a relic of column-statues. The facial expressions and gestures lack the restraint and deep spirituality of Chartres, but reflect a more homely humanity, amiable, natural, and modest.

605

605 *Head of the Virgin*, detail of fig. 604.

The Visitation group is inspired by ancient art, but certain details show quite clearly that the work is the personal creation of a Gothic artist. The beautiful young face of the Virgin does not follow the classic canon; it is individualized and treated quite freely. The sculptor, liberated from the constraint of a model, gave free range to his imagination, without any academic compulsions. The Visitation has aroused great controversy as regards its origin; the search for specific ancient models has produced nothing convincing.

607

607 *Head of Christ Teaching*, known as the *Beau Dieu*; west façade, Amiens Cathedral · French, ca. 1225–1235.

The *Beau Dieu*, set against the trumeau of the central door, is one of the great landmarks in the humanization of the type of Christ. The Chartres Christ is imbued with greater spirituality and a slight melancholy; the Beau Dieu of Amiens is more majestic, more idealized, as if to say that the Son of God can be only the most beautiful, the most perfect of creatures. His calm and perfectly regular face expresses better than any other the sense of evangelical purity. Christ is no longer a righteous and vengeful God, nor a somewhat hesitant, suffering human, but a being above human passions.

608 *The Month of May*, west façade, Amiens Cathedral · French, ca. 1225–1235.

Like those of the other great cathedrals, Paris, Reims, and Chartres, the façade of Amiens cathedral is decorated with reliefs representing the seasons and the labors of the fields, associating nature with the mysteries of the faith. Gemini, the twins, the zodiac sign for May, is illustrated here. Below it, as the Labor for the month, is a familiar and thoroughly human scene of a seated man happily contemplating blossoming trees; like the zodiac sign, the scene is neatly inscribed in a quatrefoil frame.

608

609 *Presentation in the Temple* (detail), west façade, Reims Cathedral.

The portals of the west façade show some revisions in the iconographic program. The statues of the "classicizing" atelier (see fig. 604), which had been intended for another location, were mingled with works that were more "modern" – that is, more Gothic, proceeding from the style initiated at Amiens Cathedral. This tradition will constitute the true Reims style.

609

·610

610 *The Annunciation*, west façade, Reims Cathedral · French, 1230–1240.

These figures are the work of two different workshops, both more traditional than that responsible for the Visitation group. The Virgin was carved about 1230, during the second period of activity at Reims, and the angel about 1240, when the decoration of the façade was being completed. The Virgin's head with its broad forehead and pointed chin, her sloping shoulders, and the sparse, broad folds defining her figure in large masses are in the style of Chartres, Paris and Amiens. Her facial expression and smile reveal deep psychological study. The angel is the work of the third workshop, free from both antique influence and 12th-century traditions, and it represents the style most typical of Reims.

611 *Smiling angel*, west façade, Reims Cathedral · French, ca. 1240.

The famous "smiling angel," carved about 1240, when the west façade was being finished, represents the final phase in the development of sculpture at Reims. It is a long way from the noble realism of the first years of the century; the elegant and delicate angel has become a friendly being, playful and sociable. The sacred is mixed with the profane, and the expression becomes more human; the pronounced smile, the exquisite delicacy of the face, and the refined gestures border on affectation. The sculptor's virtuosity in rendering fabrics, as in the facial modelling, displays complete technical command. Gothic art had reached the height of its possibilities and was not long to remain on this level.

611

613 *Head of a king, known as Philip Augustus* · Reims Cathedral
French, 1228–1233.

The figures on the upper part of the transept, executed between 1228
and 1253, are attributed to the workshop responsible for the west façade. In this national shrine there was a tendency to represent kings of
France rather than the kings of Judah or the fusion of profane and
biblical themes wherein historical kings were identified with legendary
figures. The head of the so-called Philip Augustus is a strikingly realistic portrait, and at the same time represents the ideal type of a statesman. The eyes are sharp and watchful beneath the strong arched
brows and they light up the thin face with its long, firm chin. (11½
feet high.) (Photograph from a cast in the Musée National des Monuments français, Paris.)

613

612

612 *Head from Reims Cathedral* · French, 13th century · Musée du
Cathédral, Reims.

After the war of 1914–1918 numerous sculptural fragments fallen from
the upper parts of the cathedral were gathered from the ruins. The
exact place this head comes from is not known, but it must have had
a simple decorative function. The freedom of the expression seems to
indicate that it was not originally part of an iconographic group but
was one of those ornamental elements in which the sculptor was
granted complete freedom and could satisfy, without constraint, a
certain naturalist verve.

614 *Head from Reims Cathedral* · French, 13th century · Musée du
Cathédral, Reims.

This head must come from the upper part of the cathedral. Many such
sculptures, fallen from the upper parts of the cathedral during bom-
bardments in the First World War, were rescued from the ruins. Set
as they were out of sight of the faithful, they reveal a realistic art
ramifying in complete freedom, whereas the sculpture groups displayed in full view on the portals adhered to accepted theological
themes. From the Romantic period on, these heads which decorated
the bosses and the cornices were called *marmousets* or grotesques. The
head reproduced here is not satirical; radiating with youth, it ranks
with the noble art of portal decorations.

614

615 *Eve*, north transept, Reims Cathedral · French, ca. 1230–1240.

Sculptors working about 1230 under the direction of Jean le Loup, the second architect to the cathedral, created the decoration around the north rose window. The sin of Adam and Eve, and its consequences, constitute the iconographic theme. Eve wears dress and veil, and fondles the serpent, who holds the apple in his mouth; the drapery style, the broken folds at the foot of the dress, and the face framed with wavy hair are characteristic of the 1230 workshop. The influence of Amiens is plainly visible. The sculptor has sought above all to express a state of mind, subtly depicting sorrow mingled with deceitfulness on the face of Eve after the fall. (Height, ca. 14 feet.)

615

616

616 *Apostle*, from the Sainte Chapelle, Paris · French, ca. 1245–1250 · Musée de Cluny, Paris.

The style of the Apostles from the Sainte Chapelle appears so advanced that they were once believed to have been carved after the building was erected. In fact, they date from the years 1245–1248. The sculptures, now in the Musée de Cluny, are examples of harmony and classical balance. In this figure, monumentality is secured by the calm and united planes of the drapery, and by the restraint of the pose. But overlying this classicism appears a Praxitelian refinement native to the Ile-de-France workshops, an elegance which perhaps had its origin in the art of the ivory carvers and the goldsmiths.

617

617 *Virgin and Child*, north portal, Notre-Dame, Paris · French, 1250–1260.

The trumeau statue of the Virgin and Child on this portal embodies a new conception of the Mother of God. Standing with her weight slightly off-center, she is an elegant, but not pretentious, figure, proudly presenting her Son to the faithful. Under the influence of courtly poetry and the developing cult of Mary, the *theotocos* element disappears: she is no longer the throne for her Son, but a mother pleased to display him. With her swaying pose and the noble beauty of her body, her robe gathered in front with a very natural gesture and falling in heavy folds, she no longer adheres to the pier in emulation of its supportive function, but stands as a freely moving figure, not subject to either architectural or iconographic strictures.

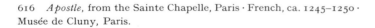

618 *Virgin and Child (The Vierge dorée)*, south transept, Amiens Cathedral · French, 1280–1288.

The decoration of Amiens was completed in the years after 1260. The *Vierge dorée* on the trumeau of the south transept portal is the most famous statue from this workshop. She is in the same tradition as the Virgin on the north portal of Notre Dame in Paris, but moves still further in the direction of humanization. A smiling young mother happily presents her son to us, with a gesture both playful and intimate. The angels supporting her halo participate in mischievous fashion in the atmosphere of homely joy. The *Vierge dorée* is the archetype of Madonnas that were to spread their graceful charm throughout Europe during the 14th century.

619 *Façade*, Bourges Cathedral · French, 1230–1265.

Begun in 1230 by the third architect to the cathedral, and finished between 1255 and 1265, the grandiose west front of Bourges Cathedral constitutes the final development of the Gothic façade. The five portals express on the exterior the cathedral's internal structure of a large central nave flanked by double aisles. Their arrangement required considerable technical ingenuity, a fact disguised by the great gables. The sculpture must have been in place by about 1275. The central theme – the Last Judgment – is treated with rare skill, but already displays a taste for the picturesque new to Gothic art.

618

619

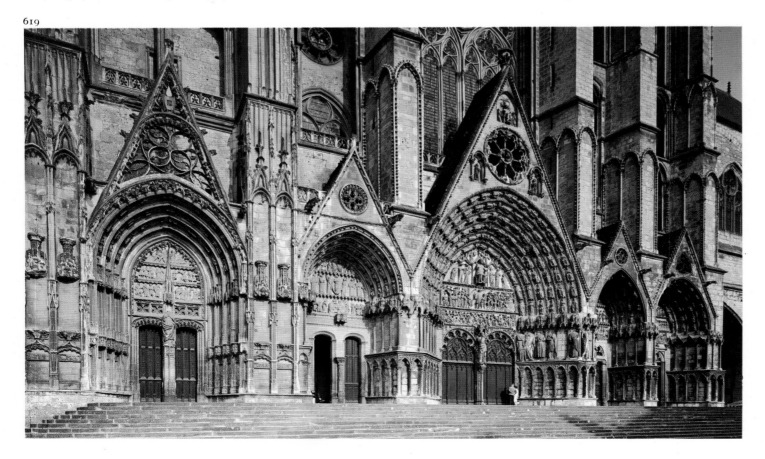

620

620 *The Archangel Michael weighing souls*: detail, tympanum of the central door, Bourges Cathedral · French, ca. 1275.

The Last Judgment was usually treated as a great drama, but here at Bourges it is picturesque and anecdotal. The composition is organized around St. Michael, who holds the scales. With a gesture full of grace and charm, he protects a frightened little soul from the feverish clutches of a devil. The archangel's smile is more marked than that of the angel at Reims and very nearly approaches a simper. At Michael's right the saved follow Peter into Paradise, a joyful scene where an angel even appears to joke with an elegant, cheerful woman among the elect. On the side depicting Hell, the sculptor shows a remarkable sense of rhythm. Charm and a feeling for narrative take precedence over awesome majesty.

621

621 *Head of the funerary statue of St. Osanna* · French, end of 13th century · Crypt, church of Jouarre.

The cenotaph of the legendary St. Osanna, probably the daughter of an Irish king, dates from the end of the 13th century. It was at that time that the portrait first appeared in western sculpture in *gisants*, the recumbent figures on tombs. The deceased woman lies at rest, in a stately dress, with her head slightly turned. Nothing here recalls the pangs of death: the saint's pose is dignified and her idealized face, less naturalistic and less set than those of the funerary sculptures at St. Denis, wears the smile of the school of Reims, as if to suggest the bliss of her sojourn in eternity.

296 of her sojourn in eternity.

622 *Guy II de Levis-Mirepoix, from his tomb*, priory of Notre-Dame de la Roche, Levis-Saint-Nom · French, ca. 1260.

The statues of the first three members of the Levis-Mirepoix family, in the priory of Notre-Dame de la Roche, provide a striking résumé of social development. Guy I, second-in-command to Simon de Montfort in the Albigensian Crusade, during which he acquired the fief of Mirepoix, has the face of a fanatic; Guy II, who died in 1260, is a knight and a courtier; Guy III, who died in 1299, has an altogether bourgeois aspect. Although a tomb figure, the statue of Guy II is carved in high relief, as if intended for a portal decoration. In accordance with 13th-century convention the deceased is shown as one of the "elect," with eyes open in contemplation of eternal bliss.

622

623 *Philip the Bold*: detail of his tomb, Abbey of St. Denis, Paris · French, ca. 1300.

The tomb of King Philip III the Bold was commissioned in 1298 by his son from Pierre de Chelles. The recumbent marble figure is treated according to 13-century tradition, but offers a clearly novel element: in this case, the face is an individualized portrait, with wide-set eyes, large mouth and strong chin. Funerary sculpture moved more and more towards the representation of the Prince as he was and not as he ought to have been; the classical idealization of tomb figures was slowly replaced by a realistic representation of the dead, often derived from funerary masks.

623

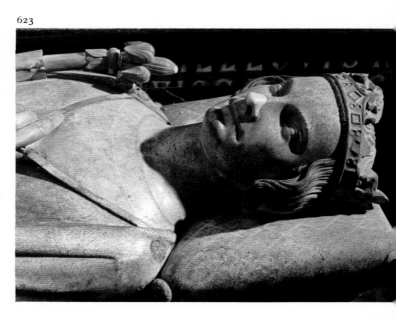

624

624 *Crocket capital* from the north portal of Chartres Cathedral.

Gothic artists created cathedral decoration *ex nihilo*, in a naturalistic and rational spirit. The "crocket" capital is repeated in the church, fitting into a strict decorative order. Starting from the changeless profile of the Corinthian capital, the sculptors move along the path of increasing naturalism. At first shaped like fern scrolls, then like buds bursting with vitality, the ornament on the capital finally broke into full leaf. Floral, springtime themes blossomed at Chartres about 1230, with scrolls decorating the very lively capitals. Gothic art completely renewed the decorative vocabulary by taking growing plants as models. (Photograph from a cast in the Musée National des Monuments français, Paris.)

625

625 *Grape-harvest capital*, nave of Reims Cathedral · French, ca. 1230.

Jean d'Orbais, architect to Reims Cathedral from 1211 to 1228, created an original design for the interior capitals. Jean le Loup, who carried on the work until 1233, used the same design from the sixth pillar onwards. The novelty consisted in treating the capitals for the pier and its attached colonnettes as a single continuous member, tying together the various elements of the compound piers at the point of the springing of the arches. The lower registers were decorated with carved scenes, here grape-harvesting and fantastic animals. The upper registers were decorated with crockets, or from 1228 on, with naturalistic foliage.

626 *Door-jamb*, south portal of the Abbey of St. Denis · French, ca. 1259.

The abbey conceived by Abbot Suger in the 12th century was completed only in the middle of the 13th century. This building campaign of 1240–1250 was formerly attributed to the famous architect Pierre de Montreuil, who was believed to have created at St. Denis a new, more refined and harmonious Gothic style. In 1965, however, Robert Branner refuted that theory, claiming that St. Denis belonged to the "Paris style," and Montreuil's role was merely that of executant. Between the jamb columns of the south transept portal, completed about 1259, surges a naturalistic forest of foliage, vine scrolls, fleur-de-lis, and crockets, all acutely observed and characteristic of the elegance and balance of Gothic at its height.

626

627 *Dormition of Mary*, tympanum, south transept portal, Strasbourg Cathedral · French, 1230–1240.

The Death of the Virgin from the south portal at Strasbourg is a Rhenish interpretation of classical French Gothic sculpture. The excitement of the Apostles, the numerous, agitated, close-set drapery folds and the sorrowful faces gazing at the Virgin with pathetic eagerness are all the work of an inspired and individual artist. If Gothic Germany adopted French iconography and composition, she nonetheless invested the scene with an expressionistic feeling that corresponded to her own deep-rooted inclinations.

627

628

628 *The Synagogue*, from the Cathedral of Strasbourg · French, ca. 1230–1250 · Musée de l'Œuvre Notre-Dame, Strasbourg.

The master masons and sculptors of Strasbourg had worked in the Reims stoneyards, whose style they brought with them to the Rhenish city. The allegory of the Synagogue is modelled after that of Reims, executed about 1225 and still impregnated with the style of the classicizing sculptors. But the Strasbourg Synagogue is more ethereal and unreal than its French prototype. The forward-stepping motion is more strongly marked in the hip movement and the gesture of the arms. The art of Reims had enormous prestige and influence during the Middle Ages, when it was considered the model of all arts by the whole of Europe.

629

630

629 *A Virtue* (detail), west front, Strasbourg Cathedral · French, beginning of the 14th century.

The Psychomachy is represented on the north door of the west façade of Strasbourg Cathedral, rebuilt after a fire in 1298. Set against the jambs is a series of female statues, each symbolizing a Virtue driving a lance through the crumpled body of a Vice on whom she stands. The influence of classical Gothic statuary is still visible in this 14th century work, but the Strasbourg sculptors succeeded in avoiding a stilted academism. In its intensely alive expression, the face displays the vitality of this peripheral art whose naturalistic realism renewed Gothic art.

630 *Virgin and Child* · Ivory · French, early 14th century · Hospice, Villeneuve-les-Avignon (France).

The tender or playful exchanges between Virgin and Christ Child provided an inexhaustible variety of themes for French Gothic sculptors from 1250 onwards. Ivory-workers reproduced this theme endlessly in statuettes for private chapels, delightful figures that contributed greatly to the spread of the elegant French Gothic style throughout Europe. The Virgin's contrapposto, counterbalancing the weight of the Child, follows quite naturally the shape of the elephant's tusk that gave the sculptor his ivory. This beautifully finished statuette touched with gold and colors retains all the natural grace of the 13th century, not yet displaying that dryness in the forms which is so characteristic of the following century.

633

633 *The Virgin fainting:* detail of an altar, Church of Notre-Dame de Louviers (Eure) · Wood · French, 14th century.

This group from a Normandy workshop forms part of an altarpiece representing Calvary. The Holy Women and St. John support the Virgin, who faints on witnessing her Son's tragic suffering. This theme was well suited to 14th-century artists, who exploited all its dramatic possibilities. Throne of God during the Romanesque period, mother during the 13th century, the Virgin now became a woman subject to terrible suffering. The broken lines, the disjointed bodies, and the artificial turbulence of the folds are characteristic of Gothic mannerism. The faces and the hands emphasize the moving sorrow of the actors in this scene.

634 *Christ Blessing*, from the tomb of Cardinal de Lagrange · French, late 14th century · Musée Lapidaire, Avignon.

During the 14th century when the papacy was established in that town, the monasteries of Avignon abounded in sculpture, of which Revolutionary vandalism has left only shattered remnants. This school of sculpture seems to have had more vitality than the Ile-de-France school, which was perhaps coarsened by a tincture of Flemish realism that failed to revitalize the Parisian formalism. Though mutilated, the surviving statues from the tomb of Cardinal Jean de Lagrange that once stood in the church of the monastery-college of the Benedictines, St. Martial, display a majesty and an eloquence in the use of drapery not to be found in contemporary sculpture in the Ile-de-France. The Cardinal's canopied tomb, which once included a large number of statuary groups arranged on seven registers, almost reached the vault of the church.

634

631

632

631 *Virgin and Child*, cemetery chapel at St. Amand-les-Pas (Pas-de-Calais) · French, late 13th century.

The Virgin in the cemetery chapel of St. Amand-les-Pas is of unknown origin. Playing with her son rather than worshipping him, she smiles with a smile like that of the *Vierge dorée* on the south portal of Amiens cathedral (fig. 618). The type of the mother of God standing and holding her child like any ordinary mother spread rapidly throughout France. Originally pleasant and gracious, the genre degenerated into affectation with the strained, unsteady poses of the mannered 14th-century Gothic Madonnas.

632 *St. Paul the Apostle*, from the funerary chapel of Jean Tessandier · French, ca. 1325–1330 · Musée des Augustins, Toulouse.

Jean Tessandier, a Franciscan friar who was Bishop of Rieux from 1324 to 1328, had a funerary chapel built onto the church of his order in Toulouse. Of the twenty statues that adorned it, including the twelve apostles, Christ and the Virgin, and several Franciscan saints, seventeen are now in Toulouse and two others are in the Musée Bonnat at Bayonne. Some of them, particularly the twelve apostles, display an expressionistic power very unusual at this stage in the development of Gothic sculpture, which for the most part was lapsing into a dry formalism. The St. Paul foreshadows Claus Sluter's Moses (fig. 673), though the Virgin and the Christ are quite conventional.

635

635 *The Bamberg Rider* (detail), Bamberg Cathedral · German, ca. 1230–1240.

The distant ancestor of this equestrian statue might have been the monument allegedly of Constantine that once stood before the Lateran Palace. Although copied from the head of a king in Reims Cathedral, the head of the Rider constitutes one of the best examples of forceful Germanic sculpture. The dry modelling emphasizing the bone structure accentuates the intensity of this almost brutal captain's face. Disregarding the idealization of Reims, which had inspired him, the master of Bamberg explored much further into realism. The rider is no king or wise man, but rather a war lord, a leader of men, a condottiere.

636 *Head of Adam*, Adam Portal, Bamberg Cathedral · German, 1235–1250.

The style of the sculptures at Bamberg is not homogeneous, diverse tendencies appearing in the sculptures from the different periods of building activity. There is a clear break between the Romanesque architecture of the Adam Portal and the sculpture ornamenting its jambs, which is ahead of its time. The primal human couple is shown naked, an iconographic innovation attributable to Germany, while the cold and melancholic beauty of Adam's face is more in keeping with the French Gothic style. The manner in which beard and hair are treated in small, patterned curls is an archaism contrasting with the restrained and subtle modelling of the face, which is marked with the tragic guilt of original sin.

636

637

637 *Last Judgment*: detail, Fürstentor, Bamberg Cathedral · German, ca. 1230–1240.

The "Counts' Portal," installed during the second building campaign, is the first entirely Gothic work at Bamberg. The tympanum is decorated with a Last Judgment, in which the figures are actually treated as sculpture in the round. The figures representing the Saved display a euphoric joy rather than an angelic and heavenly smile, and their candid, mischievous laughter suggests a Paradise filled with earthly pleasures – as the reward for a life based on those pleasures. The art of Bamberg is here clearly expressionistic, even bordering on caricature.

638 *Virgin*, from *The Visitation*, Bamberg Cathedral · German, ca. 1225.

About 1225 sculpture at Bamberg switched very suddenly from the Romanesque to the Gothic style. As at Strasbourg, the new sculpture was an adaptation of the Reims style; the Bamberg Visitation is a more dramatic version of that of Reims (fig. 604). The Virgin's contrapposto is accentuated, and the flow of close-set folds in the soft fabric at Reims has turned into a tumble of broad, thick folds, suggesting some heavy material or perhaps even leather. The artist's chisel has been irresistibly drawn by the decorative possibilities of this bunched-up material, and he achieves admirable plastic effects at the expense of anatomical rendering.

638

639

639 *Head of the Virgin*: detail of fig. 638.

The head is strongly individualized. Swathed in the mantle, the face is long and almost lean, the nose slightly turned up, the lips parted as if about to break into speech, the eyes seem to have been weeping a moment ago: this Virgin lacks completely the serene resignation of the young woman of Reims. The homage of Elizabeth, the announcement of her extraordinary destiny, have stirred her to the core. It is as if, in a single startling moment, she understood the tragedy awaiting her and her role in the divine drama: the sculptor has given us here a mother faced with suffering, not the maiden chosen by God.

640 *Ekkehard and Uta*, west choir, Naumburg Cathedral · German, ca. 1260–1270.

The "Naumburg Master," trained in France, carried his program of sculptural decoration over to the cathedral interior. In 1249, commissioned by Bishop von Wettin, he began the series of portraits of the ten founders of the church. Countess Uta, her face framed by her cloak collar and her coronet, stands next to her husband Ekkehard, the Margrave of Meissen. The modelling is restrained, and the straight folds fall in broad planes, without any ornamental effects. All the expressive force of the work is concentrated in the faces. The young Uta has an ambiguous expression, inscrutable, set and proud; Ekkehard has a soldier's face, self-confident, almost brutal.

641 *Count Wilhelm von Camburg*: detail, west choir, Naumburg Cathedral · German, ca. 1260–1270.

In the statues of the west choir, commissioned in 1249 and executed between 1260 and 1270, the Master of Naumburg sloughed off French influence to produce a typically German art. Real people, not religious figures, were portrayed: the princes who had founded the abbey. Not truly portraits – the models had been dead 200 years – these extremely realistic personages form a gallery of human temperaments, of "humors," their faces expressing the entire range of man's sentiments. Wilhelm von Camburg, his head sunk to one side, is the nostalgic, tormented poet, a melancholy Minnesinger whose gaze is lost in dream. An expressionistic art, then, which broke with Gothic classicism.

640

641

643

642 *Crucifix, Virgin, and St. John*, choir screen, Naumburg Cathedral · German, ca. 1260–1270.

A portal in the central part of the Naumburg Cathedral choir screen contains this Crucifixion group attributed to the Master of the West Choir. It is traditionally expressionistic in both the tragic intensity of the faces and the treatment of drapery, and the Master has clearly explored a new style moving decisively away from French models. The most remarkable element is the dramatic composition of the scene, in which the Virgin and St. John seem to call upon the spectators as witnesses to the sacred tragic drama. Such rhetorical pathos looks ahead, across more than a century, to the art of Sluter.

642

643 *Madonna of Seeon* · German, early 15th century · Bayerisches Nationalmuseum, Munich.

At the end of the 14th century a type of Virgin appears which was to be popular in Germanic countries throughout the 15th century. To this type belongs the early 15th-century Seeon Madonna. Richly attired, seated, she plays with her Child, to whom she offers an apple in a domestic scene tinged with preciosity. The "hip-shot" poste, so exaggerated as to seem disjointed, the angular body, the doll-like face, the brittle drapery folds, the refined clothing whose richness is emphasized by the polychromy, are characteristic of the mannered German late Gothic style – one trend in the international Gothic style, and one which spread as far as Bohemia and Czechoslovakia.

644

644 *Crucifix*, Santa Maria im Kapitol, Cologne · German, 14th century.

The great crucifix of Santa Maria im Kapitol in Cologne is one of a series of similar crucifixes from the 14th century in Germany. A tormented corpse, with hollow belly and taut arms, is nailed to a pollarded tree; Christ is an abandoned victim, body torn by suffering and wasted to emaciation. German expressionistic art renders the Passion through the physical collapse of God-made-Man. This conception, and the already tormented style, announce the excesses of 15th-century Germanic Gothic.

645

645 *Misericord of a choir stall*, from Wassemberg · Wood · German, ca. 1300 · Kunstgewerbe Museum, Cologne.

Germany, where objects of medieval art have been better preserved than in France, still offers several ensembles of 13th- and 14th-century choir stalls. The carving reproduced, from Wassemberg, is evidence of the great elegance attained by certain Gothic ateliers of the Rhine area in the second half of the 13th century, while Franconian ateliers, on the contrary, explored a more specifically Germanic expressionism.

646

646 WILLIAM TOREL · *Eleanor of Castile*, on her tomb, Westminster Abbey, London · Bronze · English, 1291–1293.

The tomb of Eleanor of Castile, wife of Edward I of England, is one of the most characteristic works of 13th-century English court art. The queen's effigy was cast in 1291–1292 by a London goldsmith called William Torel, who used the lost wax process. Torel received commissions for several tombs for the royal mausoleum in the Confessor's Chapel at Westminster Abbey. The recumbent figure of the queen, elegant and aristocratic, constitutes the final flowering of the English tradition, inspired by the royal tombs of St. Denis. The thin, refined face and the arrangement of the dress illustrate the idealizing tendency in late 13th-century portraiture.

647 *The Virgen Blanca*, west façade, Leon Cathedral · Spanish, ca. 1250–1275.

"Nuestra Señora la Blanca," the "Virgen Blanca" of the west portal of Leon Cathedral, is the masterpiece of a certain Enrico, who died in 1277. He worked at Burgos and at Leon, and though he must have been trained at Amiens, he transformed the stylized grace of his masters' 13th-century French Gothic art into something more picturesque and anecdotal. The drapery folds are more broken, more angular; the Virgin is pleasant and kindly, and her Son, a lively and mischievous *niño*.

647

648 *Christ in Majesty*, Sarmental portal, Burgos Cathedral · Spanish, ca. 1225.

Two masters influenced by the Amiens school created the sculpture for the *Puerta del Sarmental* on the south transept of Burgos Cathedral, the first specifically Gothic monument in Castile. The Christ surrounded by symbols of the Evangelists, on the tympanum, recalls the old Romanesque iconographic scheme of the Pantocrator, but the figure style and the clarity of the composition are classically Gothic. The tendency towards naturalism and the directness with which the broad surfaces are carved are more Spanish. Christ's face is exceptionally beautiful, and is comparable to the one at Amiens, although perhaps more human.

649 *Detail of portal of the Cathedral*, Burgo do Osma (Soria) Spanish, ca. 1250–1275.

The Gothic cathedral at Burgo do Osma was begun in 1232; the sculpture in the main portal was installed between 1250 and 1275. The jamb-piers are divided into two registers, the lower decorated with blind arcading, and the upper with a series of figures from the Old and New Testaments. These prophets, kings and queens are the work of an artist who knew the art of Burgos but not French cathedral sculpture. The proportions are more compact than those of contemporary French figures, the faces schematic, and the draperies coarser in treatment. This simpler, lower-keyed provincial art is at several removes from its model, the series of kings and prophets at Reims.

648

649

650　*The Queen of Swabia*, cloister, Burgos Cathedral · Spanish, late 13th century.

The sculpture of the upper cloister at Burgos Cathedral belongs to the end of the 13th century. In this case, the influence of Reims is decisive and combines with reflections of the Amiens style. The figure of Queen Beatrix of Swabia shows the Spanish Gothic sculptor typically assimilating outside influences and yet arriving at something characteristically Spanish. With its air of authority and its realism, it stands midway between the calm nobility of the Reims Queen of Sheba and the sharp Countess Uta or the harsh Gerburg at Naumburg Cathedral.

650

651

651 *Bust of Frederick II* · Italian, ca. 1225–1250 · Museo communale, Bari.

In the 13th century, while northern Italy was turning towards Gothic art, southern Italy, under Frederick II of Hohenstaufen (1194–1250) experienced a kind of primitive Renaissance, based on a direct observation of ancient art. The marble bust of Frederick, from an equestrian statue, is one of the fullest expressions of the imperial concept. The disdainful and skeptical expression of the psychologically complex prince, who was both authoritarian and liberal, is somewhat disguised by the breakages, but even in its damaged form, the bust marks the birth of a new ideal in sculpture.

652 NICCOLO DI BARTOLOMMEO DA FOGGIA (Italian, 13th century) · *Pulpit*, Ravello Cathedral · 1272.

Pisano (fig. 654) perhaps studied in the circle of the Apulian Niccolo di Bartolommeo da Foggia, who in 1272 signed his name to the pulpit in the cathedral of San Pantaleone at Ravello. The pulpit is decorated with marble sculptures conceived quite separately from the architecture. One of them is the bust of a young woman with the attributes of an empress, an allegory of the Church merged with an image of Sigilgaita della Marra, the founder of the church. Despite its late date and its overlay of classicism, Niccolo's art must be regarded as the final flowering of Apulian Romanesque sculpture. The imitation of the antique is drier and more on the surface, more formal and more systematic than in the art of Pisano.

652

653 *Pedestal* · Italian, ca. 1250–1300 · Museo Civico, Bologna.

This pedestal for a pulpit or, more probably, a paschal candelabra, comes from the old Romanesque cathedral of Bologna, which was consecrated in 1261 and later totally destroyed. Hybrid in style, it has been attributed by some to the sculptor Antelami, by others to some Lombard or Veronese artist. It must date from the second half of the 13th century, and alongside Gothic elements brought in from outside it reveals deep knowledge of antique art in the tradition of Polykleitos, especially in the plastic modelling of the anatomy. There is certainly some relationship to the art of Arnolfo di Cambio who, according to some writers, may have known it and been inspired by it.

653

654 NICOLA PISANO (Italian, active 1258–1278) · *Pulpit*, Baptistry, Pisa · 1260.

Nicola Pisano, a native of the south, introduced Gothic sculpture to Tuscany, while also displaying, in his relief scenes, a strong classicizing element no doubt linked to his Apulian training. Some art historians believe that Nicola had been to France, but this theory does not fit in with known facts. In 1260 he signed the Baptistry pulpit at Pisa. It is composed as a hexagon supported by a central column and six external columns, whose Gothic capitals are surmounted by trilobe arches. The colored marbles and the remains of polychromy create a picturesque effect. The structure of the pulpit appears to be a synthesis of elements imported from southern Italy and Tuscan elements, the whole strongly flavored with Gothic forms; but the importance given to the sculpture is something quite new.

655 NICOLA PISANO · *Adoration of the Magi*: detail of the Pisa Baptistry pulpit (fig. 654).

Nicola Pisano was directly influenced by ancient sarcophagus reliefs in carving the five relief panels of the Pisa pulpit. The model for the Virgin in the Adoration of the Magi in fact exists on a sarcophagus in the Campo Santo at Pisa. But Pisano was no mere plagiarist; he assimilated the ancient heritage and created an art that was his own. The clearly ordered composition reveals a new concern: to give a sculptural solidity to his figures, and to suggest depth by differentiating several quite distinct planes moving back into space. This definition of forms in space was to become one of the primary concerns of Italian Renaissance relief sculptors.

654

656

656 NICOLA PISANO · *Hercules*: detail from pulpit (fig. 654).

Nicola Pisano gives great emphasis to the corner statuettes, which are
treated as sculpture in the round. In them the influence of antiquity is
most clearly shown. The artist has chosen Hercules to symbolize Fortitude, a Christian virtue, and Nicola's rendering of heroic nudity
suggests how thoroughly he had absorbed the ancient forms in his
training in Apulia during Frederick II's curious proto-Renaissance
revival of antiquity (see fig. 651). The Fortitude summarizes Pisano's
vision of humanity – man elevated to the dignity of the hero – and his
conception of sculpture – firm modelling emphasizing the body's planes
and its anatomical structure.

655

657

657 NICOLA PISANO · *The Damned*: detail of the Last Judgment, pulpit, Siena Cathedral · 1265–1268.

In 1265 a contract was made between Nicola Pisano and the church authorities of Siena cathedral for the cathedral pulpit. It was stipulated that Nicola should be assisted by his son Giovanni and by Arnolfo and Lapo di Cambio; the final payments were made in 1268. The reliefs on the Siena pulpit are more narrative and more picturesque than those on the Pisa pulpit, and the whole is stylistically oriented towards French Gothic art; the influence of a Cistercian monk called Fra Melano, "operaio" of the cathedral, who had contacts with France, may explain the strong French flavor. The hand of Nicola can be recognized in the Last Judgment scene, despite the somewhat confused composition.

658 ARNOLFO DI CAMBIO (Italian, ca. 1245–1302 ?) · *Santa Reparata* · ca. 1300 · Museo dell'Opera del Duomo, Florence.

Arnolfo di Cambio is mentioned in 1265 as assistant to Nicola Pisano in Siena. His career can be traced through Rome, Viterbo, Perugia, Orvieto, until he came in 1296 to Florence, where he was made *capomaestro* of the cathedral, and produced architectural designs and also sculptures for its façade. The figure known as Santa Reparata, which may actually be an allegory of Charity, must have been one of these last. Arnolfo's sculpture is influenced by both French Gothic and the antique; however, the latter influence dominates, and there are many elements in the head of Santa Reparata that point directly to ancient sculpture.

658

659

659 GIOVANNI PISANO (Italian, ca. 1250–after 1314) · *A Sibyl*, pulpit, Sant'Andrea, Pistoia · Ca. 1300.

The pulpit of Sant'Andrea in Pistoia was completed by Giovanni Pisano in 1301. According to Vasari, he must have begun the work in 1297; according to others, in 1288. Its architecture is similar to that of Nicola's pulpit in the Baptistry of Pisa. The angles of the archivolt are decorated with sibyls, which are quite different from the angle figures at Pisa. Moving, sometimes vehement poses, expressive faces, linear rhythms, and deeply undercut relief characterize this sculpture, where pictorial values arising from the contrasting rhythms of light and shade take precedence over spatial values. Giovanni's highly expressive style illustrates the growing importance of the individual vision.

660

660 GIOVANNI PISANO · *Hercules*: detail of the pulpit, Pisa Cathedral, 1302–1310.

When compared to the Hercules figure carved by his father Nicola fifty years earlier for the Baptistry pulpit in Pisa, the figure produced by Giovanni for the pulpit of the cathedral in the same city shows the readaptation of the Gothic style in Tuscany. Nicola's Hercules has all the athletic power of antique sculpture; Giovanni's has the body of a Christian ascetic, though given a kind of restraint and composure. In the Pisa pulpit there appears to have been considerable intervention by shop hands, and the main interest lies in the large-scale figures employed as supports, like this Hercules.

663 GIOVANNI PISANO · *Head of the figure of Simeon* from the façade of Siena Cathedral · 1284–1296 · Museo dell'Opera del Duomo, Siena.

Giovanni Pisano, the son of Nicola, broke with his father's tradition. The first work for which he alone was responsible was the façade of Siena Cathedral, upon which he was employed as architect and sculptor between 1284 and 1296, holding the post of *capomaestro* from 1287. He carved a series of over life-size prophets, philosophers and sibyls which were placed above the portals, as was customary in Italy, not against the jambs, as were French Gothic figures. The poses of the figures and the carving techniques are very French – Giovanni must have been acquainted with French art, and perhaps travelled in France about 1270–75 – but there is an organic self-sufficiency and a vigor of movement in his figures that is quite un-French.

663

661   662

661–662 GIOVANNI PISANO · *Madonna della Cintola*, Prato Cathedral, ca. 1313–1314.

Over the years from about 1295 to the end of his active life, Giovanni Pisano produced a whole series of representations of the Virgin and Child. That in the Cappella del Sacro Cingolo in Prato Cathedral is one of the artist's last works. The loose and supple style of Giovanni's Madonnas reflects that of French ivories, through which the forms of later 13th-century Parisian Gothic art spread throughout Italy. Giovanni, however, added to the French grace a sense of monumentality and of pathos, arising from his figures' more broadly handled forms, firmly rooted stances, and intense expressions.

309

664

664 *Madonna and Child* · Italian, 14th century · Art Institute, Chicago.

The Campionesi were a group of sculptors, including notably Giovanni and Bonino da Campione, coming originally from Campione on Lake Lugano and from the Como district. They were active from the 12th to the 14th centuries and, assimilating different influences, created a style indigenous to Lombardy. Their work is to be found throughout northern Italy and the Alps. The 14th-century sculptor who made the seated Virgin and Child now in Chicago has fused the art of Arnolfo di Cambio and the Lombard and German traditions to produce a rather academic work in which attempts to grasp Pisan and Florentine innovations combine with recollections of the Romanesque masters.

665 *Equestrian statue* of Can Grande della Scala, from his tomb · Italian, ca. 1330 · Castelvecchio Museum, Verona.

The *arche Scaligere*, tombs of the ruling family of Verona, the Scaliger, form a group unique in Italian Gothic art. The tombs are protected by stone canopies, which were surmounted by equestrian statues of the deceased. That of the condottiere Can Grande della Scala, who died in 1329, is traditionally attributed to a nameless Maestro Campionese. In 1958, Arslan suggested that this was the work of a Tuscan; others have seen the prototypes of these sculptures in German Gothic examples. Whatever the case may be, the theme of the equestrian funerary monument became typically Veronese, and produced a flock of descendants, among which Donatello's Gattamelata (fig. 730) is supreme.

666

666 *Head of Christ*: detail from a crucifix · Italian, 14th century · Museo Nazionale, Messina.

The wood of this life-size crucifix has attained with time the color of bronze. The calm and noble work, executed with great delicacy, goes back to the 14th century, but it is difficult to attribute it to a known workshop. It was perhaps brought to Sicily from Tuscany, for Christ's ascetic and elongated body recalls the representations of Christ crucified produced by Sienese painters. However, the artist who carved this work discarded his contemporaries' dramatic violence and appears instead to have wished to stress Christ's divinity.

665

667

667 Lorenzo Maitani (Italian, ca. 1275–1330) · *Scenes from Genesis*, pier of the façade, Orvieto Cathedral · 1310–1316.

Lorenzo Maitani was first and foremost an architect. He was Master Mason of the cathedral at Orvieto from 1310 until his death in 1330 and almost surely designed, at least, the reliefs on the piers of the façade. There are in existence two drawings by him of projects for the cathedral façade in which the outline for the Tree of Jesse relief on one of the piers can be seen. The relief with scenes from Genesis appears to carry out that design and many authors attribute the execution to Maitani. A vine rising from the base subdivides the relief into smaller fields with fresh, fluent tendrils and leaves of a northern Gothic cast. In the smaller fields the scenes from Genesis are narrated with economical but telling forms and gestures, expressed principally in terms of line, and the figures are not arranged in depth, but are strung along the surface as in a frieze.

668

668 *Head of a prophet*, from Milan Cathedral · Italian, late 14th century · Opera del Duomo, Milan.

Milan Cathedral, begun during the last quarter of the 14th century, is the only Flamboyant style building in Italy; French, German and Italian architects worked on it. The sculpture is in the International Style, with a predominance of northern elements; the artists were Germans, like Walter Monich or Hans von Fernach, Frenchmen, like Roland de Banille, or Lombardians or Venetians. The prophet's head, modelled along French lines, is very conventional. The sculptor has transformed into a grimace the mystical and inspired expression of classical Gothic prophets.

670 Andrea Pisano · *Visitation*, detail of fig. 669.

Andrea was not hindered by the strictness of the quatrefoil surrounds, as is evident in the Visitation. The figures move with ease, and even the setting for the encounter, suggested by an architectural motif, is easily inserted in the frame. Andrea Pisano succeeds in composing his narrative scenes without concessions to the picturesque or to superfluous details which might have disturbed the overall balance. However, the very clarity and simplification of his presentations detracts from the rendering of spatial values. The linear style of the figures and the folds of the draperies clearly show a Gothic and French character.

669

669 Andrea Pisano (Italian, ca. 1290–1348) · *South door*, Baptistry, Florence · 1330–1336.

Andrea da Pontedera, known as Andrea Pisano, was active as an architect and as a sculptor. His biography is rather obscure before the year when his name appears in accounts relating to the Florentine Baptistry's bronze doors, which he signed with the date 1330 – the date the work was begun. The south door is divided into twenty-eight rectangular compartments within which are quatrefoils framing scenes from the life of St. John the Baptist. This rectangular disposition is inspired by Bonannus' doors at Pisa (fig. 582), while the idea for the inner quatrefoil frames must have been imported from the Ile de France. Since the cleaning of the doors, the charming coloristic contrast of the gilded relief parts against the flat bronze surfaces of the background has reappeared.

670

671

672

671 ANDREA ORCAGNA (Italian, active 1344–1368) · *Assumption of the Virgin*, Tabernacle of Or San Michele, Florence · Ca. 1355–1359.

The Florentine painter, sculptor, and architect Andrea di Cione, known as Orcagna, was probably a pupil of Andrea Pisano, as Vasari says. Orcagna was the creator of the tabernacle at Or San Michele, begun in 1355 and signed in 1359. Into the back of the richly decorated four-sided architectural framework Orcagna set his relief of the Death of the Virgin and her Assumption into Heaven. The marble figures in the Assumption stand out against a mosaic background, and a remarkable effect of contrast between the two episodes is thereby produced. The vehement, crowded figures around the Virgin on her tomb reflect the antinaturalistic style that prevailed in Florence after the Black Death, though the Assumption scene reveals a sense of volume and space pointing forward to the Quattrocento.

672 ANDREA ORCAGNA · *The Virgin Mary*: detail of the Nativity, tabernacle of Or San Michele, Florence (see fig. 671).

The quality and style of the sculptures on the tabernacle is rather uneven; the hands of less experienced assistants can be seen as well as traces of Andrea Pisano's influence. Some panels, such as the Nativity, are characteristic of the best of Orcagna, when he gives importance to the relief and to the treatment of space. The relief is synthetic, all superfluous detail eliminated in order to render the feeling of space. Orcagna's style of naturalism, which has sometimes been called academic because it is rather hieratic and set, is descended directly from the art of Giotto, and is opposed to the Gothicism of Andrea Pisano and his followers.

673

674

673–674 CLAUS SLUTER (active 1380–1406) · *Moses, with two prophets*, on the "Well of Moses," Chartreuse de Champmol, Dijon · 1395–1404.

Moses: detail of fig. 674. Of all those in western art, this head of Moses perhaps most resembles that of biblical tradition. The wrinkled face and heavy eyebrows, the forehead bearing horns in accordance with the tradition of mystery-play actors, the bifurcated, flowing beard – all these contribute to an intelligent, awe-inspiring visage full of power. This is indeed the leader of the chosen people, their law-giver and guide. Sluter's genius explores the limits of realism in the treatment of facial expression, but despite this realism, his art has a deeply moving human pathos, and although it might be termed expressionistic, it never degenerates into caricature.

The Netherlander Claus Sluter worked in a monumental, robust style that breathed new life into late Gothic sculpture, which had begun to degenerate into mannerism or academism. A native of Holland, Sluter worked first in Brussels and then for the Duke of Burgundy at Dijon. There, he carved six life-size prophets to ornament the so-called Well of Moses – actually the base of a Calvary – at the Carthusian monastery of Champmol. Treated with exceptional force, the strongly differentiated physical types of the two prophets and the boldly handled curves and broken edges in the draperies accentuate the dramatic poses and reflect the ardor and the intensity of Sluter's inspiration.

313

676 CLAUS SLUTER · *Virgin and Child*: trumeau, portal of the Chartreuse de Champmol, Dijon · Ca. 1393.

The Portal of the Virgin at Champmol was begun in 1385 by Jean de Marville, Sluter's predecessor in the employ of the Duke of Burgundy. Sluter transformed the portal composition by increasing the size of the statues and alternating standing and seated figures. The Virgin occupies the whole trumeau. She is no longer a jamb-figure, but instead a self-sufficient statue full of life and passionate movement. The baroque character of the movement, modelling, and drapery shatters the traditional conception of the Virgin. The link between mother and child has become a tragic dialogue, in which the Son, pulling away from Mary, seems to admonish her.

676

675 CLAUS SLUTER · *Tomb of Philip the Bold* · Ca. 1404–1410 · Musée des Beaux-Arts, Dijon.

The tomb of Duke Philip the Bold of Burgundy poses the difficult problem of Sluter's workshop. The tomb was commissioned as early as 1377 from Marville, the Master Mason of the Carthusian monastery. After Marville's death in 1389 Sluter took over the workshop, but abandoned the tomb for more pressing works. When the Duke died in 1404, work on the tomb was begun again; it was still unfinished when Sluter died. Some historians have tried to minimize the part played by Sluter, attributing the overall scheme to Marville and the sculptures of the mourners on the base to Claus de Werve, Sluter's nephew; however, it is almost certain that Sluter designed the models for these last.

675

677

677 CLAUS SLUTER · *A mourner*, from the Tomb of Philip the Bold (see fig. 675).

The sculptor had the original idea of transforming the traditional row of figures set in niches into a procession of mourners, moving freely behind an arcade and realistically suggesting the funeral cortege. The artist exploited the expressive possibilities of their voluminous woolen robes, into whose folds he carved the pathos of living beings confronting death. Despite their small size the mourners are works of remarkable monumentality. No volume is without function in the art of Sluter, and the powerfully built body beneath the rough homespun is clearly indicated.

314

678 SCHOOL OF JACOB DE GÉRINES · *Anne of Burgundy as Humility* ·
Bronze · Flemish, 1445–1448, or 1476 · Rijksmuseum, Amsterdam.

In the Rijksmuseum is a series of statuettes like this one, attributed
to the bronze caster Jacob de Gérines, called "of Coperslagere." They
may have come from the tomb of Jeanne de Brabant in Brussels
(executed in 1458), or from that of Louis de Mâle in Lille (dated 1455),
or from the tomb of Isabelle de Bourbon in Antwerp (cast in 1476).
Modern critics tend to the view that these figurines originally decorated the Antwerp tomb, which was begun after Gérines' death. The
figure of Anne of Burgundy, an allegory of Humility, is inspired by
15th-century Flemish painting and more particularly by the style of
Van Eyck. Northern sculpture does not show the influence of Sluter.

679

679   JAN BORMAN (Flemish, active 1479–1520) · *Two scenes of mar-
tyrdom*: detail of the St. George Altar from the church of Notre Dame,
Louvain · 1493 · Royal Museums of Art and History, Brussels.

In the 15th century, the Flemish excelled in wood carving; workshops
at Antwerp, Malines, and Brussels produced huge wooden altarpieces
which were sold throughout Europe – in France, Germany, Scandinavia and Spain. The legends of the martyrs were among the favorite
themes for their sculptured decoration, as can be seen in this typical
work by Jan Borman. His altar is divided into a series of pigeonholes
filled with statuettes, in scenes sometimes picturesque and sometimes
horrifyingly expressionistic. The essentially narrative style occasionally descends to coarse caricature. The contorted and angular forms are
an exaggeration of Van der Weyden's manner.

678

680

680   *Virgin, from Plombières-lès-Dijon* · French, ca. 1430 · The
Louvre, Paris.

The art of the Netherlander Sluter had a southern following. His Virgin
the Chartreuse of Champmol had a whole series of descendants in at
Burgundian popular imagery. Their general appearance is more mannered, the proportions sometimes so shortened that the figure appears
dwarflike, the drapery falls in limper folds, and the whole treatment
becomes heavy: Sluter's forms and techniques were applied, but the
sculptors lacked his lyrical inspiration. The Virgin from Plombières-lès-
Dijon, however, has a rustic strength not without charm, contrasting
with the supple affectations of other 15th century schools.

681 *Entombment*, Church of Notre-Dame, Semur-en-Auxois · French, end of the 15th century.

The theme of the Entombment was very much in favor during the 15th century. The Burgundian school represented it frequently and exploited all its tragic possibilities. The Entombment at Semur unites Sluter's realism and grandiloquence with more genuinely Flemish and even Rhenish influences. The French spirit of classical restraint governs the pathos and physical suffering, which are transmitted through the expressiveness of the angular faces and through the stiff fabrics with their sharp, artificial folds.

683 *Choir stalls in the Cathedral of Amiens* · Wood · French, 1508–1522.

From the 14th century onwards, the choir stalls became large, elaborate structures of carved wood, adding a rich note in the choir of the church. The greatest and most complete set of carved stalls still extant is that at Amiens. There are 4,700 figures framed within a superb flamboyant scheme of decoration. The iconography is still treated according to the medieval tradition, mingling religious and profane themes. Accompanying the figurations from the Holy Scripture are representations of trades, fools, proverbs and licentious scenes. Cabinetmakers like Boulin, Huet, le Clerc, Meurisse, Avernier, or Turpin were perhaps influenced by the anecdotal profane art of Flemish wood carvers.

681

683

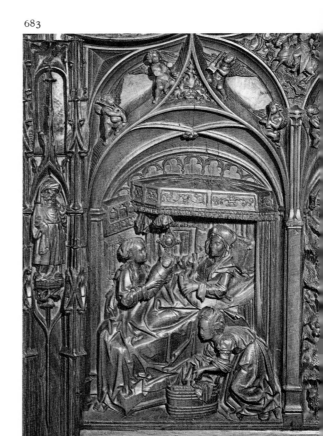

682 *Mourning angel* · French, late 15th century · Museum, Semur-en-Auxois.

This is one of a pair of mourning and praying angels that no doubt once surmounted some Crucifixion or Entombment group. They are influenced by Flemish art, and particularly by Van der Weyden, even more strongly than the Entombment group described above. The harsh gestures and the angular limbs accentuate the angel's convulsive movements of sorrow and prayer. The drapery folds are used purely for effect and the full faces surrounded by thick hair recall Sluter.

684 *Detail of the reveal of a choir stall*, Amiens Cathedral (see fig. 683).

During the High Gothic period, stall carvers indulged in a veritable orgy of fantastic forms. Expelled from capitals and pediments, the Romanesque feeling for fantasy took refuge in the misericords and the arm rests of the choir stalls. Monsters, animals, grotesque monks, and imps of all kinds were the favorite themes. In this way an extraordinary parody of society unfolds in the very choir of the church. This fantastic imagery had still to conform with the framework it ornamented; misericords and reveals have a functional use as supports, which compelled the maker to give them a shape appropriate to their use.

684

682

685

685 *Christ at the Column* (detail), Church of St. Nizier, Troyes ·
French, 15th century.

During the 15th century Christians were constantly reminded of the
Passion and death of Christ. Calvary, the Crucifixion, Ecce Homo, the
Man of Sorrows, the Flagellation – all these were frequent themes, and
became ritual images to be fervently worshipped through several
centuries. The Christ in St. Nizier at Troyes presents a tortured face.
Treated schematically in large planes, the forehead crushed by the
crown of thorns, this is no longer the visage of a willing and lucid
victim, but of a man tormented, scourged and beaten, whose bruised
face is set in an expression of overwhelming pain.

687 *Effigy of Guillaume le François* · French, 15th century · Museum,
Arras.

An obsession with death weighed heavily on the later Middle Ages,
which has left us many images depicting such subjects as the Dance of
Death and the torments of Hell. Tomb decoration best exemplifies the
realistic, almost materialistic, 15th century approach to the macabre.
The recumbent figure, the *gisant*, has become a *transi*, a rotting corpse,
such as we see on the tomb of Guillaume le François. The man is now
nothing more than a disjointed, stinking corpse, a skeleton to which
still cling a few shreds of putrefying flesh. The limits of the horrendous
are reached in this powerful reminder of the vanities of human life.

687

688 *Virgin*, Church of Notre-Dame du Marthuret at Riom (Puy-de-
Dôme) · French, 15th century.

The trumeau of the church of Notre-Dame du Marthuret is decorated
with a Virgin called "The Virgin with a Bird." It has been suggested
that it is the work of Jean de Cambrai, sculptor to the Duke of Berry.
However, the idealization of the Virgin's face, her smile, and her expression while watching the Child at play all bring to mind 13th and
14th century types. Other historians, struck by the restraint of the
sculpture, see it as a precursor to the art of Michel Colombe.

688

686

686 *Pietà*, church of Bayel (Aube) · French, early 16th century.

The school of Champagne provides another example of the change towards a less tense and fervid style at the end of the century. At the beginning of the 16th century, a workshop at Troyes became famous
under the direction of an unknown master; it is known as the Workshop of St. Martha, after its masterpiece. The Pietà from the church at
Bayel issues from this workshop. The sorrow of the resigned Virgin is
depicted with restraint, dignity, and moral force; the stiffened body of
Christ is beautiful – elegant and serene in the death that has erased
his Passion. The drapery folds are simple, the treatment straightforward; choosing simplicity, the artist rejects all the facile developments permitted by the theme.

The ambulatory and jubé at Albi are among the rare surviving examples of these grandiose structures in Flamboyant style, most of which were destroyed during the 18th century. An impressive series of statues adorns this forest of niches, arcades and pinnacles, which was completed around the end of the 15th century. Emile Mâle has pointed out the relationships between the sculpture of Albi and that of Burgundy. The workshop active at Cluny during the 15th century was probably brought by the Amboise family to work at Albi. Certainly Judith's creator was full of Burgundian memories: the full draperies, the contrasts between light and shade, the pose, the powerful treatment, all bear the stamp of Sluter's tradition.

689

690

690 *Vaulting of the jubé*, Albi Cathedral · French, ca. 1500.

The jubé of Albi Cathedral, constructed about 1500 at the instigation of Louis d'Amboise, closes off the choir completely, forming a gallery. A whole series of liernes, tiercerons and ornate pendant bosses enlivens the jubé's vault. The clear line of the ogive arch can no longer be seen; the architect gives way to the decorator and sculptor, who cover all the surfaces of the monument. At Albi the play of line and mass is conceived with a vigor not devoid of elegance, contrasting with the heaviness of other buildings in the Flamboyant style.

692 *Virgin and Child* · French, ca. 1480–1500 · Musée Rolin, Autun.

At the end of the 15th century and at the beginning of the 16th, Burgundian sculpture became subdued in its turn, but adopted a homely, gentle style quite unlike the idealistic art of the Loire region. The Virgin in the Musée Rolin at Autun is typical of the new feeling that permeated the Autun workshops in the last decades of the 15th century. Grace and charm and the softness of the modelling temper the realism that remains strong in the coloring, in the Virgin's draperies and the Child's swaddling clothes, and in the natural gesture with which the mother both protects and caresses her Son as she watches over his sleep.

692

691

691 *Virgin and Child*. French, end of the 15th century · Musée des Augustins, Toulouse.

The Virgin and Child known as Notre Dame de Grasse must come from a chapel of Notre-Dame de Grace near Toulouse. It was probably part of an Adoration of the Magi group, which would explain the curious, detached posture of the Virgin, who is turning away from the Child. Her face and her body, like those of the Child, are graceful and charming, but both the realistic treatment and the cloak cascading into heavy folds to form a pyramidal composition suggest a Burgundian inspiration. The sculpture of Toulouse in the 15th century was more deeply influenced by Burgundian art than was that of other areas.

694 *St. Mary Magdalen*, church of St. Peter, Montluçon · French, late 15th century.

After the expressions of anguish in the middle years, the 15th century ends on a note of ease and peace. The Magdalen in the Church of St. Peter at Montluçon reflects the tendency towards idealization that marks the second half of the 15th century. This delicate statue has a smooth, supple finish, and tends towards Mannerism in its aristocratic elegance and the preciosity of the drapery; its style is still within the French Gothic aesthetic, though the impact of the Italian Renaissance was soon to make itself felt in France.

694

693 *Entombment*, Abbey Church of Solesmes (Sarthe) · 1496.

The Entombment at Solesmes was formerly thought to be one of the first works of Michel Colombe. This "Sepulcher" scene has certain elements that set it apart from either the Gothic tradition or the early Italian Renaissance. The dramatic subject is treated with a reserve characteristic of the end of the 15th century. Suffering is completely interiorized, restrained with noble dignity. The disposition of the group of the Virgin, St. John and the disciples is a masterpiece of balance, and invests the work with a remarkable monumental grandeur.

693

695 *The Magdalen*: detail from fig. 693

Mary Magdalen is shown in a crouching position in the foreground, set apart from the group comprising the Virgin and the disciples, in accordance with St. Matthew's description. Overcome with grief, she restrains the sobs on her lips with her folded hands. The sculptor's reserve in no way diminishes the figure's powerful realism. This Magdalen, her physical and spiritual sorrow transcended in prayer and by an act of faith, is one of the noblest expressions of Christian mysticism. If Colombe was not in fact the creator of the Solesmes group, he certainly worked in the same vein.

695

696

697

697　Bernt Notke (German, ca. 1440–1509) · *St. George and the Dragon*, Storkyrkan, Stockholm · Painted wood · 1487.

This sculptor and painter, whose presence at Lübeck is documented from 1467 onwards, is the greatest medieval artist from the Hanseatic region. Notke is traditional in his feeling for complex composition, but a vigorous innovator in the individual qualities that he brings to the concentration of action and of figures. This terrifying confrontation of Heaven and Hell is his greatest achievement. One of the numerous works that he carved for Scandinavian towns, it was commissioned by the Swedish authorities for the national sanctuary to commemorate the victory over the Danes at Brukeberg on St. George's Day, 1471.

696　Conrad Meit (German, ca. 1480–ca. 1550) · *Sybil from the tomb of Philibert le Beau*, Church of Brou, Bourg-en-Bresse.

One of the most beautiful groups of Flemish-style sculpture is to be found in the votive church of Brou. In 1506 the hapless Margaret of Austria, Regent of Austria, built the church of Brou in memory of her husband, Philibert le Beau. A Fleming, Jean de Room, called Jean of Brussels, submitted the scheme for the sculpture in 1516; the complete scheme was finished in 1532. Conrad Meit was the main sculptor. His art is extremely refined, but the elegant gestures and the preciosity of the draperies are balanced by the ample patterns of the broken folds.

699　*Head of the Kruzlow Madonna* · Poland, Cracow school, first quarter of the 15th century · Nardowe Museum, Cracow.

Gothic art reached Poland late, at the beginning of the 15th century, and succeeded best there in painted and carved altarpieces and polyptychs. While Veit Stoss carried the art of religious scenes to a lofty perfection in the great Cracow altar, other anonymous sculptors devoted themselves to a particular theme inherited from Bohemian German sculpture, that of the *Schönen Madonnen*. In such "beautiful Madonnas" maternal love is idealized, and the Virgin's gentleness and sweetness translated by the rhythms of gentle curves and an ingenuous grace.

698　Nikolaus Gerhaert van Leyden (Dutch, active in Germany, 1463–1473) · *Man meditating* · 1462–1473 · Musée de l'Oeuvre, Strasbourg.

Outstanding among the strong personalities directing the numerous sculpture workshops in the Germanic countries is an artist of Dutch origin: Nikolaus Gerhaert van Leyden. His activity is well-authenticated at Trier, Vienna and Strasbourg between 1463 and 1473. His art owes a great deal to Sluter, but has a more marked expressive note. In this etched face and tensed hands the artist has succeeded in rendering the most intense inner emotion. The spirituality emanating from this physically stricken being demonstrates the wide scope of its author's talent.

698

699

701 GREGOR ERHART (German, active first half of the 16th century) · *St. Mary Magdalen* · Wood, polychromed · Early 16th century · The Louvre, Paris.

Little is known about this sculptor except that he was a native of Ulm who lived in Augsburg and died before 1540. After collaborating with the older Holbein on the Kaisheim altarpiece, he carved an equestrian statue of the Emperor Maximilian; the rest of his production includes crucifixes, tombs, and madonnas enveloped in full cloaks with long parallel folds. His female figures combine a realistic elegance reflecting the tastes of the German bourgeoisie and a special sweetness of countenance: they appear to hold their breath, listening to the voice of God.

700 *The Madonna of Dangolsheim* · Wood, polychromed · German, ca. 1480 · Deutsches Museum, Berlin.

Innocent of both the spirit of contemplation and conscious aestheticism, this anonymous statue embodies the taste for realism predominant at the end of the Gothic age. With its large masses and rustic verve of movement, the sculpture firmly occupies its surrounding space. The heavy draperies and the long hair tumbling over the Virgin's shoulders seem at first sight to monopolize our attention, but they guide our eyes towards the upper part and the intimacy of the two sacred beings, full of human charm. There is no feminine affectation or mystical dreaming here, but the very physical presence of a wriggling infant Jesus bounding with health, who all but twists free of his young mother's grasp.

700

701

702

702 VEIT STOSS · *Tobias and the Angel* · Wood · 1516 · Germanisches Museum, Nuremberg.

Beginning in Nuremberg, the artistic activity of Stoss, a citizen of that city, reached its peak in the gigantic Cracow altarpiece (fig. 704), then ended in the bitterness of legal disputes and professional misfortunes, again in Nuremberg, where he eventually came to be a quite isolated figure. His modernity appears in his creation of a new transparency in carving and in renunciation of polychromy, which he did not use in his later sculpture; but his outlook remained medieval, his impetuous temperament and his conception of gesture, entirely Gothic. The Tobias and the Angel was commissioned by an Italian patron.

704 VEIT STOSS (German, ca. 1477–1533) · *Dormition of the Virgin*, central scene of the high altar, Marienkirche, Cracow · 1477–1489.

The largest altar made at the end of the Gothic period (the principal figures measure 9 feet, the whole structure 39 feet high) is the masterpiece of Veit Stoss. In this, the central panel, the Virgin's death and her reunion with her Son, are conceived as so closely related that Stoss has depicted Mary upright, tenderly supported by a gigantic apostle, as she falls asleep. Some of the other apostles bend their glance on her with grave concern, while yet others lift their eyes to the scene of her glorious Assumption above. Combining a primitive violence of emotion with technical mastery over the handling of forms, Stoss created an individual style that found imitations in Bohemia, Hungary, Poland and Transylvania.

704

703

703 MICHAEL PACHER (German Tyrol, ca. 1435–1498) · *Coronation of the Virgin*, central portion of the altarpiece of the parish church, St. Wolfgang (Austria) · Wood, gilt and polychromed · 1471–1481.

In a setting of supernal radiance enraptured angels assist Divine Omnipotence and Benevolence in the courtly ceremony of welcoming human modesty, come to Paradise in the form of the Virgin Mary. Michael Pacher, a Tyrolean artist, was a master in both painting and sculpture, and combines the two techniques in some of his works. He assimilated the examples of Donatello and Mantegna while on a journey of apprenticeship in Italy, but his temperament caused him to lean more towards the northern style of sculpture, which he brought to its highest level of achievement. This altarpiece, executed between 1479 and 1481, is one of the many including scenes from the life of the Virgin produced by the great triad of German sculptors, Pacher, Stoss and Riemenschneider.

705

705 VEIT STOSS · *Head of St. John*: detail of fig. 704.

Factual information concerning the origins and schooling of this
sculptor, painter and engraver is entirely lacking; some of his forms of
expression suggest contact with Nikolaus Gerhaert. The paths by
which Sluter's principles may have come to this German master are
obscure, but Sluter's figure of St. John at least can be linked to the
Franconian tradition of Nuremberg. Borrowing the powerful and vigorous plebeian types favored by the Gothic style, Stoss so transfigures
them in his generous idealism that the craftsmanlike concern for
exactitude and tiny detail is quite submerged in the overall emotional
and plastic intensity.

706 MASTER H. L. (German, upper Rhenish, active ca. 1515–1526) ·
Coronation of the Virgin, central portion of an altarpiece at Niederrotweil (Kaiserstuhl) · Wood, polychromed · 1525.

This sculptor, whose activity can be followed between 1515 and 1526,
would appear to have come from the upper Rhine valley. It has been
conjectured that he is the same person as the engraver who hides
behind these initials. Here natural gesture is sacrificed to decorative
concerns. From the profusion of twisting locks and turning draperies,
matched in density by the foliage, and from the breeze rustling the
angels' wings and the coiling clouds, arises an overall sense of agitated
mobility almost Baroque in character. (7 feet high.)

706

707

707 MASTER H. L. *St. Michael Weighing Souls*; *Baptism of Christ*:
left wing of the Niederrotweil altarpiece · (See fig. 706.)

St. Michael weighs a soul and at the same time deals a mortal blow to
a horrid devil – recalling Netherlandish grotesques and the imagery of
engravers – who tries to pull down the scale on the side of doom. Unusual in sculpture, the scene shows its creator to be gifted with fantasy
and a remarkable feeling for life. His predilection for faithfully detailed
faces and gnarled hands and feet illustrates a typically German concern for minutiae and didactic realism. The Baptism scene takes on a
vivid emotional intensity through the surface agitation provided by
wind-flung draperies, twisting locks of hair, and a crowd of exulting
putti among whom the small image of God the Father is almost lost.

708

708 TILMAN RIEMENSCHNEIDER · *The Visitation*: detail from the
Creglingen Altar (see fig. 709).

Gradually departing from the conceptions of religious art traditional
in Wurzburg, Riemenschneider asserted his own personality, abandoning the style of virtuoso realism. The expressions of his figures are
no longer differentiated except superficially, and individuals appear
merged in a common feeling of humility; perspective effects and realistic polychromy are given up in favor of a more sculptural treatment of forms, a clearer articulation of masses and empty spaces, and
a more subtle play of light over the surfaces. He was one of the first
whose works affirm the desire, at odds with contemporary taste, to
return to simpler compositions and more natural poses.

709

709 TILMAN RIEMENSCHNEIDER (German, ca. 1460–1531) · *Assumption of the Virgin*, central panel, altar of the Herrgottskirche at Creglingen-am-Tauber · Lime-wood · 1505–1510.

Tilman Riemenschneider came from Osterode in the Harz district and was trained in Swabia; he had been a painter before settling in Wurzburg. There he was made Master in charge of the Building, then mayor of the town; he was later removed from office and persecuted for having sided with the people during the Peasants' Revolt. His work comprises tombs, statues and furniture as well as church decoration. The Creglingen altarpiece is one of the last of those thorny, visionary compositions of the German Flamboyant Gothic style, and Riemenschneider was in fact the last of the great German altarpiece sculptors.

710

Riemenschneider is one of the last great Gothic illustrators in a long line of painters and sculptors whose aim was to achieve sublime expression of the story of the Virgin. His manner is as far removed from his colleagues' artisan harshness – often bordering on brutality – as from the mannerisms of Schöngauer. He had a gift for depicting the young, and particularly the youthful feminine figure, whether in wood or stone and his art is touched with a kind of charm previously unknown in Germany.

711

710 TILMAN RIEMENSCHNEIDER · *Eve*, from the south portal of the Marienkirche, Wurzburg · 1491–1493.

The part of the portal finished by the artist between 1491 and 1493 comprised the canopy, the brackets, and the admirable statues of Adam and Eve, whose style contrasts surprisingly with the usual labored manner of the time. Although it was not immediately accepted, this rediscovered serenity and simlpified form evidently did not displease, for a contemporary text describes the work as "masterful, skilled, gracious and honestly made." Riemenschneider favored the acceptance of the Renaissance style, and without directly copying the Italians he yet moved closer to them, starting from specifically German elements.

712 *High altar* of the Cathedral of Toledo · Spanish, ca. 1498–1504.

One of the loftiest expressions of Spanish art is to be found in monumental altarpieces. That in the Toledo Cathedral was begun in 1498 from a design by Peti Juan; the Netherlanders Diego Copin de Holanda and Cristiano de Holanda, the Frenchman Bigarny de Borgona, and the Spaniard Sebastian de Almonacid worked there from 1502 to 1504; Copin completed the corners. Flemish, German and French schools are combined into a surprising Spanish mixture. This enormous polychrome and gold screen, with its proliferation of forms over which the gaze of the worshipper may wander endlessly, belongs to the very end of the Gothic tradition.

713

713 GIL DE SILOË (active 1486–1501) · *St. Catherine*: detail of the main altar, Cartuja de Miraflores (Burgos) · Spanish, 1496–1499.

Gil de Siloë, called d'Orleans or d'Anvers, was a native of northern Europe – French, Flemish or perhaps even German. He worked in and around Burgos from 1486 to 1501. Isabella the Catholic commissioned from him the great altarpiece in the Carthusian monastery at Miraflores. The polychromy and some figures are the work of Diego de la Cruz, the *dorador* appointed to Gil. The altarpiece, a symbol of the Eucharist, is constructed round a great centrally-placed circle, radiating like a rose window in a Gothic cathedral. The tortuous, allover ornament is consistent with the expressionistic style of the sculptures, which already look forward to the 16th century.

714 *Tomb of Martin de Arce*, Cathedral of Sigüenza · Alabaster · Spanish, 1486.

15th-century Castile saw the development of several schools originating in various influences. The type of tomb showing a reclining effigy was treated by a certain Master Sebastian, who succeeded Egas Cueman as the principal artist of the Toledo school. Carved by an unknown artist, the funerary monument of Martin Vasquez de Arce, called "el Doncel," has all the characteristics of this style. A profound sadness emanates from the face of the deceased, leaning on his elbow as he meditates over his reading. Framing the coat of arms on the relief below is a foliage decoration bursting with vitality, still Gothic in style, and carved with great delicacy and precision.

714

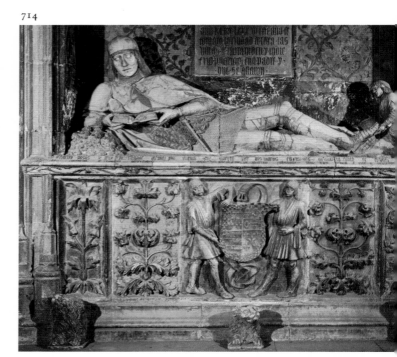

715

715 *Façade of the Colegio* de San Gregorio, Valladolid · Spanish, 1486–1496.

The façade of the Colegio de San Gregorio de Valladolid, built between 1486 and 1496, is a perfect example of the Isabelline style, the final flowering of Gothic art before the Renaissance and a direct ancestor of the Plateresque style. The sculptures are from the school of Gil de Siloë and Diego de la Cruz. Surrounding the coat of arms is a swarm of figurations echoing all aspects of the Gothic imagery. In this style, as in the later Plateresque, Spain found the very essence of its genius in the art of relief. The sculpture spreads over the architectural forms and in fact engulfs them, so that the whole façade appears to be a large relief, rather than a structure.

716

716 *Two Wild Men*, façade of the Colegio de San Gregorio, Valladolid · Spanish, 1486–1496.

A number of "wild men" line the jambs of the façade of the Colegio de San Gregorio. Their iconographic meaning is uncertain; do they represent the discovery of America, a mysterious reference to the golden age of the "noble savage," a cosmic and pantheistic yearning of man to join in creation, to immerse himself in nature? On this façade plant life is so ubiquitous that man appears to be assimilated into it, and merges into the decoration as he had done in Romanesque art. This represents the last burst of vitality in Spanish Gothic art, before the introduction of Renaissance motifs.

717 *Great window* of the chapterhouse in Tomar Abbey · Portugal, 1510–1514.

Manueline art, which owes its name to King Manoel I the Fortunate, developed in Portugal at the very end of the 15th century. The Arruda brothers are among the most ingenious proponents of this highly inventive school. Under royal patronage Diogo, the elder, directed the work at the convent of Christ in Tomar, where this ornately framed and richly crowned window testifies to his abundant imagination. Arruda combined in it memories of the Moresco and the Portuguese Mudéjar styles, nautical rope designs, cable moldings, anchor-rings mixed with foliage and naturalistic motifs. It is an original native style which evokes the seafaring traditions of Portugal.

717

718 *Atlas*: detail of fig. 717.

The medley of nautical rope, knots, rings and foliage is supported by an Atlas unique in the history of art. Diogo de Arruda has transformed an Italian type into a fantastic monster. The giant is made of rope; the supple body, the bust and the powerful arms are composed of strands of twisted cable. He is both man and ship's rigging. Nothing could be further from traditional Renaissance humanism or from the Mediterranean outlook than this curious art with its flavor of exoticism and mystery.

718

VIII Renaissance

720 LORENZO GHIBERTI (Italian, 1378–1455) · *Adoration of the Magi*, north door, Baptistry, Florence · Gilt bronze · 1410–1417.

In 1401 the Merchants' Guild of Florence organized a competition for the decoration of the second door of the Baptistry. The test-piece was the Sacrifice of Isaac, and the models submitted by the two great rivals Ghiberti and Brunelleschi have been preserved. The latter's interpretation was judged too tormented, and Ghiberti was awarded the contract because of the unquestionable maturity of his artistic conception. The style of this Adoration of the Magi suggests that it may have been one of the first works executed for the door. The composition is still rigorously symmetrical and the whole feeling is one of calm. (About 20½ x 17½ inches inside molding.)

720

719 NANNI DI BANCO (Italian, active 1419–1451) · *The Quattro Santi Coronati*, Or San Michele, Florence · 1408–1413.

Nanni di Banco received the commission for this group from the guild of masons, stoneworkers, architects and sculptors, for their tabernacle on Or San Michele. It depicts the Four Crowned Saints, martyrs of Diocletian's reign, who had become their patrons. Although the theme of his works is always Christian, Nanni di Banco, who belonged to the first generation of Quattrocento Florentines, deliberately drew his inspiration from the antique. In the attempt to escape Gothic tendencies he chose the path of formalism, and his proud and solemn figures stand firmly, with typically Roman dignity.

719

721

721 GHIBERTI · *Detail from The Story of Jacob and Esau, "Gates of Paradise"* (see fig. 722).

Following his journey to Rome in 1416, Ghiberti showed himself ever more receptive to ancient art. The models are never copied in a servile fashion, but are, rather, exploited as an inexhaustible source of inspiration, and transformed by a wholly modern, dynamic interpretation. The group of women, whose draperies move in folds revealing the forms of the body or fly in wind-lifted arabesques, appear in several scenes on the Gates of Paradise, each time in a new version. They are borrowed from antique sculpture, as is the canephore, whose ornamental potential was often to be exploited in Florentine Renaissance painting.

722

722 GHIBERTI · *Gates of Paradise*, Baptistry, Florence · Gilt bronze ·
1425–1452.

Called by Michelangelo the "Gates of Paradise" because of their sculptured themes and their great beauty, the second set of Baptistry doors
commissioned from Ghiberti was begun 1425 and finished only in 1452.

These doors mark the zenith of Ghiberti's art. To unify and lighten the
different scenes, the artist, discarding the quatrefoil frames, set them
in broad, rectangular panels that made less concession to the taste for
decoration. Using all possible gradations of relief, he suggests deep
space by combining flatly treated figures in the distance, and figures in
quite high relief, some of them almost fully in the round, in the foreground.

723

723 GHIBERTI · Decorative detail, from the surround of the *Gates of Paradise* (see fig. 722).

All his life Ghiberti retained his goldsmith's training, never neglecting the finish of his works. His taste for naturalistic detail can be seen in the garlands framing the earlier North Door, where the decorative overtones betray the artist's essentially Gothic schooling. Ghiberti's love of nature, apparent also in his writings, is fully expressed in the Gates of Paradise, where the floral species incorporated in the festoons are even more diverse, each individualized and each identifiable. However, this quasi-scientific exactitude enriches rather than diminishes the inventive originality of the floral scrolls, which are further enlivened by the presence of acutely-observed animals.

725

725 DONATELLO (Italian, 1377–1446) · *St. George* · Marble · Ca. 1415–1417 · Museo Nazionale, Florence.

Carved for the armorer's guild – the Arte dei Corazzai – the statue of St. George originally stood in a niche on Or San Michele, where a copy has replaced it. It marks the point at which Donatello's individuality begins to affirm itself. In his desire for a restrained mood, the artist has abandoned the dragon that had always accompanied the Saint in medieval representations, contenting himself with illustrating the battle between saint and dragon on the pedestal relief. Freeing the statue from the architectural frame to which it had been subordinated through the Middle Ages, he made of it a self-sufficient organism moving freely in three-dimensional space. (Figure with base about 7 feet.)

726

724

724 GHIBERTI · *Self portrait: detail from the Gates of Paradise* (see fig. 722).

Already on the north door Ghiberti had introduced a self portrait among the tiny heads in high relief at the corners of each plaque. He did it once again later, on the Door of Paradise, where he appears among the heads of the prophets which alternate with statues of biblical personages in the framework of the door. Here we can observe close up the remarkable skill of the metal sculptor. In the earlier portrait on the north door, his face is still young and not particularly individualized, still very much subservient to antique models. Here, however, the depiction is entirely realistic, and Ghiberti portrays himself as the intellectual with prominent facial features and wrinkled brow.

On St. George's face may be read the tension of the soldier alerted to imminent danger. The type of the young Christian warrior is perhaps taken from Byzantine representations, but the head is principally inspired by Hellenistic models. It is marked, however, with the pent-up energy characteristic of all Donatello's works. This is not an individual portrait like the pitilessly realistic ones which the artist was to create later, but rather a youthful symbol of controlled energy, an ideal Quattrocento soldier type.

728

727 DONATELLO · *Head of the Prophet Jeremiah* · Marble · 1423–1425 · Museo dell'Opera del Duomo, Florence.

From 1415 onwards, Donatello was engaged on a commission for eight prophets destined to occupy niches on the Campanile of the Florence Cathedral. Four of the eight statues were completed by the master himself over a period of twenty years, and the others betray a strong Donatellesque influence even though executed by other artists. The four prophets gave Donatello the opportunity to express drama in its various, but always coherent, aspects. Unlike the *Zuccone*, the last to be executed, Jeremiah remains marked with an outward realism which has not yet merged in the expression of inner conflict. (Height overall 7½ feet.)

727

728 DONATELLO · *David* · Bronze · Ca. 1440–1442 · Museo Nazionale, Florence.

Donatello's first David was a marble, now also in the Florence Museum; later he returned to the same theme for the Casa Martelli David (Philadelphia), and for this bronze David executed for the Medici family, probably about 1441. The antique concept of the beauty of the nude male figure is here revived on a large scale for the first time in Renaissance art, in pose and in the representation of the anatomy, but this figure is far removed from ancient prototypes. Standing in a relaxed contrapposto, the David has a subtle, complex mannerism in its rather sharp and angular forms which contributes to the ambiguity of the representation, suggesting a young Mercury as much as the little shepherd described in the Bible. History and myth come together in a mysterious, almost esoteric climate, which was to be still more marked in the Amor-Atys. (Height 5 feet 2 inches.)

729

729 DONATELLO · *Cantoria* · Ca. 1443–1448 · Museo dell'Opera del Duomo, Florence.

Commissioned for the Florentine cathedral, the *cantoria* (singing gallery) was Donatello's first large-scale work. The very freely treated architecture is designed to set off the figures, which move before a polychrome background treated like mosaic. Inspired by Roman sarcophagi, the putti, sweeping in a frantic dance across the gallery's front and sides, demonstrate the artist's extensive acquaintance with antique works and the complexity of the interpretations he drew from them. Two-fold incarnations, part angel, part Eros, the putti exude an elementary vitality transmitted through the impulse of their movements and the extraordinary foreshortenings. (Whole structure: 10 feet 7 inches by 18 feet 8 inches.)

731

730

730 DONATELLO · *The monument to Gattamelata* · Piazza del Santo, Padua · Bronze · Ca. 1450.

The condottiere Erasmo da Narni, known as *il Gattamelata*, spent his career in the service of the Pope and the Republic of Venice. After his death at Padua in 1443 either his son or the Venetian Senate entrusted to Donatello the task of producing a suitable funerary monument. In executing the commission the sculptor shows his dedication. He seems to have decided by himself on the idea of an equestrian monument, no doubt inspired by the antique statue of Marcus Aurelius, which he must have seen during one of his Roman sojourns. The equestrian effigy had already been employed during the Renaissance to honor a hero, but Donatello infuses into it an intellectual energy and a mood of philosophical humanism earlier unknown. (Horse and rider, about 11½ feet high.)

731 DONATELLO · *Head of Gattamelata*; detail of fig. 730.

During the fifteenth century, the equestrian statue symbolized reason overcoming the brute force of the animal. The tense-faced figure with its proud awareness personifies the *imperator*, the leader of men, borrowed from the antique by Donatello and applied to the *condottiere*, head of a band of mercenaries. The kind of force that he embodies is very different from the savage violence of the Colleoni monument, sculptured later by Verrocchio on the model of Donatello's statue. Although it is treated with profound realism, this figure radiates intelligence as well as power.

733 ANDREA DEL CASTAGNO (Italian, ca. 1423–1457) · *Niccolò da Tolentino* · Fresco · 1456 · Cathedral, Florence.

In 1436 Paolo Uccello had painted the illusionistic equestrian effigy of Giovanni Acuto, demonstrating the preoccupations that dominated Florentine painters during the first half of the Quattrocento. Twenty years later Andrea del Castagno returned to the same theme in his equestrian portrait of the condottiere Niccolò da Tolentino. Modelled with strong contrasts of light and shade, this fresco imitating a sculptured funerary monument responds to the style of Donatello, whose influence can be seen in the putti. The condottiere seems full of a pent-up energy, which is characteristic of Andrea del Castagno's figures.

733

732 DONATELLO · *Miracle of the Talking Babe*, high altar, San Antonio, Padua · 1446–1450.

In Padua, Donatello was asked to execute bronze figures and reliefs for the high altar of San Antonio; he finished them in 1450. Away from Florence, where in a climate of intellectual research artists were mainly concerned with problems of form and perspective, he was freer to explore a style attaining a high degree of dramatic intensity. In the reliefs for this altar, an electric emotional current sweeps through the swarming figures, which are often shown in drastic foreshortening, and reverberates in the vast architectural settings. In contrast to the harmony of Ghiberti, Donatello pushes his violent art to paroxysm, but the psychological and formal coherence is never lost. (About 22 x 48 inches.)

732

734

734 JACOPO DELLA QUERCIA (Italian, ca. 1374–1438) · *Creation of Eve*, central portal, San Petronio, Bologna · 1425–1438.

Although they were left unfinished at his death in 1438, and their disposition was subsequently altered, the fourteen reliefs framing the central portal at San Petronio and the lunette surmounting it constitute the masterpiece of Jacopo della Quercia, a Sienese sculptor who in 1401 had taken part in the competition for the Gates of Paradise of the Baptistry in Florence. The episode of Eve's creation, captured at its most serious moment, does not have the radiant lyricism of Ghiberti's art: two massive, naked bodies balance the dramatic figure of God, who is dressed in a vast mantle with heavy angular folds. The intensity of feeling is conveyed in the heavy forms, whose shapes and proportions are distorted for the sake of expression. (34½ x 27½ inches.)

735 JACOPO DELLA QUERCIA · *The Christ Child*, detail from a Madonna and Child, San Martino, Siena · 1425.

For the church of San Martino Jacopo della Quercia executed in gilded and polychromed wood a group comprising a Madonna and Child surrounded by four saints. Although wooden statues were rare during the Quattrocento, their production continued throughout the Renaissance in Siena, and this work belongs to the Sienese tradition. Weaknesses in the handling of form demonstrate that the saints were carved by the workshop, but the Madonna can be attributed to the Master himself. The drapery folds, still Gothic in their rendering, offer strong contrast to the taut, solid forms of the Child, who clings to his mother with a dramatic force pointing forward to Michelangelo.

735

736

736 FRANCESCO DI VALDAMBRINO (Italian, 1363–1435) · *San Crescenzio* · Wood, polychromed · Ca. 1408 · Museo dell'Opera del Duomo, Siena.

A friend and assistant to Jacopo della Quercia, Francesco di Valdambrino had also taken part in the competition of 1401 for the second Baptistry door, in Florence. Various works have been attributed to him on the basis of three documented polychromed wood busts depicting the patrons of Siena, San Crescenzio, San Savino and San Vittore, which were commissioned from him in 1408. Because of their small dimensions, these works are rather different from the large wooden statues that heve been attributed to the artist. The freshness of San Crescenzio's face is rendered with a still-Gothic preciseness combined with very rich modelling.

737

737 LUCA DELLA ROBBIA (Italian, 1399/1400–1482) · *Singing angels*: detail from a cantoria · 1431–1439 · Museo dell'Opera del Duomo, Florence.

In 1431 Luca della Robbia received the commission to carve for the Florence cathedral a marble singing gallery. His work comprises ten reliefs depicting children singing a psalm, framed in architectural elements strongly reminiscent of Brunelleschi, if not actually designed by him. Discarding all remnants of the Gothic, Luca returned to a measured classical style. Little affected by Donatello's revolutionary dynamism, he shows nonetheless the influence of the older artist's dramatic naturalism in the late reliefs of this group. The singers' faces, forcefully modelled, display sensitivity in their expressions, and the deep serenity emanating from them is characteristic of the artist.

739

739 LUCA DELLA ROBBIA · *Virgin and Child* · 1450–1460 · Museo Nazionale, Florence.

Luca della Robbia is best known as the founder of a flourishing workshop that produced enamelled terra cottas. The earlier examples were usually white-glazed in imitation of marble, but were also often polychromed or occasionally hand-painted with different colors. In this *bottega*, where the artist's family worked until the end of the Renaissance, the art of the major early Renaissance creators was translated for a kind of mass production, and a single theme might give rise to numerous variants. The Virgin and Child are united by a gentle and relaxed affection. The group stands out in front of a rose-garden which reveals the naturalistic taste of Luca, particularly noticeable in the garlands of fruit and flowers that often decorated his reliefs.

738

738 ANDREA DELLA ROBBIA (Italian, 1435–1525) · *The Visitation*, San Giovanni Fuorcivitas, Pistoia.

A nephew of Luca della Robbia, Andrea became his assistant, then his successor, but rarely rose to the level of his master. Andrea in turn soon took his son Giovanni as collaborator. For the church of San Giovanni Fuorcivitas at Pistoia, Andrea produced the free-standing Visitation group (sometimes attributed to Luca). In this work, whose iconography was inspired by Ghirlandaio, the artist attained rare dramatic conciseness. However, the faults in the white enamel highlighted with polychrome details betray the impoverishment of the della Robbia studio at the end of the 15th century.

740 ANTONIO ROSSELLINO (Italian, 1427–1479) · *Monument of the Cardinal of Portugal*, San Miniato al Monte, Florence · 1460–66.

In 1444, Bernardo Rossellino had carved the tomb of Leonardo Bruni in Santa Croce, one of the most influential of Renaissance tombs. In his funerary monument for the Cardinal of Portugal, Antonio, his younger brother, created something quite new. He appears to have been entrusted with the whole design of the ornament for a newly-constructed chapel in the church of San Miniato. Around and within the niche on one side he organized paintings (by Pollaiuolo) and sculpture to evoke a tableau within which the tomb is presented behind carved curtains. The sculpture, more suggestive of pictorial effects, is less dependent on the architecture than that in Bruni's tomb, and with its vividness and movement is freed from the wall.

740A

740A ANTONIO ROSSELLINO · *Angel*: detail from fig. 740.

Rossellino tends not to represent figures in movement. Above the tomb a calm, classicizing Virgin and Child appear in a medallion supported by two flying angels. The two putti seated on the sarcophagus also show strong influence from the antique. The design owes its animation largely to the masterful complexity of the elegant folds worked into the draperies of the two flying angels and of the two angels alighting on the tomb. The faces are imbued with a youthful grace that contrasts with the realism of the recumbent Cardinal.

740

741

741 AGOSTINO DI DUCCIO (Italian, 1418–1481) · *Angel*, Chapel of St. Sigismund, Tempio Malatestiano, Rimini · Ca. 1450.

About the middle of the century, Sigismondo Malatesta summoned architects and sculptors to redecorate the church at Rimini, desiring to transform it into a temple *all'antico*, in which the Malatesta might be quietly apotheosized. Of the ten chapels, the first on the right side, dedicated to his patron saint, was decorated by Agostino di Duccio, who shared the direction of the work as a whole with Matteo de' Pasti. Agostino had gradually moved away from the plasticity of Donatello and adopted a style in which a flowing and rather mannered line predominates over sculptural solidity. The wavy motion of the angel's wind-lifted draperies is resumed in the line of his wings, in his long, twisting locks of hair and even in the curtain that he holds back.

742 BENEDETTO DA MAIANO (Italian 1442–1497) · *Bust of Pietro Mellini* · 1474 · Museo Nazionale, Florence.

Benedetto da Maiano (brother of the architect Giuliano) executed the bust of his patron Pietro Mellini, a merchant, in 1474. Like Ghirlandaio, Benedetto belonged to a generation for whom the great problems of the 15th century were already solved, and he attained a technical skill that makes him one of the most accomplished artists of the end of the century. He paid as much attention to details of dress as to the weary, etched-in features of the face, but the portrait displays nonetheless a great nobility.

742

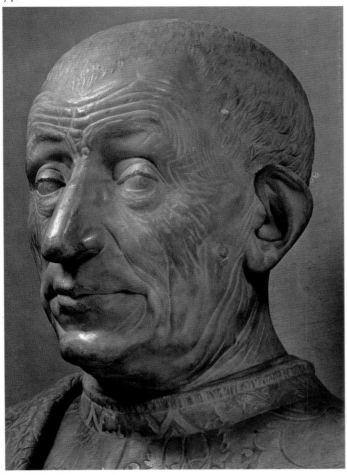

743

743 DESIDERIO DA SETTIGNANO (Italian, ca. 1430–1464) · *Laughing Child* · Ca. 1450–1460 · Kunsthistorisches Museum, Vienna.

This bust, probably an image of the Christ-child, is attributed to Desiderio da Settignano because of its similarities to the putti in a frieze on the Pazzi chapel and the putti of the Marsuppini monument. The crack round the neck, indicating an early break, was earlier hidden by a necklace. The combination of insolence and childish innocence is the mark of a new and less heroic generation working for a cultured middle class. Desiderio explores the translucent, delicate textures and evanescent surface changes in the childish flesh with miraculously soft modelling.

744

744 FRANCESCO LAURANA (Italian, ca. 1430–ca. 1502) · *Eleanora of Aragon* · Marble · Ca. 1467 · Museo Nazionale, Palermo.

The young Francesco Laurana left his native Dalmatia to work on the triumphal arch of Alfonso of Aragon at Naples, after which he moved on to the service of Sigismondo Malatesta in Rimini, then to France, and in 1467 to Sicily. It was then that he did this bust of Eleanora of Aragon for her tomb in the cloister she had founded. The art of Laurana attained its highest expression in his portraits of women. By means of an extreme purity of line, he transcended the mere surface appearances of his sitters and conferred on them an air of aristocratic mystery and princely pride.

745

745 BERTOLDO (Italian, ca. 1420–1491) · *Bellerophon* · Ca. 1480–1485 · Kunsthistorisches Museum, Vienna.

A pupil of Donatello, with whom he collaborated on the pulpits of San Lorenzo, Bertoldo specialized in small bronzes, statuettes, plaquettes and medallions. In later years he relinquished religious subjects and limited himself to pagan themes, creating an erudite but rather narrow art largely dependent on classical prototypes. The Bellerophon, one of his three signed works, has a vitality beyond mere placid imitation, although the treatment is somewhat hesitant. Bertoldo's main merit was his cultural influence, emanating from his appointment by Lorenzo de' Medici as a kind of curator for the Medici antiquities in the garden of San Marco, where, still in Bertoldo's time, Michelangelo went to study and copy the ancient sculptures.

746

746 ANTONIO POLLAIUOLO (Italian, 1431/32–1498) · *Hercules and Antaeus* · Ca. 1475–1480 · Museo Nazionale, Florence.

Pollaiuolo had already illustrated the struggle of Hercules against the giant Antaeus in one of a series of paintings done for the Medici about 1465. A decade later, he returned to the same theme, in bronze, introducing to sculpture a subject which was to be treated often during the 16th and 17th centuries. Caught at its height, the struggle of the two men allowed him to depict the adversaries in the conflicting tensions of violent movement. The principal view of the group still shows the bodies in profile, but there are subsidiary views in which may be observed a radial projection of movement in a variety of directions from the central core of the bodies. (Height 18 inches.)

747

748

747 Antonio Pollaiuolo · *Arithmetic*: relief from the Tomb of Sixtus IV, Vatican Grottos, Rome · Ca. 1490–1493.

After the death of Sixtus IV (in 1484), Pollaiuolo journeyed to Rome to execute a bronze tomb, which he signed in 1493. The monument is made up of two parts. The recumbent figure of the Pope is surrounded by reliefs showing the Virtues, probably made by Antonio's brother, Piero. The base is decorated with reliefs, framed by acanthus leaves, showing ten personifications of the Liberal Arts. In this series Antonio attained the balance of mature years. Among the compositions best illustrating this final harmony is that depicting the young woman who symbolizes Arithmetic.

748 Andrea del Verrocchio (Italian, 1435–1488) · *David* · Ca.1475 · Museo Nazionale, Florence.

In 1476, the Florentine Signoria bought from Lorenzo de' Medici the bronze statue of David recently completed by Verrocchio, and placed it in the Palazzo della Signoria (now Palazzo Vecchio), at the entrance to the Sala dei Gigli. The work strongly resembles Donatello's, but is without the inward, mysterious feeling of Donatello's statues. It was intended to be seen about eye-level, from the height of its base. The figure is still tensed from the just-won battle. Verrocchio's training as a goldsmith is revealed in the refined finish of details and the elaborately wrought forms of Goliath's head. Although it does not have the personal and original qualities of Donatello's David, Verrocchio's work had a more lasting influence. (Height about 4 feet 1 inch.)

750

750 *Rearing horse* · Italian, 16th century · Metropolitan Museum of Art, New York.

A whole series of small Italian bronzes depicting pacing or rearing horses were inspired by the numerous studies made by Leonardo da Vinci for the two equestrian statues commissioned from him, one by Marshal Trivulzio, and the other by Duke Ludovico Sforza for his father Francesco. Leonardo failed to complete either of them, but the very numerous drawings that he made for the monuments are proof of the passionate interest with which he investigated the theme. He hesitated between the calm pose of the *strategus* seated on a pacing horse, master of himself, and the pose of a general astride a rearing steed, fired by heat of battle. His drawings and models for the rearing horse, whose balance is maintained by various contrivances, must have had some influence on 17th-century equestrian monuments.

749 *Façade of the Certosa*, Pavia.

The façade of this Carthusian monastery church was contracted for in 1473 by the brothers Cristoforo and Antonio Mantegazza. The following year a half-share of the work was allotted to Giovanni Antonio Amadeo. However, the whole was finished only later, in 1560. Although the exact contribution of each of the brothers is unknown, the moving expression and powerful modelling of the Mantegazza carvings contrast with the ornamental refinements of Amadeo. With its abundance of sculptures, set off by the contrasts of white, red, and green marble in the decorative bands, the façade of the Pavia Certosa is the most perfect example of the 15th-century Lombard decorative exuberance.

749

751

751 ANTONIO (?) MANTEGAZZA (Italian, active ca. 1464–1495) · *God admonishing Adam*: detail of the façade, Certosa, Pavia · Ca. 1470 (?).

From the last phase of Cristoforo and Antonio Mantegazza's activity dates a series of Old Testament stories. They were not put in place on the façade until the Cinquecento, and the proper order of the episodes was disregarded. One of the panels, in damaged condition, depicts God admonishing Adam and Eve after their sin. It would appear that these reliefs are the work of Antonio, whose interpretations are less forceful than those of his older brother, Cristoforo (d. 1482). Nevertheless, although the figure of Adam is somewhat mannered, God's blunt gesture has a great power of expression.

753 WORKSHOP OF PIETRO LOMBARDO · *Decorative relief* on the triumphal arch of Santa Maria dei Miracoli, Venice · After 1481.

The taste for animated rinceaux was not limited to Tuscany (fig. 760). In Venice, from 1480 onwards, Pietro Lombardo and his pupils introduced into friezes and pilasters a host of diverse elements, many of them taken from the antique, mingling human, animal and plant forms. This exuberance is particularly evident in Santa Maria dei Miracoli, begun in 1481, where more than sixty pilasters are decorated with an animated relief-ornament of candelabra. The finest decoration in the church is that on the triumphal arch, carved by Pietro's sons, Tullio and Antonio Lombardo.

753

752

752 PIETRO LOMBARDO (Italian, ca. 1435–1515) · *Monument of Pietro Mocenigo* · SS. Giovanni e Paolo, Venice · 1476–1480.

Pietro Lombardo was a Venetian architect and sculptor; he presumably completed his training in Florence, for his first tomb, in Padua, shows the influence of Florentine art and in particular of Rossellino's tomb of Leonardo Bruni. Continuing his career in Venice, he specialized in funerary monuments for the Doges. In his last one, completed in 1480, that of Pietro Mocenigo, he returned to a scheme that had been used in the Gothic period, placing the deceased under an arch. In the attic, the relief depicting the Three Marys at the Tomb displays a grace reminiscent of Greece, characteristic of this artist.

754 TULLIO LOMBARDO (Italian, ca. 1455–1532) · *Adam* · Marble · Ca. 1495 · Metropolitan Museum of Art, New York.

About 1495, Tullio Lombardo, a son of Pietro, finished the monument of Doge Andrea Vendramin; it is now in the church of Santi Giovanni e Paolo in Venice. The statues of Adam and Eve adorned the lower niches of the high wall tomb, which was dismantled in the 19th century. All the figures on the monument show a study in depth of the antique. In his Adam the artist has united the influence of a head of Antinous with that of a body of Apollo. But the artist goes beyond eclecticism to attain to a cold classicism that was the dominant tone of Venetian sculpture at the end of the 15th century. (Height, 6 feet 4 inches.)

755

754

755 ANDREA SANSOVINO (Italian, ca. 1460–1529) · *The Annunciation*, Santa Casa, Loreto · 1522.

The Tuscan sculptor Andrea Contucci, known as *il Sansovino*, was active in Florence, then in Portugal, before establishing himself in Rome in 1506. Six years later he was summoned by Pope Leo X to Loreto to direct the work there on the Santa Casa. In 1522, the artist carved the Annunciation placed on the sanctuary wall. Despite its complexity, the relief's composition remains clear. In cleverly designed progession, Gabriel emerges from the circling and descending group of flying angels and moves towards the Madonna, in an elaborate architectural setting. Sansovino is especially famous for his refined and essentially pictorial style, which exerted a great influence in Florence.

756

756 ANTONELLO GAGGINI (Italian, 1478–1536) · *Madonna del Buon Riposo* · Marble · 1528 · Museo Nazionale, Palermo.

Antonello Gaggini, the finest Sicilian sculptor of the sixteenth century, carried on the traditions of his father Domenico, who had migrated from Genoa to Palermo. In 1528 Antonello executed the Madonna del Buon Riposo – the "Madonna of Sweet Rest" – for the Ansalone chapel in the church of Santa Maria dello Spasimo. The Madonna quietly holding the sleeping Child stands in a niche ornamented with seraph heads. Above the architrave, ten figures of praying patriarchs venerate a symbol of the Virgin which once crowned the monument but is now lost. There is a rather conventional sweetness in Antonello's earlier works, but at the height of his career he achieved a more convincing expression.

757

757 ANTONIO FEDERIGHI (Italian, d. 1490) · *Capella di Piazza*, Palazzo Pubblico, Siena · 1460–1468.

The chapel set against the foot of the tower of the Palazzo Pubblico in Siena was built in the 14th century, but its upper part was finished only after 1460 by the Sienese Antonio Federighi. Although this artist has often been regarded as the successor to Jacopo della Quercia, he worked largely on ornaments. The frieze of gryphons adorning the upper register of the chapel demonstrates Federighi's predilection for antique motifs. In his creations of the period 1475–1490, the artist brought together in his works many elements taken from Roman funerary altars.

758

758 ANTONIO AVERLINO, known as FILARETE (Italian, 1400–1467), and GIUNIFORTE SOLARI · *Detail of the Ospedale Maggiore, Milan* · 1456–1465.

In 1456, Duke Francesco Sforza entrusted the construction of the Ospedale Maggiore in Milan to Antonio Averlino, known as *il Filarete*. The artist went to Florence to perfect his design, and the hospital was begun the following year. All round the building he placed a portico inspired by Tuscan architecture, to which he always remained faithful. The classical rhythm of the arcades contrasts with the Gothic ogive style of the upper-story windows. The latter can be attributed to the Lombard Solari, who succeeded Filarete in 1465 and completed the work.

759 GIULIANO DA SANGALLO (Italian, 1445–1516) · *Capital* in the courtyard of the Gondi Palace, Florence · Ca. 1490.

The Gondi Palace was built in 1490 after the designs of Giuliano da Sangallo. In the courtyard especially, the artist was able to display his decorative talents. The capitals are inspired by the antique; some of the more restrained are very close to the Corinthian style, while others, decorated with a vase spilling forth flowers and foliated scrolls, demonstrate the taste for lively ornamentation that developed in the second half of the Quattrocento. The block inserted between the springing of the arch and the capital was doubtless intended to lighten the proportions.

759

760 GIULIANO DA SANGALLO · *Capital* in the sacristy of Santo Spirito, Florence, 1489–1492.

Towards the end of the 15th century, Giuliano da Sangallo furnished the designs for the capitals in the sacristy of Santo Spirito. For each group of paired pilasters there is a different decorative theme – winged sphinxes, horns of plenty, grotesque masks, leaf-borne dolphins, and chained human figures – and all are inspirited by a dynamism tending to make the compositions burst their limiting frames. This stress on ornament and this taste for fantastic elements correspond to the popularity of grotesques in Renaissance painting and foreshadow developments in Mannerist ornament.

760

761

761 *Ceiling of the "grotta" of the studiolo* of Isabella d'Este · Palazzo Ducale, Mantua.

In Isabella d'Este's apartments in the Ducal palace in Mantua, especial care was lavished on the decoration of the *studiolo* itself and the *grotta*. The carved wooden motifs on the ceiling of the latter are enlivened with gilt, against a blue background. The central rectangle is adorned with her personal arms. Around it are distributed geometric panels decorated with emblems reflecting the refined and scholarly culture of the Gonzaga court. Isabella's motto, NEC SPE NEC METU, can be read at one end. The outer part, with the marquetry panels, is attributed to the brothers Antonio and Paolo Mola.

345

763 MICHELANGELO (?) · *Crucifix*, Sacristy, Santo Spirito, Florence.

Serious considerations have led art historians to identify this work found in the sacristy of Santo Spirito with the wooden cross mentioned by early writers as having been carved by Michelangelo in 1492 for the prior of that church. The way the head and legs are treated in contrapposto suggests a search for classical harmony. The extremely soft modelling of Christ, his tender facial expression, and the complex anatomical structure have no counterpart in any of Michelangelo's youthful works, and some critics have reservations about its attribution to that artist.

762

762 MICHELANGELO · *Pietà*, St. Peter's, Rome · Marble · 1499.

Commissioned from Michelangelo in 1497 during his first Roman sojourn, this Pietà, done just after the Bacchus, is the artist's only signed work. In accordance with the medieval iconography of the *Compassio Mariae*, treated in paintings by Ercole de Roberti and others, the Virgin holds the body of Christ on her lap. Here, contrary to tradition, she does not gaze at her Son's face; with downcast eyes she submits to the divine will, offering the divine sacrifice with a gesture of resignation. Leonardo's influence appears in the gentleness of the face and in the firmly built pyramidal composition turning around a core, while the perfectly polished marble figures, especially the Madonna, belong still in the refined tradition of the Florentine Early Renaissance sculpture. (Height 5 feet 8 inches.)

764 MICHELANGELO (Italian, 1475–1564) · *David* · 1501–1503 · Accademia, Florence.

A great marble block partly cut into by Agostino di Duccio, which had lain unfinished for a number of years, was finally allotted to Michelangelo for a statue of David. Only the relative flatness of the figure, front to back, unusual in Michelangelo, suggests that he was in any way hampered by the cuts already made by the older master. The shepherd youth of the Bible appears here fused with the type of Hercules observable on Roman sarcophagi. In this heroic David – Michelangelo's version of a figure who had long symbolized the Florentine republican ideal – are expressed the *fortezza* and *ira* traditionally associated with Hercules. The duality between the classicizing ideality of the figure type and the inner spiritual tension is paralleled in the contrast between the calm stance and the nervous movements of arm and of the head, with its look of gathering resolution. (Height, 13 feet 5 inches.)

346

766 MICHELANGELO · *Dying slave* 1515–1516 · The Louvre, Paris.

In 1505, Michelangelo was summoned to Rome by Julius II, who commissioned from him a grandiose tomb destined to stand in St. Peter's. But the artist was forced to limit its scope gradually, until, many years after the Pope's death in 1513, and after at least five different projects, the matter was settled in 1545 with a much-reduced design; the tomb was partly executed by assistants and ultimately set up in San Pietro in Vincoli. The two Louvre slaves belong to the second design, from 1513. Intended for the lower level of the monument, they probably symbolize the human soul imprisoned in the brute matter of the body, according to Neo-Platonic doctrine. The so-called Dying Slave seems rather more like a sleeping man seeking escape from a nightmare. (Height, 7 feet 4 inches.)

765 MICHELANGELO · *Moses*, S. Pietro in Vincoli, Rome · Ca. 1515–1516.

The Moses was executed for Michelangelo's second project for the tomb of Julius II. Inspired perhaps by the medieval conception of man as microcosm, he brought together the elements in allegorical guise: the flowing beard suggests water, the wildly twisting hair fire, the heavy drape earth. In an ideal sense, the Moses represents also both the artist and the Pope, two personalities who had in common what is known as *terribilità*. Conceived for the second tier of the tomb, the statue was meant to be seen from below and not as it is displayed today at eye-level. (Height, 8 feet 4 inches.)

766

765

767 MICHELANGELO · *Tomb of Giuliano de' Medici*, Medici Chapel,
San Lorenzo, Florence · Ca. 1525–1530 (see also fig. 768).

Michelangelo accepted the commission for the Medici Chapel in 1520,
but the statues of the dukes were not installed until 1559 and the whole
work remained incomplete. The artist was influenced by Brunelleschi's
Sagrestia Vecchia, but he interlocked the architectural elements so as to
produce in the interior untraditional dynamic tensions that are re-
leased only in a vertical sense, giving the chapel an ascending feeling.
For the first time a total unity between symbolic and formal decorations is achieved. Against opposite walls stand the tombs of Lorenzo
and Giuliano de' Medici, depicted as patricians and captains of the
Church. (Height of central figure about 6 feet.)

769 MICHELANGELO · *Dawn*, Medici Chapel, San Lorenzo, Florence.

It would appear that in the Medici Chapel, Michelangelo wished to
represent the spiritual victory of the soul, according to the Neo-Platonic doctrine. Dawn and Dusk, reclining on either side of the sarcophagus of Lorenzo de' Medici, are symbols of the passage of time,
which corrupts the body laid in the sarcophagus, but which the spiritual element of the Duke, represented as an ideal figure, overcomes.
The figures of Night and Day on the tomb of Giuliano complete the
temporal cycle. In their poses, they are influenced by the river-gods
of ancient art. Dawn, depicted as a young woman, wakes uneasily in
the anxious circle of mortal time. (Length, 6 feet 8 inches.)

769

768

770

771

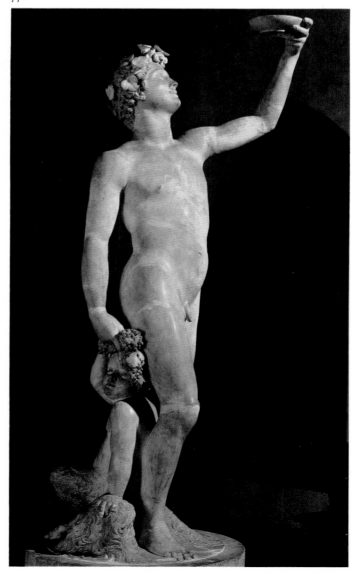

772

770 MICHELANGELO · *Virgin and Child* · Medici Chapel, San Lorenzo, Florence · Ca. 1530–1534.

Flanked by Saint Cosimo and Saint Damian, the Virgin forms the spiritual center of the Medici Chapel; the eyes of Lorenzo and Giuliano de' Medici are turned towards her. Like the first Madonna carved by Michelangelo (a relief in the Casa Buonarroti, Florence), she is suckling her child, who clings to her strongly. The dynamic interlocking spirals in space of the two figures suggest a different order of movement than that visible in the other figures, and it has been suggested that the group was originally intended for one of the earlier versions of the tomb of Julius II, and was later employed in the Medici Chapel.

771 MICHELANGELO · *Slave* · Ca. 1532 · Accademia, Florence.

Probably carved for the 1532 project for Julius II's tomb, the four slaves in the Accademia take up the theme of the Louvre versions fig. 754), but in larger dimensions. Partly emerging from the rough-hewn marble block, the naked figure is still one with the material from which the artist gradually frees it. Caught at this stage of its creation, the work illustrates the dramatic effort of the sculptor to embody an idea. (Over life-size.)

772 JACOPO SANSOVINO (Italian, 1486–1570) · *Bacchus* · Ca. 1511 · Museo Nazionale, Florence.

A disciple of Andrea Contucci, whose adoptive surname of Sansovino he took, Jacopo Sansovino carved the Bacchus after his return from Rome to Florence in 1511. It was his first important commission in marble. His figure may have been influenced by Michelangelo's Bacchus, which he could at that time have studied in Rome, but Sansovino's statue has an undulating movement quite alien to the dramatic realism of Michelangelo. Sansovino's work is marked by a calm poetry and grace which place the statue within the classicizing trend in Rome and Florence.

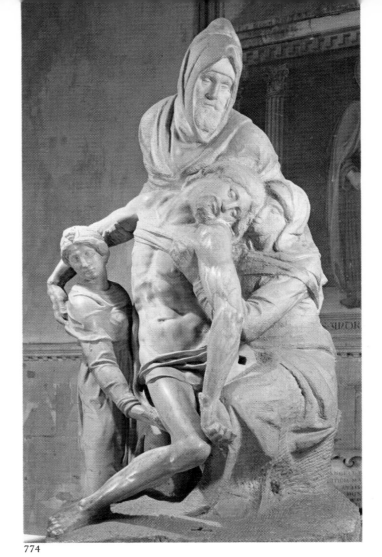

774

774 MICHELANGELO · *Pietà* · Ca. 1550 · Cathedral, Florence.

During the pontificate of Julius III (1550–1555), Michelangelo finished this Pietà, which he had meant to have on his own tomb in the church of Santa Maria Maggiore in Rome. Dissatisfied with the work, he defaced it, but his pupil Tiberio Calcagni gathered all the fragments together and restored it. Unfortunately Calcagni also finished the figure of the Magdalen, which Michelangelo had scarcely outlined, and which now appears timid and stiff, and is dwarfed by the monumentality of the other figures. In this vertically composed group of bodies united in one painful and solemn communion, the Virgin and the Magdalen support the body of Christ, while the priestly, hooded figure of Nicodemus broods over the scene. (Height about 88 inches.)

773

773 MICHELANGELO · *Rondanini Pietà* · 1550–1564 · Castello Sforzesco, Milan.

When he stopped work on the Florence Pietà, Michelangelo returned to a marble group in which clearly he had already outlined the right arm of Christ and the head of the Virgin. Re-attacking the block about 1555, he carved the smooth legs of Christ with more slender proportions. At the end of his life, the artist again modified his interpretation, again reducing the mass of the forms, and accentuating their spiritual value. Destroying the upper part of Christ's figure (the right arm remains) he re-carved it out of the Virgin's body, whose head he then placed differently. The Virgin no longer supports Christ, but leans over him in an embrace still closer than that in the Florence Pietà. (Height, 6 feet 4 inches.)

775

775 MICHELANGELO · *Head of Christ*; detail of fig. 774.

In the Florentine Pietà, Michelangelo returned to a theme which he had already treated (in drawings) for Vittoria Colonna, with whom he had been associated in a Christian and mystical friendship. The alternation of polished surfaces with a rough texture that softens the harsh light allowed the artist to express the great spirituality of the closely-bound figures. Resting against the scarcely outlined face of his mother, Christ's head is radiant with an inner light. All trace of human suffering has disappeared, replaced by heavenly bliss.

776

776 GIOVANNI DA UDINE (Italian, 1487–1564) · *Shell ornamenting an apse in the loggia*, Villa Madama, Rome · Stucco · Ca. 1520.

Giovanni da Udine, a pupil and assistant of Raphael, played a decisive role in the decorative productions of the master's workshop. Vasari says that he rediscovered the ancient formula for white stucco, permitting a very soft relief. He first used it in Raphael's Loggie in the Vatican, then at the Villa Madama, where, in the apse of the loggia, he set out little panels illustrating the story of Galatea according to Ovid. All round it run grotesques with the arms of Pope Clement VII, owner of the villa.

This tomb is the first documented work by Colombe. It was executed, on a design by Jean Perréal, by Colombe and his assistants Regnault, Jean de Chartres and Jerome Pacherot de Fiesole. The four figures of Virtues at the corners are an Italian theme. Two faces and a mirror, attributes in the Italian manner, characterize Prudence. A trace of the Gothic style remains in the idealization of the faces and in the way the draperies are handled in broad, harmonious folds. The sculptors' preoccupations were on the verge of becoming purely aesthetic.

778

779 MICHEL COLOMBE (French, ca. 1430–ca. 1515) · *St. George* · 1509 · The Louvre, Paris.

Michel Colombe was born about 1430 in Bourges, into a family of stonecarvers and illuminators. Active in Tours, where he died about 1515, he is the greatest master of the Loire valley, where artistic production enjoyed a tremendous boon as a result of the court's presence in that district. In his later years in Tours he executed a bas-relief depicting St. George, commissioned by Cardinal Georges d'Amboise for the chapel at Gaillon (Eure). An Italianate frame was carved by stonecutters from Italy. Colombe treated the legendary episode realistically, placing it in an acutely observed landscape offering no concessions to the fanciful or to the picturesque.

779

777

777 MICHEL COLOMBE (French, ca. 1430–ca. 1515) · *Tomb of Francis II of Brittany and his wife Marguerite de Foix*, Nantes Cathedral · 1502–1507.

The last Duchess of Brittany, Anne – who added her duchy to France by marrying first King Charles VIII and then King Louis XII – erected this monument to her parents. The personality of Michel Colombe cannot easily be seen in the work, since the idea for the monument came from Jean Perréal, who made the model for it. A new conception of the human form, a preoccupation with plastic qualities, a pronounced inclination towards harmony and balance, and a great refinement in execution distinguish this work as one of the great landmarks of the Renaissance in the northern countries.

780

780 FOLLOWER OF COLOMBE · *The Olivet Virgin* · 1520–1525 · The Louvre, Paris.

From Colombe's workshop in Tours emerged a string of pupils, among them Guillaume Regnault and Chalevau, who perpetuated his style. This Virgin, from the chateau at Olivet, was produced by an artist from Colombe's circle and is characteristic for the school of Tours. These Virgins from the first third of the 16th century are descended from 14th- and 15th-century examples, but they are calmer, they smile more discreetly, and they are invested with a homely tenderness. Their great charm is an exquisite gentleness. Before the revelation of Italian art in the works executed at Fontainebleau by artists from Italy, French sculpture lived on its own heritage, freed from 14th-century formalism but lacking any particular inspiration towards renewal.

781 *Virgin*, from the choir screen, Chartres Cathedral · 1525–1540.

The choir screen in Chartres cathedral was built in 1514 under the direction of Jean Texier, known as Jean de Beauce. The niches must have held scenes from the lives of the Virgin and of Christ. The sculptures were completed during the 16th and 17th centuries. The group depicting Joseph's dream, the work of an unknown artist, was installed between 1525 and 1540. The Virgin, who is sewing, is treated in a somewhat thin and anecdotal manner: the Mother of God here seems to be entirely taken up with household tasks, and she wears all the attributes of the bourgeois housewife – richly decorated garments, a purse and a bunch of keys.

781

782

782 *Ornamental panel* from the choir screen, Chartres Cathedral · 1520–1530.

The decoration of the choir screen was begun in the Flamboyant style; after a break, work was resumed in 1520, but in a hybrid style characteristic of this transitional period. Renaissance elements dominate the base, while the frame and the frieze are still in the Flamboyant style. The whole decoration must have been completed about 1530. The motifs are directly inspired by Italian *grotteschi*, to which the anonymous decorator added martial attributes, Christian symbols and recollections of Gothic plant decoration.

783 FRENCH SCHOOL · *Female bust in a medallion* · 16th century · Museum, Lyon.

Adopted from the antique by the Italian Renaissance, the motif of a bust set in a medallion was copied in France, although more rarely than in Spain. This figure, apparently in a state of ecstasy, her eyes half-closed, her bared breast depicted with sensual naturalism, evokes the voluptuous and refined poetry of Ronsard. The plumed cap crowning her head places her in the time of Ronsard, Henry III's court poet. The medallion is sculptured on a squared block, which must have been set in a façade with others of the same kind.

783

784

784 ADAM KRAFT (German, ca. 1455/60–1509) *Christ carrying the Cross* · 1506–1508 · Germanisches Museum, Nuremberg.

The new style that influenced the work of Tilman Riemenschneider about 1500 also affected Adam Kraft, a sculptor from Nuremberg. The group of seven bas-reliefs representing the stations of the cross, carved for the cemetery of St. Johann in Nuremberg, does in fact show a relaxing of the *spätgotik* style that characterized his earlier works: he renounced complicated drapery in favor of straight-falling folds, adopted shorter proportions for his figures, and simplified his compositions. Carved between 1506 and 1508, the St. Johannishof Stations of the Cross attracted the devout from all over Germany. They were commissioned by a knight from Bamberg, Heinrich Marchalk von Rauheneck.

785 PETER VISCHER (German, 1460–1529) · *St. Paul*; detail of the shrine of St. Sebald, church of St. Sebald, Nuremberg · 1507–1512.

The apostles adorning the base of this shrine show the first signs of the tendency of late Gothic art to take on soberer forms. The work was the outcome of thirty years of labor in a large workshop. Vischer, who designed the shrine, worked on it from 1507 to 1512. Remarkable in an artist who never visited Italy is the serene and unproblematic way in which Vischer was able to discard Gothic formulae in favor of broadly handled, fluid draperies clearly inspired by 15th-century Italian art.

785

786

786 GILG SESSELSCHREIBER (German 1460/65–1520) · *Cimburgis of Massovia*, Cenotaph of Maximilian, Innsbruck · 1516.

A native of Westphalia, Sesselschreiber was court painter at Munich from 1502 onwards. He designed many monumental projects and was responsible for their execution in minute detail. Forty busts and statues of rulers are known to be by him. He worked in close collaboration with the bronze workers on the tomb of Maximilian. His straightforward style, his monumental conceptions allied with a deep understanding of the themes treated – funeral escorts, ancestral figures or symbols of chivalry – brought German sculpture to a degree of perfection that it was never again to attain after this period of flowering in the early 16th century.

787

788

788 PETER VISCHER · *Theodoric the Great*; detail of fig. 787.

Like the statue of King Arthur, this is not a funerary effigy. It represents one of the deceased emperor's tutelary ancestors, whom an inscription (rather late, it is true) allows us to identify as Theodoric the Great. The impetuosity of this legendary figure is conveyed with an expressionistic note suggesting Albrecht Dürer's style rather than the Italianate style peculiar to Peter Vischer. Dürer was undoubtedly responsible for the design of this statue and of the statue of King Arthur. The two works were completed in Vischer's workshop in 1513.

789 PETER VISCHER · *King Arthur*; detail of fig. 787.

The statue of Arthur is set apart from the rest by its marked relationship with new ideas. The figure is still a medieval paladin, but its relaxed and clearly articulated pose denotes an undeniable influence of Italian Quattrocento sculpture, and a move towards a more simple and natural ideal of beauty; one has but to compare it with the ornate iron machine alongside. No crisis or personal conflict accompanied Vischer's wish to escape from German Gothic art; he never visited Italy, but he doubtless knew Italian ideas from works by the Venetian Sansovino – and he simply borrowed such elements as were required by his own artistic ideals.

787 *King Arthur, Ferdinand V of Portugal, Ernst der Eiserne, and Theodoric the Great*; Cenotaph of Maximilian, Hofkirche, Innsbruck.

For seventy-two years, from 1511 to 1583, work went on for the grandiose funerary ensemble that Emperor Maximilian I (d. 1519) ordered for his tomb – never completed. He planned forty colossal bronze statues of Hapsburg ancestors and relations or contemporaries, one hundred statuettes of saints, and thirty-four busts of Roman emperors. (Of these, actually executed were, respectively, twenty-eight, thirty-two and twenty-two. The group was set up in the Court church, built for this purpose between 1553 and 1563.) In 1507, to carry out his project, the Emperor called upon Gilg Sesselschreiber, a painter from Munich. The massive, looming armored forms of Ferdinand V of Portugal and Ernst der Eiserne are attributed to Sesselschreiber. Two statues, King Arthur and Theodoric, were executed in 1513 in Nuremberg, in the workshop of Peter Vischer, from drawings by Albrecht Dürer; these display a quality quite different from the figures attributed to Sesselschreiber or executed by his followers.

789

790 LOY HERING (German, 1485–1554) · *Virgin and St. John*; detail of a Crucifixion from the Eichstätt Mortuarium, Bavaria.

Hering, born in Kaufbeuren, Swabia, specialized in high-relief works in a fine-grained stone called Solnhofer Stein. With great enthusiasm, he adopted the Renaissance forms that he had studied in Italy; he diffused the new style widely in Swabia, leaving more than one hundred works, which embody forcefully the Germanic power of concentration and intense religiosity. His life-size tombs and crucifixions are the most sublime works of their kind produced anywhere in Germany during the Reformation and the humanist period.

790

792 BARTOLOMÉ ORDÓÑEZ (Spanish, ca. 1490–1520) · *St. John the Baptist*, tomb of Philip the Handsome and Joanna the Mad, Capilla Real, Granada Cathedral · 1519–1520.

Bartolomé Ordóñez was born in Burgos and is identified with the school of that city. However, his career took him to all parts of Europe: in 1515, he was in Barcelona; in 1517 in Italy, where he visited Florence, Genoa, and Naples. He may have met Michelangelo at Carrara. Various influences can be distinguished in his work, but especially the Italian. In 1519, Charles V ordered him to execute the tomb of Joanna the Mad and Philip the Handsome (d. 1506). To this end Ordóñez opened a workshop in Carrara and completed the tomb in one year, just before his sudden death in 1520. The saints at each corner show the restraint with which Ordóñez translated the lessons of Michelangelo.

792

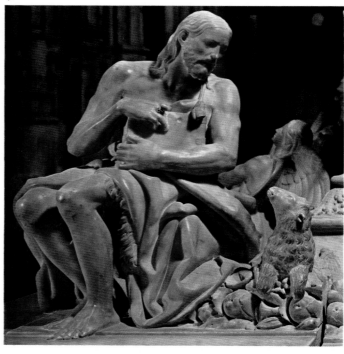

791

791 FELIPE BIGARNY (French, ca. 1470–1543; active in Spain) · *Detail from Trasaltar* from Burgos Cathedral · 1498–1513.

Felipe Bigarny or Vigarny (his name is variously spelled) is sometimes regarded as a Castilian. He appears, however, to have been a native of Champagne or Burgundy. During the first phase of his career he introduced into Castile a style related to the late French Gothic. The structure of Burgos Cathedral *trasaltar* (rear wall of the high altar), commissioned in 1498, is still Gothic; but certain details in the Christ Bearing the Cross, which reminds one of the art of Michel Colombe, announce the new style. The complete work has a hybrid character that was to typify Castilian sculpture in the first third of the 16th century.

793 FELIPE BIGARNY and DIEGO DE SILOË · *Main altar*, Du Guesclin chapel, Burgos Cathedral · 1523–1526.

The architectural elements of the Burgos altar are probably the work of Bigarny, as is also the Annunciation group, while the Holy Family must be attributed to Diego de Siloë (ca. 1495–1563). This altar exemplifies the last phase of Felipe Bigarny's art, showing that the sculptor had assimilated the Renaissance style: in both decorative elements and also in the modelling of the figures, the Italian influence is now marked. Bigarny, one of the group of artists whom Charles V gathered about him, formulated in his Burgos altar the altar-type of official art.

793

794

794 DIEGO DE SILOË (?) · *Annunciation*; detail of fig. 793.

It is difficult to distinguish the hands of Felipe Bigarny and Diego de Siloë, who together contracted for the execution of this altar. Some scholars think that the design is Bigarny's and the execution de Siloë's. One would be tempted to see the Frenchman's hand in calmer scenes like the Nativity or the Visitation, while the impulsive movement in the Annunciation appears more characteristic of the temperament of Diego de Siloë.

795 DIEGO DE SILOË · *Virgin and Child*, tomb of Canon Diego de Santander · Ca. 1524 · Burgos Cathedral.

Diego de Siloë was directly influenced by the Italian style. He travelled through Italy in his youth, was employed in Rome, where he saw the sculptures of Michelangelo, and also in Naples, where he worked with his fellow-countryman, Ordóñez. However, on his return to Spain his style became more Spanish. The relief of the seated Virgin clearly shows the influence of Michelangelo. Diego de Siloë, besides being an architect, was also the best decorator and ornamentist of the early 16th century, as evinced by the finely carved monsters, trophies, and volutes lavished tastefully around the ample architectural framework of this relief, or on the tomb as a whole.

795

796 *Façade of Salamanca University* · Spanish, early 16th century.

The Plateresque style, so called because of its resemblance to gold-smith work (*plateria*), is characterized by an exuberant decoration of Italian Renaissance inspiration covering a medieval structure. The façade of Salamanca University is the masterpiece of this style. Built by several anonymous artists, it was completed in 1533. In style, some of the reliefs suggest Lombard-Venetian influence; others appear to be influenced by the French school of the Loire.

797 *Ferdinand and Isabella*; detail of fig. 796.

The upper part of the façade, divided into three registers and crowned by a frieze, brings to mind an altarpiece, or a shrine or jewel-box. The lowest of the three registers is decorated with a central medallion enclosing portraits of their Catholic Majesties, Ferdinand and Isabella. On either side are panels of grotesques resembling those done by Michel Colombe for the chateau of Gaillon. The lavish and crowded ornamentation covers every inch of the stonework. The Spanish ornamentist hated empty spaces, and in the 16th century even more than in the Romanesque period, ornamental sculpture burgeoned at the expense of the monumental structure.

796

798 *Detail of an arcade* in patio of the Colegio Fonseca (the Irish college), Salamanca · After 1527.

In 1527 Diego de Siloë produced the plans for the most beautiful college at Salamanca – the Irish college; but, although it is probable that he worked on the door, he could not have exercised his profession of sculptor there for long, since in 1528 he was called to Granada to redesign the plans for the cathedral. Local decorators executed the admirable medallion busts on the courtyard arcade. Medallions were used endlessly by the Salamanca school, monuments in the town showing more than 1200 of them, with busts of heroes from antiquity and from modern times, of soldiers, old men, women – all the figures appearing to be overwhelmed by an unspecified emotion, their faces infused with the torments of some inner drama.

798

797

799 *Handrail of the staircase*, Salamanca University · 1500–1525.

Faced with the task of executing decorations on a monumental scale, sculptors often had recourse to engravings as models. On his handrail at Salamanca University the imitation of engravings from both Italy and the northern countries can be seen. One of its panels, depicting satirical subjects, reproduces an engraving by the German artist Israël van Meckenen, who died in 1503. The staircase, executed in the first quarter of the 16th century, illustrates the virtuosity of the Renaissance decorators at Salamanca.

801

801 Idem · *Façade of San Salvador of Ubeda* · Decorative figures · 16th century.

The two corner-stones above the porch are decorated with female figures represented as allegories of Fame. They are carved in the round and stand out freely from the wall. The grotesques are in the style of Siloé. The influence of Italian sculpture is obvious. This new decorative approach reacted against the excesses of Plateresque style by the use of accurate and harmonious proportions. The spreading of a purely Renaissance style was easier in Andalusia which had never been a great centre of Gothic art; therefore, in that region, there were no flamboyant elements to compete with the Italianate style or with the new tendencies.

799

800 *Center portion of the façade*, church of San Salvador, Ubeda Mid-16th century.

The church of San Salvador de Ubeda was erected with the financial support of Cobos, secretary to Charles V and governor of Milan. Diego de Siloë drew up the plan in 1536, and Andres de Vandelvira and Alonso Ruiz set about the construction. In 1540 work was begun on the portal, modelled after Diego de Siloë's Gate of Pardon in Granada Cathedral. Almost complete in 1556, and dedicated in 1559, the church exemplifies the architectonic style of Diego de Siloë. In composition the façade is clearer and more logical than are the Castilian Plateresque façades. The separate elements of the decoration are balanced; the sculpture no longer climbs all over the walls without any pattern but is contained and ordered by the articulating columns and niches.

802 *Vestry door in San Salvador of Ubeda* · 16th century.

Whilst the Salamanca school remained purely ornamental, the type of decoration instigated by Diego Siloé on the Gate of Pardon in Granada developed into statuary. The masterpiece of that style is the church of San Salvador of Ubeda where a whole team of sculptors worked. The Ubeda school made a great use of caryatids inside the church of San Salvador and in other monuments of the town such as the *ayutamiento* (the town hall) whose attic storey is decorated by remarkable male and female statues. The building of the vestry of San Salvador was planned in 1540. The placing of the door in an angle is a typical Plateresque feature.

800

802

803

803 DAMIAN FORMENT (Spanish, active early 16th century – d. 1540)·
Detail from the main altar of Santo Domingo de la Calzada · Ca. 1540.

Damian Forment was one of the foremost creators of Spanish altarpieces in the early 16th century. Beginning as a Gothic sculptor, he
gradually discarded the medieval style and moved towards Renaissance forms. The first stage was the introduction of Renaissance
imagery within his Gothic structure; then, from 1527, Forment worked
out an entirely new type of altarpiece. Late in the year 1537 he began
work on the altarpiece of Santo Domingo de la Calzada, in which he
employs typically Castilian themes: tritons, nereids, and nautical
themes, treated as a decorative frieze. The Castilian school had borrowed such motifs from Italian artists, incorporating them into a style
rooted in the Hispano-Flemish tradition.

804 *Main altar*, El Parral monastery church, Segovia · Spanish,
begun in 1528.

This great stone reredos, decorated with a multitude of statues, is the
most monumental piece of Renaissance sculpture in Spain. It was
undertaken in 1528 by Juán Rodríguez Blas Hernández and Jerónimo
Pellicer. In its vast triptych composition it encompasses the two tombs
of the founders of the monastery of the Hieronymites, executed by
Juán Hernández and Luis Giralde. The two sculptors were pupils of
Vasco de la Zarza, a sculptor from Avila who introduced Renaissance
art into Old Castile. The classical style of Vasco de la Zarza, continued
by his pupils, contrasts with the wild Mannerism that can be seen in
Alonso Berruguete's reredos of San Benito in Valladolid, begun at the
same time as this one.

804

805

805 NICOLAS CHANTERENE (French, active in Portugal ca. 1515–ca.
1541) · *Virgin of the Annunciation* · 1518–1520 · Museu Machado de
Castro, Coimbra.

In her natural grace and simplicity, this Virgin is very close to contemporary works of the Loire school. Insofar as statuary is concerned,
the Renaissance style was in fact introduced into Portugal by French
artists, of whom the most notable were João de Ruão (Jean de Rouen)
and Nicolas Chanterene. The latter, named *Mestre Nicolau Françês* in
contemporary documents, received the commission in 1517 for the
main door of the church of the Hieronymites at Belem, on which he
worked with eleven collaborators. He also worked at Alcobaça and
Coimbra (the university town and the great center of the Portuguese
Renaissance). The last mention of him we have is in 1541. The French
contribution in the 16th century had profound consequences in Portugal, for it drew attention to Portugal's independent nature and
helped bring about the break with Spain in the following century.

IX Mannerism: The Anti-Classical Reaction

807

807 BACCIO BANDINELLI (Italian, 1493–1560) · *Hercules and Cacus* · Marble · 1534 · Piazza della Signoria, Florence.

Shortly after Michelangelo had completed the David, he was commissioned to execute a group of two figures, representing Hercules and Cacus, intended to face the biblical hero in front of the Palazzo Vecchio. After the overthrow of the current regime, however, the work was handed on to Baccio Bandinelli, Michelangelo's great rival, who finished it in 1534. Although he originally planned a dynamic work showing Hercules tearing the giant to pieces, Bandinelli finally settled on a static composition that better suited his classicizing tendencies. Within these limitations the group shows great technical skill, though it breaks no new ground.

806

806 PIERINO DA VINCI (Italian, d. 1554) · *Samson slaying the Philistine* · Marble · Ca. 1549 · Palazzo Vecchio, Florence.

In 1548, Pierino da Vinci went to Rome to study the work of Michelangelo. On his return to Florence, he undertook the execution of a marble group inspired by a sketch for a group of Hercules and Cacus that Michelangelo had modelled for the Piazza della Signoria. The work is reminiscent of Michelangelo in the tension of the torso and the serious expression on Samson's face, but the artist interpreted his model according to his own temperament. This work inaugurated the theme of two men struggling which was to be so popular in Florence.

808

808 BENVENUTO CELLINI (Italian, 1500–1571) · *Cosimo I, Medici*; detail of a bronze bust · Ca. 1548 · Museo Nazionale, Florence.

Immediately following his return from Fontainebleau, where he had worked for Francis I, Benvenuto Cellini hastened to reproduce the features of his new patron the Grand Duke of Tuscany, Cosimo I de' Medici. As he himself relates in his autobiography, he represented the sovereign turning his head with a vivacious movement emphasized by the asymmetry of the breastplate and the movement of the curls of hair. In this bronze bust, the artist was particularly successful in portraying the individuality of the man, revealing a psychological perceptiveness exceptional among 16th-century portrait sculptors.

809

810

809 BENVENUTO CELLINI · *Perseus with the head of Medusa* · Bronze · 1554· Loggia dei Lanzi, Florence.

Completed in 1554, after the bust of Cosimo de' Medici, the bronze Perseus set the stamp on Cellini's fame in Florence. It was placed in the Loggia dei Lanzi, across the piazza from Michelangelo's David and Donatello's Judith. Placed on a high rectangular base and composed to be seen only from the basic views – front, back or profile – the statue still belongs to the Quattrocento. The artist's training as a goldsmith is revealed in the refined modelling, which recalls Donatello's David, and in the abundant ornament covering the base between the small bas-reliefs.

810 BARTOLOMMEO AMMANATI (Italian, 1511–1592) · *Nymph*; detail of the Fountain of Neptune, Piazza della Signoria, Florence · 1563–1575.

In 1560, Ammanati won the competition for the Fountain of Neptune in Florence. The colossal statue of the god brings to mind the giants of the Palazzo Ducale in Venice, executed by Sansovino, to whom Ammanati had been apprenticed. The assembly of figures around the basin, however, is typical of the erudite 16th-century Florentine culture. These sea gods and nymphs were carried out after the Neptune, with the help of many collaborators. The young nymph's elongated and mannered body shows the pictorial taste shared by Ammanati and his circle.

811

811 VINCENZO DANTI (Italian, 1530-1576) · *Venus*· Bronze · Ca. 1570 · Studiolo of Francesco de' Medici · Palazzo Vecchio, Florence.

The apartments of Francesco de' Medici in the Palazzo Vecchio were decorated in 1570 under Vasari's direction. Conceived as the setting for rare and precious objects, the *studiolo* is decorated with frescoes and paintings, with niches on the walls intended to hold statuettes. The archives identify the sculptors of seven of the statuettes, among them Giambologna and Ammanati; the eighth little bronze was executed by Vincenzo Danti from Perugia. It represents a Venus plaiting her hair, accompanied by a dolphin. (Height, 38½ inches.)

812 VINCENZO DANTI · *Venus*; detail of fig. 811.

In this bronze Vincenzo Danti drew away from the Michelangelesque style that had characterized his earlier sculptures, and developed further the tendencies already manifest in his Salome on the south door of the Baptistry in Florence. He gave the Venus a sinuous movement accentuating her tapering form and her mannered grace. Intended to be seen from the front, she turns her head in profile. This attitude displays to full advantage the incisive modelling of the facial features, modelling underlined by the wavy hair and the curves of the heavy plaits.

812

813

813 GIOVANNI DA BOLOGNA (1529–1608) · *The Neptune Fountain*, Piazza Nettuno, Bologna · 1563–1567.

Born in Douai in 1529, Giambologna left the Low Countries to complete his training in Rome. On his way back, he stopped in Florence, where the collector Vecchietti remarked his wax and clay statues, modelled from the antique. Having unsuccessfully taken part in the competition organized in Florence in 1560 for the Neptune Fountain, he was called to Bologna, where his project was accepted after being reworked. Although the face of the god betrays the influence of Michelangelo's Moses, his body reveals a characteristic, though still unformed, elegance in the pose.

814

814 GIOVANNI DA BOLOGNA · *Venus* · Ca. 1508 · Villa Medici, Petraia (Florence).

About 1560, Giovanni da Bologna made this little bronze Venus to surmount a candelabra-shaped fountain that Tribolo had designed for the Villa Castello, near Florence. In the 18th century the fountain was removed to a neighboring villa at Petraia, where it first stood in the middle of a garden. The young woman is represented drying her hair; her head is turned to her right and she holds up the ends of her long hair in the opposite direction. The work is conceived entirely in curved lines, echoed by the movements of the little satyrs who haul themselves up onto the basin.

In this work, Giambologna tackled the problem of representing a
number of figures engaged in violent action. An old man, completely
exhausted, has given up trying to defend his daughter, whom a man is
grabbing away from him. The group attracted the attention of Francesco de' Medici, who had it installed in the Loggia dei Lanzi and
christened it the Rape of the Sabine Women. In the violent movement
of the intertwined bodies may be detected the influence of the Farnese
Bull. That Hellenistic group led Giambologna to the realization of the
first truly modern sculpture, composed to be seen from all angles.

816

815

Mercury in flight was one of Giambologna's favorite subjects, which
he treated several times. The present example was sent to Cardinal
Ferdinand de' Medici around 1580. Here the sculptor shows his debt
to the refined art of Cellini, but he goes beyond it in giving an impression of extraordinary weightlessness in movement. The possibilities
of contrapposto are exploited to the full. The lifted arm anticipates the
pose of the Sabine. One leg is raised in a running movement, and the
entire weight is borne on the toes of the left foot which barely rest on
the jet of air from the mouth of a putto who symbolizes the wind that
bears up the young god.

The statue of Cosimo I was meant to represent him as the founder of
the Medici dynasty. Giambologna, who started the statue in the reign
of the Grand Duke Francesco, completed it under his successor, Ferdinand. The monument, inspired by that of Marcus Aurelius, which
the artist had studied in Rome, was the first equestrian statue erected
in Florence. Giambologna first modelled an écorché horse (now in the
Palazzo Vecchio), but the artist was no longer centrally concerned
with naturalism as was Donatello. The sovereign has been caught in
movement, while holding back his horse.

817

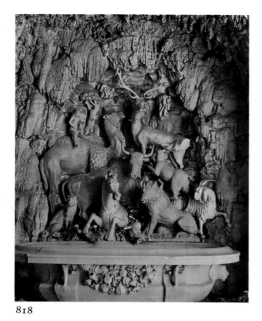

818

818 GIOVANNI DA BOLOGNA · *Grotto*, Villa Medici, Castello (near Florence) · Ca. 1540.

Giambologna was gifted with a great feeling for nature; his bronze birds seem to have been studied from life. In the Castello villa are three grottoes decorated with animals probably worked up from his drawings. The representation of a variety of species, even exotic ones, reveals a desire for an encyclopedic knowledge. Giambologna may have been influenced by his compatriot, the painter Stradano, and he may also have remembered his northern training. But under Francesco de' Medici botany and zoology were studied, and the taste for illustrated scientific works affected almost all Florentine artists.

820 GIOVANNI DA BOLOGNA · *The Appennino*, Villa Medici, Pratolino · Late 16th century.

When he was commissioned to decorate the gardens of the most famous of the Medici villas, that at Pratolino, Giambologna first modelled a reclining river-god, using a formula that Renaissance artists frequently borrowed from the iconography of antiquity. But the mountain god Appennino was substituted for the river-god, for a triangular composition was better suited to the natural setting. The giant raises himself wearily. Handled in such a way as to suggest that it was carved out of the living rock, the colossus is hardly distinguishable from the element it personifies.

820

819 *The Elephant and the Mouth of Hell*, Gardens of Bomarzo (Viterbo) · Ca. 1565.

In the region of Viterbo, at Bomarzo, Vicino Orsini, a humanist prince with a somewhat esoteric mind and a taste for the bizarre, added an enchanted garden, or *sacro bosco*, to his castle. There, natural rocks were transformed by sculptors into monsters, exotic animals, semi-gods, giants, nymphs. The images were obviously devised according to some poetical theme whose source has not been found, but perhaps was inspired by the stories of Bernardo Tasso, father of Torquato, the author of *Jerusalem Delivered*. Work was in progress on this group in 1564.

819

821

The city of Leghorn commissioned from Tacca two bronze fountains intended to flank a monument to Ferdinand de' Medici. When they were cast in 1627, however, the city refused them; later they were placed in the Piazza dell'Annunziata in Florence. The sea-monsters spitting into the water, back to back, show the artist's imaginative powers. The apish animals with shell-shaped ears, fretted wings, and muscular bodies garlanded with leaves and seaweed, forcefully renew and prolong the Cinquecento strain of fantasy.

822 PIETRO TACCA · *Moorish slave*, on the monument to Ferdinand I de' Medici, Piazza della Darsena, Leghorn · 1624.

Pietro Tacca was the most gifted disciple of Giambologna, whom he succeeded as sculptor for the Florentine court. Early in the 17th century the city of Leghorn commissioned from him a base adorned by four chained slaves for the monument to Ferdinand I de' Medici done earlier by Giovanni Bandini. The story goes that, as models for the four Moors, Tacca sketched from life the handsomest galley-slaves to be found in the port. The result is one of Tacca's finest works.

822

823 POMPEO LEONI (Italian, 1533–1608, active in Spain) · *Charles V and Isabella*, tomb of Charles V, royal mausoleum, Escorial · 1597.

In 1597, Pompeo Leoni was commissioned to carve the portrait statues for the matching tombs of Charles V and of Philip II in the chapel of the Escorial. In accordance with the iconography traditional for Spanish tombs, the figures are kneeling on their prayer-stools. Behind Charles are portrayed his sisters, Eleonora of France and Mary of Hungary, and his daughter Mary, wife of Maximilian. The faces are not studied with the idea of revealing the individuality of the sovereigns, but these official effigies compose a group of austere majesty.

824

824 GIROLAMO DA CARPI (Italian, 1501–1556)· *Courtyard façade,* Spada Palace, Rome · Ca. 1550.

The Spada Palace was built by Girolamo da Carpi, a painter and architect from Ferrara, or according to some, by Mazzoni. The ornament of the courtyard façade appears to be by Girolamo. Windows alternate with niches containing sculptures *all antico*, while higher up, garlands, caryatids and draperies surround smaller windows. The upper story dates from the 17th century. The stuccoed decoration betrays Girolamo's pictorial temperament. It is directly derived from the decoration of the Branconio dell'Aquila Palace (Rome – no longer extant), erected by Raphael in 1520, but in the mid-century Mannerist interpretation it appears archaistic.

826 *Giulio Romano* (Italian, 1492/99–1546) · *Sala degli stucchi,* Palazzo del Tè, Mantua · Ca. 1530–1535.

The *Sala degli Stucchi* in the Palazzo del Tè at Mantua is decorated with a double stucco frieze, running all the way around the room beneath the vault, representing a crowd of horsemen, foot-soldiers and chariots. This procession, inspired by Roman triumphal monuments, alludes to the journey to Mantua of Emperor Charles V. The stuccos were made about 1530 by Giovan Battista Mantovano, perhaps with the help of Primaticcio; but in their broad, energetic treatment they reveal the style of Giulio Romano, who provided the preparatory drawings for them.

826

825

825 PIRRO LIGORIO (Italian, ca. 1510–1503) · *Façade of the loggia,* Casina of Pius IV, Vatican, Rome · 1558–1562.

Pirro Ligorio, a Neapolitan archeologist and artist, built the Casina of Pope Pius IV in the Vatican gardens. Its façade, strongly influenced by ancient architecture, derives from the Spada palace, which it immediately follows in date, but the stucco elements of the Casina tend to stress the architectural design. On the loggia side, in the stuccos executed by Rocco da Montefiascone, Apollo, the nine Muses, and three bacchanal figures can be seen above the columns, while in the pediment Dawn rises from the clouds before the chariot of the Sun.

827

827 *Façade of the Otto Heinrichsbau wing,* Heidelberg Castle · German, 1553–1562.

The so-called Otto Heinrichsbau wing of Heidelberg Castle was designed by the Elector Otto Heinrich von der Pfalz (the "Magnanimous"), who thereby followed in the footsteps of the humanist princes of the 16th century. He drew his inspiration from the numerous treatises by 16th-century Antwerp decorators, and especially that by Hans Vredeman de Vries. The entire façade is carved in accordance with Mannerist canons, and the symbolism of the various figurations is very recherché; Christian virtues and an allegory of Good Government mingle with direct allusions to the Prince. The statuary is handled like ornament and fuses with the architectonic elements, the caryatids, garlands, and pediments.

828

828 WENZEL JAMNITZER (1508–1585) · *Spring* · 1578 · Kunsthistorisches Museum, Vienna.

Jamnitzer, descended from a family of Viennese goldsmiths, established himself in Nuremberg, where he worked in a courtly mannerist style. This allegorical figure in gilt bronze, the only surviving one of four Seasons that originally ornamented a table centerpiece, shows how entirely the artist had discarded German Gothic motifs in favor of a style permeated with the spirit of the Renaissance. Unfortunately, he could not transmit this new style to native artists engaged on monumental ornament, which passed into the hands of foreign, mainly Dutch, artists, while German sculptors limited themselves to the field of applied arts. (Height, 28 inches.)

369

829 HUBERT GERHART (1540/50–1620) · *Gardens of the Residenz, Munich* · 1594.

This artist, born between 1540 and 1550 at Hertogenbosch, belongs to the generation of Dutch sculptors who introduced into the German courts an international style that, fused with traditional local elements, paved the way for the great flowering of Baroque art. Raised on a base decorated with four putti, the bronze goddess wears a helmet adorned with ears of grain, symbolizing agriculture, and her shoulders are covered with the skin of an Alpine deer. At her feet is a pitcher connoting the abundance of mountain streams and a small cask symbolizing the riches of the salt mines.

829

830

830 HUBERT GERHARDT · St. Michael Slaying the Devil, St. Michael's Church, Munich.

Towards the end of the 16th century in Prague and in Munich, at the courts of the Emperor Rudolph II and the Dukes William V and Maximilian of Bavaria, two bronze-working schools were created by artists coming from the Low Countries and further formed in the great focus of Mannerist sculpture established in Florence by another northern artist, Giovanni da Bologna. Hubert Gerhardt, after a period of work in Augsburg, where he executed the Augustus fountain for the city (1594), joined the court of the Dukes of Bavaria. Under the direction of Friedrich Sustris, like Gerhardt a native of the Low Countries, he participated in the program of decoration for the Jesuit college church of St. Michael in Munich. The most beautiful piece is the group of St. Michael Slaying the Devil, which greets the worshipper on the lower level of the façade.

831 ADRIEN DE VRIES (Dutch, 1544/46–1626) · *Hercules Fountain* · Augsburg · 1596–1602.

In the course of an international career, de Vries' services were called upon by some of the greatest art patrons of the time: the Duc de Savoie, the Emperor Rudolph II, the King of Denmark, Duke Albert von Wallenstein, and the City of Augsburg. This fountain crowned by a symbol of Virtue – a statue of Hercules conquering the Hydra – is one of three fountains put up to mark the sixteen-hundredth anniversary of the city. The nude young woman washing her feet in a basin, surrounded by a group of swans and children, is one of the three beautiful female figures modelled by the artist for this monument, which turned a local market place into a dwelling place of gods.

831

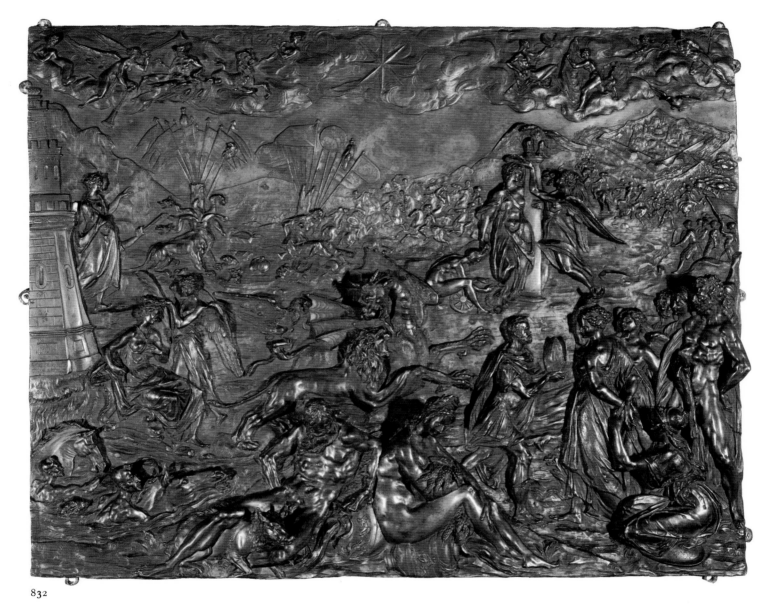

832

832 ADRIEN DE VRIES · *Victory of Rudolph II over the Turks* · 1609 ·
Hofmuseum, Vienna.

This bronze relief, a counterpart to the statue of Rudolph II as patron of
the arts, has a highly complicated iconography. On it appear allegories
of rivers, the imperial lion attacking the Ottoman dragon, and the
Emperor crowning Hungary, who has been liberated by Minerva and
Hercules; on a battlefield bristling with banners and weapons, cavalry
skirmishes at the foot of the Raab fortress, while in a sky strewn with
astrological symbols a flourish of trumpets sounds the victory. The
sensitive handling of relief links it closely with the art of Cellini, and
also shows that de Vries, not content with sculpture in bronze, was
trying to emulate the techniques of painting. (Height, 28 inches.)

833

Antoni Keller (architect) and Christoph Jelin (sculptor) ·
Portal of Tübingen Castle · 1606.

The portal framing a receding perspective exercised a strong attraction on Mannerist artists, who were inspired to treat it as an independent, monumental work. Keller, who was familiar with Italian architecture, and Jelin, a local tomb-maker who was also a gifted sculptor, wanted to create a Roman-style archway; but the sources of inspiration that they had to draw upon were the temporary triumphal arches put up for festive entries of sovereigns. They translated into stone the leather or paper scrolls and volutes of such structures, and even introduced a figure anachronistically armed with a gun.

835

834 Jörg Zürn · *Adoration of the Shepherds*; detail of fig. 836.

In the Adoration of the Shepherds, the center portion of the Überlingen altar, the figures move in a play of light and shadow against the pierced background, and the effect created repeats the mystical atmosphere of Christmas eve evoked in a picture by Altdorfer. The composition has not gone beyond the conception of a crèche scene set on a stage, but the execution is striking, revealing a liveliness rooted in the popular artistic vein and a still-Gothic feeling, despite the use of Renaissance innovations.

834

835 Jörg Zürn · *Ornament*; detail of fig. 836.

The redecoration of this church in the 16th century was largely the work of the Zürns, members of a family that produced a number of sculptors. Jörg, who was entrusted not only with the high altar, but also with the decoration of the side altars dedicated to the Holy Angels and to the Virgin, was born at Waldsee in Wurttemberg and settled at Überlingen in 1607, succeeding Virgilius Moll. Despite the upheavals caused by the Thirty Years War he achieved a synthesis of the artistic tendencies of the region, and is revealed in this masterpiece as one of the greatest artists of the first phase of the German Baroque.

836

836 JÖRG ZÜRN (1583–1635) · *High Altar*, church of St. Nikolaus, Überlingen.

Below the Adoration of the Shepherds is the Annunciation, and above it, the Crowning of the Virgin; this perpendicular transformation of the medieval altarpiece shows the daring steps that Mannerist artists took in search of new forms. The silhouette of the whole is jagged and light flickers through the pierced central area; yet the overall body of the work is vigorously and rhythmically composed, despite the profusion of decorative motifs, and the adjustment of the various component masses is an advance on previous works. In a Germany that was trying to find itself amidst religious, cultural and political upheavals, this work seems exceptional.

837

837 ALONSO BERRUGUETE (Spanish, 1480/90–1561) · *Adoration of the Magi*, from the San Benito altar · 1526–1532 · Museum, Valladolid.

Alonso Berruguete, eldest son of the painter Pedro, received a painter's training. About 1508 he was in Italy, where he certainly studied the works of Michelangelo. He returned to Spain in about 1520, entered Charles V's service and later created an important workshop in Valladolid with a number of assistants. The altar for San Benito in Valladolid was commissioned in 1526 and completed in 1532. It was later dismantled and has been partially reassembled in the Museum. The polychromed wood altarpiece was conceived as a drama, and Berruguete's talent reveals itself as pictorial rather than sculptural.

838

838 ALONSO BERRUGUETE · *The Sacrifice of Isaac,* from the San Benito altar (see fig. 828) · Museum, Valladolid.

In the group of Abraham sacrificing Isaac, originally part of the San Benito altarpiece, Berruguete's pictorial style is again visible. What traces of Italian influence remain are overlaid by a genuinely Spanish dramatic passionate feeling. Everything, including formal values, is subordinated to expressiveness. However, while Berruguete's chisel still had this element of Gothic sensitivity about it, the same was not true of his brush. He painted his sculptures with great care, and the polychromy is no longer simply a coloring, but is incorporated into the modelling and composition. It suggests a third dimension, corrects errors of carving, emphasizes the hollows and projections and accentuates the dramatic tension of the sacrificial scene.

839 ALONSO BERRUGUETE · *Eve,* on the choir stalls, Toledo Cathedral.

Between 1539 and 1561 Berruguete worked in Toledo, where he came into contact with Bigarny. He received the commission for the execution of half the choir stalls in the Cathedral. Two registers, one in alabaster and one in walnut, are decorated with panels showing figures from the Old Testament. In the panel of Eve, there is much that recalls Italian sculpture and especially Michelangelo's. The loose, supple twist of the female nude figure sets off its powerful, muscular forms without making it appear masculine. In his Toledo figures Berruguete employed more thick-set proportions and a fuller modelling than he did in those for the Valladolid altar.

839

840

840 BERRUGUETE AND STUDIO · *Lunette* of the archiepiscopal throne, Toledo Cathedral · Ca. 1543.

In 1543, after the death of Bigarny, Alonso Berruguete, who was his rival rather than his associate, received the commission for the archiepiscopal throne in Toledo. The upper part of the throne is carved with lunettes representing biblical themes. Several of these are of poor quality, since Berruguete left a great part of the work to his assistants, but the Crossing of the Red Sea, a polychromed wood panel, is a work of merit. It shows a definite Italian influence, like most of the sculptures from the later part of the artist's career. In its design, anatomy, and the suppleness of the figures tossed by the waves, it is akin to Italian Mannerist works.

841

841 JUAN DE JUNI (1506–1577) · Antigua Altar, Valladolid Cathedral.

Juan de Juni was born at Joigny in Champagne; in 1541 he was in Valladolid, where he died in 1577. He received the commission for the Antigua altarpiece in 1545 and he finished it in 1562. (It was installed in Valladolid Cathedral in 1922.) Juni tried to produce a classical work in an architectural framework – the first he ever used. Taken separately, the Corinthian columns, entablatures, and niches are based on the classical Italian arrangement, but the general organization, the relationship between the different parts, the proportions of the niches, and above all the importance given to sculpture are closer to Mannerism.

842

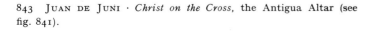

842 JUAN DE JUNI · *The Birth of the Virgin*, panel of the Antigua Altar (see fig. 841).

The iconography of the Valladolid altarpiece is somewhat confused; several statues of male and female saints are mixed with scenes of the childhood and life of the Virgin. The same confusion is found in the alternation of large statues in the round and relief panels. Juni was above all a statue maker, as can be seen from the relief representing the birth of the Virgin. His main preoccupation is the rendering of the third dimension. The carving is self-assured, the volumes well-defined in the expressive composition. The influence of Dürer's woodcuts has been suggested as the explanation for such clarity of outline.

843

843 JUAN DE JUNI · *Christ on the Cross*, the Antigua Altar (see fig. 841).

As in most Spanish altarpieces, a Christ on the Cross towers over the ensemble. Juni placed this Crucifix outside the architectural framework, above the central part of the attic, in impressive isolation. The anatomical details are masterfully rendered, but the body is distorted by Juni's dramatic genius: from head to toe, it is twisted round in a spiraling movement which expresses its last convulsion.

844

844 JUAN DE JUNI (Spanish, ca. 1506–1577) · *The Entombment* · 1544 · Museum, Valladolid.

The polychromed wood Entombment group in the Valladolid museum was executed for the Bishop of Mondonedo, Antonio de Guevara. Originally it formed the decoration of the lower part of an altarpiece. The attribution to Juni is not disputed. The artist took great pains with the composition of his group: the six life-size figures surround the body of Christ in an oval; the accentuated contrapposto and the related gestures create a dynamic balance that draws the gesticulating protagonists into a concentrated unity. The source of inspiration for this group must be in the Lombard sculpture of Milan or Bologna.

845 JUAN DE JUNI · *Head of Christ*, detail of fig. 844.

Spanish sculpture probably never reached such a degree of expressionism as in the art of Juan de Juni, whose French origins were swept aside by the feverish breath of Castilian art. The faces are violent and convulsed; thick, animated curls twist and twine in the turbulent hair and beards. This Christ has in truth experienced his Passion in human flesh, and his face retains an indelible memory of it. This Romantic conception, emphasizing the tragic sense of sorrow and death, is profoundly Spanish, foreshadowing already the Baroque art of Spain.

845

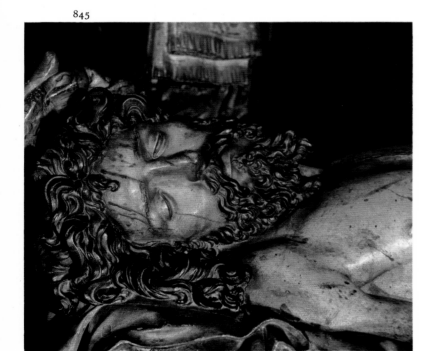

846

846 JERONIMO HERNANDEZ (Spanish, ca. 1540–1586) · *The Resurrected Christ* · Quinta Augustia, Seville.

Jeronimo Hernandez is one of the most important sculptors of the Seville school. Born in about 1540, he had established a workshop by 1567. He was above all a very skillful image-maker, and provided Spain with a complete religious iconography, principally of themes centering around the Virgin and the childhood of Christ. The Resurrected Christ at Quinta Augustia links Mannerist grace with Christian imagery. The art of Hernandez inaugurated a new trend in Spanish art towards a sweet and quiet manner that was to contribute to the style of popular religious sculpture in the 17th century.

847 ATTRIBUTED TO EL GRECO (1541–1614) · *Venus and Vulcan* (?) · Wood, polychromed · Conde de la Infantas Collection, Granada.

A few sculptures, including these two strange nudes, have been attributed to El Greco. This attribution is doubtful, however. It is based on the testimony of Pachecho, who saw in Greco's studio in Toledo a series of figurines of wax, stucco, and wood, but these may have been merely models, like those used in the Italian workshops where Greco was trained. The figures illustrated (16½ inches high) recall certain nudes in paintings by Greco in their elongated proportions, their supple postures, and their opposition in contrapposto. Nevertheless, they also evoke certain Florentine Mannerists, Sansovino or Cellini, and their naturalism and the accentuated musculature of the male figure are surprising for El Greco. The identification of the statuettes as Venus and Vulcan is also problematical.

847

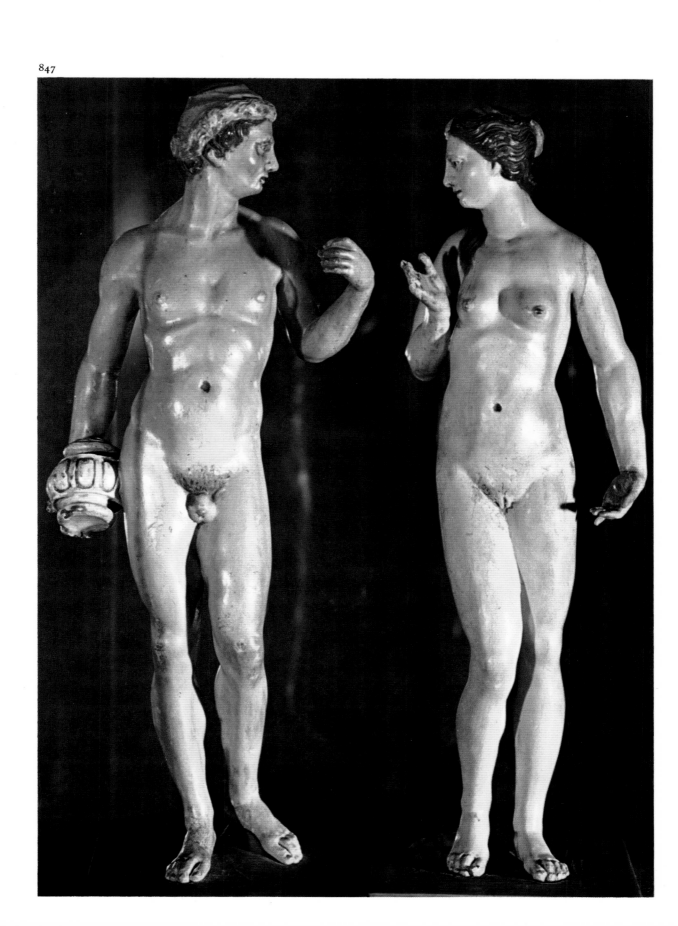

848 ESTEBAN JORDAN · *Main altar*, St. Mary Magdalen, Valladolid ·
Spanish, ca. 1571.

Esteban Jordan was a painter and sculptor, perhaps trained first in
Italy and then in Berruguete's workshop. He was a Romanist of the
Castilian school, representing the official art patronized by Philip II.
In 1571 he began work on the main altarpiece of the church of St.
Mary Magdalen in Valladolid. The architectural structure of the altar-
piece is orderly and well-balanced, and the use of sculpture restrained.
This Italianate Mannerist composition, however, suffers from a
dryness that indicates a workshop production rather than the creation
of a master.

848

849

849 ESTEBAN JORDAN · *St. Peter and St. Paul:* detail of fig. 848.

The group of St. Peter and St. Paul appealed to Esteban Jordan, who
represented it several times. These sculptures reveal the artist's dilem-
ma: attracted at the same time by the expressionism of Juni and the
grandeur of Michelangelo, he produced works either lifeless or pretentious. The conventional attitudes, the artificial draperies, show no
epic inspiration, no classic harmony. The remarkable development of
Spanish sculpture languished towards the end of the 16th century, but
Italian artists summoned by Philip II, such as Pompeo Leoni (see
fig. 823), were to revive it.

850 ODARTE (d. 1538) · *Apostle*, from a Last Supper group · 1530–
1534 · Museu Machado de Castro, Coimbra.

Though various contemporary references to him leave no room for
doubt that Odarte was of French origin, his exaggerated mannerism
is as alien as possible to the French Renaissance spirit. His style must
have been formed as a result of contacts with expressionistic Milanese
artists such as Guido Mazzini or Nicolo dell'Arca. Before coming to
Portugal, he had traveled through Spain, where we find him in Toledo,
working on the Cathedral between 1522 and 1526. This terra-cotta
statue comes from a Last Supper scene composed of life-size figures
which have reached us in a very mutilated state. The group was commissioned on October 7th, 1530 by the prior of Santa Cruz of Coimbra,
from "Odarte frances ymaginario"; on January 8th, 1534, Odarte

delivered it.

850

851 PIERRE BONTEMPS (French, active 1536–1567) · *Claude de France*; tomb of Francis I and Claude de France, Abbey Church of St. Denis, Paris.

The tomb of François Ier and Claude, daughter of Louis XII of France, is the most important 16th-century French funerary monument. The architect Delorme designed the tomb; from 1549 onwards, a team of sculptors worked on it, and in 1559 Primaticcio completed the work. Five marble statues of praying figures flank the recumbent figures. Three of these, including those of the sovereigns, are attributed to Pierre Bontemps, who executed the reliefs. Bontemps' portraits are official, neither revolutionary nor timid. His style is frank and solemn, though it occasionally lapses into a heavy softness in the modelling – a fault veiled by his technical virtuosity in the rendering of realistic details, physical characteristics, costumes and jewelry.

852 GIOVANNI BATTISTA ROSSO (Italian, 1495–1540) · *Stucco decoration*, Gallery of Francis I, Fontainebleau · 1534–1536.

The Florentine Rosso, summoned to France in 1530 at the instigation of Francis I, devised in 1534 a compartmented decoration, stuccoed and painted, for the gallery at Fontainebleau; he completed it, with the aid of numerous assistants, in 1536. Each compartment forms a self-contained composition. Framing the scene of Venus Scolding Cupid is an elaborate stucco ornament including strapwork scrolls, putti, baskets of fruit, and two graceful life-size, naked figures. At the top, in the center, appears the gilded royal emblem, the salamander. The soft, pliant modelling and the grace and femininity of the bodies are characteristic of the Fontainebleau school, representing the ideal of French Mannerism freed from the stamp of Italy.

851

852

853

853 PRIMATICCIO (Italian 1504/5–1570) · *Stucco decoration*, apartments of the Duchesse d'Étampes, Fontainebleau.

In 1532, Primaticcio, a pupil of Giulio Romano, completed the stuccos in the chamber of the Duchesse d'Étampes at Fontainebleau. Influenced by Parmigianino, Primaticcio carried to an extreme the quest for grace and elegance. Lithe, slender adolescent female figures frame medallions decorated with mythological scenes. Together with the Rosso figures, these elongated and voluptuous bodies surrounded by garlands in a fantastically elegant Olympus are the masterpieces of the Fontainebleau school. Primaticcio visited Rome again and brought back many casts from antique works; these were set out in the gardens of Fontainebleau, whence spread the taste for Greek art through France.

854 *The Diane d'Anet* · French, mid-16th century · The Louvre, Paris.

At the end of the 18th century, Alexandre Lenoir attributed the Diane from Anet, sometimes identified as Diane de Poitiers, to Jean Goujon. It is impossible that Goujon, burdened as he was by his responsibilities in Paris, could have worked at the château of Anet, which was begun in 1548 and completed in 1555 by Philibert Delorme. Du Colombier sees in this work a painter's hand, and suggests as its author Primaticcio or one of his followers, for the group, very charming but slackly modelled, is reminiscent of Italian Mannerism. The statue type itself was established in France by Cellini in 1543 at Fontainebleau. The Diane must be the work of an Italianized Frenchman.

854

855

855 JEAN GOUJON (French, active 1540–1562) · *Nymph*, Fontaine des Innocents, Paris · 1548–1549.

Jean Goujon, the greatest 16th-century French sculptor, began work on his masterpiece, the Fontaine des Innocents, at the end of 1548. Its original architecture is now greatly modified. Five nymphs personifying the rivers of France are placed between pilasters. While Goujon may have been inspired by Rosso, he rejected the Mannerism of the Fontainebleau School and devoted his masterly talents to a revival of the classical purity of later 5th-century Greek art, thus paving the way for modern French sculpture. In the figure reproduced, the supple, graceful gesture, admirably composed within the architectural frame, is counterbalanced by the delicate thrust of hips and breasts. The essence of Goujon's art is summarized in the fluid movements, subtle modelling, and rippling folds – here especially appropriate to the theme – combined with accurate drawing.

856

The Hôtel de Bagis in Toulouse was commissioned in 1537 from several architects. The decoration *all'antico* was ordered from Nicolas Bachelier, who executed the windows and the portal, his first known works. The door is framed by two bearded terminal statues supporting a heavy Ionic entablature, on whose cornice appears the coat of arms, flanked by two sphinxes. Bachelier handled antique themes with considerable power; the two robust and meditative old men are carved in broad planes. The sculptor's sober restraint and his respect for the architectural composition are noteworthy; the structure, far from being smothered by the decoration, is nobly defined. This exact balance between sculptor and architect prefigures the equilibrium of the French classical style.

857 JEAN GOUJON · *Caryatid*, Palais du Louvre, Paris · Begun 1550.

The *Tribune des Caryatides*, commissioned from Jean Goujon in 1550 for the Louvre, was reworked later, notably by Percier and Fontaine. Goujon was acquainted with this classical motif, having illustrated the caryatid figure in the 1547 edition of Vitruvius. The Louvre caryatids are Greek rather than Roman, however, and closer to those of the Erechtheion; it is likely that Goujon knew a cast from an ancient piece. Seen among the artist's other works the caryatid is a little surprising. The drapery knotted under the stomach recalls Hellenistic rather than 5th-century Greek art; furthermore, the clothing has a rather artificial elegance, contrasting with the robustness and severity of the female figure.

857

858

858 GERMAIN PILON · *A Virtue*, tomb of Henry II, Abbey Church of St. Denis, Paris · Ca. 1570.

The four bronze Virtues on the corners of the tomb of Henry II were executed by the workshop of the Grand Nesle, where a team of sculptors was working under the direction of Primaticcio. The Grand Nesle workshop was a veritable school for French sculptors, who went there to draw inspiration from the Italianized forms. Maître Ponce, and particularly Pilon, were responsible for the Virtues on Henry II's tomb. While following the plans and directions of Primaticcio, Pilon nevertheless took liberties in the execution. Pilon's figures are more robust and his forms are fuller than those of his master.

859

859 GERMAIN PILON (French ca. 1525–1590) · *Head of Henry II*; detail from his tomb, Abbey Church of St. Denis, Paris · Ca. 1570.

The art of Germain Pilon, a protégé of the court and much preoccupied with his career, was diametrically opposed to that of Goujon. Pilon combines French traditions with Renaissance influence. The tombs of Henry II and Catherine de' Medici were designed by Primaticcio. The death of various artists who had been engaged on its execution left Pilon on his own as sculptor. He gave the recumbent figures a feeling of realism without any macabre element. The king's head, thrown back, shows great concern with truthful rendering but there is no touch of vulgarity or exaggeration, and in Pilon's rather conventional idealism the tragedy of Henry II's death is muted.

860

860 HUGUES SAMBIN (French, 1515/20–1601/02) · *Door* of the Palais de Justice, Dijon · Ca. 1570.

The palace of the former Burgundian Parliament was completed at the end of the 16th century. Hugues Brouhée erected the façade in 1572, assisted by the decorator and cabinet-maker Hugues Sambin, who was also responsible for much of the interior woodwork, for which he was paid in 1583. Sambin introduced into decorative art an intricate and exuberant ornament in high relief which became characteristic of the Burgundian Renaissance: twists, trophies, foliated scrolls, mascarons, rosettes. The highly seasoned and heavily charged decoration disguises the architectural structure of this door. The sculptor enjoyed playing with the new Italian forms, as when he gratuitously frames the sloping panels of the triangular pediment with garlands of fruit.

861 *Tomb of Engelbrecht van Nassau*, Grote Kerk, Breda · Netherlands, ca. 1535.

After 1520, the art of the Netherlands looked towards Italian models, even discarding carvings in wood, the traditional material for church furniture, in favor of stone. Noble families commissioned monumental tombs modelled on French and Italian ones, and the new tradition extended well into the 17th century. One of the first such tombs was that of Engelbrecht II van Nassau, attributed to the Italian, Vincidor da Bologna, and set in place in 1535. Supporting the table on which the armor of the deceased is laid out are soldiers wearing lavishly decorated breastplates, very like those created by the Flemish Mannerist painters.

861

862 CORNELIS FLORIS (Flemish, 1518–1575) · *Jubé*, Tournai Cathedral · 1573.

The influence of Cornelis Floris, architect and sculptor from Antwerp, was decisive in the diffusion of Italian art forms in the north of Europe. The Tournai Cathedral *jubé* – or choir screen – completed in 1573, is the prototype of a series of choir screens made in Belgium and northern France. Inspired by Serlio, Floris conceived it as a triumphal arch, or rather as a tribune supported by an arcade. The framing elements of dark marble and the decoration of foliage, masks, and grotesques that covers the whole monument are directly inspired by monuments of northern Italy, and particularly by those built by Sansovino.

862

863 CORNELIS FLORIS, Crucifixion; detail of fig. 862.

Floris has subordinated the carved relief work to the effect of the architecture. He was above all a decorator and incorporated the sculptured scenes into the decorative whole. The panel representing the Crucifixion with the three Maries, set in the main face of the *jubé*, is divided by the verticals of the three crosses. The relief is quite shallow and the pictorial impression is emphasized by indications of an architectural landscape across the background of the composition, behind a wall that bounds the stage on which the action takes place. Floris was gifted with a real technical skill, but had not entirely assimilated the principles of Italian plastic art.

863

865

864

864 NICOLAS CORDIER (French, 1565–1612, active in Rome) · *Bust of Saint Peter* · Marble · 1608 · San Sebastiano fuori le mura, Rome.

In 1608 Giovanni Battista Borghese, brother of Pope Paul V, ordered from Nicolas Cordier busts of Peter and Paul, the two apostles to whom the basilica of San Sebastiano had originally been dedicated. The sculptor from Lorraine, among the most prominent of the many foreign artists who had settled in Rome, was approaching the end of his career. For this important commission he took as his inspiration Roman portrait busts of the Imperial period. However, that archeological basis took second place to a deep feeling for realism, at times not unlike that of Caravaggio, and this gave to the Saint Peter in particular a truly pathetic expressive character.

865 PIETRO BERNINI (Italian, 1562–1629) · *The Assumption*, Santa Maria Maggiore, Rome · 1607–1610.

Pietro Bernini, the Tuscan sculptor, father of Gianlorenzo, settled definitely in Rome between 1605 and 1606. At that point he was commissioned to do a relief of the Assumption for the baptismal chapel of Santa Maria Maggiore. We find in this composition the sharp linear drapery style and the extreme tenseness of the figures that characterize Pietro's art, never entirely freed from the Mannerist limitations of his training. The work, however, inspired by paintings by Ludovico Carracci, is one of the earliest examples of the pictorial relief altarpieces that were to be popular during the 17th century.

866 FLAMINIO PONZIO (Italian, 1560–1613) · *Tomb of Pope Clement VIII*, Cappella Paolina, Santa Maria Maggiore, Rome · 1605–1611.

The symmetrical tombs of Clement VIII and Paul V, executed by the Milanese sculptor Flaminio Ponzio in the Pauline chapel of Santa Maria Maggiore, reproduce the architecture of the tombs of Sixtus V and Pius V, which Fontana had done earlier in the Sistine chapel of the same church. There is, nevertheless, a strong difference between the two chapels, which provoked animated discussion in the 17th century; while Bellori declared himself in favor of the architectural clarity of Fontana, Baglione defended the ornate richness of Ponzio's carved decoration, especially noticeable in the tomb of Clement VIII.

866

867

867 FRANCESCO MOCHI (1580–1654) · *Monument to Alessandro Farnese*, Piazza Cavalli, Piacenza · 1620–1625.

When in 1612 the Piacenza authorities decided to set up twin equestrian monuments, one to Ranuccio Farnese, the ruling duke, and the other to his father, Alessandro, they did not commission the pupils of Giovanni da Bologna, who held the monopoly for equestrian statues, but called upon the young Tuscan artist Francesco Mochi. After completing the sketches, the artist had a quarrel with the founder and cast the bronzes himself. In the earlier statue of Ranuccio, Mochi is still steeped in Mannerist culture, but in the Alessandro monument he succeeded in breaking new ground, creating a powerful, moving work, whose originality was not grasped by his contemporaries.

868

868 FRANCESCO MOCHI · Detail of fig. 867.

After he had modelled the Ranuccio horse, Mochi went to Padua and Venice to study Donatello's Gattamelata, Verrocchio's Colleoni and the horses of Saint Mark's, but this cultural enrichment only brought about a few modifications in the representation of the rider. The dynamic element in the Alessandro group contrasts with the heaviness of the Ranuccio monument, which is much closer to that of Marcus Aurelius. Here the horse, foaming at the mouth, and the rider with his wind-whipped cloak form an impressive unity, vibrating with movement and light, whereby the artist achieves great stylistic coherence.

869

François Duquesnoy was trained in Brussels in the workshop of his father, Jérôme Duquesnoy the Elder, before going to Rome in 1618, where he collaborated with Poussin. St. Susanna, ordered at about the same time as his Saint Andrew, under the dome of St. Peter's, was his first important commission and perhaps his masterpiece. Though inspired by a Hellenistic statue representing the muse Urania, the figure is free of all archeological allusions and permeated with a very pure classicism, seen in the graceful attitude, the soft modelling and the delicate arrangement of the draperies.

870 GIANLORENZO BERNINI (Italian, 1598–1680) · *David* · 1623 · Galleria Borghese, Rome.

Born in Naples, Gianlorenzo Bernini, son of the Florentine sculptor Pietro Bernini, first worked under the direction of his father. Later, in Rome, his first patron was the Cardinal Scipione Borghese, for whom he executed works inspired by biblical and especially by mythological themes. Preparing to hurl the stone from his sling, David leans back to gather his strength. The old base, now transformed, must have accentuated the movement, for on it the figure appeared to be slightly off balance. Designed along a plunging diagonal, the statue frees itself from the Renaissance tradition by taking full possession of space.

870

871

871 BERNINI · *Apollo and Daphne* · 1624 · Marble · Galleria Borghese, Rome.

Bernini interrupted work on the David to do this statue. In illustrating the fable recounted by Ovid, he seized on the precise moment when the girl, to escape the unwelcome attentions of Apollo, began to metamorphose into a laurel-tree. She seems already, indeed, caught up by the winds. The works Bernini executed for Cardinal Borghese were intended to be set up against a wall rather than to be seen in the round, and in this respect he did not break with the Renaissance tradition. That, however, he was moving away from it is shown by the fact that here one forgets that the figures were carved from a block of marble, for they seem to take flight into space.

872

872 BERNINI · *Head of Daphne*; detail of fig. 871.

The subject of Apollo and Daphne was a familiar one in painting rather than sculpture, and Bernini must have drawn his inspiration from the painters, among whom he admired especially the Bolognese school and in particular Annibale Carracci. With supreme virtuosity the sculptor gave his marble the translucency of wax. His satiny smooth polished surfaces succeed in conjuring up the fresh complexion of the girl and the blondness of her hair. Although the two personages seem idealized, Bernini interprets their drama in a highly realistic manner. Daphne's face expresses all the horror of the moment when the god caught up with her and her strange metamorphosis began to cloud her human existence.

873

874

873　BERNINI · *The Ecstasy of St. Theresa*, Cornaro Chapel, Santa
Maria della Vittoria, Rome · 1645–1652.

Cardinal Cornaro commissioned Bernini to do a funerary chapel for his
family in Santa Maria della Vittoria. In the churches of the barefooted
Carmelite friars, the *Vision of St. Theresa* had often been represented
since the beginning of the 17th century. In keeping with tradition,
Bernini chose to depict that supreme moment of ecstasy when the
Saint's heart is pierced by the arrow of divine love. At either side of
the chapel, eight sculptures of members of the Cornaro family seem to
form an audience, as though watching the scene from their theater
loges.

874　BERNINI · *Head of St. Theresa*; detail of fig. 873.

With half-closed eyes and a half-open mouth, the Saint sinks in a
trance. A shudder seems to pass through her cloud-borne body, and
beneath the crushing folds of the cloak her hand and foot hang down
limply. The similarity between this mystical ecstasy and the ecstasy
of profane love has often been pointed out; but the connection is
literally made in the Saint's own account of her vision, which Bernini
followed closely. Windows concealed in a little dome diffuse a golden
light down the gilt bronze rays and over the Saint and angel, enhancing the supernatural atmosphere of the vision.

875

875   BERNINI · *Bust of Costanza Buonarelli* · Ca. 1635 · Museo Nazionale, Florence.

In about 1635 Bernini portrayed Costanza Buonarelli, a woman with whom he maintained a stormy relationship. In a Rubenesque manner, the artist sought to capture a passing expression on the face, so as to bring out its psychological nature to the full. The young woman, her shoulders hardly covered, seems to turn her head, as if to speak. Every detail suggests her wild, sensual temperament, as Bernini brings out in the marble painterly effects of light, color and movement.

876

876   BERNINI · *Bust of Francesco d'Este I* · 1650 · Galleria Estense, Modena.

In 1650 Bernini received the commission for a bust of Francesco d'Este I. He did not know his model and had to do his portrait after paintings by Sustermans; the artist complained of the difficulty, but it had the advantage nevertheless of giving him considerable freedom in the execution. He no longer sought to convey the mobility of the figure by concentrating on the smallest details of the face. The vivid turn of the head and the richly folded and agitated drapery, pulled diagonally, help to create an impression of pomp and grandeur in this state portrait.

877

877   BERNINI, *Baldacchino*, St. Peter's, Rome · 1624–1633.

Immediately after his election in 1624, Pope Urban VIII commissioned a bronze Baldacchino, which was to be raised above the supposed position of St. Peter's tomb. The monument, which cost 200.000 scudi, was inaugurated on June 29th, 1633. The twisted columns were inspired by the ancient columns (fig. 327) used to decorate the Constantine basilica of St. Peter; these Bernini reintegrated in the decoration of four great pillars of the crossing. Dramatic and filled with movement, the 92½-foot structure animates the great void under Michelangelo's dome. The bronze of the Baldacchino came in part from the letters of antique inscriptions that decorated the portico of the Pantheon. Bernini was helped by his father, Pietro, and his brother, Luigi, and also by the sculptors Nicolas Cordier and Duquesnoy. Borromini was also his assistant and, as we possess drawings by him for the Baldacchino, some people think that he may have had an influence on the design for the crowning motif.

878   Bernini · *Angel Carrying the Crown of Thorns* · Sant' Andrea delle Frate, Rome.

When Clement IX had the Ponte St. Angelo modernized, he decided to replace the fourteen stucco angels set up by Raffaello da Montelupo under Paul III with ten marble figures. Two statues were entrusted to Bernini, including the Angel Carrying the Crown of Thorns. The artist started work in 1667 and completed the two sculptures in 1669. It seems that the Angel Carrying the Crown of Thorns was partially executed by Paolo Bernini, son of Gianlorenzo, but it is difficult to point to any differences in style in the various parts of the statue. This statue and the second one commissioned from Bernini, the Angel with the Superscription, were later removed to Sant' Andrea and copies substituted on the Ponte St. Angelo.

878

879

879   Bernini · *Fountain of the Four Rivers*, Piazza Navona, Rome 1648–1651.

After Borromini had submitted to Innocent X the design for a fountain to decorate the Piazza Navona, an obelisk was discovered which the Pope wanted to use. Bernini, out of favor at the time, nonetheless managed to submit his project to the Pope, and it was immediately accepted. The artist isolated the figures of the four great rivers of the world (the Danube, the Nile, the Ganges and the Rio de la Plata) from the obelisk, which seems almost unsupported. This illusion is emphasized by the arbitrary poses of the old men symbolizing the rivers and particularly by the figure of the American river, apparently overwhelmed by fear that the fountain might collapse.

880   Bernini · *Model for the equestrian statue of Louis XIV* · 1670 · Galleria Borghese, Rome.

When the equestrian statue of Louis XIV arrived in Paris, its triumphant Baroque quality was not appreciated. Disappointed, the king relegated it to the bottom of the Versailles gardens where, soon afterwards, Girardon transformed the figure into Marcus Curtius. Fortunately, the terra-cotta model has been preserved – the one that Bernini executed personally. The galloping horse repeats the type used in his statue of Constantine the Great; Louis XIV is identified, however, with Hercules, reaching the summit of the path of Virtue and, from the top of a steep cliff, attaining glory. (Height, 30 inches.)

880

881 BERNINI · *Tomb of Pope Alexander VII*, St. Peter's, Rome ·
1671–1678.

Taking up in principle the theme of the throne of St. Peter's, Bernini
conceived the niche for the tomb of Alexander VII as a stage, setting
back in depth the allegorical figures around the Pope. Behind Charity
and Truth are Justice and Prudence. The Pope in the center is not
seated on a throne in the usual attitude of a temporal ruler; he is
kneeling and praying like the statues of Sixtus V and Paul V in the
church of Santa Maria Novella, for which the tomb had at one time
been intended. The tomb of Alexander VII was one of the greatest
undertakings of Bernini's workshop. Death with an hourglass, lifting
the drapery over the door of the sepulcher, is a dramatic reminder of
the temporality of life.

881

882

882 PADRE ANDREA POZZO (Italian, 1642–1709) · *Altar of Saint Ignatius Loyola*, Il Gesù, Rome.

Although it was carried out in the last years of the 17th century, the
Saint Ignatius altarpiece is one of the high points in Roman Baroque
sculpture. Father Pozzo provided the drawings for the ensemble and
called on a number of specialists to carry out the work. The altar
gleams with vivid colors of lapis lazuli, which covers the travertine of
the columns, gilded bronze, silver, colored alabasters and marbles.
The sculptural decoration creates powerful effects of movement. On
the urn, a masterpiece by Algardi, stands the statue of Saint Ignatius,
not the original, but a version reworked in 1814 under Canova's
direction.

883

883 JACQUES SARRAZIN (French, ca. 1588–1660) · *Temperance* · Ca.
1645 · The Louvre, Paris.

Sarrazin, born in Noyon, was chief among the sculptors working
under Louis XIII, and one of the founders of the Academy. He spent
eighteen years in Rome (1610–1628). The Temperance is one of four
medallions of the cardinal virtues that ornamented the monument of
the heart of Louis XIII, erected by his widow, Anne of Austria. The
pictorial style of the relief is expressed through forms transposed
from the antique and linked by elegant, sinuous outlines. Some of the
details give the composition a picturesque and naturalistic character.
The work is representative of the art of Sarrazin and his school.

884

884 SIMON GUILLAIN (French, 1581–1658) · *Louis XIV between Louis XIII and Anne of Austria*, from the Pont au Change · Ca. 1643 · The Louvre, Paris.

Simon Guillain, who was born and died in Paris, was one of the founders of the Academy in 1648. The statues from the monument of the Pont au Change constitute the most important examples of the artist's work. They were commissioned by the City of Paris to commemorate the presentation of the future Louis XIV to the people on April 21st, 1643. Set up at the entrance to the bridge, the group represents Louis XIV as a child, between Anne of Austria and Louis XIII. The figures were later removed to the Louvre. The style is influenced by the art of Germain Pilon and combines a rigorous realism with full monumental forms. (Height of statues: Louis XIV, 4 feet 10 inches; Louis XIII and Anne, 6 feet 6 inches.)

885

885 MICHEL ANGUIER (French, 1612–1686) · *Amphitrite* · 1680 · The Louvre, Paris.

Michel Anguier, who was born at Eu and died in Paris, was the brother of the sculptor François Anguier and worked with Simon Guillain. He spent the years 1641 to 1651 in Italy, whence he returned with some ancient models. The marble Amphitrite was executed in 1680 in an anachronistic style more closely related to the spirit of the beginning of the century than to the spirit of Anguier's own time. It once decorated the Bosquet des Dômes at Versailles, was moved to the gardens of Saint-Cloud, and then came to the Louvre. (Height, 6 feet 6 inches.)

886

886 FRANÇOIS GIRARDON (French, 1628–1715) · *Apollo tended by the Nymphs*, Grotto of Thetis, Gardens of Versailles.

Girardon became the leading figure among the sculptors at Versailles, where he collaborated closely with Lebrun. In 1666 he received the commission for the group of Apollo Tended by Nymphs, intended for the Grotto of Thetis. In the harmonious combination of the seven figures (the three nymphs in the background are by Thomas Regnaudin) there is something reminiscent of Poussin, and in particular a like desire to rival antiquity. The influence of Hellenistic art and a knowledge of nature allied to the artist's personal sensitivity make this work the most purely classical of all 17th-century sculptures.

887 GIRARDON · *Small Bronze Model of the Equestrian Statue of Louis XIV* · The Louvre, Paris.

887

Girardon executed for the Place Vendôme in Paris an equestrian statue of Louis XIV which was destroyed in 1792 but which is known from engravings and drawings, small bronze versions, and a marble bust (Troyes Museum). The king, represented as a peace-maker, is dressed in Roman style and wears a long, curled wig. The plaster model for the large version was finished in 1688; it was cast by the Keller brothers with the collaboration of Robert de Cotte in 1692. The pedestal was decorated only in 1730 by Guillaume Coustou, the first project by Mansart having been rejected.

888 ÉTIENNE LE HONGRE (French, 1628–1690) · *The River Marne*, Parterre d'Eau, Versailles · 1689.

Étienne Le Hongre was a pupil of Sarrazin. Only his works executed for Versailles are known, among them the famous statue of Air from the fountain of Diana. The figure of the Marne is one of a series of eight bronzes set about the pools on the Parterre d'Eau at Versailles that symbolize the rivers and streams of France. The whole series was cast by the Keller brothers.

888

890

890 COYSEVOX, TUBY, AND LE HONGRE · *Monument to Cardinal Mazarin* · 1689–1693 · The Louvre, Paris.

Commissioned by Mazarin's executors for the chapel of the Collège des Quatre Nations, now the Institut de France, the bronze and marble monument was executed from a drawing by J. H. Mansart. The kneeling statue of the Cardinal accompanied by a guardian genie is the work of Coysevox; it rests on a sarcophagus, around the foot of which are the seated figures of Prudence, Peace, and Fidelity, executed with the collaboration of Tuby and Le Hongre. While these three figures are still in the classical tradition of Sarrazin, the effigy of the Cardinal, with its movement, its spirited modelling and its penetrating expression, is closer to Baroque art. (Statue of the Cardinal, height 5 feet 3 inches.)

891 ANTOINE COYSEVOX · *Marie Adelaide de Savoie as Diana* · 1710 · The Louvre, Paris.

The portrait of the wife of Louis XIV's grandson, Louis, Duke of Burgundy, who died in 1712, was commissioned in 1708 by the Duc d'Antin, Directeur Général des Bâtiments du Roi, for his gardens at Petit-Bourg. Inspired by the Diana with the Stag, Coysevox's marble corresponds to Saint-Simon's description of the Duchess as a gay, flighty – and ugly – young woman. Her portrait is an early example of the representations of princesses masquerading as divinities so popular in the 18th century and in especial favor during the Régence. (Height about 6½ feet.)

889 ANTOINE COYSEVOX · (French, 1640–1720) · *Bust of the Grand Condé* · Bronze · 1688 · The Louvre, Paris.

Born in Lyons in 1640, Coysevox moved to Paris at 17 to remain there until his death in 1720. The perfect sculptor for Louis XIV, he had the most forceful temperament among the artists working at Versailles. His portraits constitute the most personal expression of his sculpture. This bust of the Grand Condé, Louis II de Bourbon, was commissioned after the Prince's death in 1686 by his grandson, the Prince de Conti. Masterpiece among French sculptured portraits, it captures with remarkable nobility and psychological penetration the traits of the Victor of Rocroy.

891

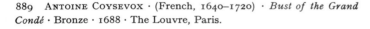

889

892 PIERRE PUGET (French, 1620/22–1694) · *Milo of Crotona* · 1671–1682 · The Louvre, Paris.

Having suggested to Colbert the idea of a statue of Milo for Versailles, Puget took an exceptionally large block of marble and carved out of it the hero, his hand caught in a split tree-trunk, about to be devoured by a lion. Completed at Marseilles after ten years' work, the sculpture, signed and dated 1682, was sent off to Versailles in 1683 and placed at the entrance of the Tapis Vert. It has been in the Louvre since 1820. Among the sculptures made for Versailles, Puget's Milo represents the irruption of the Baroque. But though it is animated by violent, twisting movements, and strong diagonals, it is nevertheless inscribed in a geometric, almost classical framework. (Height, 8 feet 10 inches.)

892

894 HENDRIK DE KEYSER (Dutch, 1565–1621) · *Tomb of William the Silent*, Nieuwe Kerk, Delft · 1614–1621.

Commissioned in 1614 by the States General from Hendrik de Keyser, William's marble and bronze tomb was finished by Hendrik's son, Pieter. Seated at the head of the white marble *gisant*, the bronze figure of the Prince of Orange, dressed in armor, presumably looks to his army. At the foot of the recumbent statue is a bronze Fame, and the corner figures of Justice, Prudence, Religion, and Liberty complete the tomb's symbolic program. Stressing his monument's architectural character, De Keyser has made his sculptures serve the structure. The figures combine a thorough understanding of Renaissance forms with the realism and modes of expression characteristic of Dutch Calvinism. De Keyser was also responsible for numerous architectural projects.

894

893 ROBERT LE LORRAIN (French, 1666–1743) · *The Horses of the Sun*, Hôtel de Rohan, Paris · Ca. 1712.

Le Lorrain was a pupil of Girardon, from whom he inherited an admirable feeling for relief. His carving of the four Horses of the Sun at their watering place, over the stable doors of the Hôtel de Rohan in Paris, can be considered as his masterpiece. The rearing, plunging horses, with tossing manes, emerge with the grooms from the clouds about the setting sun, done in very low relief. For the horses, the artist drew inspiration from those in the Thetis Grotto at Versailles, by the brothers Marsy and J. Guérin.

893

895 ARTUS QUELLIN (Flemish, 1609–1668) · *Frieze* from the marble fireplace in the Burgomaster's Room, Royal Palace, Amsterdam (formerly the Town Hall) · Ca. 1650.

The scene here reproduced shows the son of Fabius Maximus ordering his father to dismount as a sign of respect for the son's office. Quellin, from Antwerp, had received his formal training in Rubens' circle and had then been influenced by antique art, to which Duquesnoy had initiated him in Rome. Called to Amsterdam in 1650, he learned to modify his Rubensian Italianism to comply with the classicism of the architect Van Campen. He carved a number of altars in Flanders, and his busts, executed in Holland, are counted among the finest achievements in northern Baroque art.

897 LUCAS FAYDHERBE (Flemish, 1617–1697) · *Tomb of Archbishop Cruysen*, Cathedral, Mechelen (Malines) · 1660.

A sculptor, ivory-maker, and architect, Faydherbe, born in Malines, was the only leading sculptor of his generation who never went to Italy; but he collaborated closely with Rubens, hence his pictorial and theatrical style. After a series of apostles for Brussels Cathedral, he produced his most important work with this funerary monument in marble. Its central figure of the kneeling prelate is far superior to the flanking figures of Christ and Chronos. Abounding in details that are astonishing if not convincing, his production in general is very uneven.

897

898 MICHAEL ZÜRN, THE YOUNGER · (1636–1691) · *Angel from the Candida Altar*, Benedictine Church, Kremsmunster (Upper Austria) · Ca. 1682.

About 1700 Kremsmunster, which had been a flourishing center of art under the Carolingians, became a major center of Austrian Baroque art. The kneeling angel, in white marble from Salzburg, is one of the numerous figures carved by Zürn for the decoration of the side altars at Kremsmunster. Born in Wasserburg (Austria), he settled at Gmunden after having spent several years in Italy, where he was able to develop his natural inclinations towards Baroque movement and a feeling of pathos.

898

896

896 ROMBOUT VERHULST (Flemish, 1624–1698) · *Bust of Marie van Reygersberg* · Terra cotta · Rijksmuseum, Amsterdam.

A native of Malines in what is now Belgium, this aristocrat of Flemish sculpture settled in Holland where he busied himself above all with monuments to the glory of the pioneers of the young Batavian Republic. Chief collaborator of Quellin on the Amsterdam town hall, he produced for it exceptionally successful works such as the statues of Silence and of Fidelity. In his portraits he allied the sober realism typical of Holland to a supremely skillful rendering of details such as hair and clothing, and he modelled flesh with a sensitivity which seems to make hard materials malleable and expressive. This terra-cotta bust is a typical example.

899   MATTHIAS STEINL (1644–1727) · *Emperor Joseph I on Horseback* ·
Kunsthistorisches Museum, Vienna.

Steinl, a painter, sculptor, engineer and architect, was born in Bavaria
and died in Vienna. He had been living in Klagenfurt for a long time
when he was called to the Austrian court to serve as imperial ivory-
worker (*Kammerkünstler*) from 1688 to 1712. He later became profes-
sor of architecture at the Academy of Fine Arts in Vienna. A versatile
artist, he made altars, portals, furniture, and decorations for churches
and monasteries, and provided numerous designs and projects in the
various branches of art and craft. The statue of Emperor Joseph I
ranks with the equestrian statues of the Emperors Leopold I and
Charles VI as one of the most perfect of Baroque ivories.

899

900   *Column to Commemorate the Plague* (Dreifaltigkeitssäule), detail,
Vienna · 1679–1692.

The votive monument on the Graben in Vienna, dedicated to the Holy
Trinity and to the Nine Choirs of Angels, was carried out in fulfilment
of a vow made by Leopold I at the time of the plague in 1679. It was
completed in 1692 by Mathias Rauchmiller from a design by Franz
Menegatti. The whole takes the form of an obelisk, veiled in clouds and
crowned by a gilt bronze Holy Trinity by P. Strudel and J. Kilian.
The base is by Fischer von Erlach in the style of such temporary
festive decorations as those designed by Lodovico Burnacini. The
Emperor is depicted at prayer and Heresy is conquered by Religion.
The angels are by P. Strudel, M. Rauchmiller, T. Kracker, J. Frühwirt
and M. Gunst.

900

901

901   GREGORIO FERNANDEZ (Spanish, died 1636) · *Pietà* · San Martin,
Valladolid.

Gregorio Fernandez (or Hernandez) is cited for the first time in 1605,
as a sculptor in Valladolid; he died in that city in 1636. Fernandez,
one of the masters of the Castilian school, was an independent genius
who owed nothing to Italian influence. He excelled in the representation of the Christian drama – the Passion – of which he emphasized
the physical aspects. This mysticism, profound and popular, this
direct association with the divine suffering, as well as the use of
broken lines and deeply cut, angular folds, marks a return to the
Gothic spirit. The art of Fernandez had considerable influence on
popular 17th-century Castilian sculpture.

902   GREGORIO FERNANDEZ · *The Dead Christ* · El Pardo, Madrid.

The theme of the dead Christ, crucified or *gisant,* was treated frequently by Fernandez. After the 16th century the scene was reduced to the
representation of Christ alone, without the traditional mourners. Here,
anecdote is suppressed; this is the Christ of Sorrows, stiffened in the
rigor of death – the extreme expression of realism in sculpture. The
bone structure is insistently marked, the eyes hollow, the cheeks
sunken. The very realistic polychromy accentuates the physical aspect
of the Passion; streams of coagulated blood run down the cheeks and
disappear into the beard. Such conceptions emphasize the function of
image that 17th-century Spanish sculpture served.

902

904

903 JUAN MARTÍNEZ MONTÁÑEZ (Spanish, 1568–1649) · *The Merciful Christ*, Seville Cathedral · Ca. 1603.

This polychromed wood Christ on the Cross is one of the most elevated expressions of the Christian theology. Commissioned in 1603, it dates from Montáñez' early years. The contract with Montáñez survives, and in it are laid down in minute detail the smallest particulars of the iconological theme that the artist was to follow. The Christ was to be attached to the cross by four nails, as described in the Revelations of Saint Bridget, and he must be represented as "alive, just before dying, with his head leaning towards the right and looking at a faithful believer kneeling at his feet..." Impassioned with all Christological themes, the Spanish people imposed on their image-makers the task of evoking the various moments in the agony of the Crucifixion; this image conveys Christ's supreme mercy for sinners.

904 MANUEL PEREYRA (Portuguese, 1588–1683) · *San Bruno*, Cartuja de Miraflores (Burgos).

With the Portuguese artist Pereyra, Spanish art veers toward classicism. The famous San Bruno of the Carthusian house of Miraflores can be attributed safely to him on stylistic grounds. Pereyra is representative of the second trend in 17th-century Spanish art, stemming from the reform of Philip II. The San Bruno is a realistic, almost naturalistic portrait. The sculptor has completely mastered his technique, and he works in a balanced, sober, and descriptive style. The emaciated head with its hollow eye-sockets illustrates the lessons learned from the Italian Quattrocento. The polychromy by Francisco Camilo accentuates the play of light and shade in the modelling.

903

905

905 JUAN MARTÍNEZ MONTÁÑEZ · *Head of the Merciful Christ*; detail of fig. 903.

The face of the most perfect of men retains all its serene beauty in the hour of his suffering. Lowered with infinite tenderness towards the sinners, his eyes express a profound sadness, his open mouth seems about to utter the words of forgiveness. The real torment of God, who was sacrificed for man, was not his bodily pain but the tragedy of so many souls led astray in sin. The Spanish image-makers carved these works with great piety: for them, to sculpture a figure of Christ was not only to produce a work of art, but to offer a prayer; Montáñez used to take communion before setting to work.

906 JUAN MARTÍNEZ MONTÁÑEZ · *The Adoration of the Shepherds*, detail of the reredos of San Isidoro del Campo, Santiponce · 1609–1613.

A Baroque element gradually made its appearance in the style of Montáñez, and his most beautiful works are those executed in his youth. They are also more clearly stamped with his individuality, for, as time went on, his success obliged him to make use of assistants. The Santiponce Altarpiece is his masterpiece. He signed the contract for it in 1609 and completed it in 1613. In it, carvings of different saints and various scenes from the Gospel are grouped around a statue of St. Jerome. The Adoration of the Shepherds is one of the most beautiful of his classicizing compositions, with its angels and shepherds fervently gathering around the figure of Jesus in a deep silence inspired by the mystery of the divine Infant.

906

907 JUAN MARTÍNEZ MONTÁÑEZ · *St. Ignatius Loyola* (detail). Chapel, Seville University · Ca. 1610.

In celebration of St. Ignatius Loyola's beatification in 1610, Montáñez carved a statue of the saint, founder of the Society of Jesus. It was painted by Pacheco. As can be verified by the plaster death-mask, which is still preserved, the head is a very lifelike portrait. True to his own gentle temperament, however, Montáñez softened the energetic visage of the former soldier, who had conceived of his order as a militia, and gave him an expression of pity. The statue decorates the chapel of Seville University, for which Montáñez at a later date also carved a St. Francis Borgia as a counterpart.

907

908

908 ALONSO CANO (Spanish, 1601–1667) · *Eve*, Cathedral, Granada · Ca. 1667.

Alonso Cano's was a life of considerable drama; before he became a priest, he had been unjustly accused of murdering his wife. He was a painter, an architect, and a sculptor. From 1652 onwards he worked for the *capilla mayor* of the Granada Cathedral, painting pictures illustrating the life of the Virgin; and at the end of his life, when about 1666 or 1667 he returned to Granada to present his plans for the cathedral façade, he carved two colossal wooden busts of Adam and Eve as part of the same decoration. He left the Adam unfinished and it was completed by Juan Velez de Ulloa. The Eve shows Alonso Cano already in the 17th century looking forward to the effeminate, elegant imagery of 18th-century Granada. This face sparkles with intelligence and its coquettish charm has a hint of voluptuousness.

909

909 *St. Lawrence* (detail) · São Lorenzo de Los Indios, Niteroi Brazil, mid-17th century.

At the end of the 16th and the beginning of the 17th century, Brazil began to erect permanent monuments. The Jesuits played the role of pioneers by building their colleges in the towns, and farming establishments, called *aldeias*, in the country. São Lorenzo de Los Indios of Niteroi, near Rio de Janeiro, was one of the latter. Rooted in Portuguese art, Brazilian art of the 17th century emphasized still further the gravity characteristic of the Portuguese, as well as their tendency to look back from Baroque art to broadly classical principles. This polychromed wood statue of St. Lawrence is reminiscent of Florentine quattrocento sculpture. It was carved for the chapel of the São Lorenzo *aldeia*, built in 1627.

401

910 *The Holy Family*; relief from an altarpiece · Portugal, 17th century · Museu Machado de Castro, Coimbra.

In 17th-century Spain there was a division between the expressionistic Baroque style of Gregorio Fernandez in Castile and the grave classicism of Andalusia, exemplified in the sculpture of Montáñez and the painting of Zurbaran. Portugal, on the other hand, remained faithful to classicism for almost the whole of the 17th century. It followed a natural inclination which, in religious images, tended towards silent sobriety, meditation, and the expression of an inner life.

910

911 *Façade of Santa Croce*, Lecce (Apulia); detail of the upper part · Finished 1695.

While the structure of the Baroque buildings of Apulia remained impoverished, under the influence of Spanish art and also of Romanesque traditions the façades were covered with an extremely intricate ornamentation, made possible by the soft local limestone. Begun in 1549, Santa Croce was finished in 1695. Above the portals is a classicizing frieze, with thirteen consoles recalling Romanesque art; these support a balustrade decorated with vases and putti. The uppermost part of the façade, later in date, is worked in even more detail; it is surmounted by a mediocre pediment, but the harmony of the whole is saved by the central rose window.

911

912 GIACOMO SERPOTTA (Italian, 1656–1732) · *Humility*, Oratory of San Lorenzo, Palermo · Ca. 1700.

In the last years of the 17th century the Sicilian sculptor Giacomo Serpotta was commissioned to decorate the Oratory of San Lorenzo. He illustrated the lives of saints Francesco and Lorenzo in high-relief scenes, accompanying these with appropriate allegorical figures in the round. With the scenes of San Lorenzo is one of the artist's most graceful works, the figure of Humility, represented as a young woman with fluttering draperies, surrounded by four groups of flying putti. Executed, as are the reliefs, entirely in stucco – a material that demands speed in working and allows no vacillation – the group shows the artist's great virtuosity.

912

913 *Interior of the Cappella Sansevero*, Naples · Decorated in the mid-18th century.

Founded at the end of the 16th century as a funerary chapel for the Sangro di San Severo princes, the Sansevero chapel had its great period of glory in the middle of the 18th century; it was at that time that the brilliant Raimondo di Sangro, Prince of Sansevero, made his generous contributions to the development of the arts and letters in Naples. He called upon the Venetian sculptor, Antonio Corradini, who came to Naples to execute the chapel in 1750, but died there only two years later. The Prince then called in the Genoese Francesco Queirolo, who continued the work of his predecessor.

913

915 ANTONIO CORRADINI (Italian, 1668–1752) · *Modesty*, Cappella Sansevero, Naples.

When called to Naples by Raimondo di Sangro, Antonio Corradini had come to the end of a career that had taken him through Germany, Austria, and Bohemia; his Rococo style was understandably permeated with foreign influences. Corradini executed the statue of Modesty as a tribute to Cecilia Gaetani, Raimondo's mother, who had suggested to the artist that he should portray her in a new allegorical form, derived from the iconography of Spring. Taking up his favorite theme of women thinly veiled in transparent drapery, the artist concentrated almost exclusively on the surface finish, creating his last bravura piece.

915

914 LUIGI VANVITELLI (Italian, 1700–1773) · *Diana and Acteon*, gardens of the royal residence, Caserta (Naples) · Designed ca. 1770.

Luigi Vanvitelli designed simultaneously the palace and the gardens of Caserta for Charles III Bourbon. The fountains which he planned for either side of the waterfall were to illustrate ancient myths related to the theme of water. By 1773, when he died, none of them had been carried out. His son, Carlo, succeeded him, but finances were much reduced and only the Diana and Acteon group conforms to the preliminary studies. Though executed by second-rate sculptors who drew inspiration directly from Hellenistic models, they nevertheless form a charming and animated ensemble.

914

916

919 JOSÉ CHURRIGUERA (Spanish, 1665–1725) · *Main altar*, San Esteban, Salamanca · Ca. 1700.

This grandiose altar, whose construction required more than four thousand pieces of wood, inaugurated Baroque 18th-century architecture. It was designed in 1693 by José Benito Churriguera, who had won fame at Salamanca in 1689 with his design of a huge catafalque for the funeral ceremony of Doña Maria Luisa de Barbón, wife of Charles II. José belonged to a family of Salamanca architects who enriched their city with some very fine monuments. If we compare this altarpiece with that executed by Bernardo Simon de Piñeda in 1670–1673, for Santa Caridad in Seville, it is clear that the latter is still the work of a sculptor; the San Esteban altarpiece is the first example of 18th-century Baroque style *entallador*, which obtains its effects from the rhythm of the decorated surface, supported by a robust, monumental structure. (Height about 100 feet.)

916 *Neapolitan presepio* · 18th century · Bayerisches Nationalmuseum, Munich.

The art of presenting the Nativity in three-dimensional form goes back to the Middle Ages but reached its climax in the eighteenth century in Genoa and Naples especially. The heads of the figurines for these Christmas crèches were modelled either in wood or terra-cotta and eyes of glass were set in. The figures were dressed in the most sumptuous embroidered and brocaded stuffs. This became the specialty of a great many craftsmen including sculptors, waxworkers, potters, embroiderers and jewelers, but at times even distinguished artists like Lorenzo Vaccaro and his disciple Bartolommeo Granucci did not disdain to turn their hands to this humble but charming art.

917 *Feasting*; detail of a Neapolitan presepio, 18th century · Bayerisches Nationalmuseum, Munich.

Charles de Bourbon, a mystic by nature, showed a great interest in the popular, homely representations of the Nativity. The *presepio* or crèche groups were no longer confined to the religious episode but became vast scenographic compositions, often intended as ephemeral, which put on show the various aspects of Neapolitan life, in the city and in the surrounding countryside: scenes with beggars, women going to market, musicians, wood-cutters, peasants, farmyards. These humble portrayals of everyday life, often rendered with great concern for realism, form the best part of Neapolitan production in the 18th century.

917

918

918 *Portal* of the palace of the Marqués de Dos Aguas, Valencia · Alabaster · Spanish, 18th century.

In 1740–1744 the Marqués de Dos Aguas had his palace in Valencia remodelled by the painter Hipólito Rovira Brocantel and the sculptors Luis Domingo and Ignacio Vergara (1715–1776). The paintings with which Brocantel decorated the exterior walls were destroyed in the 19th century. The alabaster ensemble of the main portal by Vergara is one of the most important in Spanish 18th-century sculpture. A statue of the Virgin appears in a niche above the door, and two figures of Rivers, symbols of the name of the marquess, decorate the jambs. Everything flows in this naturalistic work, whose modelling evokes modern sculpture.

920

920 NARCISCO TOMÉ (Spanish, active 1715–1742) · *Transparente*, Cathedral, Toledo · 1721–1732.

The extraordinary *Transparente* set behind the main altar of the *capilla mayor* in Toledo Cathedral originated in the wish of Bishop Diego de Astorga y Céspedes to mark the presence of the Holy Sacrament with a glorious monument. Owing to its fantastic nature, the complexity of the forms, the mingling of stucco, painting, bronze, and all varieties of colored marbles, the quality of this decoration can not be grasped from a photograph. It is a sort of frenzy of images and symbols projected into space; of fluid, vaporous forms reminiscent of Art Nouveau but more passionate and explosive. This monument cost 200,000 ducats and provoked prodigious enthusiasm, expressed in a poem wherein it was acclaimed "the Eighth Wonder of the World."

921

921 FRANCISCO SALZILLO (Spanish, 1707–1783) · *Dolorosa* · Ermita de Jesus, Murcia.

The mundane rhetoric in the works of Francisco Salzillo (also spelled Zarcillo) might be interpreted as the expression of a decadence of religious feeling; but in fact it springs from a deep-rooted faith. While yet a child, Francisco Salzillo entered a Dominican monastery as a novice. When he was twenty, he left the monastery to assume direction of the atelier of his father, Vincente Nicolas Salzillo, who died in 1727. Vincente Nicolas had come from Naples to settle in Murcia at the end of the 17th century. Undoubtedly, the breath of Italianism which he brought with him was instrumental in dispelling some of the gravity that the Spanish sculptors typically imparted to their religious works. The workshop of Francisco Salzillo, who was helped by his brothers, was amazingly productive; Léon Bermudez has counted 1,792 works definitely by the master's hand.

922

922 JACINTO VIEIRA (Portuguese) · *St. Gertrude*, Monastery church, Aruca (Portugal) · Ca. 1725.

With the gaps that still exist in present-day scholarship, the sculptors of these numerous 18th-century religious images decorating Portuguese churches are mainly anonymous. But we do know the author of the group of Benedictine female saints decorating the *coro* of the Aruca monastery church. In 1725 payment for the figures was made to a sculptor from Braga, Jacinto Vieira. Carved in wood, the statues are painted white to simulate stone; they are exquisite examples of the cult of femininity that inspired so many 18th-century artists.

924 *Nave and main altar*, Santa Clara, Oporto · Ca. 1740.

The 17th-century Portuguese churches, generally small in size, were decorated with altars of gilded wood. During the 18th century the decoration spread to cover not just the altars, but also the walls and ceiling – in effect transforming the sanctuary into a kind of mystical golden casket. The most beautiful churches of this kind can be found in northern Portugal, at Oporto and at Braga. San Francesco at Oporto, a large Gothic church with three naves, was decorated entirely this way between 1733 and 1744, as was Santa Clara. The latter's smaller size makes it a more gem-like work.

923

923 *Two Atlantes*, main altar, Nossa Senhora da Pena, Lisbon
1720–1730.

Portuguese artists were virtuosi in this art of *talha dourada*, which
during the 17th and 18th centuries was in general confined to the
decoration of churches, though it was also used in the Coimbra University library. The columns framing the altars and supporting the
baldacchino rest on consoles often borne by angels or atlantes. If the
Lisbon school of *talha dourada* seems less rich than that of the north,
it is due to the earthquake of 1755, which destroyed a number of
important churches.

924

925 *The Holy Family* · Portuguese, second half of the 18th century · Museum, Aveiro (Portugal).

In the second half of the 18th century, the taste for the charming
images employed in Neapolitan Nativity scenes spread to Spain and
Portugal, where they gained wide popularity. They inspired little
statues in mannered attitudes and with coquettish Rococo expressions,
not unlike the porcelain statuettes from Meissen and Nymphenburg.
The figurine, often reduced to the size of a mantelpiece ornament, was
appreciated all over Europe in the 17th century. The polychromy of
18th-century Portuguese statues was particularly fine, for the country's
wealth enabled the artists to be liberal in their use of gold.

925

926 Antonio Francesco Lisboa, known as o Aleijadinho (Brazilian, 1738–1814) · *Christ Carrying the Cross*, Congonhas do Campo
(Brazil) · 1796–1799.

At the end of the Baroque era, in the state of Minas Gerais, Brazil, the
greatest artist was a mulatto architect and sculptor. A strange disease
that caused the shriveling of his hands and feet earned him the nickname of *o Aleijadinho* (the little cripple). He built churches, carved
altarpieces, and created wood and stone sculptures. The polychromed
wood Stations of the Cross in the sanctuary of Congonhas do Campo
were carved between 1796 and 1799. These images of Christ are the last
great renderings of this theme of the Passion, which had inspired masterpieces for so many centuries.

926

927

Between 1800 and 1805, Aleijadinho executed twelve stone statues of prophets, just over life-size, for the terrace in front of the Congonhas do Campo sanctuary. He took up the old theme of the Dispute of the Prophets, revivifying the exhausted topic by infusing into it an expressionistic force reminiscent of the Middle Ages. For the costumes and figure types he found inspiration in a series of Florentine copper engravings from about 1470, which retained some flavor of the oriental dress worn by the Byzantine contingent to the Council of Florence between 1439 and 1442.

929

928 O Aleijadinho · *The Bad Thief*, Sanctuary of Congonhas do Campo (Brazil) · 1796–1799.

The Stations of the Cross at Congonhas do Campo consist of sixty-six statues divided among the six chapels or *passos*; so numerous a group could only have been carried out with the collaboration of a whole workshop. The less important figures, entrusted to helpers, are on the whole rather crude in workmanship. However, the Bad Thief from the scene of the Nailing to the Cross is definitely by Aleijadinho's own hand. In the muscular body and enraged expression, the talented mulatto expresses the supreme revolt of the man who rejects God's grace.

928

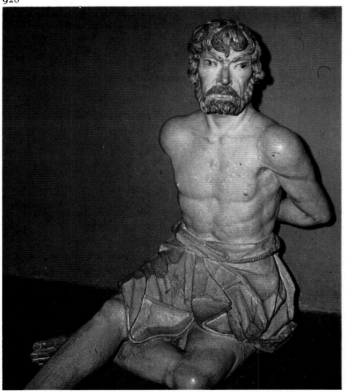

929 *Portal* of the Sanctuary of Angagua, near Paracutín (Mexico) · 1577.

The churches of the New World built by the Spanish conquerors reflect the architecture of Spain, but the native tradition of the Indian workmen is often apparent in their sculptural decoration. At Angagua, flattened, densely covered decorative fields surround the portal, contrasting with the plain surface of the façade.

930

930 *Spire*, Santa Prisca y San Sebastián, Taxco (Mexico) · 1754–1761.

Begun in 1754, the church of Santa Prisca y San Sebastián in Taxco was built (including its inside altars) in seven years; this rapid execution accounts for its unity, rare in a monument of this size. In an austere, mountainous setting it stands like a hymn to the glory of God, as proclaimed by an inscription on the outside of the tiled cupola: *Gloria a Dio en las Alturas*. It was built with funds donated by José de la Borda, a man from Aragon who had accumulated an immense fortune by exploiting the Taxco silver mines. From a base almost bare of decoration rise towers covered with a wealth of ornament and figures, reminiscent of jewelled candelabra; 18th-century Spanish Baroque art often calls to mind the spirit of the Plateresque.

931

931 ANDREAS SCHLÜTER (1664–1714) · *Equestrian statue of the Great Elector*, Charlottenburger Schloss, Berlin.

This statue was cast in bronze by Johann Jakobi and inaugurated in 1703; the base was finished in 1708. Born in Hamburg, Schlüter studied in Danzig, in Holland, Paris, and Italy. Court sculptor first at Warsaw and then in Berlin, he fell into disgrace in 1706 and died in St. Petersburg. He was a born sculptor, whose feeling for monumentality was developed to a high degree. This statue is one of the most spectacular performances of Baroque sculpture – the symbolic glorification of political absolutism. (Height, 9 feet 6 inches.)

932 BALTHASAR PERMOSER (1651–1732) *Atlante* · The Zwinger, Dresden.

A native of Kammer, in Bavaria, Permoser learned his art in Salzburg, Vienna and Italy, in particular in Venice, Rome and Florence. In 1689 he was called to the court of Dresden by Frederick Augustus of Saxony and there was set to work, in collaboration with the architect Pöppelman, on the Zwinger, a palace with ample grounds for open-air festivities. Derived from Italian sources, Permoser's art combined capricious curves with decorative exuberance in a half-pompous, half-bucolic style which became the standard for Rococo garden statuary.

932

409

933

933 EGID QUIRIN ASAM (1692–1750) · *The Assumption of the Virgin*, high altar, monastery church, Rohr (Bavaria) · 1718–1725.

E. Q. Asam, architect and sculptor, was born in Tegernsee (Bavaria) and died in Mannheim. He studied in Rome under Pietro da Cortona, then collaborated with his brother, Cosmas Damian Asam. In the work reproduced, the life-size stucco figures, lightly touched with gilt and colors, assume animated poses of wonder and awe, as the Virgin rises airily from her massive sarcophagus. In this theatrical scene, light floods from either side, its source concealed by the red marble pillars, transfiguring the actors on earth, while in the sky the Holy Trinity, bathed in a golden light, is enthroned in glory.

934 FRANZ JOSEPH IGNAZ HOLZINGER (Austrian, 1691–1775) · *Head of St. John the Baptist*, on an altar in the church of Metten (Bavaria) · 1722–24.

Holzinger was born in Attersee (Upper Austria) and died at St. Florian. He devoted most of his time to the decoration of St. Florian monastery, where he was already recorded as working in 1719 (on the common rooms, on those of the prelates, and on the imperial apartments). As a sculptor he proved himself equal to Steinl (see fig. 892), and as a stucco-worker, he was one of the most skillful practitioners of his time, but kept to the forms of the first Rococo phase. This head is from a great sculptural and decorative ensemble, including various altars and the entire interior design of the church, all by Holzinger.

934

935 *Ornament of the Spiegelsaal* (Hall of Mirrors) in the Amalienburg, Nymphenburg Park, Munich · 1734–1739.

The hunting pavilion is the most enchanting of the four pleasure retreats in the Nymphenburg park. It was built for Princess Maria Amalia, wife of Karl Albrecht, by a Frenchman of Belgian origin, François Cuvilliés, who was born at Soignies and died in Munich. The ornament and sculpture in white, silver, and pale blue were executed by the stuccoist J. B. Zimmermann and the cabinetmaker J. Dietrich, from drawings by Cuvilliés. They offer a picturesque range of Rococo variations on the theme of hunting and fishing. In the dazzling mirrors, with their reflection of the pale, silvery forms, reality appears to dissolve in shimmering wraiths of vapor. The Spiegelsaal is the climactic central element in a series of apartments creating a new ideal in interior decorations.

936 *Interior of the monastery church*, Diessen · Bavarian, 1732–1739.

This is a typical collective work of the early Rococo period and is the result of the collaboration of a number of artists: Joh. Mich. Fischer, the architect; Fr. Cuvilliés, the designer of the main altar; J. G. Bergmuller, frescoist; J. Dietrich, sculptor of the statues of the Elders of the Church; J. B. Straub, who carved the pulpit; J. G. Uebelherr and the Feichtmayr brothers, who made the stucco decoration. The last two, Franz Zaver Feichtmayr (1705–1764) and Joh. Michael Feichtmayr (1709–1772) were trained in the Wessobrunn school. The high-keyed, weightless, moving ornament is among the most sophisticated examples of German Rococo.

935

936

937 *Organ*, Benedictine abbey church of Ottobeuren · 1754–1756.

The stalls and woodwork of the organ in the "Swabian Escorial" were done by Josef Christian, sculptor, Martin Hormann, cabinetmaker and Karl Josef Riepp, organ-maker, who together created one of the most beautiful musical instruments of all time. The relationship of masses and supports on the triple-storied organ, beneath the frescoed vault, the exuberance of forms in the cabinetwork and stuccoes, the variety in the sculptural vocabulary for the atlantes and the gilded reliefs – in themselves suggesting a harmony appropriate to 18th-century musical forms – combine in the ideal, total masterpiece that was to transmit the monks' prayers to the Heavens. It is the only 18th-century organ that still preserves entire its original form.

937

938

939 JOSEF CHRISTIAN (1706–1777) · *Bust of the Prophet Ezekiel*, Benedictine abbey church of Ottobeuren · Ca. 1764.

Joseph Christian was born in Riedlingen (Württemberg) and played a major role in the decoration of this church, renovated by the Abbot Rupert Ness in 1764 for the celebration of the millennium of Ottobeuren. Christian achieved a sensitive and coherent ensemble in the decoration of the church, which offers an excellent example of successful collaboration with other artists. He exploited his gifts to the full without ever overreaching himself, working with the humility and conviction of a servant of both art and religion.

939

938 JOSEF CHRISTIAN · *St. Benedict chanting psalms*: detail of fig. 937.

Contrasting with the dynamic exuberance of the atlantes and the overall decoration is the calmer style appearing in the nine gilded wood reliefs representing scenes from the life of St. Benedict. The sculptor conveys the idea of deep space through the perspective flight of the architecture and the variation in the depth of the relief, from forms almost in outline to forms modelled in the round. The restraint and gracefulness of his subtly modelled surfaces, distantly reminiscent of Ghiberti, create an intimate atmosphere in which is revealed the Rococo feeling for the supernatural and the ecstatic. (Height 7 feet, width 4 feet 7 inches.)

940 JOSEF-ANTON FEICHTMAYR (1696–1770) · *Angel*, parish church of St. Mary, Neubirnau (Lake Constance).

This sculptor, stucco decorator, and engraver was born in Linz and spent almost the whole of his life at Minnenhausen, working alternately at Salem abbey and Neubirnau church, the former Cistercian pilgrimage church which was affiliated with the abbey. In this church by Peter Thumb, a gem of Swabian religious Baroque, Feichtmayr carried out an interior decoration of rare quality. The soft graduation of forms and colors is remarkable.

940

941 JOSEF-ANTON FEICHTMAYR · *Pietà*, St. Mary, Neubirnau (Lake Constance).

This Station of the Cross is one of eight surviving from an original fourteen attributed to Feichtmayr and his collaborators, Joh. Georg and Franz Anton Durr. The finest among his works are the stalls, confessionals, and reliefs of the life of St. Benedict at St. Gall, and these Stations, which are the most vigorous of all in style. Trained among stucco-workers at Wessobrunn, he became a typical representative of the Bavarian Rococo and achieved an international reputation.

941

942

942 DOMINIKUS ZIMMERMANN (1685–1766) · *Pulpit*, Pilgrimage Church, Wies · 1746–1756.

Most "Bavarian" of all the stucco-workers from Wessobrunn, the architect and sculptor Zimmermann spent his whole life building rural churches, and died in Wies. This pilgrimage church and the one at Steinhausen are his masterpieces, achieving a poetic rendering of space and responding to a popular demand for enchantment and religious euphoria. The pulpit, executed with the collaboration of J. and F. Steinhauser, is one of the most striking manifestations of Bavarian fantasy and illustrates the metamorphosis of the weightier religious Baroque style into the lilting, musical forms of the Rococo.

943

943 IGNAZ GÜNTHER (1725–1775) · *The Annunciation*, parish church of Weyarn (Schliersee) · 1763.

Sculptor and architect, Ignaz Günther was born at Altmannstein, was a pupil of Straub and Donner, then worked in Salzburg before becoming court sculptor at Munich in 1773. He left behind him a considerable production. His works of 1763 at Weyarn are especially interesting: they consist of the Annunciation, a Pietà, and figures of Saints, carved in wood and painted in soft, light colors. This Rococo imagery, animated by a gentle religious fervor, achieves a luminous mystical effect through its flowing grace and the lightly curving upward movements.

944

944 JOSEF THADDAEUS STAMMEL (1695–1765) · *Descent into Hell* · Wood (gilt bronzing modern), over life-size · Library of the Benedictine Abbey of Admont, Styria, Austria.

Born in Graz, this sculptor spent some time in Italy but afterwards shunned the newer currents. For the abbey of Admont he turned out his best work, in the form of sculptured decorations, medallions, statues and religious scenes. As was customary at the time, this statue was part of an overall program, in this case the Four Last Ends of Man. With strange power, Stammel ventured to carry over into sculpture a type of representation previously confined to painting, and this work constitutes a final brief flare-up of medieval expressionism.

945

945 MATTHIAS BRAUN (1684–1738) · *Garinus the Hermit*, Bethlehem Park, near Kukus (Czechoslovakia) · 1726–1731.

The idea of carving figures out of the natural rock has often been exploited in the Middle East, in India, and in China, but not so often in the West. Michelangelo used to dream of sculpturing a whole mountain of Carrara marble. The most famous western example is the enchanted garden of the Bomarzo villa, in Latium (see fig. 819). In northern Bohemia, near the sanctuary hospice of Kukus, the rocks in a park were carved into religious images by Matthias Braun between 1726 and 1731. The site is a wood, in which the pilgrim discovers sculptural groups representing scenes from the life of Christ, the penitent Magdalen, and various hermits.

946

946 FERDINAND DIETZ (1709–1777) · *Mount Parnassus*, Lake in Veitshöchheim Park (Würzburg) · 1765.

Born in Eisenberg in Bohemia, Dietz was a pupil of M. Braun in Prague. His best-known and most numerous efforts are the stone statues that he carved for the gardens of the Bamberg and Würzburg Residences, to which the Bishop-Prince Adam Friedrich von Seinsheim summoned him as court sculptor. The Parnassus group is surmounted by a Pegasus, with Apollo, the Muses, a dragon, sea-lions, and atlantes, groups of children, sphinxes, and Chinese pavilions clustered about a kind of imaginary ruin. In part owing to Dietz's sculptures, Veitschöchheim is one of the most appealing Rococo gardens in Germany.

948 MICHAEL VERVOORT (1667–1737) · *Pulpit* · 1723 · Cathedral, Malines.

After a fourteen-year stay in Rome, Vervoort returned to his native town, Antwerp. There, he specialized in carving pulpits decorated by figures and foliage, vivid and picturesque illustrations in sculpture of themes for sermons, handled with extravagant rhetoric. With an appeal to the senses intended to enhance the efficacy of religious eloquence, the sculptor here represents the dramatic conversion of St. Norbert, who has fallen off his horse at the foot of the Crucified Christ, near a cave and a storm-tossed copse. The pulpit, executed for the Leliendaal convent, was completed by J. F. Van Geel.

947

947 GEORG RAPHAEL DONNER (Austrian, 1693–1741) · *Allegory of the River Traun* · 1739 · Baroque Museum, Belvedere, Vienna.

Born at Esslingen in Lower Austria, first a metalworker and then a sculptor, Donner spent some time in Italy and then became a medal-engraver in Salzburg. After working in Pressburg for the Primate of Hungary, he returned to Vienna, where he executed this figure for the Mehlmarkt fountain, his masterpiece. Making the sculpture quite independent, he softens the Baroque style with a typical Viennese taste for playful or elegiac sweetness. He looks forward to classicism and at the same time to Romantic sensitivity.

948

949

949 LAMBERT-SIGISBERT ADAM (French, 1700–1759) · *Prometheus* · 1767 · The Louvre, Paris.

Adam's art was influenced by the Italian Baroque, which he had assimilated in Rome. Prometheus, the artist's presentation piece for the Academy in 1767, reveals a facile inspiration, great technical skill ostentatiously displayed, and a real sense for the decorative. His Triumph of Neptune and Amphitrite at Versailles, created with his brother Nicolas-Sebastian, is an exemplary work of French Rococo sculptural style.

950

Guillaume Coustou, nephew of Coysevox, worked in Versailles, Paris and Marly. The two horses, which have stood since 1794 in the Place de la Concorde at the entrance to the Champs-Elysées, were executed in 1740–1745 for the Terrasse de l'Abreuvoir in Marly, as a replacement for the Mercury and the Fame by Coysevox, which were transferred to the entrance to the Tuileries gardens in 1719. In each of the marbles by Coustou a rider tries to tame a wild horse; through the overlay of classicizing antique inspiration emerges the naturalism and impetuosity of Baroque forms.

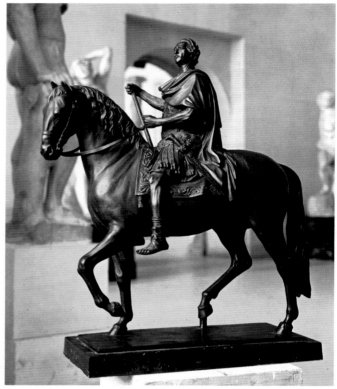

952

952 After EDMÉ BOUCHARDON (French, 1698–1762) · *Bronze model of the equestrian statue of Louis XV* · 1748–1758 · The Louvre, Paris.

Born at Chaumont, Bouchardon became a pupil of Guillaume Coustou in Paris, and then worked in Rome between 1723 and 1732. His style falls within the trend of the classical reaction against Rococo excesses. The Roman-style equestrian statue of Louis XV, commissioned by the City of Paris in 1748 for the Place Louis XV, was preceded by a number of preparatory drawings. Cast in 1758 and inaugurated in 1763 after the death of the sculptor, it was destroyed in the Revolution in 1792. It is known to us, however, through engravings and such small bronze models as one in the Louvre, made by Louis Vassé. The original pedestal was completed by Pigalle. (Height, 27 inches.)

951

951 ÉTIENNE-MAURICE FALCONET (French, 1716–1791), *Monument to Peter the Great* · Bronze · 1766–1777 · Leningrad.

Falconet, who was born and died in Paris, was, with Pigalle, the favorite sculptor of Mme. de Pompadour. His masterpiece is the statue of Peter the Great commissioned by Catherine II for St. Petersburg. This work breaks away from the traditional equestrian statue: here the horse is rearing up on a rock. The sovereign, in heroic garb, is shown as a law-maker, a reformer. His face was sculpted by Marie-Anne Collot, a pupil of Falconet. The monument is theatrical but simple in conception, devoid of allegory except for the crushed snake.

953

953 JEAN-BAPTISTE PIGALLE (French, 1714–1785) · *Mausoleum of the Maréchal de Saxe*, St. Thomas, Strasbourg · 1753–1776.

Pigalle was born and died in Paris. A pupil of Jean-Baptiste II Lemoyne, he spent the years 1736 to 1739 in Rome. The mausoleum of the Maréchal de Saxe, begun between 1752 and 1753 and resumed in 1770, was inaugurated in 1776 in the Lutheran church of St. Thomas in Strasbourg. Standing before the pyramid of Immortality, the Maréchal moves towards the sarcophagus opened by Death, while France tries to intercede; the stricken Hercules symbolizes the French army; the leopard, lion, and eagle represent conquered nations. The strongly literary flavor of the allegories, whose meaning is given in the sculptor's memoirs, does not obscure the masterly technique with which the work is executed.

954 JEAN-ANTOINE HOUDON (French, 1741–1828) · *Diana* · Ca. 1776 · Gulbenkian Collection, Lisbon.

Houdon received his earliest training in apprenticeship to Michelangelo Slodtz; he then went to the École des Élèves Protégés in Paris, before spending four years in Rome. The idea for a statue of Diana leaving for the hunt was conceived in 1776. The marble original intended for the gardens of the Duke of Saxe-Gotha was handed down to Catherine II; from the Hermitage it passed into the Gulbenkian collection in Lisbon. In the bronze version in the Louvre, the tuft of rushes used as a support for the marble statue could be eliminated, enabling Houdon to accentuate the lightness of the figure, which is entirely classical in inspiration.

954

955

The statue of Voltaire – with the Diana, one of Houdon's finest works – was executed at the request of Madame Denis, Voltaire's niece, who gave one marble version to the Comédie Française. A second marble copy was commissioned from the artist by Catherine II. The work in the Montpellier museum is a terra-cotta cast done after the original plaster model and touched up by Houdon. The sarcastic smile and sharp sparkling eyes animate the features of the old philosopher of Ferney, whom the sculptor was able to study when Voltaire visited Paris in 1778.

957

957 AUGUSTIN PAJOU (French, 1730–1809) · *Psyche Abandoned* · 1783–1790 · The Louvre, Paris.

Pajou was born and died in Paris. He was in Rome from 1751 to 1756. The marble statue of Psyche signed and dated 1790, begun in 1783, was commissioned from the artist as a counterpart to a statue of Amor by Bouchardon. Inspired by a tale of Apuleius, it represents a nude Psyche, seated, at the moment when Eros has just left her. At her feet is the dagger; by her side, the lamp with oil flowing out of it. The modelling is lively and the pose natural; the charm and sensitivity of Pajou's art are accompanied by a return to classical antiquity which is characteristic of his time. (Height a little under 6 feet.)

956

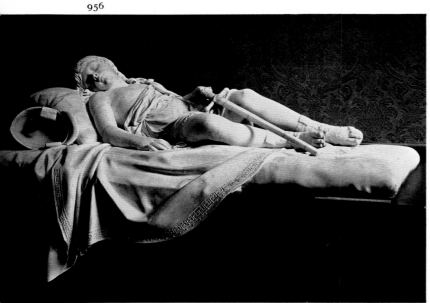

956 GOTTFRIED SCHADOW (German, 1764–1850) · *Monument of Count von der Mark*, Dorotheenstädtische Church, Berlin, 1788–1789.

Schadow, who was born and died in Berlin, is considered one of the major figures of the 19th-century German school. After several years in Rome in the 1780's, he returned to Berlin, and there, reworking a model by his teacher, Tassaert, he erected the impressive tomb of Count von der Mark in the Dorotheenstädtische Kirche. The Count, who died at the age of nine, was the illegitimate son of King Frederick-William II of Prussia. The child is shown asleep under a niche harboring the Three Fates. The work shows the sobriety and harmony of Schadow's Neoclassicism.

958

958 CANOVA · *Pauline Bonaparte as Venus Victrix* · 1808 · Galleria Borghese, Rome.

In 1804 Canova received a commission from Pauline Borghese, Napoleon's sister, for a statue portraying her as a victorious Venus, holding the apple awarded "to the most beautiful" by Paris. The marble was completed in 1808. A number of preparatory drawings show the genesis and evolution of the work, whose modelling throbs with life. The artist took his idea for the figure from a painting he owned, a Venus and Satyr inspired by Titian. The formal purity of the art of Canova, a leading artist in the early 19th-century neo-classical trend, is demonstrated in this work.

959

959 ANTONIO CANOVA (Italian, 1757–1822) · *Napoleon I* · 1811 · Courtyard of the Palazzo Brera, Milan.

Summoned to Paris in 1802 to execute a monument to Napoleon, Canova first set down the features in a plaster bust. The model for the colossal figure (over 14 feet high), portrayed in the classical manner as an idealized, heroic nude, was finished in 1808, and the marble statue was completed in 1811. Napoleon disliked it, and it was eventually sold to the English Government and placed in the Duke of Wellington's palatial house in London. The bronze version in the Brera, also completed in 1811, is reduced in size. Like some peace-bringing Mars, the Emperor holds in one hand a Victory figure balanced on a globe, and in the other, a scepter surmounted by an eagle.

419

962   JAMES PRADIER (French, 1792–1852) · *Victory*, Napoleon's tomb, Les Invalides, Paris.

Jean-Jacques (called James) Pradier was born in Geneva in 1792 and died in Rueil in 1852. The most famous sculptor during the July Monarchy, he was commissioned to execute the twelve Victory figures who stand guard around Napoleon's tomb, which was designed for the Invalides by Visconti between 1843 and 1861. Set against the columns of a circular gallery, these twelve colossal marble figures, winged and draped, have the grave expressions of Greek caryatids. They differ from each other only in some of the details. Pradier's elegant, cold style harmonizes in every way with the architecture of the tomb. (Height about 15 feet.)

962

960

960   BERTEL THORVALDSEN (Danish, 1768–1844) · *Hebe* · Marble · 1806 · Nationalmuseet, Copenhagen.

The son of an Icelandic wood-sculptor, Thorvaldsen was born and died in Copenhagen but did most of his work in Rome between 1797 and 1838 except for a brief interruption in 1818–19. There he was hailed as the successor to Canova, and his fame spread throughout Europe. For all that his statue of Hebe is rigorously subservient to imitation of the Greeks, it contrives to create an impression of calm and harmony. Lack of expressive force is compensated here by a sort of romantic revery. In 1816 Thorvaldsen took up the same subject again, treating the drapery in an even more classic manner.

961   SIR FRANCIS LEGATT CHANTREY (English, 1781–1841) · *Mrs. Siddons*, Westminster Abbey, London.

Sir Francis Legatt Chantrey enjoyed enormous popularity in England during his lifetime. Among the eleven funerary monuments that he executed for Westminster Abbey in London is that of Mrs. Siddons, the great actress, who died in 1831. Commissioned by Macready, it stands in the St. Andrew chapel in the north transept. The actress who had inspired all the English painters of the 18th century appears here as a Roman Vestal Virgin, in a stiff, cold composition lacking imagination and typical of the style of this Neoclassical sculptor.

961

963 FRANÇOIS RUDE (French, 1784–1855) · *Figure of La Marseillaise*; detail of the *Volunteers of '92*, Arc de Triomphe, Paris · 1833–1836.

Rude takes his place in the tradition of the Burgundian school. He was one of the masters of Romantic sculpture. Along with other sculptors, he worked on the decoration of the Arc de Triomphe at the Étoile in Paris; for the east face of the arch he carved the stone relief representing the *Departure of the Volunteers of 1792*, also known as *La Marseillaise*. In this epic work rooted in popular sentiment and patriotism, the shouting figure of the Marseillaise is incomparable for its passion and movement; Rude used his wife as a model, crying to her "Louder! Louder!"

963

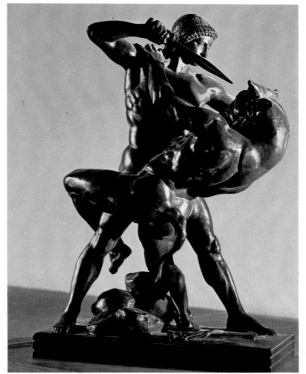

964

964 ANTOINE-LOUIS BARYE (French, 1796–1875) · *Theseus slaying the minotaur* · Bronze · 1841–1846 · The Louvre, Paris.

To familiarize himself with nature, Barye frequented assiduously the botanical and zoological gardens of his native Paris. His first success as a sculptor came in 1831. Truly excellent in his depictions of animals (he was a painter also), he has a place among the most forceful French sculptors and Romantic masters of the 19th century. This statue shows how he drew inspiration from antiquity, adding to it the profound acquaintance with anatomy, the keen sense of life, and the qualities of power and tension in expression that are characteristic of his genius. (Height, 18½ inches.)

965 ANTOINE-AUGUSTIN PRÉAULT (French, 1809–1879) · *The Killing* · 1834 · Musée des Beaux-Arts, Chartres.

Préault, who was born and died in Paris, was the pupil of David d'Angers. A typically Romantic character, he mixed 19th-century social ideas with his art. In 1834 he manifested his talent with a relief fragment (cast in bronze in 1859) called *The Killing*, a striking representation of figures larger than life, tearing at each other. This daring and nightmarish vision, possibly inspired by a popular melodrama of the time, is the work most characteristic of Préault's extremism, of his passionate concern with movement, ugliness and the colossal.

965

966 HONORÉ DAUMIER (French, 1808–1879) · *The Emigrants* · The Louvre, Paris.

Daumier was born in Marseilles in 1808 and died in Valmondois in 1879. He is best known as a caricaturist, but worked in other media as well, in which he appears as both a Romantic and a Realist. The theme of *The Emigrants*, which he treated in paintings and sculptures several times over the course of the years, first attracted him during the period of bourgeois reaction which, at the end of the year 1848, followed the February Revolution and caused the death and deportation of thousands of Republicans. Two bas-relief sketches, cast in plaster from the clay models, remain timeless symbols of suffering.

966

967 JEAN-BAPTISTE CARPEAUX (French, 1827–1875) · *The Dance* · 1869 · The Louvre, Paris.

Carpeaux was trained in the studio of Rude and also spent a few years in Rome. Upon his return to Paris in 1862 he became official sculptor for Napoleon III. In 1865 Garnier entrusted him with the execution of one of the sculptured groups for the façade of the Opéra. The result was *La Danse*, which provoked a typical Parisian scandal. The original plaster model seen here has recently been joined in the Louvre by the work itself, which was deteriorating under modern atmospheric conditions. A masterpiece of animation, rhythm and grace, this ring of nymphs around a leaping sylph reflects the round of feverish pleasure to which the Second Empire abandoned itself. (Height, 7 feet 7⅞ inches.)

967

968

968 CARPEAUX · *Mademoiselle Fiocre* · Ca. 1870 · The Louvre, Paris.

Carpeaux executed a series of brilliantly realistic busts, in the tradition of French portraiture of the 17th and 18th centuries. In the 1870 Salon he exhibited the marble bust of Eugénie Fiocre, prima ballerina at the Opéra and one of the best-loved artists of the Second Empire. (Launched by the Duc de Morny, she married the Marquis Créqui de Courtivron.) The Louvre possesses the original plaster model which, through its quick, spontaneous technique, conveys all the animated naturalness and *joie de vivre* of Carpeaux's art. (Height, 32 inches.)

969 JULES DALOU (1838–1902) · *Project for the Victor Hugo tomb*
1886 · Musée du Petit Palais, Paris.

During the 1880's Dalou's talents were fully recognized in France, and
he became much sought-after for public monuments. When Victor
Hugo died in 1885, Dalou was anxious to execute the large monument
planned for the Pantheon. However, neither his model for that project
nor the sketch shown here were ever executed. In this model Dalou
shows his strong links with the art of the mid-19th century, for his
gisant is directly under the influence of Rude's tomb for Godefroy de
Cavaignac and the accompanying mourners are descendent from the
sturdy workers and peasants of Millet and Daumier.

969

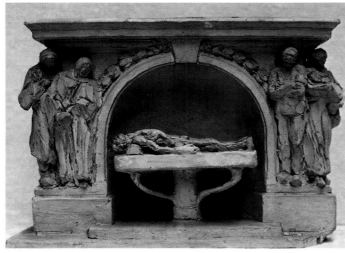

971 AUGUSTE RODIN (French, 1840–1917) · *The Thinker* · Musée
Rodin, Paris.

Rodin represents the final phase of French Romanticism, and points,
as well, to modern art. In 1880 he received a commission for a monumental door intended for the future Musée des Arts Décoratifs in Paris.
He worked at and around these grandiose, many-figured *Gates of Hell*,
inspired by Dante's poem, for the rest of his life. Some of the figures
conceived for the door he isolated and enlarged, and the bronze
Thinker is one of these. Its attitude and the powerful modelling give it
a feeling unlike the poet's image, expressing, rather, an anguished
concentration in the face of mankind's tragic destiny. (Height, 6½
feet.)

971

970 CONSTANTIN MEUNIER (Belgian, 1831–1905) · *Firedamp* · Bronze,
1893 · Musée Constantin Meunier, Brussels.

Constantin Meunier always had a feeling for the seriousness of his
subject; for two decades, in the 1860's and 1870's, he painted works
dealing with religion, poverty and death. When in the early 1880's he
discovered the coal miners in southern Belgium and the dockers of the
Antwerp port, a whole new field of expression opened up for him, and
at the age of fifty he turned seriously to sculpture. To express his
view of the dignity and the tragedy of these people's lives he developed
a strong, simple figure style, realistic but with all detail and sense of
anecdote suppressed, as we can see in this woman who bends over the
body of her son killed in a mining accident. (Height about 48 inches.)

970

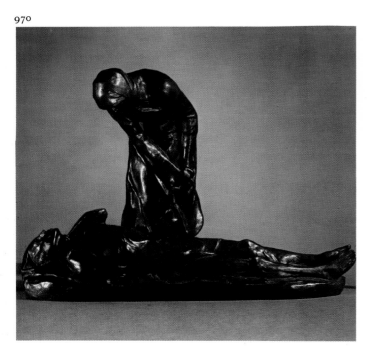

The marble *Oceanides* group, which for some time bore the title *Spring-time of Life*, was developed from a theme appearing at the base of the *Gates of Hell*. The moving, supple, feminine forms emerging from the rough marble are an example of Rodin's lyricism, but they reveal equally the element of harmony and sobriety that characterizes the last phase of his work. (Height, 22 inches.)

972

973 MEDARDO ROSSO (Italian, 1858–1928) · *Head of a Young Woman* · Wax over plaster · Ca. 1901 · Peridot Gallery, New York.

973

Rosso spent most of his life in Milan. His study at the Brera in the early 1880's was brief, as the academic atmosphere was uncongenial to his restless search. He moved quickly from a descriptive realism concentrating on sentimental and humanitarian subjects to a pictorial style dependent on the effects of chiaroscuro. The human head became his favorite vehicle through which to show the play of light on form and the color of sculpture produced by surface undulations. The importance of his work was recognized by the Futurists, and they were influenced by his manner of fusing form with surrounding atmosphere. (Height, 15¾ inches.)

974 ANTOINE BOURDELLE (French, 1861–1929) · *The Fruit* · 1907 ·
Musée National d'Art Moderne, Paris.

The style of Antoine Bourdelle, who was born at Montauban, results
from a combination of different influences. From his origins in Montauban he retained a taste for elegant contour, most likely derived
from Ingres. He worked with Rodin in Paris for a long time, but
departed from Rodin's emotive style when, after becoming acquainted
with Greek art, he began to confer on his own sculptures a classicizing
monumentality, which won him a number of commissions for public
monuments. The figure reproduced possesses a certain mannerism not
unrelated to the Art Nouveau style. In his later art, Bourdelle drew
even further away from the naturalism of Rodin, leaning towards a
somewhat dry stylization.

974

975

975 AUGUSTE RENOIR (French, 1841–1919) · *The Washerwoman* ·
1917 · Museum of Modern Art, New York.

Renoir frequented the Ecole des Beaux-Arts, then joined the Impressionist group, participating in their exhibitions. His venture into the
art of sculpture, made late in life, was exceptional. In 1907, with paralyzed hands, he modelled two portraits; in the years 1913 to 1918,
encouraged by Vollard, and employing as assistant a Spanish pupil of
Maillol's, Richard Guino, he made various other sculptures. *The
Washerwoman*, which is only a sketch, was born of this close collaboration. In its life-like attitude it exemplifies the ample forms and simplified volumes of Renoir's female type.

976

976 ARISTIDE MAILLOL (French, 1861–1944) · *L'Ile-de-France* ·
Bronze · 1920–1925 · Musée National d'Art Moderne, Paris.

Maillol devoted himself to painting and tapestry before becoming a
sculptor at the age of forty. The single, constant theme of his work is
the female body, in infinite variation, but always subjected to a formal

and monumental treatment. The *Ile-de-France*, a symbol of the district
to which the artist returned every year at Marly-le-Roi, is based on a
firm geometric framework. This bronze version, cut off below the knee,
so that it looks like a woman walking in water, is also characterized by
fullness of forms and a carefully studied balance of masses. (Height
about 6 feet.)

977 CHARLES DESPIAU (French, 1874–1946) · *Assia* · 1938 · Museum of Modern Art, New York.

Born at Mont-de-Marsan in 1874, Despiau died in Paris in 1946. He worked from 1907 to 1914 for Rodin, but his calm, reserved temperament led his art in another direction than Rodin's. Most of his production consists of portraits, which have an intense inner life, or nudes, of which the bronze Assia is a famous example. Despiau's sculpture is conceived in purely plastic terms, revealing a search for rhythms, a careful adjustment of the various planes, and subtly nuanced modelling; although based on acute observation, his figures end as types, thus carrying on the classical tradition. (Height, 6 feet 2 inches.)

977

978 WILHELM LEHMBRUCK (German, 1881–1919) · *Kneeling figure* ·
Cast stone · 1911 · Museum of Modern Art, New York.

Lehmbruck's style developed in Paris, where he was working between
1910 and 1914, coming into contact with Brancusi, Modigliani and
Archipenko. The period of his finest works begins with the *Kneeling
Figure.* Exhibited in Cologne in 1912, it was acclaimed as opening the
way to a new form of Expressionism. The profound spirituality of the
image is expressed in the predominantly linear element of the calm
figure and in the elongation and formal simplifications, which already
point towards the artist's final sculptures. (Height, 5 feet 9 inches.)

978

979

979 ERNST BARLACH (German, 1870–1938) · *The Ecstatic One* · Wood ·
1916 · Kunsthaus, Zurich.

Like many of his contemporaries in the early 20th century, Barlach's
sculptural form was dependent upon clean and simple volumes, but
unlike most he was deeply attached to the subject, to the image of
man and his spiritual state. In this sense his work has many analogies
with the Expressionist movement in painting. He worked most often
in wood, which lent itself well to the block-like character and the
material heaviness of his images. (Height, 20½ inches.)

980 CONSTANTIN BRANCUSI (1876–1957) · *Sleeping Muse* · 1909–1910 · Musée National d'Art Moderne, Paris.

Brancusi, born in Romania, arrived in Paris in 1904 and revolutionized sculpture there. The bronze *Sleeping Muse* of 1909–1910 is one of the many versions and replicas of this theme that the artist made between 1906 and 1912, endlessly purifying it and investing it with an increasingly profound spiritual intensity. The ideal, concrete form of the egg, the symbol of the origin of life and the basis for the suggested facial features, is typical of the artist's search for the essence of things. (Dimensions, $10\frac{1}{2}$ x $11\frac{3}{4}$ x $6\frac{1}{2}$ inches.)

980

981 CONSTANTIN BRANCUSI · *The Seal* · 1943 · Musée National d'Art Moderne, Paris.

Carved from a block of grey-veined marble, *The Seal* is a variation on a work of 1936, *The Miracle*. Eliminating all detail, Brancusi arrives at an essentially timeless form which is also the plastic equivalent of the animal's limber weightiness. The photographs of seals that Brancusi kept in an album testify to the artist's deep attachment to reality. The polish on the material shows prodigious craftsmanship. (Dimensions, 62 x 41 x 14 inches.)

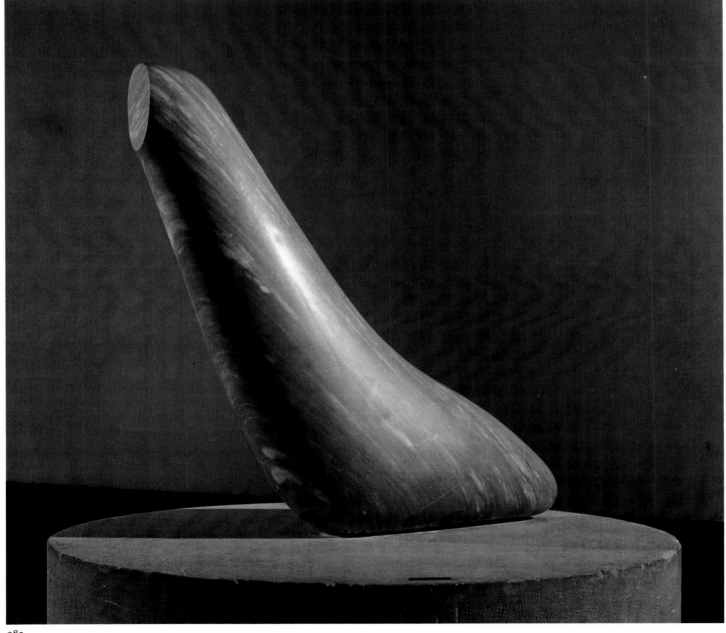

981

Matisse was the creator of French Fauvism, and besides his paintings, which were essentially dominated by line and color, he executed a number of highly original and witty sculptures. In 1910 and 1911 he sculptured five versions of Jeanne Vaderin's portrait, entitled *Jeannette*, the first two done from the model, the other three freely interpreted from these. In his search for elementary forms, in the ever-increasing isolation and contrast of the different volumes in the form studied, Matisse, sensitive to archaic and primitive art, anticipates Picasso's post-Cubist heads of 1932.

983

982

982 AMEDEO MODIGLIANI (Italian, 1884–1920) · *Female Head* · 1912 · Musée National d'Art Moderne, Paris.

The young Modigliani traveled through Italy and settled in Paris in 1906. His sculptures, of which the twenty-five known to us constitute only a part of his total production, were mostly done between 1909 and 1914. They are quite close to the art of Brancusi, to Cubism, and to Negro art. The linear style, and the stripped, dense forms in this female head carved out of a long, flat block of granular limestone, are the expression of a personal style, in which may be found an echo of ancient traditions, notably of Tuscan Mannerism. (Height, 18 inches.)

984

985 RAYMOND DUCHAMP-VILLON · *The Great Horse* · Bronze · 1914 ·
Art Institute of Chicago (Gift of Miss Margaret Fisher).

In this horse, of which several versions exist, Duchamp-Villon created
one of the most revolutionary pieces of sculpture of the time. The
rounded masses, supple and brimming with life, are animal in character and, in quite singular fashion, work in harmony with the other elements which are linear, rigid, machine-like. This union of animal and
machine gave rise to a truly expressive work which is based on Cubist
principles but also owes something to the research into the dynamics
of movement the artist was able to study in the Futurist exhibitions
of 1912 and 1913 in Paris. (Height, 39⅜ inches.)

984 RAYMOND DUCHAMP-VILLON (French, 1876–1918) · *The Athlete* ·
1910 · Musée National d'Art Moderne, Paris.

Duchamp-Villon, born at Damville (Eure) in 1876, died a premature
death in 1918 at Cannes. He renounced the study of medicine in order
to devote himself to sculpture. From 1910 onwards he belonged to the
Puteaux group, which included his brothers Jacques Villon and Marcel
Duchamp, as well as La Fresnaye, Léger, Gleizes and Metzinger.
Moving away from Rodin's example, which had influenced his early
works, he executed this bronze figure of a young man. He expresses
the violent movement that animates his subject by a skillful opposition of masses and planes; in his later works this manipulation of
forms takes on a more synthetic character. (Height, 23¾ inches.)

986

985

986 ALEXANDER ARCHIPENKO (born in Russia, 1887–died 1964) ·
Boxers · Plaster · 1914 · Guggenheim Museum, New York.

Archipenko had an early and consistent development in working with
a Cubist style in sculpture. Almost from the beginning of his career he
was interested in the void, the negative form, a new spatial concept.
His sculpture was already opening up, displaying transparency by
1912. The *Boxers* shows the kind of counterbalance of forms around a
void, the breaking up of the solids in a dynamic way that was Archipenko's most notable contribution to Cubist sculpture in its early
years. (23½ x 18 inches.)

987

987 JACQUES LIPCHITZ (1891–). *Bather* · Bronze · 1915 · Mrs. J. D. Rockefeller Collection, New York.

Lipchitz arrived in Paris from Lithuania in 1909, a boy not yet twenty. There followed swift years of learning, of trying out styles. An initial encounter with the Cubists through his friend, Diego Rivera, elicited hostility from Lipchitz, but by 1913 his work was in touch with their outlook. At first his smooth, flat planes were decorative, curvilinear and descriptive, but by 1915 with such works as the *Bather* we see that most of the semi-naturalness and the curves are gone, volume has been reduced to a minimum and what remains is a beautifully proportioned, strikingly vertical architectonic shaft. (Height, 31⅝ inches.)

988 HENRI LAURENS (French, 1885–1954) · *The Bunch of Grapes* · 1922 · Musée National d'Art Moderne, Paris.

The art of Henri Laurens, which followed its humble course without polemic or publicity, represents a sustained effort in a continuous evolution. All his life Laurens was preoccupied solely with problems of form, aiming to achieve in sculpture what the Cubists of 1910 had realized in painting. He was in fact initiated into Cubism by Georges Braque, whom he met in 1911 and whose close friend he remained all his life.

988

989 UMBERTO BOCCIONI (Italian, 1882–1916) · *Unique Forms of Continuity in Space* · 1913 · Private collection, Milan.

With the poet Marinetti, Boccioni was one of the principal ideators and signatories of the *Futurist Painters Manifesto* (1910), and he issued also *The Manifesto of the Technique of Futurist Sculpture* (1912) and *Futurist Sculpture-Painting* (1914). The bronze *Unique Forms of Continuity in Space* shows a search for dynamic form, aimed at expressing the idea of the movement of the body in space by an interpenetration of planes and the use of forms intended to suggest the turbulence of movement vibrating in space. (Height, 44 inches.)

989

990 HANS ARP (1887–1966) · *Bird in an Aquarium* · Wood · Ca. 1920 · Museum of Modern Art, New York.

The Alsatian Arp arrived in Zurich in 1915, already well acquainted with modern art in Germany and France. The following year he began his painted wood reliefs, which remain the best plastic expression of Dada from the Zurich group. These are lively abstractions made up of wavy lines and free forms assembled according to the laws of chance. They are playfully simple and tell no story, but underlying the vibrating effect is the symbolic language through which Arp expressed his feelings about growth and transformations within the organic life of nature. (9⅞ x 8 inches.)

990

991

991 MAX ERNST (German, 1891–) · *Fruit of Long Experience* · Painted wood and metal · 1919 · Collection Roland Penrose, London.

When he was a young artist in his twenties, Ernst went through several styles without finding a clear way of his own. He was particularly influenced by Picasso's collages, for in them he felt a freedom which he sought. He found his own style and the sense of liberation through Dada. *Fruit of Long Experience* dates from the high period of Dada in Cologne, when Ernst was constructing three-dimensional "objects" of scraps and bits of ready-made materials.

992 KURT SCHWITTERS (German, 1887–1948) · *MERZ Building*, Hannover · Constructed 1920's, destroyed 1943 · Photograph courtesy of Landesgalerie, Hannover.

As Dada was dying in Cologne and Berlin, it was being created by Kurt Schwitters in Hannover. His word, Merz, like Dada, was meaningless, save for the meaning that he infused into it: "Merz stands for freedom…" For sixteen years he "merzed on" new elements in constructing this three-dimensional assemblage in his own home in Hannover. It went up two stories and down one. In conceiving a work that the spectator stepped into, and in fusing architecture, painting and sculpture, Schwitters created an important ancestor of the environmental sculpture of the 1960's.

993

992

993 GEORGES VANTONGERLOO (1886–1965) · *Construction in a Sphere* · Silvered plaster · 1917 · Museum of Modern Art, New York.

After World War I, Vantongerloo, a Belgian, joined Mondrian and Van Doesburg in forming the new Dutch movement, *De Stijl*. Basic to the group's artistic objectives was the concept of an art that was totally non-objective and in which each form was universal, never personal or subjective. Vantongerloo felt that "…nature lies completely outside the sphere of art." *Construction in a Sphere* is one of his first abstractions; it is based on mathematical principles, which henceforth remained fundamental to Vantongerloo's work. We find ourselves looking at the softly rounded forms that articulate the inner space of a sphere. (Diameter, 7 inches.)

994 PABLO GARGALLO (Spanish, 1881–1934) · *The Prophet* · 1933 · Musée National d'Art Moderne, Paris.

Gargallo made several more or less extended stays in Paris (1906, 1911–1914, 1923), and his work therefore reflects the forms of contemporary French art. However, though his use of iron is avant-garde, in concept his sculptures often remain subject to the laws of the realist tradition. In the perforated figure of *The Prophet*, one of his most accomplished works, hollows substitute for forms in the round, and the mass presents itself as a silhouette. Inventiveness is coupled with a stylization most visible in the hands and feet. The figure on the whole is theatrical, but effective in its power of suggestion. (Height about 8 feet.)

995

994

996 JULIO GONZALEZ (1876–1942) · *The Angel* · Iron · 1933 · Musée National d'Art Moderne, Paris.

Born at Barcelona in 1876, Gonzalez died at Arcueil in 1942. The son of a goldsmith, he settled in Paris after 1900. Applying to sculpture the technique of wrought iron (which he had learned from his father) and the use of oxyacetylene welding, he arrived at a new form of plastic art that led him to abstraction. A sharp outline of wire defines the form of this elegant, unreal figure of an angel, and models space as the artist wishes, "thanks to the ideal trajectory of its motion." This work reveals the inventiveness and imagination of an art that had many followers. (Height, 5 feet 2 inches.)

996

995 PABLO PICASSO (born in Spain, 1881–) · *Woman in the Garden* · Bronze, after welded iron · 1929–30 · Collection of the artist, Mougins.

Perhaps it is right to think of Picasso first as a painter, but his sculpture has been an integral part of his creative life, not just a secondary consideration. Many of the artistic solutions he has sought were intimately tied to the nature of sculpture: problems of the relationship of volume to space in a non-illusionistic way, tactile qualities and primitive symbolic images. In the late 1920's he and Gonzalez worked with new techniques in metal dependent on assemblage and welding. In *Woman in the Garden* we see one of the delicate scaffold constructions of this period and the type of work that is clearly a prototype for the assemblages by sculptors in recent years. (Height, 82¾ inches.)

435

997

998 JACQUES LIPCHITZ (1891–) · *Song of the Vowels* · Bronze · 1931–32 · Kunsthaus, Zurich (Gift of Mme H. de Mandrot).

During the 1920's Lipchitz moved away from the strict Cubist geometry. His sense of rhythm reappeared and a feeling for undulating movement began to pulse again through his forms. The middle of the decade he gave over to the problem of space in sculpture and the idea of transparency. By the late 1920's he brought these interests together in a monumental series of works which include *La Joie de Vivre*, *Mother and Child* and *Song of the Vowels*. This last-named evokes the image of the played harp and connotes a sense of joyousness not only through the symbolism of the theme but through the curving lines and moving volumes. (Height, 6 feet 6¾ inches.)

997 JULIO GONZALEZ *Seated Woman* · Iron · 1935 · Collection Mme. Roberta Gonzalez, Paris.

During the 1930's Gonzalez moved away from the lightness and linearity seen in the *Angel* of 1933; his sculpture became increasingly more powerful and weighty. The human figure remained his point of departure, but it became a rougher figure, more physically present but less described. One of the themes on which he did several variants was the seated woman. Gonzalez's forms were never more severe than in the work reproduced; against the dominant rigid structure he has played two clear curves which give the figure remarkable power. We further perceive the implied strength of physical projection through the angular iron bar thrust forward and the thin sensory rods above.

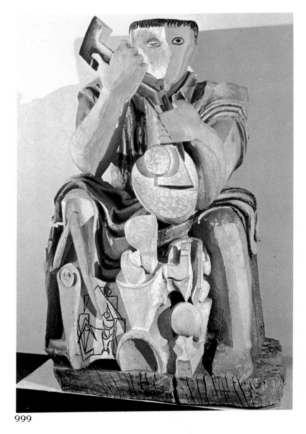

999

998

999 OSSIP ZADKINE (1890–) · *The Sculptor* · 1939 · Musée National d'Art Moderne, Paris.

Zadkine, born at Smolensk in 1890, arrived in Paris in 1909 and became integrated into the Cubist movement. As was the case with Lipchitz, Cubism served him only as a point of departure. Reverting to the practice of direct carving, he found in wood and stone a stimulus for his fertile imagination, which he employed in creating a vast repertory of subjects. *The Sculptor*, a massive polychromed wood construction of volumes and planes, mingling angles and curves, reveals the artist's stature and the lasting values of his work. (Height, 6 feet 4 inches.)

1000

1000 HANS ARP (1887–1966) · *Human Concretion* · Marble · 1934 ·
Musée National d'Art Moderne, Paris.

After 1930 Arp began to explore fully sculpture in the round and to
use the traditional processes of carving and modelling. What developed
were his smooth, white, pure forms which he referred to as Human
Concretions: "Concretion signifies the natural process of condensation, hardening, coagulating, thickening, growing together... Concretion designates solidification, the mass of the stone, the plant, the
animal, the man. Concretion is something that has grown. I wanted
my work to find its humble, anonymous place in the woods, the
mountains, in nature." (20 x 14¾ inches.)

1001 HENRY MOORE (British, 1898–) · *King and Queen* · 1952–1953 · Openhecht Museum, Antwerp.

Born at Castleford (Yorkshire), Moore is at the root of the sculptural revival in England. The son of a miner, he had a classical sculptor's training in Leeds and London. Having assimilated the most varied of cultures, from Pre-Columbian art to Surrealism, during his travels in Europe and America, he remained profoundly attached to his native land and created his work for its countryside, intending it to be displayed in the open air. The bronze *King and Queen*, which is allied with the theme of family groups that he had been developing since 1944, is distinguished from those by its mythical element. (Height 6½ feet.)

1002 ALBERTO GIACOMETTI (1901–1966) · *The Chariot* · Museum of Modern Art, New York.

Giacometti, who was born and died in Stampa (Switzerland), settled in Paris in 1922. After a period of Surrealism, his interest in sculpture and painting centered around the human figure. He tried to conjure up its reality and inner life by a process of extreme reduction in mass and equally extreme elongation of the form. The bronze *Chariot* was born from the memory of a cart that had impressed the artist in his hospital room in 1938. In 1947 Giacometti had a precise conception of what his sculpture was to be, and in 1950 he executed it: a solitary figure, vibrant and fascinating, a modern version of the antique Charioteer. (Height, 5 feet 4 inches.)

1001

1003

1003   ALEXANDER CALDER (American, 1898–) · *Mobile* · Basle Museum.

Born in Philadelphia in 1898, Calder arrived in Paris in 1926 and there first staged his famous miniature circus. Following his first abstract sculptures of 1931 (entitled by Jean Arp *stabiles*) and his motor-controlled sculptures, he created his first mobiles in 1932. Here, this assemblage of iron leaves, variegated in form, thickness, and sometimes in color, and hung on a network of wires and rods, takes possession of space with its natural, spontaneous, shifting movement. Calder's inventiveness and his exceptional gift for assembling bits and pieces give rise to a world fascinating in its ever-changing rhythms. (Height about 7½ feet.)

1004   PABLO PICASSO (1881–) · *Woman with Apple* · Bronze · 1943 · Collection of the artist, Mougins.

After 1934 Picasso neglected sculpture for a long period, but became interested in it once again during the German occupation, which he spent in Paris. The practical problems of executing sculpture under such conditions were enormous. His materials were of the widest possible choice – humble pieces of life – cardboard, metal caps, wire, matchboxes; but everything he used, through the power of his imaginative combinations, could be turned into expressive totemic beings, at once magical and witty. (Height, 70⅞ inches.)

1004

1005   PABLO PICASSO (1881–) · *Man with Sheep* · Bronze · 1944 · Vallauris.

Man with Sheep, a seven-foot figure and Picasso's most monumental work of this period, is hieratic and special. The theme had preoccupied him during the whole last year of the war. This is the ultimate successor of the Greek *Calfbearer* and the Christian *Good Shepherd*. The solemnity of the piece, as well as the rough, light-catching modelling takes us back to Picasso's own early work, the painting and sculpture of the first decade of the century, when his involvement with Man's suffering was so profoundly expressive. (Height, 86½ inches.)

1005

440

1006

1006 GERMAINE RICHIER (French, 1904–1959) · *The Storm* · Bronze · 1947–1948 · Musée National d'Art Moderne, Paris.

Germaine Richier was a pupil of Bourdelle from 1925 to 1929. In 1940, after a classical phase, she arrived at an art expressing a world of anxiety, upheaval and poetic feeling through a very personal technique that reveals her as a craftswoman of rich variety. The new image of man, as expressed in *The Storm*, is a debased creature, swollen and at the same time drawn and tense, whose forms belong also to the animal and vegetable kingdoms. In such threatening, mysterious bronze figures she evokes the powers and secrets of nature. (Height, 6½ feet.)

1007

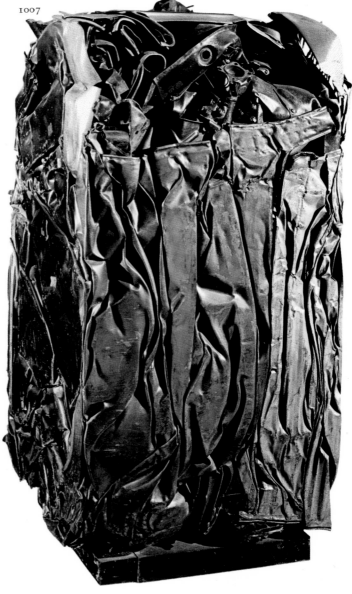

1007 CÉSAR (French, 1921–) · *Compressed Motor Car* · Ca. 1960 · Collection Countess de Noailles, Paris.

César Baldaccini, known as César, born in Marseilles of Italian parents in 1921, trained at the École des Beaux-Arts in Marseilles, then at that in Paris. Work in metal led him to an "amalgam period," during which, accumulating scrap materials, he created fantastic figures that have an authentic imaginative force and a certain humor. Through working in factories where metals were salvaged, he became sensitive to the variety and the beauty of compressed balls of metal. The discovery of the hydraulic press as a tool for formal creation led him, about 1960, to experiment freely with deliberate compressions.

1008

1008   MARINO MARINI (Italian, 1901–) · *The Angel of the City* · 1949 ·
Collection Peggy Guggenheim, Venice.

Born in Pistoia, Marini received his training in Florence and, in 1928–
1929 in Paris, where he came to know the leading tendencies in modern
art. Later he settled in Milan. Trained as a painter – an activity he
pursues along with sculpture – he has always kept a feeling for color,

as is shown by his polychrome wood statues and by his concerns with
patina. The Angel of the City done in 1949 is one of the many variations on the theme of Man and Horse which has always haunted
Marini. Its impressiveness lies in its architectonic structure and in its
movement which is abruptly halted but still charged with dramatic
tension. (Height 5 feet 5¾ inches.)

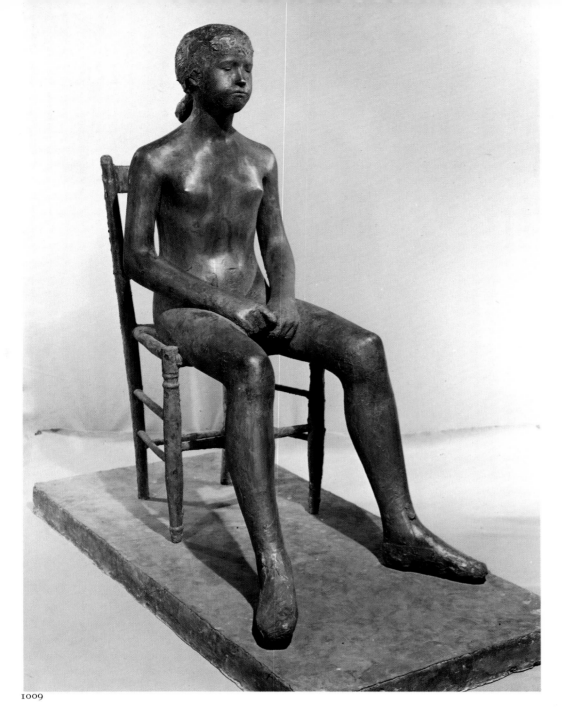

1009

1009 GIACOMO MANZÙ (Italian, 1908–) · *Young Girl on a Chair* ·
Bronze · 1955 · National Gallery of Canada, Ottawa.

Even before the war Manzù was recognized as one of Italy's leading
sculptors, and by 1948, when he won the Venice Biennale prize for
Italian sculpture, this was an established fact. Yet he has stood at
some distance from most modern movements, while being considerably
influenced by traditional western sculpture, including that of antiquity, the middle ages and the Renaissance. He has worked with religious subjects, female figures and portraits, often executing particular themes over and over again; the first study of a *Girl in a Chair*
was in 1938. His style is based on strong, simple, architectonic figures
that always display a measured degree of grace and dignity. (Height,
43¾ inches.)

1010

1010 ANTOINE PEVSNER (1886–1962) · *Project for the Monument to
the Unknown Political Prisoner* · 1955–56 · Musée National d'Art
Moderne, Paris.

Born at Orel (Russia) in 1886, Pevsner died in Paris in 1962. With his
brother, Naum Gabo, he brought a new art form into being during the
1914 war, an art "capable of utilizing emptiness and of liberating us
from solid mass," as it was defined in the *Realist Manifesto* or *Constructivist Manifesto* of 1920. Pevsner's work was done in Paris, where
settled after 1923. The bronze project for the *Monument to the Unknown Political Prisoner*, symbolizing the liberation of the spirit, is a
spatial construction achieved by the use of purely abstract forms in
which geometry is allied with poetic creation; but at the same time
the forms remind us of the control tower in a prison camp. (Dimensions, 55¼ x 54 x 35 inches.)

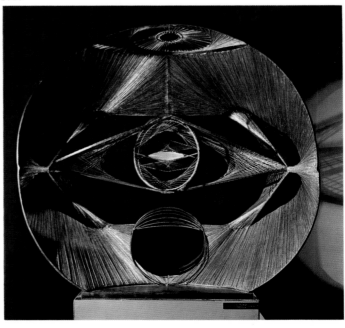

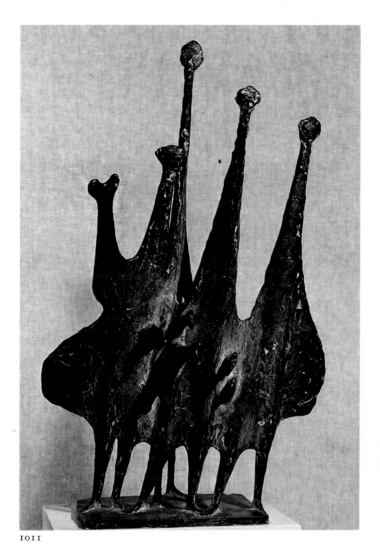

1011

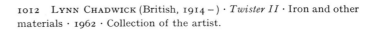
1012 LYNN CHADWICK (British, 1914 –) · *Twister II* · Iron and other materials · 1962 · Collection of the artist.

Trained as an architect, Chadwick did not begin experimenting in sculpture until after World War II. At that point his concerns were equilibrium, transparency and linearity. Many of his works were mobiles and he responded to the recent work of Calder and Gonzalez. His more developed, personal style is represented by *Twister II*, a figure that is anthropomorphic as well as architectonic. It is geometric, abstract, and yet a body on spindly legs; the planes are rough, irregular surfaces, yet they have the sense of a skin. In such works Chadwick gives us modern totemic beings; monumental, silent watchers. (Height 43 inches.)

1013

1011 KENNETH ARMITAGE (British, 1916 –) · *People in a Wind* · Bronze · 1950 · Tate Gallery, London.

Like Lynn Chadwick and Reg Butler, Armitage appeared after the war and in a parallel manner sought to establish a kind of dematerialized form in sculpture. He developed a figure style of a very summary character: people flattened-out, with thin protruding limbs, often in motion and usually collective – a pair of figures or a group joined by angular wedges of metallic drapery. Armitage is a modeller, and he creates rich surfaces to be cast in bronze, often pitted or scratched and simultaneously ugly and sensuous. (Height, 25½ inches.)

1013 ANTHONY CARO (British, 1924–) · *Mid-Day*. Steel, painted 1960 · Collection of Mr. and Mrs. Kenneth Noland.

During the 1950's Caro's sculpture dealt with the human figure in a very expressive manner. His work was modelled and cast, and in that sense traditional. 1960 was the year that marked a definite break for him, and with his monumental metal constructions he opened up a new chapter in British sculpture equivalent to the decisive step taken by Henry Moore in the 1930's. *Mid-Day* was one of Caro's first works in which he moved away from the monolith, instead assembling brightly colored fragments of steel girders. The flat, smooth, rectangular parts are loosely put together, and as the spectator moves around the work he is continually experiencing new formal combinations. (7'10½" high × 12' × 3'2").

1012

1014

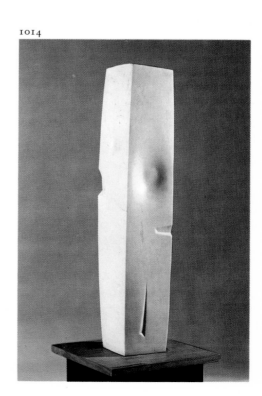

1014 ISAMU NOGUCHI (1904–) · *Integral* · Marble · 1959 · Whitney Museum of American Art, New York (Gift of the Friends of the Whitney Museum of American Art).

The diversity of images, projects, and objects that mark out Noguchi's career is always a bit surprising, but it has to do with the unique combinations in his background and the variety of influences that have deeply marked his development. Of Japanese-American parentage, he was educated in both countries. His traditional training as a sculptor in New York was followed by two years in Paris as Brancusi's assistant, where he was able to enjoy close friendship with Calder and Giacometti. He then studied in China and Japan and later worked in London and Mexico. *Integral* is a proud totem vaguely reminding us of great sculptural monuments of the past, not imitating them or nature, and yet bearing relationship to both.

1016

1015

1015 DAVID SMITH (American, 1906–1965) · *Cubi XIX* · Steel · 1964 · Tate Gallery, London.

One of the reasons for Smith's critical position in the history of modern sculpture is his early start in metal sculpture and the extraordinary diversity of ways in which he worked with it. In 1933 he made his first wrought iron sculpture with borrowed welding equipment. In the 1930's and 1940's many of his images were derived from Surrealism, and Picasso and Gonzalez strongly influenced his development. His later work was more geometric, showing greater concern for surface, as we can see in the burnished steel sides of the *Cubi* series. Through this treatment the sculpture is lightened and unified with the atmosphere: "...colored by the sky and surroundings..." as Smith saw it. (Height about 9½ feet.)

1016 RICHARD LIPPOLD (American, 1915–) · *Variation no. 7: Full Moon* · 1949–1950 · Museum of Modern Art, New York.

Born in Milwaukee, Wisconsin, of German parents, Lippold was trained as an industrial engineer and turned, self-taught, to sculpture. *Variation no. 7: Full Moon* is one of the abstract constructions that he first began making in 1942. Executed with copper rods, chrome-nickel wires and stainless steel, it expresses a "mystical feeling, without spatial limitation." (Height, 10 feet.)

1017

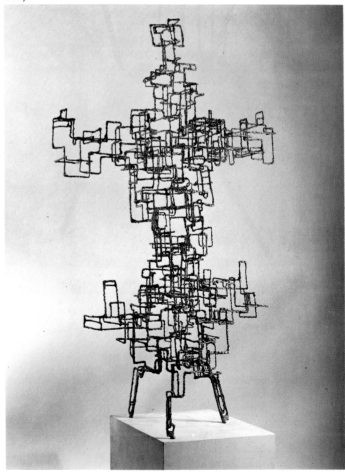

1017 IBRAM LASSAW (American, 1913–) · *Kwannon* · Welded bronze with silver · 1952 · The Museum of Modern Art, New York · (Katharine Cornell Fund).

Egyptian-born Lassaw, who studied art in New York, has been exploring constructivist forms since the 1930's. He has worked extensively in brazed metals, experimenting with new techniques and patinas. Space is gently caged by the wire tracery of his serene *Kwannon*, to which the sculptor gave the Japanese name for the Bodhisattva of Compassion.

The Futurists made modern mechanization relevant for sculpture; the Dada movement recognized objects not traditionally associated with the world of art. From these two currents many inventive works have come, particularly the assemblages of the past two decades. Stankiewicz was finding junk and welding it into new life by the early 1950's. He has taken broken machines, plumbing pipes, steam fittings, cylinder blocks, and scrap metal of all sorts as his medium, and with delicacy and a sure sense of wit that comes out through the associations we see in his works he has forged a very personal style. (Height, $80\frac{1}{4}$ inches.)

1019

1020 JOSEPH CORNELL (1903–) · *Pipe and Glass Box (Eclipse Series)*, Construction · Collection of the Artist.

Joseph Cornell is essentially a self-taught artist, but he has always been quite aware of avant-garde art; he even showed with the Surrealists in the 1930's. His boxes executed over the past four decades stand uniquely apart from all 20th-century movements, at the same time that their mysterious and personal poetry seem forever relevant to the latest phase of art. In the 1960's particularly they elicit our attention in that they stand somewhere between painting and sculpture: they are objects and contain objects, yet the box can and does act as a frame, and within it we find illusionistic painter's space as well as actual space. (Height $6\frac{1}{2}$ inches, width 12 inches, depth 5 inches).

1020

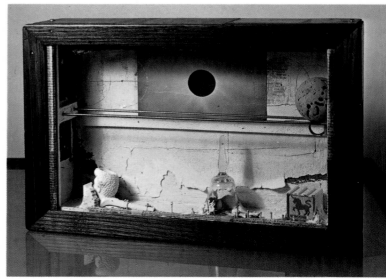

1018

1018 DAVID HARE (American, 1917–) · *Sunrise* · Bronze and steel 1953 · Albright-Knox Art Gallery, Buffalo.

Hare was not trained as a sculptor and had no previous experience when he began working with a blowtorch in the 1940's. His style has not shown a particularly consistent development: sometimes his work is figurative, sometimes it is completely abstract. He has looked for ideas through free associations in the manner of the Surrealists, by wandering through what he refers to as "the spaces of the mind." He has been quite susceptible to inspiration from nature, as seen in *Sunrise*, and works like this of the 1950's are most often executed in mixed metals with a deliberate lack of finish. (Height, 71 inches.)

1021 LOUISE NEVELSON (American, 1900–) · *Homage to 6,000,000 I* ·
Wood · 1964 · Jewish Museum, New York (on extended loan from
the Albert A. List Family).

Louise Nevelson experimented in the 1940's in all media. By the
1950's she had found that her way of expression was in wood. She
constructed shadowy, poetic images related to Surrealism, mostly
painted black and to be seen from a vast variety of points of view.
In her more recent work as represented by *Homage to 6,000,000* her
constructivist approach has become classical in feeling with the in-
sistent repetition of cubic boxes creating a strong horizontal and vertical emphasis, but bursting with energy due to the fragmentary
forms crammed into each unit. The whole is unified by the black paint,
and the breath of the two segments implies a sense of total environment, of an all-embracing nature that is also alluded to in the title.
(108 x 216 inches.)

1021

1022

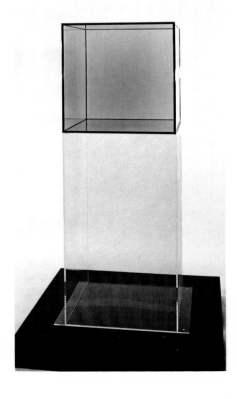

1022 LARRY BELL (1939–) · *Untitled* · Coated glass and rhodium
plated brass · 1966 · Courtesy Pace Gallery, New York.

Bell is one of the younger American artists working on the west coast
whose chrome-edged, glass cubes (here mounted on a plexiglass stand)
partake of many recent developments in sculpture. Reduction is so
complete that they have little in common with previous sculpture:
they have no interior surface divisions, all views are identical so there
is no top, no bottom or sides, they are solid and closed but unbeliev-
ably empty, they are not light-refracting but light-absorbing. The
box, done many times by Bell, is his basic unit. Like other contemporary sculptors he has borrowed from new technology in his use of an
optical coating adapted from the local Los Angeles space industry.
(20-inch cube.)

1023

1023 MARISOL (1930–) · *Women and Dog* · Wood, plaster, synthetic polymer paint and miscellaneous items · 1964 · Whitney Museum of American Art, New York · (Gift of the Friends of the Whitney Museum of American Art).

The Venezuelan-American sculptress, Marisol (she uses only her first name), had a Paris-New York education: she learned from Hans Hofmann and from what she saw in galleries and collections, especially of Pre-Columbian and Mexican art. But we do not immediately connect her very personal and original style to other art and artists even if some elements can be sorted out as related to folk art, Surrealism, and Pop. She works with life-size human figures that project wit and chic, but are not without a sense of pungent criticism toward New York life in the 1960's. They are carved and yet they share in the contemporary trend of assemblage, as seen here in the real clothes, the plaster masks of Marisol's own face, and the stuffed dog's head. (Height 72 inches, width 82 inches, depth 16 inches.)

1024 *Human head*, from Aq Kupruk (Afghanistan) · Paleolithic, ca. 20,000 B.C. · Government of Afghanistan (on loan to the American Museum of Natural History, New York).

This small piece of limestone (about 2½ inches high) is the earliest carbon-dated representation of the human face. Only two other sculptured heads in the round of comparable age have been found, and these, not yet dated by carbon-14 analysis, may be slightly later. The head reproduced was discovered in 1965 at Aq Kupruk, in northern Afghanistan, by a team of Afghan and American archeologists led by Dr. Louis Dupree and sponsored by the American Museum of Natural History. Carving at the top may represent hair or a skin cap; a beard and probably a mustache are carved near the bottom, and the right ear is roughly outlined.

1024

NOTES

969 JULES DALOU. *Project for a monument.*
Madame Annie Braunwald, curator at the Petit
Palais, has recently reidentified the sculpture previously called a project for the Victor Hugo monument. It is probably a project, never carried out, for
the Faculty of Medecine at Paris, modelled ca.
1881-1888

1024 HUMAN HEAD, *see preceding page.*
The recent announcement of this discovery permitted the inclusion of "the oldest human face" as
the final illustration. The reader will be interested
in comparing it with other Paleolithic works on
pp. 89-93.

Collaborators for the Commentaries with areas of Specialization

Armand Abel,	Professor, Université de l'Etat, Ghent, and Université Libre de Bruxelles.
Marie-Louise Bastin,	Collaboratrice scientifique, Musée Royal d'Afrique Centrale, Tervuren. Primitive cultures.
Pierre Bonenfant,	Assistant à la Faculté de Philosophie et Lettres, Université Libre de Bruxelles. Prehistoric art.
Ruth Butler-Mirolli,	Ph.D., History of Art, New York University. 19th and 20th centuries.
André Courtens,	Assistant à la Faculté de Philosophie et Lettres de l'Université Libre de Bruxelles. Medieval art.
Nicole Dacos,	Chargée de Recherches, Fond National de la Recherche Scientifique de Belgique. Italian Renaissance and Baroque.
Cecile Dulière,	Assistant à la Faculté de Philosophie et Lettres de l'Université Libre de Bruxelles. Hellenistic and Roman art.
Anne Grenez,	Licenciée en Philosophie et Lettres de l'Université Libre de Bruxelles. Egyptian art.
Pierre Grenez,	Collaborateur scientifique aux Musées Royaux d'Art et d'Histoire, Brussels. Ancient art of the Near and Middle East.
Lydie Hadermann-Misguich	Assistant à la Faculté de Philosophie et Lettres de l'Universtié Libre de Bruxelles. Early Christian art.
Jean-Pierre Müller,	Producer, Radiotélévision Belge. German art.
Claudie Neuhuys-Nisse,	Professeur, Université Ouvrière de Bruxelles. Prehistoric art.
Françoise Popelier,	Attaché aux Musées Royaux des Beaux-Arts de Belgique, Brussels. French art.
Claudine Rocmans-Donnay,	Licenciée en Philosophie de Lettres de l'Université Libre de Bruxelles. Greek art.
Maurizio Taddei,	Ispettore archeologico presso il Museo l'Arte Orientale, Rome. Oriental art.
Adolfo Tamburello,	Libero Docente di storia e civilatà dell'Estremo Oriente dell'Università di Roma.
Roland Tefnin,	Assistant à la Faculté de Philosophie et Lettres de l'Université Libre de Bruxelles

Photograph Credits

Scala, Florence, made all photographs, with the following exceptions: Photothèque, Paris, 7, 8, 76, 138, 143, 157, 217, 236, 309, 371, 373, 388, 482, 496, 692, 751, 954, 988, 1004, 1017; Ferdinand Boesch, 1023; Yves Debraine, Lausanne, 997; Courtesy Lynn Chadwick, 1012; The Hermitage, Leningrad, 353, 354. 951; Kasmin Gallery, London, 1013; Louis Loose, Brussels, 970; Photo Maier, Vienna, 828; B. Peterson, *Life*, 1024; John D. Schiff, New York, 973, 987, 1020 (courtesy Allan Stone Gallery, New York); Photo Wesemüller, Germany, 393; Jean Willemin, Paris, 969; Heinz Zinraum, *Time*, 1015.

Index

References in italics refer to the illustrations. Sculptures are listed under artist's name, when known: architectural sculpture *in situ* appears under place name (city first). Anonymous sculptures now in public collections are indexed under museum (city first), except for those very well known by popular titles (such as *Apollo Belvedere*), which appear under these titles only. Anonymous works in private collections appear under collection name.